Andreas J. Köstenberger

Studies on John and Gender

A Decade of Scholarship

PETER LANG
New York • Washington, D.C./Baltimore • Bern
Frankfurt am Main • Berlin • Brussels • Vienna • Oxford

Library of Congress Cataloging-in-Publication Data

Köstenberger, Andreas J.
Studies on John and gender: a decade of scholarship / Andreas J. Köstenberger.
p. cm. — (Studies in biblical literature; vol. 38)
Includes bibliographical references and indexes.
1. Bible. N.T. John—Criticism, interpretation, etc.
2. Sex role—Biblical teaching. I. Title. II. Series.
BS2615.52 .K67   226.5′06—dc21   00-049778
ISBN 0-8204-5275-0
ISSN 1089-0645

Die Deutsche Bibliothek-CIP-Einheitsaufnahme

Köstenberger, Andreas J.:
Studies on John and gender: a decade of scholarship / Andreas J. Köstenberger.
–New York; Washington, D.C./Baltimore; Bern;
Frankfurt am Main; Berlin; Brussels; Vienna; Oxford: Lang.
(Studies in biblical literature; Vol. 38)
ISBN 0-8204-5275-0

The paper in this book meets the guidelines for permanence and durability
of the Committee on Production Guidelines for Book Longevity
of the Council of Library Resources.

Studies on John and Gender

Studies in Biblical Literature

Hemchand Gossai
General Editor

Vol. 38

PETER LANG
New York • Washington, D.C./Baltimore • Bern
Frankfurt am Main • Berlin • Brussels • Vienna • Oxford

This collection of essays
is gratefully dedicated to
Dr. and Mrs. Paige Patterson

CONTENTS

PART I: STUDIES ON JOHN

PART II: STUDIES ON GENDER

TABLES

EDITOR'S PREFACE

More than ever the horizons in biblical literature are being expanded beyond that which is immediately imagined; important new methodological, theological, and hermeneutical directions are being explored, often resulting in significant contributions to the world of biblical scholarship. It is an exciting time for the academy as engagement in biblical studies continues to be heightened.

This series seeks to make available to scholars and institutions, scholarship of a high order, and which will make a significant contribution to the ongoing biblical discourse. This series includes established and innovative directions, covering general and particular areas in biblical study. For every volume considered for this series, we ask the question as to whether it will push the horizons of biblical scholarship. The answer must be *yes* for inclusion.

In this volume, Andreas Köstenberger brings together a series of scholarly articles that focus on central issues in the Johannine Gospel and the issue of gender in the New Testament. While the majority of the articles clearly are intended for an evangelical audience, scholars who will disagree with Köstenberger's arguments will at the same time find his scholarship engaging. Professor Köstenberger's interest goes beyond the academic, as he pursues a course which he believes needs to be refined and redirected and which he argues is essential for both the academy and the church.

In particular this volume will be a welcome source for scholars and interested students in the evangelical tradition. The horizon has been expanded.

Hemchand Gossai
General Editor

AUTHOR'S PREFACE

It is gratifying to review a decade of scholarship and to remember several special people who helped make it possible. My wife Marny has stood by me through this entire time and shares my vision of a writing ministry that exemplifies truth as well as academic excellence. It is hardly a coincidence that we were married at the end of 1989 and that the works contained in this volume were published in the years from 1991 until 2000.

I am also grateful for the excellent preparation for an academic career provided by the faculty of Trinity Evangelical Divinity School where I studied from 1990 through 1993, especially Douglas Moo, Grant Osborne, and my esteemed mentor, Don Carson. Several of the essays included in the present volume originated in doctoral seminars and were refined by sharpening discussions with fellow students and faculty.

More recently, I have had the privilege of serving at one of the finest theological institutions in North America, Southeastern Baptist Theological Seminary. The unique blend of academic work and a heart for ministry, especially outreach to the unsaved, which permeates Southeastern, continues to inspire and energize me. Special thanks are due President Paige Patterson, whose support of my writing includes a very tangible token of encouragement for the present project, and Janet Hellard, my secretary, who helped with bibliographies and other matters.

From my roots in Roman Catholic Austria to my present involvement at an evangelical, Baptist institution, God, in Christ, has been faithful to draw me to himself and to put to use the gifts he has given me. May those who read the following pages be led to see the grace of God at work, and may he receive all the glory, for he alone is worthy, yesterday, today, and forever. Amen.

Andreas J. Köstenberger
January 2001

INTRODUCTION

While the essays included in the present volume have appeared in a variety of scholarly publications, they share in common a research interest in two important fields of study: John's Gospel and gender roles in the church. With one exception (Chap. Three), all of the articles featured here were published between 1991 and 2000, hence the sub-title "A Decade of Scholarship." The eight pieces on John and the seven entries on gender proceed partially along topical and partially along chronological lines. Some have appeared in fairly well-known journals, others in publications that are less easily accessible, and no more than three have appeared in the same publication. It is hoped that bringing all of these contributions together in one volume will enhance the accessibility of these materials, both as a resource for the classroom and for further academic study and research.

John's Gospel has received a large amount of scholarly attention in the past decade. My own work has initially focused on the Johannine mission theme (see my revised dissertation, *The Missions of Jesus and the Disciples According to the Fourth Gospel*, published by Eerdmans in 1998). More recently, I have surveyed John's Gospel in the Encountering Biblical Studies series (*Encountering John*, published by Baker in 1999). A detailed treatment of the background of John's Gospel is to appear in the fall of 2001 in Vol. 2 of the four-volume *Illustrated Bible Background Commentary: The New Testament* (ed. Clinton Arnold; Zondervan). The Baker Exegetical Commentary on the New Testament on John is currently in preparation.

The present volume opens with an entry on John's Gospel for the very recent *New Dictionary of Biblical Theology*, which seemed ideally suited as an introduction also for Part I of this book. The essay lays out the historical setting (including authorship), the literary features (genre, structure, compositional flow), and the theological emphases found in John. Beyond this, there are brief discussions of John's relationship with the Synoptic Gospels, the other Johannine writings, the Pauline literature, and the rest of the New Testament. A brief section on the relevance of John's Gospel concludes the first essay.

The second piece incorporates research in the precursors of critical scholarship on John's Gospel, focusing on the period from 1790 to 1810. Usually, it is Bretschneider (1820), as well as D. F. Strauss and F. C. Baur, who are mentioned first in contemporary discussions of the history of Johannine research. However, the little-known period from 1790 to 1810 saw the emergence of critical thought applied to John's Gospel, together with conservative responses to the challenges of the Fourth Gospel's trustworthiness, which are chronicled in Chap. Two. The chapter represents the English translation of an article that first appeared in German in 1996, which should enhance the accessibility of this important, yet hard-to-locate material.

Chap. Three features the only article in the present volume that has not previously been published (though it was presented at the Regional Meeting of the Society of Biblical Literature in Toronto, Canada, in 1993). This comparative study of the anointing narrative in all four Gospels is one of the first that applies verbal aspect theory (a hypothesis on the functioning of the Greek verb) to New Testament studies. It was born out of the conviction that, now that some of the theoretical foundations have been laid, what is needed is the testing of these hypotheses in relation to concrete portions of New Testament text. The Gospels provide an ideal basis for comparison, and the anointing pericope was chosen, since it is one of the few units that is found in all four Gospels.

The following two chapters represent fairly detailed studies of two important Johannine themes: Jesus as a rabbi, and the Johannine "signs." Both were originally published in the *Bulletin of Biblical Research*. "Jesus as Rabbi in the Fourth Gospel" seeks to establish the thesis that the Fourth Gospel bears witness that Jesus was perceived by his contemporaries primarily as a Jewish teacher. This question has important implications both for the reliability of John's Gospel and for the study of the so-called "historical Jesus." "The Seventh Johannine Sign" takes its point of departure from the importance of Jesus' "signs" in Johannine theology. It is argued that these "signs" ought not to be confined to what may be called the "miraculous" but that, properly understood, they also include "signs" with a prophetic-symbolic dimension. This opens the way for the temple cleansing to be identified as the seventh Johannine sign.

Chap. Six is devoted to the reference to "greater works" of the believer found in John 14:12. Initially, it is puzzling how Jesus could predict that his followers would perform greater works even than himself after his departure and exaltation. The essay seeks to explore this saying in its primary literary context, John's Gospel, rather than domesticating it by interpreting it with immediate reference to the book of Acts, as has been regularly done.

The penultimate contribution to Johannine studies is devoted to one of the more regularly discussed lexical features of John's Gospel, the relationship between the two Johannine verbs for sending, ἀποστέλλω and πέμπω. In interaction with Rengstorf's influential entry in Kittel's *Theological Dictionary of the New Testament*, the question is discussed whether the two verbs have distinct meanings (as Rengstorf maintains) or whether they are virtual synonyms (the conclusion of the present essay). Apart from the issue at hand, the study provides an interesting case study of linguistic research as applied to New Testament studies.

Part I concludes with an essay that explores the practical implications of the study of John's Gospel, flowing from the author's full-length study of mission in the Fourth Gospel. The underlying vision of a systematized biblical theology of mission has now been realized in the book (co-authored with Peter T. O'Brien) *Salvation to the Ends of the Earth: A Biblical Theology of Mission* (IVP, 2001).

The second half of this book is given to another significant field of study, that of gender roles in the New Testament. Many (though not all) of these contributions are in one way or another related to the book *Women in the Church: A Fresh Analysis of 1 Timothy 2:9–15* (co-edited with Thomas Schreiner and Scott Baldwin; Baker, 1995). The first two studies included in Part II, however, relate to the present author's interest in engaging Roman Catholic theology. Chapter Nine features a critical review (and attempted refutation) of the thesis that priestly celibacy is of apostolic origin. Chapter Ten investigates whether or not the reference to a "mystery" (Grk. μυστήριον) indeed relates to the sacrament of marriage (as is maintained by many Roman Catholic theologians).

Chap. Eleven clears the ground by seeking to establish certain hermeneutical groundrules in the study of gender roles in the New Testament. The next three chapters are most directly related to the crucial passage in 1 Timothy 2:9–15 that also forms the subject of *Women in the Church*. "The Crux of the Matter" provides a convenient summary of the main argument of this monograph, and one that is more readily accessible (for less technical) to the average reader than the full-length treatment. Chapter Thirteen features a slightly more technical version of the present author's contribution to the study of 1 Timothy 2:12 than the one found in *Women in the Church*. Its inclusion here should make it more accessible to some readers. The research contained in this piece has proved persuasive to many, including William Mounce in his recently published commentary on the Pastoral epistles in the Word Biblical Commentary series (Word, 2000; see pp. 128–30).

Many who were aware of my work on 1 Timothy 2:12 asked me what I thought of the puzzling reference to women's "salvation by childbearing" in v. 15. For some time, all I could say was that I had never studied this issue in detail. Eventually, I did, and the essay contained in Chap. Fourteen is the result. Even for those who do not agree with my final conclusion the extensive survey of the history of research and the categorization of the major interpretive options should be helpful.

The final, and most recent, entry is "Women in the Pauline Mission," written for a volume honoring the Australian scholar Peter O'Brien. This essay is largely devoted to the study of women mentioned in narrative portions of Paul's writings (as well as the book of Acts) and thus nicely supplements the earlier treatments of didactic passages on women's roles in the church in Paul. While not everyone will agree with all of the conclusions reached in this article, the thorough inventory taken and the data amassed should prove valuable in the further scholarly discussion that will doubtless ensue.

Johannine and gender studies are both fascinating and intensely rewarding fields of scholarly inquiry. It is hoped that the essays gathered in the present volume will make a small contribution to the ongoing discussion in these disciplines, and what is more, that the truth set forth in these essays will spur many on, not only to further thought, but also to action in keeping with the injunctions of God's Word.

PART I: STUDIES ON JOHN

CHAPTER ONE

INTRODUCTION TO
JOHN'S GOSPEL[*]

John's Gospel, together with the Book of Romans, can justifiably be called "the Mount Everest of New Testament theology." From its peaks it is possible to survey much of the territory of biblical revelation, including the Old Testament, the Synoptics, and other portions of the New Testament. The following essay surveys: 1. the Fourth Gospel's historical setting; 2. its literary features; 3. its theological emphases; 4. its place in the canon; and 5. its contemporary relevance.

Historical Setting

The Gospel's internal evidence suggests that the author is an apostle (1:14 cf. 2:11; 19:35); one of the Twelve ("the disciple whom Jesus loved": 13:23 cf. 19:26–27; 20:2–9; 21, esp. vv. 24–25); John, the son of Zebedee ("the disciple Jesus loved" is associated with Peter in 13:23–24; 18:15–16; 20:2–9; 21; cf. Luke 22:8; Acts 1:13; 3–4; 8:14–25; Gal 2:9). External evidence supports this identification (Irenaeus, *Adv. Haer.* 3.1.2). The Gospel was probably written in Ephesus and aimed (like the other Gospels) at a universal readership.[1] John's original audience appears to have been made up primarily of diaspora Jews and proselytes.

The purpose statement in 20:30–31 indicates that John wrote with an (indirect) evangelistic purpose, probably expecting to reach his unbelieving audience via Christian readers.[2] The most probable occasion for writing is

---

[*]This essay is reprinted with permission from "John," *New Dictionary of Biblical Theology* (ed. T. Desmond Alexander and Brian S. Rosner; Leicester, England/Downers Grove, IL: InterVarsity, 2000), 280–85.

[1]Richard Bauckham, "For Whom Were the Gospels Written?" in *The Gospels for All Christians: Rethinking the Gospel Audiences* (Grand Rapids: Eerdmans, 1997), 9–48.

[2]Ibid., 10.

the destruction of the Jerusalem temple in 70 CE, a traumatic event that left Judaism in a national and religious void and caused Jews to look for ways to continue their ritual and worship. Seizing the opportunity for Jewish evangelism, John presents Jesus as the temple's replacement (2:18-22) and the fulfillment of the symbolism inherent in Jewish feasts (esp. chaps. 5-12). If this hypothesis is correct, the Gospel could have been written any time after CE 70. If Thomas' confession of Jesus as "my Lord and my God" is intended to evoke associations with emperor worship under Domitian (CE 81-96), a date after 81 CE would appear most likely.

Literary Features

John demonstrates that the Christ, the Son of God, is Jesus (20:30-31)[3] by weaving together several narrative strands. The prologue places the entire Gospel into the framework of the eternal, pre-existent Word who became flesh in Jesus (1:1-18). The first half of John's narrative sets forth evidence for Jesus' messiahship by way of seven selected signs (1:19-12:50; cf. 20:30-31).[4] John also includes Jesus' seven "I am" sayings (6:25-59; 8:12=9:5; 10:7=9,11; 11:25; 14:6; 15:1) and calls numerous witnesses in support of Jesus' claims (including Moses and the Scriptures; the Baptist; the Father; Jesus and his own works; the Spirit and the disciples; and the fourth evangelist himself). Representative questions concerning Jesus' messiahship serve to lead the Gospel's readers to the author's own conclusion (i.e. that Jesus is the Christ; e.g. 1:41; 4:25; 7:27, 31, 52; 10:24; 11:27; 12:34).

The second half of John's Gospel shows how the Christ ensures the continuance of his mission by preparing his new messianic community for its mission. The section opens with Jesus' farewell discourse (13-17): the new messianic community is cleansed (by the footwashing and Judas' departure; ch. 13), prepared (by instructions regarding the coming Paraclete and his ministry to the disciples; 14-16), and prayed for (ch. 17); the disciples are made partners in the proclamation of salvation in Christ (15:15-16) and taken into the life of the Godhead which is characterized by perfect love and unity (17:20-26). The Johannine passion narrative

---

[3]Cf. D. A. Carson, "The Purpose of the Fourth Gospel: Jn 20:31 Reconsidered," *JBL* 106 (1987): 639-51.

[4]Cf. Andreas J. Köstenberger, "The Seventh Johannine Sign: A Study in John's Christology," *BBR* 5 (1995): 87-103.

(18-19) presents Jesus' death both as an atonement for sin (cf. 1:29, 36; 6:48-58; 10:15, 17-18), though without the Synoptic emphasis on shame and humiliation, and as a stage in Jesus' return to the Father (e.g. 13:1; 16:28). The resurrection appearances and the disciples' commissioning by their risen Lord constitute the focal point of the penultimate chapter (20), where Jesus is cast as the paradigmatic Sent One (cf. 9:7), who has now become the sender of his new messianic community (20:21-23). The purpose statement of 20:30-31 reiterates the major motifs of the Gospel: the "signs"; believing; (eternal) life; and the identity of Jesus as Christ and Son of God. The epilogue portrays the relationship between Peter and "the disciple whom Jesus loved" in terms of differing yet equally legitimate roles of service within the believing community.

Theological Emphases

The Christ and His Mission

In keeping with its Gospel genre, John's narrative focuses on Jesus and his messianic mission. At the very outset, John's account is based on Old Testament theology. The Gospel's opening phrase, "In the beginning," recalls the beginning of Genesis, which recounts the world's creation (1:1; cf. 1:3). According to John, the Word's coming into this world and becoming flesh in Jesus constitutes an event of comparable magnitude (1:1, 14). Jesus is presented as the Word sent from heaven to accomplish a mission and, once the mission has been accomplished, to return to the place from which he came (cf. Isa 55:11). John's use of the term *logos* ("Word") with reference to Jesus also serves to contextualize the Christian message in the evangelist's culture.

Another Old Testament concept taken up in John's prologue is that of light and darkness (1:4-5, 8-9; cf. 3:19-21; Gen 1:3-4). There is a superficial parallel here with the Qumran literature. But there this contrast is set within the framework of an eschatological dualism, while in John Jesus is presented as the Word, active in creation, who has now brought final revelation from God. This revelation, in turn, is compared and contrasted with the revelation received by and mediated through Moses (1:17-18; cf. Exod 33-34). Jesus brought "grace instead of grace" (1:16): while the law given through Moses also constituted a gracious gift from God, truth—final, eschatological truth—came only through Jesus (1:17). And no one, not even Moses, truly saw God (1:18; cf. Exod 33:20, 23; 34:6-7); but now Jesus, already with God at the beginning (1:1), and always, even during his earthly ministry, at the Father's side, has "exegeted" (explained) him (1:18).

The Jewish milieu of John's Gospel and the firm grounding of its theology in Old Testament antecedents are also borne out by the various component parts of the Fourth Gospel's christological teaching. John's favorite designation for Jesus is that of the Son sent by the Father (3:17, 35-36; 5:19-26; 6:40; 8:35-36; 14:13; 17:1). This metaphor is taken from Jewish life and the halakhic concept of the *šaliah*, according to which the sent one is like the sender himself, a faithful representative of his interests (cf. 13:16, 20). The image of the descending bread from heaven develops Old Testament teaching on God's provision of manna in the wilderness (cf. Jesus as the antitype of the serpent in the wilderness, 3:14); the figure of the descending and ascending Son of Man (cf. the "lifted up" sayings in 3:14; 8:28; 12:34) probably derives from apocalyptic passages featuring "one like a son of man" (Dan 7:13). Jesus is also shown to fulfill the symbolism of the Jewish feast of Tabernacles (chs. 7-9) and the Passover (ch. 19), as well as that of Jewish institutions such as the Jerusalem temple (2:14-22; see "Historical Setting" above, and further below).

Central to John's presentation of Jesus' work (esp. in chaps. 1-12; see "Literary features" above) is the concept of signs.[5] The trajectory of antecedent Old Testament theology reaches back as far as the "signs and wonders" performed by Moses at the exodus; Jesus' signs point to a new exodus (cf. Luke 9:31). In John, however, the miraculous character of Jesus' work is blended with, and even superseded by, their prophetic symbolism (cf. Isa 20:3). As with those of Moses and later prophets, the signs' function is primarily to authenticate the one who performs them as God's true representative. People are severely criticized for demanding spectacular evidence of Jesus' authority (4:48); yet signs are offered as an aid to faith (10:38). And while blessing is pronounced on those who "have not seen and yet have believed" (20:29), Jesus' signs are clearly designed to elicit faith among his audience, and when they fail to do so, the people are held responsible.

Another crucial motif in John's theology is Jesus' fulfillment of the symbolism inherent in Jewish feasts and institutions. By pronouncing himself to be the "light of the world" (8:12; 9:5) and the source of "living water" (4:10-14; 7:38), Jesus claims to fulfil the torch-lighting and water-pouring ceremonies which formed part of the feast of Tabernacles. By dying during Passover week, Jesus is revealed as the prototype of the Jewish passover (19:14). By pointing to his own crucified and resurrected body as the true embodiment and replacement of the Jerusalem temple

---

[5]See Köstenberger, "Seventh Johannine Sign," 87-103.

(2:14-22), Jesus indicated that Judaism was merely preparatory, anticipating the coming of God's Messiah. True worship must be rendered, not in any particular physical location, but in spirit and truth (4:23-24).

One final striking feature deserving comment is John's inclusion of seven "I am" sayings of Jesus. According to John, Jesus is: 1. the bread from heaven (6:25-29); 2. the light of the world (8:12=9:5); 3. the door for the sheep and 4. the good shepherd (10:7, 9, 11); 5. the resurrection and the life (11:25); 6. the way, the truth, and the life (14:6); and 7. the vine (15:1). This terminology recalls God's self-identification to Moses at the outset of the exodus: " 'I AM WHO I AM . . . I AM has sent me to you' " (Exod 3:14). It is also reminiscent of Isaiah's consistent portrayal of the sovereign Lord God (e.g. Isa 43:10-13, 25; 45:18; 48:12; 51:12; 52:6). In places "I am sayings" and signs are linked (6:35; 11:25). Like the background to the Johannine "signs," the background to Jesus' self-designation as the "I am" is therefore to be found in a trajectory ranging from Moses and the exodus to the Old Testament prophets, particularly Isaiah (cf. also 12:38-41).

The New Messianic Community and Its Mission

Like his portrait of Jesus, John's presentation of the new messianic community follows a salvation-historical pattern.[6] In keeping with Old Testament typology, believers are described as a "flock" (ch. 10) and as "branches" of the vine (ch. 15). Yet John does not teach that the church replaces Israel. Rather, he identifies Jesus as Israel's replacement: he is God's "vine" taking the place of God's Old Testament "vineyard," Israel (Isa 5). John acknowledges that "salvation comes from the Jews" (4:22). Yet he portrays Israel as part of the unbelieving world which rejects Jesus. Jesus' "own" (i.e. "the Jews") did not receive him (1:11). In their place, the Twelve, who are now "his own," become the recipients of his love (13:1; cf. ch. 17). The Jewish leaders, on the other hand, are said not even to belong to Jesus' flock (10:26).

Another instance of John's drawing on Old Testament antecedents is Jesus' parting preparation of his followers in terms reminiscent of Moses' deuteronomic farewell discourse ("love," "obey," "keep . . . commandments," etc.; 13-17; cf. 1:17). However, at this salvation-historical juncture it is not Israel but believers in Jesus who represent the core group through which he will pursue his redemptive purposes. The community is formally

---

[6]John W. Pryor, *John: Evangelist of the Covenant People* (Downers Grove, IL: InterVarsity, 1992).

constituted in the commissioning narrative, where Jesus' breathing upon his gathered disciples marks a "new creation," recalling the creation of the first human being, Adam (20:22; Gen 2:7). Jesus' dependent and obedient relationship to his sender, the Father, is made the paradigm for the disciples' relationship with their sender, Jesus.[7]

In John's treatment of individual disciples, particular attention is given to two of Jesus' followers: Peter and "the disciple whom Jesus loved." These two characters are regularly featured together (see "Historical Setting" above):[8] in the upper room (13:23-24); in the courtyard of the high priest (18:15-16); at the empty tomb (20:2-9); and at the Sea of Tiberias subsequent to Jesus' resurrection (ch. 21). While Peter is considered to be the leader of the Twelve (cf. 6:67-79), he is presented as second to "the disciple whom Jesus loved" in terms of access to revelation (13:23) and faith (20:8). In the end, the ministry of "the disciple Jesus loved" is shown to be equally legitimate to that of Peter. The ministries of both Peter and John are portrayed by the fourth evangelist in terms which recall Jesus' ministry: in Peter's case, the analogy is found in the death by which he would glorify God (21:19; cf. 12:33); in the case of "the disciple whom Jesus loved," the parallel consists in his position "at the breast of Jesus," which qualified him supremely to "narrate" the story of his Lord (13:23; author's translations; cf. 1:18). Thus the role of (eye)witness to Jesus' ministry may take forms as different as martyrdom and writing a Gospel, but witness must be borne, according to each person's calling (15:26-27).

Place in the Canon

Relationship with the Synoptic Gospels
The relationship between John's Gospel and the Synoptics has been described in terms of mutual independence or varying degrees of literary interdependence. Historically, it seems difficult to believe that John had not at least heard of the existence of the Synoptics and read at least some portions of them. But whether or not John knew these Gospels, he clearly did not make extensive use of them in composing his own narrative. Apart from the feeding of the five thousand, the anointing and the passion narra-

---

[7]Andreas J. Köstenberger, *The Missions of Jesus and the Disciples According to the Fourth Gospel* (Grand Rapids: Eerdmans, 1998), 190-98.

[8]See Kevin Quast, *Peter and the Beloved Disciple* (JSNTSS 32; Sheffield: JSOT, 1989).

tive, and a few other thematic congruences, John has little in common with the Synoptic Gospels.[9]

Moreover, unlike the Synoptics, John has no birth narrative, no Sermon on the Mount or Lord's Prayer (but neither has Mark), no accounts of Jesus' transfiguration or the Lord's Supper, no narrative parables, and no eschatological discourse. Clearly, John has written his own book. This, however, does not make his a sectarian work apart from the mainstream of apostolic Christianity.[10] Rather, John frequently transposes elements of the Gospel tradition into a different key. The synoptic teaching on the kingdom of God corresponds to the Johannine theme of "eternal life"; narrative parables are replaced by extended discourses on the symbolism of Jesus' signs. Moreover, all four Gospels present Jesus as the Messiah fulfilling Old Testament predictions and typology. Thus the differences between the Synoptics and John must not be exaggerated.

Relationship with the Other Johannine Writings
John's first epistle is directed to defuse an early gnostic threat to the message of John's gospel by showing that Jesus has come in the flesh. John's Gospel portrays Jesus along similar lines, albeit without specific references to proto-Gnosticism. The striking similarities between John's Gospel and his first epistle include the following: the contrast between light and darkness (John 1:4-9; 3:9-21; 12:35-36; 1 John 1:5-7; 2:8-11) and the negative view of "the world" (cf. esp. 1 John 2:15-17), which must be "overcome" (John 16:33; 1 John 5:4-5); the use of the term *paraklētos* (for the Spirit, in John 14:16, 26; 16:26; 16:7; for Jesus, in 1 John 2:1); the emphasis on truth (John 1:14, 17; 3:21; 4:23, 24; 5:33; etc.; 1 John 1:6, 8; 2:4, 21; etc.); "eternal life" (John 3:15-16, 36; 4:14, 36; etc.; 1 John 1:2; 2:25; 3:15; 5:11, 13, 20) and references to believers' having already passed from death into life (John 5:24=1 John 3:14); the description of Jesus as the Christ, the Son of God (John 20:30-31; 1 John 2:22; 4:15; 5:1, 5); God's sending of his Son into the world in order that those who believe in him may have life (John 3:16-17; 1 John 4:7); and the frequent use of substantival participles ("the one who"), "just as" comparisons, and of important terms such as "know," "keep the commandments," "abide," "love," and the designations "born of God" and "children of God."

---

[9]But note the "interlocking traditions" enumerated in D. A. Carson, Douglas Douglas J. Moo, and Leon Morris, *An Introduction to the New Testament* (Grand Rapids: Zondervan, 1992), 161-62.

[10]David Wenham, "The enigma of the Fourth Gospel: another look," *TynBul* 48 (1997): 149-78.

The book of Revelation is addressed to seven churches in Asia Minor (Rev 2–3), and is intended to strengthen believers in the face of suffering at the end of the first century. Common features of John's Gospel and the Apocalypse include: the christological titles "Lamb" (John 1:29, 36; twenty-eight times in Rev.) and Logos (John 1:1, 14; Rev 19:13); the eschatological images of shepherding (John 10:1–16; 21:15–17; Rev 2:27; 7:17; 12:5; 19:15) and living water (John 4:14; 6:35; 7:37–38; Rev 7:17; 21:6; 22:1, 17); statements regarding God's dwelling with humans (John 1:14; Rev 7:15; 21:3) and the absence of the temple (John 2:19, 21; 4:20–26; Rev 21:22); the importance assigned to the number seven (in John, signs and "I am" sayings; in Rev., seals, trumpets and bowls); the identification of Satan as the chief protagonist of Jesus (John 6:70; 8:44; 13:2, 27; Rev 2:9–10, 13, 24; 3:9; 12:9, 12; 20:2, 7, 10); the contrast between believers and the world in John and between those with God's seal and those with the mark of the beast in Revelation; the quotation of Zech 12:10 in John 19:36–37 and Rev 1:7; the terminology of "witness" and "glory"; and both the necessity of perseverance and the sovereignty and predestinating counsel of God (theodicy).

Relationship with Pauline Writings
John's Gospel and Paul's epistles reflect different but not contradictory perspectives. Both emphasize love (John 13:13–14; 1 Cor 13), consider the world to be in darkness and its wisdom futile, and use the phrase "in Christ" or "in him." They also depict Israel's destiny using similar imagery, whether branches of a vine (John in ch. 15) or of an olive tree (Paul in Romans 11). Both subordinate the Law to faith in Jesus (John 1:17; Rom and Gal), and both depict God as "the Father," with John stressing the Father's role in believers' conception ("born of God") and Paul emphasizing his role in adoption. For both writers the gospel is centered on Jesus Christ crucified, buried, and risen (John 18–20; 1 Cor 15:1–4), and they both teach divine sovereignty and predestination in the context of theodicy (John 12:37–40; Rom 9–11).

But John and Paul differ in many respects. Unlike Paul, John nowhere elaborates the relationship between sin and the law; thus John lacks an equivalent to the Pauline antithesis between works and faith. The Pauline term "flesh" in contrast to the Spirit is without parallel in John (John 3:6 is no real exception). Likewise, John has no explicit doctrine of justification;[11] neither does he feature full-fledged versions of the Pauline

---

[11]Though see Andrew H. Trotter, "Justification in the Gospel of John," in *Right with God: Justification in the Bible and the world* (ed. D. A. Carson; Grand Rapids: Baker, 1992), 126–45.

corollaries to justification, such as reconciliation, calling, election,[12] adoption into sonship, and sanctification.

Relationship with Other New Testament Writings
John shares with Hebrews a high christology, particularly in the prologues. Both books stress that Jesus is the locus of God's final revelation (John 1:18; Heb 1:2), and both set God's redemptive work through Christ in parallel to his work of creation (John 1:1; Heb 1:3). Both also stress that Jesus is the last in a long series of divine emissaries and bearers of revelation (John 4:34; Heb 1:2). Both emphasize faith (John throughout; Heb 11) and portray Jesus as exalted subsequent to his suffering. But John's eschatology is mostly realized while Hebrews accentuates hope; Johannine "in Christ" language is absent from Hebrews; and Hebrews portrays the Christian life more in terms of struggle, owing to the readers' weariness and reluctance to suffer.

John and Peter are associated in ministry in the early portions of the book of Acts. It is therefore not surprising that they have similar perspectives on a number of issues. Both emphasize that the fall of Judaism is part of God's plan (John 12:37; 1 Pet 2:8). Both present Jesus simultaneously as Lamb and as shepherd (John 1:29, 36; 10:12; 21:15-19; 1 Pet 1:19; 2:25; 5:24). Both portray believers as those who are "in Christ" (1 John 2:5-6; 1 Pet 5:14) and who believe in Jesus although they do not now see him (John 20:29; 1 Pet 1:8). Both emphasize mutual love (John 13:34; 15:9, 12, 17; 17:26; 1 Pet 1:22; 2:17; 4:8), regard Jesus' death as the norm for Christian conduct (John 15:13; 1 Pet 2:21-25; 3:17-18), challenge the church to suffer joyfully for Christ (John 15:18:25; 1 Pet 2:13-4:2), and acknowledge the Spirit as the witness to Jesus (John 15:26; 1 Pet 1:11-12) and the life-giver (John 6:63; 1 Pet 3:18). Finally, neither discusses the law or the constitution of the church.

Relevance

John's Gospel accentuates Jesus' divinity more strongly than do the other Gospels (cf. esp. 1:1, 18; 20:28-29), thereby expanding the horizons of Jewish monotheism. As in John's day, his emphasis on Jesus' exclusive

---

[12]Though see Robert W. Yarbrough, "Divine Election in the Gospel of John," in *The Grace of God, the Bondage of the Will*, Vol. 1 (ed. Thomas R. Schreiner and Bruce A. Ware; Grand Rapids: Baker, 1995), 47-62.

claims and unique person and work (cf. esp. 1:18; 14:6) confronts alternative claims to (religious) truth. John's Christology, particularly regarding
Jesus' deity and his human and divine natures, has profoundly influenced
the way Christians think about their Lord, particularly through the early
church councils and creeds.

By contextualizing the good news about Jesus, John shows Christianity
to be a world religion, transcending its Jewish roots. Faith in Jesus as Messiah and Son of God is presented as entrance into a personal relationship
with God the Father in Christ and as into the messianic community, which
is no longer defined by ethnic boundaries. The most well-known verse of
the Gospel, John 3:16, tells of God's love for the (sinful) world which led
him to send his Son, so that whoever believes in him should not perish
but have eternal life.

According to the commissioning passage in 20:21–23, the church has
entered into Christ's mission and is charged to proclaim the message of
forgiveness in Jesus' name to a dark and hostile world. But as Christ has
overcome the world, believers in the exalted Christ, after having borne
testimony to the world regarding Jesus' messiahship, are certain to join
their Lord in his eternal glory (17:24).

CHAPTER TWO

EARLY DOUBTS OF THE APOSTOLIC AUTHORSHIP OF THE FOURTH GOSPEL IN THE HISTORY OF MODERN BIBLICAL CRITICISM[*]

When did doubts regarding the apostolic authorship of the Fourth Gospel first arise in the history of modern biblical criticism? The question of the authorship of the Gospels is a knotty one. As Stephen Neill points out, the Gospels belong to a class of writings that share the following characteristics: "No one of them [the Gospels] gives, in its text, the name of the author; the titles which we find in the ancient Greek manuscripts form no part of the original text. No one of them gives any indication as to the date and place of writing."[1] He asks, "If an ancient writing is of this anonymous and homeless character, by what means, if any, is it possible to fix it in time, and to establish with some probability the name of the writer?"[2]

Traditionally, the answer to Neill's question has been that a combination of internal and external evidence points to the Gospels' origin. In the case of the Fourth Gospel, the Gospel's own claims to have been written by one of Jesus' own disciples and patristic attribution to the apostle John

---

[*]This essay represents an English adaptation of "Frühe Zweifel an der johanneischen Verfasserschaft des vierten Evangeliums in der modernen Interpretationsgeschichte," *European Journal of Theology* 5 (1996): 37–46. The translation is the present author's.

[1]Stephen C. Neill and Tom Wright, *The Interpretation of the New Testament 1861–1986* (2d ed.; Oxford/New York: Oxford University Press, 1988), 41. This was already noted with regard to the Fourth Gospel by Dionysius of Alexandria, a pupil of Origen. Cf. Werner Georg Kümmel, *The New Testament: The History of the Investigation of its Problems* (trans. S. McLean Gilmour and Howard C. Kee; Nashville: Abingdon, 1972), 16.

[2]Ibid.

held the day, with very few exceptions, until the rise of historical criticism in the seventeenth and eighteenth centuries. As Neill observes, "Up to the middle of the eighteenth century, an arid theory of verbal inspiration made any scientific progress in Biblical studies almost impossible."[3] While one may differ with Neill's assessment, it must be granted that dogmatic considerations had frequently precluded a fresh assessment of the evidence in many areas of studies.

From the standpoint of contemporary scholarship, which has largely abandoned the traditional view of the apostolic authorship of the Fourth Gospel, the question arises what sparked this "paradigm shift," and how it came about. Following Kümmel's treatment, we learn that "After a few voices had been hesitantly raised against the authenticity of John's gospel as early as the last decade of the eighteenth century, several scholars at the beginning of the nineteenth questioned the Johannine authorship of the Fourth Gospel with less equivocation."[4] Kümmel names the less well known Erhard Friedrich Vogel (1750-?), Georg Konrad Horst (1767-1838), Hermann Heimart Cludius (1754-1821), and, most significantly, Karl Gottlieb Bretschneider (1776-1848), who wrote in 1820.[5]

---

[3]Ibid., 359.

[4]Kümmel, *History of Investigation*, 85. The translations from the Latin, French, and German in the following footnotes are the present author's unless noted otherwise.

[5]Ibid., and notes 109-12 on pp. 419-20. Vogel, writing anonymously in 1801-1804, contended that John's Gospel could have been written only after the apostle's death (*Der Evangelist Johannes und seine Ausleger von dem jüngsten Gericht*, 2 vols.). Horst speculated that the christological contradictions in the Fourth Gospel go back to the author's use of different sources, and that both the late attestation of the Gospel and its Alexandrian ideas make it impossible to assume that its author was one of Jesus' disciples ("Über einige Widersprüche in dem Evangelium des Johannis in Absicht auf den Logos, oder das Höhere in Christo," and "Lässt sich die Echtheit des johanneischen Evangeliums aus hinlänglichen Gründen bezweifeln, und welches ist der wahrscheinliche Ursprung dieser Schrift?" *Museum für Religionswissenschaft in ihrem ganzen Umfange*, ed. H. Ph. K. Henke, Vol. I, Magdeburg, 1804). Cludius challenged the apostolic authorship of the Fourth Gospel on the basis of its divergence from the Synoptic Gospels (*Uransichten des Christenthums nebst Untersuchungen über einige Bücher des neuen Testaments* [Altona, 1808]). He was followed by Christoph Friedrich Ammon in 1811 (Erlanger Osterprogramm, "quo docetur Johannem Evangelii auctorem ab editore huis libri fuisse diversum") who claimed that the author of the Gospel of John was someone other than the editor of the book. Another author is Johann Ernst Christian Schmidt ("Versuch über Entstehung der Katholischen Kirche," in *Bibliothek für Kritik und Exegese* [Herborn & Hadamar, 1798], 1-35; and *Kritische Geschichte der neutestamentlichen Schriften* [1804-1805]). Bretschneider's book was entitled *Probabilia de evangelii et epistolarum Joannis, Apostoli, indole et origine eruditorum Judiciis* (Leipzig,

Another writer mentioned in connection with the the criticism of the authorship of the Fourth Gospel is Heinrich C. Ballenstedt.[6]

Luthardt provides further information on the last decade of the eighteenth century only mentioned in passing by Kümmel. He names Evanson, who in 1792 attributed the Fourth Gospel to a Platonist,[7] as well as providing an extensive annotated bibliography at the end of his work, starting with Evanson.[8] However, the editor prefaces Luthardt's bibliography with the remark that one unacquainted with the history of biblical criticism might "suppose that the book of Evanson fell like a thunderbolt from a clear sky, a sky that had been cloudless since the days of the Alogi [one of the few to question the Gospel's apostolic authorship in early church history]."[9] Reference is then made to "some of the English Deists in the early part of the eighteenth century, and some of the German

---

1820). He concluded "that the Fourth Gospel could neither have been written by a Jew nor by another of the apostles, nor by a Jewish Christian but was rather put together by a Gentile Christian who wrote after John's death under John's name" (*conclusionem, evangelium quartum neque a Joanne, neque ab alio apostolorum, neque a christiano e Judaeis scribi potuisse, sed potius a christiano e gentilibus, post Joannis mortem, qui se pro Joanne probaret, confictum esse*, 114). Bretschneider claimed that "The author of the gospel . . . fell into geographical and historical errors which a native Jew would never have committed . . . and erred gravely in narrating the Passover meal" (*Scripsit auctor evangelii . . . in errores geographicos et historicos lapsus est, quos judaeus natur nullo modo commisisset, . . . eaque de causa in narranda coena paschali graviter erravit*, 113–14). Though opposed by Schleiermacher, Bretschneider's radical views were taken up by none less than David Friedrich Strauss in his *The Life of Jesus Critically Examined* (London: SCM, 1973 [1935]), who thereby inaugurated the practice of setting John aside for life of Jesus research. Cf. Kümmel, *History of Investigation*, 124–26; Christoph Ernst Luthardt, *St. John the Author of the Fourth Gospel* (Edinburgh: T. & T. Clark, 1875), 17–20. In 1847, F. C. Baur argued for a late second-century date for John (*Kritische Untersuchungen über die kanonischen Evangelien* [Tübingen]). Cf. David Friedrich Strauss, *The Christ of Faith and the Jesus of History—A Critique of Schleiermacher's* The Life of Jesus (ed. Leander E. Keck [Philadelphia, 1977]), 40, especially n. 50; and pp. 38–47; Kümmel, *History of Investigation*, 124–26; Luthardt, *St. John the Author of the Fourth Gospel*, 20–25.

[6]Cf. Luthardt, *St. John the Author of the Fourth Gospel*, 15; Howard M. Teeple, *The Literary Origins of the Gospel of John* (Evanston: Religion and Ethics Institute, 1974), 8. Teeple's work is seriously limited by its failure to engage primary sources. Cf. notes 4 and 5, p. 261, and note 3, p. 265.

[7]Luthardt, *St. John the Author of the Fourth Gospel*, 15.

[8]Ibid., 283–360; cf. also idem, *St. John's Gospel* (Edinburgh: T. & T. Clark, 1878), ix–xvii.

[9]Luthardt, *St. John the Author of the Fourth Gospel*, 283.

Rationalists towards its close" who "seem to have gone so far as to deny to the gospel of John, no less than to the other gospels, all value as original records."[10]

Using the above references as a starting point for further investigation, we will focus especially on the last decade of the eighteenth century when doubts regarding the Fourth Gospel's authorship crystallized that would cast their early shadows on the debate which has continued until this day. Our hope is that, by studying the genesis of those early doubts, we may gain a better understanding of both early historical criticism and contemporary scholarship, especially with regard to the Fourth Gospel's authorship.

---

[10]Ibid. Cf. also the helpful synopsis of early doubts of the apostolic authorship of the Fourth Gospel in Adolf Hilgenfeld, "Die Evangelienforschung nach ihrem Verlauf und gegenwärtigen Stand," *ZWT* 4 (1861): 39-40. Hilgenfeld starts with Johann Gottfried Eichhorn (1752-1827), who in his *Einleitung in das Neue Testament* defended the apostolic authorship of the Fourth Gospel (Leipzig: Weidmannsche Buchhandlung, 1810). Eichhorn finds both church tradition and internal evidence to support apostolic authorship. He views the absence of John's name in the Fourth Gospel as actually supporting the notion of Johannine authorship and calls John's practice of writing of himself in the third person "schriftstellerische Bescheidenheit" [authorial modesty; *Einleitung*, 99, 102]. Hilgenfeld then surveys Evanson in England and Eckermann in Germany and notes the opposition both of those scholars encountered (Evanson from Priestley and Simpson, Eckermann especially from Gottlob Christian Storr [1746-1805], *Ueber den Zweck der evangelischen Geschichte und der Briefe Johannis* [Tübingen, 1786] and Süsskind; see the discussion below). Hilgenfeld notes that both Eckermann and Johann Ernst Christian Schmidt ("Versuch über Entstehung der Katholischen Kirche," in *Bibliothek für Kritik und Exegese*, Vol. II, Pt. 1 [Herborn and Hadamar, 1798]) eventually retracted their doubts (Eckermann in *Erklärung aller dunklen Stellen des N. T.*, Vol. II [Kiel, 1807]; Schmidt in *Kritische Geschichte der neutestamentlichen Schriften: Historisch-kritische Einleitung in's Neue Testament*, Vol. II [Giessen, 1805], 133-60). Hilgenfeld also mentions H. Vogel, G. K. Horst, and H. H. Cludius. His survey closes with the remark that, in Eichhorn's view, Wegscheider in his *Versuch einer vollständigen Einleitung in das Evangelium des Johannes* (Göttingen, 1806) had defended the apostolic authorship of the Fourth Gospel so successfully that a further thorough refutation of doubts seemed superfluous. Another helpful summary can be found in Carl Wilhelm Stein, *Authentia Evangelii Johannis, contra S. V. Bretschneideri dubia vindicata* (Brandenburg: J. J. Wiesike, 1822), 1-21.

Early Doubts of the Apostolic Authorship of the Fourth Gospel

A Pioneer in France: Richard Simon (1638-1712)
Bacon and especially Descartes had already made doubt a central tenet of seventeenth-century scholarship. Hobbes in his *Leviathan* had disputed the Mosaic authorship of the Pentateuch. Spinoza had contended that the Bible ought to be studied like any other book. In 1695, the French critic Richard Simon, who had replaced the notion of the Mosaic authorship of the Pentateuch with his hypothesis of "public scribes" (i.e. redactors), commented regarding the apostolic authorship of the Fourth Gospel:

> La maniere dont le même Origene parle dans son Commentaire sur l'Evangile de S. Jean . . . me fait juger qu'il y avoit des doutes parmi les anciens Docteurs de l'Eglise sur la verité de ces Livres attribués aux Apôtres. Bien que le sentiment commun fût qu'ils n'en étoient point les auteurs, mais qu'ils avoient été seulement publiés sous leurs noms comme contenant leur doctrine . . .[11]

Simon was ahead of his time in expressing reservations regarding the apostolic authorship of the Gospels.[12] As Kümmel notes, Simon also pointed out that the superscriptions of the Gospels, with their specifications of authorship, do not come from the Evangelists themselves.[13]

Cotoni refers to further doubts among French New Testament scholars in the eighteenth century:

---

[11]Richard Simon, *Nouvelles Observations sur le Texte et les Versions du Nouveau Testament* (Paris, 1695), 3: "The manner in which Origen speaks in his commentary on the Gospel of John . . . leads me to believe that there were doubts among the ancient Church Fathers regarding the veracity of the books attributed to the apostles. While there was a consensus that they [the apostles] were not the authors, yet they [the Gospels] had only been published under their names as containing their teaching . . ."

[12]Cf. Barnabas Lindars, "Part III: The New Testament," in *The Study and Use of the Bible*, John Rogerson, Christopher Rowland, and Barnabas Lindars (Grand Rapids: Eerdmans, 1988), 324.

[13]Kümmel, *History of Investigation*, 43-45, quoting Simon, *Histoire critique du texte*, 14-15 (note 35). For important treatments of Simon see also John D. Woodbridge, "Richard Simon, le père de la critique biblique," in *Le Grand Siècle et la Bible*, Bible du tous les temps 6 (trans. Jean-Robert Armogathe; Paris: Beauchesne, 1989), 193-206; and id., "German Reactions to Richard Simon," in *Historische Kritik und biblischer Kanon in der deutschen Aufklärung*, Wolfsbütteler Forschungen 41 (ed. Henning Graf Reventlow, Walter Sparn, and John Woodbridge; Wiesbaden: Harrassowitz, 1988), 65-87. For an important treatment of eighteenth-century French New Testament scholarship, cf. Marie-Hélène Cotoni, *L'exegèse du Nouveau Testament dans la philosophie française du dix-huitième siècle* (Oxford: Voltaire Foundation at the Taylor Institution, 1984).

Dans *La Religion chrétienne analysée* on émet des doutes sur Jean "l'evangeliste" . . . *Les Notes* . . . indiquent les dates de . . . 97 pour Jean . . .; et les *Réflexions sur la religion* répètent encore que les faits des évangiles ne sont pas assurés par des témoins oculaires et contemporains. L'auteur de la Disserta-*tion sur la résurrection* réserve pour sa part sa critique à l'évangile de Jean, "écrit mystique que, pour de bonnes raisons, on croit très postérieur à celui dont il porte le nom" (Ms Mazarine 1168, p. 13), et à son auteur, "fourbe qui a écrit sous le nom de Saint Jean [. . .] plus de soixante ans après la mort du Christ" (p. 98). L'auteur des *Notes d'Hobbes* estime que l'évangile de Jean, d'après ses dogmes et son style, serait postérieur de trois siècles à la mort de Jésus . . .

D'autres, comme Du Laurens, sont imprégnés d'un scepticisme général . . .: "Qui nous assurera que les évangélistes ont assisté à tout ce qu'ils ont écrit?" . . . madame Du Châtelet affirme que Matthieu et Jean ne sont probablement pas les auteurs des évangiles qui portent leurs noms . . . De même, . . . en supposant le philosophe platonicien qui écrivit l' "évangile de Jean" à l'apôtre Jean, fils de pêcheur, qui ne savait peut-être pas lire, Raby veut démystifier ses lecteurs: la tradition chrétienne est non seulement incertaine mais mensongère.[14]

Eighteenth-century England

Anthony Collins vs. William Whiston (1667–1752). In the England of the early eighteenth century, *An Help for the more Easy and Clear Understanding of the Holy Scriptures: Being the Gospel of St. John* begins as follows:

As is attested by the Ancients of Best Authority, so it is generally agreed on by the more Learned among the Moderns, that St John writ this Gospel at Ephesus in Asia; namely when he was return'd thither, after his Banishment in the Isle of Patmos. And consequently it is agreed among the Learned, that He writ it A. D.

---

[14]Cf. Cotoni, *L'Exegèse*, 139. "In *The Christian Religion Analyzed* one expresses doubts about John "the evangelist" . . . The *Notes* . . . indicate the dates of . . . 97 for John . . .; and the *Reflections about Religion* repeat again that the facts of the Gospels are not assured by contemporary eye-witnesses. The author of the *Dissertation about the Resurrection* saves up for himself the critique of the Gospel of John, "written mysteriously for good reasons, one believes, much later than by him whose name it bears," and regarding its author, "pseudepigraphically writing under the name of St. John [. . .] more than sixty years after the death of Christ" (p. 98). The author of the *Notes by Hobbes* estimates that the Gospel of John, according to its teachings and style, was written three centuries after the death of Jesus . . . Others, like Du Laurens, are infected by a general scepticism . . .: 'Who assures us that the evangelists had a part in all that was written? . . . Ms Du Châtelet affirms that Matthew and John are probably not the authors of the Gospels that bear their names . . . Similarly, . . . by opposing the Platonic philosopher who wrote 'the Gospel of John' to the apostle John, son of a fisherman who could not possibly know how to read, Raby wants to enlighten his readers: the Christian tradition is not only uncertain but false."

97 or 98 or thereabout. And as it was the Last of St John's Writings; so it was the Last written of All the Books, that make up the New Testament.

The End or Design of St John in writing this Gospel was this: to put a Stop to the Heresy of Those who deny the Divinity of Christ, or that He had an Existence before his Incarnation and from all Eternity; and to supply those Passages or Parts of the Gospel History, which were omitted by the three former Evangelists.[15]

This calm consensus, however, would soon erode and make way to controversy. In 1724, Anthony Collins published his *The Grounds and Reasons of the Christian Religion,* in which he referred to the writings of William Whiston. This writer, in an "Essay on the Apostolic Constitutions wherein is proved that they are the most sacred of the canonical books of the New Testament,"[16] had argued that the books of the New Testament were all occasional books. Collins contended that Jesus or his apostles should have clearly settled the question which writings were canonical rather than leaving it up to later councils to dispute with one another "about the genuineness of all books bearing the names of the Apostles."[17] To remedy this perceived difficulty, Whiston postulated the genuineness of a document called "Apostolic Constitutions," which, he alleged, provided the kind of early support Collins demanded. However, Whiston also included other early writings such as Clement's two epistles to the Corinthians in the canon.[18] Thus, as Collins observed, Whiston in effect denied divine inspiration, since he contended that the New Testament writings had been altered and changed and were contradicting each other, and that the authors themselves might have been mistaken.[19]

With all his peculiarities, the writers of the *Cambridge History of the Bible* can still call Whiston "a traditional harmonist . . . perhaps the last wholehearted supporter of the Chillingworth thesis in his day."[20] Notably,

---

[15] Edw. Wells, *An Help For the more Easy and Clear Understanding of the Holy Scriptures: Being the Gospel of John* (London, 1719), 1.

[16] In *Primitive Christianity Reviv'd,* Vol. III (London, 1711).

[17] Collins, *Grounds and Reasons,* 17.

[18] Whiston, *Apostolic Constitutions,* 67-68.

[19] Cf. Collins, *Grounds and Reasons,* 18-19. Cf. Whiston, *Apostolic Constitutions,* 4: ". . . to examin whether this Book, when purg'd from a few Corruptions of later date, from which neither these, nor the other inspired Books of the New Testament are intirely clear, be not really deriv'd from our blessed Lord himself by the Body of his Holy Apostles . . ."

[20] *Cambridge History of the Bible—The West from the Reformation to the Present Day,* Vol. III (ed. S. L. Greenslade; Cambridge: Cambridge University Press, 1983 [1963]), 242-43, referring to William Chillingworth, *The Religion of Protestants: a Safe Way to Salvation* (Oxford, 1638), who had coined the maxim,

Whiston takes a very conservative position on the authorship of the Gospel of John, dating it in CE 63. He writes,

That this Gospel was Written so early, appears highly probable to me on the Accounts following. (1) The frequent Citation of it, and the Number of the Citations in the *Constitutions*, ne fewer than Fifty Five, plainly infer this degree of Antiquity. (2) Many of the Antient MSS, and Versions affirm that it was Written about the 30th, 31st, or 32nd Year after our Saviours Ascension: Which agrees exactly to the Time here assign'd. (3) Almost all the Commentators since Theophylact agree to the same Time. (4) John's speaking of the Pool of Bethesday, in the present Tense . . ., better agrees to the Time here assign'd, before the Destruction of Jerusalem, when that Pool and Porch were certainly in being, than to the Time afterward, when probably both were destroyed. (5) That Occasion of John's Writing his Gospel mention'd by the Antients, viz. the bringing the other Three Gospels to him, and his observing their Deficiency as to the Acts of Christ, before the Baptist's Imprisonment, does much better agree with this Time, just after the Publication of those Gospels, than with that above Thirty Years later, to which its Writing is now ordinarily ascrib'd. (6) That other occasion, of its Writing mention'd by the Antients viz. in opposition to the Heresies of Cerinthus and Ebion, which deny'd the Pre-existence and Divinity of our Savior, does also better agree with the former Time, when those Heresies first sprang up, than to that so much later, just before the end of the Century, which is usually assign'd to it. (7) No Original Writings of our Religion, which quote the other Three Gospels with any frequency, do omit this: Nay I believe no such Time of their Writing as is usually suppos'd: Which yet must in all probability have been the case, had the other Three Gospels been Publish'd between Thirty and Forty Years earlier than this before us. (8) After all, what some very Ancient Testimonies speak of, that this Gospel was Written with the Apocalypse in Patmus, a little before the Death of John, A. D. 96, is a plain mistake, since the Apocalypse itself, which was seen in Patmus, was Written not there but at Ephesus. And if that be suppos'd a mistake as to place only, but not as in time, yet will this be easily accounted for on our Hypothesis, wherein the first Twenty Chapters are suppos'd Written, A. d. 63, but the last is freely own'd to be later, and not long before the Death of John. Which indeed its Nature and Circumstances plainly imply: But so, that it appears as an evident Appendix, added after the compiling the main part of the Book: Which indeed seems to be the case, as to the greatest part of the last Chapter of Mark also. And that this is not a meer Hypothesis, made upon an emergent difficulty, in way of Evasion only, is evident, because these very *Constitutions*, which have no fewer than Fifty Five Citations or References to this Gospel, have yet not one Citation from, or Reference to that last Chapter, as will easily be observ'd on a particular Examination . . . All those Hypotheses or Solutions of difficulties, which depend on the late Writing the main of John's Gospel, after the Destruction of Jerusalem, are without Foundation, and must be laid aside unless we suppose, that when he wrote his last Chapter long afterward, he alter'd any of his former Expressions, and so suited them to those later Circumstances. Which indeed is not impossible to be suppos'd. Yet, because such an Opinion, without some Proof, must be very

---

"The Bible, I say, the Bible only, is the religion of Protestants" (ibid., 175).

weak, all those Hypotheses and Solutions, will in the meantime deserve to be esteem'd very weak also.[21]

Whiston assigned great weight to the attestation of the Fourth Gospel by the *Apostolic Constitutions*. His opinions that John 21 was a later addition and that the evangelist may at the occasion of adding chap. 21 also have altered other parts of the Gospel are worthy of note as well. Whiston indicates that the common view of his day was that the Fourth Gospel was written by John at around CE 90. Interestingly, he believes that not only the Gospel of John, but also the Apocalypse, was written in Ephesus.

Another Deist of the first half of the eighteenth century, Thomas Chubb, writing in 1738, also assumed the apostolic authorship of the Fourth Gospel:

> These propositions, for any thing that appears to the contrary, are only the private opinion of St John, who wrote history of Christ's life and ministry . . . And therefore whether Christ was the Logos or Word, whether he was with God, and was God, or whether he made all things in the sense in which St John uses those terms, or not, is of no consequence to us . . . Besides, we do not know what was the ground and foundation of St John's opinion with respect to those points, and therefore we cannot possibly form a judgment . . .[22]

Generally, the British Deists of the eighteenth century were more concerned with general philosophical and theological arguments than their detailed application to biblical studies. As Kümmel notes, "All these ideas of the Deists were the result, not of a historical approach to the New Testament, but of a rationalistic critique of traditional Christianity."[23] Yet, the spirit of "free investigation" unleashed by Descartes and embraced by Locke, Hume, and Spinoza spread irresistibly. In 1776, a volume appears in London with the title *A Liberal and Minute Inspection of the Holy Gospel*, quoting John Locke's maxim that

> We should keep a perfect Indifferency for all Opinions; so as not to with any of them true, in Preference to others; but (being indifferent) receive and embrace them according as evidence—and that alone; gives the Attestation of Truth.

First Frontal Challenge: Edward Evanson (1731-1805). Edward Evanson, a writer already mentioned above, saw himself as operating within this

---

[21]Whiston, *Apostolic Constitutions*, 38–41.

[22]Thomas Chubb, *The true gospel of Jesus Christ asserted* (London, 1738), 47.

[23]Kümmel, *History of Investigation*, 57–58.

scope of scientific freedom and objectivity. In 1792, he authored a work challenging the traditional view of the apostolic authorship of the Fourth Gospel entitled *The Dissonance of the Four generally received Evangelists and the Evidence of their Authenticity examined.*[24] Evanson notes at the outset the "striking difference" between the language of the Apocalypse and of the Fourth Gospel.[25]

Erasmus, in his *Libri duo de authoritate libri apocalypsis beati Ioannis apostoli* (Antwerp, 1530), had already expressed doubts that the same man had written the Gospel of John, the Epistles of John, and the Apocalypse of John, in light of the striking differences in style exhibited in these works.[26] Frans Tittelmans, his opponent, immediately retorted that John the Evangelist wrote all these works, but accommodated his style to his various messages, circumstances, and audiences.[27] In 1532, Erasmus agreed that, if the church pronounced John the Evangelist the author of the Apocalypse, he would drop his criticism and accept the traditional teaching regarding its authorship.[28] The Gospel of John, however, Erasmus attributed without hesitation to John the unimpeachably orthodox evangelist.[29]

Dionysius of Alexandria (bishop c. 247–265), a student of Origen, had already stressed the linguistic and stylistic differences between the Revela-

---

[24] Ipswich, 1792. References are to the 2d ed., Gloucester, 1805, 267–304.

[25] Ibid., 267.

[26] Cf. Jerry H. Bentley, *Humanists and Holy Writ—New Testament Scholarship in the Renaissance* (Princeton, NJ: Princeton University Press, 1983), 203.

[27] Ibid. Cf. also id., "New Testament Scholarship at Louvain in the Early Sixteenth Century," in *Studies in Medieval and Renaissance History*, n.s. 2 (1979): 51–79, esp. 69–79.

[28] Bentley, *Humanists and Holy Writ*, 205, referring to LB, 9:863 D–868 B.

[29] Cf. ibid., 160. In the dedicatory letter of his *Paraphrasis in Evangelium secundum Joannem* (1523), Erasmus summarizes his views on the authorship of the Gospel of John as follows: "When our Lord Jesus Christ's life and teaching had already been spread widely through the world by the preaching of the apostles and the writing of this Gospel, not so much to put together a gospel-history as to supply certain things that the other evangelists had passed over, since they seemed not unworthy of record. But the chief reason for his writing this Gospel is thought to be the desire to assert the divinity of Christ against the heresies which were already like evil tares sprouting up in the good crop; in particular those of the Cerinthians and the Ebionites, who apart from other errors taught that Christ had been nothing more than a man and had not existed at all before he was born of Mary . . ." (in *Collected Works of Erasmus*, Vol. 46; ed. Robert D. Sider, trans. Jane E. Phillips [Toronto/London: Toronto University Press, 1991], 11).

tion and the other Johannine writings. He concluded that the Revelation could not have been written by the author of the Gospel and the Epistles of John, and that the Revelation, unlike the Gospel and the Epistles, was not apostolic in origin.[30]

But let us return to Evanson. We have seen that his observation of stylistic differences between John's Gospel and the Apocalypse is hardly original. Evanson's resolution of the perceived difficulty, however, is rather interesting. He first states that,

> To remove so obvious a difficulty in the way of attributing these two works to the same writer, commentators are accustomed to insinuate, (but without any proof of the fact) that, as John wrote his Gospel many years after he had written the Apocalypse, he had acquired . . . a much better knowledge of the Greek . . . and, on that account, the style of his later work is quite unlike that of his first.[31]

Evanson immediately proceeds to state his own thesis:

> The same critics might, with equal reason . . have remarked also, that the same superior advantage of time and experience had given him a knowledge of the Platonic philosophy, of which, in his earlier days, he was entirely ignorant; for whoever the writer of this Gospel really was, it must be evident to every competent, unprejudiced judge, who reads it in the original . . . that he was well acquainted with the writings of Plato.[32]

Evanson's contention that "it must be evident to every competent, unprejudiced judge," intermingles an unconscious dogmatism with an appeal to reasonable, scientific judgment. Like Simon, who aspired to be "sans prejugé," like Spinoza, who "determined to examine the Bible afresh in a careful, impartial, and unfettered spirit, making no assumptions concerning it,"[33] Evanson basks in his supposed impartiality. While no one follows him today in seeing Platonic philosophy in the Fourth Gospel, the avenue through which Evanson came to develop his thesis should be noted. It was the observation of stylistic differences between two works traditionally attributed to the same author, the apostle John, in Revelation and the Fourth Gospel.

---

[30]Cf. Kümmel, *History of Investigation*, 15–18, quoting Dionysius' view from Eusebius, *Ecclesiastical History*, 7.25.

[31]Ibid., 267–68.

[32]Ibid., 268.

[33]Baruch Spinoza, *Tractatus Theologico-Politicus* (New York: Dover, 1951), 8.

Evanson doubts that any writer would speak of himself as John
allegedly did in John 21:24: "This is the disciple who testifies of these
things and wrote these things, and we know that his testimony is true."
Those who answer by contending that chap. 21 was a later addition by the
church of Ephesus, Evanson challenges by noting the stylistic unity of the
twenty-first with all the other chapters, so that "the whole seems to merit to
be accounted equally spurious, or equally genuine and authentic."[34]

Evanson then proceeds to investigate perceived contradictions
between the Synoptic Gospels and the Gospel of John. He observes "a
gross contradiction" between John and "the pretended Matthew" (thus
questioning the apostle Matthew's authorship of the Gospel traditionally
attributed to him as well) in John's claim "that John the Baptist declared
he did not know Jesus to be the destined Messiah, till he saw the Holy
Spirit descending on him; whereas the Gospel of Matthew, c. iii. v. 14, informs us that he knew him as soon as he came to him . . ."[35]

Later Evanson calls the resurrection of Lazarus as narrated in John 11
"a legend which, as far as I am capable of judging, has many strong marks
upon it of fictitious falsehood; but not one single feature of probability
belonging to it."[36] Evanson finds it especially difficult to see why, if Lazarus
was such a beloved friend of Jesus', "his miraculous restoration to life,
should not have been repeatedly mentioned by Luke, in both his his-
tories."[37] Evanson fails to see any "purpose whatsoever" for this miracle.[38]
It is noteworthy that Evanson strongly prefers Luke's Gospel for its historical veracity, setting aside the Gospel of John, while decades later
Schleiermacher in Germany still upholds the primacy of the Fourth
Gospel.[39] Moreover, Evanson objects to the historicity of the Lazarus
miracle, since

> . . . the very relation of the circumstances of this pretended miracle asserts an
> absolute impossibility; for it tells us, that, at our Lord's command, Lazarus came
> forth from from [sic] the sepulchre, though he was bound hand and foot, with
> grave clothes, and his face was bound about with a napkin, and that, after he was
> come forth, Jesus bid them loose him and let him go.[40]

---

[34]Ibid., 269.
[35]Ibid.
[36]Ibid., 295.
[37]Ibid.
[38]Ibid., 298.
[39]See footnote 5 above.
[40]Ibid., 298-99.

Evanson exclaims, "Such, and so very different from those recorded by Luke, are the miracles of what the orthodox receive for the Gospel according to the Apostle John!"[41] Lastly, Evanson finds the Fourth Gospel falling short of "the grand internal testimony of authenticity, indispensably necessary in every scripture, which contains the history of a supernatural revelation, predictions of future events, verified by their actual completion."[42]

Thus Evanson did not only question the apostolic authorship of the Fourth Gospel but also its historical veracity. He began by observing stylistic differences between the book of Revelation and the Gospel of John, and apparent contradictions between the Synoptic Gospels and the Fourth Gospel. His solution is to attribute the Fourth Gospel's authorship to a later Platonic writer, and to give preference especially to Luke among the Synoptists with regard to historical veracity.

Evanson's theses did not go unchallenged. A brief interchange ensued, in which Joseph Priestley and David Simpson defended the apostolic authorship of the Fourth Gospel (both in 1793), and Evanson responded to both writers in the following year (1794).[43] The prestigious Bampton lectures in 1810 were devoted to a critique of Evanson as well.[44]

Conservatism in Eighteenth-century Germany[45]

German scholarship at the middle of the 18th century still held firmly to the apostolic origin and the historical reliability of John's Gospel.

---

[41]Ibid., 299.

[42]Ibid.

[43]Priestley, "Letters to a Young Man" (1793); Evanson, "A Letter to Dr. Priestley's Young Man" (1794). Cf. Luthardt, *St. John the Author of the Fourth Gospel*, 283–84.

[44]Thomas Falconer, *Certain Principles in Evanson's "Dissonance of the Four generally received Evangelists,"' &c. examined in eight discourses delivered before the University of Oxford* (Oxford: University Press, 1811).

[45]The separate treatments of eighteenth-century France, England, and Germany should not be taken as an acknowledgment that scholars in these three countries operated in isolation from one another. It seems that the lines of influence went more from England and France to Germany than *vice versa*, to some extent due to the few number of British scholars who were able to read German. Cf. Henning Graf Reventlow, *The Authority of the Bible and the Rise of the Modern World* (trans. John Bowden; Philadelphia: Fortress, 1984), 410–14. Cf. also the brief summaries in Lindars, *Study and Use*, 326–29, and F. F. Bruce, "The History of New Testament Study," in *New Testament Interpretation* (ed. I. H. Marshall; Exeter: Paternoster, 1977), 37.

Johann Albrecht Bengel (1687–1752). The Swabian pietist and prolific textual critic Johann Albrecht Bengel considered John to be the major evangelist, whose Gospel was the most indispensable. According to Bengel (writing in 1742), "His Evangelistarum princeps est, quo omnium minime queamus carere; sed permulta, a tribus prioribus exhibita, praesupponens . . . Stilo moderno Johannis librum Supplementum dixeris historiae evangeliae per Matthaeum, Marcum et Lucam descriptae."[46] Bengel also sought to maintain a proper balance between the historical and theological aspects of Scripture:

> The historical matters of Scripture . . . constitute as it were the bones of the system; whereas the spiritual matters are its muscles, blood-vessels, and nerves. As the bones are necessary to the human system, so Scripture must have its historical matters. The expositor who nullifies the historical ground-work of Scripture for the sake of finding only spiritual truths everywhere, brings death on all correct interpretation. Those expositions are the safest which keep closest to the text.[47]

Siegmund Jacob Baumgarten (1706–1757). Baumgarten's lecture notes on the Fourth Gospel were posthumously published by his foremost student Johann Salomo Semler.[48] Baumgarten begins his discussion of the Fourth Gospel with the categorical assertion, "Der Verfasser ist Johannes."[49] Later Baumgarten discusses the "Göttlichkeit" ("divine character") of the book. He gives as the first demonstration of the Fourth Gospel's "divine character" the credibility of the author:

> Die Erzählungen haben die gröste Glaubwürdigkeit für sich a. Auf Seiten der erzählenden Person. Johannes befand sich in dem wirklichen Stande, die erzälten Dinge zu wissen, indem er theils ein Augenzeuge dessen, was er erzält, gewesen, Joh. 1,14, 19,35, 21,24, 1 Joh 1, 1.2.3; theils aber auch die göttliche Eingebung erhalten, die, als an die Apostel verheissen, Johannes ausdrücklich Joh. 16,13, 14,26, 15,26–27 und an andern Orten erwänt. Ueberdem so kan er

---

[46]Johannes Albrecht Bengel, *Gnomon Novi Testamenti, in quo ex nativa verborum vi simplicitas, profunditas, concinnitas salubritas sensuum caelestium indicatur* (3d ed.; Stuttgart: Steinkopf, 1860 [Tübingen, 1742]), 300. "He is the chief of the Evangelists, whom we could least afford to be without; he takes for granted very much that is recorded in the three former Gospels . . . In modern expression, one may call John's Book a Supplement to the Gospel History, as set forth by Matthew, Mark, and Luke."

[47]Quoted in Bengel, *Gnomon,* Vol. V (Edinburgh: T. & T. Clark, 1860), xvii.

[48]Siegmund Jacob Baumgarten, *Auslegung des Evangelii St. Johannis* (Halle, 1762).

[49]Ibid., 1. "The author is John."

keine Unwarheiten haben vortragen wollen, indem gar kein Grund zur Mutmassung angegeben werden kan, weil Johannes nicht den geringsten Vortheil davon hätte erwarten können zur Zeit der überhand nemenden heidnischen Verfolgung. Ja es ist nicht einmal möglich, daß Johannes Unwahrheiten schreiben können, da er nach den andern drey Evangelisten geschrieben, und zu einer Zeit, da noch viele lebten, die unstreitig von Christo gehöret hatten.[50]

This indeed is a very strong statement in support of the integrity and apostolic authorship of the Fourth Gospel.

Johann Salomo Semler (1725-1791). Baumgarten's student Johann Salomo Semler published his *Treatise on the Free Investigation of the Canon* in 1771-75. In it Semler distinguishes between the Word of God and Holy Scripture, and contends that not all parts of the canon are inspired or authoritative.[51] Semler also wrote a *Paraphrasis on the Fourth Gospel*.[52] Semler believed that the Gospel of John was actually the first Gospel.[53]

Hermann Samuel Reimarus (1694-1768). Prior to his death in 1768, Hermann Reimarus expressed a preference for the Synoptic Gospels by relying primarily on them in his effort to reconstruct Jesus' life. Reimarus urged the interpreter to distinguish between the teaching of the apostles and the teaching of Jesus himself. He writes:

---

[50]Ibid., 6. "The narrations can claim highest credibility: a. Regarding the narrating person. John was in the real position to know the things he told, since he was partly an eye-witness (John 1:14; 19:35; 21:24; 1 John 1:1-3), but partly also since he had received divine inspiration which John explicitly mentions as having been promised to the apostles (John 16:13; 14:26; 15:26-27). Moreover, he cannot have wanted to perpetrate untruths since no motivation can be cited, since John could not have expected the slightest advantage at the time of escalating pagan persecution. Yes, it is not even possible that John could have written untruths, since he wrote after the three evangelists, and at a time when still many were alive who had undoubtedly heard of Christ."

[51]Kümmel, *History of Investigation*, 63.

[52]Johann Salomo Semler, *Paraphrasis Evangelii Johannis* (Halle, 1771). Cf. also Gottfried Hornig, *Die Anfänge der historisch-kritischen Theologie: Johann Salomo Semlers Schriftverständnis und seine Stellung zu Luther* (Göttingen: Vandenhoeck & Ruprecht, 1961).

[53]Cf. Lange, *Schriften Johannis*, 24-25: ". . . die semlerische Hypothese, dass es das erste von allen Evangelien gewesen sey, ist mir auch nicht wahrscheinlich" ("Semler's hypothesis that it was the first of the Gospels, does not seem probable to me").

> I find ample cause, however, to separate completely that which the apostles set forth in their own writing from that which Jesus himself really spoke and taught in the course of his own life. For the apostles were themselves teachers and had therefore set forth their own teachings and never claimed that Jesus, their Master, had himself said and taught everything they had written. The four evangelists, in contrast, present themselves only as historians reporting that which was most important of Jesus' sayings and actions. Now if we want to know what the teaching of Jesus actually was, what he said and preached . . . we are asking for something that happened in history, and therefore this information has to be taken from the reports of the historical writers . . .[54]

Reimarus concludes,

> Because the apostles themselves do not claim to be historians of the teaching of their master, but wanted to be teachers themselves; consequently, after we have discovered from the four sources of the historians what the genuine teaching and purpose of Jesus was, only then is it possible to judge accurately whether the apostles really have taught the same teaching and purpose as their master.[55]

However, it is noteworthy that despite his overall skeptical stance Reimarus held on to the notion of the apostolic authorship of the Gospels (including John).[56]

Johann Gottfried Herder (1744–1803). In 1780, Johann Gottfried Herder went on record as asserting the incompatibility of the Synoptics and the Fourth Gospel. He asserted the priority of Mark and the interpretive character of the Fourth Gospel.[57] Herder was a precursor of form criticism, and his comments on the authorship of the Gospels seem astonishingly modern:

> The whole idea of our evangelists as scribes assembling, enlarging, improving, collating, and comparing tracts is strange to, and remote from, that of all ancient writings that speak of their activities, and even more foreign to conclusions drawn from observing them themselves, and most of all to their situation, their motivation, and the purpose of their Gospels . . .
>   Furthermore, their whole appearance belies the notion that they drew from one so-called Primal Gospel. Neither apostolic nor church history knows of any

---

[54]Hermann Samuel Reimarus, *The Goal of Jesus and his Disciples* (ed. George Wesley Buchanan; Leiden: E. J. Brill, 1970), 37.

[55]Ibid.

[56]Cf. ibid., 36–37, 41.

[57]In *Briefe das Studium der Theologie betreffend* (1st ed.; 1780–81; 2d ed., 1785–86). Cf. Albert Schweitzer, *The Quest of the Historical Jesus—A Critical Study of Its Progress from Reimarus to Wrede* (trans. W. Montgomery; New York: Macmillan, 1968 [1906]), 34–37; *Cambridge History of the Bible* III, 272.

such Primal Gospel; no church father in combating the false gospels appeals to such a Primal Gospel as to the fount of truth.

However, it was inevitable that in the course of their instruction these oral evangelists should acquire a circle of followers within which their message was preserved, and this circle was that which the apostles themselves possessed from the beginning of their proclamation of the Gospels.[58]

Johann David Michaelis (1717-1791). Johann David Michaelis wrote a very influential *Einleitung in die göttlichen Schriften des Neuen Bundes* in 1750, based entirely on Simon.[59] Still, Kümmel credits Michaelis with having "inaugurated the science of New Testament introduction."[60] In his *Einleitung* Michaelis was concerned with the origin of individual writings of the New Testament. He poses the question regarding the "divine character" of individual Scriptures in connection with the question of their apostolic authorship.[61] Michaelis presupposes that only those writings of the New Testament that stem from apostles are canonical and thus inspired. This question of apostolic origin is to be clarified by historical research.[62] In his *Anmerkungen zum Evangelio Johannis*, Michaelis comments on John 19:33-35, affirming John to be an eye-witness:

Für uns ist das, was Johannes hier und im Folgenden als Augenzeuge erzählt, deshalb wichtig . . . Johannes selbst macht diese Anmerkung nicht, und hat bey seiner Erzählung vielleicht gar nicht den Zweck, einem solchen Zweifel oder Einwurf gegen die Wahrheit des Todes Jesu zu begegnen: ihm wird das, was er sahe, deshalb merkwürdig, weil er darin zwey Stellen des Alten Testaments an Christo buchstäblich erfüllet findet, und darum zeichnet er es auch seinern Lesern auf.[63]

---

[58]Johann Gottfried Herder, in *Herder's Collected Works* (ed. B. Suphan; Vol. XIX, Berlin: Weidmannsche Buchhandlung, 1880 [1796-97]), quoted in Kümmel, *History of Investigation*, 81 (cf. notes 97-99, 418).

[59]Cf. Kümmel, *History of Investigation*, n. 63, 415-16, and n. 79, 417.

[60]Ibid., 69.

[61]Cf. also id., " 'Einleitung in das Neue Testament' als theologische Aufgabe," *EvT* 19 (1959): 4-16.

[62]Cf. Kümmel, *History of Investigation*, 69-70. Cf. also n. 81, 417, where Kümmel quotes Michaelis from the fourth edition of his *Introduction* (Göttingen, 1788), 277ff: ". . . the collecting of the writings that we now call the New Testament for the most part took place after the death of the apostles and must be very old, so that for this reason, it is concealed in the dark of unhistorical times."

[63]Johann David Michaelis, *Anmerkungen zum Evangelio Johannis: Anmerkungen für Ungelehrte zu seiner Uebersetzung des Neuen Testaments*, Vol. II (Göttingen, 1790), 203. "What John narrates here and subsequently as an eye-witness is important to us because . . . John himself does not note this, and he perhaps does not have the purpose in his narration to refute the objection against the truth of Jesus' death: he deems what he saw noteworthy because he finds two passages of the Old Testament literally fulfilled in Christ, and therefore records it

Later Michaelis writes, commenting on John 21:24-25,

> Dis halten einige für eine Nachschrift der Aeltesten zu Ephesus, die uns das
> Evangelium Johannis übergeben, und mit ihrem Zeugniß als wahrhaftig und
> glaubwürdig bestätigt haben. Ich glaube es nicht. Die Worte sind ganz in
> Johannis Schreibart: und wenn die Aeltesten zu Ephesus, oder was für Leute es
> sonst seyn mochten, (denn das könnte man kaum errathen) dem Evangelio ein
> Zeugniß seiner Aechtheit, und dem Evangelisten selbst ein Zeugniß daß er die
> Wahrheit schreibe, hätten geben wollen, so hätten sie wenigstens darunter
> schreiben sollen, wer sie wären, denn auf ein solch Zeugnis von einem
> Ungenannten unterschreibenden würde doch wol kein nur halb vernünftiger sich
> verlassen, sondern erst fragen, wer bist du denn selbst?
> Ich trete also denen bey, die es für Johannis eigene Worte halten, und
> denn ist, wir wissen, so viel als, ich hoffe, daß alle wissen, es ist unter uns allen
> bekannt, daß dieser Jünger glaubwürdig sey.[64]

Similarly, in his *Syntagma Commentationum* Michaelis calls John "der
einzige Augenzeuge des Leidens Christi unter den Evangelisten" ("the
only eye-witness of Christ's passion among the evangelists").[65] In discussing the different data regarding the hour of Christ's death in the Gospels,
Michaelis remarks,

> Die Schwürigkeit ist desto erheblicher, weil sie den wichtigsten Theil der Ge-
> schichte unseres Heilandes, nemlich seinen Tod, welchen zu leiden er eben in
> die Welt gesandt war, betrift. Wozu noch dieses kommt, daß dieser Zeitfehler
> dem glaubwürdigsten und grösten Zeugen des Leidens Christ selbst, und nicht
> sowol dem Evangelisten Marco beyzumessen seyn würde, als Johanni.[66]

---

for his readers."

[64]Ibid., 229. "Some consider this to be an epilogue by the elders at Ephesus
who transmit the Gospel of John and confirmed it as true and faithful by their
witness. I do not believe this. The words are wholly in John's style: and if the
elders at Ephesus, or whoever it might be, (for one could hardly guess it) had
wanted to attest to the genuineness of the Gospel, and to the evangelist's
truthfulness, they should at least have added who they were, for no somewhat
reasonable person would rely on the testimony of an unnamed, but first ask, who
are you yourself? Thus I join those who take these to be John's own words, and I
hope we all know that it is widely known that this disciple is trustworthy."

[65]Johann David Michaelis, *Syntagma Commentationum* (Göttingen,
1759-67), 44.

[66]Ibid., 45. "The difficulty is all the greater since it concerns the most
important part of our Savior's story, i.e. his death which to suffer he was sent into
the world. To which has to be added that this error of time would have been
committed by John, the most trustworthy and the greatest witness of Christ's
passion himself, rather than by the evangelist Mark." Note Michaelis' great
hesitation to charge John with error, and his effort to find an explanation that
reconciles the different ways of reckoning time by John and Mark.

Kümmel is therefore correct when he summarizes that "the very pioneer of the ground-breaking attempts to give a historical explanation of the origin of the Gospels [i.e., Michaelis] had regarded John's Gospel as an especially valuable historical work and as apostolic in authorship."[67] However, even as ardent a supporter of the apostolic authorship of the Fourth Gospel as Schleiermacher could insist that in apostolic times very probably anyone conscious of being in essential agreement with what an apostle had taught "was able to regard the publication of his writing under the apostle's name as a wholly acceptable fiction" and that Greek literature proves that such pseudepigraphy was common.[68]

Thus, while Evanson in England cast severe doubts on the apostolic authorship of the Gospel of John, scholarship in Germany was generally more conservative. As late as 1797, Samuel Gottlieb Lange (1767–1823) could write, "Daß Johannes der Verfasser dieser Schrift sey, leidet keinen Zweifel."[69] But Germany, too, had "its Evanson."

The First Doubts in Late Eighteenth-Century Germany

As in England, it was the closing years of the eighteenth century that saw the emergence of doubts regarding the apostolic authorship of John's Gospel.

Jacob Christoph Rudolf Eckermann (1754–1837). In 1796 Jacob Christoph Rudolf Eckermann writes "Ueber die eigentlich sichern Gründe des Glaubens an die Hauptthatsachen der Geschichte Jesu, und über die wahrscheinliche Entstehung der Evangelien und der Apostelgeschichte."[70] We will trace Eckermann's argumentation in detail, since his work will exercise significant influence on later studies on the authorship of the Fourth Gospel.

---

[67]Kümmel, *History of Investigation,* 85.

[68]Cf. ibid., 84, and n. 106. Kümmel also notes that as early as 1811 Schleiermacher contended that it was more important to decide if a book was canonical or not than to settle questions of authorship since the book could regardless still be canonical (ibid.).

[69]"There is no doubt that John the Evangelist is the author of this work . . ." *Die Schriften Johannis des vertrauten Schülers Jesu* (Weimar: Verlag des Industrie-Comptoirs, 1797), 2:23–24.

[70]"About the actually secure foundations of the faith in the major facts of the story of Jesus, and about the probably origin of the Gospels and Acts." In *Theologische Beyträge,* Vol. V, Pt. 2 (Altona, 1796), 106–256.

Eckermann begins by asserting that the "Hauptthatsachen der Geschichte Jesu einen so hohen Grad der historischen Gewißheit haben, als nur wenige Begebenheiten aus einer so entfernten Zeit ihrer Natur nach haben können."[71] Eckermann then discusses the question of the assessment of the credibility of witnesses. He argues that the testing of an author's trustworthiness is not an outgrowth of general historical scepticism ("einer allgemeinen historischen Zweifelsucht") but a reasonable obligation ("Weg der Vernunft").[72] Eckermann believes especially these four "Hauptthatsachen" to be beyond reasonable doubt: certain historical information regarding the setting of Jesus' life (Tiberius, Pontius Pilate, etc.); Jesus' virtue and moral life; his conducting his life according to his teachings; and that Jesus founded the Christian Church.[73] When the Church selected the four Gospels as canonical in the middle of the second century CE, it used the criterion of tradition: it required the contents of the Gospels to be in conformity with the historical and dogmatic tradition of orthodox churches.[74]

Thus, Eckermann contends, it is impossible to think of a "vorsätzliche und wissentliche Verfälschung der Wahrheit und Abweichung von der Lehre Jesu . . . bis auf die Mitte des zweiten Jahrhunderts."[75] To sum up, the Gospels were found to be in accordance with tradition at the middle of the second century CE; before that time, an adulteration of Jesus' teachings is unthinkable; thus, the Gospels deserve to be trusted.[76] So far, Eckermann's treatment is far from controversial. But, as it turns out, everything said so far is just preliminary to Eckermann's major argument which he states as follows: "Die Gewißheit der Hauptthatsachen der Geschichte Jesu in den Evangelien hängt keinesweges von dem Beweise ab, daß Matthäus, Markus, Lukas und Johannes, diese nach ihnen genannten Evangelien

---

[71]Ibid., 111. "The major facts of Jesus' history have such a high proportion of historical certitude as only few events from such a remote period can have by their nature."

[72]Ibid., 116.

[73]Ibid., 120.

[74]Ibid., 126.

[75]Ibid., 137. "It is impossible to think of a deliberate and knowing falsification of the truth and a deviation from Jesus' teaching . . . until the middle of the second century."

[76]Cf. ibid., 138 and 114-45. At this point Eckermann concurs with Johann Salomo Semler, *Beantwortung der Fragmente eines Ungenannten, insbesonders vom Zweck Jesu und seiner Jünger* (Halle, 1779), 22-23, who contended, against Reimarus, that it was preposterous to think that the disciples would distort Jesus' teachings.

wirklich und vollständig so geschrieben haben, wie wir sie jetzt besitzen!"[77]
Eckermann is quick to assure the reader that

> . . . derjenige, welcher zweifelt, ob Matthäus, Markus, Lukas und Johannes, die
> ihnen beygelegten Evangelien so geschrieben haben, wie wir jetzt sie lesen, nicht
> etwa das Zeugniß eines Apostels, sondern bloß das Zeugniß derjenigen Lehrer
> der Kirche bezweifelt, die bald nach der Mitte des zweyten Jahrhunderts auf
> ihren Konzilien diese vier Evangelien, als Evangelien des Matthäus, Markus,
> Lukas und Johannes, bestätigt und allen übrigen vorgezogen haben.[78]

Eckermann makes much of a passage in Eusebius' *Ecclesiastical History*
3.37, which he takes to support his claim that the Gospels in their
permanent form are a later product from Trajan's time. He holds to the
view of a "gemeinschaftliche Quelle" ("common source") for the first
three Gospels from which they draw in part (cf. Eichhorn). Eckermann
doubts that any of the apostles except Matthew could write.[79] He envisions
a scenario where the apostles are all dead, and only a few very old sur-
vivors of the apostolic era had "schriftliche Aufsätze" ("written essays") by
the original apostles. The term "the Gospels according to" Matthew,
Mark, Luke, and John, then, refers to the Gospels as they were written on
the basis of the reminiscences and instruction of Matthew, Mark, Luke,
and John by later redactors.

". . . und weil sie dem Hauptinhalt nach aus dem Zeugnisse dieser
Männer entstanden waren: so betrachtete man sie in der Folge als
Evangelien des Matthäus, Markus, Lukas und Johannes," Eckermann concludes.[80] He points to Papias' reference to *biblia* ("schriftliche Aufsätze"),
and his comment that oral tradition is to be preferred over written
material.[81] Eckermann notes that only Irenaeus testifies to the apostolic

---

[77]Ibid., 145. "The certitude of the major facts of Jesus' story in the Gospels
does in no way depend on the testimony that Matthew, Mark, Luke, and John did
in fact write the Gospels as we have them today!"

[78]Ibid., 148. ". . . the one who doubts that Matthew, Mark, Luke, and John
wrote the Gospels bearing their names as we read them [the Gospels] now, does
not doubt apostolic testimony but only the testimony of those teachers of the
Church that soon after the middle of the second century CE confirmed those four
Gospels to be the Gospels of Matthew, Mark, Luke, and John and preferred them
to all the other Gospels."

[79]Ib id., 152.

[80]Ibid., 156. ". . . and since they were construed in their main part after the
testimony of those men [the original apostles], they were considered to be the
Gospels of Matthew, Mark, Luke, and John."

[81]Ibid., 159.

authorship of John, and that it is only since then that the Fourth Gospel is established as canonical.[82] Eckermann adds to these objections the one that Paul does not mention the Gospels. He further notes that apostolic instruction was oral—why would the apostles have seen a need to write down their material during their own life time? And finally, in the light of the trauma of the Jews' displacement by the Romans in CE 70, it seems likely that some time passed before the Church found time to write down the Gospel records: in the time of Trajan's reign.[83] Eckermann envisions the genesis of the Gospel of John as follows:

> Dem Evangelium Johannes lagen viele eigenhändige sehr wichtige Aufsätze des Apostels Johannes zum Grunde, worin er die ihm besonders merkwürdigen Reden Jesu sich aufgezeichnet hatte. Diese wurden von einem seiner Freunde, der auch die Geschichte der Leiden Jesu aus seinem Munde gehört hatte, Joh. 19,35 oder sich wenigstens bey andern Augenzeugen nach derselben erkundigt hatte, mit andern theils aus seinem Munde, theils von Freunden der Apostel gesammelten Nachrichten in Verbindung gesetzt.[84]

Eckermann arrives at the closing criteria for authentic apostolic material in the Gospels:

> Je höher diese in den Evangelien enthaltenen Belehrungen sich über die ältern jüdischen und spätern christlichen Vorstellungen erheben, um desto gewisser kannst du seyn, daß sie nicht eine Meinung und Vorstellun gsart anderer Menschen, sondern ächte unmittelbare Lehren Jesu und seiner unmittelbaren ersten Schüler seyn.[85]

Eckermann continues,

> Denn irren konnten sich freylich die redlichen Sammler und Verfasser der Evangelien, indem sie für ächte apostolische Wahrheit hielten, was doch nur die Meinung andrer Christen, und ihre Vorstellung von den Thatsachen war, die sie

---

[82]Cf. ibid., 167, 184, and 198–99.

[83]Ibid., 209.

[84]Ibid., 213. "The Gospel of John was based on many very important essays of the apostle John where he had recorded particularly memorable discourses by Jesus. Those were connected by one of his friends who had also heard the story of Jesus' passion from his own mouth (Jn. 19:35) or who at least had inquired from other eye-witnesses about it, with other material, partially his own, partially from material collected by friends of the apostles."

[85]Ibid., 251. "The farther these instructions included in the Gospels rise above the more ancient Jewish and the later Christian concepts, the more certain can you be that they do not represent an opinion and conception of other men but genuine direct teachings of Jesus and his first disciples."

von andern, oder von den Aposteln gehört hatten. Irren konnten sie ferner in
der Wahl der eignen Art der Erzählung und Darstellung. Was ihnen die
lehrreichste und würdigste Art der Erzählung und Darstellung schien, das ist sie
darum noch nicht nothwendig für einen jeden und für alle Zeiten.[86]

Thus, Eckermann exhorts his readers to discern carefully between out-
moded ways of thought and helpful permanent teaching. In the latter, they
will hear the voice of truth. Eckermann asserts in closing that, in his
opinion, the proper use of the Gospels is actually enhanced by considering them not to be the direct works of the apostles. Otherwise one is guilty
of bibliolatry. Rather than crippling one's reason, one is to sharpen one's
discernment. The preacher will no longer be able to preach without careful selection of authentic material.[87] So Eckermann closes his plea for a
rejection of the apostolic authorship of the Gospels.[88]

Contra Eckermann: Carl Friedrich Stäudlin (1761-1826). Like Erasmus,
Reimarus, Evanson, and others before him, Eckermann did not escape
severe criticism. One of the most resolute opponents was Carl Friedrich
Stäudlin who wrote his "Bemerkungen über den Ursprung der vier
Evangelien und der Apostelgeschichte in Beziehung auf die Untersuchungen des Herrn Doctors Eckermann, in seinen theologischen
Beiträgen" in 1799.[89] After summarizing Eckermann's theory, Stäudlin
sets out to investigate the internal and external evidence to test Eckermann's hypothesis.[90]

Stäudlin especially singles out the following contentions by Eckermann: first, that Jesus' disciples probably could not write, with the excep-

---

[86]Ibid., 251-52. "For err could of course the good collectors and redactors
of the Gospels, in that they considered as genuine apostolic truth what was only
the opinion of other Christians, and their conception of the facts, which they had
heard from others or from the apostles. Err they could further in the choice of
their own way of narration and presentation. What they considered to be the most
instructive and most worthy method of narration and presentation, is therefore not
necessarily for everyone and for all times."

[87]Ibid., 254-55.

[88]Note that Eckermann later modified his views, apparently toward a more
conservative position. Cf. Jacob Christoph Rudolf Eckermann, *Erklärung aller
dunkeln Stellen des Neuen Testaments*, Vol. II (Kiel, 1807). To date I have not
been able to obtain this work.

[89]In *Beiträge zur Philosophie und Geschichte der Religion und Sittenlehre*
(Vol. V, Pt. 2; Lübeck, 1799), 147-207. Other writers opposing aspects of
Eckermann's writings are Gottlob Christian Storr (1798) and Friedrich Gottlieb
Sueskind (1800). Cf. Luthardt, *St. John the Author of the Fourth Gospel*, 285-86.

[90]Ibid., 156.

tion of Matthew; second, that the need to write the Gospels could only have arisen at the end of the first or the beginning of the second century, and Paul's silence about the Gospels; third, the negative portrayal of the disciples, which Eckermann had taken to be a sign of late composition; fourth, that the Gospels are not written in the spirit of Jesus and his immediate disciples, and that their content itself betrays a later hand.[91]

Stäudlin responds to Eckermann's arguments point by point. We will, however, focus on his conclusion in which he discusses Eckermann's contention that his theory of second-century redactors actually promotes accurate teaching and preaching.[92] Essentially, Stäudlin argues that Eckermann's theory opens the door to historical scepticism regarding both the accuracy of the Gospel records and our ability to know the historical Jesus and to distinguish his teaching from that of the apostles:

> Haben wir die Berichte der Begleiter und der Zeitgenossen Jesu vor uns; so sind diese freylich zuverläsige Hülfsmittel, um ihn und seine Lehre kenne zu lernen. Sind aber diese Berichte von später lebenden ganz unbekannten Männern, die ihre Erzählung aus mancherley ungleichen Quellen, aus ältern Nachrichten und ungewissen Sagen zusammenrafften, und auch wohl hier und da ihre eignen Einfälle einmischten; so ist es äusserst schwer auszumachen, was und wieviel wir ihnen glauben sollen.[93]

Who guarantees, Stäudlin asks, that in the hundred or so years between Jesus and the alleged composition of the Gospels the traditions were not altered? He refers to the "Fragmentisten" (Reimarus) who claimed that Jesus sought to establish an earthly kingdom and that his disciples, when Jesus' effort had failed, began talking about a spiritual kingdom. These kinds of claims are harder to sustain if one holds that the Gospels were written by close associates of Jesus within a few decades of his own lifetime.[94] Stäudlin adds that he finds everywhere in the Gospels scattered details about Jesus' teachings and character which turn suspect very

---

[91]Eckermann had contended that while Jesus had minimized his miracles, later writers had emphasized them, thus betraying their distance to the historical Jesus' intentions; here Stäudlin refers to Storr's rebuttal mentioned above.

[92]Ibid., 202–207.

[93]Ibid., 203. "If we have the reports of the companions and contemporaries of Jesus, these are indeed reliable means of getting to know his teaching. If, however, these reports are by later totally unknown men who compiled the story from various sources, from older reports and uncertain fables, and even there probably added their own ideas, it is extremely difficult to decide what and how much we should believe them."

[94]Ibid., 204.

quickly when one departs from the understanding of the apostolic author-ship of the Gospels.[95]

Stäudlin concedes that Eckermann seeks to avoid these implications by postulating "written essays" by the apostles upon which the later docu-ments are supposedly based, and by urging interpreters to distinguish between later additions and genuine information about Jesus' life and teachings. But by what criteria should one make those distinctions? "Wenn man auch alles dieses zugibt, so läst sich doch nicht leugnen, daß die Versuche zu der empfohlnen Scheidung höchst willkürlich ausfallen müssen . . . Dieser Kanon kann durchaus nicht anders als unsicher und willkührlich seyn."[96]

Lastly, Stäudlin is concerned that Eckermann's theories will weaken the appeal of the Christian faith:

> Wir wollen einmal annehmen, daß ein denkender Gegner des Christenthums sich über die von Herrn Eckermann vorgeschlagene Absonderung erklären sollte, wie würde etwa sein Urtheil ausfallen? Er wird sagen: Ich sehe wohl, daß man durch künstliche Bemühungen von der Lehre Jesu das abscheiden kann, was mir bedenklich und unrichtig vorkommt, und daß man dadurch dieser Lehre eine Gestalt geben kann, gegen die meine Vernunft nichts einzuwenden findet. Man wählt aus ihr heraus, was mit unsern Grundsätzen übereinstimmend ist; man läßt das weg, was anstößig und irrig ist. Allein wie kann man ein solches Verfahren für eine Rettung der Lehre Jesu ansehn? Ist man berechtigt, bey den Nachrichten von der Lehre Jesu nur das als wahr anzunehmen, was sich leicht vertheidigen läßt, und das als unächten Zusatz wegzuwerfen, wobey das nicht geschehen kann? Anstatt mich an eine Religion zu halten, deren Inhalt durch ein so willkührliches und zugleich unsichres Verfahren bestimmt werden soll, will ich lieber bloß bey der natürlichen Religion stehen bleiben. Da man mir zugibt, daß die Quellen der christlichen Geschichte nicht rein sind, so scheint es mir jetzt nach verflossenen Jahrhunderten unmöglich, das Reine von dem Getrübten abzusondern. Sollte man es unter diesen Umständen nicht lieber unter die unauflöslichen Probleme rechnen, was Jesus gelehrt hat, als daß man es ohne feste historische Kriterien aus den fremdartigen Zusätzen heraussuchen will?[97]

---

[95]Ibid.

[96]Ibid., 205. "Even if one were to admit all this, it cannot be denied that the attempts at the recommended separation [of genuine source material from later additions] must end up being extremely arbitrary . . . This canon can be nothing but uncertain and arbitrary."

[97]Ibid., 206–207. "Let us suppose that a thinking opponent of Christianity should consider the separation suggested by Mr. Eckermann, what would his verdict be? He will say: I understand that it is possible to abstract by artificial means from Jesus' teaching what seems questionable and incorrect, and that one can shape this teaching in a way that reason can no longer object. One chooses what is compatible with our principles; one leaves out what is offensive or false. Only how can one consider such a procedure to be the rescue of Jesus' teaching? Does one have the right to accept as true of Jesus' teaching only what can easily be

In his critique of Eckermann's position, Stäudlin drew attention to several issues that occupy New Testament scholarship to this very day: the rooted-ness of the radical dichotomization between the teaching of Jesus and the theology of the apostles in rationalism; the question regarding valid criteria for the determination of the authenticity of various Gospel traditions; and the lessening of confidence in the Gospels as reliable sources for the Christian faith.

Further Controversy in Germany between 1800 and 1820. While the debate between Eckermann and Stäudlin addressed most of the major issues regarding the authorship of John's Gospel, the first two decades of the nineteenth century witnessed a series of additional controversies on this topic.[98]

On the one hand, the rationalists Erhard Friedrich Vogel (1801) and Georg Konrad Horst (1804) registered doubts concerning the Johannine authorship of the Fourth Gospel. Vogel postulated a late date for the Gospel subsequent to the apostle's death, while Horst sought to attribute the christological "contradictions" in John to the evangelist's use of a variety of sources, noting also the relatively late references to John's Gospel in the patristic period. Hermann Heimart Cludius (1808) found in the differences between the Synoptic Gospels and the Gospel of John reason to doubt the latter's apostolic authorship. Christoph Friedrich Ammon (1811) believed he was able to distinguish between the original author and the redactor of John's Gospel (1811).

On the other hand, Johann Gottfried Eichhorn (1810) maintained that Julius Wegscheider had defended the apostolic authorship of John's Gospel so successfully that further proof had been rendered unnecessary. Eichhorn contended that both church tradition and internal evidence supported Johannine authorship. He believed that the absence of the author's name in John was indirect evidence for apostolic authorship, calling this phenomenon "authorial modesty."

---

defended, and to eliminate as inauthentic addition what cannot happen? Rather than embrace a religion whose content is determined by such an arbitrary and at the same time uncertain procedure, I would rather prefer natural religion. Since one admits that the sources of the Christian story are not pure, it seems to me impossible after all those centuries to distinguish the pure from the adulterated. Under such conditions, should one not consider the question of what Jesus taught as an insoluble problem rather than seeking to isolate Jesus' teachings from foreign accretions without sure historical criteria?"

[98]For full bibliographic data on the following two paragraphs, see notes 5 and 10 above.

By way of summary, we provide the following survey of the debate.

Table 1: Early Doubts of the Apostolic Authorship of the Fourth Gospel in the History of Modern Biblical Criticism

Scholar	Date	Major Theories regarding Fourth Gospel
Dionysius of Alexandria	247–265	Stylistic differences with Rev; FG by John
Desiderius Erasmus	1530	Stylistic differences with Rev; FG by John
Richard Simon	1695	Published under John's name; vs. superscripts
William Whiston	1711	John in Eph. AD 63; ch. 21, redaction later
Edw. Wells	1719	John in Eph AD 97 vs. heresy, add to Syn.s
Johann Albrecht Bengel	1742	Chief of evangelists; supplement to Syn.s
Hermann Samuel Reimarus	17??	Prefers Syn.s; distinction Jesus/ evangelists
Siegmund J. Baumgarten	1762	FG by John
Johann Salomo Semler	1771	FG the first Gospel
Johann Gottfried Herder	1780	Interpretive char. of FG; "apostolic circle"
Johann David Michaelis	1790	Apostolicity & canonicity; FG by John
Edward Evanson	1792	Stylistic differences with Rev.; Platonist
Joseph Priestley	1793	Vs. Evanson, FG by John
David Simpson	1793	Vs. Evanson, FG by John
Jacob Chr. R. Eckermann	1796	Mid-2d-cent. composition based on apostolic essays
Samuel Gottlieb Lange	1797	FG by John; church tradition
Gottlob Christian Storr	1798	Vs. Eckermann, FG by John
Johann E. Chr. Schmidt	1798	Doubts; no mention of FG by Papias, Justin
Carl Friedr. Stäudlin	1799	Vs. Eckermann, FG by John
Friedr. Gottl. Sueskind	1800	Vs. Eckermann, FG by John
Erhard Friedrich Vogel	1801	Written after apostles' death
Georg Konrad Horst	1804	Use of different sources; late attestation
Johann E. Chr. Schmidt	1805	Recants earlier position (see above, 1798)
Julius A. L. Wegscheider	1806	FG by John; Eichhorn: W.'s refutation decisive
Jacob Chr. R. Eckermann	1807	Recants earlier position (see above, 1796)
Hermann Heimart Cludius	1808	Vs. Syn.; writer gnostic; Jewish Christian redactor
Johann Gottfr. Eichhorn	1810	FG by John; "authorial modesty": 3d person
Christoph Friedr. Ammon	1811	Author of FG other than editor
Heinrich C. Ballenstedt	1812	Comparison with Philo
Karl Gottlieb Bretschneider	1820	Different from Synoptics; late attestation
Friedrich Schleiermacher	1832	Pseudepigraphy; FG by John
David Friedrich Strauss	1835	Myth, not history—John set aside; vs. Synoptics
Ferdinand Christian Baur	1844	Late 2nd-cent. date

Evaluation and Conclusion

The late eighteenth and early nineteenth centuries were characterized by increasing challenges to traditional paradigms. The issue of the apostolic authorship of the Gospels was no exception. While old paradigms still reigned, critical scholars advanced reasons why traditional views should be overturned. Interestingly but not surprisingly, more than one, after advancing a radical position, retreated to a more conservative stance after vehement attacks were mounted by defenders of the traditional view. The time had not yet come for an open challenge. New theories must be brought forward with great caution. Still, those thinly disguised critical hypotheses were easily recognized as "unorthodox" and rigorously exposed and countered. Not always was it "reason" that obtained the upper hand. Much argumentation was little more than mere assertion of dogmatic positions. In the clash of dogmatic traditionalism with awakening and maturing critical scholarship, genuine dialogue was rare. Power, rhetorical strategy, and demagoguery were relied on all too often. Yet the fault did not always lie with the defenders of the traditional view. Some of them, like Stäudlin, were quite able "critics' critics," sensing the writing on the wall in form of speculative departures from well-attested traditions. In the early adolescence of biblical criticism, the critical mind sought to emancipate itself all too often by reacting against all impositions of authority and tradition, failing to recognize the value of much of what had been handed down through the centuries.

In the case of the apostolic authorship of the Fourth Gospel, the traditional paradigm seemed especially strong and difficult to overturn. Scholarship until Richard Simon (1695) was almost unanimous that the apostle John was the author of the Gospel bearing his name. All the more remarkable is the fact that within about seventy years, from Reimarus (d. 1768) over Eckermann (1796), Bretschneider (1820), and Strauss (1835), the Fourth Gospel had been stripped of its authority and historical trustworthiness. While modern scholars such as Leon Morris, D. A. Carson, and John A. T. Robinson sought to stem the tide, the consensus view regarding the authorship of the Fourth Gospel is in essence a further development of the Reimarus/Eckermann/Bretschneider/Strauss trajectory. Why were even able defenders of the apostolic authorship of the Fourth Gospel such as Johann Albrecht Bengel (1742), Johann David Michaelis (1790), Carl Friedrich Stäudlin (1799), and Friedrich Schleiermacher (1832), to name but a few, unable to prevent the "paradigm shift" that overtook Johannine studies within a few decades? More importantly, what role did "reason" and sound argumentation play, and how well-founded on evidence was the change of consensus and direction?

After Gadamer and others, it is not hard to notice a major weakness of this era's scholarship: the prevalent illusion of scientific neutrality and objectivity. This form of self-deceit often fostered pride in one's—after all still fairly subjective—judgment and a degree of dogmatism that precluded meaningful dialogue with tradition or new findings respectively. The modern insight that every "interpretive community" as well as every individual interpreter is part of history and tradition had not yet been sufficiently recognized.[99]

More specifically, the question remains: What is the evidence for and against the apostolic authorship of the Fourth Gospel, and how can reasonable, sound judgments under the constraints of orthodox beliefs regarding the nature of Scripture be formed? Was the author of the Fourth Gospel the apostle John, a second-century Platonist, a circle of followers using various sources, possibly including the apostle's own "written essays"? What does it matter? Does it matter?

Our investigation has come full circle. In light of the opening statement by Stephen Neill, and Richard Simon's observation regarding the superscriptions to the Gospels, it seems important to be prepared to discuss the issue of the apostolic authorship of the Fourth Gospel with genuine openness. The fact that external and internal evidences have been evaluated in ways leading to diametrically opposed conclusions appears puzzling, yet should caution the interpreter and direct our attention to the presuppositions at work in scholarly methodology. Without impugning any one writer's motives, the recognition of the inevitable element of subjectivity in the interpretive process makes it necessary to examine what interests and consequences may be behind various conclusions regarding the authorship of the Fourth Gospel.

Here Stäudlin's cautions, expressed almost two hundred years ago, seem quite prophetic. The farther the actual composition of the Fourth Gospel is removed from its proximity to the life and person of the historical Jesus, the greater the possibility for embellishment and shifts in understanding. If the apostle John, Jesus' closest follower and an eyewitness of Jesus' life and ministry, wrote the Gospel bearing his name himself, there is a much closer connection between the source (Jesus) and the witness (John). If, on the other hand, a circle of later followers functioned

---

[99]Cf. Grant R. Osborne, *The Hermeneutical Spiral: A Comprehensive Introduction to Biblical Interpretation* (Downers Grove, IL: InterVarsity, 1991), esp. the two appendices.

as redactors, or if second-century Jewish Christians, Gnostics, or Platonists wrote or edited the Gospel, the reader's confidence in the accuracy of the Gospel would be justly diminished.

One must also acknowledge the considerable amount of tension between the apostolic authorship of the Fourth Gospel on the one hand and questions of biblical inspiration, inerrancy, and canonicity on the other. Writers in the time period under consideration were keenly aware of this connection.[100] It would do modern scholars well to recover a sense of the relationship between historical-critical theories and biblical background studies and their implications for the questions of canon, inspiration, and inerrancy.

We conclude that, while it is appropriate to draw attention to the interpretive element in all the Gospels, and especially the Fourth Gospel, it is still possible to see an essential harmony between Jesus' life and teachings and their presentation in the Gospels. The differences between the Synoptic Gospels and the Fourth Gospel, while significant, should not be exaggerated.[101] Some ideas have amazing staying power. Refuted decisively long ago, the conclusions to which these ideas led often still persist. An example of this phenomenon is David Friedrich Strauss' idea of "myth," taken up by Rudolf Bultmann in this century. While the history-of-religions school has seen a significant decline, the view of the Fourth Gospel popularized by Strauss, i.e. that of a secondary, unhistorical document, still prevails in many circles today.[102] Even after the *Leben Jesu* approach to the Gospels turned out to be a "blind alley," few lessons have been learned from the history of Gospels research and Johannine scholarship. It is to these lessons from history that we now turn in closing.

There is a need for greater openness, more dialogue, and an awareness of scholars' own presuppositions. It appears that there are still good reasons to hold to the apostolic authorship of the Fourth Gospel. No decisive evidence has been set forth that render impossible an evaluation of both external and internal evidence with the result that the Johannine authorship of the Fourth Gospel is more probable than its alternatives. It

---

[100]Cf., e.g., Schmidt, *Kritische Geschichte*, 6–8. The term used for the genuineness of a writing by German scholars of this time period is "Aechtheit." The word seems to comprise a whole cluster of concepts, such as genuineness, integrity, veracity, vs. spuriousness, and errancy.

[101]Cf. the work of scholars such as Leon Morris, *Studies in the Fourth Gospel* (Grand Rapids: Eerdmans, 1969) and D. A. Carson, *The Gospel According to John* (Grand Rapids: Eerdmans, 1991) in this regard.

[102]Cf. the work of J. Louis Martyn, and even that of C. H. Dodd.

would be an advance if scholars unpersuaded by such arguments were willing to concede that to hold to Johannine authorship is a reasonable alternative. On the other hand, it should be possible for those holding to Johannine authorship to concede that evidence allows for different conclusions, however probable (or improbable) they may seem.

It is not likely that a consensus regarding the authorship of the Fourth Gospel will be achieved in the near future, or even before our Lord returns. It is beyond the scope of this essay to launch a fresh investigation of the evidence for or against the Johannine authorship of the Fourth Gospel. If the above whirlwind tour of late eighteenth and early nineteenth-century scholarship has deepened the consciousness of standing in a centuries-old tradition of scholarly discourse and thus helped foster greater humility and openness to dialogue, our efforts will have been well rewarded.

CHAPTER THREE

A COMPARISON OF THE PERICOPAE OF JESUS' ANOINTING[*]

Introduction

Verbal aspect theory is a relatively recent development, and scholars still debate its accuracy and usefulness for understanding the Greek verb.[1] While this theory has been given a cohesive conceptual formulation,[2] much empirical testing still remains to be done in order to establish verbal aspect theory as superior to previous hypotheses on the functioning of the Greek verb.[3]

The present study seeks to make a contribution to this process by applying verbal aspect theory to comparative Gospel studies. We will briefly summarize the major components of verbal aspect theory before applying it to the study of one of the few pericopae found in all four Gospels, that of the anointing of Jesus. We will attempt to show that verbal aspect theory holds significant promise for a better understanding of the evangelists' distinctive literary and theological purposes.

---

[*]An earlier version of this essay was presented at the Regional Meeting of the Society of Biblical Literature in Toronto, Canada, 1992.

[1]Cf. the reviews of Porter, *Verbal Aspect*, and Fanning, *Verbal Aspect* (for full bibliographic references, see note 2) by Moisés Silva in *WTJ* 54 (1992): 179–83 and by Daryl D. Schmidt in *JBL* 111 (1992): 417–18.

[2]Cf. especially Stanley E. Porter, *Verbal Aspect in the Greek of the New Testament, with Reference to Tense and Mood* (New York: Peter Lang, 1989); id., *Idioms of the Greek New Testament* (Sheffield: JSOT, 1992); and Buist M. Fanning, *Verbal Aspect in New Testament Greek* (Oxford Theological Monographs; Oxford: Clarendon, 1990).

[3]Cf. Schmidt, "Review," 715: "Fanning's brief consideration of discourse features . . . needs to be demonstrated in larger narrative sections." Later in his review, Schmidt comments that "[f]uture discussion of verbal aspect will need to demonstrate greater sensitivity to narrative grammar" (p. 717).

Verbal Aspect Theory

At the heart of verbal aspect theory is the contention that a writer's choice of a given verb form is determined not by an action's objective nature (*Aktionsart*), but by the writer's subjective perception of the action.[4] This phenomenon of a writer's (or speaker's) subjective perception is called "aspect."[5] Thus it is possible for different writers to describe one and the same action while employing different verb tenses.[6]

Three Aspects

Verbal aspect theory groups these perceptions into three categories:[7]

> (1) perfective, viewing an action as complete and undifferentiated (aorist);
> (2) imperfective, viewing an action as in progress (present and imperfect); and
> (3) stative, viewing an action as a (complex) state of affairs (perfect and pluperfect).

Within these categories, the criterion of remoteness (i.e., an action's greater or lesser immediacy of impact on the writer's experience) functions to distinguish in the imperfective aspect between the present and the imperfect, and in the stative aspect between the perfect and the pluperfect. The former (i.e., present and perfect) are non-remote (i.e., more immediate) and the latter (i.e., imperfect and pluperfect) remote (less immediate).

---

[4]Cf. ibid., 717: "The starting point for all future study of verbal aspect in Greek grammar should be the clear distinction between aspect and *Aktionsart*." For a brief critique of *Aktionsart*, cf. Porter, *Idioms*, 27–28.

[5]Fanning, *Verbal Aspect*, defines aspect as "the focus or viewpoint of the speaker in regard to the action or condition which the verb describes." Porter, *Verbal Aspect*, 88, defines aspect as "a synthetic semantic category (realized in the form of verbs) used of meaningful oppositions in a network of tense systems to grammaticalize the author's reasoned subjective choice of conception of an event."

[6]Cf. Porter, *Idioms*, 24, who gives the example of the raising of Christ and its description in Rom 8:11 with the aorist (ἐγείραντος), in 2 Cor 1:9 with the present (ἐγείροντι), and in 2 Tim 2:8 with the perfect (ἐγηγερμένον).

[7]Verbal aspect theory is not as monolithic as the following presentation might suggest. While Porter distinguishes between the three aspectual categories listed below, Fanning only includes the perfective and imperfective aspects while viewing the perfect as a combination of the features of aspect, tense, and *Aktionsart*. Fanning is apparently followed by Schmidt, "Review," 717: "The starting points for all future study of verbal aspect in Greek grammar should be . . . the contrast between present and aorist aspect." As a whole, Porter's categorization seems more consistent and will therefore be followed in the survey below.

The future is viewed as grammaticalizing the writer's expectation. According to verbal aspect theory, the issue is not whether an action will actually happen (ultimately, that cannot be known since the action is still future), but whether the writer or speaker *expects* it to happen or not. What the writer using a verb in the future is saying is, "I (or someone else) expect this action to occur." Regarding moods, the indicative mood indicates the writer's assumption of a given action's reality while the other moods point to the writer's projection of an action's reality in terms of condition (subjective), direction (imperative), or wish (optative).

Verbal aspect theory does not merely substitute a different terminology for the conventional one. It rather represents an effort to capture the essence of three different ways of perceiving a given action. The extent to which these aspects were consciously employed by Greek writers and speakers is difficult to determine.[8] Like many native speakers, those speaking or writing Greek may not always have been fully aware of these various kinds of aspects. It is argued, however, that verbal aspect theory accurately describes how the Greek verb actually functions—and not just in New Testament Greek—and that writers were sufficiently conscious of verbal aspects that they could employ different verb forms to achieve their desired literary and theological purposes. But a full-fledged defense of verbal aspect theory goes beyond the scope of this paper.[9]

Visualization

We may visualize these aspects by using the illustration of different perspectives on one and the same parade.[10] As mentioned, according to verbal aspect theory a writer uses different verb tenses to describe one and the same action depending on his perspective of the action.

The perfective aspect, grammaticalized in Greek by the aorist, corresponds to the helicopter view of a television correspondent who views

---

[8]Cf. Schmidt, "Review," 717: "The notion of viewpoint as the speaker's *conscious* choice tends to be over-emphasized, especially by Porter, who talks about this choice as 'self-conscious' (pp. 325, 355), although he is aware that by its very nature subjective choice is not always explainable (p. 355). In fact, in an *ad hoc* corpus of material from a dead language there likely would be many instances where such choices have no apparent explanation."

[9]Historically, Greek (and thus also the Greek verb) has been studied as a classical language akin to Latin. However, this approach subjected the language to a grammatical paradigm that is not suitable, since it can be argued that the Greek verb may function more like the Hebrew than the Latin verb. Indeed, aspect, rather than time, is the controlling principle of the Hebrew verb. For an extensive survey of the history of Greek tense research, see Porter, *Verbal Aspect*, 17-65.

[10]Cf. Porter, *Idioms*, 23-24.

the parade as a whole (that is, as complete), without differentiating further regarding the action's characteristics. Judas' question in John 12:5, "Why was this perfume not sold (ἐδόθη) to the poor?" may serve as an example. By using aorists, that is, by casting the actions from a perfective aspect, the writer simply surveys Judas' objection without otherwise seeking to draw attention to it.

The imperfective aspect, represented by the present and imperfect tenses, expresses the perspective of a spectator who follows the parade along the road, viewing it as in progress. Martha's serving in John 12:2 (διηκόνει) or Judas' stealing in John 12:6 (ἐβάσταζεν) are both viewed from an imperfective aspect, that is, as in progress. They are viewed in such a way regardless of whether they objectively happen at a particular time (past) or in a certain way (durative); the writer perceives and casts these actions from a progressive aspect.

The stative aspect, given expression by the Greek perfect and pluperfect, reveals the perspective of the parade manager who views the parade as a (complex) state of affairs. The perfect γέγονεν in Mark 14:4, for example, refers to a complex state of affairs when some are asking, "Why this waste?" As is also indicated by the anaphoric αὕτη, the verb in the stative aspect encapsulates the complex of actions narrated previously (cf. 14:3): the woman's coming, breaking the jar, and pouring it on Jesus' head.

Planes of Discourse
Importantly, the writer's choice of one of these three aspects is determined not primarily by the time of the action (past, present, or future), nor even the kind of the action (one-time, durative, etc.), but by his literary intentions expressed in three planes of discourse.[11] For this reason verbal aspect theory is especially well-suited for discourse analysis, since verbal aspect is one of the major determining factors for various levels of discourse.[12] According to a verb's morphological bulk (i.e., according to "what the tense paradigm does to the verb stem"),[13] its

---

[11]Cf. Schmidt,"Review," 716, who quotes Porter's claim (*Verbal Aspect*, 78) that "Greek does not grammaticalize tense in any of the three major tense categories," and who sharpens this assertion as follows: "The more accurate claim would be: tense forms in the indicative do not grammaticalize *absolute time*, any more than they grammaticalize *absolute* aspect." But note Porter's own refinement on p. 98: "Greek does not grammaticalize absolute tense . . . rather, Greek maintains relative tense in all tenses and Moods."

[12]Cf. Porter, *Idioms*, 302–303.

[13]Cf. Porter, *Verbal Aspect*, 178.

specialization of meaning (lexical characteristics), and its frequency of use (the verb's "markedness"), the verb is employed by the writer in his back-grounding, foregrounding, and frontgrounding of events.[14]

As will be seen below, the anointing is generally perceived in its perfective aspect (i.e., by using aorist forms) and thus backgrounded. In other words, the anointing generally does not function as the major focus of the evangelists' versions of the anointing. It rather provides the occasion for other features of the story they choose to highlight by fore- or frontground-ing them. Such features are Judas' antagonism in John and the disciples' objection in Mark and Matthew, for which imperfective forms are used (i.e., presents and imperfects; see the analysis below). Luke alone focuses on the anointing and the woman who performs it by using stative and imperfective forms at the end of his account to mark the woman's state of salvation and forgiveness.

Generally, the perfective aspect (i.e., the aorist tense) is the least marked (i.e., it has the least morphological bulk and is most frequently used). It functions therefore as default tense, that is, it is used unless the writer finds it necessary to choose another tense form for emphasis (i.e., fore- or frontgrounding). In narratives, perfective forms are used for back-grounding. Imperfectives (remote and non-remote) are employed for fore-grounding. Statives (remote and non-remote) have the greatest mor-phological bulk and are the least frequently used (i.e., they are the least "marked"), wherefore their use indicates the writer's desire to frontground the action viewed under the stative aspect.[15]

It is our hope that by using verbal aspect theory we will discover the various perspectives with which the Gospel writers viewed the anointing of Jesus.

Verbal Aspect Theory and Time

Verbal aspect theory holds that reference to time is not the primary func-tion of the Greek verb.[16] Time, according to this view, is rather indicated

---

[14]Cf. ibid., 23.

[15]One phenomenon that can only briefly be noted here but that affects the interpretation of verbal aspect are actually vague verbs. These are verbs that have only a limited range of tense options. For example, εἰμι has no aorist. For this reason, the writer's use of the imperfect of εἰμι may be less significant.

[16]Cf. Porter, *Verbal Aspect*, 98: "It has now been established that the tense categories in Greek are not time-based, but aspectually based . . . Greek does not grammaticalize absolute tense, where the speech time is equated with the present; rather, Greek maintains relative tense in all tenses and Moods, i.e. where the time of a situation is relative to a time not necessarily the point of speaking and where any tense category may be used in any of the temporal contexts."

by so-called deictic indicators (i.e., adverbs of time, anaphora, place references, discourse deixis such as connectives and main story indicators, and social deixis, i.e., names and relationships).

Examples of deictic indicators in the anointing pericopae include the following:

- adverbs and expressions of time: πρὸ ἓξ ἡμερῶν τοῦ πάσχα; πάντοτε and οὐ πάντοτε in John 12:7;
- anaphora: τοῦτο in John 12:5 and 6; αὕτη in Matt 26:8=Mark 14:4;
- place references: εἰς Βηθανίαν, ὅπου ἦν Λάζαρος in John 12:1; ἐν Βηθανίᾳ ἐν (τῇ) οἰκίᾳ Σίμωνος τοῦ λεπροῦ in Matt 26:6=Mark 14:3;
- discourse deixis: οὖν in John 12:1, 2, 3, 7; δέ in John 12:4, 6; Matt 26:6, 8, 10, 11; Mark 14:4, 6, 7, 9; γάρ in John 12:8; Mark 14:5, 7; Matt 26:9, 10, 11, 12; and
- social deixis: the naming of Lazarus, Martha, and Mary in John 12:1, 2, 3, as well as of Judas in 12:4 and of Jesus in 12:7.

A given verb form like the aorist can be past-, present-, or future-referring, omnitemporal, or timeless. For example, λέγει in John 12:4 is a past-referring present (conventionally referred to as a "historic present"). While the present study does not afford the time or space to discuss the merits of verbal aspect theory as such, we will demonstrate the usefulness of this theory by applying it to a detailed study of the pericopae of Jesus' anointing in the four Gospels.

The Literary and Theological Purposes of the Four Evangelists

A cursory screening of the similarities and divergences of the four accounts in Matt 26:6-13, Mark 14:3-9, Luke 7:36-50, and John 12:1-8 aligns Mark's account closely with Matthew's. These two evangelists' renderings will therefore be studied jointly. While there are surface similarities between the versions of John and Luke (as there are between those of John and Mark), the circumstances surrounding the anointing of Jesus in John are in essential harmony with those described in Mark and Matthew. For this reason the accounts of Mark, Matthew, and John will be considered as referring to the same occasion, while the anointing recorded by Luke seems to represent a separate occasion.[17] We will first investigate the pericope in John, then in Mark/Matthew, and finally in Luke.

---

[17]The question of whether there are one, two, or even three anointings

John

Verbal Analysis. As Jesus enters Bethany (the verb form is ἦλθεν, backgrounded by using the aorist default tense), John sketches the proceeding action by way of remote imperfectives (i.e., imperfects): Lazarus is there (ἦν); Martha is serving (διηκόνει); Lazarus is one of those reclining with Jesus (ἦν ἐκ τῶν ἀνακειμένων; 12:1, 2). The evangelist thus sees these actions in their progressive aspect and foregrounds (i.e., emphasizes) them (cf. the above visualization of the imperfective aspect as a parade spectator along the road).

Mary's actions are sketched in the aorist default tense, viewed as complete by the writer: she takes the perfume (λαβοῦσα); she anoints Jesus' feet (ἤλειψεν); she wipes his feet with her hair (ἐξέμαξεν); the house is filled with the fragrance of the perfume (ἐπληρώθη; 12:3). This characterization corresponds to the "helicopter" perspective mentioned above. Notably, and perhaps surprisingly, the anointing itself is therefore backgrounded, that is, presented not as the actual focus of the pericope, but rather as the occasion for what is to follow in the evangelist's narration.

Three non-remote imperfectives (i.e., present tense forms) draw the reader's attention to Judas and his objection. The fourth evangelist notes that Judas speaks up (λέγει), characterizing him as "the disciple who is about to betray Jesus" (present participle ὁ μέλλων and present infinitive παραδιδόναι; 12:4). By using present tense forms, John heightens the reader's expectation of what is to follow. Judas' objection itself is presented in the aorist default tense: why was the perfume not sold (ἐπράθη) and given to the poor (ἐδόθη; 12:5)?

The writer then gradually foregrounds: Judas said this (εἶπεν; aorist), not because he was concerned about the poor (ἔμελεν; remote imperfective, i.e., imperfect), but because he was a thief (ἦν; remote imperfective),

---

recorded in the Gospels is disputed. The view that there is one anointing present in the Gospels was held by Tertullian, and more recently by Bernard, Bultmann, Dauer, Dibelius, Dodd, Elliott, Holst, Klostermann, R. H. Lightfoot, Nesbitt, O'Rahilly, D. F. Strauss, et al. The following scholars claim that there are anointings at two separate occasions found in the Gospels: Chrysostom, Tatian; Bevan, R. E. Brown, Carson, Cribbs, Drexler, Grubb, Lagrange, Legault, Lindars, I. H. Marshall, Morris, Nolland, Schnackenburg, Smalley, de Solages, et al. Origen believed that the Gospels narrate three different anointings. Many of those who hold to one anointing do so on form-critical grounds and do not necessarily affirm the historicity of the event. But careful study of the Lucan pericope and comparison between it and the anointing pericopae of the other three Gospels reveals such a substantial disparity that even form-critical considerations seem inadequate to maintain that the Gospel traditions converge in one actual story and/or event.

and having the money-box (ἔχων; non-remote imperfective, i.e., present, foregrounded), he was stealing (ἐβάσταζεν; remote imperfective) what was thrown in (τὰ βαλλόμενα; non-remote imperfective, foregrounded; 12:6). What was signalled in v. 4 is now confirmed: the writer views the anointing of Jesus from the perspective of what it reveals about Judas' attitude (i.e., his antagonism) toward Jesus.

Jesus' pronouncement is gradually foregrounded as well: he said (εἶπεν), permit her (ἄφες; aorists), so that she might keep it (τηρήσῃ; projection by the speaker, not necessarily objectively future) for the day of my burial (12:7). For the poor you always have with you (ἔχετε), but you do not always have me (ἔχετε; two non-remote imperfectives, foregrounded).

Macro-Context. In summary, the following pattern can be seen: 12:1-3 shows Jesus' friends as part of the setting: Lazarus is there and reclining with him, Martha is serving; Mary's anointing of Jesus is in the background aorist tense. 12:4-6 shows Jesus' enemy as the focus of the pericope: Judas, the betrayer, is presented by the writer as the chief antagonist of Jesus, and a thief, by using present forms. Judas, too, is featured as part of Jesus' inner circle.

The primary narrative tension is between Mary's final loving administration and Judas' dishonest questioning of her act, with the writer revealing Judas' ulterior motives. The resolution is provided by Jesus' adjudication in 12:7-8. The Lord prophetically projects his impending passion, culminating in his burial, as overshadowing the present occasion. His presence will soon be removed, a fact that his inner circle still fails to realize.

John's literary purpose is seen in the way in which he integrates this pericope into his Gospel. Prior to the anointing, he had already mentioned Mary in the introduction to Jesus' raising her brother Lazarus from the dead: "Now a certain man was sick, Lazarus of Bethany, the village of Mary and her sister Martha. And it was the Mary who anointed the Lord with ointment, and wiped His feet with her hair, whose brother Lazarus was sick" (11:1-2).

And after the anointing, John continues, "The great multitude therefore of the Jews learned that He was there, and they came, not for Jesus' sake only, but that they might also see Lazarus, whom He raised from the dead. But the chief priests took counsel that they might put Lazarus to death also . . . And so the multitude who were with Him when He called Lazarus out of the tomb, and raised him from the dead, were bearing Him witness" (12:9-10, 18).

The raising of Lazarus, Mary's brother, became a sign of Jesus' resurrection; Mary herself prepared Jesus for his burial. However, we have learned from the preceding analysis that, perhaps contrary to what one might have expected, John's account of Jesus' anointing does not focus on Mary. Rather, the anointing provides an occasion for John to expose Judas' antagonism to Jesus. This antagonism had already been referred to in 6:70-71 where Jesus had called Judas "a devil." It flares up again in 13:21-30 where Satan is entering Judas, and Judas leaves the upper room to betray Jesus.

It may be asked at this point what verbal aspect theory has contributed to an understanding of John's anointing pericope that might not have been gleaned by other tools of biblical interpretation. This is certainly a legitimate question. It may be replied, however, that the contribution of verbal aspect theory is significant indeed. Apart from providing a more accurate and measurable explanation of the functioning of the Greek verb in narratives, the theory can function as a corrective of conventional analytical methods. As mentioned, one's expectation of John's literary and theological purposes may have centered around Mary's anointing of Jesus itself and its christological significance.

Contrary to such expectations, however, verbal aspect theory, if correct, has shown that Judas (and Jesus' rebuke of Judas) occupies center stage in the pericope. Perhaps the fourth evangelist intends to communicate to his readers an indirect warning not to be like Judas in his betrayal of Jesus at a time of intense religious persecution.[18] At any rate, the evangelist's focus on Judas functions apologetically in arguing that Judas' betrayal was foreknown by Jesus and ordained by God (cf. 6:70-71; 13:10-11, 21-30; 17:12). It is theodicy, a vindication of God, and is necessary for a plot line that enters into the decisive stages of Jesus' passion. While Mary's anointing is shown to point to Jesus' burial, Judas' betrayal is instrumental in Jesus' death.

It remains now to analyze the accounts of the remaining evangelists to discover their emphases and to compare them with those of John.

Mark/Matthew

Mark sandwiches the anointing pericope between a reference to the religious leaders' hatred of Jesus (14:1-2) and a reference to Judas' intention to betray Jesus (14:10-12). The hatred surrounding Jesus is dramati-

---

[18]Cf. R. Lemmer, "A Possible Understanding by the Implied Reader, of some of the *Coming-going-being sent* Pronouncements, in the Johannine Farewell Discourses," *Neot* 25 (1991): 307-309.

cally contrasted with the woman's loving act of devotion.[19] While Mark's and Matthew's accounts are substantially the same, Matthew tends to abbreviate Mark.

Verbal Analysis. As does John, Mark views the scene primarily in its progressive aspect. In his description of the setting, Mark employs two present participles (ὄντος, κατακειμένου; Mark 14:3a), while Matthew uses an aorist participle (γενομένου, Matt 28:6). Also as in John, the actions of the unnamed woman are generally sketched in the default tense, the aorist—she comes (προσῆλθεν in Matt 26:7; ἦλθεν in Mark 14:3), breaks an alabaster jar (συντρίψασα; only in Mark 14:3), and pours its contents over Jesus' head (κατέχεεν; Mark 14:3=Matt 26:7). Only the woman's possession of the alabaster jar itself (ἔχουσα) is cast as a non-remote imperfective (present participle; Mark 14:3=Matt 26:7). Perhaps Mark and Matthew are thus drawing the reader's attention to the unusual nature of the woman's possession of such an expensive item.

In different ways, both Mark and Matthew emphasize ("foreground") the objection by "some" (Mark), i.e., "the disciples" (Matthew). Mark uses a periphrastic construction with a present participle (ἦσαν ἀγανακτοῦντες, Mark 14:4), Matthew employs an aorist (ἰδόντες) and a present participle (λέγοντες, Matt 26:8). The content of the objection is swiftly narrated in aorists (πραθῆναι, δοθῆναι; Matt 26:9=Mark 14:5), except for the imperfective ἠδύνατο (Mark 14:5) or ἐδύνατο (Matt 26:9) and especially the stative γέγονεν in Mark 14:4.

The latter form draws attention to the essence of the disciples' objection: the broken condition of the jar, the effusive waste of spilling out the precious contents rather than liquidating the asset, and doing a good deed by giving the proceeds to the poor. The scolding of the woman is also foregrounded by using a remote imperfective (i.e., imperfect; ἐνεβριμῶντο): the writer presents the disciples' attitude of dismay as in progress (Mark 14:5).

Jesus, in his response, is presented as using aorists (γνούς in Matt 26:10, εἶπεν in Matt 26:10 and Mark 14:6, ἄφετε in Mark 14:6, ἠργάσατο in Matt 26:10 and Mark 14:6), except for his reproach, "Why do you cause her trouble?" which is in the present (παρέχετε). Perhaps this continues the evangelists' previous emphasis on the disciples' dismay. As in John's account, the verbs for "having" are in the present (ἔχετε), thus

---

[19]Cf. Leon Morris, *Studies in the Fourth Gospel* (Grand Rapids: Eerdmans, 1969), 32, n. 24.

climaxing the account by drawing the reader's attention to Jesus' presence with them which is soon to be withdrawn while the poor will continue to be there (cf. also the presents θέλητε and δύνασθε in Mark 14:7, omitted by Matt, which add further emphasis to Jesus' response; and Mark 2:18-20=Matt 9:14-15 for a similar lesson).

By using imperfective verb forms, Mark and Matthew both emphasize the disciples' failure to grasp the significance of Jesus' presence with them—the unnamed woman alone rises to the occasion (Mark 14:6-8; Matt 26:10-12). In closing, Jesus projects his expectation that the woman's deed will be remembered (κηρυχθῇ, λαληθήσεται; cf. John 11:2).

Macro-Context. The pattern is as follows: Mark 14:3/Matt 26:6-7 present the setting in Simon the Leper's home and the woman's anointing; Mark 14:4-5/Matt 26:8-9 deal with the disciples' objection; and Mark 14:6-9/Matt 26:10-13 give the resolution of the event, and Jesus' explanation of the significance of the anointing to the disciples. The amount of space given to these various themes is telling: the anointing itself occupies only a small fraction of the pericope; the majority of the account is devoted to the interaction between Jesus and the disciples.

The focus in the Mark/Matthew account is on Jesus' instruction of his disciples. While John sharpens this focus to the antagonism between Judas and Jesus, the first and second Gospel writers are content to leave the pericope as a general lesson for the disciples.[20] Though they probably know the woman's name, they suppress it so as not to distract from their focus, i.e., the narrative tension between Jesus and his disciples who still fail to grasp the significance of the events about to take place. The woman is presented as unwittingly superseding them in her act of devotion.

Mark and Matthew interpret in hindsight: at the onset of passion week, his disciples still were in need of instruction concerning Christ's passion. This fits well with Mark's consistent emphasis on the disciples' failure to understand as well as with the prominence of the discipleship theme in Matthew.

---

[20]Cf. Pierson Parker, "Luke and the Fourth Evangelist," *NTS* 9 (1962): 336, comments that "John has grasped the theological implications of the gospel more profoundly than any other New Testament writer except Paul. Luke, despite his long acquaintance with Paul, is much more elementary." Indeed, at times John seems to draw out deeper connections between events than the Synoptists. Cf. also B. de Solages, *Jean et les Synoptiques* (Leiden: E. J. Brill, 1979), 172: "L'onction de Béthanie (Jo 12,1-8) mais c'est comme un prélude au récit de la Passion que Jean est bien obligé de raconter, et il y précise longuement (12,4-6) que c'est *Judas* qui protesta contre le gaspillage apparent."

Table 2: Comparison of the Anointing Pericope in John and Mark/Matthew

John	Mark/Matthew
12:1–3 Jesus' friends	14:3/26:6–7 Simon the Leper/Anointing
12:4–6 Jesus' enemy	14:4–5/26:8–9 Disciples' objection
12:7–8 Jesus' pronouncement	14:6–9/26:10–13 Jesus' explanation

Luke

The preliminary screening of the four pericopae of Jesus' anointing has already shown that the event Luke is portraying is a different one.[21] Luke probably chose to place the account of this anointing at this point in his gospel to illustrate the Pharisees' attitude toward Jesus (cf. Luke 7:30, 34). In his introduction Luke mentions "one of the Pharisees" and "into the house of the Pharisee" (7:36) while withholding the Pharisee's name, Simon, until Jesus' personal address in 7:40. This indicates that Luke is seeking to present the event as representative of the Pharisees' attitudes toward Jesus (cf. the consistent characterization as "the Pharisee" also in 7:37 and 39).

The Pharisee's namesake in the other accounts, Simon "the Leper," does not voice a single objection to the woman anointing Jesus. Those who object are "some" (Mark), "the disciples" (Matt), and "Judas" (John). However, Luke's whole account centers on the Pharisee's antagonism toward Jesus. Nevertheless, as will become evident below, Luke is the evangelist who frontgrounds the woman anointing Jesus.

Table 3: Luke's Anointing Pericope

Luke	
7:36–38	Dinner at Pharisee's, "Sinful Woman's" Anointing
7:39–47	The Pharisee's Objection and Jesus' Explanation
7:48–50	Jesus Pronounces Forgiveness and Dismisses Woman

---

[21]Regarding the question why Luke omitted the anointing pericope recorded by the three other evangelists, cf. F. Lamar Cribbs, "A study of the contacts that exist between St Luke and St John," *SBL Papers 1973*, Vol. 2 (Cambridge, MA: Society of Biblical Literature, 1973), 37=id., "St. Luke and the Johannine Tradition," *JBL* 90 (1971): 422–50. This author notes that there are only four pericopae of Matt 19:13–28:16 and Mark 10:13–16:8 lacking in Luke (cf. Luke 18:15–24:11). Luke incorporates 32 out of the 35 pericopae found in the parallel sections in Mark and Matthew, and 30 of these 32 in the same order. The four pericopae Luke chose not to include are: Mark 10:35–44/Matt 20:20–28 (John's and James' request); Mark 11:12–14, 20–24/Matt 21:18–22 (fig tree); Mark 12:28–34/Matt 22:34–40 (foremost commandment); and the Mark/Matt account of the anointing.

Verbal Analysis. The account unfolds with Luke using a remote imperfective (Ἡρώτα) and a number of perfectives (i.e., aorists; φάγῃ, εἰσελθών, κατεκλίθη, ἐπιγνοῦσα, κομίσασα, στᾶσα), viewing the actions as complete, until he narrates the woman's unusual behavior. Her weeping (κλαίουσα, present participle) and wetting Jesus' feet is foregrounded (aorist ἤρξατο + present infinitive βρέχειν), as is her wiping off (ἐξέμασσεν) and kissing his feet (κατεφίλει) and her anointing him with the perfume (ἤλειφεν; all remote imperfectives, denoting action in progress; Luke 7:36–38).

By using more highly marked verb forms, Luke is the only writer who specifically draws attention to the woman's actions. Also, his account is more detailed and longer than those of the other evangelists. It is interesting to note that Luke focuses on the woman's attitude (expressed in her weeping and wetting of Jesus' feet) even more than on her actions (i.e., her wiping off her tears and kissing of Jesus' feet).

In the ensuing interchange with the Pharisee, Jesus tells a parable and then draws out the application by directing Simon's attention to the woman (βλέπεις; non-remote imperfective, 7:44). He contrasts her behavior toward him with Simon's, using aorists throughout (εἰσῆλθον, ἔβρεξεν, ἐξέμαξεν, ἔδωκας, εἰσῆλθον, διέλιπεν, ἤλειψας, ἤλειψεν), except for the present participle καταφιλοῦσα, thus emphasizing Jesus' estimation of the woman's kissing his feet (and probably the attitude represented by this action).

What Luke frontgrounds by a string of stative verb forms, is the woman's state of forgiveness (note the repeated use of ἀφέωνται; cf. also the presents ἀφίεται and ἀγαπᾷ; 7:47–48), and her state of salvation (σέσωκεν; 7:50).[22] The recurring words "love" (cf. 7:42, 47) and "forgive" (three times in 7:47–48) are key themes in Jesus' lesson as presented by Luke. As already mentioned, it is the woman's contrite spirit, issuing in her crying and wetting of Jesus' feet even more than her actions that are emphasized by the evangelist.

Macro-Context. Luke is focusing on the contrast between a self-righteous Pharisee and a "sinful" woman, using the two characters to typify the dif-

---

[22]The perfect has given rise to the interpretation that the woman had been forgiven prior to this event, perhaps through being baptized by John the Baptist (cf. John J. Kilgallen, "John the Baptist, the Sinful Woman, and the Pharisee," *JBL* 104 [1985]: 678, following Fitzmyer; cf. Lk 7:29–30). Verbal aspect theory views the perfect form as grammaticalizing the state or condition of a person rather than referring to absolute time so that there is no need to explain the perfect form as referring to an event having taken place in the past.

ferent responses to John the Baptist's and his own ministries by the Jewish religious leaders and the tax-gatherers and "sinners" (cf. 7:24-35).[23]

An account of a number of women who traveled with Jesus and supported him out of their own means follows the present pericope (8:1-3).[24] By concluding the story with a presentation of Jesus' interaction with the woman, Luke makes the woman the heroine of the story. This emphasis is consistent with his overall literary purpose of presenting Jesus as the compassionate friend of sinners who is drawing near to the humble and lowly (cf. Mary's Magnificat in 1:51-52, the similar interchange with Pharisees upset about his fraternizing with tax-gatherers and "sinners" in 5:31-32, and the "Sermon on the Plain" in 6:20-21). The Pharisee and his muttering companions (7:49) are relegated to the sidelines, much as they are in the parable of the prodigal son in 15:11-32.

Conclusion

Verbal and Discourse Analysis
We have explored the four evangelists' presentations of the anointing of Jesus. The aorist occurred most frequently and seemed to be employed by the writer unless he desired to highlight a certain action. On the other hand, actions viewed from a stative perspective were very rare. These verbal forms, characterized by their infrequent use and their greater morphological bulk, were found only four times in all the accounts of Jesus' anointing combined (γέγονεν in Mark 14:4; ἀφέωνται in Luke 7:47 and 48; and σέσωκεν in Luke 7:50). These stative verb forms were judged to fulfill a significant function in the writer's frontgrounding of states of action in the framework of the overall discourse structure.

The assumption that verbs in the imperfective aspect are usually chosen for emphasis led to some interesting observations regarding the respective evangelists' literary and theological purposes. The evangelists' use of both remote and non-remote imperfectives (i.e., imperfects as well as presents) indicated a writer's departure from his default option, the aorist, and were found to mark emphases by way of foregrounding of an action. For example, John uses imperfects in John 12:1-2 to set the stage

---

[23]Cf. Hans Drexler, "Die große Sündnerin: Lucas 7:36-50," *ZNW* 59 (1968): 172-73 who sees a contrast between the "Selbstgerechtigkeit des Pharisäers" and the "Frau durch Sündennot zum Glauben geführt."

[24]Cf. Georg Braumann, "Die Schuldner und die Sündnerin. Luk. VII.36-50," *NTS* 10 (1963-4): 493.

for the anointing, while he uses present tense forms in 12:4 to highlight Judas' speaking up and his imminent betrayal of Jesus. In 12:5, John again employs present tense forms and imperfects to draw attention to Judas' true motives.

Regarding the literary and theological agendas of the evangelists as a whole, it has been shown that Mark and Matthew focus on Jesus' lesson to his disciples, while John's focus is sharpened to the mounting antagonism between Jesus and Judas, shortly to culminate in the latter's act of betrayal. Luke, on the other hand, uses the anointing of Jesus to illustrate the responses Jesus received during his ministry, contrasting the self-righteous religious leaders of Jesus' day with the "tax-gatherers and sinners." The evangelist was seen to highlight especially the woman's new-found state of forgiveness and salvation.

The Contribution and Potential of Verbal Aspect Theory
Verbal aspect theory has proved to be a valuable tool in the analysis of the evangelists' literary and theological strategies. We do not claim that it stands in rivalry with the conventional tools of source, tradition, and redaction criticism. To the contrary, the analysis of the anointing pericopae has shown that verbal aspect theory is able to complement and corroborate, perhaps even correct or clarify, the findings of such critical tools. This complementary relationship seems to point further to the essential accuracy of verbal aspect theory in explaining Greek verb forms.

It has also become apparent that verbal aspect theory is especially helpful in narrative and discourse analysis, thus showing significant promise for comparative Gospel studies. Together with discourse boundaries and features given prominence by other means,[25] the foregrounding and frontgrounding exposed by the analysis of verbal aspect helps set in perspective the various planes of discourse of which a pericope is composed. Verbal aspect theory provides an accurate and measurable tool for verbal and discourse analysis that has yet to be explored and employed for all its worth.

---

[25]Cf. Porter, *Idioms*, 301–304.

CHAPTER FOUR

JESUS AS RABBI IN THE FOURTH GOSPEL[*]

From Rudolf Bultmann to C. H. Dodd to the Jesus Seminar, Johannine
scholarship has emphasized the Greek background of the Fourth Gospel.
In doing so, Mandaean gnosticism, hermetic literature, and cynicism have
been postulated as likely paradigms into which the Johannine Jesus may
be fitted.[1] These contentions, however, run aground the now almost
universal recognition that Jesus must foremost of all be understood in
terms of his Jewish cultural context,[2] a conclusion aided decisively by the
terminological and theological affinity between the Fourth Gospel and the
Qumran writings.[3] But usually it is the Synoptic Gospels that are used to

---

[*]This essay first appeared in *Bulletin of Biblical Research* 8 (1998): 97–128
and is reprinted with permission.

[1]On the probable milieu of the Fourth Gospel, see esp. C. A. Evans, *Word
and Glory: On the Exegetical and Theological Background of John's Prologue*,
JSNTSS 89 (Sheffield: JSOT, 1993), chap. 1; note particularly the plethora of
bibliographical data in the notes on pp. 13–17.

[2]Cf. even R. Bultmann's own comment, "Yet in face of the entire content of
the Tradition it can hardly be doubted that Jesus did teach as a Rabbi, gather
disciples and engage in disputations." Cf. *The History of the Synoptic Tradition*
(trans. J. Marsh; Oxford: Basil Blackwell, 1963), 50. See also M. Karrer, "Der
lehrende Jesus: Neutestamentliche Erwägungen," *ZNW* 83 (1992): 1–2, who also
refers to a similar quote in Bultmann's 1926 volume, *Jesus* (Berlin: Deutsche
Bibliothek, 1926), 2, n. 5. An ardent defender of the Jewishness of John's Gospel
was A. Schlatter, *Die Sprache und Heimat des vierten Evangelisten* (BFCT 6;
Gütersloh: C. Bertelsmann, 1902) and idem, *Der Evangelist Johannes* (Stuttgart:
Calwer, 1930).

[3]Cf. esp. J. A. T. Robinson, "The New Look on the Fourth Gospel," in
Twelve New Testament Studies (SBT 34; London: SCM, 1962), 94–106, esp. 99.
Cf. also *John and the Dead Sea Scrolls*, ed. J. H. Charlesworth (New York:
Crossroad, 1990). But see now R. Bauckham, "The Qumran Community and the
Gospel of John," presentation at the Annual Meeting of the Society of Biblical
Literature (November 24, 1997), who argues, persuasively, that the Fourth Gospel
does not depend directly on the Qumran writings but that both are indebted to a
common Jewish theological and interpretive milieu. Even so, the evidence
adduced by Bauckham further aids in demonstrating the thoroughgoing Jewish

elucidate this view.[4] The Johannine Jesus, on the other hand, is often understood in terms of the Fourth Gospel's emphasis on Christ's deity, especially as portrayed in the Prologue. Works such as Marianne Thompson's *The Humanity of Jesus in the Fourth Gospel*, however, have countered the arguments of Käsemann and others that John portrays Jesus in docetic terms, that is, as a divine rather than an earthly human figure.[5]

In this debate, with its matrices of Jewish/Greek and human/divine, one important aspect of John's presentation of Jesus has been neglected in recent discussion: the evangelist's portrayal of Jesus as a Jewish rabbi. This may in part be due to the influence of M. Hengel, who, in his significant work *The Charismatic Leader and His Followers*, flatly states that "Jesus was not a 'rabbi.' "[6] While acknowledging that "Jesus was doubtless addressed as 'Rabbi,' " Hengel contends that this expression did not necessarily carry the connotation of teacher but may merely have functioned as a term of respect.[7] He himself considers Jesus primarily as an "eschatological charismatic," the focus of whose message was no longer the Old Testament.[8] For Hengel, Jesus "stood outside any discoverable uniform teaching tradition of Judaism,"[9] so that he concludes, with G. Friedrich, that "there was between him [Jesus] and the rabbis not a difference in degree as between two different teachers, but a difference in principle. He taught as someone specially authorized by God, so that his Word was God's Word, which men could not evade."[10] For this reason Hengel suggests that "we should desist altogether from the description of Jesus as a 'rabbi.' "[11]

---

provenance of the Fourth Gospel.

[4]Cf. M. M. Thompson, "The Historical Jesus and the Johannine Christ," in *Exploring the Gospel of John. In Honor of D. Moody Smith* (ed. R. A. Culpepper and C. C. Black; Louisville, KY: Westminster/John Knox, 1996), 21. Thompson helpfully contrasts the respective contents of Jesus' teaching in the Synoptics and in John on pp. 22–25 and 29–31.

[5]M. M. Thompson, *The Humanity of Jesus in the Fourth Gospel* (Philadelphia: Fortress, 1988).

[6]M. Hengel, *The Charismatic Teacher and his Followers* (Edinburgh: T. & T. Clark, 1981), 42–50. The quotation is from the heading on p. 42. Cf. also K.-H. Rengstorf, "μαθητής, κτλ.," *TDNT* 4:455: "He [Jesus] is for them [his disciples], not the rabbi/διδάσκαλος, but their Lord."

[7]Hengel, *Charismatic Teacher and His Followers*, 42–43.

[8]Ibid., 44, 46.

[9]Ibid., 49.

[10]Ibid., 50.

[11]Ibid.

In recent years, however, Hengel's treatment has been eclipsed by the magisterial work of R. Riesner on Jesus as a teacher.[12] While Riesner focuses primarily on the Synoptic Gospels, his argument remains valid that Jesus operated within the Palestinian framework of a Jewish religious teacher.[13] Nevertheless, Riesner's work remains to be supplemented by an equivalent study on Jesus as a rabbi in the Fourth Gospel. C. Evans' discussion of rabbinic terms and methods as well as targumic and midrashic traditions in John likewise is most helpful but is conducted primarily on the level of the fourth evangelist rather than that of Jesus.[14] The present study is thus designed to provide a corrective to the current debate regarding the historical Jesus as well as a modest supplement to Riesner's work by studying John's presentation of Jesus as a teacher in the Fourth Gospel. It is not argued here that this is the major, or even a major, aspect of Johannine Christology.[15] Rather, as will be seen, John reflects the common perception of Jesus among his contemporaries, friends and foes alike: that Jesus was, perhaps more, but certainly no less, than a rabbi.

---

[12]R. Riesner, *Jesus als Lehrer* (WUNT 2/7, 3d ed.; Tübingen: J. C. B. Mohr [Paul Siebeck], 1988). See also R. T. France, "Mark and the Teaching of Jesus," in *Gospel Perspectives: Studies of History and Tradition in the Four Gospels I* (ed. R. T. France and D. Wenham; Sheffield: JSOT, 1980), 101–36 and R. P. Meye, *Jesus and the Twelve* (Grand Rapids: Eerdmans, 1968), esp. 30–87.

[13]Cf. ibid., esp. 246–76; cf. also id., "Jesus as Preacher and Teacher," in *Jesus and the Oral Gospel Traditions*, ed. Henry Wansborough (Sheffield: JSOT, 1991), 185–210. Other relevant works include C. H. Dodd, "Jesus als Lehrer und Prophet," in *Mysterium Christi: Christological Studies by British and German Theologians*, ed. G. K. A. Bell and A. Deissmann (London: Longmans & Green, 1930), 67–86; E. Fascher, "Jesus der Lehrer," *TLZ* 79 (1954): 325–42; H. Riesenfeld, *The Gospel Tradition and its Beginnings. A Study in the Limits of "Formgeschichte"* (London: Mowbray, 1957); and F. Hahn, *Christologische Hoheitstitel*, FRLANT 83 (Göttingen: Vandenhoeck & Ruprecht, 1963), esp. 74–95.

[14]Cf. Evans, *Word & Glory*, 146–86, esp. 151–68. Cf. also B. D. Chilton, *A Galilean Rabbi and His Bible: Jesus' Use of the Interpreted Scripture of His Time* (GNS 8; Wilmington, DE: Michael Glazier, 1984); and E. Lohse, "ῥαββί, ῥαββουνί," *TDNT* VI: 961–65.

[15]For a more detailed investigation of John's portrayal of Jesus as the Christ see the present author's *The Missions of Jesus and the Disciples According to the Fourth Gospel* (Grand Rapids: Eerdmans, 1998) where the following three roles of Jesus are discerned in John's presentation: Jesus as the Sent Son; Jesus as the one who came into the world and returned to the Father (descent-ascent); and Jesus as the eschatological Shepherd-teacher. A survey of the history of interpretation of John's Gospel shows that while the first two aspects of Johannine Christology have been adequately recognized, the third role has often been overlooked or neglected.

It is not surprising that this aspect of Johannine Christology has not been given much attention.[16] Too striking are the more dominant aspects of John's portrayal of Jesus. Jesus is cast as Son of God (1:34, 39; 5:25; 10:36; 11:4, 27; 20:31), the eschatological Son of Man (1:51; 3:13, 14; 5:27; 6:27, 53, 62; 8:28; 9:35; 12:23, 24; 13:31), and the Christ (1:17, 20, 25, 41; 3:28; 4:25, 29; 7:26, 27, 31, 41, 42; 9:22; 10:24; 11:27; 12:34; 17:3; 20:31).[17] However, it is noteworthy that the only way Jesus is *addressed* in the Fourth Gospel is as Rabbi (ῥαββί), Teacher (διδάσκαλος), and Lord or Master (κύριος),[18] terms largely synonymous in John.[19] Thus, while the evangelist's portrayal of Jesus transcends that of Rabbi/Teacher/Master, enlarging the scope of his Christology to include terms such as Son of God, Son of Man, or Christ, his account makes clear that Jesus' contemporaries perceived and addressed Jesus primarily as a religious teacher, a rabbi.[20]

The present essay thus seeks to establish this one thesis: John's Gospel bears witness that Jesus was perceived by his contemporaries pri-

---

[16]Notably, J. Ashton, in his comprehensive survey of Johannine scholarship, *Understanding the Fourth Gospel* (Oxford: Clarendon, 1991), discusses Jesus according to John primarily as Messiah, Son of God, and Son of Man, but not as a Jewish religious teacher. R. Schnackenburg's recent biblical Christology, *Jesus in the Gospels* (trans. O. C. Dean, Jr.; Louisville: Westminster/John Knox, 1995), likewise omits reference to Jesus as a Jewish religious teacher in his discussion of Johannine Christology.

[17]To this may be added two references to Jesus as son of Joseph (1:45; 6:42), numerous references to Jesus as Lord and Master (κύριος; see further the following note), and the 244 instances of the name Ἰησοῦς in John's Gospel.

[18]Thomas' confession of Jesus as "my Lord and my *God*" (Ὁ κύριός καὶ ὁ θεός μου; 20:28) is no real exception, if for no other reason than that these words are attributed to a disciple *after* Jesus' resurrection.

[19]ῥαββί: 1:38, 49; 3:2; 4:31; 6:25; 9:2; 11:8 (translated as διδάσκαλε in 1:38 and 20:16); κύριος: 4:11, 15, 19, 49; 5:7; 6:34, 68; (8:11;) 9:36, 38; 11:3, 12, 21, 27, 32, 34, 39; 12:21, 38; 13:6, 9, 25, 36, 37; 14:5, 8, 22; 20:15, 28; 21:15, 16, 17, 20, 21. Cf. also the references to Jesus' teaching activity (διδάσκω) in 6:59; 7:14, 28, 35; (8:2;) 8:20; 9:34; 18:20. Most references are to Jesus teaching in synagogues or the Temple; moreover, the Gospel contains one reference each to the teaching activities of the Father (8:28) and the Spirit (14:26).

[20]J.-A. Bühner (*Der Gesandte und sein Weg im 4. Evangelium* [WUNT 2/2; Tübingen: Mohr-Siebeck, 1977], 428) speaks of a "rabbinisch beeinflußten Botenverständnis" in the Fourth Gospel where "der Menschensohn wird zum bevollmächtigten שׁליח Gottes, zu seinem בֶן בּית, der den geordneten Weg einer שׁליחות durchläuft, die beim Sendenden begründet wird und zu ihm zurückkehrt." But the present essay is not primarily concerned with Johannine theology or Christology as such but with historical reflections in the Fourth Gospel of Jesus' own historical role and people's perception of Jesus.

marily as a Jewish religious teacher. The validity of this assertion will be established by a demonstration of the following facts: first, "rabbi" or "teacher" is the customary address of Jesus in the Fourth Gospel; and second, John portrays the relationship between Jesus and his closest followers in terms of the customary teacher-disciple relationship in first-century Judaism. This entails Jesus' assuming the role of teacher by instructing his disciples through word and action, protecting them from harm, and providing for their needs; and the disciples' assuming the role of faithful followers, including the performance of menial tasks and the perpetuation of their Master's teaching.

By proving this thesis, the present study contributes to the study of the historical Jesus, the notion that Jesus was perceived by his contemporaries primarily as a Jewish religious teacher; to Johannine studies, the fact that Jesus' role as a rabbi constitutes the historical starting point for the fourth evangelist's presentation of Jesus, a fact that has generally been overlooked owing to a focus on John's "high" Christology and on Johannine theology rather than the historical Jesus. The results of this study should also contribute to a further rehabilitation of John's historical reliability.

Prolegomena

Before we proceed, it is necessary to address several possible objections or problem areas. First, a word must be said regarding the dating of Jewish sources. Since Judaism did not compile its traditions systematically in written form until the end of the second century CE, and since pre-CE 70 Judaism was characterized by comparatively greater variety than its later counterpart,[21] Rabbinic Judaism (post-CE 70), it is difficult to secure reliable background information for first-century CE rabbi-disciple relationships. Hence several scholars have recently issued appropriate cautions against an undiscerning use of rabbinic materials for the illumination of the background of the New Testament.[22] In the following treatment

---

[21]Cf. Chilton, *Galilean Rabbi*, 31: "The early Judaism of Jesus' time seems to have been so heterogeneous that to claim his continuity or discontinuity with the religion of his day in general terms is problematic in the extreme: in almost anything he did or said, he would have been accepted by some Jews and rejected by others."

[22]Cf. esp. P. S. Alexander, "Rabbinic Judaism and the New Testament," *ZNW* 74 (1983): 237–46; and the works by J. Neusner, *Rabbinic Literature and the New Testament: What We Cannot Show, We Do Not Know* (Valley Forge, Pa.: Trinity Press International, 1994) and *The Rabbinic Traditions about the Pharisees before 70* (3 vols.; Leiden: E. J. Brill, 1971). On criteria for the use of

every effort will be made to date a given reference, keeping in mind that an attribution to a particular rabbi may or may not be accurate.[23] At the same time, mishnaic or talmudic references, even if dated post-CE 70, may still reflect traditions current in Jesus' day.[24] In the end, the case made by the present study does not stand or fall with the dating of individual rabbinic references. The aim of this essay is rather modest. All that is needed to establish the thesis argued here is to provide a credible first-century Jewish framework for John's portrayal of Jesus and his followers, a general backdrop that makes it possible to test the contention that Jesus assumed the role of a Jewish religious teacher in keeping with Jewish practices and that he was so viewed by his contemporaries.

Second, the perception that the present study is reductionistic must be warded off at the outset. It is not argued here that rabbi is the *only* Johan-

---

rabbinic materials, see esp. Evans, *Word and Glory*, 20–28. Cf. further the essays by L. H. Silberman, "Anent the Use of Rabbinic Material," *NTS* 24 (1978): 415–17 and "Once Again: The Use of Rabbinic Material," *NTS* 42 (1996): 153–55; B. Gerhardsson, *Memory and Manuscript: Oral Tradition and Written Transmission in Rabbinic Judaism and Early Christianity* (Uppsala: C. W. K. Gleerup, 1961), 15 and 77–78; and the discussion in G. F. Moore, *Judaism in the First Centuries of the Christian Era* (Cambridge, MA: Harvard University Press, 1962), 3:17–22.

[23]Cf. here esp. H. L. Strack and G. Stemberger, *Introduction to the Talmud and Midrash* (trans. M. Bockmuehl; Minneapolis: Fortress, 1992; henceforth Str-St).

[24]For a positive attitude toward the judicious use of rabbinic materials for the purpose of establishing a framework for understanding John's portrait of Jesus, see, e.g., C. K. Barrett, *The Gospel According to St. John* (2d ed.; Philadelphia: Westminster, 1978), 33: "Great caution is necessary. No part of the rabbinic literature was written down until a date later than the composition of John. Direct literary relationship is out of the question, and some apparent parallels may be merely fortuitous. *But when all such allowances have been made it remains very probable that John himself (or perhaps the authors of some of his sources) was familiar with the oral teaching which at a later date was crystallized in the Mishnah, the Talmud, and the Midrashim*" (emphasis added). Chilton *(Galilean Rabbi*, 32–33), after issuing similar cautions, concurs: "Neither Sanders' criticisms nor others to a similar effect, however, has vitiated the essential insight which Billerbeck's monumental volumes so authoritatively convey: the Judaism of the rabbis is comparable to a great deal in the New Testament, especially when we set Jesus' teaching and ministry alongside the views and actions attributed to first century rabbis." Chilton also points out that the rabbis did not invent Judaism *de novo*. "Methodologically, they were traditionalists who handed on the views of predecessors." The verdict of M. Hengel, "The Old Testament in the Fourth Gospel," in *The Gospels and the Scriptures of Israel* (ed. C. A. Evans and W. R. Stegner; JSNTSS 104; Sheffield: Sheffield Academic Press, 1994), 395, echoes these sentiments: "One thing remains certain: . . . the Fourth Gospel is to be understood primarily from the Jewish sources of its period."

nine category for Jesus, or even the most important. Rather, it is merely contended that John reflects the fact that this was the way Jesus was primarily perceived by his contemporaries. To be sure, on the basis of this common perception speculation arose whether Jesus was the prophet like Moses or the Messianic king.[25] But if the historical starting point for John's presentation of Jesus is lost, there no longer remains any common ground on the basis of which the historical Jesus conducted the interchange with his Jewish interlocutors and the locus from which the evangelist seeks to lead his readers into a deeper understanding of Jesus' full and true identity. The present essay's focus on John's presentation of Jesus as a rabbi should in no way be viewed as an effort to diminish John's portrayal of Jesus in apocalyptic-prophetic terms, including Jesus' working of miracles. But the notion must be resisted that these elements are incompatible with John's basic presentation of Jesus as a religious teacher. As Riesner contends, a "high Christology" need not necessarily conflict with a portrayal of Jesus as a teacher, and the role of teacher and the working of miracles may complement each other rather than stand in conflict.[26] Hengel likewise notes that "prophet" and "teacher" should in no way be regarded as opposites.[27] The felt tension in this case may rather be the result of an unduly narrow concept of the category of teacher that excludes prophetic, miracle-working, or messianic notions but is incompatible with scriptural and Jewish notions in Jesus' and John's day.

Third, a distinction must be made between ῥαββί as an address for teachers prior to CE 70 and ῥαββί as a fixed title in the period of full-fledged rabbinism. The present essay uses the term "rabbi" in the former sense without implying in any way that Jesus conforms to the formalized picture of the institutionalized rabbinate after the destruction of the Jewish Temple in CE 70 and the bar Kochba revolt in CE 135.[28] Moreover, calling Jesus a "rabbi" does not necessarily imply buying into the theory that Jesus had a highly sophisticated didactic philosophy, including teaching his stu-

---

[25]Cf. esp. W. A. Meeks, *The Prophet-King: Moses Traditions and the Johannine Christology* (SNT 14; Leiden: E. J. Brill, 1967); M.-É. Boismard, *Moses or Jesus: An Essay in Johannine Christology* (trans. B. T. Viviano; Philadelphia: Fortress, 1993), esp. 1–68.

[26]Cf. Riesner, *Jesus als Lehrer*, 252.

[27]Hengel, *Charismatic Leader and His Followers*, 45.

[28]Cf. Riesner, *Jesus als Lehrer*, 274, following G. Dalman, *Die Worte Jesu mit Berücksichtigung des nachkanonischen jüdischen Schrifttums und der aramäischen Sprache* (2d ed.; Leipzig: J. C. Hinrichs, 1930), 272–80.

dents to memorize large portions of his words or other similar methods.[29]

Fourth, the effort to demonstrate that Jesus' contemporaries viewed him first of all as a rabbi in keeping with established Jewish custom does not intend to level all distinctions between the teachings and actions of Jesus and those of other Jewish rabbis. To the contrary, it will be seen that Jesus adapted this model in a number of ways and even broke common convention in his actions as well as in his teaching. In particular, Jesus' messianic consciousness led him to interpret Old Testament messianic interpretations with reference to himself, something no other rabbi of his day would have dared to do.

Fifth and last, the present essay does not view the Fourth Gospel merely as a "window" to the history of the "Johannine community," as recent influential voices have proposed.[30] This disclaimer seems justified in light of the massive recent refutation of the "Johannine community hypothesis" by M. Hengel and the equally devastating critique by R. Bauckham.[31] It is therefore not necessary to share the negative evaluation of interpreters since Bretschneider (1820), climaxing in the work of R. Bultmann, regarding the (lack of) historicity and historical accuracy of the Gospels in general and the Fourth Gospel in particular.[32] Arguably, the

---

[29]Cf. Gerhardsson, *Memory and Manuscript.* For an assessment of Gerhardsson, see esp. P. H. Davids, "The Gospels and Jewish Tradition: Twenty Years After Gerhardsson," *Gospel Perspectives I,* 75–99. Cf. also A. Schlatter, *The History of the Christ* (trans. A. J. Köstenberger; Grand Rapids: Baker, 1997): "The means by which he facilitated their work consisted merely of the free and continual access he granted them. The accounts know nothing of a formal preparation for their work, any more than they imply that Jesus used some 'method' of conversion. Therefore we do not hear anything of lessons, of sentences he had them memorize, of religious activities he drilled them in, or any other methods."

[30]Cf. R. A. Culpepper, *Anatomy of the Fourth Gospel* (Philadelphia: Fortress, 1983); J. L. Martyn, *History and Theology in the Fourth Gospel* (rev. ed.; Nashville: Abingdon, 1979). For a representative sampling of recent trends in Johannine scholarship, particularly in North America, see *"What is John?" Readers and Readings of the Fourth Gospel* (SBL Symposium Series 3; ed. F. F. Segovia; Atlanta: Scholars Press, 1996).

[31]M. Hengel, *Die johanneische Frage* (WUNT 67; Tübingen: Mohr-Siebeck, 1993); R. Bauckham, ed., *The Gospels for All Christians: Rethinking the Gospel Audiences* (Grand Rapids: Eerdmans, 1997), esp. the introductory essay on pp. 9–48. Cf. also R. G. Maccini, *Her Testimony is True: Women as Witnesses according to John* (JSNTSS 125; Sheffield: Sheffield Academic Press, 1996), esp. 144 and 240–41.

[32]Cf. the present author's essay "Frühe Zweifel an der johanneischen Verfasserschaft des vierten Evangeliums in der modernen Interpretationsgeschichte," *European Journal of Theology* 5 (1996): 37–46.

recent focus on the level of the later "Johannine community" and the negative assessment of the Fourth Gospel's historical accuracy has blinded interpreters to the truth embodied in the argument of the present essay.[33] While this cannot be fully developed here, a case can very well be made that the Fourth Gospel provides a historically reliable portrait of Jesus.[34] While the Fourth Gospel is given to more theologizing than the Synoptics, this arguably does not mean that history is treated lightly. This is already indicated, among other things, by the Johannine "witness" motif, which evidences John's concern for historical accuracy. As M. Thompson has recently put it, being left with the options of historical or unhistorical in the case of the Fourth Gospel "may finally be as futile and irresolvable as arguing that photography is superior to Impressionism."[35] The following should therefore be granted: that the purpose of John's Gospel is primarily to present the historical Jesus, not the history of a "Johannine community"; and that John's Gospel be assumed innocent of historical inaccuracies unless proven guilty, rather than vice versa.[36] In the present case, two factors in particular suggest that John's depiction of Jesus as rabbi is historically accurate: first, the observation made by Riesner that the portrayal of Jesus as a teacher cannot be explained merely by a later Jewish-Christian "rabbinization" as some have alleged in the case of Matthew;[37] and second, the agreement between all four evangelists regarding people's perception and address of Jesus as a Jewish religious teacher.

---

[33]Cf. W. D. Davies ("Reflections on Aspects of the Jewish Background of the Gospel of John," in *Exploring the Gospel of John. In Honor of D. Moody Smith* [ed. R. A. Culpepper and C. C. Black; Westminster/John Knox, 1996], 43-64), whose focus is exclusively on the level of Johannine composition.

[34]Cf., e.g., L. Morris, "History and Theology in the Fourth Gospel," in *Studies in the Fourth Gospel* (Grand Rapids: Eerdmans, 1969), 65-138; R. E. Brown, "The Problem of Historicity in John," in *New Testament Essays* (Garden City, NY: Doubleday, 1965), 187-217; C. L. Blomberg, *The Historical Reliability of the Gospels* (Downers Grove: IVP, 1987), 188-89; and now Thompson, "Historical Jesus and Johannine Christ," esp. 25-26 and 32-35. Cf. also J. D. G. Dunn, "John and the Oral Gospel Tradition," in *Jesus and the Oral Gospel Tradition* (ed. H. Wansbrough; JSNTSS 64; Sheffield: JSOT, 1991), 351-79, building on C. H. Dodd, *Historical Tradition in the Fourth Gospel* (Cambridge: Cambridge University Press, 1963); and Bauckham, "John for Readers of Mark," in *Gospels for All Christians*, 147-71.

[35]Thompson, "Historical Jesus and Johannine Christ," 35.

[36]Cf. esp. C. L. Blomberg, "Where Do We Start Studying Jesus?" in *Jesus Under Fire* (ed. M. J. Wilkins and J. P. Moreland; Grand Rapids: Zondervan, 1995), 30-36.

[37]Cf. Riesner, *Jesus als Lehrer*, 252.

The present study may now proceed in the attempt to establish the thesis that John portrays Jesus primarily as a religious teacher. The first part of this demonstration is an investigation of the instances where Jesus is addressed or referred to as "rabbi" or "teacher" in the Fourth Gospel.

The Perception of Jesus as Rabbi by His Contemporaries

Introduction

John's Gospel features eight instances where Jesus is addressed as ῥαββί: 1:38, 49; 3:2; 4:31; 6:25; 9:2; 11:8; and 20:16 (ῥαββουνί). This constitutes over half of the references in the four Gospels combined.[38] The address is attributed to Jesus' first followers (1:38), Nathanael (1:49), Nicodemus (3:2), his disciples (4:31; 9:2: 11:8), the multitudes (6:25), and Mary Magdalene (20:16). A comparison between John and the Synoptic writers shows that John frequently provides the Hebrew/Aramaic term ῥαββί while the Synoptists generally use the Greek equivalent διδάσκαλος. In the first instance where ῥαββί is used, John translates ῥαββί as διδάσκαλος (1:38).[39] He does the same at the end of the Gospel where the variant ῥαββουνί is used (20:16).[40] Even in those two instances, however, John retains the original appellation. Thus John, who is often considered to be less interested in preserving original parlance or historical accuracy, is in this instance found to be closer to the actual address of the earthly Jesus than the Synoptic writers.[41] Matthew, by contrast, seems to avoid reference

---

[38]There are two references to Jesus as ῥαββί in Matthew, four in Mark, and none in Luke.

[39]The equivalence of the terms ῥαββί and διδάσκαλος is also confirmed by the synonymous parallelism in Matt 23:8. Cf. Riesner ("Jesus as Preacher and Teacher," 186), who also refers to epigraphical evidence from pre-70 CE Jerusalem (CCII, II, 1266, 1268/69).

[40]As Karrer ("Der lehrende Jesus," 19 n. 100) points out, the correspondence between the first and the last reference to Jesus as teacher in the Fourth Gospel (1:38 and 20:16) provides evidence for the unified perspective with which the Fourth Gospel views the earthly and the resurrected Jesus.

[41]Hengel (Charismatic Leader and His Followers, 43, n. 19) ascribes this to John's "historicizing tendency." The above argument assumes that Jesus was in fact addressed as ῥαββί by his contemporaries, a contention that is rendered highly probable by the multiple attestation of all four Gospels. On this issue, see esp. the interchange by J. Donaldson, "The Title Rabbi in the Gospels—Some Reflections on the Evidence of the Synoptics," JQR 63 (1972-73): 287-91; H. Shanks, "Is the Title 'Rabbi' Anachronistic in the Gospels?" JQR 53 (1963): 337-45; and the reply by S. Zeitlin (pp. 345-49); as well as Riesner, "Jesus as Preacher and Teacher," 188.

to Jesus as ῥαββί in an effort to safeguard his uniqueness as the Jewish Messiah.[42] Of his four uses of the term, two caution Jesus' disciples against allowing themselves to be addressed as ῥαββί and two are by the traitor, Judas (26:25, 49). Luke does not use the Hebrew/Aramaic term ῥαββί at all and generally substitutes the Greek expressions διδάσκαλος or ἐπιστάτα in deference to his Gentile audience. He does this, however, without downplaying the significance of Jesus' role as a teacher.[43] Mark has three people address Jesus as ῥαββί, a blind man (10:51), Peter (9:5; 11:21), and Judas (14:45). He also features several instances where Jesus is addressed or referred to as διδάσκαλος.[44] Interestingly, Mark thus comes closest to John in reflecting the probable historical address of Jesus as ῥαββί by his contemporaries.[45] Still, John is unmatched both in the range of individuals referring to Jesus as ῥαββί and the consistency with which ῥαββί is the chosen address of Jesus.

Jesus as Rabbi in the Fourth Gospel
The next step is a brief investigation of the individual instances where Jesus is addressed as ῥαββί in the Fourth Gospel. At the outset, two preliminary remarks are in order.[46] First, the term ῥαββί, derived from the

---

[42]But see the references to Jesus as διδάσκαλος in Matt 8:19; 9:11; 12:38; 17:24; 19:16; 22:16; 22:24, 36; 26:18.

[43]Jesus is addressed as διδάσκαλος in Luke 7:40 (Peter), 9:38 (man from the multitude), 10:25 (a certain lawyer), 11:45 (one of the lawyers), 12:13 (someone in the crowd), 18:18 (a certain ruler), 19:39 (some of the Pharisees), 20:21 (scribes and chief priests), 20:28 (Sadducees), 20:39 (some of the scribes), 21:7 (disciples); to this should be added the references in 8:49 and 22:11. Riesner ("Jesus as Preacher and Teacher," 187) claims that Luke "was also careful to avoid the address διδάσκαλε in the mouth of disciples although he preserved this form of address on the lips of non-followers" for the purpose of underlining "that for him Jesus was far superior to any teacher." But this fails to consider Luke 7:40 and 21:7.

[44]Cf. Mark 4:38; 5:35; 9:17, 38; 10:17, 20, 35; 12:14, 19, 32; 13:1; 14:14. Cf. France, "Mark and the Teaching of Jesus," 101–36.

[45]This observations appears to support Markan priority. See P. M. Head, *Christology and the Synoptic Problem: An Argument for Markan Priority* (SNTSMS 94; Cambridge: Cambridge University Press, 1997), esp. 148–73; and my review in *Faith & Mission* 15/1 (Fall 1997): 76–78.

[46]Owing to the constraints of the present study, the focus will not be on the content of Jesus' teaching but on Jesus' role as teacher in relation to his disciples. Thus the question of the exact nature of Jesus' teaching role according to John will be left open. A caution must be registered, however, against categories that are too rigid, such as "teacher of wisdom" or "teacher after the manner of rabbinic authorities" (e.g., Rengstorf, "μαθητής, κτλ.," 454, n. 256), which fail to do justice to the uniqueness of Jesus as teacher.

Hebrew רבי ("my great one"), expressed considerable respect. *M. 'Abot* 4:12, a saying attributed to R. Eleazar b. Shammua (CE 130–160), student of R. Aqiba, says: "Let the fear of your teacher be as the fear of heaven."[47] According to Matthew, Jesus discouraged his disciples from appropriating the title ῥαββί (23:8),[48] which stood in contrast with contemporary Jewish practice where a student, after several years of association with his teacher, earned the right to be addressed as ῥαββί.[49] The use of ῥαββί for a Jewish religious teacher as an address rather than a title is attested for R. Eleazar b. Azariah, who addressed his teacher R. Yohanan b. Zakkai (d. c. 80 CE) as רבי when visiting him at the occasion of the death of Yohanan's son (*'Abot R. Nat.* 14). Hillel likewise was addressed as רבי (*Lev. Rab.* 34, 130d).[50] Riesner, following Cohen, notes that the term ῥαββί is confined to Palestine in the first century CE, a fact that further accentuates John's concern for historical accuracy.[51]

Second, it is significant that the address of Jesus as ῥαββί in John is confined to the time of Jesus' earthly ministry. The one instance in 20:16 where Jesus is addressed as ῥαββουνί by Mary Magdalene is no real exception. John may indicate the inappropriateness of such an address subsequent to Jesus' resurrection by translating the term and following it in short order with Thomas' confession of Jesus as "Lord and God" (κύριος καὶ θεός; 20:28). By this John draws a very important distinction in identity between the earthly and the exalted Jesus. Moreover, as will be seen below, the Farewell Discourse already portrays the exalted Jesus as transcending the identity of ῥαββί.

I proceed with a treatment of individual passages. In 1:38 and 49, it is Jesus' first followers who approach him by addressing him as ῥαββί. Only John notes the fact that some of Jesus' first followers had previously been followers of the Baptist and that the Baptist himself had pointed them to Jesus. This might explain the rather developed understanding of Jesus' mission on the part of his first followers. Interestingly, the term ῥαββί, in

---

[47]Cf. E. Schürer, *The History of the Jewish People in the Age of Jesus Christ* (rev. and ed. by G. Vermes, F. Millar, and M. Black; Edinburgh: T. & T. Clark, 1979), 2:325; and Lohse, "ῥαββί," 961–62.

[48]See the discussion in Riesner, *Jesus als Lehrer*, 259–64, 269–72.

[49]Cf. Lohse, "ῥαββί," 962, 965.

[50]Cf. Str-B 1:917, 971; Lohse, "ῥαββί," 962, n. 19; and Riesner, *Jesus als Lehrer*, 268.

[51]Cf. Riesner, "Jesus as Preacher and Teacher," 188, referring to S. J. D. Cohen, "Epigraphical Rabbis," *JQR* 72 (1982): 1–17. Cf. further Hengel, *Charismatic Leader and His Followers*, 43, n. 20.

the sole instance in John where it does not refer to Jesus, is applied to the Baptist (3:26).[52] This indicates that the Baptist was awarded the respect commensurate to a religious teacher by his disciples. The use of ῥαββί as address for Jesus in 1:38 and 49 clearly indicates that Jesus' first followers conceived of their relationship with Jesus in terms of a teacher-disciple relationship. This is not mitigated by the fact that they followed Jesus precisely because they saw in him *more* than a religious teacher, as is made clear by Nathanael's statement: "ῥαββί, you are the Son of God. You are the king of Israel" (1:49). Nathanael's statement, if historical, may well reflect an initial perception that still required growth in understanding as a result of a committed following of this ῥαββί.[53] The question addressed to Jesus in 1:38, "ῥαββί, where are you staying (μένεις)?" together with Jesus' invitation for his first disciples to "come and see" and their acceptance of Jesus' offer (ἦλθαν οὖν καὶ εἶδαν ποῦ μένει καὶ παρ' ἔμειναν τὴν ἡμέραν ἐκείνην; 1:39) indicates the closeness of relationship sustained by teacher and disciples. In the context of the Johannine narrative, it becomes the starting point for a relationship that eventually comes to transcend boundaries of time and space (compare the use of μένω in 6:56; 8:31; 12:46; and especially the eleven instances of μένω in 15:4-16). In conclusion, the two references in 1:38 and 49 indicate that Jesus' first followers transferred their allegiance from one religious teacher, the Baptist, to another, Jesus, who was more but not less than a ῥαββί. Accordingly, they expressed their perception of him as a religious teacher by addressing him as such.

In 3:2, Nicodemus, the "Teacher of Israel" (ὁ διδάσκαλος τοῦ Ἰσραήλ; 3:10), addresses Jesus as ῥαββί: "ῥαββί, we know that you are a teacher (διδάσκαλος) come from God; no one can do the signs you are doing unless God is with him." Apparently, this represents an effort by Nicodemus, the Pharisee and member of the Sanhedrin, to award Jesus similar status as a religious teacher. In this Nicodemus contrasts with the increasingly hostile reaction to Jesus on the part of the Pharisees in general (cf. 1:24; 4:1; 7:32-52; 8:3-11; 9:13-41; 11:46-57; 12:19, 42; 18:3).[54] This

---

[52]Evans (*Word and Glory*, 151) mistakenly attributes this reference to Jesus. Cf. also Luke 3:12 where the Baptist is addressed as διδάσκαλος.

[53]D. A. Carson, *Gospel According to John* (Grand Rapids: Eerdmans, 1991), 147-48.

[54]On the question of whether or not the Gospel portrait of the Pharisees is accurate, see M. Silva, "Historical Reconstruction in New Testament Criticism," in *Hermeneutics, Authority, and Canon* (ed. D. A. Carson and J. D. Woodbridge; Grand Rapids: Zondervan, 1986), 112-21. Cf. also Neusner, *Rabbinic Traditions about the Pharisees*, 1:244-48. One Pharisaic attitude reflected in the Fourth

must surely have been considered a gesture of goodwill and benevolence on the part of Nicodemus, since it was commonly recognized that Jesus lacked rabbinic credentials (cf. 7:15: μὴ μεμαθηκώς). This address of Jesus as ῥαββί also confirms that Jesus' assumption of the identity of a Jewish religious teacher provided him with common ground on which to interact with other Jewish rabbis such as Nicodemus. At the same time, the difference between Jesus and other Jewish rabbis is also highlighted: unlike the Jewish scribes, Jesus relied on his consciousness of having been sent by God and his resultant spiritual authority rather than on rabbinic training. Also, in breaking with Jewish custom, he apparently never attached himself to a particular Jewish rabbi to follow him and learn from him. Jesus does not return Nicodemus' courtesy. Rather than engaging in polite platitudes, he lectures the "Teacher of Israel" on his need for regeneration. This stands in marked contrast to Jesus' compassionate treatment of the Samaritan woman in the subsequent chapter.[55] Jesus' assertive stance toward Nicodemus strikingly demonstrates for John's readers that Jesus, while falling short of Nicodemus' rabbinic credentials, commanded spiritual authority far exceeding that of his Jewish counterpart. It was doubtless impressive to many of John's original readers that Nicodemus later in the Gospel ends up as a secret follower of Jesus (cf. 7:50–52; 19:38–42).

The next relevant passage is 4:31, where Jesus' disciples address their teacher as ῥαββί when returning from getting food. The disciples' address stands in marked contrast with the Samaritan woman's consistent reference to Jesus as κύριος (translated "sir" in the NIV and NASB; cf. 4:11, 15, 19). If it is true that Samaritans at that time addressed God as Rabbi, the woman may have wanted to avoid any such connotation with regard to Jesus, at least early in the conversation.[56] The (equivalent of the) term κύριος may also have been used by the woman to indicate respect while remaining distant, owing to the ethnic, social, and gender barriers separating her and Jesus. The disciples, on the other hand, address Jesus as ῥαββί, indicating their perception of him as their teacher. As will be fur-

---

Gospel that can be corroborated from rabbinic sources is their contempt of the scripture-illiterate masses (עם הארץ; cf. 7:49). Evans (*Word and Glory*, 166) calls this "a typical attitude toward the common people" in Jesus' day, referring also to statements attributed to Hillel ("An ignorant man cannot be holy," *m. 'Abot* 2:6) and Hanina ben Dosa (*m. 'Abot* 3:11).

[55]Cf. C. L. Blomberg, "The Globalization of Biblical Interpretation: A Test Case—John 3–4," *BBR* 5 (1995): 1–15.

[56]Cf. Lohse, "ῥαββί," 961, referring also to Dalman, *Worte Jesu*, 275.

ther discussed below, their getting food as well as their questioning of their teacher's actions (in the present case, his talking with a Samaritan woman) are entirely consistent with the pattern of Jewish teacher-disciple relationships.

The address of Jesus as ῥαββί in 6:25 is significant because it is issued by the crowds. The timing, shortly after the feeding of the multitude, is important as well, since it balances the passage in 6:14–15 where Jesus, on account of his messianic sign, is called "the Prophet" and some intend to make him king. The passage makes clear that the Jewish crowds continued to perceive Jesus first and foremost as a religious teacher, albeit one who performed remarkable feats and who taught with unusual authority.

In 7:15, reference is made to Jesus' lack of rabbinic training (Πῶς οὗτος γράμματα οἶδεν μὴ μεμαθηκώς).[57] Strack and Billerbeck note that attachment to a recognized rabbi, including being of service to him, were part of a person's religious education. This was lacking in Jesus' case; hence the question of 7:15. It was possible for someone to acquire scriptural literacy by way of self-study, but this way of obtaining knowledge did not enjoy the same esteem as formal training.[58] Nevertheless, while the people's comment is derogatory, the statement confirms the common perception of Jesus as a religious teacher. Another piece of evidence is provided by the question in 7:35, "Where does this man intend to go that we shall not find him? He is not intending to go to the Dispersion and *teach* the Greeks, is he?"

The disciples' interrogation of Jesus with regard to the cause of a man's blindness in 9:2 while addressing their master as ῥαββί fits into the pattern which by now has become a familiar one for the reader of John's Gospel (cf. 1:38, 49; 4:31). The closeness of their relationship and its purpose of providing a framework for religious instruction allow Jesus' followers to inquire regarding a matter that puzzled them. As they accompanied their master and associated closely with him, teachable moments often arose that allowed a teacher to impart his knowledge and insight to his disciples. In this case, Jesus' answer transcended the wisdom of his scribal contemporaries, who customarily attributed suffering to a person's sin. For Jesus, the man's blindness was an occasion for the revelation of

---

[57]Note the later leveling of a similar charge against Jesus' followers in Acts 4:13 where Peter and John are called "unschooled, ordinary men" (ἀγράμματοι καὶ ἰδιῶται) who nevertheless spoke with spiritual insight and authority. As in Jesus' case, people "marveled" (ἐθαύμαζον; cf. John 7:15 and Acts 4:13).

[58]Str-B 2:486.

God's glory (9:3). Again, the passage confirms John's pattern of presentation of Jesus as a rabbi.

In 11:8, Jesus' disciples fear for their master's life, asking, "ῥαββί, the Jews were just now seeking to stone you, and are you going there [Bethany near Jerusalem] again?" When Jesus insists that he must go, Thomas, perhaps with thinly veiled sarcasm but nevertheless reflecting genuine concern, remarks to his fellow disciples, "Let us also go, that we may die with him" (11:16). Similar to 4:31, where the disciples urge their master to eat, knowing that he had not had food for an extended period of time, the disciples here express concern for the physical well-being of their teacher. As will be seen further below, this, too, was a characteristic feature of first-century Jewish disciples.

Three relevant passages remain. First, Martha's statement to her sister Mary in 11:28 that "the Teacher [Jesus] is here" once again reinforces the notion that Jesus' contemporaries customarily perceived him as a religious teacher. Jesus' raising of Lazarus, of course, explodes narrow notions of the role of a religious teacher. Second, when Jesus is summoned before the Jewish high priest subsequent to his arrest, the subjects of interrogation are Jesus' *disciples and his teaching* (18:19). When it is intimated that Jesus' teaching was characterized by subversiveness, secretiveness, and exclusivism, Jesus maintains, "I have spoken openly to the world; I always taught in synagogues and in the Temple, where all the Jews come together; and I spoke nothing in secret" (18:20). This interchange, too, points to the common perception of Jesus as a religious teacher. Third, Mary Magdalene addresses Jesus as ῥαββουνί following his resurrection in 20:16. As has been noted, however, this appellation may be deemed inappropriate by the fourth evangelist subsequent to Jesus' resurrection.

Conclusion

It is now possible to summarize the cumulative thrust of the references to Jesus as ῥαββί in John's Gospel. Limited to Jesus' earthly ministry, they present a consistent picture of people's perception of Jesus as a religious teacher. This perception is not confined to the circle of Jesus' immediate followers. It extends also to the crowds (6:25; cf. 7:15, 35), other Jewish rabbis such as Nicodemus (3:2), and Jesus' friends (11:28: ὁ διδάσκαλος). For this reason it appears that the first part of the thesis of the present study has been sustained: the Fourth Gospel indeed indicates that Jesus was customarily perceived by his contemporaries as a religious teacher, a rabbi. The investigation may proceed with the second part of the argument of this essay, John's portrayal of the relationship between Jesus and his closest followers in terms of the customary teacher-disciple relationship in first-century Judaism.

The Depiction of Jesus' Relationship with His Followers in Terms
of First-century Jewish Teacher-Disciple Relationships

John's portrayal of the relationship between Jesus and his closest followers in terms of the teacher-disciple relationship customary in first-century Judaism entails depiction of Jesus as assuming the role of teacher who instructs his disciples through word and action, protects them from harm, and provides for their needs. The disciples on their part take on the role of faithful followers, including the performance of menial tasks and the perpetuation of their Master's teaching. The first part of the following discussion will investigate the various aspects of Jesus' assumption of the role of teacher according to John's Gospel.

Jesus as Teacher in the Fourth Gospel

John's Gospel portrays Jesus as providing instruction for his followers in a number of ways.[59] He does so by verbal instruction as well as action, including "mystifying gestures" followed by an explanation, and personal example. Apart from assuming responsibility for providing instruction for his followers, Jesus is also shown to provide for other needs of his disciples and to protect them from all harm, including the negative influences of false teaching. These features will briefly be surveyed in turn.

Verbal Instruction. The study of Jesus' verbal instruction entails an investigation of his use of Scripture, his "rabbinic rulings," and his style of argumentation. Regarding Jesus' reference to the Hebrew Scriptures,[60]

---

[59]On Jesus' teaching techniques, see esp. R. Riesner, "Jesus as Preacher and Teacher," 201–208.

[60]Hengel (*Charismatic Leader and His Followers*, 46) contends that the Old Testament is no longer the central focus of Jesus' message. He comments, "As a rule Jesus argues exegetically only when he is questioned or attacked by third parties about the Torah, and, in addition, also at times when his claims and authority are at stake, and here it is often methodologically difficult to distinguish between Jesus' use of scripture and that of the Christian community, as the latter again was for apologetic reasons very much more interested in proofs from scripture." But apart from Hengel's methodological skepticism, it seems precarious to brush aside instances where Jesus uses the Hebrew Scriptures "when he is questioned or attacked by third parties about the Torah, and, in addition, also at times when his claims and authority are at stake" as merely exceptional. Moreover, when Hengel claims that the new content of Jesus' teaching "was not 'scribal' and 'rabbinic' but 'charismatic' and 'eschatological,' " he seems to use the term "rabbinic" in its later, post-70 CE sense. It seems extreme to deny completely that ῥαββί carried the connotation of teacher in the instances narrated in the Gospels when applied to Jesus.

one notes five instances of particular quotations in John: in 1:51, to Gen 28:12; in 6:45, to Isa 54:13; in 10:34, to Ps 82:6; in 13:18, to Isa 41:10; and in 15:25, to Ps 35:19 or 69:5. A brief discussion of some salient features must suffice here.[61] In 1:51, Jesus claims that he transcends God's revelation to Jacob as the new, greater revelation of God.[62] Jesus' reference in 6:45 to Isa 54:13, "And they shall all be taught of God" (cf. Jer 31:31-34; Ezek 36:24-26), is remarkable for the present study in that the saying emphasizes Jesus' (and later the Spirit's) teaching role of God's new messianic community (cf. 7:37-39). According to the Johannine Jesus, his teaching ministry is in accordance with the divine promise given through the Old Testament prophets. In 10:34-36, Jesus establishes the legitimacy of his claim to deity by referring to Ps 82:6 where God extends the designation "gods" even to Israel. The reference to Isa 41:10 in 13:18 ("He who eats my bread has lifted up his heel against me") reveals that Jesus viewed even Judas' betrayal as in accordance with Scripture (cf. 17:12). Similarly, Jesus in 15:25 acknowledges that people's rejection of him fulfilled Old Testament prophecy ("They hated me without a cause"; cf. 19:28).

Moreover, Jesus occasionally refers to Old Testament types, such as when making mention of the "serpent in the wilderness" in 3:14-15 (cf. Num 21:8-9). The latter instance is particularly interesting in light of the fact that Jesus here evidences a reading of the Old Testament in light of his messianic calling, in particular the substitutionary nature of his death. Another instance of Jesus' elaborating on antecedent Old Testament types is his discourse on the "Bread of Heaven" (6:30-59). Responding to the Jews' challenge for a sign of similar proportions as God's provision of manna in the wilderness through Moses (cf. 2:18 for a similar request), Jesus points to the fruit of his own mission, again in terms of substitution-

---

[61]Cf. D. A. Carson, "John and Johannine Epistles," in *It Is Written: Scripture Citing Scripture* (ed. D. A. Carson and H. G. M. Williamson; Cambridge: Cambridge University Press, 1988), 246; Evans, *Word and Glory*, 174-75. In keeping with the purposes of the present essay, this study is only interested in, not *John's* use of the Old Testament, but *Jesus'* use of the Hebrew Scriptures according to John. Interestingly, this distinction is rarely made in the literature, perhaps owing to the prevailing skepticism regarding the ability of modern interpreters to learn anything about the historical Jesus from John's Gospel, so that all of the uses of the Old Testament in John are subsumed under "Johannine theology." Cf., e.g., G. Reim, *Studien zum alttestamentlichen Hintergrund des Johannesevangeliums* (SNTMS 22; Cambridge: Cambridge University Press, 1974).

[62]Cf. Carson, *Gospel According to John*, 163-64.

ary atonement.[63] As already mentioned, Jesus' interpretation of the Hebrew Scriptures according to John thus evidences features that transcend common interpretation in his day. Jesus' messianic consciousness causes him to read the Old Testament with references to himself, a feature not found in contemporary rabbis.[64] Nevertheless, while there are differences between Jesus' teaching and the teaching of other Jewish teachers, this does not affect the validity of the thesis postulated in the present essay that people's primary perception of Jesus was that of a religious teacher, in keeping with contemporary custom.[65]

Jesus' "rabbinic rulings" are portrayed by John, in keeping with the presentation of the Synoptics, as regularly transcending the wisdom of his contemporaries. When challenged about his healing of a man on the Sabbath, he notes that even in rabbinic interpretation the prohibition of work on the Sabbath was not without exception: if the eighth day on which a newborn male was to be circumcised fell on a Sabbath, circumcision was to proceed in order to fulfill the commandment of Lev 12:3 (cf. esp. *m. Šabb.* 19:1–3).[66] In light of this precedent, Jesus argues, what is wrong with healing an entire man on the Sabbath? On another occasion, when asked by his disciples regarding the cause of a man's blindness, Jesus rejects the customary simplistic cause-and-effect explanations of suffering and proceeds to heal the man (chap. 9).[67] It may further be noted that Jesus'

---

[63]P. Borgen, *Bread from Heaven: An Exegetical Study of the Concept of Manna in the Gospel of John and the Writings of Philo* (NovTSup 10; Leiden: E. J. Brill, 1965), emphasizes the midrashic character of the discourse. But see the critique by Carson (*Gospel According to John*, 287–88), who charges that Borgen "does not sufficiently allow for the revelatory stance that Jesus adopts in this chapter, quite unlike any of the teachers in the Jewish parallels that are commonly adduced." Cf. also R. Schnackenburg, "Das Brot des Lebens (Joh 6)," in *Das Johannesevangelium IV. Teil: Ergänzende Auslegungen und Exkurse* (HTKNT; Freiburg/Basel/Wien: Herder, 1984), 119–31.

[64]John is not the only evangelist who attributes to Jesus this kind of reading of the Hebrew Scriptures: see, for example, Luke 24:44.

[65]See further the discussion in the concluding section below.

[66]Cf. J. C. Thomas, "The Fourth Gospel and Rabbinic Judaism," *ZNW* 82 (1991): 173–74.

[67]Cf. Evans (*Word and Glory*, 154), who notes that the question of the cause of people's suffering was of interest to rabbis. Evans also points to the parallel between Jesus' saying in 9:4, "we must work the deeds of the one who sent me while it is day," and R. Simeon b. Eleazar's admonition to work while one has opportunity and life (*b. Šabb.* 151b; c. CE 200). Cf. also R. Tarphon's statement, "the day is short and the task is great" (*m. 'Abot* 2:15; c. CE 50–120; cf. J. Neusner, "A Life of Rabbi Tarfon ca. 50–120 CE," *Judaica* 17 [1961]: 141–67).

claim of God as his witness (5:32) and his comments regarding the lack of validity of self-witness (5:31–47) are both consistent with contemporaneous rabbinic discussion.[68]

Jesus also uses rabbinic style, particularly arguments from the lesser to the greater. In 3:12, he asks Nicodemus: "If I told you earthly things and you do not believe, how shall you believe if I tell you heavenly things?" In 5:46, he asks: "But if you do not believe his (Moses') writings, how will you believe my words?" In 6:27, he exhorts his audience, "Do not work for the food which perishes, but for the food which endures to eternal life." In 7:23, Jesus queries, "If a man receives circumcision on the Sabbath that the Law of Moses may not be broken, are you angry with me because I made an entire man well on the Sabbath?" And in 10:34–36, he refers to Ps 82:6 in order to legitimate his claim to deity. If in Psalm 82 God extends the designation of "gods" even to Israel, Jesus contends, how can the one chosen and sent by God be accused of blasphemy when he claims to be the Son of God?[69]

Finally, some of Jesus' sayings recorded in John's Gospel appear to reflect targumic language and tradition, such as his statement "Abraham your father rejoiced to see my day" (8:56)[70] and his words to Thomas that they are blessed who do not see but believe (20:29).[71]

Jesus' verbal instruction of his disciples and others is clearly consistent with his Jewish environment. His use of the Scriptures, his "rabbinic rulings," his style of argumentation, and even language place him squarely within a Jewish rabbinic context. This, of course, does not mean that Jesus merely conformed to the pattern of teaching used by others rabbis of his day. Rather, his teaching is devoted to establishing his messianic claims on the basis of Old Testament expectations and to distancing himself from the illegitimate heirs of God's calling to Old Testament Israel.

---

[68]Regarding Jesus' appeal to God as his witness, Evans (*Word and Glory*, 154) refers to the parallels in *m. 'Abot* 4:22 and *Exod. Rab.* 1:15 (on Exod 1:17). Regarding the lack of validity of self-witness, see the discussion by Thomas, "Fourth Gospel and Rabbinic Judaism," 174–77.

[69]Cf. Hengel, "Old Testament in the Fourth Gospel," 386.

[70]Cf. G. Reim, "Targum und Johannesevangelium," *BZ* 27 (1983): 6–7; Evans, *Word and Glory*, 162.

[71]Cf. Evans (*Word and Glory*, 154), referring to R. Yoḥanan's rebuke of a skeptical student: "Had you not seen, would you not have believed?" (*b. B. Bat.* 75a; cf. *b. Sanh.* 100a). For a more extensive discussion of targumic and midrashic traditions in John, see Evans' discussion on pp. 157–64.

Didactic Actions. Jesus' method of teaching was not limited to verbal instruction. In keeping with contemporary rabbinic practice, it also included the use of "mystifying gestures," that is, startling actions that demanded an explanation. Gerhardsson calls this kind of rabbinic teaching method "the Rabbi's didactic symbolic actions," "concrete, visible measures whereby they capture the attention of their pupils, after which they either explain what they have done or leave it to the pupils to work it out for themselves."[72] The two major examples of this in John's Gospel are Jesus' cleansing of the Temple and the footwashing, interestingly placed by the fourth evangelist at the beginning and at the end of Jesus' ministry.

Jesus' cleansing of the Temple (2:13–22) is cast by the fourth evangelist as a deliberate action designed to provoke discussion and to provide Jesus with an opportunity to present himself as the fulfillment of the symbolism represented by the Temple.[73] People's challenge of Jesus' authority in reaction to his startling act of overthrowing the tables of the moneychangers did not seek evidence of the usual type.[74] Rather, the Jews sought confirmation of Jesus' special, divine call as the Prophet or Messiah. Indeed, a rabbi's authority included both didactic and prophetic functions and was manifested by both words and actions. Jesus' miraculous healings and other amazing acts thus may be viewed, among other things, as serving the purpose of attesting to his authority as a religious teacher. In this particular instance, however, Jesus does not acquiesce to the Jews' demand for a sign. Rather, he elaborates on the significance of the act he has just done, the temple cleansing.[75] At the time, Jesus' explanation of this act as a prophetic foreshadowing of the meaning of his death and resurrection remained a mystery, not just to the Pharisees, but even to his inner core of disciples. Only much later would they understand, as the fourth evangelist duly notes (2:22; cf. 12:16).[76]

---

[72] Gerhardsson, *Memory and Manuscript*, 185.

[73] Evans (*Word and Glory*, 159–60) points out that Jesus' statement that he will build the "Temple" may represent an adaptation of the targumic tradition that Messiah will build the Temple (cf. *Tg. Isa.* 53:3; *Tg. Zech.* 6:12–13); cf. also Reim, "Targum und Johannesevangelium," 10. On John's theology of Jesus occupying "holy space," see esp. W. D. Davies, *The Gospel and the Land: Early Christian and Jewish Territorial Doctrine* (Sheffield: JSOT, 1994), 288–335.

[74] Cf. D. Daube, *The New Testament and Rabbinic Judaism* (New York: Arno, 1973), 211.

[75] On the temple cleansing as a Johannine sign, see my "The Seventh Johannine Sign: A Study in John's Christology," *BBR* 5 (1995): 87–103.

[76] Cf. D. A. Carson, "Understanding Misunderstandings in the Fourth Gospel," *TynB* 33 (1982): 59–89.

The second "mystifying gesture" performed by Jesus is the footwashing (13:1-17). Daube notes that the unfolding of Jesus' last extended time with his disciples follows the rabbinic pattern of "mystifying gesture—question—interpretation."[77] He cites the parallel of Yoḥanan ben Zakkai (d. CE 80), who sobbed on his death bed in order that his followers might inquire about the cause of his grief, thus providing the opportunity for an explanation. Similarly, Jesus performs the footwashing to teach his disciples about the need for mutual service. He gets up, girds his loins with a towel, and begins to wash the feet of his followers, a task commonly reserved in that day for household slaves. According to Jewish belief, "All manner of service that a slave must render to his master, the *pupil* must render to his *teacher*—except that of taking off his shoe" (*b. Ketub.* 96a).[78] Only a Canaanite slave performed this menial service, and a student performing it might be mistaken for such a slave.[79] Jesus' actions in the Upper Room thus dramatically run counter to contemporary Jewish convention: Jesus the *teacher* renders a service to his *pupils* rather than vice versa, and the specific task performed exceeds that from which even *pupils* in contemporary Judaism were exempt.

Owing to its startling nature and the power of personal example, Jesus' "mystifying gesture" constitutes an extremely effective teaching method. As the Johannine Jesus remarks, "Do you know what I have done to you? You call me Teacher and Lord, and you are right, for so I am. If I then, the Lord and the Teacher, washed your feet, you also ought to wash one another's feet. For I gave you an example that you also should do as I did to you. Truly, truly, I say to you, a slave is not greater than his master; neither is one who is sent greater than the one who sent him.[80] If you know these things, you are blessed if you do them" (13:12b-17).[81]

Other Provision and Protection. Among other things, the role of rabbi also entailed the provision for his disciples' various other needs and the protection of his disciples from false teaching and any harm. In keeping with this role, Jesus frequently issued warnings to his disciples regarding

---

[77]Daube, *NT and Rabbinic Judaism*, 182–83.

[78]This saying is attributed to R. Joshua b. Levi (third century CE). Cf. Str-St 92–93.

[79]Cf. M. Aberbach, "Relations Between Master and Disciple," *Essays presented to Chief Rabbi Israel Brodie* (London: Soncino, 1967), 5.

[80]Cf. Riesner, *Jesus als Lehrer*, 256–59.

[81]Cf. Matt 10:24-25; Luke 6:40. Cf. the discussion by Riesner, *Jesus als Lehrer*, 256–59.

the pervasive negative influence of the Jewish religious leadership. These issues come particularly to the fore in Jesus' shepherd allegory (chap. 10). There, in allusion to Ezekiel 34 and utilizing the familiar motif of God as Israel's shepherd, Jesus identifies the Jews' current leadership as faithless (cf. Zech 11:15-17) in contrast to himself, who is the "good shepherd." Here the image of shepherd and the role of rabbi merge in that Jesus, the shepherd-teacher, is shown to take great care to nurture a close, trusting relationship with his followers in order to protect them from any spiritual harm resulting from their exposure to false teaching.[82]

Teaching by Example. Jesus also taught by example. Reference has already been made to Jesus' statement in 13:13-15, "You call me Teacher and Lord; and you are right, for so I am. If I then, the Lord and the Teacher, washed your feet, you also ought to wash one another's feet. For *I gave you an example* that you also should do as I did to you." The issue of example also comes to the fore in 5:20, where Jesus claims that "the Father loves the Son, and shows him all things that he himself is doing" (cf. 1:18). Jesus' teaching by example has the desired result that his followers do his works: "Truly, truly, I say to you, he who believes in me, the works that I do shall he do also; and greater works than these shall he do; because I go to the Father" (14:12).[83]

As the sent Son of the Father, Jesus modeled absolute dependence, obedience, and faithfulness to his sender (cf. e.g. 4:34; 5:23, 30, 36, 38; 6:38-39; 7:16, 18, 28; 8:26; 9:4; 12:44-45, 49; 13:20; 14:10b, 24).[84] In accordance with contemporary Jewish belief, the presence of a messenger was equivalent to the presence of the sender himself (cf. 13:20; *m. Ber.* 5:5: שליחו שלאדם כמרתו).[85] How much more was this true if the one sent was the son, particularly the first-born son, of a father.[86] At the occasion of

---

[82]Cf. R. T. France, *Jesus and the Old Testament* (London: Tyndale, 1971), 208-209; Carson, "John and Johannine Epistles," 255.

[83]Cf. my "The 'Greater Works' of the Believer According to John 14:12," *Didaskalia* 6 (1995): 36-45.

[84]For a detailed discussion of Jesus as the sent Son in John, see my *Missions of Jesus and the Disciples According to the Fourth Gospel.* For a listing of representative references on agency in John, see Thompson, "Historical Jesus and Johannine Christ," 41, n. 47.

[85]For further Jewish references, see Bühner, *Der Gesandte und sein Weg,* 209, n. 1. Bühner contends that this understanding already had currency in Jesus' day. Cf. also Matt 10:40; Mark 9:37; Luke 10:16.

[86]Cf. esp. A. E. Harvey, "Christ as Agent," in *The Glory of the Christ in the New Testament. Studies in Christology in Memory of George Bradford Caird* (ed. L. D. Hurst and N. T. Wright; Oxford: Clarendon, 1987), 239-50.

the disciples' commissioning, Jesus charged his followers to emulate the same characteristics he had displayed during his earthly sojourn as the paradigmatic Sent One: "As the Father has sent me, I also send you" (20:21; cf. 9:7).

In short, Jesus the teacher sought to impart the core characteristics of his own disposition toward his mission to his closest followers as part of their preparation for ministry. This transcends even verbal instruction, the use of mystifying gestures, and other methods of teaching.

The Disciples in the Fourth Gospel

The term customarily used for Jesus' followers in the Fourth Gospel, as in the Synoptics, is μαθητής.[87] It occurs some 74 times with reference to followers of Jesus in every chapter but 5, 10, 14, and 17, the first instance being 2:2 at the wedding in Cana.[88] Linguistically, this expression is closely related to the rabbinic תלמיד.[89] The fact that the term occurs nowhere else in the New Testament outside of the Gospels and the book of Acts indicates that the early church tied the term inextricably to the historical followers of the earthly Jesus. This suggests that the term μαθήτης is part and parcel of the teacher-disciple relationship Jesus sustained with his followers during his earthly ministry.

The Disciples' Relationship with Their Teacher. The disciples of a certain rabbi would often follow their teacher wherever he went (*b. Ber.* 23a,b, 24a, 60a; *b. Šabb.* 12b, 108b, 112a; *b. ʿErub.* 30a; *b. Roš Haš.* 34b; *y. Ḥag.* 2:1; *y. B. Meṣ.* 2:3).[90] In keeping with this practice, John portrays Jesus'

---

[87]The term μαθητής is found 72 times in Matthew, 42 times in Mark, 35 times in Luke, 78 times in John, and 28 times in Acts, for a total of 259 occurrences. John, closely followed by Matthew, has the highest instance of the term, while Luke has the lowest.

[88]Μαθητής is used with reference to the Baptist's followers in 1:35, 37 and 3:25. Cf. also the expression "disciples of Moses" in 9:28.

[89]Cf. Rengstorf, "μαθητής, κτλ.," 442.

[90]Cf. Aberbach, "Relations," 7. The various passages refer to disciples of famous teachers "following" or "walking behind" them. *B. Ber.* 23a-b, 24a mentions Rabbah b. Bar Ḥana (first-generation Amoraim; cf. Str-St 94) following R. Yoḥanan (d. 279; Str-St 95) and Raba (d. 352; Str-St 104) following R. Naḥman (third-generation Amoraim); *b. Ber.* 60a refers to a disciple following R. Ishmael son of R. Jose; *b. Šabb.* 12b mentions Rabbah b. Bar Ḥanah (first-generation Amoraim; see above) following R. Eleazar (130–160; Str-St 85); *b. Šabb.* 108b refers to Rabin walking behind R. Jeremiah, and *b. Šabb.* 112a to R. Jeremiah walking behind R. Abbahu (d. c. 309; cf. Str-St 98); *b. ʿErub.* 30a mentions Rabban b. Bar Ḥana (first-generation Amoraim) following R. Yoḥanan (d. 279); *b. Roš Haš.* 34b discusses R. Abbahu following R. Yoḥanan; *y. Ḥag.* 2:1 refers to R.

disciples as accompanying their teacher at a large variety of occasions. They lived with him (e.g., 1:39; 3:22). They joined him at a wedding together with his mother and brothers (2:1–12; on Jesus' relationship with his brothers, see 7:1–10). They were the witnesses and beneficiaries of his teaching. They accompanied him when he healed the sick (4:43–54; 5:1–15; chaps. 9 and 11) and fed the multitudes (6:1–13). In this, the Johannine portrayal concurs impressively with that of the Synoptics, where the disciples' major characteristic likewise is their "following" (ἀκολουθεῖν) of Jesus, that is, their close fellowship (*Lebensgemeinschaft*) with him.[91] The following discussion will look at some of the features of the Johannine portrait of Jesus' disciples in light of their Jewish background.

One important difference between contemporary rabbinic practice and Jesus is the fact that Jesus chose his disciples, while generally disciples chose to attach themselves to a particular rabbi (cf. 15:16).[92] This had already been borne out in a statement attributed to Joshua b. Perahyah (c. 100 BCE): "Provide yourself with a teacher (רב) and get yourself a fellow-disciple" (חבר; *m. 'Abot* 1:6).[93]

Generally, Jesus and his disciples share a relationship characterized by openness that allows Jesus' followers to inquire regarding the significance of their teacher's actions or even to challenge him. An example of this is Peter's initial refusal to permit Jesus to wash his feet in the upper room (13:6–10). Throughout the Farewell Discourse, the disciples address various questions to their teacher whenever they fail to grasp an aspect of his teaching (Peter: 13:36–38; Thomas: 14:5; Philip: 14:8; and Judas, not Iscariot: 14:22). This coheres with contemporary Jewish practice. As Aberbach notes, "Students would not hesitate to question their teacher when

---

Eleazar ben Arakh walking behind Rabban Yoḥanan ben Zakkai (c. CE 70; Eleazar ben Arakh is mentioned by Str-St 74–75 as one of Yoḥanan b. Zakkai's five most important students); and *y. B. Meṣ.* 2:3 mentions someone walking behind R. Ḥalafta (c. 330? cf. Str-St 84) and Simeon b. Va walking behind R. Eleazar.

[91] Cf. Anselm Schulz, *Nachfolgen und Nachahmen. Studien über das Verhältnis der neutestamentlichen Jüngerschaft zur urchristlichen Vorbildethik* (SANT VI; München: Kösel, 1962), 137. The word ἀκολουθέω is also used in John in 1:37, 38, 40, 43; 6:2; 8:12; 10:4, 5, 27; 11:31; 12:26; 13:36, 37; 18:15; 20:6; 21:19, 20, 22.

[92] Cf. Riesner, "Jesus as Preacher and Teacher," 197; Rengstorf, "μαθητής, κτλ.," 444, 447.

[93] Cf. Lohse, "ῥαββί," 962; Str-B 1:916; Silberman ("Once Again," 155, n. 12), who provides further references; and Riesner (*Jesus als Lehrer*, 269), who dates Joshua b. Perahyah ca. 104–78 BCE.

his actions seemed to contradict his teachings or when his behaviour appeared unseemly (cf. *m. Ber.* 2:6–7; *y. Sot.* 1:4)."[94] He elaborates,

> Pupils were not supposed to ask questions irrelevant to the subject under discussion lest the teacher be put to shame (cf. *b. Shab.* 3b).[95] It was the mark of a wise disciple to confine himself to relevant questions, while the uncultured *Golem* would do precisely the opposite (cf. *m. Ab.* 5:7;[96] *Der. Ez. Zut.* 1).[97] On the other hand, students were not only permitted but encouraged to ask the master to explain whatever they had failed to grasp during the discourse. It was a well-known principle that "a shame-faced person cannot learn" (*m. Ab.* 2:5),[98] and it was further said that "he who abases himself (i.e. exposes his ignorance by asking questions) for the (sake of learning the) words of the Torah will eventually be exalted, but he who muzzles himself (i.e. refrains from asking questions) will have to put his hand to his mouth" (viz., when he, in turn, will be asked to answer

---

[94]Cf. Aberbach, "Relations," 20. *M. Ber.* 2:6–7 is attributed to Rabban Gamaliel (possibly, Paul's teacher: CE 30–40); *y. Sot.* 1:4 is attributed to R. Meir, student of R. Ishmael and R. Aqiba and among the third generation of Tannaites (ca. CE 130–160). Cf. Str-St 73, 83–84.

[95]In *b. Šabb.* 3b, R. Ḥiyya is quoted as saying to Rab (both ca. CE 200), "When Rabbi is occupied with one tractate, do not ask him a question relating to another."

[96]*M. 'Abot* 5:7 reads: "There are seven marks of the clod and seven of the wise man. The wise man does not speak before one that is greater than he in wisdom; and he does not break in upon the words of his fellow; and he is not hasty in making answer; he asks what is relevant and makes answer according to the *Halakah,* and he speaks on the first point first and on the last point last; and of what he has heard no tradition he says, 'I have not heard'; and he agrees to what is true. And the opposites of these are the marks of the clod. *"*

[97]*Der. Ez. Zut.* 1:1–2 reads: "The characteristics of a scholar are that he is meek, humble, alert, filled [with a desire for learning], modest, beloved by all, humble to the members of his household and sin-fearing. He judges a man [fairly] according to his deeds, and says 'I have no desire for all the things of this world because this world is not for me.' He sits and studies, soiling his cloak at the feet of the scholars. In him no one sees any evil. He questions according to the subject-matter and answers to the point. Be like a gourd split open that the wind may enter, like a deep furrow which retains its water, like a jar coated with pitch which preserves its wine, and like a sponge which absorbs all." Str-St 251 say that style and content permit a date in the early Amoraic period (c. CE 250); M. Ginsberg, in his introduction to *Der. Ez. Zut.* in *Hebrew-English Edition of the Babylonian Talmud: Minor Tractates* (ed. Abraham Cohen London: Soncino, 1984), notes that there may even have been an independent collection already in existence in the time of the Tannaim, as the book contains material "which is old and often quoted as Baraithoth [Tannaitic sayings outside the Mishnah] by the early authorities. *"*

[98]*M. 'Abot* 2:5 is attributed to R. Gamaliel V (ca. CE 360–380), son of R. Judah the patriarch.

questions; *b. Ber.* 63b).[99] Students could also argue freely with their teachers during discussions, which formed the essence of instruction at all higher educational institutions; but they were expected to do so not in a contentious spirit but reverently and with due restraint.[100]

This open interchange did not diminish the disciples' respect for their teacher. Rather, respect grew into love, loyalty, and deep devotion. As Aberbach continues, "In spite of the extraordinary reverence in which rabbis were held by their students, the relations between them were usually very close and far from formal. It was . . . essentially a paternal-filial relationship transcended and surpassed by the intense love master and disciple bore to each other (*Cant. Rab.* 8:7; *b. Ber.* 5b; *b. Sanh.* 101a)."[101]

As Daube points out, the relationship of master and disciples was similar to that of parents and children. However, while the parent-child relationship was based on nature, the master-disciple relationship was a matter of choice.[102] Like family members, master and disciples had responsibilities, not just *to*, but also *for* one another in the outside world.[103] This identification in the eyes of the world came into sharper focus toward the end of Jesus' ministry, when it became clear that his disciples would be held responsible for his teaching. Thus the Johannine Jesus prepares his disciples, "If the world hates you, you know that it has hated me before it hated you . . . Remember the word that I said to you, 'A slave is not greater than his master.' If they persecuted me, they will also persecute you . . . But all these things they will do to you for my name's sake, because they do not know the One who sent me" (15:18–21).

Performing Acts of Service. One of the characteristics of Jesus' disciples according to the Fourth Gospel is their rendering of service to their teacher. They are sent to buy bread (4:8) and are asked to help provide

---

[99]This saying is attributed to R. Samuel bar Naḥman, a third-generation Amoraim (second half of third century CE). Cf. Str-St 97–98.

[100]Aberbach, "Relations," 9.

[101]Ibid., 17–18. *Cant. Rab.* was composed around CE 650–750 (Str-St 342); *b. Ber.* 5b is placed at the death of R. Yoḥanan (d. CE 279); *b. Sanh.* 101a is attributed to Rabban b. Bar Hana, a first-generation Amoraim (ca. CE 250). Cf. Str-St 94–95.

[102]D. Daube, "Responsibilities of Master and Disciples in the Gospels," *NTS* 19 (1972–73), 3.

[103]Ibid., 1–15. Daube devotes his entire article to a discussion of these responsibilities.

food for the multitudes (6:5). At the feeding of the multitude, Jesus instructs them to have the people sit down, to distribute the food, and later to gather up leftover (6:10, 12). In this, they conform to the customary pattern expected of disciples in their day. Shopping, together with the preparation and cooking of food and waiting at tables were considered duties of the followers of a rabbi (*y. Šeb.* 9:9; *Lam. Rab.* 3:17,6; *y. Ber.* 8:5; *t. Ber.* 6:4-5).[104] Notably, as in the case of the footwashing, Jesus' preparing of breakfast for his disciples subsequent to his resurrection reverses the common pattern of teacher-disciple relationships in his day (21:9-13).

The disciples' duty to care for their master's various needs even transcends his death. In keeping with this, "the disciple whom Jesus loved" is given responsibility of caring for Jesus' mother (19:26-27), while Joseph of Arimathea and Nicodemus, two secret followers of Jesus from among the Pharisees, assume responsibility for Jesus' burial, as was customary for disciples. As Aberbach notes, "The death of a teacher was a major disaster for his students . . It was a matter of course for disciples to attend their master's funeral or even to bury him themselves" (cf. *y. Ber.* 3:1; *y. Mo'ed Qat.* 3:5; *b. Ber.* 42b; *b. Sanh.* 68a; end of *Semahot* 11).[105]

Also, disciples were responsible to honor their deceased teacher by following his teaching closely. "After completing their course of studies, disciples were expected, as far as possible, to follow and propagate their master's teaching. The perfect scholar was one who . . . . had 'fully absorbed his master's teaching' and 'was drawing on it to spread it abroad' (*b. Yoma* 28a)."[106] The faithful witness borne by "the disciple whom Jesus

---

[104]Cf. Aberbach, "Relations," 6. *Y. Sheb.* 9:9 contains Talmudic commentary on the Mishnaic tractate by the same name; among the teachers mentioned is R. Joshua b. Levi (third century CE; cf. Str-St 92-93). *Lam. Rab.* was compiled ca. CE 450 (Str-St 310); among the rabbis listed is R. Yehudah ben Bathyra, dated either 20/30-90 or ca. 100-160 (Str-St 83); and *y. Ber.* 8:5 provides commentary on the dispute between the houses of Hillel and Shammai regarding the order of a meal. *T. Ber.* 6:4-5 is framed in terms of contrasting rulings of Hillel and Shammai (first century CE).

[105]Aberbach, "Relations," 21. The passage in *y. Ber.* 3:1 is attributed to R. Yannai the younger, grandson of R. Yannai "the Elder," Yohanan's teacher, and R. Yose, one of the redactors of the Babylonian Talmud; *y. Mo'ed Qat.* 3:5 comments on the Mishnaic tractate *Mo'ed Qatan*, which deals with "lesser holy days" (cf. Str-St 127); *b. Ber.* 42b is placed at the death of Rab (d. CE 247; see Str-St 93); the passage in *b. Sanh.* 68a is attributed to the time of R. Aqiba (c. CE 135); and the end of *Semahot* 11 recounts the death of Rabban Gamaliel the Elder, Paul's teacher, and the words of his student and brother-in-law R. Eliezer (CE 90-130).

[106]Ibid., 18. The saying is attributed to R. Eleazar (CE 130-160; cf. Str-St 85). The reference is to R. Eleazar's explanation of Gen 24:2, where it is said that

loved" to his master's teaching in form of a written Gospel can be seen as a discharge of this responsibility.[107] As the fourth evangelist concludes, "This is the disciple who bears witness of these things, and wrote these things; and we know that his witness is true. And there are many other things which Jesus did, which if they were written in detail, I suppose that even the world itself would not contain the books which were written" (21:24-25).[108] Gerhardsson comments in this regard, "They [apostolic eyewitnesses] taught in the name of their Master, and bore witness to the words and works of their Teacher in a way which recalled—at least formally—the witness borne by other Jewish disciples to the words and actions of their teachers."[109] Strack and Billerbeck cite the parallel in Rabban Yohanan b. Zakkai (c. CE 80): "Wenn alle Himmel Pergamente und alle Bäume Schreibrohre und alle Meere Tinte wären, so würde das nicht genügen, meine Weisheit aufzuschreiben, die ich von meinem Lehrer gelernt habe."[110]

Conclusion. The Fourth Gospel provides ample evidence to sustain the second part of our thesis: Jesus is depicted in terms of first-century Jewish teacher-disciple relationships. According to John's Gospel, Jesus exercised his role by way of verbal instruction, didactic actions, other provision and

---

Eliezer, Abraham's servant, "ruled over all" his master had, which Eleazar takes to means that Eliezer ruled over [knew, controlled] the Torah of his master.

[107]It is not possible here to discuss at length the degree to which Johannine style flavors the Fourth Gospel's presentation of Jesus' teachings. But note the interesting suggestion by Gerhardsson that John, by reproducing Jesus' statements in his [John's] own words rather than verbatim, may have followed a Hellenistic rather than Jewish approach (*Memory & Manuscript*, 130). Cf. also D. A. Carson, "Historical Tradition in the Fourth Gospel: After Dodd, What?" in *Gospel Perspectives II* (ed. R. T. France and D. Wenham; Sheffield: JSOT, 1981), 122-23.

[108]I have argued elsewhere that the Fourth Gospel establishes an explicit link between the witnessing roles of Jesus and the "disciple whom Jesus loved" by the parallel phraseology of 1:18 and 13:25 (cf. *The Missions of Jesus and the Disciples According to the Fourth Gospel*, 158-61). By virtue of their close proximity to the fount of revelation (the Father or Jesus respectively), Jesus and the "disciple whom Jesus loved" are able to communicate to others the true meaning and inner substance of God's and Jesus' words. Jesus' word, in turn, is put by the fourth evangelist on the same level as Scripture in 2:22.

[109]Gerhardsson, *Memory and Manuscript*, 330.

[110]Str-B 2:587. Reim ("Targum und Johannesevangelium," 10) also refers to *Tg. Isa* 53:8: "And the wondrous things that shall be wrought for us in his days who shall be able to recount?"

protection of his followers, and teaching by example. In all of this, Jesus is cast as operating within a paradigm used by the Jewish religious teachers of his day. As has been shown, this pattern is further substantiated by the Fourth Gospel's portrayal of the disciples' relationship with Jesus in terms of contemporary rabbi-disciple relationships.

After this survey of the roles of Jesus as teacher and his followers as disciples in keeping with contemporary Jewish practice, attention may now be drawn to an important theological feature of John's portrayal of Jesus that has relevance for the present study. This will be followed by some conclusions.

The Transcending of Rabbinic Categories for Jesus in the Farewell Discourse

The Johannine Farewell Discourse (John 13-16), without parallel in the Synoptics, is devoted to Jesus' final instructions for his disciples prior to his "departure" to heaven via the cross (cf. 13:1; 16:28). The discourse is reminiscent of Moses' parting instructions to his fellow-Israelites regarding their imminent entrance into the Promised Land in Deuteronomy.[111] Jesus is here presented as the one who supersedes God's giving of the Law through Moses (cf. already 1:17). Thus he issues a "new commandment" for his disciples to love one another the way he loved them, that is, by giving his life for them (13:34–35; cf. 15:13). In the overall theological context of the Fourth Gospel, the discourse functions as one among several links between Israel, the old covenant community, and the followers of Jesus the Messiah, God's new covenant people.[112]

The previous discussion has shown that John's Gospel clearly indicates that Jesus' contemporaries customarily perceived him as a religious teacher and that his relationship with his disciples largely conformed to the pattern of Jewish teacher-disciple relationships of his day. It has also been noted that references to Jesus as ῥαββί are, with the exception of 20:16, confined to the phase of Jesus' earthly ministry in John depicted in chaps. 1–12. Thereafter, Jesus is addressed by his disciples as "Lord" (Farewell discourse: 13:6, 9, 25, 36, 37; 14:5, 8, 22; Peter and the "disciple whom Jesus loved" in the epilogue: 21:15, 16, 17, 20, 21), a sufficiently

---

[111]Cf. A. Lacomara, "Deuteronomy and the Farewell Discourse (Jn 13:31–16:33)," *CBQ* 36 (1974): 65–84.

[112]Cf. esp. J. W. Pryor, *John: Evangelist of the Covenant People* (Downers Grove, IL: InterVarsity, 1992).

ambiguous term to accomodate both notions of "master" (teacher) and "Lord" (including God worthy of worship; 20:28).

This shift in terminology suggests that, beginning in John 13, Jesus' role as religious teacher is transcended by his anticipation of his return to heaven. While this fact was already hinted at in the first part of John's Gospel (cf., e.g., 8:31), it now takes center stage. Jesus' relationship with his disciples is elevated above their physical life with him and following of him to a spiritual association and discipleship that transcends mere physical realities, including Jesus' physical departure from his followers, and reaches into eternity (cf. esp. 14:2-3).[113] The disciples are enjoined to move from a physical following of Jesus during his earthly ministry to a vital spiritual connection with him by the study of his word and prayer (cf. esp. chaps. 14-16).

Therefore Jesus' assumption of the role of rabbi during his earthly public ministry now gives way to his role as the exalted Lord.[114] As such, Jesus will be the recipient of prayer and worship while remaining involved in the disciples' ministry (cf. esp. 14:12). The Spirit will provide continuity with Jesus' ministry by serving as the disciples' teacher on behalf of Jesus (14:26; 16:13-15). Jesus' earthly pattern of a rabbi gathering around himself a circle of close followers thus is shown to serve the preparatory purpose of instructing God's new messianic community (note the number Twelve and the application of the term ἴδιοι "his own" no longer to Israel, as in 1:11, but to his disciples, in 13:1).[115]

Concluding Reflections

As the preceding discussion has shown, John's Gospel provides unmistakable evidence that Jesus was perceived as a rabbi, a Jewish religious

---

[113]Evans (Word and Glory, 158) notes that Jesus' statement that "there are many dwelling places in my Father's house" probably reflects targumic language. He particularly refers to Tg. Neof. Exod 33:13-14: "The glory of my Shekinah will accompany among you and will prepare a resting place for you." Cf. also Reim, "Targum und Johannesevangelium," 10.

[114]This is insufficiently recognized by contemporary patterns of discipleship that seek to duplicate Jesus' culture-related pattern of gathering around himself a circle of close disciples as the primary paradigm for discipleship. For important missiological implications, see my "Challenge of a Systematized Biblical Theology of Mission: Missiological Insights from the Gospel of John," Missiology 23 (1995): 445-64.

[115]Cf. Pryor, John: Evangelist of the Covenant People, 55.

teacher, by his contemporaries. While the disciples came to know Jesus as more than just a rabbi, and while Jesus' own messianic self-consciousness transcended the role of teacher, the Jewish religious leadership, the crowds, and the disciples perceived Jesus in accordance with the accepted cultural role of rabbi. Jesus, in turn, used this role as common ground with other religious teachers, be it hostile ("the Jews") or open (Nicodemus) and conducted his relationship with his disciples within the framework of a religious teacher's dealings with his students.

What are the significance and implications of the present study's finding that Jesus, according to John, assumed the role of rabbi and was first of all perceived as such by his contemporaries? First, this conclusion suggests that Johannine Christology is not a projection onto the life of Jesus but that John's "high Christology" is rooted in Jesus' earthly life and ministry. In this matter the findings of the current investigation concur with the basic argument of Gerhardsson, Riesenfeld, and Riesner, who contend that the disciples learned what they knew about Jesus first and foremost from him.[116] Second, Bultmann's extreme skepticism regarding the ability of modern interpreters to learn anything about the historical Jesus from the Gospels is unwarranted. John's Gospel shows an organic development from the earthly Jesus' instruction of his followers to their belief that Jesus continued to be present in his community by his Spirit as the exalted Lord. The relationship between the "historical Jesus" and the "Christ of faith" is not one of radical disjunction but of the gradual emergence of a realization that the disciples' relationship with their rabbi, Jesus, was to be transcended by their spiritual communion with the ascended Messiah.[117] This is the message of John's Gospel.

If these observations are correct, they confirm the emerging consensus that Jesus can only be adequately understood within a Jewish framework.[118] Moreover, a needed corrective to a conventional understanding of Johannine Christology has been supplied. Far from reflecting a docetic or otherwise idealized Christ, John's Gospel is found

---

[116]Apart from the works already cited, see also R. Riesner, "Der Ursprung der Jesus-Überlieferung," *TZ* 38 (1982): 493–513.

[117]Cf. Thompson, "Historical Jesus and Johannine Christ," 21–42. See also C. S. Evans, *The Historical Christ and the Jesus of Faith: The Incarnational Narrative as History* (Oxford: Clarendon, 1996).

[118]Cf. W. R. Telford, "Major Trends and Interpretive Issues in the Study of Jesus," in *Studying the Historical Jesus. Evaluations of the State of Current Research* (ed. B. Chilton and C. A. Evans; Leiden: E. J. Brill, 1994), esp. 70–71 and the extensive bibliography cited on p. 70, n. 129.

to reflect, in accordance with the Synoptics, Jesus' thoroughly human and cultural pattern of living and relating. As mentioned, this does not mean that Jesus was reduced to a merely human figure. It does, however, imply that Jesus' messianic claims and his disciples' understanding of Jesus as the Christ grew from his assumption of the accepted cultural role of a Jewish religious teacher.[119]

As argued, the Fourth Gospel does not present Jesus merely as a conventional rabbi. Rather, among other things, the Johannine Jesus is cast as the true reformer of Jewish religion. Jesus cleanses the Temple (2:13-22),[120] instructs the "Teacher of Israel" regarding his need for spiritual regeneration (3:3-8), teaches that true worship is spiritual (4:21-24), points to the true significance of Jewish religious feasts (7:37-38; 8:12; 9:5) or invests them with new meaning (e.g., the Passover), and supersedes Moses, through whom God had given the Law (1:17; 5:45-46) and Abraham, the Jewish patriarch (8:58).

Yet Jesus was even more than a reformer of Judaism. As E. P. Sanders asks, echoing Joseph Klausner: "How was it that Jesus lived totally within Judaism, and yet was the origin of a movement that separated from Judaism?"[121] The answer, at least in part, may be seen in the fact that Jesus, while accommodating himself to the cultural role of rabbi, at the same time transcended this role by virtue of his unique personal identity. Interestingly, difficulty for Jesus' earthly ministry seemed to arise precisely at the point where his role of rabbi was transcended, be it in terms of his implicit or explicit claims of deity, his "signs" resulting in significant popular acclaim, or other messianic manifestations. Increasingly, Jesus may have appeared to at least some of his contemporaries, including the members of his own family, as a "rabbi gone mad" (cf. Mark 3:21).

Finally, as mentioned, by pointing to John's casting of Jesus in terms of a first-century Jewish rabbi, I in no way seek to limit Jesus to being a mere marginal Galilean Jew.[122] On the contrary—the fact that Jesus' fol-

---

[119]As Riesner (*Jesus als Lehrer*, 254) points out, contra Hahn (*Christologische Hoheitstitel*, 80-81) and in agreement with Dodd ("Jesus als Lehrer und Prophet," 69), the term ῥαββί should not be understood as a christological title. As Riesner contends, the early church preserved reminiscences of Jesus' being addressed as rabbi during his earthly ministry because he in fact operated as a religious teacher.

[120]Cf. E. P. Sanders, *Jesus & Judaism* (London: SCM, 1985), 61-76.

[121]Ibid., 3.

[122]Cf. J. P. Meier, *A Marginal Jew* (2 vols.; New York: Doubleday, 1991 and 1994); G. Vermes, *Jesus the Jew* (New York: Macmillan, 1973).

lowers came to believe that their teacher was the Son of God (cf., e.g., 1:49; 20:28) shows that the humble role of an uncredentialed Jewish rabbi and that of the heaven-sent pre-existent Word could exist side by side, as in that most famous of all Johannine "oxymorons": "the Word became flesh." The Jesus of John's Gospel is therefore a religious teacher *with a difference*—issuing startling claims and performing powerful "signs"—but a religious teacher nonetheless.

CHAPTER FIVE

THE SEVENTH JOHANNINE SIGN:
A Study in John's Christology[*]

Introduction

Studies on the "signs" in John's Gospel are legion.[1] It is therefore surprising that there is no treatment of the exact number and identity of the

---

[*]This essay first appeared in *Bulletin of Biblical Research* 5 (1995): 87-103 and is reprinted with permission.

[1]On signs in the Fourth Gospel, cf. Jürgen Becker, "Wunder und Christologie. Zum literarkritischen und christologischen Problem der Wunder im Johannesevangelium," *NTS* 16 (1969/70): 130-48; Otto Betz, "Das Problem des Wunders bei Flavius Josephus im Vergleich zum Wunderproblem bei den Rabbinen und im Johannesevangelium," *Jesus. Der Messias Israels. Aufsätze zur biblischen Theologie* (WUNT 42; Tübingen: Mohr-Siebeck, 1987), 409-19; Wolfgang J. Bittner, *Jesu Zeichen im Johannesevangelium. Die Messias-Erkenntnis im Johannesevangelium vor ihrem jüdischen Hintergrund* (WUNT 2/26; Tübingen: Mohr-Siebeck, 1987); Raymond E. Brown, "Appendix III: Signs and Works," *The Gospel According to John I-XII* (New York: Doubleday, 1966), 525-32; D. A. Carson, "The Purpose of Signs and Wonders in the New Testament," *Power Religion* (ed. Michael S. Horton; Chicago: Moody, 1992), 89-118; W. D. Davies, "The Johannine 'Signs' of Jesus," *A Companion to John: Readings in Johannine Theology* (ed. Michael J. Taylor; New York: Alba, 1977), 91-115; Robert T. Fortna, *The Gospel of Signs: A Reconstruction of the Narrative Source Underlying the Fourth Gospel* (SNTSMS 11; Cambridge: Cambridge University Press, 1970); Donald Guthrie, "The Importance of Signs in the Fourth Gospel," *Vox Evangelica* V (1967): 72-83; Marinus de Jonge, "Signs and Works in the Fourth Gospel," *Miscellanea neotestamentica* 2 (ed. T. Baarda, A. F. J. Klijn and W. C. van Unnik; NovTSup 48; Leiden: Brill, 1978), 107-25; Mark Kiley, "The Exegesis of God: Jesus' Signs in John 1-11," *SBL Seminar Papers* 27 (Atlanta, GA: Scholars Press, 1988), 555-69; Eduard Lohse, "Miracles in the Fourth Gospel," *What about the New Testament? In Honor of Christopher Evans* (ed. Morna D. Hooker and Colin J. A. Hickling; London: SCM, 1975), 64-75; Leon Morris, *Jesus is the Christ. Studies in the Theology of John* (Grand Rapids: Eerdmans, 1989), 20-42; Willem Nicol, *The Semeia in the Fourth Gospel. Tradition and Redaction* (NovTSup 32; Leiden: Brill, 1972); P. Riga, "Signs of Glory: The Use of Semeion in John's Gospel," *Int* 17 (1963): 402-10; Rudolf Schnackenburg, *The Gospel According to St. John* (New York: Crossroad, 1990 [1965]), 1:515-28; Udo Schnelle, *Antidocetic Christology in the Gospel of*

Johannine signs. Such a work, however, is needed for the following reasons.

First, as will be seen, while six Johannine signs are commonly acknowledged, there is no agreement regarding possible other signs in the Fourth Gospel. Indeed, some even question whether one should look for further signs in John at all. By a thorough exploration of the alternative proposals, perhaps greater clarity, if not consensus, could be achieved.

Second, if a seventh or even other signs could be identified with a significant degree of plausibility, a closer investigation may aid in our apprehension of the characteristics of the Johannine signs in general.

Third, such a study would be important since the signs occupy a central place in John's christology (cf. 20:30–31). Clarity regarding the number and identity of the Johannine signs would therefore result in a refined understanding of the christological presentation of the Fourth Gospel as a whole.

Fourth, since the Johannine signs function as an important structural component, a precise delineation of the signs may also help clarify the structure of the Gospel.

The Six Commonly Acknowledged Signs in the Fourth Gospel

How many signs are there in the Fourth Gospel, and what are they? The Fourth Gospel explicitly identifies, and commentators generally acknowledge, the following six signs:[2]

John. An Investigation of the Place of the Fourth Gospel in the Johannine School (trans. Linda M. Maloney; Minneapolis: Fortress Press, 1992), 74–175; Marianne Meye Thompson, "Signs and Faith in the Fourth Gospel," *Bulletin for Biblical Research* 1 (1991): 89–108; id., "Signs, Seeing, and Faith," *The Humanity of Jesus in the Fourth Gospel* (Philadelphia: Fortress, 1988), 53–86; and Wilhelm Wilkens, *Zeichen und Werke. Ein Beitrag zur Theologie des 4. Evangeliums in Erzählungs- und Redestoff* (ATANT 55; Zurich: Zwingli, 1969). Cf. also the bibliography in Brown, *Gospel According to John I–XII*, 531–32, with reference to some helpful older treatments on signs in the Fourth Gospel.

[2]There are 17 occurrences of the term σημεῖον in John's Gospel: 2:11, 18, 23; 3:2; 4:48, 54; 6:2, 14, 26, 30; 7:31; 9:16; 10:41; 11:48; 12:18, 37; and 20:30. John 2:11 refers to Jesus' changing water into wine; 2:18 to the temple cleansing; 2:23 and 3:2 make general reference to "the signs" Jesus is doing; in 4:48, Jesus chastises people for their insistence on "signs and wonders" in order to believe; 4:54 refers to Jesus' healing of the nobleman's son; 6:2 talks about signs Jesus is doing upon the sick; 6:14 relates to Jesus' feeding of the multitudes; 6:30 records the Jews' request for yet another sign; 7:31 asks, in the context of discussion over Jesus' healing of the lame man (cf. 5:1–15), whether the Christ will do more signs than Jesus; 9:16 makes reference to Jesus' opening the eyes of a blind man; 10:41

(1) the changing of water into wine (2:1-11);
(2) the healing of the nobleman's son (4:46-54);
(3) the healing of the lame man (5:1-15);
(4) the feeding of the multitude (6:1-15);
(5) the healing of the blind man (chap. 9); and
(6) the raising of Lazarus (chap. 11).[3]

Whether any other work of Jesus is referred to as a "sign," however, is disputed.

Why should one look further? Should one not rest content with six Johannine signs, regarding the *number* of signs in John as merely incidental and irrelevant or possibly finding in the number six evidence for John's view that Jesus' signs are of necessity imperfect and incomplete, thus accentuating the uniqueness and significance of Jesus' resurrection?[4] Indeed, care should be taken not to press one's search for a seventh, or even other, Johannine signs unduly. On the other hand, the number seven appears to have some importance for John in the case of the seven "I am" sayings of Jesus (cf. 6:35, 51; 8:12=9:5; 10:7, 9; 10:11, 14; 11:25; 14:6; and 15:1, 5). But *regardless* of whether the number seven is significant for

---

says that John the Baptist did not do any signs; 11:47 and 12:18 refer to Jesus' raising of Lazarus; 12:37 concludes that even though Jesus did all these signs, the Jews still did not believe in him; and 20:30 notes that Jesus did many other signs, but that the evangelist selected certain signs to lead his readers to faith in Jesus. Some commentators, while acknowledging the six signs listed below, may also include additional signs. These will be treated as possible signs below.

[3]Cf. Leon Morris, *Jesus is the Christ*, 21; Stephen S. Smalley, *John: Evangelist and Interpreter. History and Interpretation in the Fourth Gospel* (Greenwood, SC: Attic, 1978), 86-87; and C. H. Dodd, *The Interpretation of the Fourth Gospel* (Cambridge: Cambridge University Press, 1953), 438; Fortna (*Gospel of Signs*, 100-101) concludes that John's source originally comprised seven signs. Fortna combines the feeding and walking on the sea miracles of chapter 6 as one sign and includes the catch of fish in chapter 21 as the seventh sign. Some have organized these σημεῖα in various ways, such as two groupings of three, each incorporating a nature and two healing miracles (cf. J. N. Sanders, *A Commentary on the Gospel According to St. John* [London: Adam & Charles Black, 1968], 5) or as three signs occurring in Galilee and three in Jerusalem and vicinity). It should be noted that until the issue of possible further signs in John is settled, such classifications remain preliminary. Since it is possible to group the Johannine signs in a number of plausible ways, the question remains which, if any, of these classifications reflects Johannine intent.

[4]Cf. Sanders, *St. John*, 5, who holds that John has six signs, not seven, and that the number six, being one less than the perfect number, points to the great sign of the resurrection.

John or not, and whether or not any symbolism is attached to the numbers six *or* seven, it is important to identify properly all the signs in John's Gospel. They are too crucial a part of John's christological presentation and, indeed, of the purpose of his entire Gospel for ambiguity regarding the number and identity of the Johannine signs to be allowed to prevail. For those still not convinced, it may be possible to adopt at least a temporary agnosticism and suspend judgment until the results of the study are known. There will still be time to evaluate whether the conclusions arrived at here show that the search for further Johannine signs was worthwhile or not and whether or not it enhanced the understanding of the Fourth Gospel.

Before seeking to identify the characteristics of a Johannine sign, it seems advisable to investigate briefly the conceptual background. John did not operate in a vacuum in formulating his theology. While there is no consensus regarding the most likely general background for John's thought (or that of his various sources), it is apparent that John is deeply rooted in Old Testament symbolism.[5] The case cannot be fully argued here, nor is it necessary to do so for the purpose of the present work. We will merely take a brief look at the Old Testament in an effort to trace the development of the "signs" concept. It is hoped that this survey will provide a general backdrop for the study of the Johannine signs.

Signs in the Old Testament

Of the roughly 120 references to "signs" in the Old Testament and apocrypha, the vast majority are clustered around two events or types of ministries: the exodus, where frequent reference is made to the "signs *and wonders*" performed by God through Moses, and the "signs" forming part of the activity of the Old Testament prophets.[6] The common element

---

[5]Regarding the Old Testament background to John in general, see especially John W. Pryor, *John: Evangelist of the Covenant People. The Narrative and themes of the Fourth Gospel* (Downers Grove, IL: InterVarsity, 1992). Cf. also D. A. Carson, "John and the Johannine Epistles," *It Is Written: Scripture Citing Scripture* (ed. D. A. Carson and H. G. M. Williamson; Cambridge: Cambridge University Press, 1988), 245–64; and C. A. Evans, *Word and Glory: On the Exegetical and Theological Background of John's Prologue* (JSNTSup 89; Sheffield: JSOT, 1993), 146–86.

[6]In the vast majority of instances, σημεῖον translates the Hebrew אות. For references to signs (and wonders) during the exodus, cf. Exod 4:8, 9, 17, 28, 30; 7:3, 8–9; 8:23; 10:1–2; 11:9, 10; 12:13; 13:9, 16; Num 14:22; 21:8 (bronze serpent; נס); Deut 4:34; 6:22; 7:19; 11:3; 13:1–2; 26:8; 29:2, 3; 34:10–12; Josh

between these two clusters of references is that in both cases the signs function to authenticate the divine messengers, whether Moses during the exodus or later Old Testament prophets.[7] While the emphasis regarding the signs performed during the exodus, however, is usually on their miraculous nature, this miraculous element later retreats into the background.[8]

There is little that is "miraculous," for example, in Isaiah's walking stripped and barefoot for three years as a sign of judgment against Egypt and Cush (cf. Isa 20:3; cf. also Ezek 4:1-3). The emphasis rather lies on the authentication of Isaiah's prophecy, and ultimately of God's sovereign power. While such prophecies were usually given on a merely verbal level, occasionally God chose to communicate by way of a visual aid, i.e., a "sign." In the case of prophetic signs, there are thus two important elements: the prophetic component and the inherent symbolism. Both aspects combine to provide a way of revelation that, once the sign has been realized, proves the prophet to be authentic and brings glory to God.

A look at the explicitly identified Johannine signs reveals that John's "signs" concept fits well within the general development from an emphasis on the miraculous to a focus on the prophetic-symbolic dimension of a "sign."[9] The "miraculous" element is certainly not missing in the signs of John's Gospel. It appears, however, that this is not where John's emphasis

---

24:5; Neh 9:10; Ps 78:43; 105:27; 135:9; Jer 32:20, 21; Bar 2:11). For signs in the ministry of the Old Testament prophets, cf. 1 Sam 2:34; 2 Kgs 19:29; 20:8, 9; 2 Chr 32:24; Ps 74:9; Isa 7:11, 14; 20:3; 38:7, 22; 44:24-25; 66:18-19; Ezek 4:3; 9:4, 6; 20:12, 20; Sir 36:6. Almost all of the remaining references can be grouped under either general category. For example, Esth 10:3 (LXX) refers to God's working of "signs and wonders" in the events commemorated in the feast of Purim. Occasionally, the term "sign" is applied to the sun, moon, and stars in the heavens (e.g., Gen 1:14).

[7]Cf. Davies, "Johannine 'Signs,' " 92, who refers to the turning of a rod into a serpent in Exod 4:1-9: "but it is not only called a wonder, but a sign (ôtl), because it points beyond itself to the power of Moses' God."

[8]Cf. Bittner, *Jesu Zeichen*, 24-27, who also points to the scholarly neglect of the question why the term "sign" gains central importance for John's christology while it is avoided by the synoptics. Cf. also F. Stolz, "Zeichen und Wunder. Die prophetische Legitimation und ihre Geschichte," *ZTK* 69 (1972): 125-44.

[9]This is inadequately recognized by Karl-Heinz Rengstorf, who claims that the Johannine signs are "theologically and fundamentally the same kind as the classical σημεῖα of the OT, the signs in Egypt in the time of Moses" ("σημεῖον, et al.," *TDNT* 7:256). Cf. also Brown, *Gospel According to John I-XII*, 528-29, who considers the exodus narrative to be the primary background for both signs and works terminology in the Fourth Gospel; and Robert Houston Smith, "Exodus Typology in the Fourth Gospel," *JBL* 81 (1962): 329-42.

lies. This seems to be suggested by the fact that the phrase "signs and wonders" which is characteristic for the types of signs performed during the exodus occurs only once in the Fourth Gospel, and there on the lips of Jesus with a strongly negative connotation (cf. 4:48). In all the other cases, the thrust of a σημεῖον reference appears to be prophetic-symbolic: the sign's symbolism is developed and the prophetic component is emphasized, in the case of John's Gospel the authentication of Jesus' Messianic claims.[10]

Whether one agrees with every detail of this reconstruction or not, the most significant insight for the purposes of the present study is that not all of the events called "signs" in the Old Testament were miraculous. If John can be shown to fall within this general conceptual framework, one should not therefore require an event to be miraculous for it to qualify as a Johannine sign. On the other hand, one may expect a possible sign to display a combination of prophetic and symbolic elements. The event thus points to the future where the symbol will become a reality, at which time God's messenger will be proved authentic and God will receive glory.

Signs in John's Gospel

As one surveys the six explicitly identified and commonly acknowledged Johannine signs in an effort to identify their common characteristics, the following observations can be made.

(1) *Signs are public works of Jesus.* In each case, the term σημεῖον in the Fourth Gospel is linked with the term ποιεῖν ("do"; cf. 2:11, 23; 3:2; 4:54; 6:2, 14, 30; 7:31; 9:16; 10:41; 11:47; 12:18; 12:37; 20:30), ἰδεῖν

---

[10]As C. K. Barrett maintains, "The אות-σημεῖον [is] a special part of the prophetic activity; no mere illustration, but a symbolic anticipation or showing forth of a greater reality of which the σημεῖον is nevertheless itself a part" (*The Gospel According to St. John* [2d ed.; Philadelphia: Westminster, 1978], 76). He contends that, seen against their most probable background, the Johannine signs are therefore "σημεῖα in the Old Testament sense, special demonstrations of the character and power of God, and partial but effective realizations of his salvation." Cf. also Schnackenburg, who refers to the symbolic actions of the prophets where the symbol was "a creative prefiguration of the future" and a "revelatory sign" (*Gospel According to St. John*, 1:527). Schnackenburg believes that John developed his notion of signs "in the course of his meditation on the Gospel tradition" while Barrett thinks that John the evangelist himself chose the term σημεῖον. Others, such as Bultmann or Fortna, conjecture that John's signs terminology stems from his use of a σημεῖα-source. However, the answer to this question does not materially affect the thesis of this paper.

("see"; 4:48; 6:26), or δείκνυμι ("show"; 2:18); the verb ἀκουεῖν is never used. This pattern of usage indicates that a "sign" is something Jesus *does* (or, in the case of 10:41, John the Baptizer has not done), not merely something he says, and something people can *see*, not merely hear. "Signs" in John are therefore *works* of Jesus, not mere words. They are events, not mere utterances.[11]

Moreover, all six commonly recognized Johannine signs are works done by Jesus not merely before his disciples but before an unbelieving world.[12] The changing of water into wine, the feeding of the multitude, and the various healings including the raising of Lazarus from the dead all share in common that they have as their audience people other than merely Jesus' followers. All these signs are collectively referred to by John's summary statement at the end of part one of his Gospel: "Even though Jesus had done all these signs *before them,* they [i.e., "the Jews"] did not believe in him." The Fourth Gospel's signs are therefore confined to the period of Jesus' public ministry (i.e., chaps. 1-12).

(2) *Signs are explicitly identified as such in the Fourth Gospel.* All six commonly acknowledged Johannine signs are called "signs": the changing of water into wine (cf. 2:1-11) in 2:11; the healing of the nobleman's son (cf. 4:41-54) in 4:54; the healing of the lame man (cf. 5:1-15) is included

---

[11]It is improper to equate completely Jesus' works and words in the Fourth Gospel, as Bultmann does when he asserts, "The works of Jesus are his words," cf. Rudolf Bultmann, *Theology of the New Testament* (trans. Kendrick Grobel; New York: Charles Scribner's Sons, 1955), 2:60; and the critique by de Jonge, "Signs and Works in the Fourth Gospel," 125. Note also that Jesus habitually refers to things he does in the Fourth Gospel as mere "works" (the only—disparaging—references made to "signs" by Jesus are found in 4:48 and 6:26) while it is John or other characters in the Gospel that use the terms "sign" or "signs" (John: 2:11, 23; 4:54; 6:14; 12:18, 37; 20:30; Nicodemus, the Jews, or people in the crowds: 2:18; 3:2; 6:30; 7:31; 9:16; 11:47). Cf. Guthrie, "what Jesus meant by works was identical with what John meant by signs" ("Importance of Signs in the Fourth Gospel," 79). Thus it appears that the term "sign" in the Fourth Gospel reflects the perspective of the audience of Jesus' works, pointing to the perceived attesting function or symbolic content of the deeds done by Jesus.

[12]Cf. 12:37: "even though Jesus had done all these signs *before them*" (ἔμπροσθεν αὐτῶν), i.e., "the Jews." In 20:30, reference is made to "many other signs Jesus did *before his disciples*" (ἐνώπιον τῶν μαθητῶν). The latter passage probably points to the disciples as the primary witnesses of Jesus' signs in relation to the Fourth Gospel's readers and should not be taken to negate the fact that Jesus' signs had a wider audience than merely the disciples. Cf. Barrett, "The stress on signs done by Jesus and beheld by his disciples is important and illuminates the structure and method of the gospel as a whole; there is no disparagement of the role of eye-witnesses" (*Gospel According to St. John,* 575).

in the reference to πλείονα σημεῖα ("more signs") in 7:31 (cf. 7:21); the feeding of the multitude (cf. 6:1–15) is called a "sign" in 6:14, 26, 30; the healing of the blind man (cf. chap. 9) in 9:16; and the raising of Lazarus (cf. chap. 11) in 11:47 (cf. 12:18). Ultimately, the only way a "sign" can be identified as such in the Fourth Gospel is by explicit reference to an event in Jesus' public ministry as a "sign."[13]

(3) *Signs, with their concomitant symbolism, point to God's glory displayed in Jesus, thus revealing Jesus as God's authentic representative.* The prominence of the signs in the two major summary sections of the Fourth Gospel underscores their centrality in John's christology. Within the framework of this sending christology, the signs are shown to authenticate Jesus as the true representative of God, revealing God's glory in Jesus. Thus people's acceptance of the genuineness of Jesus' signs should lead to their acceptance of Jesus' messianic mission. This is true both for Jesus' original audience and for the readers of the Fourth Gospel to whom testimony regarding Jesus' signs is supplied.

That the signs are works of Jesus that reflect God's glory can already be seen in John's account of the first sign: "This, the first of his signs, Jesus performed in Cana of Galilee. He thus revealed his glory, and his disciples put their faith in him" (2:11). The reader of the Fourth Gospel is almost certainly expected to draw the connection between this statement and the earlier assertion found in the prologue, "The Word became flesh and made his dwelling among us. We have seen his glory, the glory of the One and Only, who came from the Father, full of grace and truth" (1:14). John thus presents Jesus' signs as the vehicles through which God's glory is revealed in Jesus. While the word "glory" is not always used in conjunction with Jesus' working of signs, all of Jesus' signs are presented as evidence that Jesus is God's authentic representative (cf. 5:17–47; 7:14–24; 6:25–59; 9:3–5, 35–41; 11:25–27, 40). The Fourth Gospel also reflects Jewish expectations that both the coming prophet and the Messiah would perform signs to prove their divine commission (cf. 6:14; 7:31).[14]

But what kind of works are Jesus' signs according to John? Great care must be taken not to import an understanding of the term "miracle" into the Fourth Gospel that is foreign to it.[15] As has been argued above, the

---

[13]Of course, this does not mean that there may not be some ambiguity regarding the referent of a given σημεῖον passage in the Fourth Gospel. See the discussion below.

[14]See the discussion of the Old Testament background of the Johannine signs above.

[15]Contra translations such as the NIV that render σημεῖον in the Fourth Gospel regularly as "miraculous sign."

most likely background for the Johannine signs are the signs of the Old Testament prophets where the symbolic-prophetic element generally predominated over the miraculous. We agree therefore with Dodd when he maintains, "to the evangelist a σημεῖον is not, in essence, a miraculous act, but a significant act, one which, for the seeing eye and the understanding mind, symbolizes eternal realities."[16] Indeed, the signs in John "are not mere displays of power but are symbol-laden events rich in meaning for those with eyes to see."[17]

In the light of these observations, a tentative definition of a "sign" in John's Gospel can be constructed as follows: "A sign is a symbol-laden, but not necessarily 'miraculous,' public work of Jesus selected and explicitly identified as such by John for the reason that it displays God's glory in Jesus who is thus shown to be God's true representative (cf. 20:30–31)."[18]

In screening the options suggested for additional signs in the Fourth Gospel, the following criteria may therefore be used:

(1) Is a given work performed by Jesus as part of his public ministry?

(2) Is an event explicitly identified as a "sign" in the Fourth Gospel?

(3) Does the event, with its concomitant symbolism, point to God's glory displayed in Jesus, thus revealing Jesus as God's true representative?

If it can be shown that one or more events in John's Gospel fit these criteria, these should take their proper place alongside the commonly recognized six signs. If, on the other hand, no such event(s) can be identified, it can confidently be held that there are merely six signs in John.

---

[16]Cf. Dodd, *Interpretation of Fourth Gospel*, 90. Contra Schnackenburg, who understands the Fourth Gospel's "signs" as Jesus' major miracles: "The signs are important works of Jesus, performed in the sight of his disciples, miracles, in fact, which of their nature should lead to faith in 'Jesus the Messiah, the Son of God' " (*Gospel According to St. John*, 1:515); and Morris, who defines a sign simply as "a miraculous happening that points to some spiritual truth" (*Jesus is the Christ*, 22).

[17]Cf. Carson, "Purpose of Signs and Wonders," 93.

[18]This definition is not unlike that by Thompson, who describes a Johannine sign as "a manifestation, through the person of Jesus, of God's work in the world" ("Signs and Faith in the Fourth Gospel," 93–94). Cf. also George R. Beasley-Murray, "The 'signs' of the first twelve chapters are specifically actions of Jesus, generally miraculous, which find their exposition in discourses" (*John*, WBC 36 [Waco, TX: Word, 1987], 387). Note also the possible connection between the term σημεῖον and the expression λόγος in John's Gospel, an intriguing interrelation that cannot be further explored here. Likewise, it might be worthwhile to investigate further the relationship between the Johannine signs and the "I am" sayings which are sometimes, but not always, linked.

Possible Additional Signs in John's Gospel

The suggestions for additional signs in John's Gospel include the following:[19]

(1) Jesus' cleansing of the temple (cf. 2:14-17);[20]
(2) Jesus' word regarding the serpent in the wilderness (cf. 3:14-15);[21]
(3) Jesus' walking on the water (cf. 6:16-21);[22]
(4) the anointing of Jesus (12:1-8);[23]
(5) the triumphal entry (12:12-16);[24]
(6) Jesus' crucifixion and resurrection (chaps. 18-19);[25]

---

[19]While not exhaustive, the following alternatives represent the most frequently made suggestions. It should be noted that some writers define the concept of a Johannine "sign" so broadly as to include virtually everything Jesus did or said in the Fourth Gospel. Davies, for example, also includes the signs of "new birth" (John 3), "new worship" (John 4), the "light of the world" (John 7-8), and "signs that Jesus brings life through death" (11:55-12:36), including the anointing, the triumphal entry, and the grain of wheat saying ("Johannine Signs," 95-112). However, this terminology demonstrably departs from the Johannine usage. Dodd's concept of "signs" in John, too, appears to be unduly broad when he writes, "The works of Christ are all 'signs' of his finished work" (*Interpretation of Fourth Gospel*, 383). On one level that may be true, but clearly John selects certain events in Jesus' ministry by designating them as "signs" and by exposing their symbolic significance. All signs contain symbolic elements, but not every symbolic element in the Fourth Gospel is therefore a sign. To subsume various allusions to the Old Testament as well as instances of Johannine irony and double meaning under the category of "Johannine sign" fails to observe this distinction between symbolism and "signs."

[20]Cf. Beasley-Murray, *John*, 42; D. A. Carson, *The Gospel According to John* (Grand Rapids: Eerdmans, 1991), 181; Dodd, *Interpretation of the Fourth Gospel*, 300-303, 370.

[21]Cf. Brown, *Gospel According to John I-XII*, 528.

[22]Cf. Morris, *Jesus is the Christ*, 21. Cf. also Davies, "Johannine 'Signs,' " 93, calling this the traditional view.

[23]Cf. Dodd, *Interpretation of Fourth Gospel*, 438.

[24]Ibid.

[25]Cf. Betz, *Jesus*, 412-13; Carson, "the greatest sign of them all is the death, resurrection and exaltation of the incarnate Word" (*Gospel According to John*, 661); Dodd, "The death of Christ by crucifixion . . . is a σημεῖον of the reality which is the exaltation and the glory of Christ" (*Interpretation of Fourth Gospel*, 379; cf. also 438-40); J. Terence Forestell, who refers to "the supreme sign of the entire gospel, the exaltation and glorification of the Son of Man" (*The Word of the Cross. Salvation as Revelation in the Fourth Gospel* [AnBib 57; Rome: Pontifical Biblical Institute, 1974], 71); B. H. Grigsby, "it does not seem to be speculative to discuss the Johannine cross as a 'sign' " ("The Cross as a Expiatory

(7) his resurrection appearances (chaps. 20-21);[26] and
(8) the miraculous catch of fish (21:1-14).[27]

Which of the above alternatives, if any, fits the general characteristics outlined in the above definition?

(1) *Is a given work performed by Jesus as part of his public ministry?* All six commonly recognized Johannine signs occur during the course of Jesus' public ministry (chaps. 1-12). Of the suggested additional signs, only three fall into this category: the temple cleansing, the anointing of Jesus, and the triumphal entry. Jesus' word regarding the serpent in the wilderness is not an event at all but merely a word of Jesus and should therefore be ruled out from consideration.[28] The walking on the water, while being something Jesus *does,* is not a part of Jesus' public ministry but occurs privately before Jesus' disciples so that it, too, should be excluded. The remaining alternatives, i.e., Jesus' crucifixion and the resurrection, his resurrection appearances, and the miraculous catch of fish, are not a part of Jesus' ministry narrated in chaps. 1-12 and can therefore not be considered "signs" in the Johannine sense of the word. These considerations are further clarified by dealing with the second characteristic of a Johannine "sign."

(2) *Is an event explicitly identified as a "sign" in the Fourth Gospel?* Of the three events identified above that fit the first criterion, i.e., being works performed by Jesus as part of his public ministry, only the temple cleansing also appears to meet the second qualification, since neither the anointing of Jesus nor the triumphal entry is called a "sign" in the Fourth Gospel. Even in the case of the temple cleansing, the designation is somewhat indirect. When Jesus, immediately after cleansing the temple, is

---

Sacrifice in the Fourth Gospel," *JSNT* 15 [1982]: 64, n. 6); Lucius Nereparampil, *Destroy this Temple. An Exegetico-Theological Study on the Meaning of Jesus' Temple-Logion in Jn 2:19* (Bangalore: Dharmaram Publications, 1978), 92-97; Nicol, "John never directly says the resurrection is also a *semeion,* but it is significant that when the Jews ask Jesus for a *semeion* in 2:18, he answers by referring to his resurrection" (*Semeia in the Fourth Gospel,* 115); and Wilhelm Thüsing, who repeatedly refers to Jesus' exaltation at the cross as a "Glaubenszeichen" (*Die Erhöhung und Verherrlichung Jesu im Johannesevangelium* [NTAbh 21; Münster: W. Aschendorff, 1979] 289, passim).

[26]Cf. Bultmann, *Theology of NT,* 2:56; Beasley-Murray, *John,* 387.

[27]Cf. Smalley, *John: Evangelist & Interpreter,* 87; id., "The Sign in John XXI," *NTS* 20 (1974): 275-88; Fortna, *Gospel of Signs,* 87-98.

[28]Cf. Dodd, "for John a 'sign' is something that actually happens" (*Interpretation of Fourth Gospel,* 300).

asked to perform a sign, he explains the significance of what he had just done, thus apparently implying that the temple cleansing itself already constituted the sign people were asking for.[29] As one commentator has it, "Indeed, if the authorities had eyes to see, the cleansing of the temple was already a 'sign' they should have thought through and deciphered in terms of Old Testament scripture."[30] That this is a legitimate inference is suggested by the parallel in 6:30 where after Jesus' feeding of the multitude, the Jews similarly demand a sign, yet where in response Jesus offers an interpretation of what had already happened, inviting his questioners to see in the actual occurrence of the feeding of the multitude the σημεῖον they desired.[31]

Apart from the fact that the other suggested possibilities already failed to meet the first criterion, they also appear to fall short of standing the second test. None of these alternatives is called a "sign" in the Fourth Gospel. It may be objected that Jesus' crucifixion and resurrection, and perhaps even the resurrection appearances, should be included in the purview of the Johannine "signs" by virtue of being covered by the statement in 20:30.[32] This suggestion, however, while possible, should probably be ruled out for the following reasons.

First, Jesus' crucifixion and resurrection are the reality to which the signs point. Rather than symbolizing anything, they are significant in and of themselves. As Schnackenburg asserts, "An extension of the concept of

---

[29]Nereparampil objects to an inclusion of the temple cleansing under the Johannine signs by arguing that the temple cleansing cannot be a sign since it is not "miraculous." He sees the resurrection as the sign and the temple logion as the promise of a sign, maintaining that the resurrection represents "the supreme 'sign' in the full sense of the Johannine concept of *semeion*" (*Destroy this Temple*, 92–97). But Nereparampil's objection loses its force in the light of the fact that a "miraculous" element is not a necessary component of the Johannine conception of a "sign." Moreover, as has been argued, Jesus' resurrection is not a part of Jesus' public work and corresponds to the Johannine signs as reality does to symbol rather than functioning as the ultimate symbol.

[30]Cf. Carson, *Gospel According to John*, 181.

[31]Cf. Dodd, *Interpretation of Fourth Gospel*, 301. Dodd also notes the implication of the quote of Ps. 69:10 in John 2:17, i.e., "that, just as the Righteous Sufferer of the Psalm paid the price of his loyalty to the temple, so the action of Jesus in cleansing the temple will bring him to grief."

[32]Cf. e.g., Carson, who comments, somewhat tentatively, "It is possible that *miraculous signs* refers only to the miracles reported in chs. 2–12 . . . But to place this conclusion here suggests that the greatest sign of them all is the death, resurrection and exaltation of the incarnate Word . . . But however far *miraculous signs* extends . . ." (*Gospel According to John*, 661).

'sign' to take in the cross of Jesus cannot be justified."[33] The reason for this is, according to Barrett, that "in the death and resurrection of Jesus, sign and its meaning coincide."[34] Davies agrees, "The sign is not essential to the truth to which it points, but only illustrative. But the death of Jesus is not simply an illustration or a sign; it is an actual death . . . The cross—not as a symbol or an idea—but as an actual act of self-giving is, for John, the point where God's glory is actually seen. Not the sign, not the intent, but the deed is the manifestation of the glory."[35]

Second, the Fourth Gospel's "signs" are preliminary in nature. This temporary function is intrinsic to John's conception of a "sign." Once the reality to which Jesus' "signs" point has come, no further signs are needed, nor can the crucifixion and resurrection that accomplish that reality *selves* be called "signs." As de Jonge notes, Jesus' "death and resurrection . . . are *not* explicitly called signs . . . This may be because from the Evangelist's post-resurrectional viewpoint, the signs bear a preliminary character, whereas death and resurrection mark the beginning of a new period."[36] Brown writes, "Thus, the miracle is a sign, not only qualitatively (a material action pointing toward a spiritual reality), but also temporally (what happens before *the hour* prophesying what will happen after the hour has come). That is why, as we have explained, the signs of Jesus are found only in the first half of the Gospel (chs. i–xii)."[37]

Third, while the "signs" reference in 20:30 allows for the possible inference that Jesus' crucifixion and resurrection should be numbered among the Johannine "signs," this inference falls short of making the connection explicit. Other explanations are possible. As passages such as 2:22 (cf. also 12:16) indicate, even the disciples' understanding of events in Jesus' ministry was predicated upon the actual occurrences of Jesus' crucifixion and resurrection. Their reception of the Holy Spirit and their commissioning by Jesus were not possible until *after* these events. Thus the Fourth Evangelist may choose to mention Jesus' "signs" once more, not because he wants to include Jesus' crucifixion and resurrection in their purview, but because the disciples are now fit to witness to the true significance of the "signs" Jesus had performed during his public ministry. It had been necessary for Jesus' crucifixion and resurrection, the reality to

---

[33]Cf. Schnackenburg, *Gospel According to St. John*, 1:520, n. 7.

[34]Cf. Barrett, *Gospel According to St. John*, 78.

[35]Cf. Davies, "Johannine 'Signs,' " 113–14.

[36]Cf. de Jonge, "Signs and Works in the Fourth Gospel," 111 and 117, n. 24.

[37]Cf. Raymond E. Brown, *Gospel According to John I–XII*, 530.

which those "signs" pointed, to occur in order for the disciples to be able
to function as witnesses in the power of the Spirit (cf. 15:26–27). Indeed,
what the Farewell Discourse expounds is not so much the significance of
Jesus' death (which had already been foreshadowed by word and deed in
chaps. 1–12) as the *implications* of Jesus' death for the mission of his followers.[38]

Fourth, it probably would have appeared rather inappropriate (if not
blasphemous) to Jesus' own disciples, and to the author of the Fourth
Gospel, to place Jesus' crucifixion and resurrection into the same category
as the commonly acknowledged six Johannine signs. The inclusion of
Jesus' crucifixion and resurrection among the "signs" appears to run
counter to John's consistent emphasis on Jesus' salvation-historical and
personal uniqueness (cf. e.g., 1:14, 18; 3:16). The book of Acts finds the
early church preaching, not Jesus' signs, but his resurrection.

For these reasons Jesus' crucifixion, resurrection, and appearances
should not be considered Johannine "signs." They do not fit the criteria
laid out above in that they are neither a "public work" of Jesus nor called
"signs" in John. In line with the Old Testament background sketched earlier in this essay, the Johannine "signs" point symbolically to God's future
intervention. Jesus' crucifixion and resurrection, however, represent the
very reality to which the earlier signs had referred. If the raising of Lazarus
is a "sign," it may be asked, and if its symbolic significance is that Jesus is
"the resurrection and the life," how can Jesus' resurrection *itself* also be a
sign? This seems to be logically inconsistent.

Finally, the miraculous catch of fish in John 21, too, should be ruled
out from consideration, since it is neither a part of Jesus' public ministry
nor explicitly identified as a "sign" in John.

(3) *Does the event, with its concomitant symbolism, point to God's
glory displayed in Jesus, thus revealing Jesus as God's true representative?*
To some extent, this criterion is met not merely by the six commonly acknowledged Johannine "signs" but also by the various suggestions for additional "signs." In a sense, everything Jesus does and says points to God's
glory and reveals Jesus as God's true representative. Not everything Jesus
does or says, however, is selected by the Fourth Evangelist as a "sign." It
has already been suggested that the temple cleansing alone meets the first
two criteria; all that remains to be done is to discuss whether this event is

---

[38]Contra Carson, "But to place this conclusion here suggests that the greatest
sign of them all is the death, resurrection and exaltation of the incarnate Word,
the significance of which has been carefully set forth in the farewell discourse"
(*Gospel According to John*, 661).

presented in the Fourth Gospel as an incident that reveals God's glory in Jesus and that reveals him as God's authentic representative.

It has already been argued that Jesus' response to the Jews' demand for a "sign" consisted in his explication of the significance of the temple cleansing he had just performed so that the temple cleansing itself is presented as a Johannine "sign" (cf. 2:18–21).[39] It is not necessary here to discuss in detail all the implications of Jesus' temple logion in 2:19. Suffice it to say that Jesus' words were uttered in explicit response to the Jews' challenge of his authority (cf. 2:18). In Jesus' eyes, the temple cleansing was symbolic of the crucifixion and resurrection of his body which, in turn, would replace the temple's significance in the life and worship of the Jewish nation (cf. 4:21–24; cf. also already ἐσκήνωσεν in 1:14). Indeed, Jesus had the authority to lay down his life and to take it up again (cf. 10:18). In this, Jesus is confirmed to be God's authentic representative.

If the temple cleansing is indeed the seventh sign of John's Gospel, the question arises why interpreters have generally failed to identify it as such. A few possible reasons come to mind. Scholarship on the temple cleansing in John has frequently focused on its placement at the beginning of Jesus' public ministry in John's Gospel in contrast with the synoptic placement at the end of Jesus' work. Moreover, the temple cleansing is not a "healing miracle" as are four of the other Johannine signs, nor is it a "nature Miracle" as are two other signs in John. Therefore the temple cleansing does not seem to fit the common stereotype of a Johannine sign. Indeed, signs in John have often been understood in terms of the miraculous in line with the synoptic portraits of Jesus' miracles. The six commonly acknowledged Johannine signs appear to fit the stereotype of a synoptic-style miracle very well: they are amazing feats, displays of Jesus' power over nature, indeed, even over sickness and death. The temple

---

[39]Note also the connection between the changing of water into wine and the temple cleansing. What the first sign indicates, i.e., that Jesus replaces Judaism in its various features, is applied in the case of the temple cleansing to the Jewish temple. Cf. Dodd, "it seems clear that both the Miracle of Cana and the Cleansing of the Temple are σημεῖα which signify the same foundational truth: that Christ has come to inaugurate a new order in religion" (*Interpretation of Fourth Gospel*, 303). Cf. also Nereparampil, *Destroy this Temple*, 89; and Pryor, who likewise emphasizes the close connection between Jesus' first sign at the wedding in Cana and the temple cleansing: "the two pericopae form an impressive and united introduction to the ministry of Jesus. Both point to the passing away of the old religion (signified by water and temple), and its replacement by the newness and superiority of Christ. He is the wine of the new age, he is its temple, the focus of worship and devotion" (*John: Evangelist*, 17). On the Johannine replacement motif, cf. especially Carson, *It Is Written*, 254–56.

cleansing, on the other hand, if measured by those characteristics, appears to fall short.

While providing a number of possible explanations for the failure of some to identify the temple cleansing as the seventh Johannine sign, however, none of these obstacles is insurmountable.[40] Once one substitutes the Johannine concept of "signs" for the synoptic framework of "miracles," the temple cleansing fits the category of "Johannine sign" very well indeed. As has been argued, what John considers a "sign" is not primarily an amazing feat of power but an event in Jesus' public ministry that has special symbolic significance in attesting to Jesus as God's authentic representative. Not the so-called "miraculous" element but the christological symbolism and Jesus' messianic authority are significant for John. Ultimately, all signs point to *Jesus* as the true messenger of God, the giver of life, a reality that finds its fullest expression in Jesus' resurrection from the dead, but a reality that is already given preliminary expression in the signs performed during Jesus' public ministry. According to John, the "signs," including the temple cleansing, are revelatory pictures of Jesus' true identity: he is the Christ, the Son of God (cf. 20:30–31).

Implications for the Structure of the Fourth Gospel

The identification of the temple cleansing as an additional Johannine sign would have significant implications for one's understanding of the structure of the Fourth Gospel. The inclusion of the temple cleansing has two important effects on the structure of the Fourth Gospel: first, it makes the raising of Lazarus the seventh climactic sign, providing the ultimate sign of Jesus' own resurrection; second, it reveals the probable division of the first six Johannine signs into two categories, i.e., three inaugural signs, and three further signs which are characterized by mounting controversy.

Jesus' raising of Lazarus, of course, is linked with Jesus' saying, "I am the resurrection and the life," and shortly followed by the conclusion of the Fourth Evangelist that "even though Jesus had done all these signs, they would not believe." It appears that after Jesus' raising of Lazarus no greater sign could be given. The Jews' unbelief in the face of such evidence for Jesus' messianic identity made it clear that they would not believe Jesus' own resurrection either. The number seven, indicating complete-

---

[40]Note also that there have been a significant minority of scholars, including C. H. Dodd, D. A. Carson, or G. R. Beasley-Murray, who have identified the temple cleansing as a Johannine sign.

ness and perfection, shows that Jesus' performance of a resurrection provides a climax in the number of the Johannine signs.

John himself gives some clues that signs 1 and 3, and then signs 4 and 6, form the outer parameters of two groupings of three signs each. In the case of signs 1 and 3, John numbers them as having both been performed in Cana of Galilee (4:54). The two healings in chaps. 5 and 9 contain numerous textual connections. The sequence of locations for the six signs would reflect Jesus' continued movement from Galilee to Judea and back again in the Fourth Gospel. The progression would be as follows: Galilee/Judea/Galilee; Judea/Galilee/Judea. The climactic sign, finally, occurs in Judea.

With all seven signs taking place during Jesus' public ministry in chaps. 1–12, the references to Jesus' signs in the concluding sections of parts one and two of the Fourth Gospel appear to relate to one another in the following way. The conclusion in 12:37 shows that Jesus' messianic signs had been rejected by the old covenant community. The conclusion in 20:30 indicates that Jesus' messianic signs would be witnessed to by the new covenant community. Between these two conclusions, one finds sections on the implications of Jesus' exaltation for the new covenant community (chaps. 13–17); on the reality to which the signs point, i.e., Jesus' crucifixion and resurrection (chaps. 18–19); and on the resurrection appearances and commissioning of the new covenant community (chaps. 20–21).

On a different note, it is crucial to view the Fourth Gospel's signs, not in an isolated fashion, but in their interrelationships with one another. All Johannine signs *jointly* point to various aspects of Jesus' messianic identity, authority, and mission. Any one sign may only reveal a *part* of this mission. Taken together, the signs provide a complete picture of the Christ who is Jesus.

Finally, why are the messianic signs of Jesus emphasized in the Fourth Gospel? One reason may be John's expectation that a focus on Jesus' messianic signs would add persuasiveness to the portrait of a crucified and risen Messiah, especially if Jews were at least part of his envisioned audience.[41] The added emphasis on the earthly ministry of Jesus points also to the abiding value of Jesus' works, demonstrating that Jesus' works are reflections of who he is. Thus for John, christology is not limited to

---

[41]This, of course, is hotly disputed. The point cannot be argued here, but in the light of the internal clues provided in the Fourth Gospel itself, there appears no good reason why Jews (diaspora Jews as well as proselytes) could not have been the intended audience of the Fourth Gospel.

soteriology, and Jesus' crucifixion and resurrection are shown to be in continuity with his earthly ministry.

Conclusion

It appears that the temple cleansing, and it alone, meets all the criteria for inclusion in the Johannine signs. It is a work performed by Jesus as part of his public ministry, it is identified as a "sign" in the Fourth Gospel, and it symbolically points to God's glory displayed in Jesus, thus revealing Jesus as God's true representative.[42] Jesus' crucifixion and resurrection, on the other hand, should not be considered as signs, since they relate to the seven signs featured in chaps. 1–12 as does reality to symbol.

If the thesis argued here is correct, greater clarity regarding one's understanding of the signs in John's Gospel may indeed be achieved. The discussion of the Old Testament background and the investigation of the characteristics of a Johannine sign have illuminated not only John's concept of a sign but also his entire christological presentation. The identification of the temple cleansing as an additional sign also provided a proposed clarified structure for the Fourth Gospel. While not everyone may agree with the thesis argued here, it is at least hoped that the plausibility of an additional Johannine sign in the temple cleansing has been established.

---

[42]If the temple cleansing is a Johannine sign, this would also provide an antecedent sign, notably in Jerusalem, for references to "the signs" Jesus was doing shortly thereafter in the Gospel narrative (cf. 2:23; 3:2). It appears that the reference to "the second sign" in 4:54 merely pertains to Jesus' working of signs *in Galilee*, though this is disputed.

CHAPTER SIX

THE "GREATER WORKS" OF THE BELIEVER ACCORDING TO JOHN 14:12[*]

Introduction

The reference to the "greater works" of the believer in John 14:12 is one of the most puzzling passages in the entire Gospel. Indeed, one wonders in what sense Jesus' followers could be said to accomplish greater things than their Lord. Surely this assertion is so startling that it is hard to imagine the later community having produced it.[1] In the light of the dif-

---

[*]This essay first appeared in *Didaskalia* 6 (1995): 36–45 and is reprinted with permission.

[1]The idea that Jesus' followers will be given power to perform marvelous works is found in many New Testament writings (cf. e.g. Mark 11:23–24 par. Matt 21:21–22; Matt 17:20; Luke 17:6; Acts 3:6; 5:1-11; 9:34, 40; etc.; cf. also Mark 16:17-18). The standard commentaries generally seem to assume the authenticity of the logion in John 14:12. Even J. Louis Martyn, in contending that "[t]he paradox presented by Jesus' promise that his work on earth will be continued because he is going to the Father is 'solved' by his return in the person of the Paraclete," appears to presuppose the saying's genuineness (*History and Theology in the Fourth Gospel* [2d ed.; New York: Harper & Row, 1979], 148). Barnabas Lindars, *The Gospel of John* (NCBC; Grand Rapids: Eerdmans, 1992 [1972]), 48 identifies the logia introduced by the formula "Truly, truly, I say to you" as traditional. He notes that scholars as diverse as Joachim Jeremias and Ernst Käsemann maintain that this formula certainly goes back to Jesus himself. This has been challenged by Victor Hasler, *Amen: Redaktionsgeschichtliche Untersuchung zur Einführungsformel der Herrenworte "Wahrlich, ich sage euch"* (Zurich/Stuttgart: Gotthelf, 1969) and Klaus Berger, *Die Amen-Worte Jesu. Eine Untersuchung zum Problem der Legitimation in apokalyptischer Rede* (BZNW 39; Berlin: W. de Gruyter, 1970). Lindars concludes, however, that these logia "preserve very primitive, and for the most part certainly authentic, tradition of the words of Jesus." R. F. Collins, *These Things Have Been Written. Studies on the Fourth Gospel* (Grand Rapids: Eerdmans, 1991), 144 considers these sayings a "Johannine trademark" indicating that "the evangelist is passing along a saying acknowledged within the Johannine community as a logion traditionally ascribed to Jesus." Cf. also the discussion by Gary M. Burge, *The Anointed Community.*

ficulties the present passage creates for interpretation, it is surprising that there is only one recent article on the "greater works" reference in John 14:12.[2] Moreover, a perusal of commentaries on John's Gospel suggests that the "greater works" reference in the Fourth Gospel is frequently interpreted in the light of the description of the early church's mission in the book of Acts. This practice, however, tends to obscure the function of the "greater works" passage within Johannine theology. As will be seen, when placed in the larger framework of the Gospel's depiction of Jesus' and of the disciples' task, the passage retains a distinctness that refuses to be facilely harmonized with the narrative of the book of Acts.

A second observation renders the present passage extremely relevant for the life of the contemporary church. In recent discussion, the "greater works" have often been understood in terms of "signs and wonders," with interpreters finding in Jesus' prediction of his disciples' "greater works" support for the expectation of frequent miraculous acts performed by believers.[3] The question arises whether such a theology is in fact set forth by John. In order to determine this, one has to study the passage itself in greater detail, as well as to ascertain its place within the larger framework of Johannine "signs" and "works" terminology and theology. The answer to this question will have a significant bearing on how the church today conceives of its mission and of the nature of its life and calling.

The present essay takes its starting point from the intertextual relationships linking the "greater works" passage with other passages in John's Gospel with similar wording or similar theological or terminological content. After a brief survey of the history of interpretation of the reference to believers' "greater works" in John, an effort will be made to develop an interpretation of the passage that is unencumbered by extratextual presup-

---

The Holy Spirit in the Johannine Tradition (Grand Rapids: Eerdmans, 1987), 62–67; and the following note.

[2] Christian Dietzfelbinger, "Die größeren Werke (Joh 14.12f.)," *NTS* 35 (1989): 27–47. This author's contribution is severely limited by the fact that he denies entirely the historicity of the statement given in John 14:12, attributing it instead to the post-Easter community (38). The criterion of dissimilarity, however, strongly suggests this to be an authentic dominical logion. Cf. also D. A. Carson, *The Gospel According to John* (Grand Rapids: Eerdmans, 1991), 496, n. 1; and id., "Historical Tradition in the Fourth Gospel: After Dodd, What?" in *Gospel Perspectives. Studies of History and Tradition in the Four Gospels* (Vol. II; ed. R. T. France and David Wenham; Sheffield: JSOT, 1981), 83–145, esp. 126–29.

[3] Cf. D. A. Carson, "The Purpose of Signs and Wonders in the New Testament," in *Power Religion* (ed. Michael S. Horton; Chicago: Moody, 1992), 89–118.

positions stemming from a reading of the book of Acts or from contemporary ecclesiological paradigms. Subsequently, implications will be
drawn from the present study's findings for the self-understanding and
practice of the contemporary church's task and mission.

The Larger Framework for Interpreting John 14:12

History of Interpretation
From the patristic period onward, the "greater works" have been interpreted as the missionary successes of the disciples.[4] The Fathers as well as
medieval commentators understood the "greater works" as referring to the
miracles performed by the apostles accompanying their missionary
activities. Later the idea of the extension of faith and salvation gained
greater prominence. Thus Augustine and Aquinas saw in the "greater
works" a reference to justification and sanctification.

As a screening of commentaries written in this century shows, this
tendency of reading John's "greater works" reference in relation to the
book of Acts persists. Only occasionally, voices have been raised calling
for an appreciation of the passage in its own right. Before considering the
reference in greater detail, it will be helpful to look briefly at the Fourth
Gospel's larger description of the disciples' task and mission in relation to
those of Jesus.[5]

Signs and Works Terminology in John
While Jesus' task is referred to in John's Gospel in terms of "work(s)" or
"signs," the range for the disciples' task is much more limited. The disciples do not perform any "signs," nor is there mention of their "work"
(sg.). Even reference to the disciples' "works" (pl.) is limited to the passage
at hand (14:12). The question therefore arises what is the significance of
John's more extensive characterization of Jesus' task, and especially of his
restriction of the working of "signs" to Jesus.[6] This is captured well by
Schnackenburg who writes,

---

[4]Cf. Rudolf Bultmann, *The Gospel of John* (Oxford: Basil Blackwell, 1971),
610; Rudolf Schnackenburg, *The Gospel According to St. John* (Vol. 3; New
York: Crossroad, 1990 [1975]), 412, n. 76.

[5]For a more thorough treatment, see Chapter 4 of my *The Missions of Jesus
and the Disciples According to the Fourth Gospel* (Grand Rapids: Wm. B.
Eerdmans, 1998).

[6]For a thorough treatment of the Johannine signs, see my "The Seventh
Johannine Sign: A Study in John's Christology," *BBR* 5 (1995): 87–103; for

Thus the later heralds of the faith can only recount, attest and recall the revelation given by Jesus in "signs" (and words), which becomes thereby "present" in their own day. It is presupposed implicitly that he who once wrought these "signs" on earth has in the meantime been glorified, that he still lives and still effects the salvation of believers. But his revelation, as a historical and eschatological event, is closed, and it only remains to explain it further, disclose its riches and explicitate [sic] its full truth.[7]

John appears to perceive Jesus' working of "signs" from a salvation-historical vantage point that views these "signs" as primarily directed toward the Jewish nation. Since Jesus' exaltation is presented in John as the event that makes possible the universalization of the gospel message, the "signs" are confined to the time prior to Jesus' "hour," i.e. his "glorification" at the cross.[8]

The "signs" also have an important revelatory function that is inextricably related to Jesus' function in making the Father known (cf. 1:14, 18 with 2:11). Thus there appears to be a relationship between the Fourth Gospel's signs and the characterization of Jesus as "the Word," i.e. God's self-expression (cf. 1:1, 14), as well as with Jesus' "I am" sayings (cf. 6:35, 51; 8:12=9:5; 10:7, 9; 10:11, 14; 11:25; 14:6; and 15:1, 5). In a variety of ways, Jesus' signs point to his Messianic mission, especially to his Messianic authority, demonstrating kaleidoscopically Jesus' person and work which are of unique and decisive salvation-historical significance.

Moreover, in their function of authenticating God's messenger (i.e. his agent, prophet, the unique Son), the Fourth Gospel's signs build upon the prophetic-symbolic dimension of the "signs" that had increasingly moved into the foreground in the development of this concept in Old Testament revelation.[9] While Moses' working of "signs and wonders" at the exodus gave significant attention to the miraculous nature of such works, "signs" during the later prophetic era focused more on the symbolic content of such events, with the miraculous element retreating into the background (cf. e.g. Isa 20:2-3; Ezek 4:1-3).[10] Seen against this backdrop, the Messiah is shown in John to perform signs that include predictive as well as sym-

---

bibliographical references, see there note 1. Only the most salient features of John's "signs" theology can be given here.

[7]Cf. Schnackenburg, *The Gospel According to St. John* (Vol. 1; New York: Crossroad, 1990 [1965]), 524.

[8]Cf. Köstenberger, "Seventh Johannine Sign."

[9]Cf. ibid.

[10]Cf. F. Stolz, "Zeichen und Wunder. Die prophetische Legitimation und ihre Geschichte," ZTK 69 (1972): 125-44.

bolic elements and thus, if fulfilled, have the potential of authenticating Jesus as God's true messenger, indeed as the Christ, the Son of God (cf. 20:30-31). Johannine "signs" are thus foreshadowing the fulfillment, or reality, to which they point. The changing of water into wine looks forward to Jesus' bringing of Messianic joy to his community; the temple cleansing indicates both the judgment of the Jewish nation and the replacement of the temple as the central place of worship with worship directed toward the crucified and risen Lord;[11] Jesus' feeding of the multitude anticipates his provision of eternal life through his substitutionary sacrifice; and Jesus' raising of Lazarus points to Jesus' own resurrection.

One further notes a dynamic in the Fourth Gospel from initial to ever greater demonstrations of Jesus' Messianic authority, so that the final sign, i.e. Jesus' raising of Lazarus, provides climactic evidence for Jesus' Messianic claims. The signs thus play an important part in John's emphasis on the Jews' obduracy and the divine sovereignty displayed in Jesus' Messianic mission (cf. John 1-12).[12]

In the light of these observations, it becomes clear why John did not extend the working of "signs" to Jesus' followers. The signs' sole purpose in John is their authentication of Jesus as God's Messiah (cf. esp. 20:30-31; cf. also 7:31). They are therefore linked inextricably to Jesus, and to Jesus alone, during this particular phase of salvation-history, with special reference to Jesus' mission to the Jews (cf. 12:37-43). After Jesus' ascension, there will be room for the working of "signs (and wonders)" by the apostles in order to authenticate their own function in preaching the gospel of the resurrected Jesus (cf. the book of Acts), but this era is not in John's view in his presentation of the Messianic "signs."

While John is indeed concerned to show the relevance of Jesus' earthly ministry for the later community, he does not therefore blend these eras in such a way as to blur salvation-historical lines.[13] By applying "signs" terminology also to the disciples, however, John would have opened up the possibility of transfering the Messianic overtones resonat-

---

[11]Cf. Köstenberger, "Seventh Johannine Sign."

[12]Cf. Craig A. Evans, "Obduracy and the Lord's Servant: Some Observations on the Use of the Old Testament in the Fourth Gospel," in *Early Jewish and Christian Exegesis: Studies in Memory of William Hugh Brownlee* (ed. Craig A. Evans and William F. Stinespring; Atlanta: Scholars Press, 1987), 221-36; D. A. Carson, *Divine Sovereignty and Human Responsibility. Biblical Perspectives in Tension* (Atlanta: John Knox, 1981).

[13]Cf. D. A. Carson, "Understanding Misunderstandings in the Fourth Gospel," *TynB* 33 (1982): 59-89; Eugene E. Lemcio, *The Past of Jesus in the Gospels* (SNTSMS 68; Cambridge: Cambridge University Press, 1991).

ing with his "signs" terminology in reference to Jesus also to Jesus' followers, a transfer that he made every effort to avoid. In fact, John
emphasizes that the disciples would reap what they did *not* sow (cf. 4:38),
disavowing them any part in making possible their own mission and
maintaining a clear distinction between the eras of Jesus' predecessors, of
Jesus, and of the apostolic mission.

Other references to the disciples' future task, likewise, accentuate the
foundational nature of Jesus' work. Thus Jesus' commissioning of his disciples to go and bear fruit (15:16) depends on their remaining in the
"vine," i.e. Jesus, while Jesus' sending of his followers in 20:21 is predicated upon his own work, i.e. his death and resurrection (cf. 20:19-20). For
John, the disciples' mission consists, not in duplicating Jesus' mission or
task, but in bearing witness to it as Jesus' representatives (13:16, 20;
15:26-27; 16:8-11; 17:18; 20:21-23).

The care taken by John in nuancing his terminology in such a way as
to avoid any improper theological implications needs to be kept in mind
when one considers John's reference to the disciples' "greater works" to
which we now turn. It is apparent that "works" terminology in John is con-
siderably broader than the "miraculous" (cf. e.g. 5:36; 9:3-4; 10:25, 38;
14:11; 15:24). Indeed, in Jesus' own consciousness, there is no dichotomy
between the natural and the supernatural, a distinction so dear to post-
Enlightenment thought. In John, Jesus' "works" are therefore, together
with his "words" (cf. e.g. 14:10-12; 15:22-24), part of Jesus' overall ministry. While Jesus' works frequently have a miraculous component, John
deemphasizes this element by focusing on the symbolism inherent in
those works and by labelling certain works of Jesus as "signs."

The Greater Works of the Believer

Two elements require a decisive recasting of the interpretation of the present passage over against the traditional understanding which conceives of
the "greater works" as the disciples' missionary successes narrated in the
book of Acts: (1) passages with similar wording and import, such as 1:50
or 5:20; and (2) the phrase immediately following the reference, i.e.
"because I am going to the Father" in 14:12c.[14] Both of these elements

---

[14]Cf. Dietzfelbinger, "Größeren Werke," 28, who observes the common
deficiency of older German interpretations to be their failure to grasp the
eschatological dimension undergirding the statement in John 14:12: "Sie klären
den Begriff 'größere Werke' nicht oder nicht konsequent genug aus dem
johanneischen Sprachgebrauch (s. vor allem 5.20ff.) und sie lassen die Wendung

bring into sharp focus the need to view the reference within the framework of Johannine eschatology.

The Eschatological Framework
In 1:50, Jesus is quoted as prophesying that Nathanael, the true Israelite, will see "greater things than these" (μείζω τούτων), a phrase similar to 14:12. This reference to eschatological events regarding the Son of Man appears to reveal a significant conceptual similarity with Matt 11:11 where Jesus is quoted as maintaining that, "Among those born of women no one greater has arisen than John the Baptist; yet the least in the kingdom of heaven is greater than he."[15] These parallels suggest that the "greater works" of the believer in 14:12 should be understood within an eschatological framework, i.e. as part of a new salvation-historical period inaugurated by Jesus' own completed work (cf. 17:4; 19:30).

Another important parallel is 5:20, the "parable of the apprenticed son." There it is said that the son will do the works of his master, and that Jesus' audience will see him do even greater things than the ones it had already witnessed (μείζονα τούτων).[16] The statement in 14:12 likewise indicates that the disciples will do the works of their master once their time of apprenticeship is completed. Significantly, they will not merely do the same works, but even greater works than their master, because Jesus will have gone to the Father.[17]

The reason elicited in the passage itself for Jesus' pronouncement of believers' "greater works" is his own "going to the Father," an euphemism for his crucifixion and resurrection (14:12c).[18] This statement points to the fact that Jesus' "glorification" would inaugurate a new order, i.e. that of his followers' mission carried on in the power of the Spirit. As Barrett comments, "The death and exaltation of Jesus are the condition of the

---

'denn ich gehe zum Vater' und den in ihr sich aussprechenden Zukunftsaspekt nicht mit dem nötigen Nachdruck zur Geltung kommen."

[15]Cf. F. F. Bruce, *The Hard Sayings of Jesus* (Downers Grove, IL: InterVarsity, 1983), 112-14; D. A. Carson, *The Farewell Discourse and Final Prayer of Jesus* (Grand Rapids: Baker, 1980), 42.

[16]Cf. Lindars, *Gospel of John*, 475.

[17]Note also the Fourth Gospel's "forerunner motif" which connects John the Baptist with Jesus, and Jesus with the Spirit and the disciples. See also 13:16; 15:13, 20. Cf. Burge, *Anointed Community*, 23-25.

[18]Cf. esp. Godfrey Carruthers Nicholson, *Death as Departure. The Johannine Descent-Ascent Schema* (SBLDS 63; Chico, CA: Scholars Press, 1983).

church's mission."[19] In fact, as this author maintains, "Thus the 'greater works' are directly dependent upon the 'going' of Jesus, since before the consummation of the work of Jesus in his ascent to the Father all that he did was necessarily incomplete. The work of the disciples on the other hand lies after the moment of fulfillment . . . Their works are greater not because they themselves are greater but because Jesus' work is now complete."[20]

Thus the disciples' "greater works" are not simply *more* works; nor are they merely *more spectacular* works or "miracles" (this would be hard to imagine in the light of the care taken by John to accentuate the amazing nature of Jesus' works). Neither is the primary reference in John to raw numbers of converts made or to the larger geographical dimension of the disciples' mission.[21] John's focus is rather on the substantially superior quality of works performed in the era subsequent to the period of the earthly Jesus, without elaborating upon the specific shape such works will take. Indeed, as Brown notes, John's emphasis is less on the marvelous character of the "greater works" and more on their eschatological dimension.[22]

The Disciples' Mission in Relation to
the Missions of Jesus and the Spirit
Remarkably, the reference in 14:12 elevates the future work of the believer, in a sense, above Jesus' "signs" narrated in John 1–12.[23] Setting Jesus' own work in relation to that of his followers subsequent to Jesus' crucifixion and resurrection, John emphasizes the foundational significance of Jesus' work for the church's mission. Indeed, Jesus is the sower of the eschatological harvest (cf. 4:34–38), the grain of wheat that falls into the ground and dies (cf. 12:24). Only in the age of the Spirit, however, will Jesus' followers reap the fruit of Jesus' work and gather the eschatological harvest made possible by it, thus accomplishing "greater works" even than Jesus himself during his earthly mission.

---

[19]Cf. C. K. Barrett, *The Gospel According to St. John* (2nd ed.; Philadelphia: Westminster, 1978), 460.

[20]Ibid.

[21]Cf. George R. Beasley-Murray, *John* (WBC; Waco, TX: Word, 1987); Bultmann, *Gospel of St. John*; Carson, *Gospel According to John, ad loc.*

[22]Cf. Raymond E. Brown, *The Gospel According to John* (Vol. 2; New York: Doubleday, 1970), 633.

[23]Note that the reference to "greater works" in 14:12 is not limited to the followers of the earthly Jesus but pertains to every believer (ὁ πιστεύων).

Significantly, the primary distinction in 14:12 is not between Jesus and his followers, but between the mission of the earthly and of the exalted Jesus. As Beasley-Murray contends,

> The contrast accordingly is not between Jesus and his disciples in their respective ministries, but between Jesus with his disciples in the limited circumstances of his earthly ministry and the risen Christ with his disciples in the post-Easter situation. Then the limitations of the Incarnation will no longer apply, redemption will have been won for the world, the kingdom of God opened for humanity, and the disciples equipped for a ministry in power to the nations.[24]

This author points to John's emphasis on "the continuing ministry of the Lord with and through his disciples, by whom the glorification of the Father in the Son will be continued."[25] Indeed, "the disciples go forth to their mission and seek the Lord's aid therein, and in response to their prayers *he* will do through them 'greater things' than in the days of his flesh, 'that the Father may be glorified in the Son'—in the powerful mission that *he* continues!"[26]

John's acknowledgment of the disciples' misunderstandings before the giving of the Spirit underscores the fact that it is the *Spirit* who accounts for the disciples' later understanding and ability. It is he who continues the revelation and work of Jesus who is now exalted. This keeps the Messiah from being just a past chapter of history that fades forever from living memory. The Spirit's mission will be manifold: he will teach the disciples all things and bring to their remembrance all that Jesus had said to them (14:26); he will bear witness to Jesus (15:26); he will convict the world regarding its sin of unbelief in Jesus, its lack of righteousness, and its judgment (16:8–11);[27] he will guide the disciples into all truth and declare to them the things to come (16:13); thus he will glorify Jesus by taking what is Jesus' and declaring it to his followers (16:14). Consequently, the Spirit ensures that Jesus' work continues in his disciples, legitimizing their work owing to their association with Jesus the Messiah who is now exalted.[28]

---

[24]Cf. Beasley-Murray, *John*, 255.

[25]Ibid.

[26]Ibid., 380.

[27]Cf. D. A. Carson, "The Function of the Paraclete in John 16:7–11," *JBL* 98 (1979): 547–66.

[28]Dietzfelbinger, "Größeren Werke," 44–46, unduly dichotomizes "the old Jesus tradition" and the new revelation provided for the community by the Paraklete. The Fourth Gospel rather suggests that it is the task of the Spirit *both* to remind the disciples of Jesus' words *and* to guide them into all truth, thus pointing to a deep underlying continuity between Jesus' words and the Spirit's teaching.

It may be concluded that the "greater works" of John 14:12 are the activities of believers, still future from the vantage point of the earthly Jesus, that will be based on Jesus' accomplished Messianic mission. Viewed from an eschatological perspective, these works will be "greater" than Jesus', since they will take place in a different, more advanced phase of God's economy of salvation. At the same time, there is an essential continuity between Jesus' earthly mission *for* his followers and the mission of the exalted Jesus *through* his followers. The "greater works" are thus works *of the exalted Christ* through believers.

Implications for the Fourth Gospel's Structure and Authorship
The interpretive insights gained above have important structural implications for John's Gospel. Since the purpose statement in 20:30-31 sets chaps. 13-20 in the context of chaps. 1-12, one should view chaps. 13-20 as well as chaps. 1-12 as seeking to show that the Messiah is Jesus.[29] To the "signs" of the earthly Jesus are thus added the "greater works" of the exalted Jesus through his followers. John closes the gap between 30 and 90 CE by interpreting the work of the Christian community as the continued work of the exalted Messiah. Nevertheless, he begins his presentation by setting forth the earthly Jesus' Messianic signs for the Jewish people. Indeed, it is impossible to believe in the exalted Christ operative in the contemporary community without believing in the Son sent from the Father, the heaven-sent, "signs"-working, Coming and Returning One, the "lifted-up" Son of Man who descended from heaven and who ascended back into heaven.

Finally, the profound reflection on the limitations of following the earthly Jesus *before* his being "lifted up" appears to reveal an acquaintance both with the time and person of the earthly Jesus. It suggests that the author was one who himself followed Jesus during his earthly ministry, and that he now functions as a "witness" who experienced the limitations of this kind of following and who was subsequently led by the Spirit into an understanding of the true identity of Jesus as the Messiah. The Fourth Gospel may therefore be taken to represent the product of a disciple who knew from his own experience the difference between the pre- and the post-glorification eras, and who for this reason is able to emphasize, for

---

[29]Regarding this rendering, see D. A. Carson, "The Purpose of the Fourth Gospel: Jn 20:31 Reconsidered," *JBL* 106 (1987): 639-51; and the critique by Gordon D. Fee, "On the Text and Meaning of John 20.30-31," in *The Four Gospels 1992. Festschrift Frans Neirynck* (BETL C; ed. F. van Segbroeck, C. M. Tuckett, G. van Belle, J. Verheyden; Leuven: University Press, 1992), 2193-2205.

later believers, the importance of understanding the true significance of
Jesus' person, words, and works (cf. esp. 20:17, 29; cf. also 2:22; 12:16;
14:26).

Implications for the Contemporary Church

If the above interpretation is correct, the emphasis in John's reference to
the believer's "greater works" is eschatological. Works done in the era
subsequent to that of the earthly Jesus are greater, not because of the
human being doing them, but owing to Jesus' exalted position with the
Father and to his complete authority, as well as on account of Jesus' answering of the disciples' prayers in his name and his sending of the Spirit as
a helping presence for his followers.

In the light of John's avoidance of "signs" terminology with reference
to the disciples, and in the light of the fact that the emphasis of "works"
terminology likewise is not necessarily, nor even primarily, on the
miraculous (as in "signs and wonders"), one should caution against using
John 14:12 in support for a theology that advocates the expectation of a
believer's working of miracles today. The issue is not so much that is it
possible to exclude this notion entirely from the Johannine reference as to
demonstrate that such a theology was clearly not central in John's intention.

His concern rather lay in showing that the works of a believer would
of necessity be superior to those of the earthly Jesus since they would be
based on Jesus' finished work and thus be able to administer its full
benefits while drawing on the full range of spiritual resources made available by the exalted Jesus in answer to prayer through the Spirit. The church's understanding of its own mission should thus glean from the present
passage the importance of an individual believer's, and the entire church's,
full reliance on Jesus in the gospel proclamation and the need to draw
consistently on the spiritual resources required for the church's mission.

The passage should also foster a better understanding of the church's
position in salvation-history. Believers should conceive of their roles, not
in terms of their own, but in relation to Jesus. They are to witness to *him*,
expounding the significance of Jesus' work and the forgiveness available
for repentant sinners, humbly pointing to the work *Jesus* has done rather
than focusing on their own. This stands in marked contrast to the subjectivism, sensationalism, and self-centeredness found in some segments
of the North-American church.

Indeed, John 14:12 reflects Jesus' consciousness of his own salvation-historical position. With amazing humility, he predicts that his followers' works will be, at least in some respect, greater than his own. May we today be inspired by, and emulate, our Lord's humility as we seek to bring the gospel to a sinful world, a world that is, despite its sin, loved by God who sent his only Son to offer it salvation.

CHAPTER SEVEN

THE TWO JOHANNINE VERBS FOR SENDING:
A Study of John's Use of Words with Reference to General Linguistic Theory[*]

Is there a distinction in meaning between the two words used for "sending" in the Fourth Gospel, ἀποστέλλω and πέμπω? Not only does the answer to this question prove to be significant for the exegesis of several important passages in John's Gospel, the history of the debate surrounding this issue also provides an interesting case study of developments in linguistic theory as applied to New Testament Greek in this century.

A notable proponent of an earlier stage of this development is Kittel's *Theological Dictionary of the New Testament*. In it Karl-Heinz Rengstorf argues for an important semantic difference in John's use of ἀποστέλλω and πέμπω.[1] Rengstorf's views, however, have not gone unchallenged. Nigel Turner has maintained that the terms constitute a "pointless variety in style," "a needless synonym," contending that "[t]here is no apparent point in these synonyms beyond the avoiding of monotony, however hard one looks for a subtle distinction."[2]

---

[*]This essay is reprinted with the permission of Sheffield Academic Press from "The Two Johannine Verbs for Sending: A Study of John's Use of Words with Reference to General Linguistic Theory," *Linguistics and the New Testament: Critical Junctures* (ed. Stanley E. Porter and D. A. Carson; JSNTSup 168; Studies in New Testament Greek 5; Sheffield: Sheffield Academic Press, 1999), 125–43.

[1]Cf. Karl-Heinz Rengstorf, "ἀποστέλλω, et al.," *TDNT* 1:398–446.

[2]Cf. Nigel Turner, *Vol. IV: Style*, in James Hope Moulton, *A Grammar of New Testament Greek* (Edinburgh: T & T Clark, 1976), 76. Some would argue that there is no such thing as a "needless synonym," since, in the words of Levinsohn, "Choice implies meaning . . . when an author has the option of expressing himself or herself in either one of two ways, the two differ in significance; there are reasons for the variations." Cf. Stephen H. Levinsohn, *Discourse Features of New Testament Greek* (Dallas, TX: SIL, 1992), 8.

On a general linguistic level, Barr's well-known critique of the *TDNT* exposes the common fallacy of projecting one's own theology onto biblical words, a tendency from which Rengstorf may not be exempt.[3] This mindset, exposed by Barr, which frequently fails to distinguish between word meanings and concepts and attempts to establish a writer's theology on the basis of word studies, remains remarkably persistent to this day.[4] Indeed, as will be seen, numerous attempts have been made to modify Rengstorf's theses while leaving his basic approach intact.

The present study will seek to explain John's use of ἀποστέλλω and πέμπω within the framework of general linguistic theory. After a brief survey of the history of the debate, Rengstorf's theory will be tested against extrabiblical evidence. Modifications of Rengstorf's hypothesis will also be subjected to close scrutiny. This will be followed by a search for alternative explanations for John's use of ἀποστέλλω and πέμπω.

The History of the Debate

The issue of "Johannine synonyms" in general was first addressed by Abbott (1905, 1906) at the beginning of this century.[5] Abbott maintained, "The whole of this Gospel is pervaded with distinctions of thought, represented by subtle distinctions of word or phrase-words and phrases so far alike that at first the reader may take the thought to be the same, though it is always really different."[6] This view was challenged by C. C. Tarelli (1946) who concluded that

[t]he Johannine usage . . . is dependent not upon difference of meaning, but upon difference of tense or mood, upon a preference for one verb in certain of

---

[3]Cf. James Barr, *The Semantics of Biblical Language* (Oxford: University Press, 1961), 206–62.

[4]This is lamented, amongst others, by Moisés Silva, *Biblical Words and their Meaning. An Introduction to Lexical Semantics* (Grand Rapids: Zondervan, 1983), 18–22. Cf. also id., *God, Language and Scripture. Reading the Bible in the light of general linguistics* (Grand Rapids: Zondervan, 1990); Peter Cotterell and Max Turner, *Linguistics and Biblical Interpretation* (Downers Grove, IL: InterVarsity, 1989), 106–28.

[5]Edwin A. Abbott, *Johannine Vocabulary: A Comparison of the Words of the Fourth Gospel with Those of the Three* (London: Adam and Charles Black, 1905) and *Johannine Grammar* (London: Adam and Charles Black, 1906).

[6]Cf. Abott, *Johannine Grammar*, 645.

its grammatical forms and for the other in other forms. It is probable also that this preference was not personal, but dictated by popular usage.[7]

Freed (1964), in an article written half a century after Abbott's assessment, took issue with him, maintaining, "I fail to see these differences in most cases."[8]

In the more recent history of the debate, the spectrum of opinions has spanned the following range: a first group essentially follows Abbott in his contention that there are significant theological differences behind John's use of ἀποστέλλω and πέμπω (especially Rengstorf and many others following him); a second group, siding with Freed, fails to see any distinction at all (e.g. Turner); a third group embraces a mediating position similar to the one proposed by Tarelli, pointing to grammatical forms as explaining the different usage of the two "sending" words in John (e.g. Mercer); and a fourth group argues that these terms, though synonyms, play a part in John's stylistic variation in the framework of his construction of entire discourses (Louw).[9] It should be noted that the second, third, and fourth groups, while differing in their particular explanations, are united in believing that the two Johannine words for "sending" are essentially synonymous.

In interaction with the major studies on the subject, the ensuing discussion will seek to explain John's varied use of ἀποστέλλω and πέμπω by answering the following questions: (1) Do the words ἀποστέλλω and πέμπω themselves differ in meaning? (2) If they do not, is John's use of ἀποστέλλω and πέμπω based on grammatical, stylistic, or other considerations, or is a combination of these factors at work?

Semantic Difference?

Rengstorf, in a very influential study, believes to have found a clear distinction in John's use of ἀποστέλλω and πέμπω, maintaining,

---

[7]Cf. C. C. Tarelli, "Johannine Synonyms," *JTS* 47 (1946): 175.

[8]Cf. Edwin D. Freed, "Variations in the Language and Thought of John," *ZNW* 55 (1964): 167. To the writers referred to here should be added those commenting on John's use of a specific pair of words such as terms for "loving," "knowing," or others. Cf. e.g. D. A. Carson, *Exegetical Fallacies* (Grand Rapids: Baker, 1984), 52–53.

[9]Cf. Abbott, *Johannine Vocabulary* and *Johannine Grammar*; Freed, "Variation," 167–97; Turner, *Style*, 76; Calvin Mercer, "'Αποστέλλειν and Πέμπειν in John," *NTS* 36 (1990): 619–24; J. P. Louw, "On Johannine Style," *Neot* 20 (1986): 5–12.

There is also a significant difference from πέμπειν. In the latter the point is the sending as such, i.e., the *fact* of sending, as in the transmission of an object or commission or the sending of a man. ἀποστέλλειν, however, expresses the fact that the sending takes place from a specific and unique standpoint which does not merely link the sender and recipient but also, in virtue of the situation, *unites* with the sender either the person or the object sent. To this extent it is only logical that ἀποστέλλειν should also carry with it the significance that the sending implies a commission bound up with the *person* of the one sent.[10]

Essentially, Rengstorf argues that in ἀποστέλλω the emphasis is on the sender and his relationship with the one sent (i.e. unity, authority), while in πέμπω the focus is on the fact and the task of sending: "[W]e can say in general that when πέμπειν is used in the New Testament the emphasis is on the sending as such, whereas when ἀποστέλλειν is used it rests on the commission linked with it."[11]

Generally, Rengstorf believes that the "sending" words were "taken out of their ordinary meaning . . . and filled with religious significance."[12] He deems his observations of a semantic difference between ἀποστέλλω and πέμπω to be very significant not merely linguistically, but also theologically: "We can hardly overestimate the significance of this fact for the linguistic expression of the early Christian awareness of mission."[13]

The use of words for "sending" in John, Rengstorf finds "[a]t first sight . . . extremely odd."[14] He concludes:

> In John's Gospel ἀποστέλλειν is used by Jesus when his concern is to ground His authority in that of God as the One who is responsible for His words and works and who guarantees their right and truth. On the other hand, He uses the formula ὁ πέμψας με (πατήρ) to affirm the participation of God in His work in the *actio* of His sending.[15]

When such a distinction cannot be sustained in the use of a given writer, such as Luke, Rengstorf concludes that this author was insuffi-

---

[10]Cf. Rengstorf, "ἀποστέλλω," 1:398 (emphasis added).

[11]Ibid., 404.

[12]Ibid.

[13]Ibid., 399–400.

[14]Ibid., 405.

[15]Ibid. Cf. also Josef Blank, *Krisis. Untersuchungen zur johanneischen Christologie und Eschatologie* (Freiburg im Breisgau: Lambertus, 1964), 70, n. 61, who essentially follows Rengstorf, albeit with slight modifications; Rudolf Bultmann, *Das Evangelium des Johannes* (Göttingen: Vandenhoeck & Ruprecht, 1950), 30, n. 2; and Jan-Adolph Bühner, *Der Gesandte und sein Weg im 4. Evangelium. Die kultur- und religionsgeschichtliche Entwicklung* (WUNT 2/2; Tübingen: J. C. B. Mohr [Paul Siebeck], 1977), 412–14, also following Rengstorf.

ciently aware of such a distinction: "Lk. . . . also [like Josephus] seems to use the words as synonyms," but this, according to Rengstorf, is due to the fact "that neither Lk. nor Josephus has any true feeling for the special nature of ἀποστέλλειν."[16] However, to charge a writer such as Luke—who displays a significant degree of literary sophistication in his writings—with linguistic incompetence, claiming he was ignorant of the proper use of ἀποστέλλω (a word Luke uses twenty-six times, not counting compounds), in order to be able to maintain the validity of one's own general theory, as Rengstorf does, seems precarious indeed.

Moreover, Rengstorf's thesis is contradicted by the frequent synonymous use of ἀποστέλλω and πέμπω in Greek writings preceding and contemporary with the New Testament.[17] A study of Thucydides' *Historiae* (fifth century BCE.), for example, yields a number of instances where ἀποστέλλω and πέμπω are demonstrably used synonymously (cf. *Hist.* 1.90, 91, 128-129; 3.4-7, 115; 4.16-17, 50, 80-81; 6.93; 7.7, 19; 8.28).[18] Compare, for example,

3.4: καὶ ἀνοκωχὴν ποιησάμενοι *πέμπουσιν* ἐς τὰς Ἀθήνας οἱ Μυτιληναῖοι . . . ἐν τούτῳ δὲ *ἀποστέλλουσι* καὶ ἐς τὴν Λακεδαίμονα πρέσβεις ("So the Mytilenaens, having concluded an armistice, *sent envoys* to Athens . . . Meanwhile they also *sent envoys* to Lacedaemon");

3.115: τὸν μὲν οὖν ἕνα τῶν στρατεγῶν *ἀπέστειλαν* Πυθόδωρον ὀλίγαις ναυσί, Σοφοκλέα δὲ . . . ἐπὶ τῶν πλειόνων νεῶν *ἀποπέμψειν* ἔμελλον ("Accordingly they *dispatched* one of their generals, Pythodorus, with a few ships, and were planning later on to *send* Sophocles . . . with the main body of the fleet"); or

---

[16] Ibid., 403-404. Other writers, such as Tarelli, also seem to have difficulty in subsuming Luke's use of ἀποστέλλω and πέμπω under their general theory. Tarelli, while referring to Matthew and Mark, completely ignores the references to "sending" in Luke/Acts.

[17] It should be acknowledged that, strictly speaking, *absolute synonymy* hardly ever occurs. For the present discussion, it is sufficient to argue for a substantial semantic overlap between the two Johannine words for "sending" that amounts to virtual synonymy. At any rate, these technicalities do not materially affect the argument below. On synonymy, see especially Cotterell and Turner, *Linguistics and Biblical Interpretation,* 159-61; Anthony C. Thiselton, "Semantics and New Testament Interpretation," in *New Testament Interpretation* (ed. I. Howard Marshall; Exeter: Paternoster, 1977), 90-93; and standard linguistic texts.

[18] Cf. Tarelli, "Synonyms," 175, who refers to Thucydides, 1.90-91. The various passages in extrabiblical Greek literature cited here and below were located by using the TLG data base of the IBYCUS system.

7.19: μετὰ δὲ τούτους Κορίνθιοι . . . πεντακοσίους ὁπλίτας . . .
ἀπέπεμψαν. ἀπέστειλαν δὲ καὶ Σικυώνιοι διακοσίους ὁπλίτας ὁμοῦ τοῖς
Κορινθίοις ("the Corinthians *sent out* five hundred hoplites . . . The Sicyonians
also *dispatched* at the same time as the Corinthians two hundred hoplites").

In all these instances, the uses of ἀποστέλλω and πέμπω seem to be a
function, not of different word meanings, but of stylistic variation. This is
further underscored by the fact that in two of the three above cited examples ἀποστέλλω and πέμπω are used in parallel fashion in the same grammatical form (3.4: pres. act. ind. 3d pl.; 7.19: aor. act. ind. 3d pl.), so that
the author's preference for a certain grammatical form of ἀποστέλλω or
πέμπω demonstrably does not play a part. Rather, these are clear instances
of stylistic variation. A screening of Greek literature from the second
century BCE to the first century CE yields similar conclusions. Polybius
(202–120 BCE), Diodorus Siculus (first century BCE), and Josephus
(37–100 CE) all use the two terms synonymously in close proximity to one
another.[19]

It may therefore be concluded that the data from extrabiblical Greek
literature invalidate Rengstorf's thesis that ἀποστέλλω and πέμπω differ
semantically, not just in John, but in general Greek language use. If no
such semantic differences can be found in Greek language in general,
however, John would have had to be exceedingly idiosyncratic to deviate
from general current usage. Since, as has been shown, ἀποστέλλω and
πέμπω occur frequently in Greek literature preceding and contemporary
with John's Gospel in close proximity to one another with no apparent difference in meaning, these two terms should be viewed as virtual synonyms.

Excursus: Modifications of Rengstorf's Thesis
Despite the weaknesses just noted, Rengstorf's view has been very influential. Even the most ingenious efforts to eliminate the weaknesses of Rengstorf's theory while maintaining its core tenet, however, cannot remedy its
fundamental flaws. Rengstorf's thesis was adopted, among others, by
Radermakers, who asserts,

---

[19]Cf. Polybius, *Historiae*, 1.53, 67; 3.69, 75, 97; 4.10, 19, 22, 49, 52, 72;
5:27, 28, 35, 102, 110; 7.2–3; 8.19; 19.42; 14.1; 18.19; 20.3, 9; 21.37; 22.13–14;
25.6; 27.4; 28.15; 29.3, 24; 30.9, 19; 31.32; 32.15; 33.8; Diodorus Siculus,
Bibliotheca historica, 2.22, 26; 4.10; 11.21, 30, 92; 12.30, 41, 46–47, 60, 77; 13.1,
6–7, 9, 36; 14.8, 12, 20, 30, 35, 82, 109; 15.5, 13, 29, 45–46, 67, 73, 77, 82;
16.17–18, 27, 39, 44, 59, 65, 84; 17.12, 55, 73, 86; 18.12, 49–50; 19.61–62, 68,
71, 77, 79, 85, 97; 20.14–15, 19, 49, 79, 82; Josephus, *Antiquities*, 1.255;
6.167–68, 222–23; 7.175; 8.50–51, 332–33; 9.24, 289–90; 11.317; 13.23, 45, 278;
14.126; 16.138–40; 18.112; 20.37.

To emphasize the source, the origin, the Father, in Johannine vocabulary is to speak of apostolic "mission" (πέμπω): the sent one is the reflection of the one who sent him. To put the development, the unfolding, in perspective, the active outworking of the life of love and the faithful adherence to that expansive and transforming presence of God, is to speak of a missionary "apostolate" (ἀποστέλλω): the sent one is completely obedient to the one who sent him.[20]

As Radermakers contends, "The instances of πέμπω . . . stress the close bond uniting Son and Father. Those of ἀποστέλλω add to this a relationship with people; what is at issue is the ministry performed by the sent one in their midst."[21] Quite apart from the question whether Radermakers is correct in his reconstruction of the Johannine concepts of ἀποστέλλω and πέμπω, he confuses word meanings with the concepts which are elucidated by their respective discourse contexts.

Another attempt to modify Rengstorf's hypothesis has recently been made by Mercer.[22] This author, while finding fault with Rengstorf's emphasis on authority in John's use of ἀποστέλλειν, contends that the distinctiveness of this term lies in the idea of a special commission.[23] Mercer rightly maintains, contra Rengstorf, that "[u]tilizing the two categories suggested by Rengstorf, we find numerous instances of both ἀποστέλλειν and πέμπειν in which the fact of sending stresses the authority of the Father who sent Jesus."[24] However, when Mercer contends that ἀποστέλλειν in John focuses on a special commission from God while πέμπειν focuses on God himself, he fails to convince. Thus, for example, there is no commission statement in 1:24 where ἀποστέλλειν is used. Conversely, one finds a commission statement in 1:33 (ὁ πέμψας με βαπτίζειν; cf. 1:8: ἀπεσταλμένος . . . ἵνα μαρτυρήσῃ; cf. also 4:38: ἀπέστειλα ὑμᾶς θερίζειν). The identification of the sender detected by Mercer in John's use of πέμπειν seems bound up with the (participial) formula ὁ πέμψας με (πατήρ) rather than with the term πέμπειν itself. That the issue is syntactical and not merely lexical is borne out by 5:36–38, where the phrases ὁ πατήρ με ἀπέσταλκεν (v. 36) and ὃν ἀπέστειλεν ἐκεῖνος (v. 38)

---

[20]Cf. J. Radermakers, "Mission et Apostolat dans l'Évangile Johannique," *SE* II/1 (TU 87; ed. Frank L. Cross; Berlin: Akademie, 1959), 120. Cf. also Johannes Riedl, *Das Heilswerk Jesu nach Johannes* (FTS 93; Freiburg im Breisgau: Herder, 1973), 55, concurring with Radermakers.

[21]Ibid., 111.

[22]Cf. Mercer, "Ἀποστέλλειν and Πέμπειν," 619–24.

[23]Ibid., 123.

[24]Ibid. Mercer lists for ἀποστέλλειν 3:34; 6:57; and 17:18; and for πέμπειν 4:34; 5:30; 7:16, 29; 8:16, 26; 12:49; 14:24; 15:26; and 20:21.

are used parallel to ὁ πέμψας με πατήρ (v. 37). Mercer, by focusing on the morphology of individual words, neglects to consider syntax as a possible explanation for the different uses of the two "sending" verbs in John. Moreover, he does not deal with the possibility of stylistic variation.

Kuhl's assessment is more cautious.[25] He concedes that both Johannine terms for sending are frequently used for Jesus' sending by the Father and are therefore substantially equivalent. However, he still maintains that the different grammatical forms (participial or indicative forms) and the respective contexts in which the terms are found may point to nuances in meaning. At the same time, Kuhl seems to approve of Rengstorf's thesis that πέμπειν refers to the origin of the sending and the unity between sender and sent one while ἀποστέλλειν accentuates the authority of the sent one in his being sent.[26] Kuhl observes that in John 17 (which is strongly shaped by a spirit of unity between sender and sent one) ἀποστέλλειν is used (and that seven times), not πέμπειν (as Rengstorf's theory would require). He also finds it difficult to fit 6:57 (ἀποστέλλειν) or 13:20 (πέμπειν) into Rengstorf's scheme. One wonders how, in the light of such serious difficulties, Kuhl can still give a qualified endorsement of Rengstorf's thesis.

Finally, Seynaeve, too, sees a marked distinction in John's use of ἀποστέλλω and πέμπω. However, his reconstruction is different than Rengstorf's. Seynaeve concludes, "[W]hereas the verb ἀποστέλλω insists on the fact of Christ's coming as sent one, that is, on his actual presence, the verb πέμπω suggests the task or work to be accomplished."[27] He elaborates,

> On the one hand, ἀποστέλλω rather points to the sent one himself having come, the Messiah's appearance in the world. Through the Father's free, sovereign initiative, Jesus has been sent; he finds himself being there, among human beings . . . On the other hand, πέμπω brings out more the service Jesus renders in his

---

[25]Cf. Josef Kuhl, *Die Sendung Jesu und der Kirche nach dem Johannes-Evangelium* (St. Augustin: Steyler, 1967), 54.

[26]William Loader, *The Christology of the Fourth Gospel* (BET 23; Frankfurt am Main: Peter Lang, 1992), 238, n. 54, seems to misjudge Kuhl's position at least partially, when he cites him as believing that there is no difference in meaning between ἀποστέλλω and πέμπω.

[27]Cf. J. Seynaeve, "Les verbes Ἀποστέλλω et πέμπω dans le vocabulaire théologique de Saint Jean," *L'Évangile de Jean. Sources, Rédaction, Théologie* (BETL XLIV; ed. Marinus de Jonge; Leuven: Gombleux, 1977), 389: "[A]los que le verbe ἀποστέλλω. insiste sur le fait de l'envoi-venue du Christ, sur le fait qu'Il est là, le verbe πέμπω suggère la tâche, l'oeuvre à être accomplie."

role as sent one: that he performs, that he accomplishes the commission he received from the Father.[28]

Despite Seynaeve's efforts to refine Rengstorf's thesis, his theory likewise fails to explain the use of the two Johannine "sending" words in passages such as John 20:21 (cf. 17:18). According to Seynaeve's view, 20:21a refers to Jesus' being sent into the world (ἀποστέλλω) while 20:21b focuses on the quality of the relationship between sender and sent ones (πέμπω). However, the question arises as to how one should explain the switch of sending words in 20:21 theologically. Is the meaning of the passage, "Just as the Father commissioned me to go into the world, I want you to live in a dependent relationship with me as your sender"? It seems that the presence of καθώς already implies that ἀποστέλλω and πέμπω are used synonymously in 20:21.[29]

In light of the evidence from extrabiblical Greek literature, and the mutually contradictory explanations forwarded by those who argue for a semantic difference between the two Johannine verbs for "sending," one is inclined to conclude with Okure, "It is not evident that a different shade of meaning is intended in the use of each of these two verbs."[30] As another writer elaborates, "Both words are used for the sending of Christ by the Father, and for the sending of the disciples by Christ . . . This is an instance of John's penchant for minor stylistic variations."[31] However,

---

[28]Ibid., 388.

[29]Cf. Tarelli, "Johannine Synonyms," 175: " '*As* the Father hath sent me, even so send I you' surely suggests assimilation, not differentiation."

[30]Cf. Teresa Okure, *The Johannine Approach to Mission* (WUNT 31; Tübingen: Mohr-Siebeck, 1988), 2, n. 4. Overall, Okure's treatment of the possibility of distinctions between ἀποστέλλω and πέμπω is rather cursory. Among those who do not see a distinction between these two terms in the Fourth Gospel are also C. H. Dodd, *The Interpretation of the Fourth Gospel* (Cambridge: Cambridge University Press, 1953), 254: "The verbs πέμπειν and ἀποστέλλειν, used apparently without any difference of meaning . . ."; C. K. Barrett, *The Gospel According to St. John* (2d ed.; Philadelphia: Westminster, 1978), 569; Ferdinand Hahn, *Mission in the New Testament* (SBT 47; London: SCM, 1965), 158, n. 2: "the two words are closely related to each other and are clearly synonymous and interchangeable in John"; and James McPolin, "Mission in the Fourth Gospel," *ITQ* 36 (1969): 113, n. 4: "it seems that a distinction in their meaning[i.e. of the two Johannine verbs for sending] has not been clearly proved."

[31]Cf. D. A. Carson, *The Gospel According to John* (Grand Rapids: Eerdmans, 1991), 648, n. 1. Cf. Barrett, *Gospel According to St. John*, 569; Leon L. Morris, *Studies in the Fourth Gospel* (Grand Rapids: Eerdmans, 1969), 293–319; Loader, *Christology of the Fourth Gospel*, 30.

while we may concur that ἀποστέλλω and πέμπω are virtually synonymous, is John's use of the respective "sending" verbs best accounted for by "stylistic variation"?

The Search for Alternative Solutions

Since there appears to be no semantic difference between ἀποστέλλω and πέμπω, it is necessary to explore alternative explanations for the Johannine use of "sending" words. Can this usage be accounted for by a preference for those words in certain grammatical forms? Should one view the usage as serving the purpose of stylistic variation? Is John's use of ἀποστέλλω and πέμπω completely arbitrary? Or is there a combination of these or other factors at work?

Preference for Grammatical Forms and Possible Obsolescence
That John uses πέμπω more frequently in certain grammatical forms than ἀποστέλλω and vice versa is undeniable. As a matter of fact, John's preference for a given "sending" word is absolute, for he never employs the alternative grammatical form of a "sending" verb, even where it was available to him through general usage. Specifically, John uses ἀποστέλλω twenty-one times in the aorist active indicative (75 per cent of all uses of ἀποστέλλω in John), four times in the adverbial or periphrastic perfect passive participle (15 per cent), and three times in the perfect active indicative (10 per cent). The term πέμπω is used by John twenty-seven times in the substantival aorist active participle (84 per cent of all uses of πέμπω in John), once in the aorist subjunctive (3 per cent), once in the present active indicative (3 per cent), and three times in the future active indicative (10 per cent).[32]

These data cause one to ask whether or not John's preference for the two "sending" words in certain grammatical forms was predetermined by

---

[32]Note also that all four instances of πέμπω in Matthew feature the aorist participle πέμψας (Matt 2:8; 11:2; 14:10; cf. Mark 6:27: ἀποστείλας; and 22:7). Luke exhibits greater variety in his use of πέμπω. One finds, for example, the aorist passive indicative (Luke 4:26) and participle (7:6). Interestingly, in the pericope of the parable of the wicked tenants, Mark uses ἀποστέλλω five times (cf. Mark 12:1-6) while Luke uses ἀποστέλλω just once while featuring πέμπω three times (Luke 20:10-13). These observations suggest that, within certain boundaries, there remained room for individual writers to choose either "sending" word based on their personal preference.

the obsolescence of certain forms at the time of writing, as Tarelli contends, or whether other reasons should be found.

Table 4: Grammatical Forms of Sending Verbs in the New Testament

Form	Matt		Mark		Luke		Acts		John		Paul		Total	
	ἀ.	π.	ἀ.	π.	ἀ.	π.	ἀ.	π.	ἀ.	π.	ἀ.	π.	ἀ.	π.
P A I	4	0	6	0	3	0	1	1	0	1	0	1	14	3
P A S	0	0	1	0	0	0	0	0	0	0	0	0	1	0
P A Ptc	0	0	0	0	0	0	0	1	0	0	0	0	0	1
P A Inf	0	0	1	0	0	0	0	0	0	0	0	0	1	0
A A I	10	0	7	0	12	3	8	2	21	0	2	8	60	13
A A S	0	0	1	0	0	1	1	0	0	1	0	0	2	2
A A Ptc	2	4	3	0	3	0	4	2	0	27	0	1	12	34
A A Inf	0	0	0	0	1	2	0	3	0	0	0	3	1	8
A A Impf	1	0	0	1	0	1	1	2	0	0	0	0	2	4
A P I	1	0	0	0	3	1	1	0	0	0	0	0	5	1
A P S	0	0	0	0	0	0	0	0	0	0	1	0	1	0
A P Ptc	0	0	0	0	0	1	0	0	0	0	0	0	0	1
Pf A I	0	0	0	0	1	0	5	0	3	0	1	0	10	0
Pf P Ptc	1	0	0	0	2	0	2	0	4	0	0	0	9	0
F A I	3	0	1	0	1	1	1	0	0	3	0	2	6	6
Total	22	4	20	1	26	10	24	11	28	32	4	15	124	73

(NT: 132 79)

Going no further than the New Testament, one notes that other New Testament writers use the alternative grammatical forms to those used most frequently by John, that is, the aorist active indicative of πέμπω (cf. Luke in Luke 7:6, 19; 15:15; Acts 10:33; 23:30; Paul in 1 Cor 4:17; 2 Cor 9:3; Eph 6:22; Phil 2:28; 4:16; Col 4:8; 1 Thess 3:2, 5) as well as the substantival aorist active participle of ἀποστέλλω (cf. Matt 10:40=Mark 9:37=Luke 9:48; Luke 10:16; Acts 15:33). John's preference for ἀποστέλλω in the aorist active indicative, while following the general preference of the Synoptic writers, is contrasted by Paul's preference for πέμπω in the same grammatical form, which is probably due to Paul's epistolary context and literary convention. John's preference for πέμπω in the substantival aorist active participle differs from Luke.

Regarding the less frequent forms, John's exclusive use of πέμπω in the future active indicative (14:26; 15:26; 16:7) is parallel to Paul's preference while running counter to the Synoptists so that personal style, not the obsolescence of forms, appears to be the determinative factor. Similar things can be said about John's one-time use each of πέμπω in the present active indicative (20:21) and in the aorist active subjunctive (13:20). In both cases, John's usage differs from that of at least some of the other New Testament authors and cannot be attributed to the obsolescence of forms. John's preference for the perfect passive participle of ἀποστέλλω, on the other hand, appears to be due to the obsolescence of the equivalent form of πέμπω.[33] Finally, obsolescence, or at least very infrequent usage, also appears to provide the explanation for John's exclusive use of ἀποστέλλω in the perfect active indicative (cf. 5:33, 36; 20:21; with the later passage possibly "echoing" the two earlier ones), since πέμπω never occurs in this form in the entire New Testament.[34]

I conclude that John's preference for ἀποστέλλω and πέμπω in particular grammatical forms is an important factor in his choice of "sending" verbs. Tarelli's proposed rationale for John's preference of the two verbs for "sending" in certain grammatical forms, that is, the obsolescence of the respective alternative grammatical form, however, only appears to apply to John's use of ἀποστέλλω in the perfect active indicative and possibly also to the periphrastic aorist passive participle of ἀποστέλλω. It does not furnish a rationale for the forms most commonly used in John, such as the aorist active indicative of ἀποστέλλω or the substantival aorist active participle of πέμπω, so that other explanations must be found.

Stylistic Variation?
If ἀποστέλλω and πέμπω are virtual synonyms and John displays a preference for certain grammatical forms of the respective terms that is often not due to the obsolescence of alternative forms, does John perhaps at times use stylistic variation? Louw writes, "Though there seems to be no difference in lexical meaning however hard one looks for a subtle distinction, this tendency to variety in the use of similar words should rather be understood as a Johannine device to give flavor to a discussion which is syntactically very simple in structure."[35]

Louw argues, against N. Turner, that stylistic variation is not "pointless" but that it rather fulfills an important linguistic function, that is, that

---

[33]A search of the TLG data base found no instances of the use of the perfect passive participle of πέμπω in the centuries surrounding the writing of John's Gospel.

[34]A search of the TLG data base yielded 11 uses of the perfect active indicative of πέμπω in the centuries surrounding the writing of John's Gospel: Polybius, *Hist.* 1.67; 4.49; Plutarch, *Quaest. Conv.* 612; Dio Chrysostom, *Orat.* 13.8; 1 Esdr 2:20; 2 Macc 2:11; Josephus, *Ant.* 12.56; 13.45; 14.191; *Vit.* 55.5; 95.1.

[35]Cf. Louw, "Johannine Style," 7.

of "flavoring" (Louw's term) a discourse that otherwise would be repetitive and monotonous. He contends, "Perhaps the most notable [significant stylistic feature] is the tendency in the Gospel of John to employ relatively close synonyms with essentially the same meaning . . . John seems to be very fond of varying his diction for the sake of aesthetic embellishment."[36]

Louw cites as one example the use of two different words for "love" in 21:15-17 which, according to Louw, "seems to reflect simply a rhetorical alteration designed to avoid undue repetition."[37] He adds, "Style is not only concerned with individual words and phrases, but should also be considered in terms of a larger stretch of language such as the paragraph, and for this matter, even the total discourse . . . style involves both syntactic and semantic features, that is, the arrangement of words and of thought."[38]

Louw gives the following examples in John where an alteration between ἀποστέλλω and πέμπω occurs in the same discourse:

- 1:19-24: ὅτι ἀπέστειλεν . . . (v. 19) τοῖς πέμψασιν . . . (v. 22) καὶ ἀπεσταλμένοι (v. 24);
- 5:36-38: ὅτι ὁ πατήρ με ἀπέσταλκεν. καὶ ὁ πέμψας με πατήρ . . . (vv. 36-37) ὅτι ὃν ἀπέστειλεν ἐκεῖνος (v. 38); and
- 20:21: καθὼς ἀπέσταλκέν με ὁ πατήρ, κἀγὼ πέμπω ὑμᾶς.[39]

To these examples adduced by Louw, the following passages could be added:

- 7:28-33: ὁ πέμψας με . . . (v. 28) κἀκεῖνός με ἀπέστειλεν (v. 29) . . . ἀπέστειλαν οἱ ἀρχιερεῖς (v. 32) . . . ὑπάγω πρὸς τὸν πέμψαντά με (v. 33); and perhaps also
- 9:4, 7: τὰ ἔργα τοῦ πέμψαντός με . . . ἀπεσταλμένος.[40]

Is John's varied use of "sending" words in these examples best explained by stylistic variation, as Louw maintains? While this appears

---

[36]Ibid., 6.

[37]Ibid.

[38]Ibid., 10,12.

[39]Ibid. Cf. 17:18 where ἀποστέλλω is used twice in an otherwise very similar passage.

[40]For other New Testament examples of the use of ἀποστέλλω and πέμπω in the same discourse, see Matt 22:3, 4 (ἀ.), 7 (π.); Mark 5:10 (ἀ.), 12 (π.); Luke 7:3 (ἀ.), 6, 10, 19 (π.), 20 (ἀ.); 20:10 (ἀ.), 11, 12, 13 (π.), 20 (ἀ.); Acts 10:32, 33 (π.), 36 (ἀ.); 12:29 (π.), 30 (ἀ.); 15:22, 25 (π.), 27 (ἀ.); Rev 1:1 (ἀ.), 11 (π.); 22:6 (ἀ.), 16 (π.).

possible at a first glance, a closer look indicates that in each case more probable explanations can be found. To demonstrate this claim, it will be best to group the relevant passages into categories of usage. The first category is made of instances where John uses a "sending" word in a set, stereotypical phrase. This may be ὁ πέμψας με (cf. 1:33; 4:34; 5:23, 24, 30, 37; 6:38, 39, 44; 7:16, 18, 28, 33; 8:16, 18, 26, 29; 9:4; 10:44, 45; 12:49; 13:16, 20; 14:24; 15:21; 16:5) or ὃν ἀπέστειλεν ἐκεῖνος or a similar phrase (cf. 3:34; 5:38; 6:29, 57; 7:29; 8:42; 10:36; 11:42; 17:3, 8, 21, 23, 25). As will be argued below, this usage of "sending words" in fixed patterns should probably be viewed as an instance of John's tendency toward stereotyping, a practice that appears to be the exact opposite of stylistic variation. Leaving aside the three uses of πέμπω in the future active indicative in 14:26, 15:26, and 16:7 with reference to the expected sending of the Spirit, neither of which is adduced by Louw as an example of stylistic variation, and which has to be explained on other grounds, we are left with the following passages: 1:6, 19, 22, 24; 3:17, 28; 4:38; 5:33, 36; 7:32; 9:7; 11:3; 13:20; 17:18; 18:24; and 20:21.

Two initial observations can be made. First, one notes that in fourteen of these sixteen passages, ἀποστέλλω is used (except for 1:22; 13:20). This general preference for ἀποστέλλω, of course, is not only analogous to the New Testament usage in general (but see Paul), it also conforms to usage in the LXX where ἀποστέλλω is used almost exclusively (of the twenty-six uses of πέμπω, only five are in the canonical books: Gen 27:42; 1 Kgs 20:20; 28:24; Neh 2:5; Esth 8:5; twelve of the other references are in 1 Maccabees). With regard to genre boundaries, one observes that ἀποστέλλω appears to be preferred in narratives while πέμπω is used more frequently in epistolary contexts. Secondly, there are also instances in John where, according to Louw's theory, one might expect John to use stylistic variation, but where such is not used (cf. 13:20; and esp. 17:18). Was John therefore inconsistent or arbitrary at occasions, or are there more plausible ways to account for his use of "sending" words than stylistic variation?

What, then, are the most likely explanations for John's usage in the sixteen passages given above? Genre (i.e. narrative) may account for the uses of ἀποστέλλω in about a third of these passages, i.e. 1:19, 24; 7:32; 11:3; and 18:24. In 13:20, one of only two passages left where πέμπω is used, this term is probably required to match the phrase ὁ πέμψας με later in the same sentence. The only remaining use of πέμπω in 1:22, while not as stereotypical as the other uses of the substantival aorist active participle, is in accordance with John's tendency to use only one "sending" verb in a given grammatical form. As already suggested, the use of the perfect passive participle ἀπεσταλμένος and the perfect active indicatives of ἀποστέλλω are explained by the obsolescence or rare usage of πέμπω in these forms. Three passages remain: 3:17; 4:38; and 17:18. Notably, 3:17 and 17:18, together with 10:36, are the only passages in the entire Gospel where the phrase ἀποστέλλω εἰς τὸν κόσμον is found. John 3:17 may echo the tradition enshrined in Gal 4:4 where the wording is virtually identical: ἐξαπέστειλεν ὁ θεός τὸν υἱὸν αὐτοῦ; 17:18 may echo both 4:38 and especially 3:17 and 10:36 (see further below).

If these detailed observations are correct, it is possible to account for John's use of "sending" verbs in each and every case without resorting to the (rather vague and generalizing) explanation of stylistic variation (at least as a primary or exclusive factor in John's usage). Rather, general factors, such as genre or grammar (including verbal aspect; see further below), as well as personal style characteristics, such as stereotyping or echoing, provide more plausible explanations of the detailed instances where a "sending" verb is used. This, of course, does not deny that the use of "sending" verbs by certain writers in Greek may have been due merely to stylistic variation; we have already seen instances in Thucydides' *Historiae* above where this is demonstrably the case. What it does suggest, however, is that the issue may be more complex and that "stylistic variation" should not be used prematurely as a catch-all phrase to describe a writer's (in the present case, John's) use of virtual synonyms. Synonyms they may be, but a writer may still have had other reasons for choosing one term over against the other in a given context than mere stylistic variation (see further below).

We may return briefly to the three examples adduced by Louw to see how the above analysis alternatively explains John's usage. In the first example, 1:19-24, ἀπέστειλεν is used in v. 19 due to the passage's narrative genre; τοῖς πέμψασιν in v. 22 conforms to John's preference for πέμπω in the substantival aorist active participle; and John's choice of ἀπεσταλμένοι in v. 24 is probably due to both genre and grammatical considerations (obsolescence of πέμπω in this particular form). In the second example, 5:36-38, ἀπέσταλκεν in v. 36 is probably used owing to the obsolescence of the perfect active indicative of πέμπω; and both ὁ πέμψας με πατήρ in v. 37 and ὅτι ὃν ἀπέστειλεν ἐκεῖνος in v. 38 are set phrases due to stereotyping. Finally, John's use of the perfect ἀπεσταλκέν together with πέμπω in 20:21, likewise, rather than being due to stylistic variation, appears to be merely a function of the limitations imposed upon John when wanting to use a perfect active indicative form, that is, the obsolescence of πέμπω. Thus while a first glance may suggest mere stylistic variation, a closer look indicates that in each case other factors may have been ultimately determinative.

One final point should be made. Of the sixty uses of "sending" verbs in John combined, no less than forty-nine instances, or almost eighty per cent, feature various forms of the aorist (ἀποστέλλω: twenty-one out of twenty-eight; πέμπω: twenty-eight of thirty-two instances). It appears therefore that verbal aspect provides another parameter for John's use of "sending" verbs. This also means that attention is focused on the eleven instances where John chooses to deviate from his usual preference, especially the three uses each of the perfect (5:33, 36; 20:21) and also of the future (14:26; 15:26; 16:7), his use of the perfect passive participle of ἀποστέλλω (1:6, 24; 3:28; 9:7), and his one use of the present (20:21).

It is now possible to present the findings of the above analysis. A model will be used that is designed to do justice to the complexity of the issue at hand.

John's Use of "Sending" Verbs

Generally, genre and grammar, including verbal aspect, provide parameters for language use. Within these parameters, there is room for individual characteristics of style to be displayed, be it stereotyping, echoing, or stylistic variation. A few words should be said here about the stylistic characteristics of stereotyping and echoing. "Stereotyping" may be defined as a writer's, or speaker's, tendency to use words or phrases in fixed grammatical forms due to his own personal style for the sake of reinforcing a given massage or other reasons. In John's Gospel, it is especially the substantival aorist active participle ὁ πέμψας that takes on an almost technical force. Convenience, consistency, clarity of expression, and other factors may have contributed to the development of the Johannine sending terminology. The phenomenon of "stereotyping" is characterized well by Kraft, who writes on various "protective devices built into human experience":

> A fourth factor contributing to communicational success and closely related to the habitual nature of our cultural activities is the fact that *what we do and say has a high level of predictability or, more technically, redundancy.* One aspect of this redundancy is the fact that we tend to deal most of the time with familiar subjects and in a way that finds us frequently saying the same or similar things over and over again. The content of many conversations and a large number of books is, in fact, so highly predictable that it is often possible to get almost all of the important content in a conversation by listening no more than half the time. We can also fairly well master the content of certain books by barely skimming them. Indeed, speed reading courses are based on this fact.
>
> Such predictability leads to the energy-saving propensity of human beings that we call *stereotyping.* Though there are many negative things to be said about

stereotyping, a positive one is that stereotypes enable us to guess fairly accurately most of the time many of the things we need to know in order to interpret properly. Stereotyping at its best is merely the categorizing of people, places, times, things, and so forth in such a way that the factors held in common by the members of any given category are kept in focus and, in a communicational situation, do not need to be restated. Such predictability and the reflective way in which we respond to it play an important part in our ability to accurately interpret communicational phenomena.[41]

By repeatedly featuring Jesus as the one who calls God "the one who sent me," and by using the term πέμπω in each case, John uses the linguistic phenomenon of "stereotyping" with considerable skill and effect in the way just described.

"Echoing" may be understood as a writer's deliberate specific reference to another similar or identical phrase, usually, but not necessarily, earlier in the book. The difference between "stereotyping" and "echoing" is that the former practice is rather general and almost subconscious, while the latter is specific and deliberate. Examples of possible echoes of "sending" verbs in John include the following: (1) 1:6 may echo (signal) 3:28; which may in turn be echoed by 9:7; (2) 3:17, which may itself "echo" Gal 4:4, may be echoed in 17:18, with a possible secondary echo of 4:38 in 17:18; and (3) 20:21 may echo 5:33, 36. It should also be noted that stereotyping, echoing, and stylistic variation seem to function along a continuum ranging from a high degree of determinacy of forms (stereotyping) to a high degree of flexibility (stylistic variation). While it is possible to find a combination of both stereotyping and stylistic variation in the same writing, one should generally expect one or the other characteristic to predominate.

The following outline describes John's use of "sending" verbs.

---

[41]Cf. Charles H. Kraft, *Communicating Theory for Christian Witness* (rev. ed.; Maryknoll, NY: Orbis, 1991), 104–105. Note that there is another, more narrow, use of the term "stereotype," usually bearing a negative connotation, which is touched upon by Kraft earlier in his book, i.e. with reference to the labelling of a *person* in a way which becomes a barrier to communication. The example Kraft provides is that of a student saying to him, "You don't act like a professor," thus implying that all professors are the same and act alike, plus the connotation that the way professors usually act is in accordance with their formal status and thus impersonal (p. 19). But the way the term "stereotyping" is used in the present essay is to describe the linguistic phenomenon illustrated by the quote in the text above.

I. General Parameters
  A. Literary Genre
    1. ἀποστέλλω (cf. LXX) commonly used especially in narratives
    2. πέμπω occurs more frequently in epistolary contexts
  B. Grammatical Form
    1. the perfect of πέμπω is very rare: generally ἀποστέλλω is used
    2. the periphrastic perfect passive participle of πέμπω is obsolete (or very rare)
    3. verbal aspect: the aorist is used in 49 out of 60 instances; other: 3 perfect active indicatives; 4 perfect passive participles, 3 future active indicatives, 1 present active indicative

II. Style Characteristics
  A. Stereotyping
    1. ὁ πέμψας με (πατήρ)
    2. ὃν ἀπέστειλεν ἐκεῖνος or similar phrase
    3. exclusive usage of given "sending" verb in certain grammatical form
  B. Echoing
    1. 1:6 echoing 3:28, which is echoed by 9:7
    2. 3:17, echoing Gal 4:4, is echoed in 17:18, which also echoes 4:38 and 10:36
    3. 20:21 echoing 5:33, 36
  C. Stylistic Variation
    may function in John's use of "sending" verbs as a supplementary (but not necessarily primary or ultimately determinate) factor

Conclusion

It has been argued that ἀποστέλλω and πέμπω are virtual synonyms (contra Rengstorf and those following him). As a study of extrabiblical Greek literature from the fifth century BCE to the first century CE has suggested, ἀποστέλλω and πέμπω often occur in similar or identical grammatical forms in close proximity to one another with no evident difference in meaning.

John's use of "sending" verbs was found to be largely determined by the author's preference for a given word in a certain grammatical form. This, however, was only in a few instances traced to the obsolescence of the alternative form. It was suggested that, within the general parameters of literary genre and grammar (including verbal aspect), various style characteristics were determinative for John's use of "sending" verbs, specifically "stereotyping" and "echoing." Stylistic variation thus was found not to play the exclusive or predominant role assigned to it by conventional wisdom in the relevant literature.

More work needs to be done to explore the linguistic and extra-linguistic phenomena guiding a writer's choice of words and phrases in general, and of John in particular, such as studies of other potential Johannine synonyms (such as words for "love" or "know"). It will be important to face the complexity of the linguistic phenomena involved and to avoid dogmatism and monolithic theories. In this context, Stanley Porter's statement, made in his essay in this volume, is certainly confirmed by the results of this present study: "We have asked too many theological and not enough linguistic questions." It is hoped that the present essay may contribute to such a discussion both a general framework and a case study of a particular pattern of usage.

CHAPTER EIGHT

THE CHALLENGE OF A SYSTEMATIZED BIBLICAL THEOLOGY OF MISSION:
Missiological Insights from the Gospel of John[*]

Introduction

Missiology currently appears to be suffering from an acute identity crisis.
This crisis is exacerbated by at least two major factors: the increasing inter-
disciplinary nature of missiology and the rapid pace of change in the world
around us. Each of these has significant implications for the church's missionary task. While few would oppose in principle the efforts made to
draw upon the valid findings of the various social sciences, there is a
mounting concern among missiologists and other Christian thinkers that
missiology, as a discipline, should be rescued from drifting (and drowning!) in a sea of social science data and be anchored once again to its
theological foundation.[1]

---

[*]This essay first appeared in *Missiology* 23 (1995): 445-64 and is reprinted
with permission.
[1]Cf. David J. Bosch, "Reflections on Biblical Models of Mission," in *Toward
the Twenty-first Century in Christian Mission: Essays in Honor of Gerald H.
Anderson* (ed. James M. Phillips and Robert T. Coote; Grand Rapids: Eerdmans,
1993), 175-92; D. A. Carson, "Church and Mission: Reflections on
Contextualization and the Third Horizon," in *The Church in the Bible and the
World* (ed. D. A. Carson; Grand Rapids: Baker, 1987), 213-57; David J.
Hesselgrave, *Today's Choices for Tomorrow's Mission* (Grand Rapids:
Zondervan, 1988), 139-44; Edward Rommen, "Missiology's Place in the
Academy," *Trinity World Forum* 17/3 (1992): 1-4; idem, "The De-Theologizing
of Missiology," *Trinity World Forum* 19/1 (1993): 1-4; David Wells, "The D-
Min-Ization of the Ministry," in *No God but God: Breaking with the Idols of Our
Age* (ed. Os Guinness and John Seel; Chicago: Moody, 1992), 175-88.

External trends and changes, such as the world's urbanization, globalization, modern computer technology, and the pervasive influence of the mass media, have also presented Christian missions with unprecedented challenges and opportunities. While the potential for global Christian outreach has never been greater, these external pressures have led to a rising degree of secularization in the church's self-understanding and strategizing.[2] Lured away from its theological moorings by the explosion of knowledge in the social sciences and overwhelmed by the breathtaking pace of technological and sociological changes, missiology, after gaining much the world has to offer, needs to save its soul.[3]

How can the church's reflection on its missionary task be again properly grounded? The answer lies in a carefully constructed biblical theology of mission that is hermeneutically sound, yet oriented toward the challenges facing the contemporary church. It has been increasingly recognized in recent years that it is inadequate to quote the great commission passages of the New Testament in an isolated fashion.[4] Instead, one ought to understand a given biblical writer's teaching on mission *as a whole*, first within the framework of his overall theology and then within the context of the entire canon.[5]

----

[2]Thus, John Piper writes his book, *Let the Nations Be Glad! The Supremacy of God in Missions* (Grand Rapids: Baker, 1993), "for college and seminary classes on the theology of missions that really want to be *theo*logical as well as anthropological, methodological and technological" (p. 8; emphasis Piper's). Peter Beyerhaus, *Shaken Foundations: Theological Foundations for Mission* (Grand Rapids: Zondervan, 1972), 30, already had written over 20 years ago, "Our one-sided concern with man and his society threatens to pervert mission and make it a secular or even a quasi-atheistic undertaking. We are living in an age of apostasy where man arrogantly makes himself the measuring rod of all things. Therefore, it is part of our missionary task courageously to confess before all enemies of the cross that the earth belongs to God and to His anointed."

[3]This perhaps hyperbolic statement is not intended to discredit missiology as an entire discipline nor to label negatively the efforts of all current missiologists. The assessment is also not intended to detract from the efforts by noted writers to stem the trend of a "de-theologizing of missiology" (Edward Rommen's term), such as Johannes Blauw, *The Missionary Nature of the Church: A Survey of the Biblical Theology of Mission* (Grand Rapids: Eerdmans, 1974 [1962]); J. Herbert Kane, *Christian Missions in Biblical Perspective* (Grand Rapids: Baker, 1976); and Donald Senior and Carroll Stuhlmueller, *The Biblical Foundations for Mission* (Maryknoll, NY: Orbis, 1983).

[4]Cf. Mortimer Arias and Alan Johnson, *The Great Commission. Biblical Models for Evangelism* (Nashville: Abingdon, 1992).

[5]Cf. Rudolf Schnackenburg, "Der Missionsgedanke des Johannesevangeliums im heutigen Horizont," in *Das Johannesevangelium. IV. Teil. Ergänzende Auslegungen und Exkurse* (HTKNT; Freiburg: Herder, 1984),

To reconstruct the mission theology of the Scriptures in this more sophisticated manner requires a considerable amount of effort. It is necessary to study, for example, the mission theology (not just terminology) of John as well as the mission theologies of Luke-Acts, Matthew, Mark, Paul, and others individually before attempting to synthesize these various biblical theologies into a systematized biblical theology of mission that gives adequate consideration to the various perspectives contributed by the respective biblical writings.[6]

The present article seeks to contribute to such a project some insights from a detailed study of John's mission theology.[7] After a discussion of John's concept of mission and of its relation to the purpose of the Gospel of John, we will explore some of the more salient features of John's mission theology. This will be followed by a discussion of a number of important missiological implications. Here we will deal with the question

---

58-72; Gerald Anderson, ed., *The Theology of the Christian Mission* (Nashville: Abingdon, 1961).

[6]While the constraints of this article do not permit a defense of this position, the apostle John, the son of Zebedee, is held to be the author of the Gospel bearing his name. If this thesis is correct, the mission theology presented in the Fourth Gospel represents apostolic authority as well as an essentially single authorial intent. If the author were, for example, John "the elder," as Martin Hengel has recently sought to demonstrate (*Die johanneische Frage: Ein Lösungsversuch* [WUNT 67; Tübingen: Mohr-Siebeck, 1993]), the former, apostolic authority, would not characterize the document while the latter, a single authorial intent, would be safeguarded. Many redaction-critical theories, however, yield both aspects. They place the responsibility for the final form of the Fourth Gospel into the hands of a committee so that the document becomes a conglomerate of disparate sources and redactions. According to those scholars, whatever unity can be found in the Gospel of John as we now have it, resides in the collective mind of the final board of editors. In this case, it would appear to be precarious to speak of a coherent, consciously set forth "mission theology" of John's Gospel.

[7]The essay is based on the author's dissertation (Andreas J. Köstenberger, "The Missions of Jesus and of the Disciples According to the Fourth Gospel" [Deerfield, IL, 1993]), published as *The Missions of Jesus and the Disciples According to the Fourth Gospel* (Grand Rapids: Eerdmans, 1998). It is unfortunate that the magnum opus of the late David J. Bosch, *Transforming Mission: Paradigm Shifts in Theology of Mission* (Maryknoll, NY: Orbis, 1991), while claiming to be comprehensive, treats only the mission theology of three New Testament writers, viz., Matthew, Luke, and Paul. Bosch justifies the omission of John by maintaining that these authors "are, on the whole, representative of first-century missionary thinking and practice" (p. 55). While Bosch's work is generally admirable in its scope, his neglect of John's teaching on mission is a serious deficiency which is an instance of the frequent neglect of John as a relevant document for mission in favor of Luke-Acts or Paul's writings.

of what constitutes the proper theological focus for the church's mission (i.e., whether John's mission theology is theocentric or Christocentric). We will also examine the frequent claim that John teaches an "incarnational" concept of mission.

While the scope of the present treatment is primarily theological, it is hoped that those interested in the church's mission will find some of the insights presented from the Gospel of John foundational, practical, and relevant for formulating the missionary task of the church today.

Preliminary Issues

John's Concept of Mission

The term "mission," while frequently used, is rarely defined in academic studies on the subject. DuBose's assessment still holds true:

> Despite the excellent studies on the subject, most writers who in some way deal with the meaning of mission reflect the following weaknesses: 1) some assume rather than give a definition; 2) some give or imply definitions but do not employ them consistently in the development of their material; 3) some imply more than one working definition without clearly demonstrating their conceptual relationship; 4) some state a definition but do not give any biblical basis for it; 5) some use biblical words but define them in terms of concepts of traditional North Atlantic mission administration.[8]

This lack of precision has contributed to a certain amount of ambivalence in recent discussion. Part of the difficulty may be traced to the fact that the term *mission* itself does not appear in Scripture.[9] Nevertheless, as John Stott rightly maintains, "Although 'mission' is not, of course, a biblical word (any more than 'trinity' and 'sacrament' are), yet the concept is biblical."[10] Indeed, properly defined, the term *mission* is "a useful piece of shorthand for a biblical concept."[11]

---

[8]Francis M. DuBose, *God Who Sends* (Nashville: Broadman, 1983), 15.

[9]The term ἀποστολή is no real exception, since in its four occurrences in the the New Testament it is always used in a technical sense to denote "apostleship" (cf. Acts 1:25; Rom 1:5; 1 Cor 9:2; and Gal 2:8).

[10]John R. W. Stott, "An Open Letter to David Hesselgrave," *Trinity World Forum* 16/3 (1991): 1. In his very influential earlier work, *Christian Mission in the Modern World* (London: Church Pastoral Aid Society, 1975), 30, Stott defines mission as "everything the church is sent into the world to do." Whether Stott is correct in defining mission as broadly as he does, is another question. Cf. David J. Hesselgrave, "Holes in 'Holistic Mission,' " *Trinity World Forum* 15/3 (1991): 3.

[11]John R. W. Stott, *The Contemporary Christian: Applying God's Word to Today's World* (Downers Grove, IL: InterVarsity, 1992), 342.

Hermeneutically, one must take care not to impose one's own definition of mission onto a book of Scripture, nor should one expect one general definition of mission to fit all the biblical writings.[12] One should therefore primarily speak of John's concept of mission, or Luke's concept of mission, rather than of the biblical concept of mission. Only secondarily might one be able to relate the various concepts of mission found in the respective biblical books and thus arrive at a biblical concept of mission, as long as one keeps in mind that such a concept will of necessity be rather broad and general.

How should one go about tracing the concept of mission in a given book of Scripture? The task is one of a careful inductive study of the terminology of a given writer (here John) while remembering that the concept of mission may still be found where certain words are not present (cf., e.g., 4:1–30).[13] What then is John's concept of "mission"? An inductive study of John's Gospel suggests that mission in John may be understood as *the specific task which a person or group (as sender or sent ones) seeks to accomplish, involving various modes of movement*.[14] This suggests that

---

[12]This is inadequately considered by DuBose, *God Who Sends*, 37, who fails to distinguish clearly between the distinct conceptions of mission by the different New Testament writers. Defining mission simply as sending, he writes, "No matter how it is used, the word send always has a threefold idea: 1) an intelligent sending source, 2) a sending medium or agent, either personal or impersonal, 3) a sending purpose . . . The language and idea of the sending convey exactly what the language and idea of mission convey. A mission always has a source, a medium, and a purpose."

[13]This invalidates studies that equate "mission" with "sending," as if one word could adequately and comprehensively express a biblical writer's thought on mission as a whole. Note that Scripture references in this article are to the Gospel of John unless indicated otherwise.

[14]John uses words occupying two semantic fields to develop his mission theology: for the mission task, ἔργον or infrequently κόπος ("work") and related verbs as well as σημεῖον ("sign"); for modes of movement, the two Johannine words for sending, ἀποστέλλω and πέμπω, as well as various words for "come" and "go" (ὑπάγω, ἔρχομαι and cognates); and the metaphorical equivalents "descend" and "ascend" (ἀνα- and καταβαίνω); "follow" (ἀκολουθέω); and "lead" or "gather" (ἄγω or συνάγω). For a complete account, see my *Missions of Jesus and the Disciples*, 27–41; see also my "The Two Johannine Verbs for Sending: A Study of John's Use of Words with Reference to General Linguistic Theory," in *Linguistics and the New Testament: Critical Junctures* (ed. Stanley E. Porter and D. A. Carson; JSNTSup 168; Studies in New Testament Greek; Sheffield: Sheffield Academic Press, 1999), 125–43. For these categories, cf. Johannes P. Louw and Eugene A. Nida, *Greek-English Lexicon of the New Testament Based on Semantic Domains*, 2 vols. (2d ed.; New York: United Bible Societies, 1988, 1989). Note also that the term "missionary" is used in this essay merely as the noun (a "mission-ary") or adjective ("missionary") to "mission" as defined here

John does not limit mission to the *cross-cultural* proclamation of the gospel. A mission is rather accomplished whenever a person or group seeks to carry out a certain task or purpose.

This general conceptual framework of mission is fleshed out in John's Gospel in the following way. In Jesus' case, his task is one of revelation (cf., e.g., 1:18; 17:6-8, 14) as well as redemption (cf. 1:29, 36; 6:51, 53-58; 10:15, 17-18).[15] Regarding the latter aspect of Jesus' mission, John's favorite expression is the giving of life (cf. 3:16; 6:57; 10:10; 17:2; cf. also 14:6).[16] In the case of Jesus' followers, their task is that of continuing Jesus' mission by re-presenting Jesus' revelation and redemption through their proclamation of the gospel (cf. 18:20; 20:23).

Making use of his terminological framework, John constructs his treatment of mission along certain theological lines.[17] Thus, John's Christology has an important missiological dimension. Jesus is the Son sent from the Father; he came into the world and returned to the Father; and he is the eschatological shepherd-teacher who called others to follow him in order to help gather the eschatological harvest. John's concept of discipleship, too, is missiologically constrained. Jesus' disciples are to follow him (even past his earthly mission; cf. 21:10, 22) and are sent by Jesus into the world as he was sent into the world by his sender (17:18; cf. 20:21).

It may appear that an inordinate amount of space has been given to definitional matters. However, diligence and precision in delineating one's terms are imperative. In the light of the considerable terminological confusion that still exists in missiological discussions, it seems appropriate to call for greater methodological rigor and accountability. Before John's mission theology can be examined in greater detail, one more preliminary issue should be briefly considered: the relationship between John's concept of mission and the purpose of John's Gospel.

---

without necessary implications regarding the cross-cultural nature of the work (as is the usual practice; the exception to this use is the rare occasion where we accomodate our usage to current conventions as in the opening paragraph). The term "mission" is generally avoided.

[15]J. Terence Forestell, *The Word of the Cross: Salvation as Revelation in the Fourth Gospel* (AnBib 57; Rome: Biblical Institute Press,1974), following Bultmann, claims that the notion of a substitutionary atonement is absent from John's Gospel; cf. the helpful critique by Max Turner, "Atonement and the Death of Jesus in John: Some Questions to Bultmann and Forestell," *EQ* 62 (1990): 99-122.

[16]Cf. James McPolin, "Mission in the Fourth Gospel," *ITQ* 36 (1969): 118: "the primary purpose, to which all others are subordinated, is to confer life."

[17]See note 14 above.

Mission and the Purpose of John's Gospel

How does John's emphasis on mission function within the intention of John's Gospel as a whole? Some have argued that the missionary theme in John seeks to counteract a tendency among John's audience to neglect their own mission.[18] Perhaps, it has been speculated, the Johannine Christians were recovering from their traumatic expulsion from their Jewish parent synagogue and needed to reconfigure the understanding of their mission in the surrounding world.[19] Others have sought to locate John's mission theology within the framework of an evangelistic purpose for his Gospel, directed especially toward diaspora Jews and Gentiles.[20] In that case, John would have sought to show prospective converts that to be incorporated into the new Messianic community means to have a part in its mission to the world. While it is not possible here to give a full-fledged defense, the last alternative appears to be the most plausible.

Reconstructions of the life setting of a so-called Johannine community underlying the Fourth Gospel must of necessity remain highly speculative, especially since there is no shred of evidence for as much as even its existence either in the Church Fathers or in documents of the community itself (as is the case for the Qumran community).[21] Moreover, the argu-

---

[18]Teresa Okure, *The Johannine Approach to Mission: A Contextual Study of John 4:1–42* (WUNT 2/31; Tübingen: Mohr-Siebeck, 1988), 232. Perhaps the best recent study of mission in John's Gospel, Okure's work is nevertheless flawed in at least two ways: first, she arbitrarily limits the focus of her study to John 4:1–42 rather than treating mission in John more comprehensively; and second, she occasionally sets forth rather eccentric views on the supposed background of the Fourth Gospel such as the one referred to in the text above.

[19]Takashi Onuki, *Gemeinde und Welt im Johannesevangelium: Ein Beitrag zur Frage nach der theologischen und pragmatischen Funktion des johanneischen "Dualismus."* (WMANT 56; Neukirchen-Vluyn: Neukirchener, 1984); David Rensberger, *Overcoming the World: Politics and Community in the Gospel of John* (London: SPCK, 1988).

[20]W. C. van Unnik, "The Purpose of St. John's Gospel," in *Studia Evangelica I* (TU 73; ed. Kurt Aland et al.; Berlin: Akademie, 1959), 382–411; John A. T. Robinson, "The Destination and Purpose of St. John's Gospel," *NTS* 6 (1959–60): 127–31; D. A. Carson, *The Gospel According to John* (Grand Rapids: Eerdmans, 1991), *passim*.

[21]Cf. the recent assault on the "Johannine community hypothesis" by Martin Hengel, *Johanneische Frage* (1993) and this author's forthcoming review in *JETS.* Of course, the identity of the community behind the Qumran documents, after a time of apparent consensus, is itself again the subject of debate: cf. Robert Eisenman and Michael Wise, *The Dead Sea Scrolls Uncovered* (New York: Penguin, 1992).

ment that John could not have written an evangelistic Gospel to diaspora Jews and proselytes at a time when Christian-Jewish relations were severely strained remains far from convincing. If Jesus was indeed the Messiah, the gospel message would be perennially relevant for Jews, even at a time when Jewish sentiments toward Christians were generally rather hostile. But we must move on to a more detailed discussion of John's presentation of the missions of Jesus and of his followers.

Theological Observations on Mission in John's Gospel

The Sent Son Carries Out His Mission

Even a cursory reading of John's Gospel reveals that it is the mission of *Jesus* that is central in John's presentation. Jesus is shown to carry out faithfully the mission given him by God, his sender. The metaphor of the sent son would have been well understood in its original Jewish setting. A father, when wanting to ensure the faithful execution of a commission, would send not a slave or other messenger, but his son, especially his first-born, oldest son (cf. Mark 12:1–11, especially v. 6).[22] Thus, Jesus claims to be the unique Son of the Father, fully obedient to this charge.

In carrying out the commission entrusted to him "by the Father who sent" him, Jesus provided his followers with a missionary paradigm, i.e., that of complete obedience and dependence on their sender.[23] In the Johannine commissioning passage, John 20:21, the resurrected Jesus, up to that point the "sent one," becomes the one who sends; his followers are to emulate the sender-sent relationship Jesus had modelled with the Father.

This relationship encompasses the following components.[24] The sent one is to:

---

[22]Anthony E. Harvey, "Christ as Agent," in *The Glory of Christ in the New Testament: Studies in Christology in Memory of George Bradford Caird* (ed. L. D. Hurst and N. T. Wright; Oxford: Clarendon, 1987), 239–50; Helen S. Friend, "Like Father, Like Son: A Discussion of the Concept of Agency in Halakah and John," *Ashland Theological Journal* 21 (1990): 18–28

[23]Compare the occurrences of the phrase "the Father who sent me" in 4:34; 5:23, 24, 30, 37; 6:38, 39, 44; 7:16, 18, 28, 33; 8:16, 18, 26, 29; 9:4; 12:44, 45, 49; 14:24; 15:21; and 16:5.

[24]Jan-Adolph Bühner, *Der Gesandte und sein Weg im 4. Evangelium: Die kultur- und religionsgeschichtliche Entwicklung* (WUNT 2/2; Tübingen: Mohr-Siebeck, 1977); Josef Kuhl, *Die Sendung Jesu und der Kirche nach dem Johannes-Evangelium* (St. Augustin: Steyler, 1967); Juan Peter Miranda, *Der Vater der mich gesandt hat: Religionsgeschichtliche Untersuchungen zu den johannei-*

- bring glory and honor to the sender (5:23; 7:18);
- do the sender's will (4:34; 5:30, 38; 6:38–39) and works (5:36; 9:4);
- speak the sender's words (3:34; 7:16; 12:49; 14:10b, 24);
- be accountable to his sender (chap. 17);
- bear witness to his sender (5:36; 7:28=8:26);
- represent him faithfully (12:44–45; 13:20; 15:18–25);
- exercise delegated authority (5:21–22, 27; 13:3; 17:2; 20:23);
- know the sender intimately (7:29; cf. 15:21; 17:8, 25);
- live in a close relationship with the sender (8:16, 18, 29; 16:32);
- follow the sender's example (13:16).

To fulfill their God-given role as sent ones of Jesus, Jesus' followers need the Spirit (20:22). Using Jesus' followers as his instruments, the Spirit will convict people in the world of their sin, (un)righteousness, and judgment (cf. 16:8–11).[25] The mission of the Messianic community is that of extending to unbelievers the forgiveness of sins made possible through Jesus' completed work (see 17:4; 20:23).[26] The roles of individuals within the overall Messianic mission will differ: Peter is assigned a shepherding role and will die a martyr's death; John will witness in his own way (21:15–23).[27] The community of believers as a whole is to be united in

---

schen Sendungsformeln: Zugleich ein Beitrag zur johanneischen Christologie und Ekklesiologie (EHS 23/7; Frankfurt am Main: Peter Lang, 1976); idem, Die Sendung Jesu im vierten Evangelium: Religions- und theologiegeschichtliche Untersuchungen zu den Sendungsformeln (SBS 87; Stuttgart: Katholisches Bibelwerk, 1977); Yu Ibuki, "Die Doxa des Gesandten—Studie zur johanneischen Christologie," in Annual of the Japanese Bible Institute XIV (ed. Masao Sekine and Akira Satake; Tokyo: Yamamoto Shoten, 1988), 38–81.

[25]Cf. D. A. Carson, "The Function of the Paraclete in John 16:7-11," JBL 98 (1979): 547-66.

[26]Contra Barry Sullivan, "Ego Te Absolvo: The Forgiveness of Sins in the Context of the Pneumatic Community" (Th. M. thesis; Grand Rapids Theological Seminary, 1988).

[27]This is not the place to argue for an identification of the "beloved disciple" with the apostle John (though such a case can be convincingly made). The issue is, in any case, marginal for the point made here. More substantially, note the similarities in wording between John's description of the missions of Jesus (12:33: "he was saying this to indicate the kind of death by which he was to die") and Peter (21:19: "now this he said, signifying by what kind of death he would glorify God"), on the one hand, and between John's presentation of the missions of Jesus (1:18: "the one who is in the bosom of the Father, he has explained him") and the "beloved disciple" (13:23: "there was reclining on Jesus' bosom one of his disciples, whom Jesus loved"), on the other. While the analogies should not be stretched too far, these similarities nevertheless underscore the aspect of continuity between the missions of Jesus and those of his followers.

love, not as an end in itself, but for the purpose of witnessing to Jesus (chap. 17).[28]

What are the implications from these observations for the contemporary church's apprehension of its task? The general contours are the same: obedience and dependence on Jesus as well as unity and love toward one another remain the essential prerequisites and characteristics of the church's missionary mandate. In his role as the Sent Son, Jesus lived out before his followers the role he wanted them—and us—to fulfill, i.e., that of a faithful messenger who carries out his commission humbly and dependably. However, a discussion of John's presentation of Jesus' mission would be incomplete without also highlighting the importance assigned to the exalted Jesus in the mission of his followers.

The Exalted Jesus Continues His Mission

The Gospel of John falls rather neatly in two distinct parts. The first 12 chapters present the earthly Jesus' mission to the Jews while chapters 13 through 21 depict the mission of the exalted Jesus to the world. The sent one turns sender (20:21); the one who came now returns to where he came from (16:28); and the shepherd appoints an under-shepherd (21:15-19). This perspective is not unique to John. In an often-overlooked aspect of Matthew's great commission passage, Jesus assures his followers that he will be with them until the end in their discipling of all nations (Matt 28:20).[29] Jesus does not say, "The Holy Spirit will be you." He says "*I* will be with you." Likewise, Jesus asserts, "*I* will build my [Messianic] community" (Matt 16:18).

Luke, too, in his two-volume work, presents "what Jesus *began* to do and teach" (cf. Acts 1:1) in his Gospel and, by implication, "what Jesus *continued* to do and teach" in the book of Acts. Thus, for Luke, Jesus is not absent during the mission of the early church.[30] Through his Spirit, Jesus directs the mission of the church. In Saul's conversion, Jesus took an even more active part (Acts 9:3-6). And the entire book of Acts is presented by Luke as the fulfillment of Jesus' prediction uttered shortly before the ascension that his followers would be his witnesses "unto the ends of the earth" (Acts 1:8).

---

[28]Contra Wiard Popkes, "Zum Verständnis der Mission bei Johannes," *Zeitschrift für Mission* 4 (1978): 63-69.

[29]But see Bosch, "Reflections on Biblical Models of Mission," 185.

[30]Oscar Cullmann, *Der johanneische Kreis* (Tübingen: Mohr-Siebeck, 1975), 14-15.

This emphasis on the mission of the *exalted* Jesus in the second part of John's Gospel accounts for the absence of much of the shame-language in John's passion narrative that is found in the synoptic Gospels.[31] John's is not, as Käsemann has speculated, a docetic Christ, "a god striding upon the earth."[32] John's mission theology is rather pervaded by the understanding that, from a post-resurrection perspective, Jesus' cross-death is not shameful but glorious, since it constitutes the culmination of Jesus' obedient fulfillment of his mission (cf. 19:30).

John claims that it is only after Jesus' resurrection, with the aid of the Spirit, that Jesus' disciples understood the true significance of Jesus' mission. In this, John concurs with the other evangelists, especially Mark (cf. e.g. Mark 8:31-33; 9:32; 10:35-40; cf. John 2:22; 12:16). What John therefore gives us is not merely a historical narrative of Jesus' passion, but a theological interpretation of it. It is true that Jesus' contemporaries saw in his cross a shameful curse. In hindsight, however, the cross was a place of glory and exaltation where the Son of Man was "lifted up," not humiliated (cf. 3:14; 8:28; 12:32; see also 17:1, 4-5).

As the Son of Man would soon be glorified, Jesus instructs his followers regarding their identification with him in this world (13:16, 20), particularly in their suffering of persecution (15:18-25). He also urges them to demonstrate love and unity for the sake of carrying out their mission to the world (13:34-35; 17:20-23). The mission of Jesus' followers shares with Jesus' own mission a profound spiritual dimension. Like Jesus, the Messianic community is to live a spiritually separated life in a world hostile to God and Jesus (17:13-19). Moreover, Jesus' followers, too, are to embark on a mission while remembering that God's love is not merely to be experienced personally, nor even merely to be expressed toward fellow-believers, but is a message to be carried into a world that is spiritually dark and dominated by the evil one (cf. 17:18, 20; 20:21-23).

The Universal Scope of the Gospel and John's View of the Jews

John places the missions of Jesus and of his followers squarely in the framework of salvation history. In his opening statement, John asserts that

---

[31] Cf. Grant R. Osborne, "Redactional Trajectories in the Crucifixion Narrative," *Evangelical Quarterly* 51 (1979): 92; Godfrey Carruthers Nicholson, *Death as Departure: The Johannine Descent-Ascent Schema* (SBLDS 63; Chico, CA: Scholars Press, 1983).

[32] Ernst Käsemann, *The Testament of Jesus in the Light of Chapter 17* (trans. Gerhard Krodel; Philadelphia: Fortress, 1968). But see Marianne Meye Thompson, *The Humanity of Jesus in the Fourth Gospel* (Philadelphia: Fortress, 1988).

Jesus' "own," i.e., the Jewish people, "did not receive him" (1:11). He concludes the first part of his Gospel by maintaining that even after Jesus had done a number of "signs," the Jews would still not believe in him (12:37).[33] In the important allegory of the vine in chap. 15 (cf. Isa 5), John presents Jesus as Israel's representative. Now Jesus is the vine whose branches constitute the new Messianic community. John's frequent use of covenant language for Jesus' followers amply substantiates such a conclusion).[34]

John's movement from Old Testament Israel over Jesus to the Messianic community climaxes in the assertion that the scope of the gospel has now taken on universal dimensions. Everyone who receives Jesus becomes a child of God (1:12); everyone who believes will be saved (3:16); again and again, mere believing is presented as the characteristic criterion for the one who has come to Jesus and received his message. Indeed, Jesus also has other sheep which he must bring as well (10:16, a probable reference to the Gentiles who, by the will of God, would be incorporated into the Messianic community by the exalted Jesus); the scattered children of God will be gathered (11:51–52).

What then is John's view of the Jews? Is the writer of the Fourth Gospel anti-Jewish, as some have suggested?[35] This contention is hardly credible in a Gospel where an acknowledgment is made that "salvation comes from the Jews" (4:22) and where there is no lack of positive Jewish identification figures, such as Nicodemus, the twelve, or several individual disciples (e.g., Peter or the Beloved Disciple; Martha, Mary, and Lazarus). John rather makes an important theological point: Jews must not presume upon their Jewishness; belonging to God's old covenant people by itself is not enough. Faith, not ethnicity, is the indispensable characteristic of a true member of God's people (cf. also Rom 2:28–29; 9:6b–8). Rather than presuming upon their ethnic heritage, a Jewish person should acknowledge his or her innate sinfulness which can only be taken away by the Lamb of God, Jesus, the Son of God, the Messiah (cf. 8:21–59; 1:29, 36; 20:30–31).

Placing one's descent from Abraham and one's discipleship of Moses in necessary antithesis to one's acceptance of Jesus as Messiah, amounts to

---

[33]Cf. Andreas J. Köstenberger, "The Seventh Johannine Sign: A Study in John's Christology," *BBR 5* (1995): 87–103.

[34]Cf. John W. Pryor, *John: Evangelist of the Covenant People: The Narrative and Themes of the Fourth Gospel* (Downers Grove, IL: InterVarsity, 1992); Edward Malatesta, *Interiority and Covenant* (AnBib 69; Rome: Biblical Institute Press, 1978).

[35]Cf. Erich Grässer, *Der Alte Bund im Neuen: Exegetische Studien zur Israelfrage im Neuen Testament* (WUNT 35; Tübingen: Mohr-Siebeck, 1985).

rejecting God's final revelation (1:18; cf. Heb 1:1-4). What is attacked in the Fourth Gospel, therefore, is not the Jews *as Jews*, but the Jews' ethnic presumption which represented a major stumbling block in acknowledging the legitimacy of Jesus' Messianic claims. This was motivated not by hatred and anti-Semitism (which is hardly conceivable of Jews like Jesus or John), but by love that agonized over this powerful obstacle to faith which was unique to the members of God's old covenant people (cf. also Rom 9:1-5). Ultimately, according to John, the Jews, in their rejection of their own Messiah, are representatives of the unbelieving world (1:10-11).[36]

Finally, for my part, I remain unpersuaded that the so-called anti-Jewish polemic allegedly found in John's Gospel stems from the dialogue between a non-Messianic Jewish synagogue and believing Jewish Christians at the end of the first century.[37] It appears that there is ample evidence from the other Gospels (especially Matthew; cf., e.g., 21:23-23:39) that Jesus during his earthly ministry repeatedly confronted the Jewish leadership. It appears therefore at least equally plausible that John urges his readership to do better than the Jewish religious leadership during Jesus' earthly mission and to believe in the Messiah they so stubbornly rejected.[38]

---

[36]On the Fourth Gospel's alleged anti-Semitism, cf. especially Carson, *Gospel According to John*, 92, 141-42, 575-76; Reinhold Leistner, *Antijudaismus im Johannesevangelium? Darstellung des Problems in der neueren Auslegungsgeschichte und Untersuchung der Leidensgeschichte* (Bern: Herbert Lang, 1974); and Urban C. von Wahlde, "The Johannine 'Jews': A Critical Survey," *NTS* 28 (1982): 33-60.

[37]Contra J. Louis Martyn, "Glimpses into the History of the Johannine Community," in *L'Évangile de Jean: Sources, rédaction, théologie* (ed. Marinus de Jonge; Louvain: University Press, 1977), 149-75; idem, *History and Theology in the Fourth Gospel* (2d ed.; Nashville: Abingdon, 1979 [1968]); and Raymond E. Brown, " 'Other Sheep Not of This Fold': The Johannine Perspective on Christian Diversity in the Late First Century," *JBL* 97 (1978): 5-22; idem, *The Community of the Beloved Disciple* (New York: Paulist, 1979).

[38]In this context it is very significant that John, like the other evangelists, as well as Paul, argues that even this rejection of the Messiah by the Jewish nation fulfilled biblical prophecy (cf. 12:37-41, quoting Isa 6:9; cf. also the parallels in the other Gospels as well as Acts 28:25-28 and Rom 9:6-33). Just like Stephen in his speech to the Sanhedrin (cf. Acts 7:2-53) and Jesus in his parable of the wicked tenants (Mark 12:1-11 par.), John challenges the Jews' own version of salvation history wherein they are featured as righteous and pious. Not so, John argues: the Jews, in accordance with biblical prophecy, already resisted Isaiah's message, just as they now reject the evidence that Jesus is the Messiah sent from God. To identify with such a spiritual heritage is undiscerning. Even Abraham and Moses are mistakenly claimed by the Jews as their own. If they truly want to follow those great men of faith, let them believe in the Messiah who antedates Abraham (8:58) and who was anticipated by Moses (5:46; cf. Deut 18:18).

Missiological Implications from John's Mission Theology

Equipped with a better understanding of John's mission theology, we are now able to explore some missiological implications. It has been shown that John's mission theology focuses on Jesus, especially on his role as the Son sent from the Father. At the same time, it has become apparent that, in John's perspective, Jesus is now exalted and continues his mission through believers. The scope of Jesus' mission is universal so that Jews as well as Gentiles enter his Messianic community by believing in Jesus as Messiah, i.e., the Son of God sent by God (cf. 20:30–31). If the purpose of John's Gospel was in the first place primarily evangelistic, the message to prospective (Jewish) believers would have been that every person who chooses to believe also joins the community's mission to the world.

From this apprehension of the first horizon of the text we must now move to our own, second horizon. What can we learn from John's teaching on mission? While it is impossible to be exhaustive here, we will attempt to deal briefly with the following questions. First, regarding the focus of mission, should the church consider the focus to be theocentric or Christocentric? Second, regarding the model of mission, does John teach an incarnational or a representational model of mission, or are there elements of both? Third, regarding the scope of mission, does John conceive of the church's outreach as universal or as ethnically constrained? And what are the missiological implications of these issues for today?

The Focus of Mission: Theocentric or Christocentric?
Is God or Jesus the central figure in John's mission theology? This is an important question, since in the recent past frequent attempts have been made to provide an ecumenical agenda that deemphasizes the centrality of Jesus Christ in the church's mission. A case in point is the recent gatherings and resolutions of the World Council of Churches as well as the World Parliament of Religions held in Chicago in the late summer of 1993.[39] It may be argued that the question just raised is largely a matter of a proper perspective. Surely *both* God *and* Christ are to be central. Nevertheless, the issue must be probed further in order to identify more precisely the relationship between God and Christ in the way the church conceives of its role in the world.

---

[39]Cf. David J. Hesselgrave et al., "The 1993 Parliament of the World's Religions—Our Response to Invitations to Participate," *Trinity World Forum* 18/2 (1993): 1–5; John Zipperer, "The Elusive Quest for Religious Harmony," *Christianity Today* 37/11 (1993): 42–44.

At the outset, it is apparent that, indirectly, John emphasizes God's mission, since Jesus constantly refers to the Father as his sender. Nevertheless, in a very important sense it is Jesus' mission that is John's focus, since John's purpose is to show that Jesus is the Messiah, the Sent One par excellence (cf. 20:30-31; 9:7). The Jews, during Jesus' earthly ministry as well toward the end of the first century when John wrote, already believed in God—the key question was whether Jesus was God's authentic authorized representative or not.[40]

The church faces a similar situation today. Generally, it is not the message of God's existence or of God's love that is offensive, but whether God's love has found its decisive and ultimate expression *in Jesus*. Any ecumenism that is achieved at the expense of lessening the centrality of Jesus' work, claims, and requirements is not only of little value but is actually misleading and deceptive. The church's (missionary) proclamation must be theocentric by being Christocentric, since according to Scripture, God's revelation and redemption were ultimately and finally accomplished in Jesus (cf. 1:18; 14:6; cf. also Heb 1:1-3). Thus it is clearly illegitimate to re-imagine God and replace Christ as the center of Christian worship with the goddess Sophia, as recent participants at an ecumenical conference attempted to do.[41]

In interaction with adherents of other religions, we should not be embarrassed by Jesus, trying to keep references to him to an absolute minimum in order not to offend non-Christians. Rather, following the example of the early church (cf. the sermons in Acts), we should accentuate Jesus' relevant characteristics when communicating to a given target culture. John, in his interaction with diaspora Jews and proselytes, contextualized the message about Jesus in terms of Greek philosophy (Jesus as the "logos"; 1:1, 14) and Jewish Messianic expectations (the Christ is Jesus; 20:30-31). What is the appropriate Christocentric emphasis in our respective mission contexts? There is room for exploration, experimentation, flexibility, and creativity in adapting our message to a given audience.

---

[40]Thus, I disagree, at least in part, with C. K. Barrett, "Christocentric or Theocentric? Observations on the Theological Method of the Fourth Gospel," in *Essays on John* (Philadelphia: Westminster, 1982), 3 and 8, who contends that "John is writing about, and directing our attention to, God" in the sense that "For John . . . Jesus is central; yet he is not final." Barrett's essay appears to be primarily systematic in nature while giving perhaps insufficient consideration to the Fourth Gospel's purpose and life setting.

[41]Cf. Susan Cyre, "Fallout Escalates Over 'Goddess' Sophia Worship," *Christianity Today* 38/4 (1994): 74.

At the same time, we must beware not to drain our proclamation of its distinctively Christian character (cf. Rom 1:1-4, 16; 1 Cor 1:22-24; 2:1-2).

The Model of Mission: Incarnational, Representational, or Both?
Recent missiological discussion of John's Gospel has focused on John's alleged incarnational model for the church's mission. Indeed, the term *incarnational* has become a buzzword in missions circles. While there appears to be some diversity, if not confusion, regarding the sense in which the term is used, the following definition seems to be representative: "incarnational mission" is "an identification that transcends the superficial material culture and behavior roles and focuses on the underlying attitudes that should characterize missionaries as servants."[42]

The commissioning passage of John 20:21, "As the Father sent me, so send I you," often functions as the point of departure in such discussions.[43] In his incarnation, it is argued, Jesus identified with humanity. He condescended to our level and came to serve us, and in this he became our model. In our mission, we should therefore emulate Jesus' example and become like those we seek to serve (cf. Mark 10:45; Luke 22:27; 1 Cor 9:19-22; Phil 2:7-8).

It should be stated at the outset that the underlying concern for the missionary's Christlikeness in going about cross-cultural ministry is highly commendable. Clearly, there are plenty of New Testament passages that support such a notion, as they do for all believers. The question that occupies us here, however, is not merely whether the concern underlying an "incarnational model" of mission is worthy, but whether the model itself as is it usually propagated properly reflects biblical teaching. In the ultimate analysis, the issue is not merely one of mission strategy, or pragmatics, but also, more importantly, one of biblical theology and terminology.

The rationale for an "incarnational model" presented above sounds plausible enough, but can it be substantiated from John's Gospel? Can it be shown that it was John's intent to teach an incarnational missiology? Is the incarnational model a case of getting "the right doctrine from the wrong texts"?[44] Or should John's—and the New Testament's—teaching on

---

[42]Cf. Kenneth McElhanon, "Don't Give Up on the Incarnational Model," *EMQ* 27 (1991): 391.

[43]Cf. Stott, *Christian Mission in the Modern World*, idem, *Contemporary Christian*, 264-65, 341-43, 357-74; Hesselgrave, "Holes," 1-5; idem, "Surrejoinder," 3-4; and Stott, "Open Letter," 1-2.

[44]This is the title of Greg K. Beale, ed., *The Right Doctrine from the Wrong Text?* (Grand Rapids: Baker, 1994).

the subject be understood differently altogether so that it may be advisable to drop the term and to replace it with a more appropriate expression?

Does John teach an incarnational model of mission? Does he present the Word-become-flesh as a missiological paradigm to be emulated by Christians as they go about their mission? As a study of the relevant passages in the Fourth Gospel indicates, John's concern in his treatment of Christ's incarnation is demonstrably to highlight Jesus' uniqueness, not to set forth a model that links Christ's incarnation with the way every Christian should missionize (1:14, 18; cf. also 3:14, 18).[45] Likewise, in the Fourth Gospel's commissioning passage (20:21), it is *the kind of sender-sent relationship maintained by Jesus during his earthly ministry* (i.e., his obedience, dependence, and faithfulness) that functions as a model for his disciples to follow, not Jesus' incarnation.

Believers thus are not enjoined in John's Gospel to emulate Jesus' incarnation, but to witness to him (15:26–27) and to spread the message of the good news of forgiveness of people's sins through Jesus (17:20; 20:23). If anything provides a pattern for the believing community's outreach, it is the Father-Son relationship of mutual love and unity (cf., e.g., 17:21–23).[46] In one word, they are to be his representatives, sent by him into an unbelieving world to re-present his unique personal characteristics and his exclusive claims and requirements of discipleship.

In a narrow sense, therefore, the Gospel of John does not appear to teach an incarnational model of mission.[47] John seems far too concerned to preserve Jesus' ontological uniqueness (i.e., his unparalleled personal characteristics) to make his incarnation the model for the church's mission.[48] The role of Jesus' followers is rather presented as that of being representatives, messengers, and witnesses to their sender, Jesus, while great care is taken not to blur, much less obliterate, the ontological gap that forever separates Jesus and believers.[49]

---

[45]Cf. Köstenberger, *Missions of Jesus and the Disciples*, Chaps. 3–5.

[46]Jesus' love for his disciples is presented by John as a model for the relationships of believers with one another, not as a model for their mission to the world (cf. 13:14–15).

[47]Whether other New Testament writers do, is doubtful, but an investigation of this issue is beyond the scope of the present essay.

[48]Note also the fine distinction preserved in 20:17: "I have not yet returned to the Father . . . I am returning to my Father and your Father, to my God and your God."

[49]See the section *Theological Observations on Mission in John's Gospel* above. Cf. also Carson, *Gospel According to John*, 566, commenting on 17:18: "Use of the phrase *into the world* for the mission of the disciples shows that there is no *necessary* overtone of incarnation or of invasion from another world. Only

Where does that leave the contemporary discussion? As mentioned above, it appears that the term *incarnational* is often used in missiological circles in a broad sense that transcends biblical-theological categories, as connoting the need to identify with people who should be reached with the gospel. On its basis, missionaries are encouraged to become, in a sense, like those they are seeking to evangelize by voluntarily adopting certain customs or other external cultural conventions in order to build common ground, remove needless obstacles, and to facilitate the kinds of relationships within which the gospel can be best communicated, both by way of verbal proclamation and by the example of a godly, Christlike life.

While these concerns are legitimate, however, and while the procedure itself is unobjectionable, yes, desirable, it must be maintained that this kind of incarnational model is never taught in the Scriptures in those terms. The analogy between the theological necessity of Christ's becoming a man in order to be able to atone for the sins of the world and a contemporary missionary's practical expediency to build common ground between himself or herself and prospective converts to Christianity simply breaks down. Indeed, one is hard pressed to find even one New Testament passage where the connection between Christ's incarnation and human mission procedure is made explicit in this way. To the contrary, as has been argued, writers like John jealously guard the theological uniqueness of Christ's incarnation.

What then are we to make of the Pauline principle of "becoming all things to all men" (1 Cor 9:19-23)? it may be asked. While it is not the purpose of this paper to examine Paul's writings thoroughly, a look at this passage indicates that Paul does not mention Christ's incarnation at all, but rather provides a primarily pragmatic rationale for this procedure: "that I may by all means save some" (v. 22). Paul contends that while all distinctions between Jews and Gentiles have been obliterated in Christ, it is part of his Christian liberty to retain, or to forego, characteristics that would present unnecessary obstacles in his gospel proclamation. This simply makes good sense and maximizes the opportunities for preaching the gospel effectively. It does not, however, involve resorting to Christ's incarnation as a theological or missiological model.

The other passage frequently adduced as proof for an incarnational model in Scripture, Phil 2:5-11, likewise hardly supports such an interpretation. First, the context is not one of mission, but of relationships

---

the broader descriptions of the coming of the Son 'into the world' betray the ontological gap that forever distances the origins of Jesus' mission from the origins of the disciples' mission."

among believers. Second, Paul here exhorts Christians to emulate the humility expressed supremely in Christ's incarnation, rather than patterning their entire lives or mission after the Word-become-flesh. The focus is thus much more narrow and specific (i.e., the humility expressed by Christ's incarnation, rather than the incarnation as a whole) than advocates of an incarnational model would appear to suggest.

It would, therefore, seem to be advisable to drop the term "incarnational model" owing to the virtually inevitable ambiguity and theological imprecision created by its use. Why not replace the term by an expression such as "culture accomodation" or the like? This may not satisfy those who seek a closer tie-in along sacramental lines between Christ and his people today, but it is questionable in any case whether this kind of theology is in fact taught in the New Testament.

The Scope of Mission: Ethnically Constrained or Universal?

The universal scope of the gospel message and John's view of the Jews have already been discussed. It remains, therefore, merely to probe further some of the implications of these aspects of John's mission theology for contemporary missiological thought and practice. Current approaches to mission tend to give significant attention to the different ethnic groups that need to be reached with the gospel. Interestingly, John focuses primarily on the universality of the Christian message and the non-discriminatory requirement of "believing" for Jew and Gentile alike (cf., e.g., 3:16).

John insists that, for Jews as for everyone else, the way of salvation is through believing in Jesus only—"no one can come to the Father except through me" (14:6). At the same time, John affirms that the Jews have not ceased to be God's covenant people. Specifically, individual believing Jews are incorporated into Jesus' new Messianic community. While John does not develop the intricacies of these issues to the same extent as Paul (see Rom 9–11), his theology in this regard does in no way contradict Paul's.

In fact, John's emphasis on the universal scope of the gospel resembles Paul's dictum that in Christ "there is neither Jew nor Greek, slave nor free, male nor female" (Gal 3:28). This universal dimension of the gospel precludes any ethnocentrism or parochialism in the way the contemporary church carries out its missionary task. Just like God did not inappropriately favor the Jews in John's day, he does not favor the Western world, nor America, today.

At the same time, anti-Semitism cannot be supported from the Gospel of John.[50] John's comments regarding the Jews pertain to the religious and political leadership of the Jewish nation, not to the Jews as a race. Nevertheless, according to John, the rallying point for Jewish and Gentile Christians alike is to be Jesus the Messiah, not Abraham or Moses (cf., e.g., 1:17; 5:45-47; 8:37-58). Therefore non-Messianic Judaism, in John's day as well as in ours, should be challenged to consider the Messianic mission, claims, and demands of Jesus.[51]

Conclusion

While John's Gospel does not provide us with detailed answers for specific contemporary missionary challenges, it can be used to help establish a more biblical foundation for the church's mission. John's mission theology draws our attention to the exalted Jesus who is present today in order to continue his mission, working through the Spirit and his Messianic community. John alerts us to our need for obedience, dependence, and faithfulness to Jesus and his commission. He also stresses our need for mutual love and unity. Are these emphases too vague and general? Are they too idealistic and simplistic?

To the contrary, we would do well to reflect on John's mission-theological message today. Only such reflection is able to fill the spiritual

---

[50]See already the discussion and bibliographical references given above. See also Samuel Sandmel, *We Jews and Jesus* (Oxford: Oxford University Press, 1965).

[51]The position advocated here runs counter to the World Council of Churches which, in a reversal of its founding position, declared in 1988, "The next step may be to proscribe all proselytism of Jews on the theological ground that it is a rejection of Israel's valid covenant with God" (Allan Brockway et al., *The Theology of the Churches and the Jewish People* [Statements by the World Council of Church {*sic*} and Its Member Churches; Geneva: World Council of Churches, 1988], 186, quoted by Arthur Glasser, "Evangelical Missions," in *Toward the Twenty-first Century in Christian Mission: Essays in Honor of Gerald H. Anderson* [ed. James M. Phillips and Robert T. Coote; Grand Rapids: Eerdmans, 1993], 18). This "Sonderweg" (German for "special way") or "bi-covenant" theology is frequently supported by reference to Rom 11:25-28, a passage whose import appears to be that "all Israel" (i.e., at least a substantial portion of ethnic Israel) will acknowledge Jesus as Messiah at the occasion of his second coming (regarding the issue of two ways of salvation for non-Jews and Jews, cf., e.g., H. J. Schoeps, *Paul. The Theology of the Apostle in the Light of Jewish Religious History* [trans. Harold Knight; Philadelphia: Westminster, 1961]; Rosemary Radford Ruether, *Faith and Fratricide: The Theological Roots of Anti-Semitism* [New York: Seabury, 1974]). It must be maintained, however, that the terms of acceptance before God are the same for Jews as for Gentiles, i.e., faith in Jesus.

void often characteristic of the church's outreach today. The world will be confronted effectively with the claims and demands of Christ, not by an activism that elevates human need and the urgency of the task while finding little time to contemplate the truths of God's word, not by a can-do approach that confidently seeks to "manage" mission as if it were a merely human enterprise, but by a renewed reflection on the glory of God in Jesus.

Do we understand ourselves as Christ's emissaries, under his orders, or as actually in charge of the missionary enterprise? The spirit in which we carry out our mission ought to be one of humility and submissiveness to our sender, Jesus. Do we make room in our missionary practice for the exalted Jesus? Are we aware of his active efforts to provide us, from his exalted position, with all the resources needed for accomplishing his mission? Are we depending on his power by persistent prayer?

John's mission theology reminds us that to be a follower of Jesus means also to be sent into the world by Jesus, not merely individually, but as a member of the new Messianic community. It challenges us to reflect on the great privilege that is ours to be chosen by the exalted Jesus to continue his mission. It rebukes us when we think the mission is ours rather than treating it as a charge to re-present Jesus by preaching *his* message, nor ours, in *his* name, not ours.

The task of reconstructing a truly biblical theology of mission has the potential of bringing together scholars in the fields of biblical studies and of missiology in fruitful cooperation. A focus on the biblical foundation of mission is also the major, if not only, hope for greater unity between Christians from various denominational and confessional backgrounds in mission. May the glorious, exalted Jesus be continually present in our hearts and minds as we carry out his mission in a world which has no other hope but Jesus.[52]

---

[52]On this final point, see the helpful chapter entitled "The Supremacy of Christ as the Conscious Focus of All Saving Faith" in Piper, *Let the Nations Be Glad*, 115–66.

PART II: STUDIES ON GENDER

CHAPTER NINE

ON THE ALLEGED APOSTOLIC ORIGINS OF PRIESTLY CELIBACY[*]

Introduction

The Roman Catholic church requires celibacy of all its priests.[1] The term "celibacy" may be defined as a person's voluntary pledge to refrain from marriage for religious reasons.[2] Although this obligation is currently the subject of vigorous discussion, I will not directly address this issue.[3]

---

[*]This essay is the English translation of "Review Article: The Apostolic Origins of Priestly Celibacy," *European Journal of Theology* 1 (1992): 173-79 (with permission). The translation from the German is the present author's.

[1]Bishops likewise have an obligation to celibacy, because they are selected from among priests. The most important Roman Catholic documents regarding celibacy are: *Presbyterorum Ordinis* (December 7, 1965); *Optatam Totius* (October 28, 1965); *Sacerdotalis Caelibatus* (Paul VI, June 24, 1967); *Novo Incipiente Nostro* (John Paul II, April 6, 1979); and *Ultimis Temporibus* (November 30, 1967). I will not address the few exceptions of the universal celibacy requirement, such as those for certain deacons. My subject is a critique of the Roman Catholic rationale for its requirement of celibacy. The Vatican documents referred to in the present article are found in ET in Austin Flannery, *Vatican Council II*, 2 vols. (Northport, NY: Costello, 1988 [2d ed.] and 1982).

[2]The Orthodox Church permits married priests, as long as they observe continence, i.e. refrain from sexual marital relations. However, only celibate priests are named bishops (cf. *Sacerdotalis Caelibatus*, in Flannery 2:296-97). The Eastern church recognized celibacy and continence at the Quinisext Council (Trullo) in the year 691 (Christian Cochini, *The Apostolic Origins of Priestly Celibacy* [San Francisco: Ignatius, 1990]. 429; Roman Cholij, *Clerical Celibacy in East and West* (Leominster, Herefordshire: Fowler Wright, 1988]). However, the Roman Catholic celibacy requirement and the obligation to continence in the Orthodox Church are based on the same premises. For this reason I will limit myself to the Roman Catholic celibacy requirement.

[3]Cf. *Sacerdotalis Caelibatus* (June 24, 1967) and *Ultimis Temporibus* (November 30, 1967) in Flannery, 2:285-317 and 687-90. Concerning the contemporary debate, see also Joseph Blenkinsopp, *Celibacy, Ministry, Church* (New York: Herder & Herder, 1968); Thomas Bokenkotter, *Essential Catholicism—Dynamics of Faith and Belief* (New York: Doubleday, 1985), 268-72; Georg Denzler, *Das Papsttum und der Amtszölibat. Päpste und das*

Neither is the history of the celibacy debate the subject of investigation.[4] The Roman Catholic church maintains that the celibacy requirement is essentially of apostolic origin and that it was therefore binding on priests from early church history. If this claim of an apostolic origin for the Roman Catholic celibacy requirement can be refuted, celibacy is rendered without adequate foundation. The question of whether or not the Roman Catholic church will change the requirement of celibacy is secondary to the issue of whether or not there exists an adequate theological and historical basis for such a requirement.

The Alleged Apostolic Origins of Celibacy

The *magnum opus* of the Italian Jesuit Christian Cochini, *The Apostolic Origins of Priestly Celibacy* is considered by the eminent church historian Alfons Stickler to be "the best scholarly volume [about priestly celibacy] from a Roman Catholic perspective." Cochini attempts to relate references to the celibacy requirement in conciliar documents of the 4th century CE with the person and ministry of Jesus Christ himself in order to bridge the gap of three intervening centuries. Cochini is astutely aware that

---

Papsttum, Vol. 5, I & II (Stuttgart: Anton Hiersemann, 1973); Joseph Henry Fichter, *The Pastoral Provisions—Married Catholic Priests* (Kansas City, MO: Sheed & Ward, 1989); George H. Frein, *Celibacy: The Necessary Option* (New York: Crossroad, 1988); Uta Ranke-Heinemann, *Eunuchen für das Himmelreich—Katholische Kirche und Sexualität* (Munich: Knaur, 1989); Edward Schillebeeckx, *Clerical Celibacy under Fire* (London/Sidney: Sheed & Ward, 1968); A. W. Richard Sipe, *A Secret World: Sexuality and the Search for Celibacy* (New York: Brunner-Mazel, 1990); Leo Waltermann, ed., *Über den Zölibat der Priester* (Cologne: J. P. Bachern, 1970).

[4]For a survey of the history of the debate in the 19th and 20th centuries, cf. Cochini, *Apostolic Origins*, 18–46. As the title of his work indicates, the author concludes that priestly celibacy is actually of apostolic origin. Written from an entirely different perspective is Peter Brown, *The Body and Society—Men, Women and Sexual Renunciation in Early Christianity* (New York: Columbia University Press, 1988). Brown, similar to Cochini, investigates the practice of permanent sexual continence from the apostolic period until Augustine. He concludes that clerical celibacy, though eventually finding some proponents, was practiced very differently from the way in which it is exercised today in the Roman Catholic church (xv). Brown has a different concept of church tradition than Cochini; he does not presuppose at the outset that tradition is invested with a certain degree of authority. Tradition can err. See also Joseph Coppens, *Sacerdoce et Célibat. Etudes Historiques et Théologiques* (Louvain: Editions Duculot, 1971) and Henry C. Lea, *The History of Sacerdotal Celibacy in the Christian Church* (New York: Russell & Russell, 1957).

the main question is whether or not the Roman Catholic celibacy requirement is of apostolic origin and thus possesses a biblical foundation.[5]

The case, as it is presented by Roman Catholic theologians, is based
on a hermeneutic that underscores the continuity between the Old and the
New Testament. Moreover, Roman Catholic theology holds to the notion
of a dual authority for Roman Catholic dogma, according to which
ecclesiastical tradition (Tradition) as well as the Bible are drawn upon in
the formation of church dogma.[6] In the case of the celibacy requirement,
three aspects are closely interrelated: Roman Catholic teaching on the
sacrament of "holy Communion"; the Roman Catholic conception of the
nature of the priesthood; and Roman Catholic requirements for priests,
particularly celibacy.[7]

As mentioned, Roman Catholic hermeneutics stresses the continuity
between the Old and the New Testament. Consequently, the nature of the
sacrament of "holy Communion" is understood in continuity with the Old

---

[5]In the Roman Catholic church's long history it was frequently political or
pragmatic considerations that exercised great pressure on questions of dogma. If,
however, the celibacy requirement cannot be shown to be derived from holy
Scripture itself or is even found to be in contradiction with biblical theology, the
celibacy requirement must be repudiated, regardless of political or pragmatic
considerations. For this reason the Roman Catholic rationale for the celibacy
requirement must be subjected to close scrutiny. The result of such an
investigation can then be used to inform the contemporary debate.

[6]Cf. *Dei Verbum* (Vatican Council II; in Flannery, 1:750–65), where
"Tradition" is regularly written with a capital "T" and is often called "sacred." The
footnotes are half scriptural quotations and half references to the Fathers or papal
and conciliar documents, a fact that further underscores the fact that the Roman
Catholic church's teaching is based on tradition as well as the Bible. "Sacred
Tradition and sacred Scripture [note the order], then, are bound closely together
. . ., flowing out from the same divine well-spring . . . Thus it comes about that the
Church does not draw her certainty about all revealed truths from the holy
Scriptures alone. Hence, both Scripture and Tradition must be accepted and
honored with equal feelings of devotion and reverence" (Flannery, 1:755). ". . . in
the supremely wise arrangement of God, sacred Tradition, sacred Scripture and
the Magisterium of the Church are so connected and associated that one of them
cannot stand without the others" (p. 756). Cf. Cochini, *Apostolic Origins*, xiv, who
likens the evolution of Catholic dogma to the growth of a seed into a tree, initially
inconspicuous but eventually taking on clearer contours, so that the inconspicuous
beginnings can be interpreted in light of later developments. He refers to
Newman, who taught, "The whole question boils down to whether we can
faithfully be guided by the strong light coming from the 4th and 5th centuries in
order to explore the still pale, though sharp, outlines of the previous centuries"
(*Apostolic Origins*, 17).

[7]Cf. Cochini, *Apostolic Origins*, 429–39.

Testament sacrifical system. The "Communion" elements, particularly the "body" and the "blood" of Christ, are set in analogy to the sacrificial animals in the Levitical system.

The Roman Catholic emphasis on the continuity between the testaments also has implications for the manner in which the nature of priesthood is conceived. Essentially, Roman Catholic priests are viewed in correspondence to the Old Testament Levitical system. Their primary role is the mediation between God and believers. The priests' most important ministry is their service at the altar, particularly the observance of the sacraments, and here again particularly "holy Communion."

According to Roman Catholic teaching, the holders of such an office must be "ritually pure," so that they are able to represent Christ effectively to the believing community and in order to be able to render sacrifices to a holy God that are acceptable to him. For their prayers to be heard and their "sacramental sacrifices" to be effective, priests must therefore not "defile themselves" through sexual intercourse. For this reason celibacy is required of all priests in the Western church; the Eastern church requires celibacy or continence for its priests.[8]

Although ceremonial purity constitutes an important requirement for priests, Roman Catholic theologians emphasize that this requirement must not become an end in itself. Celibacy is rather seen as rooted directly in Christ's life and person. In the ultimate analysis, the celibacy requirement is substantiated and defended christologically. A celibate life is therefore understood as an integral part of the incarnation and sacrifice of Christ. As Christ's representative, the Roman Catholic priesthood must be *celibate* in

---

[8]Cochini claims that celibacy is the one requirement that remains valid of the Levitical code pertaining to sexual abstinence during priestly service at the altar (cf. e.g. Zachariah in Luke 1:8-25). While other Levitical requitements are no longer valid, sexual abstinence was not only kept, but even *extended* from continence during the course of one's service at the altar (Levites) to permanent sexual abstinence in the case of Roman Catholic priests, since they perform their service at the altar and occupy their mediatorial role between God and the believing community continuously. The argument runs *a minori ad maius* ("from the lesser to the greater"): if Levites must refrain from sexual relations during the course of their ceremonial duties, how much more must Roman Catholic priests must refrain from sexual relations *all their lives*, since they were called by Christ to a greater, more lasting priesthood. Cf. D. Callam, "Clerical Continence in the Fourth Century: Three Papal Decretals," *Theological Studies* 41 (1980): 31, who conjectures that at a time where daily mass was customary, continence for the sake of "ceremonial purity" became an absolute necessity. He concludes that arguments for priestly continence were primarily substantiated by ceremonial requirements.

order to participate effectively in Christ's mediatorial office.[9]

Cochini provides both patristic and biblical arguments for the apostolic origin of priestly celibacy.[10] He concedes that there were married priests in the first few centuries CE but claims that they were from the beginning required to remain continent (i.e. that married men must abstain from marital sexual relations subsequent to their ordination to the priesthood). A decree of the Council of Carthage (CE 390) stipulated that married individuals must observe continence in their marital relationships, because this is rooted *in apostolic tradition*.[11] The Roman Catholic con-

---

[9]Cf. Paul VI in *Sacerdotalis Caelibatus* (June 24, 1967) on the christological significance of celibacy (Flannery, 2:290-92): "The Christian priesthood . . . can be understood only in the light of the newness of Christ, the Supreme Pontiff and eternal Priest, who instituted the priesthood of the ministry as a real participation in his own unique priesthood. The minister of Christ and dispenser of the mysteries of God, therefore, look up to him directly as his model and supreme ideal. . . . Being entirely consecrated to the will of the Father, Jesus brought forth this new creation . . . Christ, the only Son of the Father, by the power of the Incarnation itself was made mediator between heaven and earth, between the Father and the human race. Wholly in accord with this mission, Christ remained throughout his whole life in the state of celibacy, which signified his total dedication to the service of God and men. This deep connection between celibacy and the priesthood of Christ is reflected in those whose fortune it is to share in the dignity and in the mission of the Mediator and eternal Priest; this sharing will be more perfect the freer the sacred minister is from the bond of flesh and blood. . . . Thus, they [priests] intend not only to participate in Christ's priestly office, but also to share with him his very condition of living." The argument can be summarized as follows: Christ himself is the ideal of every priest. He is the perfect mediator between God and people. Jesus' celibacy is necessary not only for him personally in order to fulfill his mission but is normative for all of those who follow him in his mediatorial office. The priestly calling thus entails not merely participation in Christ's priestly office but also identification with him in his manner of life (i.e. celibacy!).

[10]Cochini refers to pope Pius XI in *Acta Apostolicae Sedis* (1936), 25 and to pope John Paul II in *Acta Apostolicae Sedis* 71 (1979), 406. Pius XI claims that the 4th century stipulations regarding celibacy presuppose an older and similar tradition. John Paul II relates priestly celibacy to the example of the Lord Jesus Christ, the teaching of the apostles, and the entire tradition of the church.

[11]Cochini maintains that both the Council of Trent and Pius IV in his reply to the German princes cited the Council of Carthage (p. 4). The conciliar document indicates that "it is fitting that the holy bishops and priests of God as well as the Levites, i.e, those who are in the service of the divine sacraments, observe perfect continence, so that they may obtain in all simplicity what they are asking from God; what the apostles taught and what antiquity itself observed, let us also endeavor to keep. The bishops declared unanimously: It pleases us all that bishop, priest, and deacon, guardians of purity, abstain from [conjugal intercourse] with their wives, so that those who serve at the altar may keep a perfect chastity" (p. 5).

cept of "sanctification" teaches that a man who is promoted to the order of a "holy person" must be elevated from the rank and file of "ordinary believers" in order to be able to exercise his "holy occupation." This is how performance of the sacraments and sexual abstinence are related.

Cochini further refers to a decret of Siricius (*Directa*, CE 385), and *Cum in Unum* (CE 386), in which Siricius' requirement of clerical continence is supported by Pauline teaching (1 Cor 7:5; 1 Tim 3:2; Titus 1:6). Cochini maintains that the Pauline requirement of an *unius uxoris virum* ("husband of one wife") ought to be interpreted in light of the continence requirement for married "priests." Cochini contends that this is how monogamous marriage thus became an important requirement for the candidate for the priestly office. If he was faithful to his earthly wife, he would also remain faithful to his heavenly "wife" in Christ, the Church (cf. Eph 5:21–33, esp. 25–27).[12]

Paul's teaching in 1 Cor 7:5, Cochini explains as follows. Paul permits husband and wife temporary sexual abstinence for the purpose of prayer. This concession establishes the principle of temporary sexual abstinence for the purpose of spiritual activity. Again, Cochini argues *a minori ad maius*: if *the temporary* sexual abstinence of husband and wife for the purpose of *temporary* spiritual activity is taught by the apostles, should not *permanent* sexual abstinence of priests for the purpose of the discharge of a *permanent* spiritual vocation *all the more* be seen as part of apostolic teaching?[13]

Even the apostles, claims Cochini, observed continence subsequent to their being called by Christ. He refers to the passage where the apostles claim to have left "everything" for Christ (Matt 19:27). Jesus himself had spoken of "eunuchs for the kingdom" (Matt 19:12).

---

[12]Cochini cites Ambrosius and Epiphanius, who derive the inadmissibility of remarried widowers to priestly ordination from 1 Tim 3:2 and Titus 1:6 (p. 248). But see the Vatican II document *Presbyterorum Ordinis* (Flannery, 1:892): "It is true that it is not demanded of the priesthood by its nature. This is clear from the practice of the primitive Church (cf. 1 Tim. 3:25; Tit. 1:6) and the tradition of the Eastern Churches where in addition to those—including all bishops—who chose from the gift of grace to preserve celibacy, there are also many excellent married priests." It appears that Vatican Council II and Cochini represent different viewpoints here. Cf. also D. Callam, "Clerical Continence in the Fourth Century: Three Papal Decretals," 28, who cites Siricius (4th cent. CE): "For this reason [the purity of Christ's church] we priests are constrained to continence from the day of our ordination . . ." The purity of the "Bride of Christ" (i.e. the Church, cf. Eph 5:25-27) is here related to the continence (or celibacy) of her ministers.

[13]Cochini, *Apostolic Origins*, 10, with reference to Siricius' *Directa* (CE 385).

Finally, Mary's "perpetual virginity" can be seen as logical necessity within the framework of Roman Catholic teaching. Mary herself served as mediatrix between God and people, when she gave birth to the Savior of the world. How, argues Roman Catholic dogma, could Mary have exercised this mediatorial office, apart from fulfilling the necessary requirements of perfect purity?

Roman Catholic theologians reject the charge that the celibacy requirement diminishes the significance and legitimacy of marriage. They point out that marriage is one of the seven sacraments of the Roman Catholic church. Yet they also note Jesus' own teaching that there will be no marriage in heaven (Mark 12:25). Marriage is therefore a temporary institution while the priest's relationship with Christ's church is eternal.[14]

The Roman Catholic celibacy requirement is viewed as being rooted in Christ's celibate life itself, as well as in the apostolic practice of continence (refraining from sexual relations in marriage). Paul's "husband of one wife" requirement and the Pauline principle of sexual abstinence for the purpose of exercising a spiritual ministry are noted as well. The Roman Catholic argumentation is based on a hermeneutic of continuity between Old and New Testament and on the assigning of joint authority to holy Scripture and church Tradition. The nature of the sacraments, particularly of "holy Communion," the nature of the priesthood, and the celibacy requirement are integral and mutually interdependent parts of Roman Catholic dogma.

Critique

In the following discussion, the Roman Catholic systematic-theological interconnections and the implications regarding the celibacy requirement for priests will be subjected to a more detailed investigation.

---

[14]Siricius, who is enlisted by Cochini as an important witness, is cited by Peter Brown, *The Body and Society*, 358, as follows: "To Siricius, the issue seemed clear: service at the altar was only for those who were prepared henceforth to be perpetually free from at least one of the many strains of worldly life: the stain of intercourse. Those who stood before God to offer up the Eucharist must practice continence. Siricius cited Saint Paul's Letter to the Romans: 'for those who are in the flesh canno please God' [Siricius, *Letter* 1.7.10: 1139A]." Brown aptly notes, "Siricius' ruling was one of the first, but by no means the last, occasion in the history of the Latin Church when Paul's might notion of the flesh, as all that was opposed to the Spirit of God, was whittled down to more manageable proportions, by being referred exclusively to sexual activity" (ibid.). This appears to support the impression that the Roman Catholic celibacy requirement was influenced at least in part by an unbiblical contrast between flesh and Spirit.

We begin with the Roman Catholic hermeneutic that undescores the continuity between the testaments and the joint authority of holy Scripture and ecclesiastical Tradition. These foundational issues have important implications on the formation of Roman Catholic dogma and thus also for the formulation of the celibacy requirement for Roman Catholic priests.

While there are elements of continuity between the testaments, the discontinuity between Old and New Testament must in no way be diminished. Roman Catholic theologians cite Jesus' saying that he did not come to abolish the old covenant but to fulfill it (Matt 5:17). However, the contrast here is not between "abolish" and "uphold," but between "abolish" and "fulfill and thus set aside."[15] Jesus did not abolish the old covenant; he fulfilled it. His mission, however, was thereby not yet accomplished. He rather instituted a new covenant in the place of the old that differs from the old covenant in important respects. As Roman Catholic theologians themselves acknowledge (cf. Mark 7:19), Jesus indeed set aside many aspects of the old covenant. What is of even greater significance, Jesus set aside the entire Old Testament sacrificial system through his once-for-all, permanently valid sacrifice at the cross (cf. Heb 7:27). For this reason one must be careful in drawing parallels between the testaments. As mentioned, however, it is precisely these kinds of parallels, such as between the Old and the New Testament priesthood, that constitute the basis for Roman Catholic teaching on celibacy.

The place and authority of ecclesiastical Tradition in the formation of dogma tends to interpret holy Scripture in such a way that a certain kind of interpretation is invested with infallible authority, even when the original passage allows a variety of interpretations. Thus the emphasis shifts from holy Scripture itself to "sacred Tradition." But human tradition must always be subjected to holy Scripture itself. When Cochini therefore draws upon historical documents in order to support the requirement of celibacy, he may be successful within the framework of the Catholic understanding of Tradition. But he will hardly persuade the theologian who deems it possible that misunderstandings and wrong turns in the formative stages of doctrinal development in church history have obscured or supplanted biblical teaching. Succinctly put, a theologian who subjects tradition to Scripture will in all likelihood arrive at conclusions that differ from the one who assigns to Tradition a "sacred" place within the framework of the Roman Catholic history of dogma. In this way Cochini's argument takes on a certain circularity.

---

[15]Cf. D. A. Carson, *Matthew*, in EBC 8 (Grand Rapids: Zondervan, 1984), 143–44.

An example of this dynamic is Cochini's interpretation of 1 Cor 7:5. Cochini gives virtually no consideration to the circumstances that occasioned Paul's letter. He also appears to ignore certain qualifications Paul registers regarding his remarks. In fact, Paul replies to particular questions raised by the Corinthians. He intermingles binding teaching (7:11-12) with personal opinion (7:12, 25-26, 40). He notes that both marriage and singleness are a gift of God (7:7).[16] Paul assumes that marriage is the usual calling of a Christian (7:2).[17] Moreover, Paul places his remarks into an eschatological framework (7:29-31). It is his concern that the Corinthians—and all Christians—live in light of eschatological realities. The external form of earthly things is perishable, so that we must focus on heavenly realities—including the spiritual significance of our marital relationships! The idea that singleness as such can lead a Christian to a higher form of spirituality is foreign to Paul. Medieval monastic asceticism or Eastern religions may view abstinence from earthly activities as virtues *per se*, but not Paul (see also 1 Tim 4:3-5). Roman Catholic theologians may interpret Paul's remarks in 1 Cor 7:29-31 concerning chastity and poverty in a celibate sense. But does Paul also teach that priests in this life must never weep or laugh (1 Cor 7:30)? Consistent exegesis would require this interpretation.

Further arguments for celibacy may be answered as follows: Jesus' pronouncement regarding "eunuchs for the kingdom" (Matt 19:12) was made in the context of questions concerning the admissibility of divorce (cf. 19:3). When Jesus' disciples are shocked owing to his harsh-sounding limits on divorce, they gush out that it would be better in that case for people not to marry (19:10). In reply to his followers' statement, Jesus refers to certain individuals who may voluntarily forego marriage. But this

---

[16]For this reason it appears illegitimate to play off one calling (singleness) against another (marriage), and singleness ought not to be made an indispensable requirement for a certain class of believers (priests). Roman Catholic theologians contend that no one is compelled to celibacy. Rather, candidates for the priesthood are encouraged during the course of their preparation for priestly ordination to seek "the gift of celibacy" from God. Because he is gracious and good, God will certainly not deny their request. However, there is no biblical teaching indicating that all "priests" or full-time religious officers must live a celibate life (cf. 1 Tim 3:2 and Titus 1:6 and the discussion above). Moreover, by requiring all of its priests to meet the celibacy requirement, the Roman Catholic church indeed requires singleness. To label priestly celibacy a free "choice," as Paul IV in *Sacerdotalis Caelibatus* (Flannery, 2:300) and John Paul II (Flannery, 2:356-57) do, thus does not do full justice to the Roman church's actual practice.

[17]Cf. Werner Neuer, *Man and Woman in Christian Perspective* (trans. Gordon Wenham; Wheaton, IL: Crossway, 1991), 105-107.

renunciation is *voluntary*, as Jesus' final sentence, "He who can accept this, let him accept it" (19:12), makes clear. It is therefore illegitimate to apply this passage of Scripture to the Roman Catholic church's *requirement* of celibacy. Moreover, Jesus' statement does not pertain to *priestly* celibacy in a Roman Catholic sense.[18]

Another passage that is often adduced in the context of the Roman Catholic celibacy requirement is the apostolic claim to have left "everything" in order to follow Jesus (Matt 19:27-29; Mark 10:28-30; Luke 18:28-30). "Everything," according to Roman Catholic theologians, includes sexual relations with the apostles' wives or marriage itself. However, it is probable that the apostles resumed their familial obligations after three years of intensive following of Jesus. This seems to be indicated by Paul's statement in 1 Cor 9:5, "Do we not have the right to bring along a believing wife, as do the other apostles and the Lord's brothers and Cephas?" There is no good reason to assume that the individuals mentioned by Paul observed continence.

Jesus' own celibate state can hardly be considered decisive for the celibacy requirement. After all, following Jesus does not entail identification with him in every conceivable aspect of his life. Should every one of Jesus' disciples who is serious about following him die on a cross? Should such a one not write any books, serve as itinerant preacher, and begin his public ministry at age thirty? Is it even possible for anyone but Jesus to die *for the sin of the world*? Or should every Christian be conceived by the Holy Spirit in his mother's womb apart from collaboration by his physical father? Jesus' "celibate" life-style could be explained in a number of ways. That the Lord sought to elevate "priestly" celibacy by his example to the normative life-style of his followers is by far not the only possible explanation, or even the best. If celibacy (or marital continence) was such a strong concern of Jesus, why do we not have a single, clear statement of Jesus on this topic? Rather, it appears that self-imposed celibacy is a kind of "poverty" that renders certain experiences in life impossible that facilitate ministry to others in the case of married followers of Jesus. The continence legislation of the fourth century (and of following centuries), far from reflecting biblical teaching on God's own will, rather seems to represent a religious aberration and perversion that robbed existing marriages of their central core, complete union in a physical *as well as* spiritual sense.

Finally, as far as Mary's "perpetual virginity" is concerned that is often seen as related to celibacy, this teaching on Mary, as others, is not taught

----

[18]Cf. ibid., 89-90, 130.

in holy Scripture. The doctrine rather seems to represent a logical consequence of other Roman Catholic dogmas. It can hardly be used to help answer the question regarding the nature of the priesthood in relation to its mediatorial role.

Conclusion

In the above discussion, we have attempted to demonstrate that the Roman Catholic interpretation of Scripture in cases such as 1 Corinthians 7 and 1 Tim 3:2/Titus 1:6 is inadequate. Likewise, Roman Catholic views on the Lord's Supper and the nature of the priesthood reflect Roman Catholic hermeneutics and Tradition but are not actually based on biblical exegesis. The Lord's Supper is nowhere in the New Testament presented as "sacrifice." Christ's sacrifice is shown to be unique and unrepeatable (Heb). For this reason we do no longer need Levite-style priests today, who celebrate the "sacrifice of Mass" (in an Old Testament sense). Moreover, the regulations concerning ritual purity pertaining to the priesthood must be modified. A New Testament "Levitical priesthood" in place of the Old Testament priesthood is not taught anywhere in Scripture. The celibacy requirement is therefore theologically unnecessary in every respect. In whichever way this requirement originated historically in the Roman Catholic church, "priestly" celibacy is not in keeping with biblical teaching, nor is it of apostolic origin.

CHAPTER TEN

THE MYSTERY OF CHRIST AND THE CHURCH:
Head and Body, "One Flesh"[*]

Introduction

Ephesians 5:22-33 has been an important passage in recent debates on headship and submission in marriage.[1] An important aspect of this passage that has not received proper attention, however, is the reference to a "great mystery" in Eph 5:32. As the term μυστήριον occurs consistently throughout Ephesians, an understanding of Paul's use of the term will help in the interpretation of Eph 5:22-33. How is the term μυστήριον used? What does it refer to in the present passage? Is it the "sacrament" of marriage? Is it the typological relationship between marriage and the union of Christ and the church? Or is it the union of Christ and the church itself?

Depending on how one answers these questions, one will come to different understandings of the biblical view of marriage. If one adopts the "sacramental" view, one will see marriage as a relationship which symbolizes, in a "mystical" way, Christ's relationship with the church. One's focus will be on the inscrutable, transcendent nature of marriage and its "sacramental" nature in the church.

If one holds to a typological view, one will view marriage according to the way in which its various elements are related to Christ's union with the

---

[*]This essay first appeared in *Trinity Journal* 12 NS (1991): 79-94 and is reprinted with permission.

[1]Cf. Wayne Grudem, "The Meaning of κεφαλή ('Head'): A Response to Recent Studies," *TrinJ* 11 NS (1990): 3-72, for an interaction with recent literature on the issue of headship and submission. Cf. now also the recent compendium edited by John Piper and Wayne Grudem, *Recovering Biblical Manhood & Womanhood—A Response to Evangelical Feminism* (Wheaton, IL: Crossway, 1991).

church. The following will all be seen as connected by typology, allegory, or some other form of "deeper meaning": Adam and Christ, Eve and the church, and marriage and Christ's union with the church. The marriage partners will understand their relationship in the context of these connections and attempt to live out their roles accordingly.

If, however, μυστήριον is taken as referring to Christ and the church, and not directly to marriage, there will still be important implications for the marriage relationship. One will see marriage in the larger framework of God's purpose "in Christ": the restoration of a united body under one head, Jesus Christ. One will view Paul's use of Gen 2:24 as indicative of God's purpose to restore marriage to its original design, in analogy to Christ's union with the church.

The Term Μυστήριον

The background of Paul's use of μυστήριον has been the subject of considerable scholarly debate.[2] Even though some see Paul's use of μυστήριον as influenced by Hellenistic mystery religions,[3] most commentators prefer a background in the Old Testament concept of God's disclosing his secrets to men, a concept that was further developed in Jewish literature.[4]

Interest in (hidden) wisdom was widespread in the ancient world. Semitic and Hellenistic peoples were no exception. The Greek world used

---

[2]The Pauline authorship of Ephesians is assumed in this paper. Cf. Donald Guthrie, *New Testament Introduction* (revised ed.; Downers Grove, IL: InterVarsity, 1990), 496–528, for a survey of the argument and a defense of the Pauline authorship of Ephesians. The epistle shares a significant amount of terminology and theology with Colossians (which is usually regarded as Pauline) including the use of the term μυστήριον. For example, the first chapter of Colossians forms a close parallel to Paul's theology in Ephesians. Cf. Col 1:18 with Eph 5:23, and Col 1:25-27 with Eph 3:3-10. Cf. also Bruce Metzger, "Paul's Vision of the Church," *TToday* 6 (1949): 49, n. 1.

[3]So A. H. Harvey, "The Use of Mystery Language in the Bible," *JTS* 31 (1980): 320–36; cf. also Chrys C. Caragounis, *The Ephesian Mysterion: Meaning and Content* (Lund: C. W. K. Gleerup, 1977).

[4]Cf. George Ladd, *A Theology of the New Testament* (Grand Rapids: Eerdmans, 1974), 383–86; Raymond E. Brown, *The Semitic Background of the Term "Mystery" in the New Testament* (Philadelphia: Fortress, 1968); and Markus N. A. Bockmühl, *Revelation and Mystery in Ancient Judaism and Pauline Christianity* (Tübingen: Mohr, 1990).

μυστήριον with regard to "mystery religions."[5] The most famous were the "Eleusinian mysteries" which took place about twenty-five miles west of Athens, near the Isthmus of Corinth. The "mystery religions" were still commonly observed in New Testament times. The term μυστήριον was used for the religious rites performed in these "mystery religions," as well as for the sacred objects used during the various ceremonies.[6] The primary denotation of μυστήριον, however, was that of a secret knowledge of the ineffable, incomprehensible, impenetrable, "divine," a knowledge which was reserved for religious initiates. If Paul were using μυστήριον in this way, he would refer to the spiritual insights into transcendent divine truths given to a group of Christian "initiates."

On the other hand, μυστήριον is the term used in the LXX to translate the Aramaic רז in Dan 2:18, 19, 27, 28, 29, 30, 47, and 4:6. The term occurs in the context of Daniel's interpretation of King Nebuchadnezzar's dream. God, a "revealer of mysteries" (Dan 2:28), disclosed the dream and its meaning to Daniel, and Daniel interpreted it to the king. The divine truths here related to the unfolding of world history and the eventual establishment of God's kingdom on earth. The notion of "something *intrinsically* ineffable" which is so prominent in the Hellenistic use of μυστήριον is absent here. The obstacle to human knowledge and understanding of the "mysteries" is not their ineffability but their undisclosedness by God at the time.

The same word also plays a very important role in the Qumran writings (in Hebrew).[7] Besides referring to "mysteries of divine providence" (1QS 3:20-23; 4:18; 1QH 9:23-24; 1QM 14:14; 17:8-9; 1QpHab 2:1-2; 7:8, 13-14), cosmic (1QH 1:11-12, 21) and evil mysteries (1QS 5:36), רז also refers to the sect's interpretation of the Hebrew Scriptures (1QS 4:6; 5:1; 6:5; 9:18-19; 11:5-8; 1QH 5:11-12; 8:4-36; CD 3:12-14, 18-20). Similar to the use in Daniel is the reference to knowledge of divine truth

---

[5]Cf. Everett Ferguson, *Backgrounds of Early Christianity* (Grand Rapids: Eerdmans, 1987), 197-240. This author categorically states, "The New Testament did not use the technical vocabulary of the mysteries" (p. 240). Cf. also Joscelyn Godwin, *Mystery Religions in the Ancient World* (New York: Harper & Row, 1987).

[6]Cf. Caragounis, *Ephesian Mysterion*, 14ff., for a detailed reconstruction of the "Eleusinian mysteries."

[7]Cf. J. Coppens, "Le 'mystère' dans la théologie paulinienne et ses parallèles qumrâniens," *Littérature et théologie pauliniennes* (Recherches bibliques 5 [1960]), 142-65; E. Vogt, " 'Mysteria' in textibus Qumran," *Bib* 37 (1956): 247-57; Béda Rigaux, "Révélation des Mystères et perfection à Qumran et dans le Nouveau Testament," *NTS* 4 (1958): 237-62.

that had previously been hidden but now revealed. Im Qumran, it was the "Teacher of Righteousness" who had the prerogative to interpret the Scriptures with regard to the sect's contemporary situation.[8] The Semitic background of μυστήριον thus accentuates the revelation of previously hidden divine truth through divinely commissioned interpreters. The difference between Paul's usage and Qumran's, however, is that Paul does not resort to the often far-fetched "contemporizing" hermeneutic methodology so common in the Dead Sea Scrolls.[9]

A survey of the uses of μυστήριον in the Pauline writings shows that it is the Old Testament usage that is most consistent with Paul's use of the term. Paul does not teach that there is a body of religious truths that is reserved for Christian "initiates." Divine truth can be known by all Christians. It is not, as in the mystery religions, considered as communication with the intrinsically ineffable. It is therefore inaccurate to equate the meaning of the modern English term "mystery" with the Greek term μυστήριον. Even if μυστήριον in Eph 5:32 refers to marriage, it would be anachronistic to render the expression as "the mystery of marriage."[10] Rather, μυστήριον consistently denotes a divine truth which was once hidden but has now been revealed. Ephesians contains the largest number of references to μυστήριον in the New Testament. The term occurs throughout the letter (1:9; 3:3, 4, 9; 5:32; 6:19)[11] and consistently refers to God's eschatological purpose in Christ. It is usually related to aspects of ecclesiology.[12]

Once the interpreter has decided on the background of Paul's use of μυστήριον in Eph 5:32, the question still remains: what does the term

---

[8]Cf. 1QpHab.

[9]Concerning Paul's use of the OT, see footnote 37 below.

[10]As does, for example, the Anglican writer Mike Mason in *The Mystery of Marriage* (Portland, OR: Multnomah, 1985).

[11]Of the twenty-seven or twenty-eight times μυστήριον is used in the New Testament (there is a textual variant in 1 Cor 2:1), twenty or twenty-one are by Paul. The other references are: Rom 11:25; 16:25; 1 Cor 2:1 (variant μαρτύριον); 2:7; 4:1; 13:2; 14:2; 15:51; Col. 1:26, 27; 2:2; 4:3; 2 Thess 2:7; 1 Tim 3:9, 16. The non-Pauline references are found in the Synoptics (Matt 13:11 = Mark 4:11 = Luke 8:10) and Revelation (1:20; 10:7; 17:5, 7).

[12]Eph 1:10: "an administration suitable to the fulness of the times, the summing up of all things in Christ"; 3:1–10: "the μυστήριον of Christ" (v. 4) which was revealed "to his holy apostles and prophets in the Spirit" (v. 5) is that "the Gentiles are fellow heirs and fellow members of the body" (v. 6), "in order that the manifold wisdom of God might now be made known through the church to the rulers and the authorities in the heavenly places" (v. 10); 6:19: "the mystery of the gospel."

refer to in the present context? There are three kinds of approaches to the interpretation of μυστήριον in Eph 5:32.[13] The first sees μυστήριον as the symbol or "sacrament" of the human marriage relationship. Here, the term is understood in a similar way to its usage in the Hellenistic "mystery religions." The second approach maintains that the μυστήριον of Eph 5:32 is the typology found in the human marriage relationship, a relationship that points to the union between Christ and the church. In this view, μυστήριον is interpreted similar to its usage in the Dead Sea Scrolls. The third approach holds that μυστήριον relates marriage to the union of Christ and the church by way of analogy. In the analogical view, the term is understood as it is used in the Old Testament (as translated in the LXX).[14]

These three approaches differ in the degree of emphasis they place on the two elements of Paul's discussion (marriage and the union of Christ and the church). The sacramental approach understands Paul's emphasis to be on marriage. The typological interpretation views Paul as relating various elements in marriage with their corresponding elements in the union between Christ and the church (emphasis equally on both). The analogical approach sees Paul's primary reference to be to the union between Christ and the church in the light of which marriage is now to be understood (emphasis on the union of Christ and the church). Before critically evaluating these approaches, I will present a synopsis of Paul's theology in Ephesians as it is relevant for an interpretation of the present passage. Some general observations on Eph 5:22-23 will follow.

---

[13]For a survey of the history of interpretation of Eph 5:22-33, cf. J. Cambier, "Le grand mystère concernant le Christ et son Eglise Ephésiens 5,22-33," *Bib* 47 (1966): 43-90. He cites as proponents of the "sacramental approach" Ambrose, Augustine, Chrysostom, and Aquinas. The view that μυστήριον refers to the union of Christ and the church was held by Erasmus, Luther, and Calvin.

[14]Besides the three approaches outlined in this paper, there are various mediating positions. John Paul Sampley (*And the Two Shall Become One Flesh: A Study of Traditions in Ephesians 5:21-33* [Cambridge: University Press, 1971] 146-47) holds that "the author of Ephesians interprets Gen 2:24 to refer *not only* to the human marriage *but also* to the marriage of Christ and the Church." Sampley, however, still needs to answer the question, "*Which of these two* does Paul call a 'mystery'?" Are there *two* mysteries, a "lesser" and a "greater" one, marriage and Christ's union with the church?

Paul's Theology in Ephesians as Relevant for Interpreting 5:22-33

John Stott, in his helpful exposition *The Message of Ephesians*, points out that the phrase "in Christ" encapsulates the message of the book.[15] He defines this phrase as the believer's state of being "organically related to him [Christ] by faith."[16] In Christ, God has bestowed on the believer a multitude of spiritual blessings (1:3-14). Paul defines God's program in 1:9-10 as "the summing up (ἀνακεφαλαίω) of all things in Christ." The term μυστήριον is first used in this context.

In chap. two, Paul gives the first example of God's breaking down barriers in Christ. Jews and Gentiles are "reconciled *both in one body* (2:16)."[17] The term μυστήριον is used in 3:3, 4, and 9 to describe this divine truth which had been hidden but has now been revealed. Stott writes,

> To sum up, we may say that the "mystery of Christ" is the complete union of Jews and Gentiles with each other through the union of both with Christ. It is this double union, with Christ and with each other, which was the substance of the "mystery."[18]

As far as the Gentiles were concerned, they had been alienated, but were now brought near (2:12, 13). Paul develops the theme of unity at great length in chap. four. He describes God's purpose for the church as its attaining to "the unity of the faith," growing up "in all aspects into Him, who is the head, even Christ" (4:13, 15).

In chap. five, the Christian life is sketched as an essentially new life "in Christ." The believers are to be filled with the Spirit (5:18) in their marriages, their parenting, and their work relationships (5:21-6:9). As is argued below, the term μυστήριον is used in 5:32 with reference to Christ's union with the church. Paul, according to this view, quotes Gen 2:24 because it describes God's original design for marriage. It is this union which can be restored in the light of the μυστήριον of the union of

---

[15]John R. W. Stott, *The Message of Ephesians* (Downers Grove, IL: InterVarsity, 1979), 25. The phrase ἐν (τῷ) Χριστῷ or ἐν αὐτῷ with reference to Christ occurs in Ephesians twenty-five times: 1:1, 3, 4, 7, 9, 10, 11, 12, 13 (twice), 15, 20; 2:6, 7, 10, 13, 16, 21, 22; 3:6, 11, 12, 21; 4:21, 32. Other forms of Χριστός occur frequently as well, as does the phrase ἐν κυρίῳ.

[16]Ibid.

[17]Cf. the phrases τοὺς ἀμφοτέτους ἐν ἑνὶ σώματι (2:16) and οἱ ἀμφότεροι ἐν ἑνὶ πνεύματι (2:18) with οἱ δύο εἰς σάρκα μίαν (Eph 5:31 = Gen 2:24).

[18]Stott, *Message of Ephesians*, 117.

Christ and the church. The μυστήριον is the ground for the restored relationship between husband and wife, much like it is the ground for the restored relationship between Jews and Gentiles (cf. Gal 3:28).

General Observations on the Passage [19]

Paul adapts the *Haustafel* pattern to relate the Christian marriage relationship to the union of Christ and the church.[20] The sections of Eph 5:22-24 and 5:25-28a are subunits of the *Haustafel*. Both units are structured in a similar way. First, a command is given (to "wives" and "husbands," respectively); then Christ's relationship to the church is presented as the model to emulate ("as . . . Christ" [v. 24]; "just as Christ" [v. 25]); lastly, the command is reiterated ("so also wives . . ." [v. 24]; "in this same way . . ." [v. 28]). The only significant variation is that Paul elaborates in more detail about Christ's relationship to the church in the second section than he does in the first.

In 5:28b, Paul expands the *Haustafel* format. The section does not start with a command (as the previous units), but with a participle stating a general principle. Also, a change of grammatical subject and a shift of subject matter are detectable. While the example of Christ ("just as Christ also" [v. 29c]) provides continuity with the previous section, the summary statement is quite different: ὅτι μέλη ἐσμὲν τοῦ σώματος αὐτοῦ ("because *we* [change of subject] are *members of his body* [change of subject matter]"). Thus the immediate antecedent of the Gen 2:24 quotation in Eph 5:31 is not the marital relationship, but the union of Christ and the church, his "body."

The quotation has three parts: (1) ἀντὶ τούτου καταλείψει ἄνθρωπος τὸν πατέρα καὶ τὴν μητέρα ("for this reason a man shall leave his father and his mother"); (2) καὶ προσκολληθήσεται πρὸς τὴν γυναῖκα αὐτοῦ ("and shall cleave to his wife"); and (3) καὶ ἔσονται οἵ δύο εἰς σάρκα μίαν ("and the two shall be one flesh"). Paul then comments, τὸ μυστήριον

---

[19]Cf. Sampley, *One Flesh*, 86-108. Sampley discusses the "Hermeneutical Problems in Eph 5:31-32" (pp. 86-102), and "The Movement of Thought in Eph 5:31-32" (pp. 103-108).

[20]Cf. Guthrie, *New Testament Introduction*, 919-20. The origin of this genre is still the subject of much scholarly debate. The general format is a series of addresses to various family members and participants in relationships ("wives . . . husbands"; "children . . . parents"; "slaves . . . masters"), usually moving from the subordinate part to the one(s) placed in a role of authority. Cf. also Col 3:18-4:1; 1 Pet 3:1-7.

τοῦτο μέγα ἐστίν ("this mystery is a great one"). The statement could refer to the whole quotation, part of it, or the explanation immediately following it. It may be significant that Paul agrees with the LXX in an instance where it differs from the Hebrew text. The phrase "the two" is added before the words "will become one flesh."[21] Paul may here accentuate the paradox of "the two" becoming "one." If so, τὸ μυστήριον τοῦτο should be seen primarily as tying the third part of the quotation, "the two shall be one flesh," to the explanation that follows: "now I am speaking about Christ and the church."[22]

The whole section Eph 5:22–33 is concluded with a summary statement to husband and wife. Verse 33 combines the exhortations given to the individual marriage partners in vv. 24b and 28a. This concluding verse ties in Paul's adaptation of the *Haustafel* format (5:22–28a) with his excursus on the union between Christ and his church (5:28b–32).[23]

Structurally, the relationship "Christ"/"church" is the constant of Eph 5:22–33. The question is: is the marriage relationship used to illustrate the union between Christ and the church or vice versa? Paul first uses the union between Christ and the church as a pattern for the marital partners to follow. However, at Eph 5:28b he starts shifting focus and emphasis. What was the model, i.e., the union of Christ and the church, now becomes the primary subject. The marital union, which had been the subject, now briefly retreats into the background.

---

[21]Cf. Markus Barth, *Ephesians 4–6* (AB; New York: Doubleday, 1974), 720.

[22]Cf. also the discussion below. The wording λέγω εἰς is unusual. Usually λέγω uses περί or the dative. The phrase is otherwise only found in Luke 22:65 ("*against* Him") and in Acts 2:25. In the latter reference Peter quotes Ps 16:8–11 and introduces his quotation by "For David said *of* Him [Christ]" (Δαυὶδ γὰρ λέγει εἰς αὐτόν). The preposition indicates the *reference* of David's statement. The quotation could be paraphrased as, "David spoke *with reference to* Him." Paul's statement in Eph 5:32 can similarly be rendered as, "But I am referring to Christ and the church." Cf. A. T. Robertson, *A Grammar of the Greek New Testament in the Light of Historical Research* (Nashville: Broadman, 1934), 595, for a use of εἰς like a dative with the connotation "with reference to."

[23]Cf. Sampley, *One Flesh*, 147. Note that the *Haustafel* continues in Eph 6:1–9 with exhortations to children and parents, slaves and masters. Common subordination to God and proper subordination to one another in the church are to reflect a proper (creation) order of God in Christ. Cf. Paul's exhortation in 1 Cor 11:3: θέλω δὲ ὑμᾶς εἰδέναι ὅτι παντὸς ἀνδρὸς ἡ κεφαλὴ ὁ Χριστός ἐστιν, κεφαλὴ δὲ γυναικὸς ὁ ἀνήρ, κεφαλὴ δὲ τοῦ Χριστοῦ ὁ θεός.

Table 5: Shift of Primary Subjects in Eph 5:22-32

Verses	Marital Union	Union of Christ & Church
Eph 5:22-28a	Primary Subject	Illustration
Eph 5:28b-32	Illustration	Primary Subject

Evaluation of Alternate Approaches to the Interpretation of Eph 5:32

Evaluation of Interpretation of Μυστήριον Referring to Marriage

The view that μυστήριον refers to the marriage relationship is often taken by Roman Catholic theologians, who view the term within the framework of their "sacramental" ecclesiology. Roman Catholic dogma holds that the institution of marriage conveys grace. Marriage in this view "indicates participation in ultimate reality, the operation of grace in an effective sign, the permanence received in sacredness."[24] As Barth notes,

> The Christians who support the equation of marriage with a sacrament intend to say that marriage is a means of grace by which man and woman participate in the mystery of creation, incarnation, redemption, reconciliation, perfection.[25]

Eph 5:22-33, according to this view, teaches the "mystical" nature of marriage. Barth's criticism is helpful. He charges the "sacramental view" of marriage with the following inaccuracies:

(1) It neglects the singularity of Christ's betrothal to the church by making every marriage a reenactment of Christ's union with the church. Marriage is this-worldly, "not a semiheavenly repetition of Christ's romance."

(2) The thesis that marriage is a sacrament amounts to a sacralization or mystification of a structure or institution in human society.

(3) There is a syncretistic element introduced from pagan religion where partners use each other to come closer to the divine.[26]

Marriage is just part of Paul's theological presentation in Ephesians. His focus is on the doctrine of the church as the "body of Christ." Thus it would be more consistent with Paul's overall argument to see μυστήριον

---

[24]Barth, *Ephesians*, 4-6, 747.

[25]Ibid.

[26]Ibid., 748-49.

as a reference to his larger theme, the union of Christ and the church, and view marriage as one of a number of applications of this "great mystery." There is no obvious reason for Paul in the present context to call marriage a μυστήριον. Considering that the term in Ephesians usually connotes a truth that was previously hidden but has now been revealed, marriage can hardly be seen as a previously hidden "mystery."

The structure of Eph 5:22–33 indicates a shift in emphasis from the marital union to the church as the "body of Christ" in 5:28a–32, thus making Christ and the church the most natural referent of μυστήριον. Note that the immediate antecedent of the Gen 2:24 quotation is the clause "for we are members of his body," which gives the reason for Christ's nurture of his church. One would expect Paul to continue this train of thought through the Gen 2:24 quotation.

On exegetical grounds, the demonstrative pronoun τοῦτο likely points only to a certain aspect of the marital union—i.e., "the two becoming one flesh"—for the purpose of relating this aspect to the relationship between Christ and the church.[27] Also, ἐγὼ δὲ λέγω ("but I am speaking") indicates a change in subject matter from marriage to the relationship between Christ and the church.

Historically, the interpretation of μυστήριον in Eph 5:32 as referring to marriage has been based on an equation of the term with the Latin *sacramentum*[28] in line with Catholic theology. Jerome's Vulgate used this term to translate μυστήριον. When Roman Catholic theology began to develop, with the element of mysticism expressed in its "sacraments," the original meaning of μυστήριον began to fade in favor of the meaning that the term *sacramentum* had begun to acquire. This use, however, is foreign to the New Testament.[29]

There is nothing in marriage itself as an institution that "mystically" dispenses divine grace. It is not the case, as the Roman Catholic Church

---

[27]Cf. Sampley, *One Flesh*, 86, citing BAGD, 66, for support, who comment that "τοῦτο . . . could conceivably refer to any *part* or *parts* of the section beginning with 5:21." The use of τοῦτο in Eph 5:32 is somewhat ambivalent because Paul immediately redirects the demonstrative pronoun from its original referent (the aspect of the two becoming one flesh), as in the antecedent quotation, to a new referent (the union of Christ and the church).

[28]*Sacramentum* originally referred to a military oath of allegiance (cf. Webster's *Ninth New Collegiate Dictionary*, 1035). Later the term's meaning was changed to denote "a formal religious act that is sacred as a sign or symbol of a spiritual reality, especially one believed to have been instituted or recognized by Jesus Christ" (ibid.).

[29]Cf. Hans von Soden, "ΜΥΣΤΗΡΙΟΝ und sacramentum in den ersten zwei Jahrhunderten der Kirche," *ZNW* 12 (1911): 188–227.

maintains, that when marriage is entered into under the auspices of the Church it is in itself an institution where Christ is "personally present" in a mystical way. There is no intrinsic power in the oath or marriage vows themselves. The prerequisite for a Christian marriage is not the "sacramental blessing" of the institutionalized church, but becoming "new creatures" in Christ (cf. 2 Cor 5:17; Eph 4:23-24), by being regenerated, "born again" in him (cf. Titus 3:5).

Evaluation of Interpretation of Μυστήριον as a Typology

The view that μυστήριον refers to the typology found in the human marriage relationship as pointing to the union between Christ and the church is more difficult to evaluate. The term "typology" is used in different ways.[30] A "type" may be an example, i.e., a pattern, found in one instance and related to a later instance in Scripture. Usually an eschatological advance in the New Testament antitype over against the Old Testament type is considered essential to true typology. But is the typology *prospective* or *retrospective*? Does the Old Testament type have a genuinely predictive function, or is typology simply a way of looking back at the Old Testament and drawing out resemblances?[31] If Paul uses typology in the present passage at all, it is a retrospective form of typology: Paul uses a principle regarding marriage found in Gen 2:24 and relates it to his contemporary reference, the union of Christ and the church.[32]

A variant of the typological approach is the view that Paul finds a "deeper meaning" in Gen 2:24, as if there were a hidden meaning under the surface that awaited its revelation in the "last days" (*sensus plenior*).[33]

---

[30]Cf. the discussion by Douglas J. Moo, "The Problem of Sensus Plenior," in *Hermeneutics, Authority, and Canon* (ed. D. A. Carson and John D. Woodbridge; Grand Rapids: Zondervan, 1986), 175-212. Moo cautions against the assumption that certain exegetical methods (in his context, Jewish methods like *pesher*) "necessarily result in a perversion of the meaning of the text" (p. 193). Moo quotes E. Earle Ellis explaining Paul's procedure in using the OT: "His idea of a quotation was not a worshiping of the letter or 'parroting' of the text; neither was it an eisegesis which arbitrarily imposed a foreign meaning upon the text. It was rather, in his eyes a quotation-exposition, a *midrash pesher*, which drew from the text the meaning originally implanted there by the Holy Spirit and expressed that meaning in the most appropriate words and phrases known to him" (p. 195).

[31]Cf. ibid., 195-98.

[32]Cf. footnote 40 below.

[33]Cf. again Moo, "Sensus Plenior," 201-204. He quotes Brown as distinguishing *sensus plenior* from typology in that the former has to do with the deeper meaning of *words*, and the latter with the extended meaning of *things* (p. 202). I would argue, if at all, for typology rather than *sensus plenior* in Eph 5:32. Moo's criteria of "whether it is necessary and adequate to explain the phenomena"

Gen 2:24, though literally referring to marriage, is believed to be typologically structured so that husband and wife function as the type of which Christ and the church are the antitype. Paul, as an inspired New Testament author, is seen to make this latent typology explicit.[34] Similarly to the practice of the Qumran community, Paul is represented as using a *midrash pesher* type of approach.[35] If such is understood to involve a "reading into" an Old Testament text of what is not there explicitly,[36] one should note that there is no indication in the present passage for this kind of practice. The view is based on inference. It seems presumptuous to maintain that Gen 2:24 is typologically structured based on Paul's use of it in Eph 5:31-32. *Sensus plenior* is not required to make sense of Paul's statement.[37] A better explanation for the way Paul uses the quotation, if

---

and "whether it coheres with an acceptable theory of inspiration" (p. 203) seem to apply.

[34]For interpretations in the direction of *sensus plenior*, cf. Barth (*Ephesians 4-6*, 734), who contends that " 'the secret meaning' (5:32) of the verse in Genesis is *the promise that Christ will elect the church to be his own.*" Barth continues by elaborating on the union of Christ and the church as "one flesh" (ibid., 736-37). While I reject the "hidden sense" part of Barth's interpretation, I agree with his focus on the "one flesh" aspect of Christ's union with the church. Similarly, Brown (*Semitic Background*, 65-66), who says that the reference to μυστήριον in Eph 5:32 is "to a scriptural passage [i.e., Gen 2:24] which contains a deeper meaning than that which appears at first sight." Cf. also F. F. Bruce (*The Epistle to the Ephesians* [London: Pickering & Inglis, 1961], 119) who comments that "the words of Gen 2:24 *enshrine a greater truth than that which lies on the surface,*" i.e., " 'I am treating the man as *symbolic* of Christ and the woman as *symbolic* of the Church.' " Cf. also A. Skevington Wood (*Ephesians* [EBC, Vol. 11; Grand Rapids: Zondervan, 1978], 32), who states, "Gen 2:24 *enunciates a more profound truth than was realized* till Christ came to win His bride, the church, by giving Himself for her on the cross." Cf. also Bockmühl, *Revelation and Mystery*, 205. Bockmühl interprets Eph 5:32 as "an exegetical mystery: a deeper (in this case either allegorical or prophetic) meaning of a Scriptural text which has been elicited by means of some form of inspired exegesis. In other words, the deeper meaning of Gen 2:24 points typologically to Christ and the church."

[35]Cf. Moo, "Sensus Plenior," 193, and 400-401, notes 54 and 57, for bibliographical information regarding this interpretational practice.

[36]Ibid., 193.

[37]Concerning Paul's use of the OT, cf. D. Moody Smith, "The Old Testament in the New Testament: The Pauline Literature," in *It Is Written: Scripture Citing Scripture* (ed. D. A. Carson and H. G. M. Williamson; Cambridge: University Press, 1988), 265-91. The author remarks: "there is a kind of unpredictability about Paul's use of the OT, except that he almost always reads it in light of the events of Christian revelation" (p. 278). He continues: "there are unmistakable signs of his originality as his own exegetical work develops" (ibid.). Ethical application [e.g., Eph 5:31], typology, allegory, categories of promise and fulfillment are all part of Paul's repertoire in using the Old Testament for his

there is typology at all, is to regard the reference as retrospective typology. In that case, Paul would look for a way to illustrate the union of Christ and the Church and use the principle enunciated in Gen 2:24 regarding the "one flesh" marital union.

Others call Paul's interpretive method "allegorical." This interpretation is similar to the typological approach. Moo differentiates typology from allegory as follows: "While allegory looks for meaning *behind* the text, typology bases meaning on events narrated in the text itself."[38] Similar criticisms as the ones just raised against the typological view apply also to the allegorical approach. When Paul is speaking allegorically in Gal 4:21–31, he gives a lengthy exposition of the counterparts in his allegory: Hagar and Sarah are two covenants, the Sinaitic and the New Covenant. When Jesus tells the allegory of the vine and the branches in John 15:1–8, he establishes the allegorical correlations as well: the Father is the vinedresser, Jesus is the vine, and his disciples are the branches. In Eph 5:31–32, no such allegorical connections are established. The allegorical approach to the interpretation of μυστήριον in Eph 5:32 is thus an argument from silence. One would expect that Paul would have made his allegory more explicit if it was indeed his intention to draw one. How else would his readers have known how to interpret it?

Rather than focusing on typology or allegory, however, Paul takes the Gen 2:24 quotation literally as referring to the fact that "the two" become "one flesh" in human marriage.[39] He then implies that, in the union

---

theological argument (p. 279). Ephesians is the only "prison epistle" to include Old Testament quotations. Of the six references, only two are formally introduced. In 4:8 (quoting Ps 68:18) and 5:14 (Isaiah?), Paul uses the rather informal διὸ λέγει. In the other four instances, Paul interweaves the Old Testament into his argument: in 4:25, 26 (quoting Zech 8:16; Ps 4:4); 5:31 (Gen 2:24); and 6:2 (Exod 20:12; Deut 5:16). Cf. 4:25, 26, commenting on ὅτι μέλη ἐσμὲν ἀλλήλων μέλη and 5:32 elaborating on ὅτι μέλη ἐσμὲν τοῦ σώματος αὐτοῦ. Cf. also Paul's quoting Gen 2:24 in 1 Cor 6:16 and his conclusion (v. 17): ὁ δὲ κολλώμενος τῷ κυρίῳ ἓν πνεῦμά ἐστιν. Note also that Paul adds οἱ δύο, which is not found in the Hebrew MT (for emphasis?—cf. Barth, *Ephesians 4–6*, 720–21, for a thorough discussion of the various textual issues).

[38]Cf. Moo, "Sensus Plenior," 195. For an allegorical interpretation, cf. G. Bornkamm, *TDNT* 4 (1967): 823: "Since an exhortatory conclusion regarding marital life is drawn from the *text* and its *exposition*, μυστήριον refers to the text and not to the institution of marriage itself. The μυστήριον is thus *the allegorical meaning of the Old Testament saying*, its mysteriously concealed prophecy of the relationship of Christ to the ἐκκλησία. . . . The eschatological marriage of Christ and the Church is mysteriously prefigured in Gen 2:24."

[39]A detailed discussion of the expression "one flesh" is beyond the scope of this paper. Cf. A. Skevington Wood (*Ephesians*, 78), who limits the term to sexual intercourse; Barth (*Ephesians 4–6*, 734–35), who includes social and spiritual

between Christ and the church also, "the two" become "one flesh." It is this spiritual union itself that Paul calls a "mystery," not the typological correspondence between marriage and the relationship between Christ and the church.[40] Paul himself does not elaborate on any typological connection.[41] The interpreter thus should be careful to avoid fanciful developments.[42]

---

components; and cf. also Richard Batey, *New Testament Nuptial Imagery* (Leiden: Brill, 1971), 30–37; idem, "The *mia sarx* union of Christ and the Church," *NTS* 13 (1966–67): 270–81.

[40]At best, it is not marriage as a whole that is related typologically to the union between Christ and the church, but only the paradoxical principle of "two becoming one flesh." That this kind of typology is present in this passage is not impossible. However, there are no clear contextual cues to confirm this contention. Unlike in other places where Paul uses typology (Rom 5:12–21; 7:1–6; 1 Cor 15:45–47; Gal 4:21–31), he does not elaborate on the typological relationships he seeks to establish. Furthermore, there seems to be no compelling reason for Paul to use typology in the present passage. It is true that Paul had available a rich typological imagery from both Old Testament and intertestamental Judaism picturing God's relationship with his people in marital terms. Paul was no doubt aware of this imagery and uses it in other places (e.g., 2 Cor 11:2, 3). To argue for Paul's use of typology in Eph 5:22–33, however, is based on inference rather than explicitly found in the text. It is true that Paul compares the marital union with Christ's union with the church in Eph 5:23–24, and especially 5:25–27, but note that he always uses ὡς (v. 23) or καθώς (vv. 25, 29). The construction in 5:32, however, is different (λέγω εἰς.

[41]Cf. Sampley (*One Flesh*, 89–90), who argues that the reason why Paul can be so brief in his discussion of the μυστήριον in Eph 5:31–32 is that he has already set forth his interpretation of Gen 2:24 in Eph 5:21–30. Another possibility is that Paul could be using deliberate ambiguity in his phraseology. It is important to remember that Ephesians is not a formal exposé, but an epistle. It may well be that as Paul wrote the letter he gradually digressed from his initial subject of marriage into a brief treatment of the union of Christ and the church.

[42]Cf. Richard A. Batey (*Nuptial Imagery*, 31), who elaborates and cautions: "This verse has frequently been allegorized to refer to Christ's leaving of his Father and his Mother, the heavenly Jerusalem in order to come to earth and be joined to the church. . . . Those who view the coming [of Christ] as being the historical Jesus are eager to find parallels in Hellenistic mystery cults, where a dominant motif was the descent of the savior-god into the cosmos in order to establish order and save mankind. To see in this Old Testament quotation a reference to either the ἱερος γάμος of the mystery religions, of the return of the Son of Man on 'the clouds of glory' is an unnecessary intrusion. . . . Since the Ephesian writer makes no other use of the passage than to express the unity established by marriage, efforts to find other meanings distort the purpose of the quotation." Batey interprets μυστήριον in Eph 5:32 as "not an enigma, but the revelation of a secret which was once hidden but now revealed" (ibid.).

Evaluation of Interpretation of Μυστήριον as a
Reference to the Union of Christ and the Church

The third kind of approach considers μυστήριον in Eph 5:32 a direct reference to the union of Christ and his church. This seems to be the most straightforward reading of the text. After all, does not Paul himself say, "But I am speaking with reference to Christ and the church"? As husband and wife are "one flesh," Paul argues, Christ and the church are "one flesh": "head" (5:32) and "body" (5:30). Thus, in one sense, Paul envisions Christ and his church as one person, inextricably united in this world, just like husband and wife (cf. Gen 2:24).[43]

This interpretation is the most consistent with regard to the content of the term μυστήριον in Ephesians and the other Pauline writings. The divine truth that once had been hidden but now, in the train of Christ's coming and work, is revealed, is God's oneness with His people as realized to a far greater degree than in the OT. While God's faithful love for his wayward people was revealed through the prophets, it was Jesus Christ who took on human flesh and redeemed the Church as his own body on earth. This body, he would nurture (cf. Eph 5:30: "for we are members of His body"). Paul, a "steward of God's mysteries (cf. 1 Cor 4:1)," was the herald of the μυστήριον.[44]

The interpretation that μυστήριον in Eph 5:32 refers to the union of Christ and the church fits well with Paul's overall theology in Ephesians and his other letters.[45] It is true that this is the only place where Paul uses the marital union to teach about the union of Christ and the church. It is also true that this is the only place where Paul calls the union between Christ and the church a "mystery." Yet, Paul had been in the process of

---

[43]Concerning Paul's very first experience of Christ's close identification with his church, cf. Acts 9:4, where Christ asks him, "Saul, Saul, why are you persecuting *Me?*" To persecute the church is to persecute her Lord.

[44]Note that even though Paul's theology of the church as the body of Christ and their "one flesh" union is new, it is certainly not a *creatio ex nihilo.* The Old Testament frequently uses the metaphor of husband and wife for God and his people (cf. Ps 45; Isa 50:1; 54:1-8; 62:3-5; Jer 2:32; 3:1-18; 31:31-34; Ezek 16; Hosea 1-3; 11:8; 14:4). For New Testament references, cf. Matt 9:15; Mark 2:18ff; John 3:29; 2 Cor 11:2; Rev 19:7; 21:2, 9.

[45]Note, for example, the close relationship of Col 1:18, 22, and 28 to Paul's theology in Eph 5:22-33. For an advocacy of an interpretation of Eph 5:32 consistent with the other Pauline usages of μυστήριον in Ephesians, cf. Sampley, *One Flesh,* 94-95. He writes: the usual referent is "something that was hidden, but now is revealed. Does this apply to 5:21-33? What might be at stake in this context is *a heretofore undisclosed relationship that now subsists between Christ and the church.*"

developing his theology of the church as the body of Christ in his previous letters to the Romans and Corinthians.[46] In Ephesians, Paul applies this theology to his development of the μυστήριον theology.[47] Thus, Paul's theology of the church as the body of Christ culminates in his explanation that there is a union between Christ and the church like the union between husband and his wife in the marriage relationship.

This interpretation is also the most natural one exegetically. It is the one that is most coherent with Paul's movement of thought in Eph 5:22–33 (see "General Observations on the Passage" above). While the Catholic "sacramental" interpretation fails properly to identify both the content and referent of μυστήριον, the typological interpretation is largely based on inference and cannot clearly be demonstrated from the text. The interpretation that μυστήριον in Eph 5:32 refers to the union of Christ and the church is the only one that correctly identifies both the content and referent of μυστήριον, and adequately accounts for the text of the passage without resorting to unnecessary extratextual explanations.

Conclusion

The referent of μυστήριον in Eph 5:32 is the union of Christ and the church. Paul, in seeking to teach about the union of the two entities, Christ and the church, draws on the paradox present in the marital union, where two entities, husband and wife, become "one flesh." The "great mystery" Paul reveals is that just as the marital partners are "one flesh," so are Christ and the church, as "head" and "body."

Eph 5:32 cannot properly be used to support a view of marriage as a "sacrament" or "mystery" in the modern sense of the word. Neither can

---

[46]Cf. Rom 12:4, 5; 1 Cor 12:12-27. Note that there are two aspects to the metaphor of the church as "the body of Christ": (1) the Church is animated by the Spirit of Christ, and the Christians are the various members of his "body"; and (2) Christ is the "head" and the church the "body." In Eph 5:21–33, the second aspect is in view.

[47]Paul has demonstrated the way in which Christ cares for his church (Eph 5:29) by using another Old Testament quotation in Eph 4:8. In Eph 4:7-16, Paul applies this quotation to the church: Christ gave to the church apostles, prophets, evangelists, and pastor/teachers, to the building up of the body of Christ (4:11). God's purposes are the unity, maturity, and "fulness" of the "body of Christ" under its "head, Christ." Thus, structurally as well as theologically, the interpretation of μυστήριον as a new divine truth concerning the spiritual union of Christ and his church is consistent with Paul's argument in Ephesians.

the passage be cited as evidence for the typological significance of marriage.

While the focus in Eph 5:22-28a is on the actual roles to be taken in marriage, Paul's discussion in Eph 5:28b-32 puts marriage in perspective.[48] As follows from the discussion here, the primary application of the latter passage is to God's plan of restoration "in Christ" as worked out in the marriage relationship. While marriage is not the primary focus, there are still significant implications for how to view and live out the marital union. Eph 5:28b-32 helps one to think of marriage in relation to God's larger purposes. Marriage is not an end in itself; it is part of a life under God in the church and in the world. Marriage is a relationship in the process of restoration. To the extent that a married couple sees itself as part of the global eschatological movement toward "summing up all things in Christ" (Eph 1:9), it will experience fulfillment and share the perspective on marriage Paul presents in the passage at hand.

The contemporary debate on the biblical view of marriage has witnessed a polarization of positions. It seems that both—those who stress headship and submission and those who emphasize equality—are affirming biblical truths. The proponents of these positions, however, should take care not to neglect (or deny) the balancing, corresponding truths. Headship and submission, as well as God's plan to restore the original design of the husband/wife relationship without (post-fall) barriers, are both taught in Eph 5:22-33. It is erroneous to "separate what God has joined together": a restored marriage relationship, and a pattern of headship and submission between the marriage partners. Yet it is important to recognize

---

[48]Contra George W. Knight III, "Husbands and Wives as Analogues of Christ and the Church," in *Recovering Biblical Manhood & Womanhood*, 175-76. Knight assumes that Paul's primary subject in 5:30-32 is still marriage. He considers Christ and the church as the analogy (section heading on p. 175; but the title of his article seems to suggest the reverse). Knight seems to combine the symbolic and typological (and analogical? [s.a.]) approaches when he calls marriage a "picture" (pp. 175, 176) and a "parable" (p. 175) of Christ and the church. He maintains that "mystery" in Eph 5:32 refers to the symbolism invested in marriage by God at creation regarding Christ and the church, which was revealed through Paul to the Ephesians (similarly John Piper, ibid., p. 476, n. 16: "the 'mystery' of marriage is the truth that God designed male and female from the beginning to carry different responsibilities on the analogy of Christ and his church"). But why would Paul teach this to the Ephesian church? How does the teaching fit into the passage's flow of thought and Paul's theology of μυστήριον? A preoccupation with the contemporary agenda of male/female roles must not be permitted to cloud an unbiased reading of the text in its larger biblical theological framework.

that Paul's teaching on headship and submission is given in the larger framework of his theology of the breaking down of old barriers and the restoration of united relationships. In that sense, then, "there is neither Jew nor Greek, neither male nor female" in God's new community. The marriage relationship shares in God's μυστήριον as it is revealed through Paul: the "heading up again" of all things under Christ.

CHAPTER ELEVEN

GENDER PASSAGES IN THE NEW TESTAMENT:
Hermeneutical Fallacies Critiqued[*]

The pre-fall bliss man and woman enjoyed in the Garden has given way to much confusion regarding man's and woman's place in God's world, in Christ's church, and in relation to one another. North American culture, with its emphasis on equality and the advances of feminism in this century, has pressed hard upon the church to conform its teachings to new societal standards. As is customary in American public life, special interest groups have been formed representing different sides of the "gender issue" in an effort to influence the various segments within American evangelicalism toward their respective viewpoints.[1]

The last few decades have witnessed an increasing awareness of the importance of hermeneutical procedure in interpreting the gender passages in the New Testament. Grant Osborne contended in 1977 that "the determining factor in the discussion [of gender passages in the New Testament] is hermeneutical."[2] Already in 1958, Krister Stendahl had investigated *The Bible and the Role of Women—A Case Study in Hermeneutics*.[3] Robert Johnston in 1978 and again in 1986 attributed the differences in approach regarding the role of women in the church taken

---

[*]This essay first appeared in *Westminster Theological Journal* 56 (1994): 259–83 and is reprinted with permission.

[1]The reference is to *The Council on Biblical Manhood and Womanhood* and *Christians for Biblical Equality*, cf. their respective publications, *Recovering Biblical Manhood & Womanhood—A Response to Evangelical Feminism* (ed. John Piper and Wayne Grudem; Wheaton, IL: Crossway, 1991) and Alvera Mickelsen, ed., *Women, Authority & the Bible* (Downers Grove, IL: IVP, 1986).

[2]Cf. Grant R. Osborne, "Hermeneutics and Women in the Church," *JETS* 20 (1977): 337.

[3]Krister Stendahl, *The Bible and the Role of Women—A Case Study in Hermeneutics* (Philadelphia: Fortress, 1966).

by evangelicals to "different hermeneutics," calling the study of women's roles a "test case" of evangelical interpretation.[4]

If Johnston is correct, evangelical hermeneutics seem to have failed the test, since the existing exegetical conclusions on the New Testament gender texts vary widely. What is perhaps even more disturbing is the apparent lack of consensus regarding a proper methodology.[5] The authors referred to above provide some constructive suggestions regarding hermeneutical procedure in dealing with gender issues.[6]

However, at times their suggestions are too superficial or otherwise unhelpful. For example, Johnston distinguishes between "obscure" and "plain" passages on gender issues.[7] He cites as an example "the difficult text" in 1 Tim 2 which, according to Johnston, "needs to be read in the light of . . . Gal 3:28."[8] But surely this categorization is inadmissibly subjective.[9] Moreover, Johnston illegitimately merges the ancient and the contemporary contexts. The mere fact that a passage is difficult to understand

---

[4]Robert K. Johnston, "Biblical Authority & Interpretation: the Test Case of Women's Role [sic] in the Church & Home Updated," in *Women, Authority & the Bible* (ed. Alvera Mickelsen; Downers Grove, IL: IVP, 1986), 30–41. This essay is a revised version of "The Role of Women in the Church and Home: An Evangelical Testcase in Hermeneutics," in *Scripture, Tradition, and Interpretation* (ed. W. Ward Gasque and William Sanford LaSor; Grand Rapids: Eerdmans, 1978), 234–59. Cf. also Gordon D. Fee, "Issues in Evangelical Hermeneutics, Part III: The Great Watershed—Intentionality & Particularity/Eternality: 1 Timothy 2:8-15 as a Test Case," *Crux* 26 (1990): 31–37.

[5]Cf. Geoffrey W. Bromiley, "The Interpretation of the Bible," in *The Expositor's Bible Commentary* (ed. Frank E. Gaebelein; Grand Rapids: Zondervan, 1979), 1:78–79.

[6]Cf. also the recent article by Terrance Thiessen, "Toward a Hermeneutic for Discerning Moral Absolutes," *JETS* 36 (1993): 189–207. Thiessen enumerates five hermeneutical principles for discerning universal moral absolutes: (1) their basis in the moral nature of God; (2) their basis in the creation order; (3) transcendent factors and lack of situational limitations; (4) consistency in progressive revelation; (5) consistency in the progress of redemption. Thiessen often refers to the role of women in the church. His discussion of 1 Cor 14:34 and 1 Tim 2:11-14 unfortunately deals with both passages simultaneously, oscillating back and forth between them (pp. 195-96).

[7]Cf. Johnston, "Test Case," 31.

[8]Ibid.

[9]Cf., e.g., George W. Knight, *The Role Relationship of Men & Women* (rev. (rev. ed.; Phillipsburg, N. J.: Presbyterian and Reformed, 1985), 17, who considers 1 Tim 2:11-15 to be the passage which "most clearly" gives Paul's teaching on the role of women in the church—the opposite verdict of Johnston's! Cf. also Thiessen, who distinguishes between "clear" and "less obvious" passages but admits that "this often-cited principle is not easily applied" ("Hermeneutic," 202).

at the end of the twentieth century does not mean that the original audience considered the same passage "obscure" or "difficult." A similar charge can be brought against the distinction drawn by Osborne between "passages which deal with an issue systematically" and "incidental references."[10]

The present essay therefore seeks to readdress some of the issues taken up in earlier treatments, taking into account developments since these studies appeared. It also attempts to sharpen further the discernment of improper methodology. It is hoped that the critique of fallacious methodologies will contribute to better hermeneutical procedures. This, in turn, might lead to a greater convergence of exegetical conclusions. In the following article, the usual procedure will be first to identify the fallacy and then to illustrate it by concrete examples found in the interpretations of various writers. After the critique of a given fallacy, a few constructive comments will seek to point the way toward a better hermeneutical approach.

It should also be pointed out that the fallacies treated below are not necessarily mutually exclusive. For example, one's use of an imbalanced methodology may be due to an underestimation of the power of presuppositions, or an imbalanced hermeneutic may consist in an interpreter's improper elevation of alleged background data over the explicit text.

Underestimating the Power of Presuppositions

Twentieth-century hermeneutical emphases such as the impossibility of presuppositionless exegesis and the reality of the horizon and preunderstanding of the interpreter have still not been sufficiently applied to the contemporary enterprise of biblical interpretation.[11] In the case of the interpretation of biblical gender texts, every writer has preconceived notions of how male-female relationships are properly conducted. An illusory notion of hermeneutical objectivity will render genuine dialogue

---

[10]Cf. Osborne, "Hermeneutics and Women," 338 (referring to Letha Scanzoni and Nancy Hardesty, *All We're Meant to Be* [Waco: Word, 1974], 18).

[11]Cf. Rudolf Bultmann, "Is Exegesis without Presuppositions Possible?" in *Existence and Faith* (ed. S. Ogden; London: Hodder and Stoughton, 1961), 289–96; Hans-Georg Gadamer, *Truth and Method* (2d ed.; New York: Crossroad, 1982). Cf. also the good survey on the preunderstandings of the interpreter by William Klein, Craig Blomberg, and Robert Hubbard, *Introduction to Biblical Interpretation* (Dallas: Word, 1993), 98–116.

with both the text and other interpreters and interpretive communities much more difficult.[12]

Johnston evaluates positively the recent trend from "the myth of objectivity" in interpretation to what he calls "a controlled subjectivism."[13] He rightly chastises evangelicals who, "in their desire to escape the supposed relativity of such reader-oriented perspectives, have too often attempted to hide themselves behind the veneer of objectivity."[14] Whether the kind of "new hermeneutic" advocated by Johnston provides the answer remains another question. Johnston himself seems to see the dangers of such an approach when he searches for ways "[t]o protect against a destructive subjectivism" in order to practice "a reader-sensitive criticism."[15]

Of course, the existence of presuppositions does not mean that all presuppositions are equally valid or that an interpreter's prior convictions in approaching the text cannot become more and more consistent with biblical teaching.[16] Nevertheless, it is helpful to be aware of the way in which one's experience, interpretive and denominational traditions, cultural and social backgrounds, vocation, gender, education, and other factors influence the way in which Scripture is interpreted.[17]

An example of presuppositions that remain largely unacknowledged is the recent article "Why God is Not Mother" by Elizabeth Achtemeier.[18] In an article that purportedly critiques the radical feminist movement, she

---

[12]Cf. Anthony C. Thiselton, *The Two Horizons: New Testament Hermeneutics and Philosophical Description* (Grand Rapids: Eerdmans, 1980); id., *New Horizons in Hermeneutics* (Grand Rapids: Zondervan, 1992); Grant R. Osborne, *The Hermeneutical Spiral: A Comprehensive Introduction to Biblical Interpretation* (Downers Grove, IL: IVP, 1991).

[13]Cf. Johnston, "Test Case," 32 and 38.

[14]Cf. ibid., 35.

[15]Ibid., 40–41. Johnston lists (1) the wider insights of the Christian community, past and present; (2) the whole canon of Scripture; (3) reliance on the Holy Spirit; and (4) the witness of multiple cultures in interpreting the Bible.

[16]Cf. Grant Osborne, *Hermeneutical Spiral*, esp. p. 324.

[17]For a commendable instance of an awareness and acknowledgment of their personal limitations, cf. Piper and Grudem, *Recovering*, 84: "We have our personal predispositions, and have no doubt been influenced by all the genetic and environmental constraints of our past and present. The history of exegesis does not encourage us that we will have the final word on this issue, and we hope we are not above correction."

[18]Cf. Elizabeth Achtemeier, "Why God is Not Mother," *Christianity Today* 37/9 (1993): 16–23.

states at the outset of her essay what she considers to be the general evangelical consensus:

> The Scriptures *clearly proclaim* that both female and male are made in the image of God (Gen. 1:27), that husband and wife are to join flesh in a marital union of *mutual helpfulness* (Gen. 2:18), that the ancient enmity between the sexes *and the subservience of women* are *a result of human sin* (Gen. 3), that *such enmity and subservience have been overcome* by the death and resurrection of Jesus Christ (Gal. 3:28), and that all women and men are called equally to discipleship in the service of their risen Lord. The Scriptures further show that our Lord *consistently treated women as equals* and *that the New Testament churches could have women as their leaders.*[19]

However, except for the statements that both female and male are made in the image of God and that women and men are equally called to discipleship, all of the above assertions, far from representing an evangelical consensus, are strongly disputed.[20] What, according to Achtemeier, the Scriptures "clearly proclaim" are in fact Achtemeier's own interpretive conclusions.

At times ambiguous wordings conceal the actual thrust of the author's views. Is the phrasing used in Gen 2:18 best rendered as "mutual helpfulness"? Whatever the term "helper" may denote, it is *the woman* who is said to be *the man's* helper and not vice versa (cf. 1 Cor 11:9). What does Achtemeier mean by her contention that Jesus treated women "as equals"? She cannot mean "equal *in every respect*," including women's being fellow-Messiahs. At the same time, she seems to argue for more than simply contending that Jesus treated women with respect and dignity. Achtemeier's point presumably is that Jesus treated women as "equal *to men.*" But by wording her contention ambiguously she seems to allow deliberately for a double meaning of the term "equal." And how does Achtemeier define the term "leaders" in her final assertion? Would she include pastors and teaching and ruling elders in this definition? If so, she can hardly point to an evangelical consensus on this issue.

Finally, by subsuming both the enmity and "subservience" (another ambiguous term) of women under the consequences of human sin that were "overcome" in Christ, Achtemeier misleadingly suggests that this is

---

[19]Ibid., 17. Emphasis added.

[20]Cf., e.g., Thiessen, "Hermeneutic," 197: "In particular there is lack of consensus concerning the effect of the fall upon the relationship. Whether hierarchy within the marital relationship is of the created order and hence universal, or whether it was the result of the curse and hence removed in the order of redemption, is still a matter of contention."

the only interpretation allowed by the scriptural data. Is Achtemeier
inadequately aware of her own presuppositions? Is she deliberately using
ambiguous language in order to disguise them? Or does she not mention
alternative interpretations for other reasons? In any case, her article is a
fine example of the power of presuppositions and the importance of
acknowledging one's own preconceived notions as well as those of
others.[21]

Generally, the practice of seeking to substantiate a theological point by
way of appeal to "hard" lexical, morphological, or syntactical data when
the available evidence itself seems far from conclusive may reveal a selective appraisal of the data which may be a result of an interpreter's conscious or unrecognized presuppositions.[22]

Lack of Balance in Hermeneutical Methodology

In principle, most students of the New Testament gender passages would
probably agree that the process of interpreting a biblical passage should
include the following components: an identification of the book's genre, a
reconstruction of the historical and cultural background of a document,
lexical and syntactical studies, and a survey of the passage's literary context
and the flow of the argument. However, interpreters do not always live up
to their best hermeneutical intentions. As the examples below will attempt
to demonstrate, a lack of balance in hermeneutical methodology (i.e., the
giving of inadequate weight to one element of the hermeneutical process at
the expense of other components) accounts for varying degrees of distor-
tion in interpreters' exegetical results.

With regard to balance in hermeneutical methodology, the important
questions are: (1) What is the *relative weight* given to the various elements
of the interpretive process by an interpreter? (2) Which of these factors is
judged decisive by a given author? And (3) what *criteria* are used to arrive
at one's judgment among alternative interpretive options?

For example, an interpretation of 1 Tim 2:8–15, conducted properly,
should incorporate the use of all of the hermeneutical procedures listed

---

[21]Cf. also the positive example of the acknowledged presuppositions of
Elisabeth Schüssler-Fiorenza, "Toward a Feminist Biblical Hermeneutics: Biblical
Interpretation and Liberation Theology," *Readings in Moral Theology IV: The
Use of Scripture in Moral Theology* (ed. C. E. Curran and R. A. McCormick;
Ramsey, NJ: Paulist, 1984), 376.

[22]Cf. regarding this the classic work by James Barr, *Semantics of Biblical
Language* (Oxford: University Press, 1961).

above in proper balance. What is the genre of the Pastorals? Granted that it is an occasional writing, does that necessarily mean that the letter cannot contain any injunctions of permanent validity? What is the most probable historical-cultural background for 1 Tim 2:8–15?[23] What are significant words or important syntactical constructions that need to be studied? And what is the passage's function in its immediate and larger contexts? Ideally, the results of these various analyses are properly related in order to arrive at a balanced interpretation of the passage. However, one's overall interpretation will only be as strong as its weakest link. An improper emphasis on one element in the interpretive process or a wrong judgment in one area of study will weaken, if not invalidate, one's entire interpretation.

Thus a given writer may give preeminence to lexical study. George W. Knight, finding no instances of αὐθεντεῖν with a negative connotation in extrabiblical literature, believes he can exclude the possibility that the term can take on a negative connotation in any imaginable context.[24] However, while the lack of extant references to that effect may suggest a certain (some might say high) *plausibility* of Knight's thesis, it seems much harder, if not impossible, to prove the *impossibility* of a term's taking on a certain connotation in a given context.

Other cases of an imbalanced hermeneutical procedure may be treatments that place undue emphasis on word studies. Especially the recent extensive interchange on the meaning of κεφαλή in the New Testament and especially in Eph 5:21–33 comes to mind.[25] Most would agree that there is some value to the study of a term's usage in extrabiblical Greek literature. But these efforts need to be placed in proper perspective and their limitations recognized. Specifically, while such a survey may help

---

[23]Note that it is not enough merely to reconstruct the general milieu of a given area. What needs to be demonstrated is the plausibility, even probability, that a given background is relevant for the writing of the respective biblical document. See further the discussion of the improper use of background data below.

[24]Cf. Knight, "Role Relationship," 18, n. 1. Cf. also Knight's article, "Αὐθεντέω in Reference to Women in 1 Tim 2:12," *NTS* 30 (1984): 143–57.

[25]Cf. the interchange between Wayne Grudem, "Does *kephalē* ('Head') Mean 'Source' or 'Authority Over' in Greek Literature? A Survey of 2,336 Examples," *TrinJ* 6 NS (1985): 38–59; Richard S. Cervin, "Does *kephalē* Mean 'Source' or 'Authority over' in Greek Literature? A Rebuttal," *TrinJ* 10 NS (1989): 85–112; and Wayne Grudem, "The Meaning of *kephalē* ('Head'): A Response to Recent Studies," *TrinJ* 11 NS (1990): 3–72. Cf. also the recent article by Joseph Fitzmyer, "*Kephalē* in I Corinthians 11:3," *Int* 47 (1993): 52–59, siding with Grudem (for further bibliographical references, Fitzmyer, "*Kephalē*," 57–58, n. 2).

determine the term's range of meaning, ultimately the use of κεφαλή in the context at hand will be decisive.

To preclude misunderstandings, it should be emphasized once again that word studies are indeed helpful since they set general parameters for what words can be expected to mean in various contexts. However, the issue addressed here is not the value of word studies *themselves* but a (false) confidence that they all but settle a term's meaning before one has seriously looking for intertextual reference points of a given passage. This confidence, of course, is rarely expressed explicitly. But it seems often *implied* in the relative weight assigned to word studies in certain writers' discussions of a gender passage in relation to their study of intertextual reference points in the book under consideration. For example, in the view of this writer, recent discussion of Eph 5:21-33 has placed too much emphasis on the meaning of the word κεφαλή *in extrabiblical literature* and comparatively not enough attention has been given to the text and other uses of κεφαλή *in Ephesians.*

Specifically, in one's interpretation of Eph 5:21-33, one may profitably consult Eph 1:21-23, where word clusters and concepts similar to Eph 5:21-33 are found (cf. ὑποτάσσω, κεφαλή, ἐκκλεσία, σῶμα). Likewise, Eph 4:15-16 surely should be considered. This is not to suggest that the use of κεφαλή, even in the same letter, is rigidly uniform.[26] The point is simply that one should immerse oneself in the theology of a given writer (in the present case, the author of Ephesians). Thus, on balance, in the study of the use of κεφαλή in Eph 5:21-33 the ultimate emphasis should be placed on the contexts and conceptual interrelationships in the same book, with word studies in extrabiblical literature providing a helpful framework for contextual exegesis. But at times, when reading articles on gender issues in which word studies are prominently featured, one gets the impression that these writers believe the work has essentially been completed when all that has been done is a setting of some basic parameters, with the major exegetical and biblical-theological work still to be accomplished.

When engaging in literary-theological analysis, contextual and syntactical factors should be carefully balanced with lexical considerations. This can be illustrated in the case of 1 Tim 2:12. Word studies of the term αὐθεντεῖν ("to have or exercise authority") in extrabiblical literature (1 Tim 2:12 is the only instance where the word is used in the New Testa-

---

[26]Cf. Edmund P. Clowney, "The Biblical Theology of the Church," in *The Church in the Bible and the World* (ed. D. A. Carson; Grand Rapids: Baker, 1987), 54.

ment) are able to supply a range of possible meanings. As one considers the term's meaning in its specific context in 1 Tim 2:12, one should seek to determine the *probable* meaning of αὐθεντεῖν with the help of contextual and syntactical studies.

Contextually, it is apparent that 1 Tim 2:11–12 is framed by the phrase "in quietness" or "in silence" (ἐν ἡσυχίᾳ), while "teaching" (διδάσκειν) and "exercising authority" (αὐθεντεῖν) in verse 12 correspond to "learning" (μανθανέτω) and "in full submission" (ἐν πάσῃ ὑποταγῇ) in verse 11.[27] This juxtaposition already suggests that αὐθεντεῖν means "to have or exercise authority" rather than "to usurp authority," as has been suggested by some.[28] Recent lexical analyses have confirmed this interpretation.[29] Moreover, the question may be asked whether the syntax of the passage helps to clarify further the meaning of αὐθεντεῖν in 1 Tim 2:12.[30] The following syntactical considerations may be relevant:

(1) What is the relationship between "teach" (διδάσκειν) and "have authority" (αὐθεντεῖν) in 1 Tim 2:12?

(2) What kind of connection is indicated by the word οὐδέ ("nor") that binds διδάσκειν and αὐθεντεῖν together?

(3) How close is the connection between the two terms in the light of the fact that intervening words separate them?

(4) What significance should be given to the fact that the infinitive διδάσκειν is placed first in the sentence and comes before the

---

[27]Contra Andrew C. Perriman, who argues that verse 12 is parenthetical ("What Eve Did, What Women Shouldn't Do: The Meaning of Αὐθεντέω in 1 Timothy 2:12," *TynBul* 44 [1993]: 129–30, 139–40).

[28]Cf. especially Philip Barton Payne, "Libertarian Women in Ephesus: A Response to Douglas J. Moo's Article, '1 Timothy 2:11–15: Meaning and Significance,' " *TrinJ* 2 NS (1981): 169–97; and id., "οὐδέ in 1 Timothy 2:12" (paper read at the 1988 annual meeting of the Evangelical Theological Society). Cf. also John R. Stott, *Decisive Issues Facing Christians Today* (Old Tappan, NJ: Revell, 1990), 269, 277–80; Carroll D. Osburn, *"Authenteo* (1 Timothy 2:12)," *ResQ* 25 (1982): 1–12; Johannes P. Louw and Eugene A. Nida, *Greek-English Lexicon of the New Testament Based on Semantic Domains* (New York: United Bible Societies), 1:474; and the KJV and the NEB.

[29]Cf. especially the extensive study by H. Scott Baldwin, "A Difficult Word: αὐθεντέω in 1 Timothy 2:12," Chap. 3 and App. 2 in *Women in the Church: A Fresh Analysis of 1 Timothy 2:11–15* (ed. Andreas J. Köstenberger, Thomas R. Schreiner, and H. Scott Baldwin; Grand Rapids: Baker, 1995).

[30]Cf. especially Douglas J. Moo, "1 Timothy 2:11–15: Meaning and Significance," *TrinJ* 1 NS (1980): 62–83.

finitive verb (ἐπιτρέπω, "I permit") which governs it?[31]

While lexical analysis can provide the basic parameters for a term's meaning (i.e. its range of meaning), contextual and syntactical studies may be able to provide further help for the interpretation of a difficult Pauline gender passage. With regard to the syntactical questions posited above, detailed analyses of the New Testament and extrabiblical Greek literature conducted by the present writer have shown that διδάσκειν and αὐθεντεῖν are linked in 1 Tim 2:12 by the coordinating conjunction οὐδέ in a way that requires them to share either a positive or negative force. Thus 1 Tim 2:12 could either be rendered as "I do not permit a woman to teach nor to exercise authority over a man" (both terms share a positive force) or "I do not permit a woman to teach *error* nor to *usurp* a man's authority" (both terms share a negative force). Moreover, since διδάσκειν in the Pastorals always has a positive force (cf. 1 Tim 4:11; 6:2; and 2 Tim 2:2), αὐθεντεῖν, too, should be expected to have a positive force in 1 Tim 2:12 so that the rendering "I do not permit a woman to teach nor to *exercise authority* over a man" is required. Other instances of διδάσκειν in the Pastorals indicate that if a negative connotation or content is intended, the word ἑτεροδιδάσκαλειν or other contextual qualifiers are used (cf. 1 Tim 1:3-4; 6:3; Tit 1:9-14).

Thus it has been demonstrated in the case of the interpretation of 1 Tim 2:12 that a balanced use of various hermeneutical tools can best supply solid exegetical results. Of course, to the lexical, contextual, and syntactical studies similar analyses of the Pastorals' genre and the historical-cultural background of 1 Timothy (and specifically of 2:8-15) should be added. The hermeneutical questions of normativity versus relativity and of the contemporary application of the passage should also be addressed.[32]

---

[31]For a detailed treatment of the syntax of 1 Tim 2:12, cf. my "Syntactical Background Studies to 1 Timothy 2.12 in the New Testament and Extrabiblical Greek Literature," in *Discourse Analysis and Other Topics in Biblical Greek* (ed. Stanley E. Porter and D. A. Carson; JSNTSup 113; Sheffield: JSOT, 1995), 156-79; and Chap. 4 in *Women and the Church.* The material was originally presented at the ETS and SBL annual meetings in San Francisco in November 1992. Only a brief synopsis of the results of this study can be given here.

[32]Cf. the various chapters in the volume *Women and the Church,* to which reference has been made in the previous note.

Underrating the Importance of the Use of the OT in the NT[33]

There is general agreement regarding what the relevant passages on gender issues in the New Testament are. The references usually listed are 1 Cor 11:2-16; 14:33b-36; Gal 3:28; Eph 5:21-33; Col 3:18-19; 1 Tim 2:8-15; and 1 Pet 3:1-7.[34] To this may be added a number of instances in the Gospels where Jesus relates to or teaches regarding women.[35] It is also commonly recognized that Genesis 1-3 is a foundational passage for the gender passages of the New Testament.[36] It seems, however, that more could be done in studying the exact way in which Genesis 1-3 is used in the respective New Testament gender passages.[37]

Consider, for example, the following relationships between Genesis and the Pauline gender passages:

---

[33]It has been suggested that it may be better to entitle this section "Underrating *or Overrating* the Importance of the Use of the Old Testament in the New Testament." However, in the opinion of this writer, it seems hard to *overrate* this element in the interpretation of gender passages in the New Testament (see the discussion below). However, as a survey of the recent literature on New Testament gender passages indicates, the fallacy committed much more frequently is indeed that of not giving the New Testament writer's use of an Old Testament passage the weight it appears to deserve.

[34]See Osborne, "Hermeneutics and Women," 337; Piper and Grudem, *Recovering*; Mickelsen, *Women*.

[35]See further the discussion of *Isolationist Exegesis* below.

[36]See especially the excellent article by Raymond C. Ortlund, Jr., "Male-Female Equality and Male Headship: Gen 1-3," in Piper and Grudem, *Recovering*, 95-112.

[37]But cf. the articles by A. T. Lincoln, "The Use of the Old Testament in Ephesians," *JSNT* 14 (1982): 16-57, and A. T. Hanson, "The Use of the Old Testament in the Pastoral Epistles," *IBS* 3 (1981): 203-19 which deal, albeit incidentally, with the use of the Old Testament in some of the gender passages in the New Testament. In departure from the usual procedure in this essay, no direct effort will be made to present specific instances in the literature on New Testament gender passages where this fallacy is committed. Rather, in the light of the significant complexity of the issue of Paul's use of Genesis 1-3 when dealing with gender issues, a series of questions will be raised that should be dealt with in order to avoid the fallacy under consideration, i.e. an underrating of the importance of the use of the Old Testament in the New.

Table 6: Old Testament References in New Testament Gender Passages

NT passage	*OT reference or allusion*
1 Cor 11:2–16 (cf. 14:33b–36)	Gen 2:18, 21–23
Gal 3:28	Gen 1:27
Eph 5:21–33 (par. Col 3:18–19)	Gen 2:24
1 Tim 2:8–15 (cf. 3:1–5)	Gen 2:7, 21–22; 3:1–6

Evangelical hermeneutics affirms the significance of authorial intention in determining meaning. If one seeks to understand the Pauline gender passages with regard to authorial intent, one must not take lightly the fact that Paul in virtually every instance refers to one or the other passage from Genesis 1–3. This, as noted above, has of course not gone unnoticed. However, fundamental hermeneutical questions remain to be asked and answered.

First, regarding authorial intention: What does this consistent reference to some aspect of Genesis 1–3 reveal about authorial intention? That is to say, why did Paul refer or allude to Genesis? Did he do so simply to establish a connection with antecedent Scripture? Did he resort to "prooftexting" to bolster his arguments? Did he use Genesis merely as illustrative material? Did he believe in the authority of the Old Testament Scriptures and use them to establish equally authoritative New Testament principles? Or did he have any other purposes in mind? How did he craft his arguments?

Second, regarding reader response and the dynamics of the communicative context: How did Paul want his references to Genesis to be received by the recipients of their correspondence? How did he desire his audience to respond? What was his readers' perception of scriptural authority? What were these readers' perceptions of apostolic authority, especially in regard to Paul's interpretation and use of the Old Testament? How were those writings in fact received and responded to? What impact did Paul's use of the Old Testament have, especially compared with the impact his teachings on gender issues would have had without reference to the Old Testament?

Of course, this question is a hypothetical one. Still, it is a legitimate question to ask. One should face the fact that the Old Testament, particularly the opening chapters of Genesis, is commonly referred to when Paul deals with gender issues. This procedure should be understood in relation to the possibility that Paul might have used other points of reference or grounds of appeal, such as a direct reference to their contemporary context, community standards, their own personal views, or other forms of argumentation. While these alternative procedures are not completely absent (cf. 1 Cor 11:2, 16), one must give proper weight to the fact that Paul commonly referred to the fundamental passages in Genesis 1–3 as his ultimate reference point in his respective contemporary contexts.[38]

Third, regarding the text itself: What does the text say explicitly, especially in connection with Old Testament references? Does Paul himself give an Old Testament principle as the reason for his argument in a certain contemporary context, as he does in 1 Tim 2:13 and 14? What is the relationship between references to the Old Testament and to contemporary practice or community standards? Are those reference points of equal weight and authority and thus to be placed side by side or is one more important than the other? Does the contemporary context ever override Old Testament principles? Or is the Old Testament principle the fundamental ground of appeal, with contemporary practice as a corroborating aspect? How the questions posed above are answered will largely determine the final outcome of an interpreter's historical exegesis as well as her contemporary application.

There seem to be instances where Paul makes the whole force of his argument rest on principles derived from the Old Testament. In 1 Tim 2:8–15, he draws significance from both the historical sequence of the creation of man and woman (v. 13; cf. also 1 Cor 11:8) and from the way in which the historical fall of man occurred, i.e. by a reversal of the created order (v. 14).[39] Finally, by way of synecdoche, Paul assures his readers that

---

[38]Regarding 1 Cor 11:16, see the recent article by Troels Engberg-Pedersen, "1 Corinthians 11:16 and the Character of Pauline Exhortation," *JBL* 110 (1991): 679–89. Engberg-Pedersen argues that Paul does not want to be contentious and thus leaves the decision of what to do about head coverings up to the Corinthians themselves. This rather unconventional conclusion aside, Endberg-Pedersen's article is representative of much recent scholarship in focusing his interest on rhetorical criticism to the extent that he completely fails to address the references to the Old Testament found in the passage he discusses. A balanced hermeneutical consideration should do both.

[39]The introductory γάρ ("for") can be simply explanatory or illustrative, or give the reason or logical grounds for Paul's injunction. Walter L. Liefeld and Ruth A. Tucker *(Daughters of the Church: Women in Ministry from New Testament Times to the Present* [Grand Rapids: Zondervan, 1987], 461) seem to lean toward taking the conjunction in the former sense, following Payne ("Response," 175–77). But cf. the arguments for the latter force given by Moo ("Rejoinder," 202–204), who notes that the explanatory use of γάρ is not only quite rare, but that it makes little sense in the context of 1 Tim 2:12–14. He shows that the movement in Paul's writings from command or prohibition to the *reason* for the command or prohibition is common. Such a construction appears twenty-one times in the Pastorals alone (1 Tim 3:13; 4:5, 8, 16; 5:4, 11, 15; 2 Tim 1:7;

the woman will be saved "by the bearing of children," i.e. by adhering to her God-ordained role.[40]

The interpretive conclusion and implication Paul draws from the narrative accounts in Genesis 2 and 3 is that both creation order and fall have in fact abiding significance for male-female relationships.[41] For the man, to have been created first means that he has first responsibility for the stewardship entrusted to him by God. The role reversal at the fall is a further argument, according to Paul, that the final responsibility and authority legitimately rest with the man. Thus Paul in 1 Tim 2:8–15 draws from the Old Testament narratives abiding principles for male-female relationships and applies them to his contemporary context. It seems that Paul's appeal to the Old Testament as well as his own apostolic office were, in his mind, definitive, at least in the context at hand.[42]

Probably the most difficult passage in this regard is 1 Cor 11:2–16, since reference is made both to the Old Testament and to contemporary practice.[43] The way man and woman were created (cf. Gen 2:22) as well as the purpose for which they were created (cf. Gen 2:18) form the basic framework for Paul's reasoning (vv. 8–9). According to Paul, the creation

---

2:7, 16; 3:6; 4:3, 6, 10, 11, 15; Titus 1:10; 2:11; 3:3, 9, 12).

[40]See Thomas R. Schreiner, "An Interpretation of 1 Timothy 2:9–15: A Dialogue with Scholarship," in *Women in the Church: A Fresh Analysis of 1 Timothy 2:9–15* (ed. Andreas J. Köstenberger et al.; Grand Rapids: Baker, 1995), 151.

[41]In the context of 1 Tim 2:8–15, Paul's application is to male-female relationships in the church.

[42]Note the rather categorical "I do not permit" (οὐκ ἐπιτρέπω) in 1 Tim 2:12. Note in this context, and with regard to the interpretation of 1 Tim 2:8–15 as a whole, the interchange between Douglas J. Moo, "1 Timothy 2:11–15: Meaning and Significance," 62–83, and Philip B. Payne, "Libertarian Women in Ephesus: A Response to Douglas J. Moo's Article, '1 Timothy 2:11–15: Meaning and Significance,' " *TrinJ* 2 NS (1981): 169–97, and Moo's response to Payne, "The Interpretation of 1 Timothy 2:11–15: A Rejoinder," *TrinJ* 2 NS (1981): 198–222. The term ἐπιτρέπω is discussed in Moo's first article (pp. 65–66), Payne's response (pp. 170–73), and Moo's rejoinder (pp. 199–200). Regardless of the question whether permanent validity of Paul's injunction can be construed from the wording οὐκ ἐπιτρέπω alone, it seems clear that Paul wrote with the consciousness of one who had been commissioned as an apostle with concomitant authority (1 Tim 1:1) and thus would have perceived his injunction to be authoritative at least in this present context. His use of the Old Testament should also be seen from that perspective.

[43]For a survey of the relevant issues and pertinent bibliographical references, cf. Thomas R. Schreiner, "Head Coverings, Prophecies and the Trinity: 1 Corinthians 11:2–16," in *Recovering*, 124–39.

narrative clearly indicates "that the husband is the head of (over) his wife" (cf. v. 3). Perhaps it is appropriate here to distinguish between the principle inherent in the way man and woman were created and the way in which Paul desired this principle to be expressed in the churches of his day (cf. vv. 2 and 16). As in other instances (cf. 1 Corinthians 7), Paul's authority does not rest exclusively in himself but is tied to the basis for the respective teaching invoked by Paul. The Old Testament passages referred to in 1 Cor 11:8-9 establish absolute parameters; Paul's authority regarding the application of this principle, while extending to the churches subject to his apostolic jurisdiction, does not necessarily extend to churches in other cultures and times. In any case, the important difference between 1 Cor 11:2-16 and 1 Tim 2:8-15 is that in the latter passage it seems impossible to separate the principle (i.e. the woman's functional subordination to the man in creation) from the way in which this principle is to be applied (i.e. for woman not to teach nor to exercise authority over man in the context of a congregation gathered for worship); neither are there any contextual cues limiting the application of 1 Tim 2:12 to the circumstances at hand.

The question of authorial intent has great significance for the proper interpretation of the passages in the New Testament that cite the Old. Paul, Peter, and their fellow-apostles perceived the Old Testament, as well as the evolving New Testament writings, as authoritative.[44] Thus it can be argued that when those writers quoted the Old Testament in their arguments, they did so because they were considering it to be authoritative. Furthermore, the canonical process itself guarded and selected those writings of the apostolic era which had continuing value because they were able to transcend contemporary situations. Now it should be acknowledged that the inclusion of a book into the canon does not imply that this book transcends its original occasion *in every respect*. But one should at least consider the issues of apostolic authority and canonicity in the interpretation of the New Testament gender passages—and that has rarely been done in recent discussion. To be sure, to disregard the results of the

---

[44]Paul writes in 2 Tim 3:16 that "All Scripture is God-breathed and profitable for teaching, reproof, correction, and training in righteousness." Peter notes about Paul's own writings, "our beloved brother Paul . . . wrote to you, as also in all his letters, speaking in them of these things, in which are some things hard to understand, which the untaught and unstable distort, *as they do also the rest of the Scriptures* . . ." (2 Pet 3:15b-16). Furthermore, Peter, Paul, and John also thought *of themselves* (i.e. of their own writings) as authoritative (cf. John 21:24; 1 Cor 4:1; 2 Cor 10:10-11 with 11:2-3; and the openings of the Pauline and Petrine correspondences).

canonical decisions entirely is not impossible, but it does remove one from the stream of historic Christianity.

Moreover, since the apostles were given a unique role by God in the progress of formulating the New Testament, the contemporary interpreter should submit to the apostolic interpretation of the Old Testament where such is available.[45] Evangelicals should be prepared to assign a proper role to tradition. Apostolic tradition is given a very positive role in the New Testament. The current trend towards individualism and subjectivism in interpretation testifies to the imbalance between the contemporary interpreter's judgment and his link with apostolic tradition. Rather than islands adrift on a sea of relativity, contemporary interpretive communities should be branches of the tree of apostolic tradition.

Improper Use of Background Data

While certain writers appear to devote too little attention to background matters, others allow their own reconstruction of the ancient cultural milieu to control almost entirely their exegesis of a given gender passage. An example of the latter extreme is the work by Richard Clark and Catherine Clark Kroeger on 1 Tim 2:12.[46] As Yarbrough rightly contends, there is virtually no basis for the existence of the gnostic heresy that the Kroegers allege forms the background to 1 Tim 2:12.[47] Throughout their book, the Kroegers are so predominantly concerned with the ancient cultural milieu supposedly underlying 1 Tim 2:12 that there is little room in their treatment for contextual exegesis.

---

[45]The opposite attitude to a submission to the apostolic interpretation of a given Old Testament passage is the effort to interpret the reference independently by the modern interpreter, with the subsequent attempt to make the New Testament conform to one's own interpretation of the Old Testament passage. For this kind of approach, cf. Joy L. E. Fleming, *A Rhetorical Analysis of Genesis 2–3 with Implications for a Theology of Man and Woman* (Ph.D. diss.; Strasburg, 1987). Fleming variously ignores or distorts the context of the Pauline arguments and theology to substitute her own views based on an independent interpretation of the Old Testament.

[46]Cf. Richard Clark and Catherine Clark Kroeger, *I Suffer Not a Woman: Rethinking 1 Tim 2:11–15 in Light of Ancient Evidence* (Grand Rapids: Baker, 1992) and the reviews by Robert W. Yarbrough, "I Suffer Not a Woman: a Review Essay," *Presbyterion* 18 (1992): 25–33; id., "New Light on Paul and Women?" *Christianity Today* 37/11 (1993): 68–69; and Albert Wolters, "Review: *I Suffer Not a Woman*," *Calvin Theological Journal* 28 (1993): 208–13.

[47]Cf. Yarbrough, "New Light," 68.

Moreover, not only do the Kroegers use late sources to establish the background of a New Testament writing, there also remains widespread disagreement regarding the interpretation of the available evidence. For example, Steven Baugh has recently argued that "there is not the slightest evidence that there was a feminist movement at Ephesus."[48] He contends that the worship of goddesses alone does not constitute sufficient evidence for the presence of feminism in a given society.[49] These findings sharply contradict the Kroegers' assertions, also made by other recent interpreters.[50] In any case, a general reconstruction of the Ephesian milieu in the first century CE must not be used indiscriminately in one's reconstruction of the circumstances prevailing in the Ephesian church that occasioned the writing of 1 Timothy.

Now it is one thing to argue that 1 Tim 2:12, for example, no longer applies due to changed cultural circumstances, or even that the author of that passage inconsistently and wrongly restricts the ministry of women.[51] It is quite another issue to reinterpret the textual evidence by selective use of background data.[52] The procedure followed by the Kroegers focuses on what may at best be implicit in Paul's reasoning at the expense of the explicit argumentation and wording of the text.[53] Specifically, Paul explicitly adduces two reasons from the Old Testament creation account to substantiate his injunction regarding women's teaching of men (cf. 1

----

[48]Cf. Steven M. Baugh, "Feminism at Ephesus: 1 Timothy 2:12 in Historical Context," *Outlook* 42/5 (May 1992): 10. See now Baugh's recent article, "The Apostle among the Amazons," *WTJ* 56 (1994): 156-71.

[49]Baugh, "Feminism at Ephesus," 9.

[50]Cf. especially Kroegers, *I Suffer Not a Woman.*

[51]Cf. Osborne, "Hermeneutics and Women," 337-52; Paul K. Jewett, *Man as Male and Female* (Grand Rapids: Eerdmans, 1975), 112-13, 119.

[52]Besides the work by the Kroegers, see also John Temple Bristow, *What Paul Really Said About Women. An Apostle's Liberating Views on Equality in Marriage, Leadership, and Love* (San Francisco: Harper & Row, 1988).

[53]Cf. David M. Scholer, "1 Timothy 2:9-15 and the Place of Women in the Church's Ministry," in Mickelsen, *Women,* 193-219; id., "Women in the Church's Ministry. Does 1 Timothy 2:9-15 Help or Hinder?" *Daughters of Sarah* 16/4 (1990): 7-12. Cf. also S. H. Gritz, *Paul, Women Teachers, and the Mother Goddess at Ephesus. A Study of 1 Timothy 2:9-15 in Light of the Religious and Cultural Milieu of the First Century* (Lanham, MD: University Press of America, 1991); Catherine C. Kroeger, "Women in the Church: A Classicist's View of 1 Tim 2:11-15," *Journal of Biblical Equality* 1 (1989): 3-31; Kroegers, *I Suffer Not a Woman.* Of these writers, only Gritz considers the Old Testament background. The authors are united in giving priority to the presumed religious and cultural background of 1 Tim 2:8-15.

Tim 2:13-14). The Kroegers, however, hardly discuss these Old Testament references, while they give ample attention to their own reconstruction of this passage's contemporary background.

On the other side of the spectrum, it is sometimes alleged by those who emphasize the importance of their reconstructed historical-cultural background for the interpretation of a given gender passage that interpreters who view that reference as indicating a permanent universal injunction have *by necessity* no regard for the passage's background. Scholer, for example, uses 1 Tim 2:15 as a launching pad for reconstructing the contemporary context of 1 Timothy. He argues that this verse is the climax of the argument and infers behind the verse a certain kind of heresy. At the same time Scholer charges those who in his view give insufficient consideration to 1 Tim 2:15 with "irresponsible and symptomatic neglect of reading texts in their contexts."[54]

However, while this charge may apply to certain writers, it is certainly an inappropriate one for *any* interpretation of 1 Tim 2:12 that considers the passage to have normative character. It is possible to give adequate consideration to the contemporary context of 1 Timothy and still find Paul's injunction universal and permanently binding for the Church.[55] As has already been noted, the occasional nature of a writing by itself is insufficient to establish the non-normativity of a given teaching. To insist fallaciously that occasionality equals cultural relativity renders in the ultimate analysis any divine revelation to humanity impossible, since such revelation by necessity occurs in a cultural, circumstantial context. Thus the question is not whether a given teaching is *occasional* in nature but whether it is *limited to the occasion* by the biblical writer or other textual or contextual factors.

Again, the neglect to consider adequately a text's explicit argumentation in favor of a preoccupation with questions of cultural background lacks balance. It is certainly appropriate to seek to illumine a text with relevant background information. But to all but ignore explicit textual material and to allow the text to be superseded by background information fails to meet the standard of a hermeneutical methodology that properly employs *all* the tools at its disposal and does so with proper balance.

---

[54]Cf. Scholer, "1 Timothy 2:9-15," 195.

[55]Cf. the contention by Douglas J. Moo in *Recovering*, 193: "It is surely not enough simply to suggest local or cultural factors that may restrict the application of a text, for with such a methodology any teaching in Scripture could be dismissed . . . we are justified in requiring very good reasons *from the text itself* to limit the application of this text in any way."

An Arbitrary Distinction between "Paradigm Passages"
and "Passages with Limited Application"

A hermeneutical fallacy that is quite common in the discussion of gender passages in the New Testament is the arbitrary distinction between passages conveying a "general principle" and those of "limited application." Specifically, Gal 3:28 is often viewed as establishing Paul's general parameters and thus providing the paradigm into which "passages of limited application" such as 1 Tim 2:8-15 or 1 Cor 11:2-16 and 14:33b-36 have to be fitted.

As Osborne writes, "Feminists are quick to argue that Gal 3:28 is the theological and hermeneutical key to the issue."[56] "On that basis," Osborne continues, "the Galatians statement, 'there is no male and female,' becomes the *crux interpretum*, and women in the new dispensation are completely equal to men."[57] On the other hand, those who do not share the view that Gal 3:28 is the paradigm for the interpretation of all the gender passages in the New Testament are at times said to "de-emphasize the importance of the verse for understanding male and female relations in this age."[58]

Indeed, as Snodgrass charges, "For them, it is not the primary passage for discussing the relation of male and female. In fact, it is not even a key text. Focus is usually placed instead on 1 Corinthians 11 and 14 and 1 Timothy 2."[59] Snodgrass concludes, "I view 1 Corinthians 14:33b-36 and 1 Timothy 2:11-15 as statements necessitated by specific problems in Corinth and Ephesus, respectively, and as shaped by an ancient culture.

---

[56]Cf. Osborne, "Hermeneutics and Women," 348, referring to Hardesty and Scanzoni, *All We're Meant To Be*, 18-19.

[57]Ibid. Note that Osborne is using the expression *crux interpretum* in a novel way. The term usually is taken to refer to an interpretive crux, i.e. a passage that is extremely difficult to interpret in its own right and context. Osborne, however, uses *crux interpretum* in the sense that how one takes Gal 3:28 becomes rather important in the entire debate.

[58]Cf. Klyne R. Snodgrass, "Galatians 3:28: Conundrum or Solution?" in Mickelsen, *Women*, 164-65.

[59]Ibid. Snodgrass cites Richard N. Longenecker, *New Testament Social Ethics for Today* (Grand Rapids: Eerdmans, 1984), 84-86 and Scott Bartchy, "Power, Submission, and Sexual Identity among the Early Christians," *Essays in New Testament Christianity* (ed. C. Robert Wetzel; Cincinnati: Standard Publishing, 1978), 58-59 as examples of scholars who view Gal 3:28 as a normative text while texts such as 1 Corinthians 14 and 1 Timothy 2 are descriptive or deal with problems in the early church.

These texts do not become less important than Galatians 3:28, but they are less direct in their application."[60]

However, the question arises whether or not Galatians 3:28, too, could be seen as "necessitated by specific problems" in the Galatian church. Moreover, it appears that Snodgrass uses the term "necessitated" in an unduly limited sense, i.e. as meaning "limited to the instance which occasioned a teaching." It is also unclear what Snodgrass means when he calls the texts in 1 Corinthians and 1 Timothy "less direct in their application." Snodgrass also fails to provide convincing evidence that would allow one to limit the application of 1 Tim 2:12 to the Ephesian context.

It may be argued that this writer underestimates the fact that the interpretation of Gal 3:28 needs to be just as sensitive to the occasion at which the teaching was given as the interpretation of the texts Snodgrass considers "less direct in their application." Indeed, one may contend that, insofar as Paul appeals to contemporary practice, 1 Cor 11 and 14 have no direct application for today. It seems more difficult to find such qualifying or limiting factors in 1 Timothy 2. Thus one may legitimately wonder what warrants Snodgrass' inclusion of it among culturally limited passages.

But Snodgrass' statements seem restrained compared to unequivocal statements such as the following comment by W. Ward Gasque: "*Galatians 3:28 is the necessary theological starting place for any discussion on the role of women in the church*. . . . Other texts must not be used to undermine this fundamental theological affirmation."[61] Gasque also refers to F. F. Bruce who comments, "Paul states the basic principle here [Gal 3:28]; if restrictions on it are found elsewhere in the Pauline corpus, as in 1 Cor. 14:34f. . . . or 1 Tim. 2:11f., they are to be understood in relation to Gal. 3:28, and not vice versa."[62]

This decision regarding "paradigm passages" tends to predetermine one's exegetical conclusions.[63] As Gasque summarizes, "By taking

---

[60]Ibid., 180.

[61]W. Ward Gasque, "Response," in Mickelsen, *Women*, 189.

[62]Ibid., 89–90. The reference is to F. F. Bruce, *The Epistle to the Galatians* (Grand Rapids: Eerdmans, 1982), 190.

[63]It must be said in all fairness that those who uncritically assume 1 Timothy 2 to be the central New Testament teaching on gender issues likewise need to take care to substantiate this contention rather than merely asserting it. But it seems that generally writers are less aggressive in arguing that 1 Timothy 2 is a "paradigm passage" than those who assign central importance to Gal 3:28. As a matter of fact, it is often those writers focusing on Gal 3:28 who isolate 1 Timothy 2 as the only passage of its kind in the New Testament, thus dichotomizing between different kinds of gender passages of the New Testament and seeking to marginalize and relativize 1 Timothy 2. But for the reasons adduced in this section, this practice

Galatians 3:28 as the starting place for Paul's view on women, it becomes extremely difficult, if not impossible, to come to the traditionalist conclusion."[64] Interestingly, it is not just writers who argue for the cultural limitation of a passage like 1 Tim 2:8-15 who show a preference for Gal 3:28. Thus George W. Knight introduces his discussion of New Testament gender passages by contending, "The momentous words of Galatians 3:28 provide us with the framework within which any and all differences or role relationships must be seen and considered . . ."[65]

In order to resolve the tension between teachings on gender issues in the respective Pauline writings, some postulate a development in Paul's thought. According to these writers Paul, while holding to an egalitarian position at the time of writing Galatians, retreated to a more conservative position in dealing with problems at Corinth or Ephesus. Betz compares Paul's comments on gender issues in 1 Corinthians and Galatians as follows:

> 1 Corinthians is different and emphasizes the subordination of the woman. The parallel to Gal 3:28 in 1 Cor 12:13 does not contain this line [i.e. "neither male nor female"]; instead we find the woman "under man" in a hierarchy of beings (1 Cor 11:2-16). The question arises, furthermore, whether the extraordinary space given to the women's issues in 1 Corinthians . . . reflects difficulties which arose from the emancipation of the women proclaimed in Gal 3:28c. *This may imply that in 1 Corinthians Paul has retracted the Galatian position.* 1 Cor 11:11-12 may still use similar words, but in fact Paul argues in the opposite direction compared with Gal 3:28c.[66]

Betz concludes, "While Paul admits the radical implications in Galatians, he has obviously changed his position in 1 Corinthians, and it may not be accidental that the whole matter is dropped in Romans."[67] But besides the obvious negative implications these views have on issues of inerrancy, inspiration, and canonicity, one may wonder whether Betz's evaluation is based on a fundamental misreading of Gal 3:28.

Again, modern presuppositions regarding gender issues may raise their head. When Snodgrass remarks, "Being in Christ did not change a Jew into a Gentile, rather, it changed the way that Jews and Gentiles relate

---

must be rejected.

[64]Gasque, "Response," 190.

[65]Cf. Knight, *Role Relationship*, 7.

[66]Cf. Hans Dieter Betz, *Galatians: A Commentary on Paul's Letter to the Churches in Galatia* (Hermeneia; Philadelphia: Fortress, 1979), 200.

[67]Ibid., 201.

to each other," and again, "Being in Christ does not change a woman into a man any more than it changes Gentiles into Jews, but it changes the way that men and women relate to each other just as it changed the way Jews and Gentiles relate," does he represent Paul accurately or are his statements flavored by his contemporary concerns?[68] Was it really Paul's point in Gal 3:28 to address the issue of how Christ "changes the way that men and women relate to each other"? A reading of the passage in its context of chapters 3 and 4 makes this interpretation rather dubious. As the ensuing discussion details, Paul's concerns are salvation-historical rather than relating to social, racial, or gender issues as such.

Similarly, when Gasque comments, "In Galatians 3:28, Paul opens wide the door for women, as well as for Gentiles and slaves, to exercise spiritual leadership in the church,"[69] one may legitimately ask whether this is *really* Paul's point in the text's context or an implication drawn by Gasque himself. If the latter, it would be advisable to distinguish more clearly between historical exegesis and contemporary application. A failure to draw this distinction unnecessarily confuses the issues.

A hermeneutical procedure that assigns certain passages into "paradigmatic" categories and others as passages with "limited application" is highly suspect. The superimposition of a topical grid onto a cluster of "gender passages" is probably one of the major culprits for the development of such arbitrary distinctions. To use Gal 3:28 as an example, the interpreter who puts aside his interests in gender issues, at least temporarily, when approaching Gal 3:28 will discover that the verse is linked with Gal 3:16.

There Paul argues that Gen 12:7 pointed not to Abraham's *many* offsprings, but "to one [ἐφ' ἑνός] which is Christ." Thus the statement in Gal 3:28b, "For you are all one in Christ Jesus," refers back to the divine promise made to Abraham of which all believers are indiscriminately heirs. This is made clear by v. 29 which draws this exact conclusion: "And if you are Christ's, then you are Abraham's offspring, heirs according to promise."

The other important contextual reference point of Gal 3:28 is Gal 3:26. The statements in vv. 26 and 28 are parallel, as can easily be seen: "For you are all sons of God through faith in Christ Jesus" (v. 26: Πάντες γὰρ υἱοὶ θεοῦ ἐστε διὰ τῆς πίστεως ἐν Χριστῷ Ἰησοῦ) and "For you are all one in Christ Jesus" (v. 28: πάντες γὰρ ὑμεῖς εἷς ἐστε ἐν Χριστῷ

---

[68]Cf. Snodgrass, "Galatians 3:28," 176–77.
[69]Gasque, "Response," 192.

Ἰησοῦ). The two parallel elements are "sons of God" in v. 26 and "one" in v. 28. This further underscores the conclusion reached with regard to the relationship of Gal 3:28 with 3:16 and 29 above. "You are all one in Christ Jesus" means essentially, "You are all *sons of God* in Christ Jesus."[70]

In the context of the divine promise to Abraham, Paul's point is that in the one Son of the promise, Jesus Christ, all believers are indiscriminately heirs of God's promise to Abraham. There is no discrimination in that promise between Jew or Gentile, slave or free, male or female, as Paul proceeds to develop in chapter four of Galatians.

Thus an interpretation that starts with the assumption that Gal 3:28 relates directly to contemporary gender issues will have difficulty entering into Paul's argument in the context of the passage. Contrary to the assertion that Gal 3:28 contains "an unequivocal statement of absolute equality in Christ in the church" where "Paul excludes all discrimination against Gentiles, slaves or women,"[71] Gal 3:28 in fact contains the salvation-historical demonstration that the divine promise to Abraham includes Jews as well as Gentiles, slaves as well as free, and men as well as women. That is Paul's point in Gal 3:28 in the context of chapters 3 and 4, and, indeed, the whole epistle.

Of course, some insist that Paul's statements in Gal 3:28 *imply* a change in human relationships. But whether a change in human relationships is implied in Gal 3:28 or not, this does not appear to be the point Paul actually intended to make. The interpreter should take care to distinguish between authorial intention and possible implications. Moreover, it seems questionable to focus on the implications of Paul's statements to the extent that the point Paul actually intended to make all but retreats into the background.

It is also interesting that the same commentators who view Gal 3:28, a passage that is clearly part of a polemical context, as a paradigmatic passage for gender roles, tend to be the ones who seek to limit the applicability of 1 Timothy 2, a passage that is much less clearly polemical but rather seems to be self-consciously and explicitly grounded on antecedent Old Testament Scripture.

Finally, I. H. Marshall contributes a yet different, rather nuanced approach that is nevertheless not without its problems.[72] In a very helpful

_____

[70] Cf. for a similar pattern of parallelism where one phrase is explicated by the other John 3:3, 5.

[71] Gasque, "Response," 189.

[72] Cf. I. H. Marshall, "An Evangelical Approach to 'Theological Criticism,'" in *The Best in Theology Volume Three* (ed. J. I. Packer; Carol Stream, IL: Christianity Today, 1989), 45–60. The article first appeared in *Themelios*.

article that addresses many of the hermeneutical concerns dealt with in the present essay, Marshall deals with apparent theological contradictions in the New Testament. He introduces a distinction between "what a writer actually says and what may be presumed to be his real intention."[73] According to Marshall, one has to form a judgment as to "which texts are to be taken as expressing the real intention of a writer or the main thrust of the Scripture and how they are to be interpreted."[74] But no clear criteria are given. Also, the introduction of the concept of a writer's "real intention" seems rather artificial.

Marshall subsumes the teaching of the Pastorals on gender issues under "teaching which appears out of date or untrue for the church today." Arguing that the Pastorals' "refusal to allow women to teach" is a "local, situation-bound restriction," Marshall maintains that "what seems to me to be a central part of the concern of the New Testament, namely the principle expressed in Galatians 3:28, overrules it," as well as that "we do actually see women fully engaged in ministry in the New Testament itself."[75] Marshall concludes, "there is a contradiction within the New Testament message itself if this passage is judged to be normative for all time, including New Testament times."[76]

It appears that this discussion is based on Marshall's definition of "biblical authority" earlier in the same essay. Marshall writes, "When we speak of the supreme authority of Scripture, we speak of *the authority of Scripture taken as a whole* rather than of isolated texts within it. This means that we assume that Scripture as a whole is harmonious in its teaching, and therefore we can take its total message as our guide."[77] This, according to Marshall, has an important implication, "namely that isolated texts taken on their own may convey a message which is at variance with that of Scripture as a whole."[78]

Marshall recognizes that the Pastorals do not allow women to teach men (albeit the specific reference in 1 Tim 2:12 is to teaching men in the context of public worship). But Marshall's analysis is flawed on a number of counts. It is not necessary to respond in detail to Marshall's contention that the New Testament portrays women "fully engaged in ministry." Few

---

[73]Ibid., 48–50.

[74]Ibid., 50.

[75]Ibid., 58.

[76]Ibid.

[77]Ibid., 51.

[78]Ibid.

would deny this; the question is whether the New Testament elsewhere portrays women *in the capacity of overseers or pastors*. Since it does not seem to do so (even though this is, of course, hotly debated), Marshall's alleged contradiction has been resolved. The New Testament portrays women fully engaged in *ministry* but not in the role of a *public, church-recognized proclamation of the Word* so that 1 Tim 2:12 is not at odds with other parts of the New Testament.

Marshall's contention that the Pastorals are incompatible with the central principle enunciated in Gal 3:28 has already been dealt with above. By adding "it seems to me," Marshall already indicates the subjective nature of this judgment. What makes Marshall's discussion profitable is his thoroughly hermeneutical focus, a feature which in turn makes more transparent the hermeneutical foundation from which interpreters arrive at their exegetical judgments. While there may be residual presuppositions that remain unacknowledged in Marshall's analysis, he sets the example in frankly dealing with evangelical presuppositions and difficult issues such as development and diversity in the New Testament.

Isolationist Exegesis

The danger of fragmentary exegesis has already become apparent in the discussion of Betz's view of a development in Paul's thinking from an "egalitarian" position in Galatians to a "subordinationist" stance in 1 Corinthians. The pendulum has swung too far in the direction of diversity in recent scholarship. While the interpreter should avoid forced, dogmatic, or superficial harmonization, there should be at least an openness to explore the possibility that the various gender passages in the Old and the New Testament cohere and mutually inform each other.

A caricature of the various parts of the canon may look as follows. The Old Testament reflects a patriarchal approach though perhaps one that is progressive in comparison with the surrounding cultures. Jesus is the great liberator who treated women equally. Paul, on whom recently much emphasis has been placed, is variously characterized as a misogynist or, to the contrary, a champion of equality, or as one who regressed from the latter disposition to the former.

Into this state of affairs, it seems appropriate to issue a call to courage. Rather than simplistically caricaturing the different biblical writers, interpreters should set out to explore the underlying continuity among the teachings on gender issues by the Old Testament, Jesus, and Paul in his earlier and later writings. What is needed is a systematized biblical theology of manhood and womanhood that is based on a careful exegesis of the relevant passages but transcends such exegesis by integrating interpretive insights into a systematic whole.[79] Here we agree wholeheartedly with Johnston who contends, "The Bible has an overarching consistency despite its multiple theological foci. Thus, all interpretations of given texts can be productively correlated."[80]

Frequently the study of gender passages in the New Testament focuses on the Pauline epistles. However, Jesus' own example and teaching need to be given proper attention as well. As Osborne contends,

> Too often discussions on women in the church center only upon Paul and ignore the formative example of Jesus' attitude toward and use of women in his own ministry. For this reason several recent works on women and ministry have stressed Jesus' relationship with women. However, they often simply categorize Jesus and Paul as separate models and fail to note the very real correspondences that exist between the two.[81]

But how is one to relate Jesus' and Paul's teachings with one another and both to the Old Testament? Longenecker proposes a "developmental hermeneutic."[82] He enumerates four implications of such an approach: (1) the priority of redemptive over creation categories; (2) Jesus in the Gospels and the Pauline epistles as proper starting points; (3) a distinction

---

[79]An example of a good basic treatment along these lines is Werner Neuer, *Man & Woman in Christian Perspective* (Wheaton: Crossway, 1991), though much more thorough study needs to be done.

[80]Cf. Johnston, "Test Case," 31.

[81]Cf. Grant R. Osborne, "Women in Jesus' Ministry," *WTJ* 51 (1989): 259; see also this author's conclusions regarding the relationship between Jesus' and Paul's teachings on pp. 288–91. For separate studies on women in Jesus' and the early church's ministries, cf. Ben Witherington, *Women in the Ministry of Jesus* (SNTSMS 51; Cambridge: University Press, 1984); id., *Women and the Genesis of Christianity* (Cambridge: University Press, 1990); and id., *Women in the Earliest Churches* (SNTSMS 59; Cambridge: University Press, 1988).

[82]Cf. Richard N. Longenecker, "Authority, Hierarchy & Leadership Patterns in the Bible," in Mickelsen, *Women*, 80–85, and the responses to Longenecker's proposal on pp. 87–96. Cf. also the same author's essay, "On the Concept of Development in Pauline Thought," in *Perspectives on Evangelical Theology* (ed. Kennety S. Kantzer and Stanley N. Gundry; Grand Rapids: Baker, 1979), 195–207; and id., *New Testament Social Ethics for Today* (Grand Rapids: Eerdmans, 1984). See also the critique of Longenecker's "developmental hermeneutic" by Thiessen, "Hermeneutic," 203–206. Thiessen writes, "My major point of discomfort with Longenecker's proposal is the disjunction it introduces between creation and redemption and the suggestion that there is an unresolved tension in Paul's own ethical teaching that later Christians must resolve" (p. 206).

between the proclamation of gender principles and their actual implementation in the first century AD; and (4) a recognition of the effect of circumstances on Christians in the first century as they sought to implement the gospel.[83] Longenecker's burden is that contemporary interpreters "stress the redemptive notes of freedom, equality and mutuality."[84]

While his proposal has not gained widespread support, Longenecker should be commended for his effort to lay out a program for integrating the various biblical teachings on gender in a framework that is conscious of the development from the Old Testament to Jesus and to Paul. However, it remains unclear why "redemptive categories" should be given priority over "creation categories." Are these two sets of categories, whatever they may contain, necessarily in disagreement so that one has to prioritize?

Leveling the Distinction between Historical Exegesis and Modern Contextualization

The importance of maintaining a distinction between historical exegesis and modern contextualization has already become apparent in the discussion up to this point.[85] The power of presuppositions, however, tends to inject at least some elements of the modern interpreter's contemporary horizon into the interpretive process. Openness to correction by the ancient horizon of the text is required in this "hermeneutical circle" (or, hopefully, "spiral") in order for this tendency to be counteracted. In practice, as has been seen in the examples given above, the line between the ancient and the contemporary horizons is often blurred. Topical concerns with modern "gender issues" often supersede in effect biblical-theological considerations, resulting in superficial systematizations. Moreover, contemporary social and cultural concerns exert pressure on one's exegetical endeavors so that at times one may forget that modern concerns regarding gender roles in the church are not necessarily addressed directly in the various contexts where biblical teaching on male and female roles is found.

---

[83]Ibid., 81–84.

[84]Ibid., 84. The similarity between this slogan and the motto of the French revolution, "Liberté, égalité, fraternité," may be accidental.

[85]Cf. especially the discussion of the interpretation of Gal 3:28 above, under the heading, An Arbitrary Distinction between "Paradigm Passages" and "Passages with Limited Application."

Thus, having come full circle from the way in which this essay started, it is clear that the modern interpreter has to distance himself to a certain extent from his own contemporary personal or cultural concerns as he approaches the biblical passages where the issue of gender roles in the church is addressed. Foremost of all, it appears that while contemporary Western culture is preoccupied largely with sociological, economic, and psychological concerns, the New Testament, including Paul, is written primarily with a view toward biblical-theological and salvation-historical categories. What therefore is of primary interest in the present discussion on gender issues may at times be found in Paul's writings at best on the level of *implications* rather than as the primary focus of the apostle's teaching. Certain interpretations of Gal 3:28 that were discussed above may be among the best examples of this kind of reversal between ancient and contemporary priorities. A naive evolutionary perspective on the social "progress" made in Western culture may tend to elevate the modern culture over the ancient one. But it is exactly at this point that the Scriptures must be allowed to challenge contemporary developments, if indeed the Scriptures are believed to provide transcultural and permanent principles for human relationships.

For these reasons it is important not to level the distinction between historical exegesis and modern contextualization. Of course, once the interpreter has determined the authorial intention in the ancient context and reconstructed the historical message, his task still remains unfinished. While it is essential to distinguish clearly between historical exegesis and contemporary application, both are required for the process of interpretation to be complete. R. T. France calls for "the priority in biblical interpretation of what has come to be called 'the first horizon,' i.e. of understanding biblical language within its own context before we start exploring its relevance to our own concerns, and of keeping the essential biblical context in view as a control on the way we apply biblical language to current issues."[86]

If France's call were heeded, perhaps a greater consensus could be reached at least on the level of historical exegesis, i.e. what the text *meant* to its original recipients. It would then be easier to draw appropriate applications for the diverse contemporary contexts various interpreters find themselves in. Unfortunately, however, modern hermeneutics has wit-

---

[86]R. T. France, "The Church and the Kingdom of God: Some Hermeneutical Issues," in *Biblical Interpretation and the Church: The Problem of Contextualization* (ed. D. A. Carson; Nashville: Nelson, 1984), 42, quoted in Grant R. Osborne, *Hermeneutical Spiral*, 415.

nessed a radical shift toward the subjective element in interpretation. A pluralism that affirms the legitimacy of "feminist hermeneutics," "liberation hermeneutics," "African-American hermeneutics," and, it may be supposed, "white Anglo-American hermeneutics," contains within itself the seeds of a subjectivism that denies the priority of what France calls the "first horizon." The reader's response, not the author's intent, decisively shapes the interpretation of the text.[87]

Conclusion

The following hermeneutical fallacies were critiqued: (1) underestimating the power of presuppositions; (2) lack of balance in hermeneutical methodology; (3) underrating the importance of the use of the Old Testament in the New; (4) improper use of background information; (5) an arbitrary distinction between "paradigm passages" and "passages with limited application"; (6) isolationist exegesis; and (7) leveling the distinction between historical exegesis and modern contextualization. As the various examples have shown, each of these fallacies distorts an interpreter's understanding of the New Testament's gender passages. Perhaps by raising these hermeneutical issues to a conscious level this essay can make a contribution toward the avoidance of these fallacies and toward a greater degree of methodological consensus in the study of New Testament gender passages. It is hoped that even those who disagree with some parts of this essay may gain a renewed appreciation for the crucial role hermeneutics plays in the contemporary discussion of the biblical teaching on gender issues.[88]

---

[87]Cf. the two appendices in Osborne, *Hermeneutical Spiral*, 366–415. Note in this context also E. D. Hirsch's distinction between "meaning" (i.e. what the text *says*) and "significance" (i.e. what the text *means to me today*) in *Validity in Interpretation* (New Haven: Yale University Press, 1967). Thiselton, in *The Two Horizons*, has tried to mediate between Hirsch and reader-response models. This a wide-open field. The final word has not been spoken. Only genuine dialogue will make it possible to find the proper balance between the various elements in the process of interpretation: the author, the text, and the reader.

[88]I would like to express my appreciation to Drs. D. A. Carson, Grant R. Osborne, and Thomas R. Schreiner for their suggestions for improvement of an earlier draft of this essay.

CHAPTER TWELVE

THE CRUX OF THE MATTER:
Paul's Pastoral Pronouncements Regarding Women's Roles in 1 Timothy 2:9–15*

The issue of women's roles in the church spans cultures, times, denominations, and, of course, genders. It spans cultures: believers in North America may not always realize that this issue is not merely an in-house debate among American evangelicals. "Es hat ja Priesterinnen gegeben" ("There were indeed female priests") trumpets a recent headline in an Austrian national newspaper, arguing for the apostolic origins of the priesthood of women.[1] "More than three years after they cracked the stained-glass ceiling to become priests, Australia's female Anglican clergy say they still are fighting against the church's male leadership," reads a current report from Australia.[2] "Female priests may be church's salvation," opines a contemporary assessment of the situation in the Anglican church in Great Britain.[3] American Episcopalians ordained their first female bishop in 1989, Anglicans in England followed suit in 1994, and Germany saw the ordination of its first female Lutheran bishop in 1992.[4] Indeed,

---

*This essay first appeared in *Faith & Mission* 14 (1997): 24–48 and is reprinted with permission.

[1]Maria Regina Pisa in *Die Presse* (November 13, 1995): 2.

[2]Listed under "International News in Brief" in a 1995 issue of the *Chicago Tribune*.

[3]Veronique Mistiaen, *Chicago Tribune*, August 13, 1995, 6/1, 8.

[4]Werner Neuer, *Mann und Frau in christlicher Sicht* (5th ed.; Gießen: Brunnen, 1993), 6. Regarding the German Lutheran scene, see esp. "Wer 'verläßt den Boden der in der evangelischen Kirche geltenden Lehre'?: Zur EKD-Stellungnahme von 1992 'Frauenordination und Bischofsamt' " (Gr. Oesingen: Harms, 1995). Cf. also Manfred Hauke, *Die Problematik um das Frauenpriestertum vor dem Hintergrund der Schöpfungs- und Erlösungsordnung* (KKKTS 46; Paderborn, 1982; 3rd ed. 1991); idem, *God oder Goddess? Feminist Theology: What is it? Where does it lead?* (San Francisco: Ignatius,

the role of women in the church, and in particular the issue of women's ordination, is a world-wide phenomenon.[5]

The issue spans times: as Daniel Doriani demonstrated in a thorough recent survey, we must avoid the notion that we are here confronted with an unprecedented issue in the history of the church.[6] The issue of women's roles in the church is not a new one. This renders it all the more remarkable that the "progressive" reading of biblical texts such as 1 Tim 2:9–15 is a comparatively recent phenomenon. In a current essay, Robert Yarbrough argues persuasively that radical egalitarianism regarding gender roles mirrors societal developments more than it issues from an exegesis of the biblical texts themselves.[7] While there were precursors of egalitarianism, an egalitarian school of biblical interpretation did not fully take hold until a few decades ago. However, nineteen centuries of virtual unanimity in this matter constitute strong presumptive evidence that the "historic" reading of the relevant texts is valid.[8]

The issue spans denominations: Roman Catholics, Anglicans, Lutherans, Presbyterians, Baptists, Episcopalians, and many other denominations around the world have recently had to wrestle with the issue of whether women should be placed in positions of ultimate responsibility in their respective bodies.[9] For now, the Roman Catholic hierarchy stands firm in its opposition to women's ordination, not merely on biblical, but primarily on traditional and dogmatic grounds.[10] Anglicans and

---

1995).

[5]Cf. Paige Patterson, "The Meaning of Authority in the Local Church," in *Recovering Biblical Manhood and Womanhood—A Response to Evangelical Feminism* (ed. John Piper and Wayne Grudem; Wheaton, IL: Crossway, 1991), 248–59.

[6]"Appendix 1: A History of the Interpretation of 1 Timothy 2," in *Women in the Church: A Fresh Analysis of 1 Timothy 2:9–15* (ed. Andreas J. Köstenberger, Thomas R. Schreiner, and H. Scott Baldwin; Grand Rapids: Baker, 1995), 209–67.

[7]Robert W. Yarbrough, "The Hermeneutics of 1 Timothy 2:9–15," in *Women in the Church*, 167–71.

[8]Cf. Köstenberger et al., *Women in the Church*, 209.

[9]"Positions of ultimate responsibility" may bear a variety of designations: bishop, priest, (senior) pastor, elder, or deacon (in some denominations).

[10]Pope John Paul II issued an encyclical on qualifications for the priesthood entitled "Ordinatio Sacerdotalis" on May 22, 1994. For a discussion of the Roman Catholic stance toward women's ordination and for a complete list of recent Catholic texts pertaining to the women's issue, see "Emanzipiert oder diskriminiert?," *Die Furche* 8 (February 22, 1996): 13. See also the compendium edited by Helmut Moll, *The Church and Women. A Compendium* (San Francisco: Ignatius, 1988) for valuable contributions by Catholic authors.

(German) Lutherans have recently begun to ordain women.[11] Presbyterians and Baptists have been divided over the issue, which continues to be hotly debated in their respective circles.[12] And no consensus appears to be on the horizon.

Finally, the issue spans genders: what constitutes proper roles for women in the church is, of course, a topic of vital interest to every Christian woman who cares to know the will of God on the subject. But this matter affects men as well, since women and men are to serve Christ together in the church, and to settle the issue of God-pleasing role distinctions is vital for an effective ministry carried out harmoniously by representatives of both genders. Some men seem afraid to appear chauvinistic by teaching that positions of ultimate responsibility in the church are reserved for qualified men. But in the end the issue is not conformity to cultural norms but fidelity to Scripture. When a leading American journalist excoriates a complementarian understanding of male-female roles as contemptible, even inhuman, "doctrinaire reductionism," proponents of the church's historic position on male-female relationships must not be intimidated.[13] Sadly, many churches have already surrendered to the enormous pressure brought to bear on them in this regard; yet other congregations are in the process of intense, even divisive, debates over the issue and its implications.[14]

How can this difficult question be brought closer to a satisfactory solution? Different answers have been given by egalitarians that may be divi-

---

[11]For a recent treatment from an Anglican perspective, see Michael Harper, *Equal and Different: Male and Female in Church and Family* (London: Hodder & Stoughton, 1994). Regarding the German Lutheran scene, see Jobst Schöne, "Hirtenbrief zur Frage der Ordination von Frauen zum Amt der Kirche" (Groß Oesingen: Verlag der Lutherischen Buchhandlung Heinrich Harms, 1994).

[12]Regarding the Baptist scene, see esp. Jesse C. Fletcher, *The Southern Baptist Convention: A Sesquicentennial History* (Nashville: Broadman & Holman, 1994), 249-50, 271-72, 292-93. Apparently the first Baptist woman to be ordained was Addie Davis by the Watts Street Baptist Church in Durham, NC. But in 1984, a resolution opposing women's ordination was passed. The ordination of women is one of the major planks in the Southern Baptist moderates' platform.

[13]Lance Morrow in *TIME*, October 3, 1994, p. 71.

[14]For a perceptive critique of the feminist movement, see Mary Kassian, *The Feminist Gospel: The Movement to Unite Feminism with the Church* (Wheaton, IL: Crossway, 1992; note also Kassian's essay in this present issue). For recent radical egalitarian works and further bibliography, see Carol E. Becker, *Leading Women* (Nashville: Abingdon, 1996) and Sally B. Purvis, *The Stained Glass Ceiling* (Louisville, KY: Westminster John Knox, 1995).

ded into secular, liberal, and "biblical" feminists on the one hand and complementarians and traditionalists on the other.[15] I myself have argued in a recent essay that the issue is ultimately not merely the interpretation of biblical texts, but that the underlying interpretive assumptions may influence views on the matter.[16] In the final analysis, the problem even extends to one's stance toward Scripture as a whole and to the issue of what constitutes one's final point of reference in answering the question of whether women should be put in positions of ultimate responsibility over men in the church or not.[17] Despite extreme assertions to the contrary in recent years, this does not render biblical exegesis irrelevant, impossible, or unnecessary.[18] It merely means that it is illusory to hope to persuade someone of one's position *solely on exegetical grounds* while this person is committed to a grid of contrary hermeneutical presuppositions and a worldview that *a priori* excludes particular exegetical outcomes.

---

[15]For a helpful discussion of different kinds of feminists, see Guenther Haas, "Patriarchy as an Evil that God Tolerated: Analysis and Implications for the Authority of Scripture," *JETS* 38 (1995): 321, n. 1, who distinguishes between (1) "evangelical (or biblical) feminists" who claim to hold to the authority of Scripture (R. Tucker); (2) "mainline (or liberal) feminists" who accept as authoritative in Scripture only those elements that promote the full liberation of women (R. Ruether, P. Trible); (3) "radical feminists" who reject the Bible entirely as divine revelation owing to the pervasive influence of patriarchy; among these, some continue to consider themselves as Christians (E. S. Fiorenza) while others do not (M. Daly).

[16]Andreas J. Köstenberger, "Gender Passages in the NT: Hermeneutical Fallacies Critiqued," *WTJ* 56 (1994): 259-83.

[17]It seems helpful to frame the crux of the question regarding women's roles in the church in these terms. This must not be the end of the discussion of women's ministries, which are varied and of vital importance to the function of God's people. As Satan asked Eve in the garden, however, "Indeed, has God said, 'You shall not eat *from any tree* in the garden?,' " thus twisting God's word, those who appear satisfied with nothing less than radical egalitarianism today appear obsessed with claiming as legitimate the *only* ministry apparently reserved for men in the church for women while charging their opponents with "devaluing the ministry of women."

[18]See David L. Thompson, "Women, Men, Slaves and the Bible: Hermeneutical Inquiries," *Christian Scholar's Review* 25 (1996): 326-49, who claims that "attempts either to support or to deny egalitarian relationships between men and women solely on the basis of the interpretation of individual biblical texts in their contexts *lead inevitably to eisegesis* [emphasis added]—to reading the interpreter's agenda into the text" (327). This extreme argument, however, denies both the necessity and possibility of genuine biblical exegesis. For a decisive rebuttal of Thompson, see Wayne Grudem, "Asbury Professor Advocates Egalitarianism but Undermines Biblical Authority: A Critique of David Thompson's 'Trajectory' Hermeneutic," *CBMW News* 2/1 (1996): 8-12.

Having stressed the importance of these larger considerations, however, and armed with a healthy dose of realism regarding the likelihood of persuading adherents of opposing views to one's position, we may therefore venture on the interpretation of 1 Tim 2:9–15, arguably the "crux of the matter." It is the most difficult passage for those who *on biblical grounds* argue for radical egalitarianism, and the most important ground of appeal for those who claim that Scripture limits women from assuming positions of ultimate authority and responsibility in the church.[19] In light of the fact that the recent book *Women in the Church: A Fresh Analysis of 1 Timothy 2:9–15*, co-edited by the present author, lays out the various aspects of the interpretation of 1 Timothy 2 in considerable detail, we will follow the procedure of summarizing some of the most salient arguments made there, supplemented where appropriate, with further material for discussion. We will conclude with an appraisal of the possibility of tracing a biblical theology of women's roles in the church.[20]

The Ancient Background: The Goddess Artemis and Ephesian Women

Battles have raged with little respite regarding the most proper reconstruction of the ancient background for 1 Timothy 2.[21] How this background is

---

[19]This is acknowledged by Stanley Grenz: "I think the strongest argument that the complementarian has is the argument that the Bible indicates that God ordained a hierarchy of male over female from the beginning—that is, in creation. And that this understanding then lies beneath the 1 Timothy 2 text. You can use that presupposition to make sense out of some very difficult texts . . ." and Denise Kjesbo: "[T]he 1 Timothy 2 passage . . . that text can nag at me . . . it's a hard passage." See "Putting Women in Their Place," *Academic Alert* 5/1 (Winter 1996): 2.

[20]In order not to exhaust the reader and to prolong the discussion unnecessarily, documentation below will be representative and illustrative rather than exhaustive. For detailed bibliographic references, see the various essays and the bibliography in *Women in the Church*, ed. Köstenberger et al.

[21]Cf. esp. Catherine Clark and Richard Clark Kroeger, *I Suffer Not a Woman: Rethinking 1 Timothy 2:11–15 in Light of Ancient Evidence* (Grand Rapids: Baker, 1992) and the decisive response by Steven M. Baugh in *Women in the Church*, ed. Köstenberger et al., 13–52. See also the devastating critiques of the Kroegers' work by Robert W. Yarbrough, "I Suffer Not a Woman: A Review Essay," *Presbyterion* 18 (1992): 25–33; Albert Wolters, "Review: *I Suffer Not a Woman*," *Calvin Theological Journal* 28 (1993): 208–13; and Steven M. Baugh, "The Apostle Among the Amazons," *WTJ* 56 (1994): 153–71. For hermeneutical observations regarding the use of background data, see Köstenberger, "Gender Passages," 271–73.

construed is indeed significant for the interpretation of the present passage, since in recent debate it has been argued that the relevance of this text is limited to the original occasion. It must be noted, however, that, in the final analysis, this is a question of *hermeneutics*, not background. In other words, a limited application of 1 Timothy 2 cannot be established *on the basis of a particular reconstructed background* of this text, but only on the basis of proper hermeneutical considerations, such as the genre of the Pastoral Epistles, the nature of the normativity of biblical commands, and other such factors. The relevance of the message of 1 Timothy 2 to the issue of contemporary women's roles is therefore not contingent on a solution (or the lack thereof) of the debate regarding the most plausible background to 1 Timothy 2. If it is decided on hermeneutical grounds that the text transcends its immediate occasion and therefore possesses perennial pertinence for the church, it should be applied today.

Nevertheless, the background to 1 Timothy 2 remains significant in order to elucidate the text. Before providing a brief overview of the issue, however, one more word of caution must be registered: it must not be assumed that every piece of evidence regarding life in ancient Ephesus in the latter half of the first century CE will of necessity be *relevant* background information *for 1 Timothy 2*. It is not enough for so-called progressive interpreters to postulate a given feature of ancient life in the city of Ephesus. What must further be demonstrated, ultimately in terms of the most plausible reconstruction of the epistle's occasion *from the text*, is that a given feature of ancient life in Ephesus *was relevant for the writer of 1 Timothy in addressing the issue of women's teaching or assuming authority over men in the church*. Only this system of checks and balances retains ultimate authority for Scripture and guards the latter from an undue domestication in light of extrabiblical data that are used to supersede statements found in the biblical texts themselves.

What, then, is the nature of the debate regarding the background to 1 Timothy 2? It has been argued that Ephesus was "a bastion and bulwark of women's rights" in the midst of a uniformly unfeminist Graeco-Roman world, in which Democritus' saying, "For a man to be ruled by a woman is the very height of hubris" ruled the day.[22] Artemis Ephesia is said to have been "a powerful female deity who elevated the status of women," "a symbol of Women's Liberation" and "matriarchy."[23] On the strength of this

---

[22]Baugh, "Foreign World," 14, n. 4.

[23]Cf. Catherine Clark Kroeger, "1 Timothy 2:12–A Classicist's View," in *Women, Authority and the Bible* (ed. Alvera Mickelsen; Downers Grove, IL: InterVarsity, 1986), 227–28; Marcus Barth, "Traditions in Ephesians," *NTS* 30 (1984): 16; Kroegers, *I Suffer Not a Woman*, passim.

assessment, it is argued that Paul's prohibition against women teachers extended only to *Ephesian* women in his day, since they were infected by an anomalous cultural outlook.[24] But in a comprehensive, well-informed piece of painstaking scholarly reconstruction based on the first-hand study of thousands of inscriptions from first-century Ephesus, Steven M. Baugh lays this theory of "feminist Ephesus" to rest once and for all.[25] What makes his contribution particularly valuable is that it is not merely written in reaction to egalitarian views but in an effort to provide an independent, all-encompassing survey of Ephesian society during the second half of the first century CE.

When all is said and done, the society described by Baugh turns out to be nothing like the "feminist Ephesus" alleged by egalitarians but rather a city very much in keeping with other Graeco-Roman metropolitan centers of its day. As Baugh sums up his discussion, "Ephesus was in most ways a typical Hellenic society."[26] He even argues that Paul was more "liberal" than the Roman writer Plutarch, who wanted a virtuous wife to be hidden away when not accompanied by her husband and not to make her own friends but be content with her husband's (*Mor.* 139C, 140D), while Paul encourages them to learn in the church, to exercise their gifts in form of public good works and in the discipleship of younger women.[27] Baugh concludes, "If this chapter has added anything concrete to [the] discussion of 1 Timothy 2:9–15, it is that exegetical treatments can proceed with the assumption that Ephesus was not a unique society in its era. Specifically, it was not a feminist society [as commonly alleged]."[28] Thus it seems inadmissible to rule 1 Tim 2:12 out from consideration by the argument that the women in this church were unusually unruly or emancipated.

But were women perhaps prohibited from teaching men merely because of the presence of heretical female teachers in the congregation? If this had been Paul's intent, he arguably would have said so: there is a perfectly good Greek word for "teaching error," that is ἑτεροδιδασκαλεῖν

---

[24]Cf. Kroegers, *I Suffer Not a Woman*, 93; Sharon Hodgin Gritz, "The Role of Women in the Church," in *The People of God: Essays on the Believers' Church* (ed. Paul A. Basden and David S. Dockery; Nashville: Broadman, 1991), 308.

[25]Cf. Baugh, "Foreign World," 14–52, who on p. 15 mentions that there are almost four thousand extant inscriptions from Ephesus, more than from any other city in the region.

[26]Ibid., 49.

[27]Ibid., 49–50.

[28]Ibid., 50.

used in 1 Tim 1:3 and 6:3), which could have been used in 1 Tim 2:12. Moreover, why would Paul merely forbid *women* the teaching of false doctrine and not also men? This seems strange, especially since all the *explicitly named* false teachers in the Ephesian church are male (Hymenaeus and Alexander in 1 Tim 1:20; Hymenaeus and Philetus in 2 Tim 2:17; Demas in 2 Tim 4:10), with women featuring, not primarily as *perpetrators*, but as *victims* of false teaching (1 Tim 2:14; 2 Tim 3:6).

Were women then disqualified from teaching men merely owing to their lack of proper education?[29] The evidence provided by Baugh from ancient Ephesus explodes the myth of women's general lack of education in that day.[30] While women were indeed less involved in formal public education in the ancient world, that does not necessarily imply that they were uneducated. According to Baugh, other avenues of learning were available to women, particularly private lectures in salons (cf. 2 Tim 3:6). Still more important, all interpretations limiting the application of 1 Tim 2:12 on the basis of alleged background information ultimately flounder on the stubborn fact that they substitute unstated rationales in the place of the reasons actually supplied by the text (cf. 1 Tim 2:13-14). Finally, women are not barred by 1 Tim 2:12 from teaching altogether, but only from the teaching of *men* (ἄνδρος), which in context refers to the authoritative doctrinal instruction of a local church gathered for worship.

As argued above, none of these background considerations precludes the actual exegesis and hermeneutical evaluation of the passage. It does, however, exclude the setting aside of 1 Tim 2:9-15 *solely on the basis of background considerations*. And so we may proceed with an assessment of the genre of the Pastoral Epistles and the issue of the normativity of biblical injunctions.

The Genre of the Pastorals and the Nature of the Normativity of Biblical Injunctions

It is of some importance for the interpretation of 1 Timothy 2 whether or not the Apostle Paul penned the epistle or whether a later follower of Paul is responsible for the composition of 1 Timothy. Even the alleged pseudo-

---

[29]Craig S. Keener, *Paul, Women and Wives: Marriage and Women's Ministry in the Letters of Paul* (Peabody, MA: Hendrickson, 1992), 107-13, is an influential recent advocate of this position.

[30]See the section on "Women and Education" in Baugh, "Foreign World," 45-47.

nymity of this letter, however, would not by itself remove it from the sway of normativity for the universal church since, whether from Paul or not, the passage is part of the church's canonical Scriptures, which provide the framework for its faith and practice. Nevertheless, if the "I" of "I do not permit a woman to teach or exercise authority over a man" is the Apostle Paul, this would add significant weight to the injunction, since the New Testament indicates that the church is founded on the foundation of the apostles and their teaching (cf. Eph 2:20; Acts 2:42). This is not the place to argue for the Pauline authorship of the Pastorals, though such a case can be, and recently has been, convincingly made.[31] The epistle's overt claim of having been penned by Paul (1:1) and the presence of several autobiographical pieces of information throughout the epistle (e.g. 1:2-4, 12-16 or 4:13) must be given full weight, especially since there is no evidence that pseudonymous *epistles* were an established genre in the first century AD, and even if this were the case, that the church would ever have incorporated such a document into its canon. For these reasons we may proceed on the basis of the assumption that 1 Timothy 2:12, like the entire epistle, has Paul as its author.

It is often argued that, as a "difficult" text "of limited application," 1 Timothy 2 should be interpreted in the light of "clear" texts "of universal applicability" such as Gal 3:28.[32] But a closer look reveals that the converse is true. To begin with, the text in Galatians is likewise part of an epistle that was written to confront a very specific heresy plaguing the Galatian churches, so that it cannot be said that the Galatian passage is free from concrete conditions that faced a local church at a particular time. Hence both 1 Tim 2:12 and Gal 3:28 need to be interpreted in light of the circumstances that occasioned a given teaching. Moreover, the argument can be made on the basis of *genre* that, since 1 Timothy 2 is part of a *Pastoral Epistle*, whose very nature is that of apostolic instruction regarding the organization of the apostolic and postapostolic churches, the

---

[31]See Stanley E. Porter, "Pauline Authorship and the Pastoral Epistles: Implications for Canon," *Bulletin of Biblical Research* 5 (1995): 105-23. Cf. also T. David Gordon, "A Certain Kind of Letter: The Genre of 1 Timothy," in *Women in the Church*, ed. Köstenberger et al., 53-55. Gordon also provides further bibliography on pp. 53-54, n. 1 in his article.

[32]For a survey of the relevant issues, see Köstenberger, "Gender Passages," 260 and 273-79. See also Gordon D. Fee, "The Great Watershed—Intentionality & Particularity/Eternity: 1 Timothy 2:8-15 as a Test Case," in *Gospel and Spirit: Issues in New Testament Hermeneutics* (Peabody, MA: Hendrickson, 1991), 52-65 and the response by Bruce K. Waltke, "1 Timothy 2:8-15: Unique or Normative?" *Crux* 28/1 (1992): 22-27.

injunctions *of 1 Timothy 2* should be considered *paramount*, exceeding in their finality even texts in earlier Pauline epistles or the Gospels in their authority for the church of all time. In other words, while the purpose of a letter such as Galatians was demonstrably *not* primarily to lay down permanent guidelines on the organization of the church in terms of qualifications for elders or the roles of men and women in the church, the injunctions of 1 Timothy 2 are part of an epistle whose entire purpose for writing is wrapped up in the purpose of providing such normative instruction. This is the power and significance of genre identification: it sets the parameters for interpretation by providing a framework for exegesis.[33] Genre precedes exegesis as a vital part of hermeneutics.

As David Gordon contends, the canonical Pastoral Epistles "contain norms that are especially germane to the issues of life in the church, 'the household of God' " (cf. 1 Tim 3:15).[34] He lists the following pronouncements:

- instructions regarding the duties and qualifications of officeholders (1 Tim 3:1-13; 5:1-2; 2 Tim 2:1-26; 4:1-5; Titus 1:5-9; 2:1-15; 3:1-11);
- instructions regarding the enrolling of qualified widows for diaconal assistance (1 Tim 5:3-16);
- instructions regarding public prayer (1 Tim 2:1-15);
- instructions regarding remuneration of the ministers of the Word (1 Tim 5:17-19);
- instructions regarding the suppression of heresy (1 Tim 1:3-7; 2 Tim 4:3-4; Tit 1:10-11)

Gordon's primary contribution, however, lies in his clarification of the issue of the normativity of biblical injunctions. He shows that the occasional nature of the New Testament epistles in no way precludes the abiding normative force of injunctions contained therein. What is crucial in this regard, according to Gordon, is *the distinction between the actual injunction and the underlying norm informing the injunction.* In other words, Paul may issue a particular command to a given church and substantiate it by stating a particular norm that informs it. But while the specific formulation of the injunction may be occasional, *the informing*

---

[33]See esp. E. D. Hirsch, Jr., "3. The Concept of Genre," *Validity in Interpretation* (New Haven and London: Yale University Press, 1967), 68–126.

[34]Gordon, "Certain Kind of Letter," 60.

norm is not. This is precisely what makes it a *norm* : that it is an abiding principle that is capable of an unlimited number of specific applications to a variety of occasions and circumstances. Moreover, while it is possible to make such a distinction in certain instances, such as 1 Cor 11:2–16, where the wearing of a veil is but one possible concrete cultural expression of a woman's submission to male authority in the church, there are other occasions where the injunctions are so inextricably tied to the norms informing them that the injunctions themselves assume permanent validity beyond the original context to which they were addressed.

Arguably, this is the case in 1 Timothy 2. There the command, "I do not permit a woman to teach or to exercise authority over a man" is substantiated in the following verses both by the order of creation and the scenario of the Fall.[35] The informing norms, positively the order of creation (i.e. Adam first, then Eve), and negatively the inappropriate role reversal at the Fall (i.e. Eve first, then Adam), ground the apostle's pronouncement that, in God's household, it should likewise be the man, not the woman, who bears ultimate responsibility for the church.[36] While there may be some room for discussion as to exactly what roles would therefore be inadmissible for women in the church, it seems clear that this includes at a minimum the role of overseer, as is made clear in the verses immediately following 1 Tim 2:9–15, when one of the qualifications of an overseer is that of "being the husband of one wife" (μιᾶς γυναικὸς ἄνδρα; 1 Tim 3:2).[37] Thus read, 1 Tim 2:9–15 and 3:1ff provide a close-knit argument that coheres very well indeed.

---

[35]This runs counter to the claim of egalitarians who argue that male-female role distinctions are merely a function of the fall. Cf. e.g., "Men, Women & Biblical Equality," a statement issued by the organization called "Christians for Biblical Equality": "The Bible teaches that the rulership of Adam over Eve resulted from the Fall and was therefore not a part of the original created order."

[36]Grant R. Osborne, "Hermeneutics and Women in the Church," *JETS* 20 (1977): 347, maintains that the normative principle is the woman's submissiveness and the cultural application, not to teach but to be silent. But it is hard to see how Paul would substantiate a mere temporary cultural application with a rationale from both creation order and the Fall, events of abiding relevance for humanity even after Christ's provision of redemption. Moreover, the text of 1 Tim 2:11–12 presents "submission" and "not teaching or having authority over a man" as two sides of the same coin rather than respectively as normative principle and cultural application, as Osborne asserts.

[37]This expression probably refers to a "faithful husband," i.e., a "one woman-kind of man." Not the parallel phrase found in 1 Timothy 5:9, "wife of one husband" (ἑνὸς ἀνδρὸς γυνή), which hardly serves to exclude those widows who were subsequently married to more than one husband, but merely requires eligible widows to have been faithful wives, "one husband-kind of women."

Moreover, it is significant that the norm explicitly stated in 1 Tim 2:13-14 as informing Paul's injunction in 2:12 is that of Adam's temporal priority over Eve in creation and the latter's priority over the former at the Fall. As Gordon incisively comments, this effectively waylays the contention that the thrust of Paul's teaching is here directed toward women's lack of education, their teaching of heresy or unruly behavior in the Ephesian church, or other matters.[38] In other words, if Paul had stated that he did not want women to teach men *because he wanted the church to conduct itself in an orderly fashion or because he wanted to ensure the teaching of sound doctrine*, the state of orderliness or education of the Ephesian woman in Timothy's church would be significant. But Paul, of course, states nothing of this sort. To the contrary, the norm explicitly stated in the text is that of preeminence and ultimate responsibility, which, according to the apostle, would be violated if women taught men or exercised authority over them in the church. Hence he enjoins them to refrain from doing so.

The Word "Assume Authority" and the Sentence Structure of 1 Tim 2:12

We may briefly survey jointly the issue of the meaning of the word αὐθεντέω and the sentence structure of 1 Tim 2:12.[39] Here it has been the contention of egalitarians that the word may have a negative connotation, such as "domineer," so that Paul merely forbids the *inappropriate* exercise of authority by women rather than their exercise of authority altogether. Apart from the fact that this already flies in the face of mere logic—why would Paul only forbid *women* to exercise authority inappropriately, especially since it is clear from the text that it was men in particular who were responsible for heretical teaching?—this can also not be sustained from the meaning of the word itself in the light of the sentence structure of 1 Tim 2:12.

Scott Baldwin, in a recent comprehensive study of the term αὐθεντέω, leaves no stone unturned in examining all the available instances of this

---

[38]The question of whether women were teaching false doctrine in the Ephesian church is therefore ultimately not decisive. Apparently, however, Paul's primary concern was, not with women as the *perpetrators* of false teaching, but as its *victims* (cf. e.g., 2 Tim 3:6).

[39]For a detailed discussion, see H. Scott Baldwin, "A Difficult Word: αὐθεντέω in 1 Timothy 2:12," and Andreas J. Köstenberger, "A Complex Sentence Structure in 1 Timothy 2:12," both in *Women in the Church*, ed. Köstenberger et al., 65-103.

term in ancient literature. In short, he concludes that there is not a single unambiguous reference where the word means "domineer." Demonstrating that a negative connotation of the word has frequently been postulated owing to the fallacy of linking the meaning of the noun *authentes* (αὐθεντής) with the verb αὐθεντέω, the author does prove that αὐθεντεῖν does not ordinarily have a negative meaning. Nevertheless, it can, of course, not be excluded that the term could conceivably be supplied with a negative connotation in a given context, so that Baldwin's study, while doubtless supplying a solid foundation for the *plausible* meaning of αὐθεντέω in the present passage, falls short of absolute proof.[40] Moreover, while Baldwin surveys a total of eighty-two instances of αὐθεντέω in ancient Greek literature, only two (!) date prior to the writing of First Timothy, a sample size so small as to preclude any certainty regarding the meaning of the word at the time the epistle was written.[41]

For this reason it appeared necessary to look for additional, alternative strategies at arriving at a definitive conclusion regarding the meaning of the word αὐθεντέω in 1 Tim 2:12.[42] Sophisticated computer searches of large amounts of ancient Greek literature[43] yielded, strikingly, a fixed pattern in the Greek language, according to which the two elements of a "neither/nor" construction (two verbs connected with οὐδέ) share the same force with one another, be it positive or negative. This finding renders a translation of αὐθεντέω with "to teach in a domineering way" or the like impossible and in violation of the rules of Greek grammar. Rather, it suggests that the phrase be understood in terms of the exercise of any kind of authority, not just an inappropriate one. Consider the following words of Jesus as further examples of this kind of grammatical con-

---

[40]This he frankly acknowledges in a section entitled "The Limitations of Word Studies," 69–71.

[41]These two references are: Philodemus (1st cent. BCE): "Ought we not to consider that men who incur the enmity of *those in authority* (σὺν αὐθεντοῦσιν) are villains, and hated by both gods and men"; and BGU 1208 (27 BCE): "I *exercised authority* (Κἀμοῦ αὐθεντηκότος) over him, and he consented to provide for Catalytis the Boatman on terms of full fare, within the hour." For full Greek texts and translations, see Baldwin, "Appendix 2" in *Women in the Church*, 275–76.

[42]Cf. Köstenberger, "Difficult Sentence Structure," chap. 4 in *Women in the Church*, ed. Köstenberger et al.

[43]For a detailed account of the methodology used in those computer searches, see Andreas J. Köstenberger, "Syntactical Background Studies to 1 Timothy 2.12 in the New Testament and Extrabiblical Greek Literature," in *Discourse Analysis and Other Topics in Biblical Greek* (ed. Stanley E. Porter and D. A. Carson; JSNTSS 113; Sheffield: Sheffield Academic Press, 1995), 165–66.

struction: "Look at the birds of the air: they neither sow nor reap, nor gather into barns, and yet your heavenly Father feeds them" (Matt 6:26); "sow," "reap," and "gather into barns" all are legitimate activities, even though the subjects of Jesus' discourse (birds) are said not to engage in them for particular reasons. An example of the converse can be found in Matt 6:20, where Jesus is quoted as saying, "But lay up for yourselves treasures in heaven, where neither moth nor rust destroys, and where thieves do not break in nor steal." In this instance, both "breaking in" and "stealing," while not synonymous (thieves first break in and then steal), possess an intrinsically negative connotation. In other words, two verbs conjoined by οὐδέ always relate either in terms of +/+ or -/-, never +/- or -/+.

The significance of this axiomatic feature of ancient Greek language for the interpretation of 1 Timothy 2 is that it settles conclusively the meaning of αὐθεντέω, which can only be approximated on other grounds (such as word studies, see above). The two verbs conjoined by οὐδέ ("or") in 1 Tim 2:12 are διδάσκειν ("to teach") and αὐθεντεῖν, and since it is demonstrable that διδάσκειν here has a positive force as elsewhere in the Pastorals, it follows that αὐθεντέω does as well.[44] Thus, far from connoting merely the *negative* exercise of authority by women, the term in 1 Tim 2:12 can therefore be shown to pertain *to any* such exercise of authority (which by itself is positive), owing to considerations adduced in the context (cf. 1 Tim 2:13-14). Thus the egalitarian position, as in the case of background and genre, again founders on the hard evidence based on the text itself.

The Exegesis of 1 Tim 2:9-15

The previous discussions of the background of 1 Timothy 2, the genre of the Pastorals and the issue of normativity, and the meaning of αὐθεντέω in 1 Tim 2:12, have prepared the way for a full-fledged exegesis of the passage. Extensive research has cleared away improper assumptions such as that of first-century "feminist Ephesus," the restriction of the application of

---

[44]Cf. esp. 1 Tim 4:11; 6:2; 2 Tim 2:2. In cases where a negative connotation is intended, the term is usually ἑτεροδιδασκαλεῖν, as in 1 Tim 1:3 and 6:3. In Titus 1:11, the heretical nature of teaching is made abundantly clear by contextual qualifiers ("They must be silenced, because they are ruining whole households by teaching *things they ought not to teach*—and that for the sake of dishonest gain"). Contra Kroegers, *I Suffer Not a Woman*, 81.

1 Timothy 2 to the original context on larger hermeneutical grounds, or the giving of a negative connotation to the term αὐθεντέω. It remains now to build on these insights and to illumine the passage as a whole. In what follows, we will not attempt to be comprehensive. Tom Schreiner, in a very thorough chapter in *Women in the Church*, has already rendered us this service.[45] In our survey, we will merely focus on the most significant issues, beginning with earlier verses, and occasionally suggest alternative detailed interpretive conclusions.

We begin with an observation regarding the structure of 1 Timothy. The key question presents itself as follows: is 1 Tim 2:12 part of the author's negative polemic directed toward the false teachers and aspects of their heretical teaching? If so, this would support the notion that 1 Tim 2:12 was written likewise to combat a specific abuse or error in the Ephesian church. If not, however, the teaching in 1 Tim 2:12 may be viewed as more programmatic and constructive rather than narrowly constrained by the correction of a current heresy. Indeed, commentators differ on the extent to which the statement in 1:3-4 is determinative regarding 1 Timothy as a whole. Some believe that the reference places the entire letter in the purview of correcting heresy, seeking to find a specific heretical teaching behind every positive instruction in the epistle. Others believe that 1:3-4 provides the general occasion for the correspondence, without, however, limiting Paul's teaching in 1 Timothy completely to the refutation of specific aspects of heresy.

While it is clear that the author returns to this issue in 4:1, it is less clear whether the section of 2:1-3:16 is to be subsumed under the refutation of heresy. Fee thinks so; on the strength of the introductory preposition οὖν in 2:1, he seeks to identify a specific heresy in relation to virtually every single positive statement made by Paul. When prayers are urged for people in authority, this is mirror-read as an indication that heretics counseled against such prayers (2:1); when Paul asserts that God wants *all* to be saved, it is conjectured that this statement is designed to refute the false teachers' claim that salvation was intended only for *some* (2:4); when Jesus is called the only mediator between God and men, this is to counter the notion that there are other mediators as well (2:5), and so forth.[46] But it is far from clear whether οὖν should be taken to tie in the entire con-

---

[45]Thomas R. Schreiner, "An Interpretation of 1 Timothy 2:9-15: A Dialogue with Scholarship," in *Women in the Church*, ed. Köstenberger et al., 105-54.

[46]Gordon D. Fee, *1 and 2 Timothy, Titus* (NIBC; Peabody, MA: Hendrickson, 1988), *ad loc.*

tents of 2:1–3:16 narrowly with 1:3–4. Hence the NASB, for example, translates the term "first of all, then," in the sense of starting a new section that is not merely to be subsumed under what precedes.

Several arguments support the thesis that Paul in 2:1–3:16 moves beyond a narrow concern of refuting specific heresies to a pattern of more positive instruction regarding how Timothy should organize the church entrusted to him: first, the absence of specific explicit references to heresy in chapters 2 and 3; and second, the conclusion of this section in 3:15: "I write so that you may know *how one ought to conduct himself in the household of God,* which is the church of the living God, the pillar and support of the truth." This conclusion implies that Paul views the instructions in this section as befitting the church of all times, not merely for the Ephesian church in Timothy's day—note the solemn description of the church—and that his purpose is more positive and constructive than merely rebutting false teachers.[47]

Moreover, it stretches credulity to argue, as hermeneutical consistency would appear to require Fee and others to do, that behind every attribute that is to be characteristic of an overseer stands a heresy: when Paul requires him to be prudent, some argued he was to be foolish; when he expects him to be uncontentious, heretics taught overseers should be contentious; when Paul demands the overseer to have a good reputation with outsiders, the false teachers contended that his reputation did not matter; and so forth. At the very least it should be agreed that if Paul had had a specific heresy regarding, for example, women's teaching men in mind, he could have made it explicit rather than leaving it for his readers to draw this out. In the end, it should be noted that the arguments made by egalitarians regarding particular heresies underlying Paul's injunction particularly in 2:12 are arguments *from silence*—a fact that makes them not only unverifiable but often doubtful. As a result, we will tread lightly on supplying extra-textual information in order to interpret the explicit statements of the text, relying rather primarily on the latter to tell us what we need to know to understand Paul's message.

---

[47]If 1 Timothy 2 is to be set aside as merely addressed to correct abuses in the Ephesian church, hermeneutical consistency would demand that 1 Timothy 3, with its instructions on what requirements are "necessary" (δεῖ) for "anyone" (τις) aspiring to the office of overseer, likewise be set aside from universal application, since 1 Timothy 2 and 3 form a close-knit unit. This, however, even most egalitarian interpreters are unwilling to do. But if 1 Timothy 3 is accepted as normative, 1 Timothy 2 should be afforded the same treatment.

We need not tarry unduly at the introductory verses in 1 Tim 2:8-10.[48] Suffice it to say that Paul's desire for men "everywhere" to pray should be taken to imply that his instructions for women in the following verses are likewise pertinent for women "everywhere," not merely in Ephesus.[49] His exhortation for women not to be unduly concerned with their external appearance but rather to focus on inner beauty is very much in keeping with New Testament instruction elsewhere (cf. e.g., 1 Pet 3:1-6) as well as with Old Testament wisdom (Proverbs 31) and insights from the surrounding culture.[50] The underlying norm is that of a proper spiritual focus for women, to be exhibited in modest external adornment. The charge must therefore be rejected that conservative interpreters are inconsistent when they do not apply the words of verses 8 and 9 "literally" while taking seriously the injunction in verse 12.

But what does the crucial verse 12 itself mean? It should be stated at the outset that, especially in the light of the above findings regarding the meaning of αὐθεντεῖν in 1 Tim 2:12, the presumption lies heavily in favor of interpreting the text to mean what it actually says: "I do not permit a woman to teach or to exercise authority over a man." As Robert Yarbrough states perceptively, he is no fool who is slow to reject the overt message of a biblical text in favor of more "sophisticated readings."[51] The Reformation hermeneutical principle of the preferred status of the "natural" reading still stands. Clearly, the burden of proof lies with those who urge a reading other than this natural reading, and as has been shown, research regarding the passage's background, normativity, lexis, and syntax, all join in supporting the notion that the natural reading is indeed the correct one.

This, however, is not the end of the story. Some "biblical feminists" would agree with this interpretation. They concur that Paul indeed meant to restrict women from teaching men. Rather than arguing that Paul was wrong in doing so, they merely contend that, for a variety of reasons, the contemporary situation differs from the one in Paul's day, so that his command should no longer be considered applicable today. We have already addressed this issue in our discussion of genre and normativity above and need therefore merely briefly remind the reader of our conclusion there.

---

[48]See Schreiner, "Interpretation," 112-21.

[49]Contra Fee, *ad loc.*

[50]Baugh ("Foreign World," 52) quotes Joannes Stobbaeus: "A woman's particular virtue is modesty (σωφροσύνη), for by it she is enabled to honor and love her husband."

[51]Yarbrough, "Hermeneutics," 155-56.

The key, apart from the wording of verse 12 itself, is the reasons given in verses 13 and 14, stating as the informing norms for Paul's teaching in verse 12 not culture-relative circumstances but realities rooted in the very order of creation and, conversely, the role reversal occurring at the Fall.[52] Efforts to marginalize or explain away the force of this connection (such as efforts to minimize the force of the conjunction "for" [γάρ]) completely fail to convince.[53]

We may therefore conclude that the verse means what it says, and that efforts to limit its applicability to Paul's day do not do justice to the force of the text itself. If the text is reasonably clear, how should one account for sustained efforts to limit the verse's applicability? We will need to address this issue in the next section. Before tackling this question, however, we may briefly deal with the reference to women's "salvation by childbearing" in verse 15.

Women's Preservation by the Bearing of Children

In another article I argue that none of the current proposals for the interpretation of 1 Tim 2:15 is entirely adequate.[54] There is no need here to provide a long list of proposed interpretations only to discount them and to find them wanting.[55] At this point we will confine ourselves to arguing for what appears to be the most plausible understanding of this admittedly complex passage.

There are two primary difficulties in this verse: the meaning of σῴζω ("saved"? "preserved"?), and the import of τεκνογονία ("childbearing").

---

[52]Cf. Köstenberger, "Gender Passages," 267–71. We take exception to the contention by Schreiner, "Interpretation," 145–46, following Doriani, "Appendix 1: A History of the Interpretation of 1 Timothy 2," in *Women in the Church*, ed. Köstenberger et al., that Paul in 1 Timothy 2:14 teaches that women are to be excluded from positions of ultimate responsibility in the church owing to their greater relational and nurturing nature, which would inhibit them from confronting people regarding doctrinal error. It is unclear how this conclusion could be drawn on the basis of an exegesis of the biblical text itself.

[53]See the discussion in Schreiner, "Interpretation," 134–35, including bibliographic information on p. 134, n. 132.

[54]Andreas J. Köstenberger, "Ascertaining Women's God-ordained Roles: An Interpretation of 1 Timothy 2:15," *Bulletin of Biblical Research* 7 (1997): 107–44. I disagree here with the interpretation presented in Schreiner, "Interpretation," 146–53.

[55]Cf. ibid., 8–12 (orig. ms.).

Regarding both issues, recourse to a close parallel passage in the same epistle proves most illuminating. In 1 Tim 5:14–15, Paul writes, "Therefore, I want younger widows to get married, bear children (τεκνογονεῖν), keep house, and give the enemy no occasion for reproach; for some have already turned aside to follow Satan." Two observations may be made: first, the bearing of children is in the latter passage presented as part of a package that also includes one's marital relationship and the managing of one's household; second, evidently, Paul's primary concern underlying his command to young widows in this passage is their preservation from Satan. Arguably, 1 Tim 5:14–15 thus makes explicit what appears to be implied in 1 Tim 2:15: "childbearing" is merely a *pars pro toto* (a "part standing for the whole"), encompassing a woman's entire range of marital, familial, and domestic responsibilities; and by adhering to this role, women will be "preserved," i.e. *from Satan*, contrary to Eve, who, when stepping outside her God-ordained sphere, was *not* preserved from the serpent but fell into transgression (verse 14). People's preservation from Satan is indeed a constant, albeit thus far overlooked, theme in the Pastorals (for brevity's sake, only references in 1 Timothy are listed below):

- Hymenaeus and Alexander are handed over to Satan in order not to blaspheme (1:20);
- new converts should not be appointed as overseers, lest they become conceited and fall into the condemnation incurred by the devil (3:6);
- an overseer must have a good reputation with those outside the church so that he might not fall into reproach and the snare of the devil (3:7);
- the false teacher's forbidding of marriage and command to abstain from certain foods are doctrines of demons (4:1–5);
- those who want to get rich fall into temptation and a snare and many foolish and harmful desires which plunge men into ruin and destruction (6:9–10; cf. 2 Tim 2:26).

In other places, Paul warns against unresolved anger (Eph 4:27) or a married couple's ill-advised, prolonged abstinence from sexual intercourse (1 Cor 7:5), both of which would make people vulnerable to Satan.

This reading also makes best sense of the flow of the argument in the entire passage. After telling women to focus on inner rather than external beauty, and after enjoining them not to step outside their proper role and teach or exercise authority over men in the assembly—which would violate creation order and reenact the scenario that led to the Fall—Paul concludes his instruction on this issue by elaborating on what women's role positively entails. By adhering to their God-ordained sphere involving their marital, familial, and domestic responsibilities, they will not make themselves vulnerable to Satan. This they would do, like Eve, if they stepped outside their proper domain by assuming public teaching or ruling functions in the church, thus being found in positions of ultimate authority over men. Arguably, this represents the reading of verse 15 that requires the least injection of additional information into the text. Moreover, this interpretation avoids the tendency of an inappropriate reading of the passage in the light of unrelated Pauline theology elsewhere, a fallacy frequently committed by evangelical commentators who take σῴζω as a reference to women's eschatological salvation in order to avoid making Paul teach "salvation by works."[56]

What Seems to Be the Problem? Reasons for the Rejection of the Natural Reading of the Passage

If 1 Tim 2:12 means what it says, why then have people, especially in recent years, had such difficulty accepting the message of this verse? Robert Yarbrough lists three primary factors: (1) Western culture's liberalized views of women; (2) the putative meaning of Gal 3:28; and (3) an alleged tie between women's subordination and slavery. We refer readers to the able treatment by Yarbrough.[57] A few comments on the each ques-

---

[56]Cf. e.g., Schreiner, "Interpretation," 152, who strains to make this point: "The term σωθήσεται is used rather loosely here, so that Paul does not specify in what sense women are saved by childbearing and doing other good works. I think it is fair, though, *since Paul often argues elsewhere that salvation is not gained on the basis of our works* [emphasis added] (e.g., Rom. 3:19–4:25; Gal. 2:16–3:14; 2 Tim. 1:9–11; Titus 2:11–14; 3:4–7) to understand the virtues described here as *evidence* that salvation is genuine."

[57]Yarbrough, "Hermeneutics," chap. 6 in *Women in the Church.* Thompson, "Women, Men, Slaves, and the Bible," 326–49, has recently argued that "slavery provides a hermeneutical paradigm sufficiently parallel" to male-female relationships, with the implication that, since slavery has been found wanting and abolished, hierarchical male-female relationships should likewise be obliterated. But slavery is nowhere in Scripture presented as rooted in creation order, while the male-female relationship clearly is cast in such terms (cf. 1 Cor 11:8–9; 1 Tim 2:12–13). Moreover, Thompson's contention that Scripture moves toward an egalitarian target (pp. 338–39) fails to account for the crucial text of 1 Timothy 2:12: if the Bible's thrust is toward egalitarianism, why does the last word in the canon pertaining to the issue represent a clear affirmation of men's bearing of ultimate responsibility for the church?

tion may, however, be helpful for the reader. Regarding the first issue, Yarbrough demonstrates that it has only been recently, after the rise of feminism, that the "progressive" interpretation of 1 Timothy 2 has emerged. Harold O. J. Brown echoes Yarbrough's concern when he asks, "Did God suddenly permit 'more light to break forth from his holy Word'?"[58] He observes, "[W]hen opinions and convictions suddenly undergo dramatic alteration, although nothing new has been discovered and the only thing that has dramatically changed is the spirit of the age, it is difficult to avoid the conclusion that that spirit has had an important role to play in the shift."[59] Indeed, it is difficult to avoid the conclusion that there is more at work in egalitarian readings of the relevant gender passages in the New Testament than mere exegesis of the biblical texts.

As Brown argues in a sweeping indictment against the profound rebellion of modern culture against God, the rejection of distinct gender roles ordained by the Creator is only one symptom of the world's defiance of the very notion of external, binding standards. Sinful man prefers to think of himself as an autonomous, rational individual, who is accountable to no one but himself and who has no other obligations than to maximize his own liberty, personal peace, and happiness—even as Francis Schaeffer characterized Western man decades ago. And in their rebellion against the Creator, men and women suppress the truth in unrighteousness and pervert God-ordained patterns of relating between genders, leveling distinctions and preferring sameness over complementarity—was that not Paul's verdict writing to the Roman church in the midst of the excesses of the Roman Empire? Indeed, more than biblical exegesis is at work here. The present issue entails an entire culture's stance toward its Creator.

Regarding the second issue, the putative meaning of Gal 3:28 and its relation to 1 Tim 2:12, Yarbrough builds on the observations of David Gordon pertaining to genre and normativity which were already discussed above.[60] There it was observed that many egalitarian interpreters assign permanent validity to Gal 3:28 on the basis of its alleged universality of application while relegating 1 Tim 2:12 to a temporary and culturally relative status. However, we maintained that full weight must be given to the genre of the writing in which 1 Tim 2:12 is found, i.e., that of a Pastoral

---

[58]Harold O. J. Brown, "The New Testament Against Itself: 1 Timothy 2:9–15 and the 'Breakthrough' of Galatians 3:28," in *Women in the Church*, ed. Köstenberger et al., 197.

[59]Ibid., 199.

[60]For a thorough discussion of the relationship between Gal 3:28 and 1 Tim 2:12, see also Köstenberger, "Gender Passages in the NT," 273–79.

epistle. Yarbrough in his treatment traces the now customary egalitarian interpretation of Gal 3:28 to the Swedish bishop and Harvard professor Krister Stendahl, who used it with great effect to argue for the ordination of women in Scandinavia.[61] Essentially, Stendahl distinguishes between what is absolute and enduring in Scripture and what is ephemeral and nonbinding. Based on what criterion? On that of worldview.

According to Stendahl, Jesus, Paul, and the early church were part of a patriarchal society, which makes it necessary to reinterpret their teachings for modern society in keeping with its "enlightened," egalitarian values and principles. Thus Gal 3:28 becomes for Stendahl the "breakthrough verse," against which all other statements in Scripture must be measured. "There is neither . . . male nor female, for you are all one in Christ Jesus" is elevated as Scripture's "Magna Carta of gender equality." But Stendahl's use of Gal 3:28 is not constrained by the passage's original context in Paul's argument in the Galatian Epistle; his primary concern is rather the verse's potential for modern-day application. Christians dare not play "First-Century Semites," accepting some "static 'biblical view' " of the past no longer applicable in our day, nor pursue a "nostalgic attempt to play 'First-Century' " or "First-Century Bible Land.' "[62]

In Stendahl's case, then, it is no longer the biblical text that is the measure of biblical interpretation but the values of contemporary culture. While Stendahl was quite explicit regarding his motivation and method of interpretation, however, some of his followers have been less forthcoming, which has lent Stendahl's arguments a significant amount of credibility. In fact, none less than F. F. Bruce, one of the most respected evangelical scholars of this century, adopted and advocated Stendahl's position, and many less-recognized authorities as well.[63] By uncovering the background of the interpretation that elevates Gal 3:28 above all other biblical injunctions pertaining to gender roles including 1 Tim 2:12, Yarbrough has

---

[61]Krister Stendahl, *The Bible and the Role of Women* (trans. Emilie T. Sander; Facet Books 15; Philadelphia: Fortress, 1966 [1958]).

[62]Ibid., 34–35, quoted by Yarbrough, "Hermeneutics of 1 Timothy 2:9–15," 181.

[63]See F. F. Bruce, "Women in the Church: A Biblical Survey," in *A Mind for What Matters* (Grand Rapids: Eerdmans, 1990), 259–66, 323–25; Paul K. Jewett, *Man as Male and Female* (Grand Rapids: Eerdmans, 1975); Richard Longenecker, *New Testament Social Ethics for Today* (Grand Rapids: Eerdmans, 1984); John W. Cooper, *A Cause for Division? Women in Office and the Unity of the Church* (Grand Rapids: Calvin Theological Seminary, 1991); Clarence Boomsma, *Male and Female, One in Christ* (Grand Rapids: Baker, 1993); and Rebecca Groothuis, *Women Caught in the Conflict* (Grand Rapids: Baker, 1994).

rendered a service to those who thus far may not have recognized that at the root of such arguments is an elevation of contemporary culture above the biblical text itself.

Third, Yarbrough tackles the alleged tie between women's subordination and slavery. What is the background to this supposed analogy? Since "slave and free" and "male and female" are both mentioned in Gal 3:28, the argument has been made with increasing frequency that, just as slavery was abolished, female subordination should likewise be, and egalitarianism should be put in its place. On the surface, this argument sounds plausible enough—but does it withstand closer scrutiny? First of all, it should be noted that, unlike female subordination, slavery is never in Scripture substantiated from the created order. In other words, slavery is considered by the biblical writers as a socioeconomic institution, albeit flawed, while the principle of female subordination is supported, not merely by an appeal to societal conventions, but by pointing to creation (cf. esp. 1 Cor 11:8-9; 1 Tim 2:12-13). Hence the authors of Scripture do not consider slavery and female subordination to be built on the same foundation.

But what about the juxtaposition of "slave and free, male and female" in Gal 3:28? All depends on the organizing principle underlying the reference. What is this principle? It is stated explicitly in the text itself: "All are one in Christ Jesus." Note that it does not say, "All are *equal* in Christ Jesus," but "All are *one* in Christ Jesus." In other words, there is no difference in how anyone comes to Christ: all must approach him the same way, that is, by faith (note that the word "faith" is used in every verse from Gal 3:22 to 26). Nothing is said about gender roles in relation to each other here. Manifestly, this is not the author's present concern; for this, we must turn to Eph 5:21-33 or similar passages, including 1 Tim 2:12. Hence the analogy between slavery and female subordination is shown to be born in the mind of the modern egalitarian interpreter and imposed on the biblical text rather than found in the text itself.

Yarbrough's response to such arguments, most recently revived by Kevin Giles,[64] is much more thorough that can be summarized here. We must conclude by noting that Giles himself bases his interpretation on the claim, "The Bible is authoritative in matters of faith and conduct but not necessarily in science, or on how to order social relations."[65] But if the Bible is not authoritative with regard to social relations, what is? And how

---

[64]Kevin Giles, "The Biblical Case for Slavery: Can the Bible Mislead? A Case Study in Hermeneutics," *EQ* 66 (1994): 3-17.

[65]Ibid., 4.

can Giles claim to take Scripture seriously at all in his interpretation if he discards it as authoritative revelation concerning the ordering of human relationships? May the reader judge for himself or herself. We must conclude with some reflections of an integrative nature.

Reflections on a Biblical Theology of Women's Roles in the Church

Stanley Grenz and Denise Kjesbo recently ventured to construct a biblical theology of women's ministry.[66] Kjesbo makes the historical observation that women generally have been very involved in ministry and leadership during religious revivals. She contends that the transition from the charismatic to the credentialing phase in revival movements tends to lead to the loss of leadership for women. Her recommendation is therefore to ordain women as pastors to keep the church in a state of revival. But even if Kjesbo's historical research were correct, her argument is merely pragmatic and fails to engage Scripture seriously. Moreover, she does not adequately distinguish between "leadership" and pastoral ministry. The conclusion of the present essay is that women should not be placed *in positions of ultimate responsibility and authority over the church,* not that they should not engage in responsible positions of leadership in the church.

This tendency to equate "leadership" with "pastoral ministry" can frequently be observed in egalitarian circles. For example, the title of a recent essay asks, "The Ordination of Women—Thirteen Years Later: Do we Really Value the Ministry of Women?"[67] The implication is, of course, that the only way to "value the ministry of women" is to ordain them to pastoral ministry. Wendy Cotter, in an article entitled "Women's Authority Roles in Paul's Churches: Countercultural or Conventional?" asks the question whether or not women occupied positions of leadership and authority in the Pauline churches.[68] She finds five women in this cate-

---

[66]Stanley J. Grenz with Denise Muir Kjesbo, *Women in the Church: A Biblical Theology of Women in Ministry* (Downers Grove, IL: InterVarsity, 1995); cf. also the summary in Stanley J. Grenz, "Anticipating God's New Community: Theological Foundations for Women in Ministry," *JETS* 38 (1995): 595-611. See the perceptive review by Mary A. Kassian in *Christian Week*; the extensive review by Thomas R. Schreiner in *TrinJ* 17 NS (1996): 114-24; and my review in *JETS* 41 (1998): 489-91.

[67]Klyne R. Snodgrass, "The Ordination of Women—Thirteen Years Later: Do we Really Value the Ministry of Women?" *Covenant Quarterly* 48/3 (1990): 26-43.

[68]Wendy Cotter, "Women's Authority Roles in Paul's Churches: Countercultural or Conventional?" *NovT* 36 (1994): 350-72. See further the

gory: Chloe, who was "a patroness of some kind" (1 Cor 1:11), Prisc(ill)a, who operated in tandem with her husband Aquila (Rom 16:3; 1 Cor 16:19), Euodia and Syntyche who "visited friends and set up networks for 'evangelization' " (Phil 4:2), and Phoebe, a "benefactress and guardian" and a deaconess (Rom 16:1–2).[69]

It may be concluded that (some) women functioned indeed in spheres of genuine, significant responsibility in the Pauline churches. The intriguing thing is that while Cotter appears to insinuate that all leadership positions should be opened to women in the churches indiscriminately, none of the women she identifies actually were overseers or pastor-teachers! Thus, while women were involved in exercising some sort of leadership, they do not seem to have occupied places of ultimate responsibility for God's church. This evidence from the narrative portions of Paul's epistles stands in perfect harmony with his explicit injunctions in passages such as 1 Tim 2:12. Rather than disproving the complementarian thesis, Cotter actually aids in establishing it. And once again, one is struck by the importance of defining one's terms carefully, in the present case the term "leadership."

In the remainder of the above-mentioned book, Grenz then presents the scriptural arguments for an egalitarian position. Apart from significant flaws in his discussion of individual texts which have adequately been exposed elsewhere,[70] the major weakness of Grenz's and Kjesbo's contribution lies in the fact that they present women's "teaching, leading, and exercising authority in the church as an all-or-nothing proposition."[71] Misleadingly, these authors fail to acknowledge "that there is a whole spectrum of ministry outside of the ordained office of pastor/elder wherein these gifts can be exercised."[72] This kind of presentation unduly dichotomizes the issue and also tends to misrepresent the alternative, complementarian position, which fully affirms women's exercise of spiritual gifts in a variety of responsible ministries, while, on the grounds of passages such as 1 Tim 2:12, holding that the pastoral ministry is an improper forum for women to do so.

---

present author's review of Cotter in *CBMW News* 1/4 (1996): 14.

[69]On the women mentioned in Philippians, see also A. Boyd Luter, "Partnership in the Gospel: The Role of Women in the Church at Philippi," *JETS* 39 (1996): 411–20.

[70]See esp. the reviews by Schreiner and Köstenberger referred to above.

[71]Kassian, "Review."

[72]Ibid.

Rather than embracing the radical feminist agenda and subscribing to the notion that women will only be able to live up to their potential if exactly the same church functions are open to them as to men, we affirm that Scripture teaches that man and woman are equally created in God's image; that man and woman are equally saved by grace through faith in Christ; that man and woman are fellow-heirs of grace, of equal worth in the sight of God. None of these affirmations does, however, imply *sameness in role.* For at the same time Scripture calls woman a "weaker vessel" whom husbands are to treat "in an understanding way" (1 Pet 3:7). As their "head," husbands are in positions of authority over their wives, and wives are to submit themselves voluntarily to their husbands (Eph 5:21-33; 1 Cor 11:2-16). As in the home, so in the church, for both spheres are to reflect God's creative design and are dignified by Christ. The church, made up largely of families, is to be conducted by the same principles that are to govern the home.[73] For the church is "*God's* household" (1 Tim 3:15), so that the one who does not manage his own household well should not preside over God's as an overseer or deacon (1 Tim 3:5, 12; Tit 1:6).[74]

---

[73]Cf. Vern Sheridan Poythress, "The Church as Family: Why Male Leadership in the Family Requires Male Leadership in the Church," in *Recovering Biblical Manhood and Womanhood,* 233-47. See also Egbert Schlarb, *Die Gesunde Lehre: Häresie und Wahrheit im Spiegel der Pastoralbriefe* (Marburg: N. G. Elwert, 1990), 321-56, esp. the section entitled "Das Verhältnis von οἶκος ἀνθρώπων und οἶκος θεοῦ" on pp. 342-56.

[74]Ironically, egalitarians appear to fall prey to the very error committed by Paul's opponents in 1 and 2 Timothy: an over-realized eschatology (cf. the cautious endorsement of Philip H. Towner, *Goal of Our Instruction* [JSNTSup 34; Sheffield: JSOT, 1989], 21-45, by Schreiner, "Interpretation," 111. Cf. also Philip H. Towner, *1-2 Timothy & Titus* [IVPNTCS; Downers Grove, IL: InterVarsity, 1994], 22-26 and 75-76). In 2 Tim 2:17-18, we are told that "Hymenaeus and Philetus, men who have gone astray from the truth *saying that the resurrection has already taken place,* and thus they upset the faith of some." And notably, in 1 Tim 1:18-20, Paul exhorts Timothy to "fight the good fight, keeping faith and a good conscience, which some have rejected and suffered shipwreck in regard to their faith. Among these are Hymenaeus and Alexander." Thus the same heretic, Hymenaeus, is mentioned in both 1 and 2 Timothy as one of the targets of Paul's refutation, with the reference in 1 Timothy immediately preceding chapter 2. Likewise, contemporary egalitarians argue that, in Christ, "there is neither male nor female," which they take to mean that the paradigm of new creation in Christ replaces the old paradigm of man and woman under the Fall (cf. the critiques of Richard N. Longenecker's position as developed in *New Testament Social Ethics for Today* [Grand Rapids: Eerdmans, 1984] by Köstenberger, "Gender Passages," 280; and Terrance Thiessen, "Toward a Hermeneutic for Discerning Moral Absolutes," *JETS* 36 [1993]: 203-206). But even the vast majority of egalitarians do not take this passage literally. They

Conclusion

Two professors, one an egalitarian, the other a complementarian, recently debated each other at a prestigious seminary in the United States. Afterwards, the student newspaper wrote up a brief account of their interchange. "The egalitarian professor," it reported, "affirmed that God created man and woman equal, that man and woman are of equal worth before God, and that they both have been called to exercise their spiritual gifts actively in the church." "The complementarian professor," the paper continued, "also affirmed all these things. Beyond this, however, he contended that men and women were created different and that they have been assigned different roles within which they are to fulfill their callings in the home and the church." What a wonderful way to summarize the essence of the argument! Egalitarians are largely correct in what they affirm but wrong in what they deny. It is not enough to affirm *part* of God's truth: the imbalanced emphasis of *partial* biblical truth often results in dangerous distortions of Scripture. We must affirm *all* of God's truth, and do this in proper balance.[75] Only then can we claim to live by the *whole* counsel of God and credibly contend that Scripture is the sole and final authority for our faith and practice.

---

acknowledge that the distinction between male and female still remains in place in this life. Salvation in Christ does not transform men and women instantaneously into genderless, androgynous creatures devoid of sexually distinct, yet complementary characteristics. Paul's statement in Gal 3:28 only refers to spiritual *access* to and *position* in Christ, not to an obliteration of male and female biological or other functions in this life. To deny this duplicates the error of an over-realized eschatology.

[75]For a plea for hermeneutical balance in the interpretation of New Testament gender passages, see Köstenberger, "Gender Passages," 263–67.

CHAPTER THIRTEEN

SYNTACTICAL BACKGROUND STUDIES TO 1 TIMOTHY 2:12 IN THE NEW TESTAMENT AND EXTRA-BIBLICAL GREEK LITERATURE[*]

Introduction

The injunction in 1 Tim 2:12, "I do not permit a woman to teach or to exercise authority over a man," occupies a central position in the contemporary debate on the role of women in the church. To this day, no agreement has been reached regarding the proper rendering of this passage. While exegetical and hermeneutical issues cannot be dealt with here, this study will seek to establish an accurate translation of the text.[1] A new methodological approach will be taken, utilizing the Ibycus system. A search of extrabiblical Greek literature in the relevant time period will provide a significantly enlarged data base that will aid in the study of the syntactical construction found in 1 Tim 2:12. It is hoped that the clarified translation of this text will advance its proper interpretation.

---

[*]This essay is reprinted with permission of Sheffield Academic Press from "Syntactical Background Studies to 1 Tim 2.12 in the New Testament and Extrabiblical Greek Literature," *Discourse Analysis and Other Topics in Biblical Greek* (ed. Stanley E. Porter and D. A. Carson; JSNTSup 113; Sheffield: Sheffield Academic Press, 1995), 156–79.

[1]For a treatment that incorporates the findings of this study into a comprehensive interpretation of 1 Tim 2:12, see the various chapters in *Women and the Church: A Fresh Analysis of 1 Timothy 2:11–15* (ed. Andreas J. Köstenberger, Thomas R. Schreiner, and H. Scott Baldwin; Grand Rapids: Baker, 1995).

The Recent Debate

The most disputed translational matter in 1 Tim 2:12 is the meaning of αὐθεντεῖν. It is this which occupies the bulk of this paper. Since this is the only instance in the entire New Testament and since the expression is also very rare in extrabiblical literature, certainty regarding its meaning remains elusive. Should αὐθεντεῖν be rendered as "to have or exercise authority" (NIV, NRSV, and NASB) or "to domineer or usurp authority" (NEB and KJV; cf. CEV)? If it is the former, this passage could be seen as supporting the claim that women should not be permitted to exercise authoritative teaching functions over men in the church. If it is the latter, 1 Tim 2:12 would only prohibit women from teaching men "in a domineering way."

Word Studies

The primary approach taken to resolve this issue has been that of word studies.[2] The most recent study by Baldwin, using the Ibycus system, concludes that "to assume authority over" and "to rule" are the only meanings for αὐθεντεῖν that are unambiguously attested for the period surrounding the New Testament. However, due to the following factors word studies of αὐθεντεῖν need to be complemented by another approach.

First of all, the number of occurrences of αὐθεντεῖν in literature roughly contemporary with the New Testament is very small. Baldwin gives only three references from the first century BCE to the second century CE where the verb αὐθεντεῖν occurs: Philodemus' *Rhetorica* (first century BCE), Ptolemy's *Tetrabiblos* (second century CE), and a non-literary papyrus dated 27 BCE (BGU 1208). The scarcity of data should keep one from claiming certainty regarding the meaning of αὐθεντεῖν based on word studies alone.

Also, word studies are not the hard science they are sometimes made out to be. They can help establish the lexical core of a given term, but they should not be used to exclude the possibility that a word can take on a certain connotation, i.e. in the case of αὐθεντεῖν a negative one, as some have sought to argue.[3]

---

[2] Cf. C. D. Osburn, *"Authenteo* (1 Timothy 2:12)," *ResQ* 25 (1982): 1–12; G. W. Knight, "Αὐθεντέω in Reference to Women in 1 Timothy 2.12," *NTS* 30 (1984): 143–57; L.E. Wilshire, "The TLG Computer and Further Research to Αὐθεντέω in 1 Timothy 2.12," *NTS* 34 (1988): 120–34; and H. S. Baldwin, Chap. 3 and App. 2 in *Women in the Church: A Fresh Analysis of 1 Timothy 2:9–15* (ed. A. J. Köstenberger et al.; Grand Rapids: Baker, 1995).

[3] Cf. e.g. G.W. Knight, *The Role Relationship of Men and Women* (Phillipsburg, NJ: Presbyterian and Reformed, rev. edn, 1985), 18, n. 1.

Finally, modern linguistics cautions against absolutizing any one lexical equivalent for a given term. It is agreed that, ultimately, a word's context is determinative for its meaning. Since word studies deal with a finite number of contexts, they should not be expected to settle with certainty the meaning of a word in any possible context. Due to the limited contribution of word studies, other creative approaches need to be explored. Is it possible that οὐδέ as a coordinating conjunction joins two words in a particular syntactical pattern which could shed light on the meaning of these words?

Syntactical Analyses

The need for syntactical background studies to understand 1 Tim 2:12 has been recognized by Payne and Moo, who engaged in a detailed interchange on the syntactical significance of οὐδέ in 1 Tim 2:12.[4] Payne has argued that οὐδέ connects the two infinitives διδάσκειν and αὐθεντεῖν "in order to convey a single coherent idea," i.e. as a hendiadys, so that the rendering of the passage should be: "I do not permit a woman to teach *in a domineering manner.*"[5] Moo, however, has maintained that, while οὐδέ "certainly usually joins "two *closely related* items," it does not usually join together words that restate the same thing or that are mutually interpreting."[6] He has concluded that, while teaching and having authority are closely related, "they are nonetheless distinct," referring also to 1 Tim 3:2, 4–5 and 5:17 which distinguish those concepts.[7]

Indeed, Payne's study is subject to improvement at several points:

1. Payne studies only Paul. A more comprehensive study of οὐδέ in the entire New Testament seems desirable to broaden the data base available for comparison.

2. Payne studies all the occurrences of οὐδέ in Paul, even where it joins nouns, not verbs. However, one should sharpen the focus by study-

---

[4]Cf. P. B. Payne, "οὐδέ in 1 Timothy 2:12," presented at the Annual ETS Conference, November 21, 1986; D. J. Moo, "1 Timothy 2:11–15: Meaning and Significance," *Trin*/NS 1 (1980): 62–83; and *idem*, "The Interpretation of 1 Timothy 2:11–15: A Rejoinder," *Trin*/NS 2 (1981): 198–222.

[5]Cf. Payne, "οὐδέ," 10.

[6]Cf. D. J. Moo, "What Does It Mean Not to Teach or Have Authority Over Men? 1 Timothy 2:11–15," in J. Piper and W. Grudem (eds.), *Recovering Biblical Manhood & Womanhood—A Response to Evangelical Feminism* (Wheaton, IL: Crossway, 1991), 187.

[7]Cf. ibid.

ing the passages where οὐδέ joins verbs, since that is the construction found in 1 Tim 2:12.[8]

3. Payne does not consider uses of μηδέ in Paul or elsewhere in the New Testament. Only seven instances remain where Paul uses οὐδέ to connect verbs (1 Cor 15:50; 2 Cor 7:12; Gal 1:17; 4:14; Phil 2:16; 2 Thess 3:8; 1 Tim 6:16). References including μηδέ in writings traditionally attributed to Paul provide eight further examples alone (Rom 9:11, 16b; 14:21; 2 Cor 4:2; Col 2:21; 2 Thess 2:2; 1 Tim 1:3-4; 6:17). Two of these, 1 Tim 1:3-4 and 6:17, occur in the same letter.

4. Payne starts with the assumption that αὐθεντεῖν means "domineer." However, the meaning of αὐθεντεῖν in 1 Tim 2:12 should not be merely asserted, but be established by an inductive study of all the instances of οὐδέ joining verbs in the New Testament and extrabiblical Greek literature.

5. Since Payne presupposes that αὐθεντεῖν means "domineer," he concludes that "teach" and "domineer" by themselves are conceptually too far apart to be joined by οὐδέ —which usually joins closely related terms—in a coordinating manner. Thus Payne views the second term joined by οὐδέ in 1 Tim 2:12, αὐθεντεῖν, as subordinate to the first, διδάσκειν. However, if αὐθεντεῖν were to mean "to have authority" rather than "to domineer," it would be quite closely related to διδάσκειν, "to teach." In that case, consistent with Payne's own observations on how οὐδέ generally functions, οὐδέ could well link the two closely related terms, "to teach" and "to have authority," in a coordinating fashion. Payne's argument is circular, and his conclusion is unduly predetermined by his presupposition regarding the meaning of αὐθεντεῖν.

6. Payne's terminology is ambiguous when he calls two terms "closely related." He seems to use this terminology in the sense of "essentially one" so that he can conclude that in 1 Tim 2:12 "οὐδέ joins together two elements in order to convey a single coherent idea." However, as will be shown below, two terms can be "closely related" and yet be distinct. For example, Matt 6:20 refers to heaven "where thieves neither break in nor steal." While "breaking in" and "stealing" are sequentially related and may be seen as components of essentially one event, i.e. burglary, the two activities are not so closely related as to lose their own distinctness. The burglar first breaks in, and then steals.

7. Payne's terminology categorizing the use of οὐδέ is inconsistent. At the beginning of his study, he terms his second category "those which spe-

---

[8]Studies of passages where οὐδέ links nouns yield similar results as studies of instances where οὐδέ connects verbs.

cify with greater clarity the meaning of one word or phrase by conjoining it with another word or phrase."[9] Yet in his conclusion, he calls the same category "οὐδέ joins together two elements in order to convey a single coherent idea."[10] From beginning to end, Payne has subtly shifted from one definition of this crucial category to another. While his initial definition allows for terms to be closely related and yet distinct, Payne's later categorization unduly narrows his earlier definition so that now closely related yet distinct terms seem excluded.

8. Payne only notes translations that support his own understanding of 1 Tim 2:12, i.e. those that render αὐθεντεῖν with "domineer" or similarly negative connotations.[11] However, he fails to observe that neither NASB, NRSV, nor NIV render the term with a negative connotation. The NASB has "exercise authority," the NIV and NRSV translate αὐθεντεῖν with "to have authority."[12]

Summary

The recent history of the debate has been dominated by word studies. However, the scarcity of αὐθεντεῖν and other factors limit the potential contribution of word studies in the present case. A syntactical analysis should therefore supplement such studies. As shown, the major syntactical study on the passage is subject to improvement. Therefore a fresh analysis of New Testament syntactical parallels to 1 Tim 2:12 in biblical and extrabiblical literature should be conducted.[13]

---

[9]Cf. Payne, "οὐδέ," 1.

[10]Ibid., 10.

[11]Ibid.

[12]R. C. and C. C. Kroeger, *I Suffer Not a Woman: Rethinking 1 Tim 2:11-15 in Light of Ancient Evidence* (Grand Rapids: Baker, 1991), 83-84 and 189-92, have recently argued for the presence of an "infinitive of indirect discourse" in 1 Tim 2:12. These authors translate the passage as "I do not permit a woman to teach *that she is the author of man*," finding here an allusion to gnostic teaching. However, none of the instances of "infinitives of indirect discourse" cited by the Kroegers includes οὐδέ. Moreover, a use of οὐδέ similar to ὅτι is unsubstantiated in the New Testament or elsewhere.

[13]A few constraints should be noted. Although the title of this paper is "*Syntactical* Background Studies," the conclusions drawn from the syntax as found in 1 Tim 2:12 will involve *semantic* judgments (especially in the two patterns of the usage of οὐδέ which will be identified). There are also other syntactical and semantic issues raised by 1 Tim 2:12 that will not be dealt with in this study, such as the question whether ἀνδρός should be read with both διδάσκειν and αὐθεντεῖν or exactly how the ἀλλά-clause at the end of v. 12 relates to the preceding clause and which verb should be supplied there. Even the verbal aspect or verb tense of the verbs involved will not be dealt with at this stage of this investigation since, as will become evident, the major thesis of this paper is not materially affected by the

Syntactical Parallels to 1 Tim 2:12 in the New Testament

The passage reads as follows: διδάσκειν δὲ γυναικὶ οὐκ ἐπιτρέπω οὐδὲ αὐθεντεῖν ἀνδρός, ἀλλ' εἶναι ἐν ἡσυχίᾳ. One can lay out the syntactical pattern found in 1 Tim 2:12 this way: (1) negated finite verb + (2) infinitive + (3) οὐδέ + infinitive, and, if available, + (4) ἀλλά + infinitive.[14]

Strictly speaking, there is only one close syntactical parallel to 1 Tim 2:12 in the New Testament, Acts 16:21, where the same construction, a negated finite verb + infinitive and οὐδέ + infinitive, is found.[15] However, if one allows for verbal forms other than infinitives to be linked by οὐδέ, fifty-two further passages can be identified. These can be grouped into two patterns of the usage of οὐδέ.

- *Pattern #1* : two activities or concepts are viewed positively in and of themselves, but their exercise is prohibited or their existence denied due to circumstances or conditions adduced in the context.

- *Pattern #2* : two activities or concepts are viewed negatively and consequently their exercise is prohibited or to be avoided or their existence is denied.

---

aspect or tense of the verbs.

[14]This syntactical pattern is not necessarily always found in this particular chronological order. For example, in 1 Tim 2:12, the first infinitive precedes the negated finite verb so that the order there is (2), (1), (3), and (4). However, a study of preceding infinitives in Pauline literature indicates that it is hard to find any consistent significance in preceding rather than following infinitives. Cf. the nineteen instances of preceding infinitives in Pauline writings, Rom 7:18; 8:8; 1 Cor 7:36; 14:35; 15:50; 2 Cor 8:10; 11:30; 12:1; Gal 4:9,17; Phil 1:12; 2 Thess 1:3; 1 Tim 2:12; 3:5; 5:11, 25; 6:7, 16; 2 Tim 2:13. At any rate, the central thesis of this paper is not affected by whether the first infinitive precedes or follows the negated finite verb. Likewise, the presence or absence of element (4) does not substantially affect the thesis of this paper.

[15]This is one major reason why, after screening less close syntactical parallels, this study will proceed to search extrabiblical Greek literature for more exact parallels involving, as in 1 Tim 2:12, two infinitives governed by a negated finite verb. However, the fact that, strictly speaking, there is only one close syntactical parallel to 1 Tim 2:12 in the New Testament, does not mean that New Testament passages where a negated finite verb governs two verb forms other than infinitives are without value for identifying general patterns of the usage of οὐδέ. Rather, the New Testament allows one to identify basic patterns of the usage of οὐδέ that can then be tested and refined by resorting to extrabiblical Greek literature. This is the approach followed in the present study.

In both patterns, the conjunction οὐδέ coordinates activities of the same order, i.e. activities that are either both viewed positively or negatively by the writer or speaker. The instances of *Pattern #1* in the New Testament can be diagrammed as follows.

Table 7: Pattern #1 in the New Testament

Pattern #1: two activities or concepts are viewed positively in and of themselves, but their exercise is prohibited or their existence denied due to circumstances or conditions adduced in the context.

Matt 6:26	οὐ σπείρουσιν (sow)	οὐδὲ θερίζουσιν (harvest)
		οὐδὲ σψνάγουσιν εἰς ἀποθήκας (gather into barns)
Matt 6:28	οὐ κοπιῶσιν (labor)	οὐδὲ νήθουσιν (spin)
Matt 7:6	Μὴ δῶτε (give)	μηδὲ βάλητε (throw)
Matt 7:18	οὐ δύναται ποιεῖν (can yield)	οὐδὲ ποιεῖν (yield) *
Matt 10:14	μὴ δέξηται (receive)	μηδὲ ἀκούσῃ (listen)
Matt 13:13	οὐκ ἀκούουσιν (hear)	οὐδὲ συνίουσιν (understand)
Matt 22:46	οὐδεὶς ἐδύνατο ἀποκριθῆναι (could answer)	οὐδὲ ἐτόλμησέν ἐπερωτῆσαι (dared to ask)
Matt 23:13	οὐκ εἰσέρχεσθε (enter)	οὐδὲ ἀφίετε εἰσελθεῖν (permit to enter)
Mark 6:11	μὴ δέξηται (receive)	μηδὲ ἀκούσωσιν (listen; cf. Matt 10:14) **
Mark 8:17	οὔπω νοεῖτε (understand)	οὐδὲ συνίετε (understand)
Mark 13:15	μὴ καταβάτω (go down)	μηδὲ εἰσελθάτω (enter)
Luke 6:44	οὐ συλλέγουσιν (pick)	οὐδὲ τρυγῶσιν (gather)
Luke 12:24	οὐ σπείρουσιν (sow)	οὐδὲ θερίζουσιν (harvest; cf. Matt 6:26)
Luke 12:27	οὐ κοπιᾷ (labor)	οὐδὲ νήθει (spin; cf. Matt 6:28)
Luke 17:23	μὴ ἀπέλθητε (depart)	μηδὲ διώξητε (follow)
Luke 18:4	οὐ φοβοῦμαι (fear [God])	οὐδὲ ἐντρέπομαι (care [about man])
John 14:17	οὐ θεωρεῖ (behold)	οὐδὲ γινώσκει (know)
Acts 4:18	μὴ φθέγγεσθαι (speak)	μηδὲ διδάσκειν (teach)
Acts 9:9	οὐκ ἔφαγεν (eat)	οὐδὲ ἔπιεν (drink)
Acts 16:21	οὐκ ἔξεστιν παραδέχεσθαι (accept)	οὐδὲ ποιεῖν (practice)
Acts 17:24-25	οὐκ κατοικεῖ (dwell)	οὐδὲ θεραπεύεται (be served)
Acts 21:21	μὴ περιτέμνειν (circumcise)	μηδὲ περιπατεῖν (walk [in customs])
Rom 9:11	μήπω γεννηθέντων (born)	μηδὲ πραξάντων (done)
Rom 9:16	οὐ τοῦ θέλοντος (wishing)	οὐδὲ τοῦ τρέχοντος (running)
Rom 14:21	μὴ φαγεῖν (eat)	μηδὲ πιεῖν (drink)
1 Cor 15:50	κληρονομῆσαι οὐ δύναται (can inherit)	οὐδὲ κληρονομεῖ (inherit) *
Gal 1:16-17	οὐ προσανεθέμην (consult)	οὐδὲ ἀνῆλθον (go up)
Col 2:21	μὴ ἅψῃ (touch)	μηδὲ γεύσῃ μηδὲ θίγῃς (taste, handle)

(Table continued on following page.)

(Table continued from preceding page.)

1 Tim 2:12	διδάσκειν οὐκ ἐπιτρέπω (teach)	οὐδὲ αὐθεντεῖν ἀνδρός (have authority over a man)
1 Tim 6:16	εἶδεν οὐδεὶς (see)	οὐδὲ ἰδεῖν δύναται (can see)
Heb 10:8	οὐκ ἠθέλησας (desire)	οὐδὲ εὐδόκησας (be well-pleased)
1 John 3:6	οὐχ ἑώρακεν (see)	οὐδὲ ἔγνωκεν (know)
Rev 12:8	οὐκ ἴσχυσεν (prevail)	οὐδὲ τόπος εὑρέθη (place be found) *

Abbreviations: *=change of subject; **=change from sg. to pl. verb form; ***=used substantivally

A few examples illustrate this pattern. In Acts 16:21, the closest syntactical parallel to 1 Tim 2:12 in the New Testament, the two terms in the infinitive, παραδέχεσθαι and ποιεῖν, are conceptual parallels. Neither "accepting" nor "practicing" carry negative connotations in and of themselves. However, due to circumstances indicated in the context, "being Romans," the exercise of these otherwise legitimate activities is considered "not lawful." In Acts 21:21, Paul is told that there are reports that he forbids Jews living among Gentiles to carry out two activities viewed positively by the speakers, circumcising their children and walking according to Jewish customs. And in Gal 1:16–17, Paul insists that, upon his conversion, he did not immediately consult with others nor go up to Jerusalem, two activities which are not intrinsically viewed negatively, to underscore that he had been divinely commissioned.

The New Testament occurrences of *Pattern #2* present themselves as follows.

Table 8: Pattern #2 in the New Testament

Pattern #2: two activities or concepts are viewed negatively and consequently their exercise is prohibited or their existence denied or to be avoided.

Matt 6:20	οὐ διορύσσουσιν (break in)	οὐδὲ κλέπτουσιν (steal)
Matt 12:19	οὐκ ἐρίσει (quarrel)	οὐδὲ κραυγάσει (cry out)
Luke 3:14	μηδένα διασείσητε (extort money)	μηδὲ συκοφαντήσητε (accuse falsely)
Luke 12:33	κλέπτης οὐκ ἐγγίζει (thief come near)	οὐδὲ διαφθείρει (destroy; cf. Matt 6:20) *
John 4:15	μὴ διψῶ (thirst)	μηδὲ διέρχωμαι ἀντλεῖν (come to draw)
John 14:27	μὴ ταρασσέσθω (be troubled)	μηδὲ δειλιάτω (be afraid)
Acts 2:27	οὐκ ἐγκαταλείψεις (abandon)	οὐδὲ δώσεις ἰδεῖν διαφθοράν (give to see decay)

(Table continued on following page.)

(Table continued from preceding page.)

2 Cor 4:2	μὴ περιπατοῦντες ἐν πανουργίᾳ (distort)	μηδὲ δολοῦντες (walk in deceit)
2 Cor 7:12	οὐκ ἕνεκεν τοῦ ἀδικήσαντος (the wrongdoer)	οὐδὲ ἕνεκεν τοῦ ἀδικηθέντος (the injured party)***
Gal 4:14	οὐκ ἐξουθενήσατε (treat with contempt)	οὐδὲ ἐξεπτύσατε (scorn)
Phil 2:16	οὐκ εἰς κενὸν ἔδραμον (run in vain)	οὐδὲ εἰς κενὸν ἐκοπίασα (labor in vain)
2 Thess 2:2	μὴ σαλευθῆναι (become unsettled)	μηδὲ θροεῖσθαι (become alarmed)
2 Thess 3:7-8	οὐκ ἠτακτήσαμεν (be idle)	οὐδὲ ἐφάγομεν (eat another's food)
1 Tim 1:3-4	μὴ ἑτεροδιδασκαλεῖν (teach error)	μηδὲ προσέχειν μύθοις (pay attention to myths)
1 Tim 6:17	μὴ ὑψηλοφρονεῖν (be arrogant)	μηδὲ ἠλπικέναι ἐπὶ πλούτου (put hope in wealth)
Heb 12:5	μὴ ὀλιγώρει (despise)	μηδὲ ἐκλύου (consider lightly)
Heb 13:5	οὐ μή ἀνῶ (leave)	οὐδ' οὐ μή ἐγκαταλίπω (forsake)
1 Pet 2:22	ἁμαρτίαν οὐκ ἐποίησεν (commit sin)	οὐδὲ εὑρέθη δόλος (deceit be found)*
1 Pet 3:14	μὴ φοβηθῆτε (be afraid)	μηδὲ ταραχθῆτε (be disturbed)
Rev 7:16	οὐ πεινάσουσιν (hunger)	οὐδὲ διψήσουσιν (thirst)

Abbreviations: *=change of subject; **=change from sg. to pl. verb form; ***=used substantivally

The following examples demonstrate the second pattern, the prohibition or denial of two activities which are viewed negatively by the writer or speaker. In John 4:15, the Samaritan woman expresses her desire to avoid two things she views negatively, thirsting and having to come to the well to draw water. In 1 Thess 3:7-8, Paul denies that, at his previous visit, he had engaged in two activities which he views negatively, being idle and eating another's food. A passage in the epistle under consideration, 1 Tim 1:3-4, indicates the instruction to Timothy to command certain ones to avoid two activities the author views negatively, teaching error and holding to myths and endless genealogies. Later in the same epistle, in 1 Tim 6:17, one finds the instruction to Timothy to command the rich in his congregation to avoid two things viewed negatively by the writer, being arrogant and setting their hope on the uncertainty of riches.

These examples set forth the New Testament evidence that οὐδέ joins terms that denote activities that are either both viewed positively or negatively by the writer or speaker.[16] The implications of this observation

---

[16]The following subcategories of this basic pattern may be identified: 1. Synonymous Concepts: Matt 7:18; Mark 8:17; John 14:27; Acts 2:27; 1 Cor

for 1 Tim 2:12 will be explored after the extrabiblical parallels preceding or contemporary with the New Testament have been considered as well.

Syntactical Parallels to 1 Tim 2:12 in Extrabiblical Greek Literature

The Ibycus system provides the modern scholar with unprecedented opportunities in the study of ancient literature. Without the Ibycus system, this study would not have been possible. The more common use of the Ibycus traces the occurrence of a certain term in a large number of ancient writings, usually for the purpose of word studies and comparisons. However, this system has the capacity of producing more than word searches. Although the word entries are not tagged, i.e. not semantically defined, the Ibycus, properly managed, is capable of string searches (the search for two or more terms used in conjunction with one another in a given writing).

In the present scenario, the search pattern presented itself as follows: οὐ, οὐκ, or οὐχ and οὐδέ. The system thus flags all instances where a negative and οὐδέ are used in the same context. Since the Ibycus system operates with a context of about three lines, some of the references have the negative and οὐδέ occur too far apart or even in different clauses altogether, so that a manual weeding out of the references is necessary. Furthermore, since it seemed wise to limit the search to negated *finite* verbs + infinitive + οὐδέ + infinitive, instances where the negative modifies, say, a participle, also need to be eliminated. Most importantly, however, only a small fraction of the passages printed out by the Ibycus system are instances where the negated finite verb as well as οὐδέ are governing infinitives (as opposed to, for example, two finite verbs, or a finite verb and two or more nouns). Finally, the system also gives references of the relative

---

15:50; Gal 4:14; Phil 2:16; 2 Thess 2:2; 1 Tim 6:16; Heb 10:8; 12:5; 13:5; 1 Pet 3:14; 2. Conceptual Parallels: Matt 6:28=Luke 12:27; Matt 7:6; 10:14=Mark 6:11; Matt 12:19; Luke 3:14; 6:44; 18:4; John 14:17; Acts 4:18; 17:24-25; Rom 9:16; 2 Cor 4:2; Col 2:21; 2 Thess 3:7-8; 1 Pet 2:22; 1 John 3:6; Rev 12:8; 3. Complementary Concepts: Acts 9:9; Rom 14:21; 2 Cor 7:12; Rev 7:16; 4. Sequential Concepts: Matt 6:20,26=Luke 12:24; Matt 13:13; Mark 13:15; Luke 12:33; 17:23; John 4:15; Rom 9:11; 5. Ascensive Concepts: Matt 22:46; 23:13; Acts 16:21; 6. Specific to General or General to Specific: a. Specific to General: Acts 21:21; 1 Tim 2:12; b. General to Specific: Gal 1:16-17; 1 Tim 1:3-4; 6:17. Note that there may be some overlap between these categories so that they should not be understood to be totally mutually exclusive but rather as indicating the most likely emphasis on the relationship between the two concepts linked by οὐδέ.

pronoun οὖ, and instances where the subjects tied to οὐ and οὐδέ are different.

An extraordinary amount of work is required to extract from the initial printout the references relevant for the present study. In order to arrive at the forty-eight syntactical parallels to 1 Tim 2:12, about three hundred pages of data had to be sifted, with each page including about ten passages, for a total of about three thousand references. Thus only one out of sixty references, or about 1.5 %, were true syntactical parallels to 1 Tim 2:12. While this may appear to be an excessive amount of data and work for a relatively small collection of passages, the results are worth the effort, since this study provides for the first time exhaustive background data for the syntactical study of 1 Tim 2:12. The Ibycus system has enabled the researcher to study all the extant Greek literature directly relevant for the study of the syntax used in 1 Tim 2:12 (i.e. literature from the third century BCE until the end of the first century CE)—the LXX, the papyri and inscriptions available on the Ibycus, and all the extant works of Polybius, Dionysius Halicarnassensis, Diodorus Siculus, Josephus, Philo, and Plutarch.

Following is the list of syntactical parallels to 1 Tim 2:12:

LXX:
1. 1 Macc 15:14: καὶ ἐκύκλωσεν τὴν πόλιν, καὶ τὰ πλοῖα ἀπὸ θαλάσσης συνῆψαν, καὶ ἔθλιβε τὴν πόλιν ἀπὸ τῆς γῆς καὶ τῆς θαλάσσης, καὶ (1) οὐκ εἴασεν οὐδένα (2) ἐκπορεύεσθαι (3) οὐδὲ εἰσπορεύεσθαι.[17]
2. Sir 18:6: (1) οὐκ ἔστιν (2) ἐλαττῶσαι (3) οὐδὲ προσθεῖναι, καὶ οὐκ ἔστιν ἐξιχνιάσαι τὰ θαυμάσια τοῦ κυρίου.[18]
3. Isa 42:24b: οὐχὶ ὁ θεός, ᾧ ἡμάρτοσαν αὐτῷ καὶ (1) οὐκ ἐβούλοντο ἐν ταῖς ὁδοῖς αὐτοῦ (2) πορεύεσθαι (3) οὐδὲ ἀκούειν τοῦ νόμου αὐτοῦ;[19]
4. Ezek 44:13: καὶ (1) οὐκ ἐγγιοῦσι πρός με τοῦ (2) ἱερατεύειν μοι (3) οὐδὲ τοῦ προσάγειν πρὸς τὰ ἅγια υἱῶν τοῦ Ισραηλ οὐδὲ πρὸς τὰ ἅγια τῶν ἁγίων μου καὶ λήμψονται ἀτιμίαν αὐτῶν ἐν τῇ πλανήσει, ᾗ ἐπλανήθησαν.[20]

---

[17]He surrounded the city, and the ships joined battle from the sea; he pressed the city hard from land and sea, and (1) permitted no one (2) to leave (3) or enter it. This translation is taken from Bruce M. Metzger, *The Apocrypha of the Old Testament* (New York: Oxford University Press, 1977).

[18][Who can measure his majestic power? And who can fully recount his mercies?] (1) It is not possible (2) to diminish (3) or increase them, nor is it possible to trace the wonders of the Lord (trans. Metzger, *Apocrypha*).

[19][Who gave Jacob up for spoil, and Israel to plunderers?] Was it not God, against whom they have sinned, and in whose ways (1) they were not willing (2) to walk (3) nor to obey my law (own trans.)?

[20]And (1) they shall not come near to Me (2) to serve as a priest to Me, (3) nor to approach any of the holy things of the sons of Israel, nor to the holiest of my holy things; but they shall bear their dishonor in their shame by which they

5. DanTh 5:8: καὶ εἰσεπορεύοντο πάντες οἱ σοφοὶ τοῦ βασιλέως καὶ (1) οὐκ ἠδύναντο τὴν γραφὴν (2) ἀναγνῶναι (3) οὐδὲ τὴν σύγκρισιν γνωρίσαι τῷ βασιλεῖ.[21]

Inscriptions:
6. Attica.IG II(2).11589 (third century BCE): . . . (1) οὐκ ἄνσχετο (2) δῶρα δέχεσθαι (3) οὐδὲ κλύειν ἱκέτου Τισαμενοῖο πατρός.[22]
7. PZenPestm.21 (246 BCE): Νίκων δὲ ὁ κρινόμενος πρὸς Ἀντίπατρον (1) οὐκ ἔφατο (2) εἰληθέναι τὸ παιδάριον παρ' αὐτῶν (3) οὐδὲ ἔχειν αὐτὸ παρευρέσει οὐδεμιᾶι.[23]

Polybius (202-120 BCE):
8. *Hist.* II.56.10: (1) δεῖ τοιγαροῦν οὐκ (2) ἐκπλήττειν τὸν συγγραφέα τερατευόμενον διὰ τῆς ἱστορίας τοὺς ἐντυγχάνοντας (3) οὐδὲ τοὺς ἐνδεχομένους λόγους ζητεῖν καὶ τὰ παρεπόμενα τοῖς ὑποκειμένοις ἐξαριθμεῖσθαι, καθάπερ οἱ τραγῳδιογράφοι, τῶν δὲ πραχθέντων καὶ ῥηθέντων κατ' ἀλήθειαν αὐτῶν μνημονεύειν πάμπαν, κἂν πάνυ μέτρια τυγχάνωσιν ὄντα.[24]
9. *Hist.* V.10.5: (1) οὐ γὰρ ἐπ' ἀπωλείᾳ δεῖ καὶ ἀφανισμῷ τοῖς ἀγνοήσασι (2) πολεμεῖν τοὺς ἀγαθοὺς ἄνδρας, ἀλλ' ἐπὶ διορθώσει καὶ μεταθέσει τῶν ἡμαρτημένων, (3) οὐδὲ συναναιρεῖν τὰ μηδὲν ἀδικοῦντα τοῖς ἠδικηκόσιν, ἀλλὰ συσσῴζειν μᾶλλον καὶ συνεξαιρεῖσθαι τοῖς ἀναιτίοις τοὺς δοκοῦντας ἀδικεῖν.[25]
10. *Hist.* VI.15.8: . . . τούτους (1) οὐ δύνανται (2) χειρίζειν, ὡς πρέπει, ποτὲ δὲ τὸ παράπαν (3) οὐδὲ συντελεῖν . . .[26]

---

were deceived (own trans.).

[21]Then all the king's wise men came in, but (1) they could not (2) read the inscription (3) [n]or make known its interpretation to the king (trans. Metzger, *Apocrypha*).

[22]. . . (1) he did not stand up (2) to receive gifts (3) nor to give ear to the suppliant, Tisamenoios the father [or: the father of Tisamenoios] (own trans.).

[23]Nikon the judge (1) did not say to Antipater (2) to take the boy from them (3) nor to hold him under any pretense (own trans.).

[24]A historical author (1) should not (2) try to thrill his readers by such exaggerated pictures, (3) nor should he, like a tragic poet, try to imagine the probable utterances of his characters or reckon up all the consequences probably incidental to the occurrences with which he deals, but simply record what really happened and what really was said, however commonplace (this and the following translations are taken from the Loeb Classical Library series).

[25]For good men (1) should not (2) make war on wrong-doers with the object of destroying and exterminating them, but with that of correcting and reforming their errors, (3) nor should they involve the guiltless in the fate of the guilty, (4) but rather extend to those whom they think guilty the mercy and deliverance they offer to the innocent.

[26][For the processions they call triumphs, in which the generals bring the actual spectacle of their achievements before the eyes of their fellow-citizens,] (1) cannot (2) be properly organized and sometimes even cannot (3) be held at all, [unless the senate consents and provides the requisite funds.]

11. *Hist.* XXX.5.8.4–6: . . . (1) οὐκ ἐβούλοντο (2) συνδυάζειν (3) οὐδὲ προκαταλαμβάνειν σφᾶς αὐτοὺς ὅρκοις καὶ συνθήκαις, (4) ἀλλ᾽ ἀκέραιοι διαμένοντες κερδαίνειν τὰς ἐξ ἑκάστων ἐλπίδας.[27]

12. *Hist.* XXX.24.2.3–4: . . . (1) οὐ δοκοῦσι δὲ (2) γινώσκεσθαι παρὰ τοῖς ἀπαντῶσιν (3) οὐδὲ συνορᾶσθαι διότι λέλυνται σαφῶς, ἐὰν μή τι παράλογον ποιῶσι καὶ τῶν ἄλλων ἐξηλλαγμένον.[28]

13. *Hist.* XXXI.12.5–6: . . . τὴν δὲ σύγκλητον (1) οὐ τολμήσειν ἔτι (2) βοηθεῖν (3) οὐδὲ συνεπισχύειν τοῖς περὶ τὸν Λυσίαν τοιαῦτα διεργασαμένοις.[29]

Dionysius Halicarnassensis (first century BCE):

14. *De Thucydide* 7.13–15: Θουκυδίδη δὲ τῷ προελομένῳ μίαν ὑπόθεσιν, ᾗ παρεγίνετο αὐτός, (1) οὐκ ἥρμοττεν (2) ἐγκαταμίσγειν τῇ διηγήσει τὰ θεατρικὰς γοητείας (3) οὐδὲ πρὸς τὴν ἀγάτην ἁρμόττεσθαι τῶν ἀναγνωσομένων, ἣν ἐκεῖναι πεφύκασι φέρειν αἱ συντάξεις, (4) ἀλλὰ πρὸς τὴν ὠφέλειαν . . .[30]

15. *Antiqu. Rom.* 10.12.3–5: . . . ἢ ὡς (1) οὐ δεῖ (2) κοινωνεῖν (3) οὐδὲ παρεῖναι τῇ ζητήσει τοὺς ἀνειληφότας τὴν τοῦ δήμου ἀρχήν.[31]

16. *De Comp. Verb.* 23:2–5: (1) οὐ ζητεῖ καθ᾽ ἓν ἕκαστον ὄνομα ἐκ περιφανείας (2) ὁρᾶσθαι (3) οὐδὲ ἐν ἕδρᾳ πάντα βεβηκέναι πλατείᾳ τε καὶ ἀσφαλεῖ οὐδὲ μακροὺς τοὺς μεταξὺ αὐτῶν εἶναι χρόνους.[32]

Diodorus Siculus (c. 40 BCE):

17. *Bibl. Hist.* 3.30.2.8–9: (1) οὐ χρὴ δὲ (2) θαυμάζειν (3) οὐδὲ ἀπιστεῖν τοῖς λεγομένοις, πολλὰ τούτων παραδοξότερα κατὰ πᾶσαν τὴν οἰκουμένην γεγονότα διὰ τῆς ἀληθοῦς ἱστορίας παρειληφότας.[33]

---

[27][As they wished none of the kings and princes to despair of gaining their help and alliance,] (1) they did not desire (2) to run in harness with Rome (3) and engage themselves by oaths and treaties, (4) but preferred to remain unembarrassed and able to reap profit from any quarter.

[28][The inhabitants of Peraea were like slaves unexpectedly released from their fetters, who, unable to believe the truth, take longer steps than their natural ones] and (1) fancy that those they meet will (2) not know (3) and see for certain that they are free unless they behave in some strange way and differently from other men.

[29][For the Syrians would at once transfer the crown to him, even if he appeared accompanied only by a single slave,] while the senate (1) would not go so far as (2) to help (3) and support Lysias after his conduct.

[30]Thucydides, however, chose a single episode in which he personally participated: (1) it was therefore inappropriate for him (2) to adulterate his narrative with entertaining fantasies (3) or to arrange it in a way which would confuse his readers, as his predecessors' compositions would naturally do. (4) His purpose was to benefit his readers . . .

[31] . . . or that the magistrates of the populace (1) ought not (2) to take part in or (3) be present at the inquiry.

[32][The polished style of composition, which I placed second in order, has the following character.] (1) It does not intend each word (2) to be viewed from all sides, (3) nor that every word shall stand on a broad, firm base, nor that the intervals of time between them shall be long . . .

[33](1) Nor is there any occasion (2) to be surprised at this statement (3) or to distrust it, since we have learned through trustworthy history of many things more astonishing than this which have taken place throughout all the inhabited world.

18. *Bibl. Hist.* 3.37.9.1–4: διόπερ τηλικούτου μεγέθους ὃ φεως εἰς ὄψιν κοινὴν κατηντηκότος (1) *οὐκ ἄξιον* (2) *ἀπιστεῖν* τοῖς Αἰθίοψιν (3) *οὐδὲ μῦθον* (4) *ὑπολαμβάνειν* τὸ θρυλούμενον ὑπ' αὐτῶν.[34]

Josephus (37–100 CE):

19. *Ap.* 2.6.1–3: (1) ἔστι μὲν οὖν *οὐ ῥάδιον* αὐτοῦ (2) *διελθεῖν* τὸν λόγον (3) *οὐδὲ* σαφῶς *γνῶναι* τί λέγειν βούλεται.[35]

20. *Ap.* 2.212.1–2: (1) *οὐ* γὰρ *ἐᾷ* τὴν γῆν αὐτῶν (2) *πυρπολεῖν* (3) *οὐδὲ τέμνειν* ἥμερα δένδρα, ἀλλὰ καὶ *σκυλεύειν* ἀπείρηκε τοὺς ἐν τῇ μάχῃ πεσόντας καὶ τῶν αἰχμαλώτων προυνόησεν.[36]

21. *BJ* 5.199.3–5: κατὰ γὰρ τὰς ἄλλας (1) *οὐκ ἐξῆν* (2) *παρελθεῖν* γυναιξίν, ἀλλ' (3) *οὐδὲ* κατὰ τὴν σφετέραν *ὑπερβῆναι* τὸ διατείχισμα.[37]

22. *Ant.* II.116.3–5: ὡς (1) *οὐ προσῆκε* μὲν αὐτὸν περὶ τἀδελφοῦ (2) *δεδιέναι* (3) *οὐδὲ* τὰ μὴ δεινὰ δι' ὑποψίας *λαμβάνειν* . . .[38]

23. *Ant.* VI.20.3–5: (1) *οὐκ* (2) *ἐπιθυμεῖν* ἐλευθερίας (1) δεῖ μόνον, ἀλλὰ καὶ *ποιεῖν* δι' ὧν ἂν ἔλθοι πρὸς ὑμᾶς, (3) *οὐδὲ βούλεσθαι* μὲν ἀπηλλάχθαι δεσποτῶν ἐπιμένειν δὲ πράττοντας ἐξ ὧν οὗτοι διαμενοῦσιν.[39]

24. *Ant.* VI.344.5–6: . . . (1) *οὐκ ἔγνω* (2) *φυγεῖν* αὐτὸν (3) *οὐδὲ* φιλοψυχήσας προδοῦναι μὲν τοὺς οἰκείους τοῖς πολεμίοις *καθυβρίσαι* δὲ τὸ τῆς βασιλείας ἀξίωμα, ἀλλά . . .[40]

25. *Ant.* VII.127.1–3: Τοῦτο τὸ πταῖσμα τοὺς Ἀμμανίτας (1) *οὐκ ἔπεισεν* (2) *ἠρεμεῖν* (3) *οὐδὲ* μαθόντας τοὺς κρείττονας *ἡσυχίαν ἄγειν*, (4) *ἀλλὰ* πέμψαντες πρὸς Χαλαμάν . . .[41]

26. *Ant.* XIV.346.1–3: ὁ δὲ Ὑρκανὸν (2) *ἀπολιπεῖν* (1) *οὐκ ἠξίου* (3) *οὐδὲ* παρακινδυνεύειν τἀδελφῷ.[42]

---

[34]Consequently, in view of the fact that a snake of so great a size has been exposed to the public gaze, (1) it is not fair (2) to doubt the word of the Ethiopians (3) or to assume that the report which they circulated far and wide was a mere fiction.

[35]His argument (1) is difficult (2) to summarize and his meaning (3) to grasp.

[36](1) He does not allow us (2) to burn up their country (3) or to cut down their fruit trees, and forbids even the spoiling of fallen combatants . . .

[37]For women (1) were not permitted (2) to enter by the others (3) nor yet to pass by way of their own gate beyond the partition wall.

[38][Judas, ever of a hardy nature, frankly told him] that (1) he ought not (2) to be alarmed for their brother (3) nor harbour suspicions of dangers that did not exist.

[39]. . . (1) ye ought not to be content (2) to yearn for liberty, but should do also the deeds whereby ye may attain it, (3) nor merely long to be rid of your masters, while continuing so to act that they shall remain so.

[40][For he, although he knew of what was to come and his impending death, which the prophet had foretold,] yet (1) determined not (2) to flee from it (3) or, by clinging to life, to betray his people to the enemy and dishonour the dignity of kingship; instead . . .

[41]This defeat (1) did not persuade the Ammanites (2) to remain quiet (3) or to keep the peace in the knowledge that their enemy was superior. (4) Instead they sent to Chalamas . . .

[42]Phasael, however, (1) did not think it right (2) to desert Hyrcanus (3) or to endanger his brother.

27. *Ant.* XV.165.3-4: ὁ μὲν γὰρ Ὑρκανὸς ἐπιεικείᾳ τρόπου καὶ τότε καὶ τὸν ἄλλον χρόνον (1) *οὐκ ἠξίου* (2) *πολυπραγμονεῖν* (3) *οὐδὲ νεωτέρων ἅπτεσθαι*.[43]

Philo (c. 25 BCE–40 CE):
28. *Posterity and Exile of Cain* 84.5-7: (1) *οὐ γὰρ* (2) *ἀναπτῆναι*, θησίν, εἰς οὐρανὸν (3) *οὐδὲ πέραν θαλάσσης ἀφικέσθαι* (1) *δεῖ* κατὰ ζήτησιν τοῦ καλοῦ.[44]

Plutarch (40–120 CE):
29. *Rom.* 9.2.4-5: ὅτι γὰρ (1) *οὐκ ἠξίουν* οἱ τὴν Ἄλβην οἰκοῦντες (2) *ἀναμιγνύναι* τοὺς ἀποστάτας ἑαυτοῖς (3) *οὐδὲ προσδέχεσθαι* πολίτας . . .[45]
30. *Cor.* 27.4.1: τὰ γὰρ ἄλλα πάντα λυμαινόμενος καὶ διαφθείρων, τοὺς ἐκείνων ἀγροὺς ἰσχυρῶς ἐφύλαττε, καὶ (1) *οὐκ εἴα* (2) *κακουργεῖν* (3) *οὐδὲ λαμβάνειν* ἐξ ἐκείνων οὐδέν.[46]
31. *Tim.* 37.2.1: ὧν Λαφυστίου μὲν αὐτὸν πρός τινα δίκην κατεγγυῶντος (1) *οὐκ εἴα* (2) *θορυβεῖν* (3) *οὐδὲ κωλύειν* τοὺς πολίτας.[47]
32. *Comp. Arist. et Cat.* 4.2.1: (1) *οὐ γὰρ ἔστι* (2) *πράττειν* μεγάλα φροντίζοντα μικρῶν, (3) *οὐδὲ πολλοῖς δεομένοις βοηθεῖν* πολλῶν αὐτὸν δεόμενον.[48]
33. *Pyrrh.* 33.6.4: σπασάμενον γὰρ τὸ ξίφος ἢ κλίναντα λόγχην (1) *οὐκ ἦν* (2) *ἀναλαβεῖν* (3) *οὐδὲ καταθέσθαι* πάλιν, ἀλλ᾿ ἐχώρει δι᾿ ὧν ἔτυχε τὰ τοιαῦτα πάντα, καὶ περιπίπτοντες ἀλλήλοις ἔθνησκον.[49]
34. *Ages.* 32.3.3-4: ἐπεὶ δὲ φιλοτιμούμενος ὁ Ἐπαμεινώνδας ἐν τῇ πόλει μάχην συνάψαι καὶ στῆσαι τρόπαιον (1) *οὐκ ἴσχυσεν* (2) *ἐξαγαγεῖν* (3) *οὐδὲ προκαλέσασθαι* τὸν Ἀγησίλαον, ἐκεῖνος μὲν ἀναζεύξας πάλιν ἐπόρθει τὴν χώραν.[50]

---

[43]Now Hyrcanus because of his mild character (1) did not choose either then or at any other time (2) to take part in public affairs (2) or start a revolution . . . (Note that "to take part in public affairs" is not as neutral as this translation might suggest. Cf. Liddell & Scott, 1442: πολυπραγματέω: "mostly in bad sense, to be a meddlesome, inquisitive busybody; esp. meddle in state affairs, intrigue.")

[44]'For (1) it is not necessary,' he says, (2) 'to fly up into heaven, (3) nor to get beyond the sea in searching for what is good.'

[45]For that the residents of Alba (1) would not consent (2) to give the fugitives the privilege of intermarriage with them, (3) nor even receive them as fellow-citizens [is clear].

[46]For while he maltreated and destroyed everything else, he kept a vigorous watch over the lands of the patricians, and (1) would not suffer anyone (2) to hurt them (3) or take anything from them.

[47]Of these, Laphystius once tried to make him give surety that he would appear at a certain trial, and Timoleon (1) would not suffer the citizens (2) to stop the man (3) by their turbulent disapproval [lit.: nor to prevent him].

[48](1) It is impossible for a man (2) to do great things when his thoughts are busy with little things; (3) nor can he aid the many who are in need when he himself is in need of many things.

[49]For when a man had drawn his sword or poised his spear, (1) he could not (2) recover (3) or sheathe his weapon again, but it would pass through those who stood in its way, and so they died from one another's blows.

[50]Epaminondas was ambitious to join battle in the city and set up a trophy of victory there, but since (1) he could (2) neither force (3) nor tempt Agesilaus out of his positions, he withdrew and began to ravage the country.

35. *Quom. Adul.* 64.E.7–8: Ὁρᾷς τὸν πίθηκον; (1) οὐ δύναται τὴν οἰκίαν (2) φυλάττειν ὡς ὁ κύων, (3) οὐδὲ βαστάζειν ὡς ὁ ἵππος, οὐδ᾽ ἀροῦν τὴν γῆν ὡς οἱ βόες.[51]

36. *Cons. ad Apoll.* 115.E.3.: ἀνθρώποις δὲ πάμπαν (1) οὐκ ἔστι (2) γενέσθαι τὸ πάντων ἄριστον (3) οὐδὲ μετασχεῖν τῆς τοῦ βελτίστου φύσεως (ἄριστον γὰρ πᾶσι καὶ πάσαις τὸ μὴ γενέσθαι).[52]

37. *Reg. et Imp. Apopht.* 185.A.2: πρὸς δὲ τοὺς θαυμάζοντας τὴν μεταβολὴν ἔλεγεν ὡς "(1) οὐκ ἐᾷ με (2) καθεύδειν (3) οὐδὲ ῥᾳθυμεῖν τὸ Μιλτιάδου πρόπαιον."[53]

38. *Act. Rom. et Graec.* 269.D.8–9: (1) οὐ δεῖ δὲ τῶν ἡμερῶν τὸν ἀκριβέστατον ἀριθμὸν (2) διώκειν (3) οὐδὲ τὸ παρ᾽ ὀλίγον συκοφαντεῖν . . .[54]

39. *Act. Rom. et Graec.* 273.E.9–10: Διὰ τί τοῖς μὴ στρατευομένοις μὲν ἐν στρατοπέδῳ δ᾽ ἄλλως ἀναστρεφομένοις (1) οὐκ ἐξῆν ἄνδρα (2) βαλεῖν πολέμιον (3) οὐδὲ τρῶσαι;[55]

40. *Act. Rom. et Graec.* 291.B.3–4: Διὰ τί τοῖς ἱερεῦσι τούτοις ἀρχὴν (1) οὐκ ἐφεῖτο (2) λαβεῖν (3) οὐδὲ μετελθεῖν;[56]

41. *De E Apud Delph.* 385.A.9: . . . (1) οὐκ ἦν εὐπρεπὲς (2) παράγειν (3) οὐδὲ παραιτεῖσθαι.[57]

---

[51]You must have noticed the ape. (1) He cannot (2) guard the house like the dog, (3) nor carry a load like the horse, nor plough the land like oxen.

[52]But for men (1) it is utterly impossible (2) that they should obtain the best thing of all, (3) or even have any share in its nature (for the best thing for all men and women is not to be born).

[53][Themistocles while yet in his youth abandoned himself to wine and women. But after Miltiades, commanding the Athenian army, had overcome the barbarians at Marathon, never again was it possible to encounter Themistocles misconducting himself.] To those who expressed their amazement at the change in him, he said that "the trophy of Miltiades (1) does not allow me (2) to sleep (3) or to be indolent."

[54]But (1) we must not (2) follow out the most exact calculation of the number of days (3) nor cast aspersions on approximate reckoning [since even now, when astronomy has made so much progress, the irregularity of the moon's movements is still beyond the skill of mathematicians, and continues to elude their calculations].

[55]Why were men who were not regularly enlisted, but merely tarrying in the camp, (1) not allowed (2) to throw missiles at the enemy (3) or to wound them?

[56]Why were these priests (1) not allowed (2) to hold office (3) nor to solicit it?

[57][On many other occasions when the subject had been brought up in the school I had quietly turned aside from it and passed it over, but recently I was unexpectedly discovered by my sons in an animated discussion with some strangers, whom, since they purposed to leave Delphi immediately,] (1) it was not seemly (2) to try to divert from the subject, nor was it seemly for me (3) to ask to be excused from the discussion [for they were altogether eager to hear something about it].

42. *De Def. Orac.* 426.B.1: (1) οὐ γὰρ ὡς σμήνους ἡγεμόνας δεῖ (2) ποιεῖν ἀνεξόδους (3) οὐδὲ φρουρεῖν συγκλείσαντας τῇ ὕλῃ μᾶλλον δὲ συμφράξαντας.[58]

43. *De Tranqu. Anim.* 474.A.12: (1) οὐ δεῖ τοῖς ἑτέροις (2) ἐξαθυμεῖν (3) οὐδ' ἀπαγορεύειν.[59]

44. *De Tranqu. Anim.* 475.D.3: ὅθεν (1) οὐ δεῖ παντάπασιν (2) ἐκταπεινοῦν (3) οὐδὲ καταβάλλειν τὴν φύσιν . . .[60]

45. *Quaest. Conviv.* 706.D.5: ἐρῶντι μὲν γὰρ πολυτελοῦς (1) οὐκ ἔστι τὴν Πηνελόπην (2) προσαγαγεῖν (3) οὐδὲ συνοικίσαι τὴν Πάνθειαν.[61]

46. *Quaest. Conviv.* 711.E.3: ὥσθ' ὁ οἶνος ἡμᾶς (2) ἀδικεῖν (1) οὐκ ἔοικεν (3) οὐδὲ κρατεῖν.[62]

47. *Aetia Phys.* 918.B.4: . . . ἡ δ' ἄγαν περίψυξις πηγνύουσα τὰς ὀσμὰς (1) οὐκ ἐᾷ (2) ῥεῖν (3) οὐδὲ κινεῖν τὴν αἴσθησιν;[63]

48. *Brut. Rat.* 990.A.11: . . . καὶ (1) οὐκ ἐᾷ (2) θιγεῖν (3) οὐδὲ λυπῆσαι τὴν γεῦσιν ἀλλὰ διαβάλλει καὶ κατηγορεῖ τὴν φαυλότητα πρὶν ἢ βλαβῆναι.[64]

These instances also suggest that the construction "negated finite verb + infinitive + οὐδέ + infinitive" is used to link two infinitives denoting concepts or activities which are either both viewed positively or negatively by the writer. The same two patterns of the usage of οὐδέ are found: Pattern #1 where two activities or concepts are viewed positively in and of themselves, but where their exercise is prohibited or their existence denied due to circumstances or conditions adduced in the context, and Pattern #2

---

[58][Yet such an organization is altogether appropriate for the gods.] For (1) we must not (2) make them unable to go out, like the queens in a hive of bees, (3) nor keep them imprisoned by enclosing them with matter, or rather fencing them about with it . . .

[59](1) We should not (2) be disheartened (3) or despondent in adversity [but like musicians who achieve harmony by consistently deadening bad music with better and encompassing the bad with the good, we should make the blending of our life harmonious and conformable to our own nature].

[60]Therefore (1) we should not altogether (2) debase (3) and depreciate Nature [in the belief that she has nothing strong, stable, and beyond the reach of Fortune, but, on the contrary, . . . , we should face the future undaunted and confident . . .].

[61]If a man has a passion for a costly harlot, (1) we cannot (2) bring Penelope on stage, (3) nor marry Pantheia to him [but it is possible to take a man who is enjoying mimes and tunes and lyrics that are bad art and bad taste, and lead him back to Euripides and Pindar and Menander, 'washing the brine from the ears with the clear fresh water of reason,' in Plato's words].

[62]The wine (1) seems not (2) to be harming us (3) or getting the best of us.

[63][Why is ground that has become dewy unfavourable for hunting so long as the cold lasts? . . . A spoor does this when there is warmth to free and release it gently] whereas excessive chill freezes the scents and (1) does not allow them (2) to flow (3) and affect [i.e. move] our perception.

[64][It (our sense of smell) admits what is proper, rejects what is alien] and (1) will not let it (2) touch (3) or give pain to the taste, but informs on and denounces what is bad before any harm is done.

where two activities or concepts are viewed negatively and where consequently their exercise is prohibited or their existence denied or to be avoided. The following survey chart documents the first pattern.

Table 9: Pattern #1 in Extrabiblical Literature

Pattern #1: two activities or concepts are viewed positively in and of themselves, but their exercise is prohibited or their existence denied due to circumstances or conditions adduced in the context.

1. LXX: 1 Macc 15:14	ἐκπορεύεσθαι (leave)	εἰσπορεύεσθαι (enter)
2. LXX: Sir 18:6	ἐλαττῶσαι (diminish)	προσθεῖναι (increase)
3. LXX: Isa 42:24b	πορεύεσθαι (walk)	ἀκούειν (obey)
4. LXX: Ezek 44:13	ἱερατεύειν (serve as priest)	προσάγειν (come near)
5. LXX: DanTh 5:8	ἀναγνῶναι (read)	γνωρίσαι (make known)
6. Inscr.: Attica	δέχεσθαι (receive gifts)	κλύειν (heed suppliant)
10. Polyb., *Hist.* VI.15	χειρίζειν (be organized)	συντελεῖν (be held at all)
12. Polyb., *Hist.* XXX.24	γινώσκεσθαι (know)	συνορᾶσθαι (see)
13. Polyb., *Hist.* XXXI.12	βοηθεῖν (help)	συνεπισχύειν (support)
15. D. Hal., *Ant. R.* 10.12	κοινωνεῖν (take part in)	παρεῖναι (be present at)
19. Jos., *Ap.* 2.6.1–3	διελθεῖν (discern)	γνῶναι (know)
21. Jos., *B. J.* 5.199	παρελθεῖν (enter)	ὑπερβῆναι (pass by)
23. Jos., *Ant.* VI.20	ἐπιθυμεῖν (yearn for)	βούλεσθαι (want) *
25. Jos., *Ant.* VII.127	ἠρεμεῖν (remain quiet)	ἡσυχίαν ἄγειν (be quiet)
28.Philo, *Post.* 84.5	ἀναπτῆναι (fly up)	ἀφικέσθαι (go beyond) *
29.Plut., *Rom.* 9.2	ἀναμιγνύναι (intermarry)	προσδέχεσθαι (receive as citizen)
32.Plut., *Comp.* 4.2	πράττειν (do great things)	βοηθεῖν (help)
33.Plut., *Pyrrh.* 33.6	ἀναλαβεῖν (take again)	καταθέσθαι (resheathe)
35.Plut., *Adul.* 64.E	φυλάττειν (guard)	βαστάζειν (carry)
36.Plut., *Apoll.* 115.E	γενέσθαι (obtain)	μετασχεῖν (have a share)
38.Plut., *Act.* 269.D	διώκειν (follow)	συκοφαντεῖν (approxim.)
40.Plut., *Act.* 291.B	λαβεῖν (hold office)	μετελθεῖν (solicit office)
45.Plut., *Conv.* 706.D	προσαγαγεῖν (bring on stage)	συνοικίσαι (marry)
47.Plut., *Phys.* 918.B	ῥεῖν (flow)	κινεῖν (move)

Abbreviation : *=preceding infinitive

Pattern #1 can be illustrated by the following instances. Polybius writes (10.) that victory processions cannot be properly organized or sometimes be held at all unless the senate consents and provides the requisite funds. While "organize" and "hold" are both viewed positively in and of themselves by the writer, Polybius indicates that the holding of these processions is not possible unless certain conditions are met, the senate's consent and the requisition of appropriate funds. At another occasion (13.) Polybius writes that "the senate would not go so far as to help or support Lysias after his conduct." Again, the writer views the two activities (here synonyms), "helping" and "supporting," positively in and of them-selves, but the help is denied because of Lysias' unacceptable conduct. Josephus writes (23.) that "you ought not to be content to yearn for liberty . . . nor merely long to be rid of your masters." While the writer views his readers' yearning for liberty and their longing to be rid of their masters positively in and of themselves, he indicates in the context why these long-ings by themselves are insufficient unless accompanied by action and change in behavior.

The following chart lists the instances of the second pattern:

Table 10: Pattern #2 in Extrabiblical Literature

Pattern #2: two activities or concepts are viewed negatively and consequently their exercise is prohibited or to be avoided or their existence is denied.

7. Inscr.: PZenPestm.	εἰληθέναι (take away)	ἔχειν (hold in pretense)
8. Polyb., *Hist.* II.56	ἐκπλήττειν (thrill)	ζητεῖν (seek to imagine)
9. Polyb., *Hist.* V.10.5	πολεμεῖν (make war)	συναναιρεῖν (involve guiltless)
11. Polyb., *Hist.* XXX.5	συνδυάζειν (run in harness)	προκαταλαμβάνειν (engage)
14. D. Hal., *Thuc.* 7.13	ἐγκαταμίσγειν (adulterate)	ἁρμόττεσθαι (confuse)
16. D. Hal., *De Comp.* 23	ὁρᾶσθαι (be viewed)	βεβηκέναι (stand)
17. Diod. Sic., *B.H.* 3.30	θαυμάζειν (be surprised)	ἀπιστεῖν (distrust)
18. Diod. Sic., *B.H.* 3.37	ἀπιστεῖν (doubt)	ὑπολαμβάνειν (view as fictional)
20. Jos., *Ap.* 2.212.1	πυρπολεῖν (burn)	τέμνειν (cut down)
22. Jos., *Ant.* II.116	δεδιέναι (be alarmed)	λαμβάνειν (harbor suspicions)
24. Jos., *Ant.* VI.344	φυγεῖν (flee)	προδοῦναι (betray)
26. Jos., *Ant.* XIV.346	ἀπολιπεῖν (desert)	παρακινδυνεύειν (endanger)*
27. Jos., *Ant.* XV.165	πολυπραγμονεῖν (intrigue)	ἅπτεσθαι (start revol.)
30. Plut., *Cor.* 27.4	κακουργεῖν (hurt)	λαμβάνειν (take from)
31. Plut., *Tim.* 37.2	θορυβεῖν (stop)	κωλύειν (hinder)
34. Plut., *Ages.* 32.3	ἐξαγαγεῖν (force)	προκαλέσασθαι (tempt)
37. Plut., *Apoph.* 185.A	καθεύδειν (sleep)	ῥαθυμεῖν (be idle)
39. Plut., *Act.* 273.E	βαλεῖν (throw missiles)	τρῶσαι (wound)
41. Plut., *De E* 385.A	παράγειν (try to divert)	παραιτεῖσθαι (be excus.)
42. Plut., *Orac.* 426.B	ποιεῖν ἀνεξ. (make unable)	φρουρεῖν (keep imprisoned)
43. Plut., *Tran.* 474.A	ἐξαθυμεῖν (be disheartened)	ἀπαγορεύειν (be despondent)
44. Plut., *Tran.* 475.D	ἐκταπεινοῦν (debase)	καταβάλλειν (depreciate)
46. Plut., *Conv.* 711.E	ἀδικεῖν (harm)	κρατεῖν (get the best of)*
48. Plut., *Brut.* 990.A	θιγεῖν (touch)	λυπῆσαι (give pain to)

Abbreviation: *=preceding infinitive

A few examples of Pattern #2 will demonstrate instances where two activities or concepts are both viewed negatively by the writer and where consequently their exercise is prohibited or their existence is denied or to be avoided. An inscription (7.) indicates that a judge ordered Antipater not "to take the boy from them or to hold him under any pretense." Clearly both activities, taking the boy away from them as well as holding him under any pretense, are viewed negatively by the judge who consequently denies the exercise of these activities. Josephus writes (27.) that "Hyrcanus because of his mild character did not choose . . . to meddle in state affairs or start a revolution." "Meddling in state affairs" and "starting a revolution" are both viewed negatively by the writer who asserts that it was Hyrcanus' "mild character" that kept him from engaging in these undesirable activities. In a writing by Plutarch (46.), the existence of two negative effects of wine is denied: "The wine seems not to be harming us or getting the best of us."[65]

Conclusion

It has been shown that the data from the New Testament and extrabiblical Greek literature equally display a clearly delineated use of οὐδέ. It was found that this conjunction always coordinates activities of the same order, i.e. activities that are either both viewed positively or negatively by the writer or speaker. The following conclusions and implications for the interpretation of 1 Tim 2:12 can be drawn.

---

[65]These passages may be categorized as follows: 1. Synonymous Concepts: Isa 44:24b (LXX); Ezek 44:13 (LXX); Polybius, *Hist.* XXXI.12; Dionysius Halicarnassensis, *Antiqu. Rom.* 10.12; Josephus, *Apion* 2.6.1-3; *Ant.* II.116; VI.20; VII.127; Plutarch, *Tim.* 37.2; *Apoph.* 185.A; *Orac.* 426.B; *Tran.* 474.A; 475.D; *Conv.* 711.E; 2. Conceptual Parallels: Polybius, *Hist.* II.56; V.10.5; XXX.5,24; Dionysius Halicarnassensis, *Thuc.* 7.13; *De Comp.* 23; Diod. Sic., *Bibl. Hist.* 3.37; Josephus, *Ap.* 2.212.1; *B.J.* 5.199; *Ant.* VI.344; XIV.346; Philo, *Post.* 84.5; Plutarch, *Comp.* 4.2; *Ages.* 32.3; *Adul.* 64.E; *Act.* 269.D; *De E Apud Delph.* 385.A; *Conv.* 706.D; 3. Complementary Concepts: 1 Macc 15.14 (LXX); Sir 18.6 (LXX); 4. Sequential Concepts: DanTh 5.8 (LXX); PZenPestm. 21; Plutarch, *Pyrrh.* 33.6; *Phys.* 918.B; *Brut.* 990.A; 5. Ascensive Concepts: Attica.IG II (2).11589; Polybius, *Hist.* VI.15; Diodorus Siculus, *Bibl. Hist.* 3.30; Josephus, *Ant.* XV.165; Plutarch, *Rom.* 9.2; *Apoll.* 115.E; *Act.* 291.B; 6. Specific to General or General to Specific: a. Specific to General: Plutarch, *Act.* 273.B; b. General to Specific: Plutarch, *Cor.* 27.4.

1. Syntactically, there are only two acceptable ways of rendering 1 Tim 2:12: (a) "I do not permit a woman to teach or to have authority over a man," or (b) "I do not permit a woman to teach error or to domineer over a man." In the first instance, both "teaching" and "exercising authority" would be viewed positively in and of themselves, yet for reasons to be gleaned from the context the writer does not permit these. In the latter case, both "teaching error" and "domineering over a man" would be viewed negatively by the writer.

2. Since οὐδέ is a coordinating and not a subordinating conjunction, it is not permissible to make αὐθεντεῖν subordinate to διδάσκειν so that it in effect functions adverbially ("to teach in a domineering way"). Furthermore, while "teaching" and "exercising authority" may be perceived jointly in 1 Tim 2:12, these concepts do not blend to the extent that they become one concept where the two constituent elements are no longer distinguishable.

3. A distinction should be made between the fact that two activities or concepts are viewed positively in and of themselves and that they may be prohibited due to circumstances. In 1 Tim 2:12, the phrase "I do not permit" has by some been taken to mean that the writer views the two activities, διδάσκειν and αὐθεντεῖν, themselves negatively, in the sense of "teaching in a domineering way." However, it remains a legitimate possibility for a writer to deny someone for certain reasons the exercise of activities he otherwise views positively.

4. 1 Tim 2:12 can legitimately be seen as an example of the first pattern, i.e. the denial of two activities which are viewed positively in and of themselves, under contextually adduced circumstances. This is strongly suggested by the fact that the term διδάσκειν is consistently viewed positively in the New Testament when used absolutely, i.e. unaccompanied by contextual qualifiers.[66] In passages such as 1 Tim 4:11; 6:2; and 2 Tim 2:2, διδάσκειν is viewed positively by the writer and linked with activities such as encouraging, exhorting, and the passing on of apostolic tradition.[67]

---

[66]Contra Kroegers, *I Suffer Not a Woman*, 81. See also Payne, "οὐδέ," 6–8, who argues that teaching is an activity viewed positively in and of itself in the New Testament and in Paul's writings.

[67]Notably, in instances in the same letter where reference is made to *false* teaching, the term ἑτεροδιδάσκαλειν is used (cf. 1 Tim 1.3–4; 6.3), while in Titus 1.9–14 there is ample contextual indication that false teaching is in view, a feature that is absent from the context of 1 Tim 2:12. Contra Kroegers, *I Suffer Not a Woman*, 81.

5. Since the term διδάσκειν is used absolutely in the New Testament for an activity that is viewed positively in and of itself and since οὐδέ coordinates terms which are either both viewed positively or negatively, αὐθεντεῖν should be seen as denoting an activity that is viewed positively in and of itself as well. Thus 1 Tim 2:12 is an instance of the first pattern where the exercise of two activities is prohibited or the existence of two concepts is denied by the writer due to certain circumstances. Since the first part of 1 Tim 2:12 reads "But I do not permit a woman to teach" and the coordinating conjunction οὐδέ requires the second activity to be viewed correspondingly by the writer, αὐθεντεῖν should also be regarded positively and thus be rendered "to have authority" and not "to domineer."

6. The immediate context of the passage supports the conclusion just stated. Framed by the *inclusio* of ἡσυχία at the beginning of 2:11 and at the end of 2:12, there are two corresponding pairs of terms: "learning" in 2:11 corresponds to "teaching" in 2:12, and "full submission" in 2:11 relates to "having authority" in 2:12. The author first expresses his desire for a woman to learn in full submission. He then registers his prohibition of the opposite, a woman's teaching or being in authority over a man. He closes by reiterating his desire for a woman to learn in submission. "Learning" and "teaching," "full submission" and "having authority" are contrasted, the former terms in the pair being viewed positively in the case of women, the latter ones negatively. Thus syntax and context join in suggesting that 1 Tim 2:12 be rendered as "I do not permit a woman to teach or to have authority over a man."

CHAPTER FOURTEEN

ASCERTAINING WOMEN'S GOD-ORDAINED ROLES:
An Interpretation of 1 Timothy 2:15[*]

"But women will be saved through childbearing" (1 Tim 2:15; NIV)—this pronouncement of the writer of 1 Timothy[1] has puzzled commentators of

---

[*]This essay first appeared in *Bulletin of Biblical Research* 7 (1997): 107-44 and is reprinted with permission.

[1]The question of the authorship of the Pastorals has no direct bearing on this paper, even though the date of writing may alter the possible contemporary backdrop for 1 Tim 2:15 in terms of the respective stage of gnosticism at the time of writing. While the problems attached to Pauline authorship are several, the problems related to non-Pauline authorship are also very significant (cf. Stanley E. Porter, "Pauline Authorship and the Pastoral Epistles: Implications for Canon," *BBR* 5 [1995]: 105-23; for a helpful general summary of the issues involved, see Thomas D. Lea, "Pseudonymity and the New Testament," in *New Testament Criticism and Interpretation* [ed. David Alan Black and David S. Dockery; Grand Rapids: Zondervan, 1991], 533-59, esp. 553-56). Bruce M. Metzger, "A Reconsideration of Certain Arguments Against the Pauline Authorship of the Pastoral Epistles," *ExpTim* 70 (1958): 91-94, has persuasively argued that the Pauline authorship of the Pastorals cannot merely be proven by statistical analysis (see also Donald Guthrie, "Appendix," in *The Pastoral Epistles* [TNTC; Grand Rapids: Eerdmans, 1957; repr. 1984], 211-28; and Eta Linnemann, "Pauline Authorship and Vocabulary Statistics," a paper presented at the 47th Annual Meeting of the Evangelical Theological Society, Philadelphia, November 17, 1995). Likewise, the presence of pseudonymous epistles in New Testament times is as uncertain as the question whether the church would have chosen to include pseudonymous epistles in the New Testament canon. Cf. E. Earle Ellis, "Pseudonymity and Canonicity of New Testament Documents," in *Worship, Theology and Ministry in the Early Church: Essays in Honor of Ralph P. Martin* (ed. Michael J. Wilkins and Terence Paige; Sheffield: JSOT, 1992), 212-24; and idem, "Pastoral Letters," in *Dictionary of Paul and His Letters* (ed. Gerald F. Hawthorne, Ralph P. Martin, Daniel G. Reid; Downers Grove, IL: InterVarsity, 1993), 658-66, esp. 659. Thus the book's inclusion into the New Testament canon appears to imply early recognition of apostolic (Pauline) authorship, which, in turn, when coupled with the explicit reference to Paul in 1 Tim 1:1, seems to make a strong case for the fact that the implied author (Paul) is to be identified with the apostle Paul. Interestingly, the dual rationale of 1 Tim 2:13 and 14 is

all ages to no end, and consensus can be found in one thing only: that this passage has consistently defied attempts to interpret it, and that consensus on the passage's meaning is therefore as elusive today as it ever has been. Could the writer of 2 Peter have had this passage in mind when he wrote, "So also our beloved brother Paul wrote to you according to the wisdom given him, speaking of this as he does in all his letters. There are some things in them hard to understand, which the ignorant and unstable twist to their own destruction, as they do the other Scriptures" (2 Pet 3:15b-16)? Others may agree with a recent writer who laments, "Just as the first half of this chapter showed us the author at his best, so the second half seems to show him at his worst. Christians are under no obligation to accept his teaching on women."[2] The same writer paraphrases the content of the present passage as follows: "woman, a weak, gullible creature, should find her natural vocation in a life of domesticity in subordination of her husband."[3] Another commentator finds the reference "almost unbearable."[4]

A mere cursory glance at the available English translations reveals a confusing array (or disarray?) of alternatives, ranging from the provocative "women will find their salvation in motherhood" (TCNT) over the daring "women will get safely through childbirth" (Moffat) to "she shall be preserved through the bearing of children" (NASB). The interpretation of this passage even cuts across partisan lines on the "women's issue," so that commentators otherwise on opposite sides of the spectrum may find themselves in agreement on the verse's meaning. In the light of this unsettled situation, are we seeking to do the impossible by writing yet another piece on this inscrutable verse? Perhaps, but one might be

---

already found in the unquestionably Pauline Corinthian correspondence (cf. 1 Cor 11:8-9; 2 Cor 11:3; see Leopold Zscharnack, *Der Dienst der Frau in den ersten Jahrhunderten der christlichen Kirche* [Göttingen: Vandenhoeck & Ruprecht, 1902], 14) which may suggest, to the mind of some, the Pauline authorship of the Pastorals, and to others the effort by a later follower of Paul to replicate his theology. In the following argument, Pauline authorship will be considered probable, but the thesis of this paper is not materially affected by it.

[2]Anthony Tyrrell Hanson, *The Pastoral Letters* (Cambridge Bible Commentary; London: CUP, 1966), 38.

[3]Idem, *The Pastoral Epistles* (NCBC; Grand Rapids: Eerdmans, 1982), 74.

[4]Otto Michel, "Grundfragen der Pastoralbriefe," in *Auf dem Grunde der Apostel und Propheten: Festgabe für Landesbischof D. Theophil Wurm zum 80. Geburtstag* (ed. Emil Brunner et al.; Stuttgart: Quell-Verlag der Evangelischen Gesellschaft, 1948), 94, quoted in Gottfried Holtz, *Die Pastoralbriefe* (THKNT; 3d ed.; Berlin: Evangelische Verlagsanstalt, 1980 [1966]), 70-73.

forgiven a little foolishness when the topic is as significant as that addressed by the present passage, i.e., women's God-ordained roles. It should also be acknowledged that this issue, like few others, has enormous implications on the social, and political domain.

In light of the formidable challenge presented by the phrase "saved by childbearing," we will narrow our focus to the three component parts of this expression and discuss (1) the meaning of σωθήσεται ("be saved" or "be preserved") in 1 Tim 2:15; (2) the preposition διά ("by" or "through") in the present context; and (3) the meaning of τεκνογονία ("childbearing," literally or as synecdoche for a woman's "domestic calling").[5] We will first present a survey of the history of the interpretation of the present passage, focusing on patristic, Reformation, and modern writers, and categorize the major interpretations proposed for 1 Tim 2:15. Based on this survey, we will discuss the phrase "saved by childbearing" word for word, considering also possible references to gnostic teaching and to Gen 3:15 or 16. The essay will conclude with a brief effort to integrate the interpretation of 1 Tim 2:15 presented here into a coherent reading of 1 Tim 2:9-15.

The History of the Interpretation of 1 Timothy 2:15[6]

The Fathers[7]

We begin our survey with two instances of Messianic typology in Justin and Tertullian.[8] In Justin Martyr's *Dialogue with Trypho* (CE 114-165), we find the following passage:

---

[5]We thus will not attempt to include a discussion of the conditional clause in the latter half of the verse. While this is certainly a limitation, it seems to be a necessary and reasonable one that does not negatively affect our ability to arrive at a valid interpretation of the passage, as we hope to demonstrate below.

[6]For a survey of the history of the interpretation of 1 Timothy 2:9-14, see Daniel Doriani's Appendix in *Women in the Church: A Fresh Analysis of 1 Timothy 2:9-15* (ed. Andreas J. Köstenberger, Thomas R. Schreiner, and H. Scott Baldwin; Grand Rapids: Baker, 1995).

[7]For surveys of the history of interpretation of 1 Tim 2:15, see Ceslaus Spicq, *Saint Paul. Les Épîtres Pastorales* I (ÉBib; 4th ed.; Paris, 1969), 382-83; Jürgen Roloff, *Der erste Brief an Timotheus* (EKKNT; Zürich/Neukirchen-Vluyn: Benziger/Neukirchener, 1988), 142-46.

[8]Cf. Robert Falconer, *The Pastoral Epistles* (Oxford: Clarendon, 1937), 132: "The Greek fathers in general gave no place to this interpretation, but in the Latins this mystical sense was general."

... and that He became man by the Virgin, in order that the disobedience which proceeded from the serpent might receive its destruction in the same manner in which it derived its origin. For Eve, who was a virgin and undefiled, having conceived the word of the serpent, brought forth disobedience and death. But the Virgin Mary received faith and joy, when the angel Gabriel announced the good tidings to her that the Spirit of the Lord would come upon her, and the power of the Highest would overshadow her: wherefore also the Holy Thing begotten of her is the Son of God; and she replied, "Be it unto me according to thy word." And by her has He been born, to whom we have proved so many Scriptures refer, and by whom God destroys both the serpent and those angels and men who are like him; but works deliverance from death to those who repent of their wickedness and believe upon Him.[9]

Some claim this passage as evidence that the Fathers, and here Justin, interpreted 1 Tim 2:15 in terms of a Messianic typology. While the above passage clearly reveals Justin's use of Messianic typology, however, it is less clear that the author depends on 1 Tim 2:15.

Tertullian (CE 145–220), arguing for the full incarnation of Christ, writes this regarding Christ's birth of Mary:

... it was by just the contrary operation that God recovered His own image and likeness, of which He had been robbed by the devil. For it was while Eve was yet a virgin, that the ensnaring word had crept into her ear which was to build the edifice of death. Into a virgin's soul, in like manner, must be introduced that Word of God which was to raise the fabric of life; so that what had been reduced to ruin by this sex, might by the selfsame sex be recovered to salvation. As Eve had believed the serpent, so Mary believed the angel. The delinquency which the one occasioned by believing, the other by believing effaced. But (it will be said) Eve did not at the devil's word conceive in her womb. Well, she at all events conceived; for the devil's word afterwards became as seed to her that she should conceive as an outcast, and bring forth in sorrow. Indeed she gave birth to a fratricidal devil; whilst Mary, on the contrary, bare one who was one day to secure salvation to Israel, His own brother after the flesh, and the murderer of Himself. God therefore sent down into the virgin's womb His Word, as the good Brother, who should blot out the memory of the evil brother. Hence it was necessary that Christ should come forth for the salvation of man, in that condition of flesh into which man had entered ever since his condemnation.[10]

What has been said about Justin's theology also applies to Tertullian. It is unclear whether either writer had 1 Tim 2:15 in mind as he penned the

---

[9]Justin Martyr, *Dial.* 100, in *Ante-Nicene Fathers* 1:249. Some also refer to Ignatius, *Eph.* 19, but it is unclear whether this refers to a Messianic typology or not, and even more doubtful that this represents an effort at interpreting 1 Tim 2:15. The same must be maintained regarding Iren., *Haer.* 3.22 and 5.19.

[10]Tertullian, *De Carne* 17, in *Ante-Nicene Fathers*, 3:536.

respective passages. Moreover, even if Tertullian and Justin thought of 1 Tim 2:15 as they wrote, it can hardly be argued that this provides a confirmation of 1 Tim 2:15's teaching of a Messianic typology along the lines they suggest. This must be demonstrated on other grounds.

Clement of Alexandria (CE 153-217), an eclectic Christian theologian, wrote a work directed against gnosticism entitled *Stromateis* between CE 192-202, presenting Christianity as the true gnosis. In his previous book, he had argued that marriage is a holy estate and consistent with the perfect person in Christ. In the current work, he refutes the gnostics' licentious tenets that despised the ordinances of the Creator, resulting in grossest immorality in practice. Clement first cites 1 Tim 5:14-15, leading up to a reference to 1 Tim 2:15:

> He is applying the idea of defilement to a partnership involving an alien body rather than the body given away in marriage for the purpose of producing children. This is why the Apostle says, "So it is my wish that younger women should marry, have children, and be mistresses of their homes, without giving any opponent an opportunity to criticize. There are some already who have taken the wrong course and followed Satan." In fact, he expresses approval of the man who is husband of a single wife, whether elder, deacon, or layman, if he gives no ground for criticism in his conduct of his marriage. He "will be preserved by the generation of children."[11]

We note the following: (1) Clement links 1 Tim 2:15 with 1 Tim 5:14-15, alluding also to 1 Tim 3:2; (2) he applies the passage not (merely) to women, but (also) to men; (3) he uses the passage for the purpose of refuting gnosticism.

Gregory of Nyssa (CE 335/6-395), in a work entitled *De Virginitate* written in Basil's monastery before CE 365, interprets the reference to "children" in 1 Tim 2:15 metaphorically as relating to good works, defending the spiritual superiority of virginity:

> Everyone knows that the propagation of mortal frames is the work which the intercourse of the sexes has to do; whereas for those who are joined to the Spirit, life and immortality instead of children are produced by this latter intercourse; and the words of the Apostle beautifully suit their case, for the joyful mother of such children as these "shall be saved in child-bearing"; as the Psalmist in his divine songs thankfully cries, "He maketh the barren woman to keep house, and to be a joyful mother of children (Ps 113:9)." Truly a joyful mother is the virgin

---

[11]Clement of Alexandria, *Stromateis* 3.12.89-90. Cf. *Clement of Alexandria* (trans. John Ferguson; Washington, D.C.: Catholic University of America Press, 1991), 312.

mother who by the operation of the Spirit conceives the deathless children, and who is called by the Prophet barren because of her modesty only.[12]

Chrysostom (CE 347–407), preaching on the present passage, comments as follows:

> Shall not women then be saved? Yes, by means of children. For it is not of Eve that he says, "If they continue in faith and charity and holiness with sobriety." . . . It is as if he had said, "Ye women, be not cast down, because your sex has incurred blame. God has granted you another opportunity of salvation, by the bringing up of children, so that you are saved, not by yourselves, but by others. See how many questions are involved in this matter." "The woman," he says, "being deceived was in transgression." What woman? Eve. Shall she then be saved by child-bearing? He does not say that, but, the race of women shall be saved. Was not it then involved in transgression? Yes, it was, still Eve transgressed, but the whole sex shall be saved, notwithstanding, "by childbearing." And why not by their own personal virtue? For has she excluded others from this salvation? And what will be the case with virgins, with the barren, with widows who have lost their husbands, before they had children? will they perish? is there no hope for them? yet virgins are held in the highest estimation. What then does he mean to say?
>
> Some interpret his meaning thus. As what happened to the first woman occasioned the subjection of the whole sex, (for since Eve was formed second and made subject, he says, let the rest of the sex be in subjection,) so because she transgressed, the rest of the sex are also in transgression. But this is not fair reasoning; for at the creation all was the gift of God, but in this case, it is the consequence of the woman's sin. As all men died through one, because that one sinned, so the whole female race transgressed, because the woman was in the transgression. Let her not however grieve. God hath given her no small consolation, that of childbearing. And if it be said that this is of nature, so is that also of nature; for not only that which is of nature has been granted, but also the bringing up of children. "If they continue in faith and charity and holiness with sobriety"; that is, if after childbearing, they keep them in charity and purity. By these means they will have no small reward on their account, because they have trained up wrestlers for the service of Christ. By holiness he means good life, modesty, and sobriety.[13]

Chrysostom thus appears to take 1 Tim 2:15 to refer to women's reward from rearing Christian offspring. This interpretation appears to be echoed by Jerome (CE 345–420), who writes in a letter, "We read of Eli the priest that he became displeasing to God on account of the sins of his children (1 Sam 2:27–36); and we are told that a man may not be made a bishop if his sons are loose and disorderly (1 Tim 3:4). On the other hand it is writ-

---

[12]Gregory of Nyssa, *De Virginitate* Chap. 4 in *Nicene and Post-Nicene Fathers* Second Series 5:350.

[13]St. Chrysostom, *Homilies on Timothy* 9 in *Nicene and Post-Nicene Fathers,* First Series, 13:436.

ten of the woman that 'she shall be saved in childbearing, if they continue in faith and charity and holiness with chastity.' "[14]

Finally, Augustine, writing between CE 400–428, provides a figurative interpretation of the present passage similar to that of Gregory of Nyssa, taking "children" to refer symbolically to good works:

> For that the Apostle Paul, when speaking outwardly of the sex of male and female, figured the mystery of some more hidden truth, may be understood from this, that when he says in another place that she is a widow indeed who is desolate, without children and nephews, and yet that she ought to trust in God, and to continue in prayers night and day (1 Tim 5:5), he here indicates, that the woman having been brought into the transgression by being deceived, is brought to salvation by child-bearing; and then he has added, "If they continue in faith, and charity, and holiness, with sobriety (1 Tim 2:15)." As if it could possibly hurt a good widow, if either she had not sons, or if those whom she had did not choose to continue in good works. But because those things which are called good works are, as it were, the sons of our life, according to that sense of life in which it answers to the question, What is a man's life? that is, How does he act in these temporal things? . . . what the apostle meant to signify is plain, and in so far figuratively and mystically . . .[15]

It may be concluded that, while Justin and Tertullian teach a Messianic typology that links Eve and the fall with Mary and the birth of Christ, this is not clearly presented as an interpretation based on 1 Tim 2:15. Even if that were their point of reference, it would not be the only, or even predominant, interpretation in the patristic period. Gregory of Nyssa and Augustine use a symbolic or allegorical approach, taking "childbearing" as a reference to women's bearing of spiritual children, i.e., good works. This, of course, opens the door to find in 1 Tim 2:15 the teaching of salvation by works, an interpretation that has been combated ever since, both during the time of the Reformation and in the modern era. Yet other ancient interpreters took 1 Tim 2:15b to refer, not to women themselves, but to their children and to women's contribution to their children's godly conduct (Chrysostom, Jerome). Finally, 1 Tim 2:15 was understood as affirming the propriety of marriage, even for overseers (with reference to 3:2), with the present passage referring to the woman's preservation within the marital and familial bond (Clement of Alexandria).

---

[14]Jerome, Letter 107 in *Nicene and Post-Nicene Fathers,* Second Series, 6:192.

[15]Augustine, *De Trinitate* Book 12 in *Nicene and Post-Nicene Fathers,* First Series, 3:159.

The Reformers

Almost a millennium later, Martin Luther wrestled with the question whether or not the bearing of children constituted a good work, concluding that it is to be an outgrowth of a woman's faith:

> It is a very great comfort that a woman can be saved by bearing children, etc. That is, she has an honorable and salutary status in life if she keeps busy having children. We ought to recommend this passage to them, etc. She is described as "saved" not for freedom, for license, but for bearing and rearing children. Is she not saved by faith? He goes on and explains himself: bearing children is a wholesome responsibility, but for believers. To bear children is acceptable to God. He does not merely say that bearing children saves; he adds: if the bearing takes place in faith and love, it is a Christian work . . . This is the comfort for married people in trouble: hardship and all things are salutary, for through them they are moved forward toward salvation and against adultery.[16]

Luther's discussion is clearly informed by systematic concerns, particularly the great Reformation issue of salvation by faith vs. works. Without detailed study of the passage, he interprets it in the light of these concerns in the larger framework of Genesis 3.

John Calvin provides a sensitive and seasoned discussion that has set the standard for treatments of this passage ever since:

> To censorious men it might appear absurd, for an Apostle of Christ not only to exhort women to give attention to the birth of offspring, but to press this work as religious and holy to such an extent as to represent it in the light of the means of procuring salvation. Nay, we even see with what reproaches the conjugal bed has been slandered by hypocrites, who wished to be thought more holy than all other men. But there is no difficulty in replying to these sneers of the ungodly. First, here the Apostle does not speak merely about having children, but about enduring all the distresses, which are manifold and severe, both in the birth and in the rearing of children. Secondly, whatever hypocrites or wise men of the world may think of it, when a woman, considering to what she has been called, submits to the condition which God has assigned to her, and does not refuse to endure the pains, or rather the fearful anguish, of parturition, or anxiety about her offspring, or anything else that belongs to her duty, God values this obedience more highly than if, in some other manner, she made a great display of heroic virtues, while she refused to obey the calling of God. To this must be added, that no consolation could be more appropriate or more efficacious than to shew that the very means (so to speak) of procuring salvation are found in the punishment itself.[17]

---

[16]In *Luther's Works*, Vol. 28: *Commentaries on 1 Corinthians 7, 1 Corinthians 15, Lectures on 1 Timothy* (ed. Hilton C. Oswald; St. Louis: Concordia, 1973 [Jan. 13, 1528]), 279.

[17]John Calvin, *Commentaries on the Epistles to Timothy, Titus, and Philemon,* (trans. William Pringle; Grand Rapids: Eerdmans, 1948), 71.

Overall, Calvin shows remarkable balance in his interpretation. Most notably, he refers "childbearing" also to the raising of children and to anything else that belongs to a woman's duty (synecdoche). In one of his sermons, Calvin summarizes the message of 1 Tim 2:15 as follows: "Let us who know to what end we are made learn to bear the yoke God has laid upon us, i.e. let everyone of us follow his vocation."[18] Calvin found ample parallels in his own day to the original background of the present passage:

> As amongst the Papists, to have a household seems to be a polluted state of the world . . . And this is a shameful thing that a Pope, that Antichrist, spews out this blasphemy, 'That those who are in the flesh cannot please God,' i.e. they that are married . . . If nuns and friars boast of their chastity and lie in idleness and call this a spiritual state, God shows that it is a detestable and cursed kind of life. Let us learn therefore that if a woman be among her household and be busied about her children . . . if she bears it patiently, knowing that it is God's good appointment, . . . this is a sweet smelling sacrifice to him. Let the nuns therefore tarry still in their convents and cloisters and in their brothel houses of Satan . . .[19]

In sum, Luther and Calvin move away from an allegorical to a more literal rendering of the passage. However, this does not of itself solve the problem, since the appearance of teaching salvation by works, i.e., the bearing of children, remains. Even an appeal to the teaching of the Pastorals in general or to the Pauline epistles by Calvin and many modern interpreters does not really solve the problem.[20] While it is thus ruled out that the passage means what it appears to mean since it cannot mean that on grounds of systematic theology, this hardly is a constructive interpretation or explanation of the passage on its own terms. After an analysis of 1 Tim 2:15, we may, of course, conclude that this passage speaks of the woman's eschatological salvation with reference to her God-ordained function centering on her role in the domestic sphere. But whatever theological presuppositions we may hold based on Pauline theology elsewhere should not preclude an open-minded study of the present passage, which should entail the acknowledgment of the possibility that Paul (or whoever

---

[18]In *Sermons of John Calvin on the Epistles of S. Paule to Timothie and Titus* (trans. L. T.; London: Banner of Truth Trust, 1983 [1579]), 233.

[19]Ibid., 231.

[20]Cf., e.g., I. Howard Marshall, "Salvation in the Pastoral Epistles" (paper presented at the annual conference of the Society of Biblical Literature, November 1994), 4: "The reference can hardly be to conversion but to the attaining of final salvation, and it can hardly be to doing good works in order to be saved, since the Pastoral Epistles teach quite clearly that we are not saved by works."

wrote 1 Timothy) in 1 Tim 2:15 presents a teaching different from the central thrust of his theology regarding salvation in his earlier writings.

The Modern Era

As mentioned, there is considerable diversity in the interpretation of the present passage in recent times. Some interpreters merely list the different options without taking a position themselves[21] or refrain from comment altogether,[22] others present a variety of interpretive insights without ever presenting a coherent interpretation of the passage,[23] yet others primarily display a concern to rehabilitate women in the light of contemporary concerns. Hermeneutically, it may be observed that emphases often vary according to the predominant underlying paradigm of a given interpreter: if religion-historical, the gnostic background may be weighted heavily; if salvation-historical, the role of Genesis 3 and of a possible Messianic typology is considered important; if systematic-canonical, reconciliation with Pauline teaching on salvation elsewhere will be a particularly serious concern; if contemporary issues are a driving motivation, one's views on women's roles in the church and in society will tend to affect one's approach. For convenience's sake, the different kinds of interpretation proposed in the modern era may be summarized and briefly critiqued below.[24]

---

[21]Cf. John Temple Bristow, *What Paul Really Said About Women* (San Francisco: Harper & Row, 1988), 75–77; Stephen B. Clark, *Man and Woman in Christ* (Ann Arbor, MI: Servant, 1980), 205–208; Letha Scanzoni and Nancy Hardesty, *All We're Meant to Be* (Waco, TX: Word, 1974), 133–34; Willard M. Swartley, *Slavery, Sabbath, War, and Women* (Scottdale, PA: Herald, 1983), 179–80; Philip H. Towner, *1-2 Timothy & Titus* (IVPNTC; Downers Grove, IL: InterVarsity, 1994), 79–80.

[22]The works by Bonnidell and Robert G. Clouse, eds., *Women in Ministry* (Downers Grove, IL: InterVarsity, 1989); Michael Harper, *Equal and Different* (London: Hodder & Stoughton, 1994); Mary Hayter, *The New Eve in Christ* (Grand Rapids: Eerdmans, 1987); and Ruth A. Tucker and Walter Liefeld, *Daughters of the Church* (Grand Rapids: Zondervan, 1987) do not contain any discussion of the present verse.

[23]Cf. Richard Clark and Catherine Clark Kroeger, *I Suffer Not a Woman* (Grand Rapids: Baker, 1992), 26, 144, 171, 176, 181.

[24]For summaries, see George W. Knight, *The Pastoral Epistles* (NIGTC; Grand Rapids: Eerdmans, 1992), 144–46; Sharon Hodgin Gritz, *Paul, Women Teachers, and the Mother Goddess at Ephesus. A Study of 1 Timothy 2:9-15 in Light of the Religious and Cultural Milieu of the First Century* (Lanham, MD: University Press of America, 1991), 140–44; Mary A. Kassian, *Women, Creation and the Fall* (Westchester, IL: Crossway, 1990), 78–81; and David R. Kimberley, "1 Tim 2:15: A Possible Understanding of a Difficult Text," *JETS* 35 (1992):

First, women's salvation may be taken to refer to the bearing of "spiritual children," i.e., good works. While this interpretation was held by Gregory of Nyssa and Augustine, it is hardly ever held today. While the importance of women's good works is stressed in New Testament and Pauline teaching, this approach resorts to a symbolic interpretation that appears inconsistent with the epistolary genre and the passage's context.

Second, women's salvation may be contingent on their physical children's perseverance in holy lives of faith. Chrysostom and Jerome held this view. While a detailed discussion of 1 Tim 2:15b is beyond the scope of this paper, it should be noted that the shift from a singular to a plural subject from the first to the second half of the verse is a sign of incongruence characteristic of paraenetic style, and that there is therefore no reason to interpret this shift as connoting a change of subject.[25] The change from singular to plural subject in verse fifteen may simply reverse the movement from plural to singular from verse nine (γυναῖκας) to the following verses.[26] In any case, few today hold to this interpretation.

Third, some detect in the present passage a reference to Messianic typology. 1 Tim 2:15 is taken to mean that women will be saved by *the* childbirth, i.e., Mary's giving birth to Jesus the Messiah, thus reversing the consequences of Eve's fall into deception. Clark (?), Ellicott, Fairbairn, Falconer, Huizenga, Kassing, Knight, Payne, Roberts, and Spencer, amongst others, favor this interpretation.[27] At the outset, it should be

---

481-86. The survey focuses on the major types of interpretation proposed over the history of interpretation and does not intend to be comprehensive. Thus some argue that 1 Tim 2:15 teaches that a woman's salvation depends on rearing her children to become good Christians (cf., e.g., J. H. Ulrichsen, "Noen bemerkninger til 1. Tim 2,15," *NorskTeolTids* 84 [1983]: 19-25). There are also minor variants of the interpretations given below. For example, James Hurley and Mary Kassian hold to variations of the sixth interpretation: women will be kept safe from seizing men's roles (James B. Hurley, *Man and Woman in Biblical Perspective* [Grand Rapids: Zondervan, 1981], 321-23), or women will be saved from loss of leadership (Kassian, *Women, Creation, and the Fall*, 78-80).

[25]Cf. Roloff, *Der erste Brief an Timotheus*, 142, referring to Peter Trummer, "Corpus Paulinum—Corpus Pastorale. Zur Ortung der Paulustradition in den Pastoralbriefen," in *Paulus in den neutestamentlichen Spätschriften. Zur Paulusrezeption im Neuen Testament* (ed. Karl Kertelge; QD 89; Freiburg: Herder, 1981), 149, n. 184.

[26]Cf. Spicq, *Épitres Pastorales*, 1:384, who cites other possible reasons for the shift such as the Semitic practice of oscillating between the collective and the individual.

[27]Cf. Clark, *Man and Woman in Christ*, 205-208; Charles J. Ellicott, *The Pastoral Epistles of St. Paul* (London: Longmans, Green, Reader, & Dyer, 1869), 38-39; Patrick Fairbairn, *Pastoral Epistles* (Minneapolis: James & Klock, 1976 [1874]), 130-34; Falconer, *Pastoral Epistles*, 132; Hilde Huizenga, "Women,

noted that some, though certainly not all, interpreters holding to this view, tend to overstate, if not misrepresent, their case, by giving the impression, when appealing to early patristic support for their interpretation, that the Messianic typology they find taught in 1 Tim 2:15 is the one alluded to in certain Fathers.[28] This, however, is debatable and should certainly not be assumed without argument.[29] Moreover, while the preceding verses (i.e., 1 Tim 2:13-14) refer to Genesis 2 and 3, they do so to illustrate Paul's prohibition of women's teaching in verse twelve by pointing to the order of creation and to the scenario of the fall rather than by establishing a Messianic typology. While verse fifteen may allude to Gen 3:16, there is absolutely no hint in the text that the author of the Pastorals intends to refer to a Messianic rendering of Gen 3:15, the so-called "proto-evangelion." It must also be noted that the presupposed understanding of Gen 3:16 as the "proto-evangelion" is only found in the second century and nowhere occurs in the New Testament.[30] The same is true for the Messianic typology linking Eve and the fall with Mary and the birth of the Messiah (cf. also 2 Cor 11:2-3 where such is manifestly absent). The presence of the definite article in the original Greek (τῆς τεκνογονίας) merely indicates the generic nature of childbirth rather than pointing to a specific birth of a child. An elaborate salvation-historical typology would be unexpected in the present context, especially in the light of the sparse use of the Old Testament in the Pastorals in general. Moreover, it is not merely women who are saved through the birth of the Messiah. One is reminded of the classic statement by Guthrie who commented, "[I]f that

---

Salvation, and the Birth of Christ: A Reexamination of 1 Timothy 2:15," *SBT* 12 (1982): 17-26; P. Altfrid Kassing, "Das Heil der Mutterschaft," *Liturgie und Mönchtum* (1958): 39-63; George W. Knight, *Pastoral Epistles*, 144-48; Philip B. Payne, "Libertarian Women in Ephesus: A Response to Douglas J. Moo's Article, '1 Timothy 2:11-15: Meaning and Significance,' " *TrinJ* 2 n.s. 2 (1981), 177-81; Mark D. Roberts, "Women Shall Be Saved: A Closer Look at 1 Timothy 2:15," *TSF Bulletin* (1991): 4-7; Aída D. B. Spencer, "Eve at Ephesus (Should Women Be Ordained as Pastors according to the First Letter to Timothy 2:11-15?)," *JETS* 17 (1974): 215-22.

[28]Cf., e.g., Payne, "Libertarian Women," 177-78; Knight, *Pastoral Epistles*, 146. It appears that many commentators merely quote earlier writers without direct recourse to the patristic references themselves (cf., e.g., Ben Witherington, *Women in the Earliest Churches* [SNTSMS 59; Cambridge: Cambridge University Press, 1988], 265, n. 228, who refers to Payne, "Libertarian Women," and Lock's commentary).

[29]See already the discussion under the history of interpretation of 1 Tim 2:15 above.

[30]Cf. Roloff, *Der erste Brief an Timotheus*, 140-41.

were the writer's intention he could hardly have chosen a more obscure or ambiguous way of saying it."[31]

Fourth, the term "saved" is sometimes taken in its literal meaning and applied to women's physical preservation through (during) childbirth. Barrett, Bernard, Guthrie, Hanson, Jeremias, Keener, and Moffat's translation are representatives of this view.[32] The effort to render σώζω literally probably stems from a desire to avoid the teaching of a woman's spiritual salvation by the bearing of children. However, it may be objected by some that the meaning "to be preserved physically" for σώζω would be unusual (cf. the use of ῥύομαι in 2 Tim 3:11; 4:18).[33] Besides, many Christian women have died during childbirth and thus were not physically preserved during it. Finally, the rendering of διά with "during" is unusual as well.

Fifth, it has recently been argued that 1 Tim 2:15 means exactly what it says (or at least seems to say on the surface): women will be saved by the bearing of children (so Gritz, Kimberley, Motyer, Porter).[34] It is suggested that the author may here, as Paul does in 1 Corinthians, pick up on a slogan used by his opponents, in this case gnostics who forbid marriage (cf. 1 Tim 4:3, 7-8; 6:20-21). This interpretation has the virtues of a literal rendering and of an attention to a possible gnostic backdrop to this epistle. On the other hand, this view, similar to the closely related sixth type of interpretation discussed below, appears to conflict with Pauline teaching on salvation elsewhere. In the light of the considerable semantic range of σώζω in the New Testament and in Pauline literature (cf., e.g., 1 Cor 6:17; 1 Tim 4:16; 2 Tim 4:18), alternatives to a literal rendition of the term should be explored.

Sixth, the view that has found considerable support among commentators in recent years is the one that interprets the reference to "child-

---

[31]Cf. Guthrie, *Pastoral Epistles*, 78.

[32]Cf. C. K. Barrett, *The Pastoral Epistles* (London: Oxford University Press, 1963), 56-57; J. H. Bernard, *The Pastoral Epistles* (Grand Rapids: Baker, 1980 [1899]), 49-50; Guthrie, *Pastoral Epistles*, 77-79; Hanson, *Pastoral Epistles*, 72-74; Joachim Jeremias, *Die Briefe an Timotheus und Titus* (NTD 9; 8th ed.; Göttingen: Vandenhoeck & Ruprecht, 1963), 22; Craig S. Keener, *Paul, Women, and Wives* (Peabody, MA: Hendrickson, 1992), 118-20.

[33]Cf. Gordon D. Fee, *1 and 2 Timothy, Titus* (Peabody, MA: Hendrickson, 1988), 31.

[34]Cf. Gritz, *Paul, Women Teachers, and the Mother Goddess*, 140-44; Kimberley, "1 Tim 2:15: A Possible Understanding of a Difficult Text," 481-86; Steve Motyer, "Expounding 1 Timothy 2:8-15," *Vox Evangelica* 24 (1994): 91-102; Stanley E. Porter, "What Does it Mean to be 'Saved by Childbirth' (1 Timothy 2.15)?" *JSNT* 49 (1993): 87-102.

bearing" in 1 Tim 2:15 as a synecdoche. Women, it is held, will be spiritually saved by adhering to their God-ordained role in the domestic sphere. The future tense of σωθήσεται is usually taken to refer to women's eschatological salvation at Christ's second coming. As has been seen above, this was essentially the view of John Calvin, and many conservative interpreters such as Alford, Barclay, Bowman, Foh, Hendriksen, Kelly, Moo, Schreiner, Scott, White, and Witherington follow this approach (see also the variations by Hurley and Kassian).[35] Of all the interpretations surveyed thus far, this reading perhaps does most justice to the text in context. Moreover, this view is attractive particularly for conservative (and here especially Reformed) interpreters since it appears to harmonize well with Pauline theology elsewhere. This strength, however, may also be the greatest weakness, since it may betray presuppositions that unduly prejudge certain elements of the interpretation of 1 Tim 2:15. At the same time, the interpretation of "childbearing" in terms of a synecdoche appears well-founded in the light of the close parallel passage in 1 Tim 5:14 where "the bearing of children" (τεκνογονεῖν) is part of a series of verbs including "to marry" (γαμεῖν) and "managing their household" (οἰκοδεσποτεῖν). The eschatological interpretation of σώζω with reference to the second coming of Christ, however, is not corroborated, to say the least, by any further eschatological references in the context. In fact, the future tense, if time-referring, may refer to any point in time future to the writer of 1 Timothy, not just the end of time, including the immediate future.[36] Moreover, the future tense of σωθήσεται need not be taken to refer to a real event at a future time (such as the woman's future salvation

---

[35]Cf. William Barclay, *The Letters to Timothy, Titus and Philemon* (3d ed.; Edinburgh: Saint Andrew, 1965 [1960]), 79; Ann J. Bowman, "Women in Ministry: An Exegetical Study of 1 Timothy 2:11–15," *BibSac* 149 (1992): 207–209; Susan J. Foh, *Women and the Word of God* (Grand Rapids: Baker, 1979), 128; William Hendriksen, *Exposition of the Pastoral Epistles* (NTC; Grand Rapids: Baker, 1957), 111–12; J. N. D. Kelly, *A Commentary on the Pastoral Epistles* (Grand Rapids: Baker, 1963), 69–70; Douglas J. Moo, "What Does It Mean Not to Teach or Have Authority Over Men? 1 Timothy 2:11–15," in *Recovering Biblical Manhood and Womanhood* (ed. John Piper and Wayne Grudem; Wheaton: Crossway, 1991), 179–93; Thomas R. Schreiner, "An Interpretation of 1 Timothy 2:9–15: A Dialogue with Recent Scholarship," in *Women in the Church*; E. F. Scott, *The Pastoral Epistles* (MNTC; London: Hodder & Stoughton, 1936), 23–29; Witherington, *Women in the Earliest Churches*, 123–24. On Hurley and Kassian, see already note 24.

[36]Cf. K. A. Van der Jagt, "Women are Saved through Bearing Children (1 Timothy 2.11–15)," *BibTrans* 39 (1988): 207: "The salvation is not purely eschatological, that is, it is not only in the future but also a reality of the present."

at Christ's return) at all but may more properly be understood as a gnomic future, i.e., of the projected result of an event on the basis of the meeting of a certain condition (in the present case, the woman's continuing in faith, love, and holiness with all sobriety; cf. 1 Tim 2:15b).[37] Nevertheless, while certain tensions remain in this interpretation, if no other more satisfying approach emerges, this is a reading of the text that is certainly possible and perhaps correct. In the light of the above survey, our search for an alternative, entirely satisfying interpretation of the present passage may focus on determining the possible renderings and the most plausible meaning of the term σωθήσεται in the present context.

Seventh, it is held that the present passage indicates that women shall be preserved (or shall escape from) Satan (or the consequences of the curse) by adhering to their God-ordained role in the domestic sphere. The perceptive discussion by Brox and brief but suggestive articles by R. Falconer and S. Jebb and, more recently, an article by A. Padgett point in this direction (cf. also the NASB: "But she shall be preserved through the bearing of children").[38] The advantage of this interpretation is that it links v. 15

---

[37]For the gnomic use of the future tense in Greek, cf., e.g., Stanley E. Porter, *Idioms of New Testament Greek* (Sheffield: Sheffield Academic Press, 1992), 44; James Brooks and Carlton Winbery, *Syntax of New Testament Greek* (Wilmington: University Press of America, 1979), 98; Wesley J. Perschbacher, *New Testament Greek Syntax* (Chicago: Moody, 1995), 293. These authors list the following instances of a gnomic use of the future in the New Testament: Matt 7:16; 12:37; 15:14; Mark 2:22; Luke 12:34; Rom 5:7; 7:3; Gal 6:5; Eph 5:31 (cf. Matt 19:5; 1 Cor 6:16). But see also the remarks on the four references involving a future passive of σώζω contemporaneous to 1 Timothy discussed below. As will be seen, none of these instances involve a reference to a distant future point in time.

[38]Cf. Norbert Brox, *Die Pastoralbriefe* (Regensburger NT; 8th ed.; Regensburg: Friedrich Pustet, 1969), 136: "Der vorausgehende Vers hatte ihre Position recht aussichtslos gezeichnet, hier wird ein 'Ausweg,' eine Möglichkeit, ein Heilsweg gezeigt . . . Der apodiktische Satz mag an Merkwürdigkeit verlieren, wenn man annimmt, daß das 'Kindergebären' (nach Tit 2,4) die Erziehung der Kinder und die Führung des häuslichen Lebens einbegreift, also für die Ehe und das Verheiratetsein als ganzes steht"; Robert Falconer, "1 Timothy 2:14, 15: Interpretative Notes," *JBL* 60 (1941): 376: "Σωθήσεται δὲ διὰ τῆς τεκνογονίας: here 'she shall be saved' must mean escape from the effects of the transgression"; S. Jebb, "A Suggested Interpretation of 1 Ti 2.15," *ExpTim* 81 (1970): 221-22. Alan Padgett, "Wealthy Women at Ephesus. 1 Timothy 2:8-15 in Social Context," *Int* 41 (1987): 19-31: "I believe that Paul means to say that Eve was saved from the snake, that is, from Satan" (28). Padgett argues that Paul was in the present passage dealing with a particular problem with certain women in Ephesus who supported false teachers. Paul's response, according to Padgett, was to limit these women's authority, so that there is nothing in the text that limits the role of women in the church today. Our agreement with certain aspects of Padgett's exegesis does not imply that we are following all of Padgett's sociological

particularly well with the preceding verse (v. 14) where the fall and the serpent's temptation of the woman are explicitly mentioned. A possible reference to the woman's preservation from Satan is also given added probability by the explicit mention of Satan in the close parallel passage in 1 Tim 5:14. Moreover, as will be seen below, the concern for believers' preservation from Satan pervades the Pastorals. On the other hand, some may object that "to be preserved" is an unusual, or at least infrequent, rendering of σώζω in the New Testament and in Paul, and that Satan (or the curse) is not explicitly referred to in v. 15 but needs to be implied from the context.

An Interpretation of 1 Timothy 2:15a

The Meaning of σωθήσεται διά in 1 Timothy 2:15a

The preceding survey of interpretations of 1 Tim 2:15 has indicated that determining the intended meaning of σωθήσεται may well be the key to a correct interpretation of the passage.[39] Should the term be taken to connote physical preservation (fourth view), spiritual salvation (fifth view), eschatological salvation (sixth view), or spiritual preservation from Satan (or the curse) (seventh view)? Moreover, there are further issues that pertain to the interpretation of the term: (1) What is the implied subject? (2) What is the range of meaning of σώζω in the New Testament, in Paul's writings, and in the Pastorals, and what light is shed on the meaning of σωθήσεται by the immediate and larger context? (3) What is the force of διά in the present passage? (4) Does the writer allude here to Gen 3:15 or 16 and is there a reference to the author's gnostic opponents? (5) How does σωθήσεται relate to the phrase διὰ τῆς τεκνογονίας? These ques-

---

conclusions regarding the background of 1 Tim 2:15. Likewise, his typological approach to the present passage appears too ingenious to be a plausible interpretation of the text as it stands.

[39]We presuppose a hermeneutic that will not make extratextual information functionally determinative of the text's meaning to the extent that it actually sets aside the plain reading of the text and other hermeneutical fallacies that have particularly beset the study of the New Testament gender passages. On this, see Andreas J. Köstenberger, "Gender Passages in the NT: Hermeneutical Fallacies Critiqued," *WTJ* 56 (1994): 259–83. In the case of the interpretation of the present passage, care should be taken lest issues such as the alleged gnostic background or a putative allusion to Gen 3:15 or 16 or both take effective control of the passage's entire interpretation. The challenge is to provide an interpretation that does not unnecessarily import extratextual information nor adds extensively to the explicit statement but is a plausible interpretation of the text as it stands.

tions will provide the framework for the discussion below. While they cannot be dealt with independently so that there will be a certain amount of overlap in our treatment of these issues, these questions are the ones that will need to be answered in the course of the present study.

The Implied Subject of 1 Timothy 2:15a. We may begin by determining the implied subject of σωθήσεται. This subject appears to be the term "(the) woman" (ἡ γυνή) from the previous verse, as informed by the addition in the latter part of the verse (see below). While the author had referred to the man and the woman at creation by their names, i.e., Adam and Eve (v. 13), he refers in v. 14 to Adam and to "the woman" (rather than Eve), thus apparently pointing to Eve's representative role for womankind in general at the fall.[40]

In the present verse, based on the transitional ἡ γυνή in v. 14, the writer completes his change of reference from Eve as a historical person to Eve "the woman" as representing womankind at the fall to the women addressed in the present correspondence and thereafter as indicated by the omission of any explicit subject in v. 15. It should be noted that the statement in verse 15b narrows the reference to *Christian* women, i.e., those who "continue in faith and love and holiness, with modesty."[41] The generic reference to women also seems to favor taking the future tense of the verb as gnomic, i.e., used without reference to time.

Finally, the sequence of passive forms in vv. 13, 14, and 15 requires explanation. The reference in v. 13 to Adam's creation clearly implies God as the agent, an instance of the so-called *passivum divinum* ("divine passive"; ἐπλάσθε). Conversely, the terms of being deceived in verse 14 (ἠπατήθη, ἐξαπατηθεῖσα) point to Satan as the implied agent, an instance of what may be called a "diabolical passive."[42] This may explain the fact that Satan is not explicitly referred to in v. 15 as the implied threat from which the woman is saved: as in v. 14, Satan is understood to be the potential danger from which the woman is to be "saved." The passive form in v. 15 (σωθήσεται) itself, then, may be another instance of a "divine passive," with God as the implied agent of the woman's salvation, or be taken as a quasi-deponent form where stress is laid on the woman's own participa-

---

[40]See already Sir 25:24: "From a woman sin had its beginning, and because of her we all die."

[41]Cf. Spicq, *Épitres Pastorales*, 1:382. On taking the plural reference in v. 15b as pertaining to the women addressed in v. 15a, see already the brief discussion above. But this subject can and need not be fully dealt with here.

[42]This category is, at least at present, not found in most Greek grammars!

tion in her salvation or preservation from the implied threat of v. 15 (e.g., "the woman will escape"). These possibilities must be kept in mind in the course of the remaining study.

The Range of Meaning of Σώζω and Σωθήσεται in 1 Timothy 2:15a. We may proceed as follows. We will first sketch out the range of meaning of σώζω in the New Testament at large. This is followed by an identification of the most compatible passages in the Pauline writings and particularly in the Pastorals. Extending our scope beyond the New Testament to extrabiblical literature preceding or contemporaneous to the Pastorals, we will survey instances, first of future passives of σώζω, and then of (future) passives of σώζω plus δία plus the genitive.

Introduction. Two major implications emerge from the study of σώζω, in the New Testament and in Paul: first, the term's range of meaning is broader than is often acknowledged, even in the Pauline literature, and even in the Pastorals; and second, the effort at illuminating the probable meaning of σώζω, in 1 Tim 2:15a needs to be narrowed to instances of σώζω, in the (future) passive plus δία plus the genitive.

Our comments regarding the range of meaning of σώζω in the New Testament, Paul, and the Pastorals in general, can therefore be brief.[43] In classical Greek, the term generally referred to the averting of life-threatening danger or, where no immediate danger was mentioned, to a person's keeping or preservation. This usage is comparatively rare in the New Testament; is is, however, found in Acts 27–28 (σώζω: 27:20, 31; διασώζω: 27:43, 44; 28:1, 4). In the LXX, σώζω translates as many as fifteen different Hebrew words. Regarding the range of meaning of σώζω relevant for 1 Tim 2:15a we survey the three most pertinent lexicons:

Bauer, Arndt, and Gingrich sketch the range of meaning of σώζω as follows:

1. preserve or rescue from natural dangers and afflictions;
2. save or preserve from eternal death;
   a. active: so. or sthg.;
   b. passive: be saved, attain salvation;
3. combination of 1. and 2.[44]

---

[43]Cf. I. Howard Marshall, "Salvation in the Pastoral Epistles." Marshall's discussion reflects that 1 Tim 2:15 is not a central passage in the epistle's teaching regarding salvation. He takes the passage to refer to eschatological salvation, "since the Pastoral Epistles teach quite clearly that we are not saved by works."

[44]Cf. BAGD, 798–99.

Category 2. b. appears to be the most likely meaning of the present term in 1 Tim 2:15a within this range.

Liddell and Scott provide the following outline (partial):

1. of persons: save from death, keep alive;
    pass. to be saved, kept alive, preserved;
    keep a whole skin, escape destruction;
    to be healed, recover from sickness;
    also, save oneself, escape[45]

We note that the relevant renditions include those of "be preserved," "escape destruction," and "escape."

Louw and Nida include σώζω with three different meanings in two different semantic domains:

I. Physiological Processes and States
        1. heal;
II. Danger, Risk, Save, Safe
        A. to cause to be safe, free from danger
            2. rescue; and
        B. to save in a religious sense
            3. save[46]

The meaning "to heal" is frequently found in the Gospels; it is transparently not the meaning of σώζω in the present passage. This leaves the meanings of "to rescue" (i.e., keep safe, preserve from danger) and "to save" (in terms of religious salvation) as possible renderings.

What are we to learn from these categorizations? It appears that much confusion has resulted from the fact that interpreters sought to reconcile the connotation of religious salvation with Pauline teaching elsewhere (viz. the Reformation). However, the meaning "to rescue" in the sense of safekeeping or preservation is perfectly possible and, as will be seen, highly probable in 1 Tim 2:15. Perhaps even meanings such as "escape from destruction" (see Liddell and Scott) are conceivable in the present passage. Moreover, Louw and Nida comment that preservation implies "not only rescue from danger but a restoration to a former state of well-being and safety."

In general, it should be noted that, while a term's range of meaning sets the outer parameters for a given occurrence of this expression in con-

---

[45]Cf. LSJ, 1748.
[46]Cf. Louw and Nida, *Greek-English Lexicon,* 1:241–42, 269.

text, it functions primarily as an excluding criterion of what a term *cannot* mean rather than indicating what it *does* mean. Specifically, the occurrence of σώζω in the future passive, i.e., σωθήσεται, in 1 Tim 2:15a should primarily be compared with similar uses of σώζω elsewhere in the New Testament, Paul, or the Pastorals, as well as with the occurrence of similar forms, i.e., (future) passives, in other writings contemporary to 1 Timothy. Moreover, in the present case, the usage of σώζω, even in the future passive, is demonstrably so different from its use in Paul and the Pastorals that we may safely exclude the Gospels as the source of possible close parallels to 1 Tim 2:15.

Similar Passages to 1 Timothy 2:15a in the Paulines and Pastorals. The term σώζω occurs in the Pastorals in 1 Tim 1:15; 2:4, 15; 4:16; 2 Tim 1:9; 4:18; Tit 3:5. In the remaining Paulines, there are these additional references: Rom 5:9, 10; 8:24; 9:27; 10:9, 13; 11:14, 26; 1 Cor 1:18, 21; 3:15; 5:5; 7:16; 9:22; 10:33; 15:2; 2 Cor 2:15; Eph 2:5, 8; 1 Thess 2:16; 2 Thess 2:10. Also, the term σωτήρ is found in the Pastorals in 1 Tim 1:1; 2:3; 4:10; 2 Tim 1:10; Tit 1:3, 4; 2:10, 13; 3:4, 6; and the term σωτήριος in Tit 2:11. Of those references, the following may be identified as possible parallels to the use of σώζω in 1 Tim 2:15:

- 1 Cor 3:15: "If it is burned up, he will suffer loss; he himself will be saved, but only as one escaping through the flames" (NIV footnote: "Perhaps a Greek proverbial phrase, meaning 'by a narrow escape' "); εἴ τινος τὸ ἔργον κατακαήσεται, ζημιωθήσεται, αὐτὸς δὲ σωθήσεται, οὕτως δὲ ὡς διὰ πυρός);
- 1 Cor 7:16: "For how do you know, woman, if you will save your husband? Or how do you know, man, if you will save your wife?" (τί γὰρ οἶδας, γύναι, εἰ τὸν ἄνδρα σώσεις; ἢ τί οἶδας, ἄνερ, εἰ τὴν γυναῖκα σώσεις;);
- 1 Tim 4:16: "Watch yourself and your teaching; persevere in them. For by so doing you will save both yourself and those who listen to you" (ἔπεχε σεαυτῷ καὶ τῇ διδασκαλίᾳ, ἐπίμενε αὐτοῖς· τοῦτο γὰρ ποιῶν καὶ σεαυτὸν σώσεις καὶ τοὺς ἀκούοντάς σου);
- 2 Tim 4:18: "The Lord will rescue me from every evil work and bring me safely into his heavenly kingdom" (ῥύσεταί με ὁ κύριος ἀπὸ παντὸς ἔργου πονηροῦ καὶ σώσει εἰς τὴν βασιλείαν αὐτοῦ τὴν ἐπουράνιον).

1 Cor 3:15 is the closest formal New Testament parallel to the present passage. Here the future passive of σώζω is used to denote an escape through danger. But differences between 1 Cor 3:15 and 1 Tim 2:15 must

be noted as well: unlike 1 Tim 2:15, the context in 1 Cor 3:15 is clearly eschatological; and in 1 Cor 3:15, the phrase οὕτως δὲ ὡς is interjected between σωθήσεται and διὰ πυρός, while no adversative conjunction is found between σωθήσεται and διὰ τεκνογονίας in 1 Tim 2:15. In the next two passages, 1 Cor 7:16 and 1 Tim 4:16, it is evident that the addressees will not be the direct cause for a person's salvation.[47] 1 Tim 4:16 should be seen as an instance of the "preservation" theme (from Satan) in the Pastorals which will be discussed further below.[48] Timothy's teaching of sound doctrine will help preserve his hearers from falling into error. Finally, in 2 Tim 4:18, reference is made, not to first-time salvation, but to preservation and safe passage. Interestingly, the similar term ῥύομαι is used in the first part of the clause, denoting deliverance, while σώζω focuses, not on a one-time act, but on a process of preservation and safekeeping. While this passage clearly has an ultimate eschatological reference point, the emphasis is at least in part on the author's confidence of his safekeeping *in this life* until that final day. But whether the above passages are parallel to the present one or not and whether or not they are to be interpreted eschatologically or with primary reference to the here and now, ultimately the context of 1 Tim 2:15 itself remains determinative for the term's meaning there. Moreover, in light of the paucity of New Testament parallels, it will be desirable to extend our scope of reference to contemporaneous extrabiblical literature.

Σώζω in the Future Passive. There are twenty instances of the future passive of σώζω in the New Testament of which one in the longer ending of Mark (16:16) can be omitted: Matt 9:2=Mark 5:28; Matt 10:22=24:13= Mark 13:13; Luke 8:50; John 10:9; 11:12; Acts 2:21=Rom 10:13 (OT); 11:14=16:31; Rom 5:9, 10; 9:27 (OT); 10:9; 11:26; 1 Cor 3:15; and 1 Tim 2:15. In these nineteen references, the term σώζω refers either to healing (four times; only in the Gospels: Matt 9:21=Mark 5:28; Luke 8:50; John 11:12) or religious salvation, usually conceived of in eschatological terms

---

[47]Cf. Adolf Schlatter, *Die Kirche der Griechen im Urteil des Paulus* (2d ed.; Stuttgart: Calwer, 1958 [1936]), 92, n. 1, who names 1 Tim 4:16 as a close conceptual parallel to 1 Tim 2:15. This author also refers to 1 Corinthians 7 as a similar instance where Paul refutes the improper disparagement of sexual relations, even within marriage, among his readers.

[48]Thomas Schreiner, in a personal correspondence dated September 15, 1995, objects that in "1 Tim. 4:16 human actions are the instrumental cause for [eschatological] salvation." This interpretation is possible, but hardly seems to do justice to the major concern here and elsewhere in the letter for people's present preservation from false teaching.

(fourteen times; Matt 10:22=24:13=Mark 13:13; John 10:9; Acts 2:21; 11:14=16:31; Rom 5:9, 10; 9:27; 10:9, 13; 11:26; 1 Cor 3:15; in both Acts and Romans, Old Testament quotations may set the overall framework). It should be noted that these passages need to be looked at individually and that they are confined to a relatively small number. Arguably, the reference in 1 Tim 2:15 stands apart from either category (but cf. the discussion of 1 Cor 3:15 above). The occurrence of διεσώθησαν in 1 Pet 3:20 should also be noted.[49]

Finally, the future passive indicative of σώζω occurs once in each of the following writers: Philo (*LA* 3.190); Diodorus Siculus (*Hist.* 1.80); Dionysius Halicarnassensis (*Thuc.* 26.107); and Josephus (*BJ* 2.201). The passage in Philo may best be rendered actively (as does the Loeb Classical Library Series) as "to preserve her" (σωθήσεται):

> καὶ μὴν ἔμπαλιν ἡ ἡδονὴ τοῦ μὲν ἄφρονος διατηρεῖ τὴν ἐπίβασιν, τοῦ δὲ σοφοῦ λύειν καὶ ἀναιρεῖν ἐπιχειρεῖ τὴν ἐνστὲον, ἡγουμένη τὸν μὲν κατάλυσιν αὐτῆς μελετᾶν, τὸν δ' ὧν μάλόϋα σωθήσεται ("Pleasure on the other hand watches over and preserves the procedure of the foolish mind, but endeavours to break up and destroy the way of life of the wise mind, holding that the latter is planning her ruin, while the former is devising the best means to preserve her").

The usage in Diodorus Siculus is brought over into English by the phrase "would be recovered" (σωθήσεται): ἀδυνάτου γὰρ ὄντος τοῦ πάντας ἀποστῆσαι τῆς κλοπῆς εὗρε πόρον ὁ νομοθέτης δι' οὗ πᾶν τὸ ἀπολόμενον σωθήσεται μικρῶν διδομένων λύτρων ("For as it was impossible to keep all mankind from stealing, the lawgiver devised a scheme whereby every article lost would be recovered upon payment of a small ransom").

The references in Dionysius Halicarnassensis and Josephus are best rendered as "save themselves" (σωθήσονται) and "saving myself" (σωθήσομαι), indicating the verb's possible deponent force in the passive. The former reference reads as follows: ἄλλοι δὲ καὶ οἱ πλεῖστοι ἤδη περὶ σφᾶς αὐτοὺς καὶ ὅπη σωθήσονται διεσκόπουν (". . . while the remaining and most numerous part already began to consider how they should save themselves"). Finally, the passage in Josephus has: ἢ γὰρ τοῦ θεοῦ συνεργοῦντος πείσας Καίσαρα σωθήσομαι μεθ' ὑμῶν ἡδέως, ἢ παραξυνθέντος ὑπὲρ τοσούτων ἑτοίμως ἐπιδώσω τὴν ἐμαυτοῦ ψυχήν ("Either, God aiding me, I shall prevail with Caesar and have the satisfaction of saving myself as well as you, or, if his indignation is roused, I am ready on behalf of the lives of so many to surrender my own").

---

[49]See the discussion below.

Thus some fluidity regarding the rendering of this verb in the passive voice remains: the future passive once carries an active force, is once used passively, and twice as a middle. Moreover, the future tense does not appear to carry strong weight in any of these passages.

The Force of Διά in 1 Timothy 2:15a. We may take up this question in relation to one further element, i.e., the usage of σώζω in the (future) passive with the preposition διά plus the genitive. The general categories of usage of διά are listed by Harris as (1) means or instrument; (2) attendant circumstance; (3) cause or ground; and (4) purpose.[50] Regarding the meaning of διά in 1 Tim 2:15, reference may be made to Harris' citation of the present passage as an instance of double entendre similar to 1 Peter 3:20.[51] In the latter case, διεσώθησαν δι' ὕδατος may mean both "they were brought safely through water" (local διά) and "they were preserved by means of water" (instrumental διά). The translation "they were saved through water" preserves the deliberate ambiguity in English. Harris appears to imply that διά in 1 Tim 2:15, likewise, may be understood both in terms of physical preservation throughout the process of childbirth (temporal) and childbirth as the means by which salvation (preservation) occurs (instrumental). The double entendre may well be intended in 1 Peter 3:20; but is 1 Tim 2:15 a comparable example?

The study of passive instances of σώζω with the preposition διά in literature surrounding the time period of the writing of 1 Timothy reveals the following passages. Josephus provides this reference in his autobiography:

Ἐπεὶ δὲ προελθὼν ὀλίγον ὑπαντιάζειν ἔμελλον τὸν Ἰωάννην ἰόντα μετὰ τῶν ὁπλιτῶν, δείσας ἐκεῖνον μὲν ἐξέκλινα, διὰ στενωποῦ δέ τινος ἐπὶ τὴν λίμνην σωθεὶς καὶ πλοίου λαβόμενος, ἐμβὰς εἰς τὰς Ταριχαίας διεπεραιώθην ἀπροσδοκήτως τὸν κίνδυνον διαφυγών ("I had not proceeded far when I found myself nearly facing John, advancing with his troops. I turned from him in alarm, and, escaping by a narrow passage to the lake, seized a boat, embarked and crossed to Tarichaeae, having, beyond all expectation, come safe out of this perilous situation.").[52]

In this instance, the passive of σώζω plus διά is used to denote an escape by way of a narrow passage. Thus the passive form is to be rendered

---

[50]Murray J. Harris, "Appendix: Prepositions and Theology in the Greek New Testament," *NIDNTT* 3:1181–84. Cf. also BAG, 180, who list under the category entitled "means, instrument, agency": 1. means or instrument; 2. manner; 3. attendant circumstance; 4. efficient cause; 5. occasion.

[51]Ibid., 3:1177.

[52]Josephus, *Vita* 304.

actively, i.e. "escape," as if the verb were functioning as a deponent, and the preposition points to a place through which the escapee passed on his way out of danger.

The geographer Strabo supplies us with a similar usage. He writes,

τῶν δὲ Ῥωμαίων ἐπακολουθούντων ναυκλήρῳ τινί, ὅπως καὶ αὐτοὶ γνοῖεν τὰ ἐμπόρια, φθόνῳ ὁ ναύκληρος ἑκὼν εἰς τέναγος ἐξέβαλε τὴν ναῦν, ἐπα γαγὼν δ᾽ εἰς τὸν αὐτὸν ὄλεθρον καὶ τοὺς ἑπομένους, αὐτὸς ἐσώθη διὰ ναυαγίου καὶ ἀπέλαβε δημοσίᾳ τὴν τιμὴν ὧν ἀπέβαλε φορτίων ("And when once the Romans were closely following a certain ship-captain in order that they too might learn the markets in question, out of jealousy the ship-captain purposely drove his ship out of its course into shoal water; and after he had lured the followers into the same ruin, he himself escaped by a piece of wreckage and received from the State the value of the cargo he had lost.").[53]

Once again, the passive of σώζω is to be rendered with the active term "escape," and a piece of wreckage becomes the means of the escapees' transition into safety.

Another instance from Strabo's writings reads thus:

οἱ δὲ τοῦ Ἀδράστου συντριβῆναι τὸ ἅρμα φεύγοντός φασιν ἐνταῦθα, τὸν δὲ διὰ τοῦ Ἀρείονος σωθῆναι. Φιλόχορος δ᾽ ὑπὸ τῶν κωμητῶν σωθῆναί φησιν αὐτόν . . . ("[O]thers say that the chariot of Adrastus, when he was in flight, was smashed to pieces there, but that Adrastus safely escaped on Areion. But Philochorus says that Adrastus was saved by the inhabitants of the village . . .").[54]

The passive form of σώζω is again to be rendered with the term "escape" and a horse becomes the means of the warrior's flight into safety.[55]

Finally, reference should be made to 1 Cor 3:15 and 1 Pet 3:20. It appears that the phrases διεσώθεσαν διὰ πυρός and διεσώθησαν δι᾽ ὕδατος ("were preserved/escaped through water") resemble closely the usage of σώζω in the present passage, similar to the references cited above.

What these examples illustrate, is that the passive of σώζω plus διά was in literature surrounding the writing of the Pastorals regularly used in

---

[53]Strabo, *Geog.* 3.5.11.

[54]Strabo, *Geog.* 9.2.11.

[55]This passage adds an interesting element, i.e., the occurrence of a passive form of σώζω with the preposition ὑπό. The latter phrase denotes a person's being saved by one or several agents (in the present case, "the inhabitants of the village)." Rather than constituting parallel uses, the two phrases thus rather seem to be of a contrasting nature.

the context of a person's escape or preservation from danger by way of a given route (circumstantial use; cf. also Rom 2:27; 14:20; 1 Cor 3:15; 2 Cor 2:4; 3:11; 6:8; 1 Pet 3:20).[56] There seems to be therefore no need to resort to double entendre on the part of the author of the Pastorals as is suggested by Harris.[57] 1 Tim 2:15, likewise, should therefore be understood as a reference to the woman's escape or preservation from a danger by means of childbearing. Moreover, as in the above examples, what a person is saved *from* is implied rather than explicitly stated; merely the way of escape is given. But the context always suggests a given danger, be it death by drowning or by the hand of the enemy. What is therefore the most likely danger or enemy from which the woman escapes or is preserved in the present context? Arguably, it is the serpent, or Satan, and perhaps the temptation provided by it. Three factors combine to render this reading probable:

(1) the reference to the woman's being deceived at the fall in the preceding verse (1 Tim 2:14);

(2) the explicit mention of Satan in the close parallel passage later in the same epistle, i.e., 1 Tim 5:14-15 which reads: "Therefore I want younger widows to get married, bear children (τεκνογονεῖν), keep

---

[56]Cf. Roloff, *Der erste Brief an Timotheus*, 147; Spicq, *Épîtres Pastorales*, 383: "διά avec le génitif n'introduit jamais le complément du passif, il marque souvent l'état ou la condition dans laquelle s'insère une personne ou une action (au milieu, les circonstances, l'occasion)"; both of these writers also refer to C. F. D. Moule, *An Idiom Book of New Testament Greek* (Cambridge: Cambridge University Press, 1953), 56 (c); and H. Bürki, *Der erste Brief des Paulus an Timotheus* (Wuppertaler Studienbibel; Wuppertal: R. Brockhaus, 4th ed., 1980 [1974]), 92-93. But see, for example, Knight, *Pastoral Epistles*, 147: "διά with the genitive is used here to express means, instrument, or agency (cf. BAGD s.v. A. III. 1d [180]). There are seven occurrences in the New Testament of the verb σώζω with διά (Acts 15:11; Rom. 5:9; 1 Cor. 1:21; 3:15; 15:2; here; 1 Pet. 3:20), all except 1 Cor. 1:21 passive and all except 1 Cor. 3:15 and 1 Pet. 3:20 indicating with διά the means through which salvation is brought, accomplished, or appropriated." But, inexplicably, Knight fails to mention that BAGD itself places διά in A. III. 1c attendant circumstances, not 1d as he himself does. No more need be said.

[57]Porter et al. suggest that σωθήσεται in 1 Tim 2:15 may be an instance of a so-called "divine passive," with God being the unexpressed but implied agent of the woman's "salvation" (cf. Porter, "What Does It Mean?" 94). In context and in light of the uses documented above, the quasi-deponent force of σώζω in the passive ("escape," "be kept safe") may provide a better explanation. On this, see already the discussion under II. A. 1. on the implied subject of 1 Tim 2:15a above.

house (οἰκοδεσποτεῖν), and give the enemy no occasion for reproach, for some have already turned aside to follow Satan (Σατανᾶ);" in this passage, the author appears to make explicit both elements that are merely implied in 1 Tim 2:15: the larger scope connoted by the term "bearing of children," i.e., "keeping house," and his desire to preserve women from Satan;

(3) the consistent concern for believer's preservation from Satan or demonic forces in the Pastorals (or at least insinuations in this regard) and the presence of this motif elsewhere in Pauline writings (references will be to 1 Timothy unless noted otherwise):

- the writer has delivered Hymenaeus and Alexander over to Satan in order not to blaspheme (1 Tim 1:20);
- Eve fell into deception at the fall, women will escape by childbirth (1 Tim 2:14–15);
- new converts should not be appointed as overseers, lest they become conceited and fall into the condemnation incurred by the devil (3:6);
- an overseer must have a good reputation with those outside the church so that he might not fall into reproach and the snare of the devil (3:7);
- the author finds evidence for the presence of deceitful spirits and doctrines of demons in the environment of the recipients of his letter, particularly the forbidding of marriage and abstinence from certain foods (4:1–5);
- younger widows should remarry, bear children, keep house, and give the enemy no occasion for reproach, for some have already turned to follow Satan (5:14–15);
- those who want to get rich fall into temptation and a snare and many foolish and harmful desires which plunge men into ruin and destruction (6:9–10; cf. 2 Tim 2:26);
- Timothy should guard what has been entrusted to him, avoiding the opposing arguments of what is falsely called "knowledge" which some have professed and thus gone astray from the faith (6:20–21; cf. 6:9–10);
- in 2 Timothy, the author expresses the hope that kind, patient, and gentle correction of one's opponents may lead to their repentance and a coming to the knowledge of the truth so that they may come to their senses and escape from the snare of the devil, having been held captive by him to do his will (2 Tim 2:26);
- in 1 Cor 7:5, it is a married couple's ill-advised prolonged abstinence from sexual intercourse that makes them vulnerable to Satan;

- in Eph 4:27, it is unresolved anger;
- and numerous references in 1 and 2 Timothy speak of a person's need to guard (φυλάσσω) what has been entrusted to him (cf., e.g., 1 Tim 6:12; 2 Tim 1:12, 14; 4:7, 15, 18)

The consistency with which the theme of preservation is sounded particularly in 1 and 2 Timothy is indeed remarkable. References to preservation from Satan (or the lack thereof) in the context of the present passage include 1 Tim 1:20 on the one hand and 1 Tim 3:6 and 7 on the other. It should also be noted that 2 Timothy is framed by significant "preservation" passages, i.e., 2 Tim 1:12 and 4:18. The Pastorals' "preservation theme" may be considered to be a subcategory of perseverance versus apostasy, involving also numerous exhortations to Timothy to "escape" and "pursue" (φεῦγε, δίωκε; cf., e.g., 1 Tim 6:11; 2 Tim 2:22). The above list of references to people's preservation from Satan (a positive concern) may be supplemented (with some overlap) by a list of the negative corollary in the Pastorals, i.e., references to people's "wandering away from the faith," their "straying" or "turning aside," or their "being shipwrecked" and similar terms. This fills out the preservation (or lack thereof) theme in the Pastorals and further underscores its significance by providing us with the following references in 1 Timothy:

- some were straying (ἀστοχήσαντες), turning aside (ἐξαπατηθεῖσαν; 1:6)
- some have rejected (ἀπωσάμενοι) and suffered shipwreck (ἐναυάγησαν; 1:19)
- not Adam (ἠπατήθη), but woman deceived (ἐξαπατηθεῖσα; 2:14)
- be blinded (τυφωθείς) and fall into condemnation of devil (ἐμπέσῃ; 2:14)
- fall into reproach and snare of devil (ἐμπέσῃ; 3:7)
- some will fall away from the faith (ἀποστήσονται; 4:1)
- incurring judgment, setting aside previous pledge (ἔχουσαι κρίμα, ἠθέτησαν; 5:12)
- go around from house to house (περιερχόμεναι τὰς οἰκίας; 5:13)
- some have already turned aside to follow Satan (ἐξετράπησαν ὀπίσω; 5:15)
- reference to "elect angels" implies some are fallen (5:21)
- those who want to get rich fall into temptation and a snare (ἐμπίπτουσιν; 6:9)
- some have wandered away from the faith (ἀπεπλανήθησαν) and pierced themselves (περιέπειραν; 6:10)

• some have professed "knowledge" and thus gone astray from the faith (ἠστόχησαν; 6:21; inclusio with 1:6; cf. also 2 Tim 2:18 with reference to Hymenaeus and Philetus' teaching that resurrection had already taken place)[58]

We may sum up the argument thus far. In the light of the reference to the fall in 1 Tim 2:14, the explicit reference to Satan in the close parallel of 1 Tim 5:14-15, and the impressive and substantial evidence for a "preservation from Satan" theme in the Pastorals, it appears more than justified to view Satan as the one from whom women will escape or be preserved by childbearing according to 1 Tim 2:15. Thus the phrase σωθήσεται διά in 1 Tim 2:15 may be rendered as "She (i.e., the woman) escapes (or is preserved; gnomic future) [from Satan] by way of τεκνογονία."

Allusions to Gnostic Teaching or to Genesis
Gnosticism. If this is the likely rendering of this verse, may we here find an allusion to the teaching of the opponents of the writer of 1 Timothy? These opponents have often been uncritically identified as gnostics (see especially 1 Tim 6:20). However, as has increasingly been realized, utmost caution must be taken not to impose on the present text a later, more developed form of gnosticism.[59] The primary clues should, at any rate, be taken from the text of 1 Timothy itself. Generally, it is apparent that the antagonists of the writer of this epistle represent a blend of Jewish and pagan religious features.[60] Thus one finds an interest in genealogies and

---

[58]One notes that the author of 1 and 2 Timothy frequently uses the vague expression "some" to refer to his opponents in the first epistle while naming some of his adversaries explicitly in his second letter (e.g., Hymenaeus and Philetus in 2:18 [but cf. already 1 Tim 1:20: Hymenaeus and Alexander], Demas in 4:10, and Alexander in 4:14; cf. Egbert Schlarb, *Die gesunde Lehre: Häresie und Wahrheit im Spiegel der Pastoralbriefe* [Marburg: N. G. Elwert, 1990], 129). Also, verbs relating to "wandering away" or "straying" are less common in the second epistle, which may indicate a more confirmed situation at the time of writing 2 Timothy: in the author's mind, teachers are either confirmed as true or false.

[59]Cf. esp. E. M. Yamauchi, "Gnosis, Gnosticism," in *Dictionary of Paul and His Letters*, 353.

[60]Cf. Oskar Skarsaune, "Heresy and the Pastoral Epistles," *Them* 20/1 (October 1994): 9: "Most commentators conclude that the adversaries were Judaizing Christians with a Gnostic leaning, or gnosticizing Christians with a Judaizing tendency." Skarsaune himself argues on the basis of 2 Tim 2:18 that these gnosticizing opponents despised the material aspect of creation, had no use for a resurrection of the body, and thus ended up with a one-sided stress on realized eschatology (cf. also Towner, *1-2 Timothy & Titus*, 22-26). But it seems

matters of the law (Jewish; 1:4, 7; 4:7; cf. Tit 1:10, 14; 3:9) and a contempt for marriage (pagan; 4:3: κωλυόντων γαμεῖν) existing side by side among the doctrines of the false teachers.[61] Since it is therefore apparent that the antagonists' concept of spirituality demeaned procreation, it is certainly possible, if not likely, that the writer of 1 Timothy seeks to counter this false dichotomy by linking the term σώζω with the term τεκνογονία, a juxtaposition that surely would have made the writer's opponents cringe. Indeed, the currency of the term σώζω in contemporary religious terminology may well explain the use of this expression by the writer of 1 Timothy with the less common meaning "to be preserved" rather than "to be saved." Similar to instances in 1 Corinthians and Colossians, the author may turn slogans by his opponents against them by redefining them within a Christian framework. A Christian woman, he maintains, is "saved" (σωθήσεται), not by knowledge and communion with the divine in neglect of her physical functions, but by adhering to her proper biological and societal role centering on her function in procreation and the domestic sphere. This coheres well with the emphasis on orderly family relations in the Pastorals (cf. 1 Tim 3:4, 12; 5:4; Tit 1:6).

Another factor that is seldom given proper weight is the fact that the writer of the Pastorals' primary concern regarding women is not with them as perpetrators but as victims of false teaching (cf., e.g., 2 Tim 3:6; but see Rev 3:20-23).[62] Thus a desire to protect women from harmful teaching

---

questionable to use a passage in 2 Timothy as the primary evidence to determine the background of the false teachers in 1 Timothy.

[61]For second-century gnosticism, cf. Irenaeus, *Haer.* 1.24.2–3, on the gnostics and Saturninus: "they consider marrying and childbearing to be from Satan" (*nubere autem et generare a Satana dicunt esse*). Cf. also the fragmentary apocryphal *Gospel of the Egyptians* cited in patristic literature which quotes Jesus as saying, "I have come to destroy the works of the woman" or answering the question of how long death will continue to reign by remarking, "As long as women bear children." If similar attitudes were present among the false teachers in Ephesus at the time of writing of 1 Timothy, an over-realized eschatology could have combined with asceticism owing to the gnostic negative evaluation of physical functions as the backdrop to the injunction in 1 Tim 2:15. A further poignant passage regarding women is found at the end of the *Gospel of Thomas* (before CE 200?): "Simon Peter said to them, 'Let Mary leave us, for women are not worthy of life.' Jesus said, 'I myself shall lead her in order to make her male, so that she too may become a living spirit resembling you males. For every woman who will make herself male will enter the kingdom of heaven" (logion 114).

[62]Robert J. Karris ("The Background and Significance of the Polemic of the Pastoral Epistles," *JBL* 92 [1973]: 554) cites as a parallel to this situation the example of Lucian's tirade against the wandering Cynic philosophers: "The thing would not be so dreadful if they offended against us only by being what they are. But although outwardly and in public they appear very reverent and stern, if they

seems to be the underlying motive for much of the instruction found in the Pastorals. This, of course, harmonizes perfectly with the scenario at the fall alluded to in 1 Tim 2:14, where Eve was not a perpetrator of false teaching but the victim of the serpent's deception.[63]

The effect of subverting natural family structures appears to have been a major characteristic of the heresy behind 1 Timothy. The author of this epistle counteracts this aberration by maintaining that true Christianity undergirds and dignifies rather than subverting or obliterating the natural order. What is more, he explicitly establishes a connection between the church as God's "household" and people's own households (cf. 3:4-5, 12, 15; 5:10, 12-15).[64] Thus he strongly refutes a certain proto-gnostic libertinism which apparently denied the effects of the fall (cf. 1 Tim 2:14?; 1 John 15:2-2:2) and taught that Christians were no longer bound by the natural family order. Especially if it is true that an over-realized eschatology accounts for certain aspects of the heresy refuted in 1 and 2 Timothy (cf. esp. 2 Tim 2:17-18; cf. 1 Tim 1:19-20), the teaching of 1 Tim 2:15 should be understood as providing a corrective against such extremism.[65]

This significant proto-gnostic backdrop to the present passage raises the question to what extent 1 Tim 2:15 should be tied to the original context that occasioned its teaching. On one level, of course, all epistles, even all biblical documents, are occasional in nature, since their composition was prompted by particular circumstances that led to their writing. To equate occasionality with historical relativity would thus lead to the radical conclusion that all biblical teaching, indeed all human communication, is

---

get a handsome boy or a pretty woman in their clutches or hope to, it is best to veil their conduct in silence. Some even carry off the wives of their hosts, to seduce them after the pattern of that young Trojan, pretending that the women are going to become philosophers . . ." (*De Fugitivi* 18-19). Contra Martin Dibelius and Hans Conzelmann, *The Pastoral Epistles* (trans. Philip Buttolph and Adela Yarbro; Philadelphia: Fortress, 1972), 48: "2 Tim 3:6 shows that women played some kind of role among the opponents of the Pastoral Epistles."

[63]Cf. also 2 Cor 11:3 where an analogy is established between Eve's deception by Satan and the possible deception of the Corinthian church (not merely women) by Satan, and 11:14-15 where Paul develops lines of analogy between the false teachers and Satan. Note, however, that there is no trace of a Messianic typology in 2 Cor 11:3 but that the relationship is merely between Eve and the church.

[64]On this, see Schlarb, *Gesunde Lehre*, 321-56, especially the section entitled "Das Verhältnis von οἶκος ἀνθρώπων und οἶκος θεοῦ," on pp. 342-56.

[65]Cf. Philip H. Towner, *The Goal of Our Instruction: The Structure of Theology and Ethics in the Pastoral Epistles* (JSNTSup 34; Sheffield: JSOT, 1989), 29-42; idem, *1-2 Timothy & Titus*, 23-24, 72-81.

contingent and relative to its historical and cultural context.[66] Few evangelicals go to this extreme.[67] The question remains, however, what criteria should be used to distinguish clearly time-bound injunctions (such as Paul's request to Timothy to bring his coat and scrolls in 2 Tim 4:3) from passages that carry normative, authoritative weight beyond the original context that occasioned their teaching.

This is not the place to tackle this issue comprehensively.[68] Reference should, however, be made to T. David Gordon's helpful suggestion to distinguish between underlying absolute ethical norms and the specific formulation given to them in a particular context, with the implication that the former are timeless while the latter is subject to variation.[69] In our specific context the writer refers immediately prior to the present reference both to creation order, clearly of permanent validity, and to the fall, likewise of lasting consequences, both as narrated in the authoritative Hebrew Scriptures, in order to underscore his teaching regarding the

---

[66]But see, for example, J. I. Packer, "The Adequacy of Human Language," in *Inerrancy* (ed. Norman L. Geisler; Grand Rapids: Zondervan, 1979, 197-226; Vern S. Poythress, "Adequacy of Language and Accommodation," in *Hermeneutics, Inerrancy, and the Bible* (ed. Earl D. Radmacher and Robert D. Preus; Grand Rapids: Zondervan, 1984), 349-76.

[67]For a survey of relativism as it relates to modern biblical interpretation, see William J. Larkin, Jr., *Culture and Biblical Hermeneutics: Interpreting and Applying the Authoritative Word in a Relativistic Age* (Grand Rapids: Baker, 1988), especially 18-21.

[68]For helpful general introduction to some of the relevant issues, see Grant R. Osborne, *The Hermeneutical Spiral: A Comprehensive Introduction to Biblical Interpretation* (Downers Grove, IL: InterVarsity, 1991), 318–38, especially 326–32; and William W. Klein, Craig L. Blomberg, and Robert L. Hubbard, Jr., *Introduction to Biblical Interpretation* (Dallas: Word, 1993), 401–26, especially 409-10 (but see the present writer's review in *TrinJ* 15 NS [1994]: 251–52). We dissent, however, from Osborne's treatment of the present passage, where he concludes, despite the presence of supracultural indicators in the context of 1 Tim 2:13-14, that while "[t]his points toward normative force," it does not solve the issue in itself (p. 329). However, as the following discussion will seek to demonstrate, a number of factors combine that appear to make a compelling case for the presence of norms underlying 1 Tim 2:11-15 that transcend the occasion of 1 Timothy. For an advanced treatment of some of the relevant hermeneutical issues pertinent to the present discussion, see further Anthony C. Thiselton, *New Horizons in Hermeneutics* (Grand Rapids: Zondervan, 1992), whose index curiously does not include a single reference to the Pastorals.

[69]T. David Gordon, "A Certain Kind of Letter: The Genre of 1 Timothy," chap. 2 in *Women in the Church*.

woman's place in the Christian congregation (1 Tim 2:12-14).[70] Immediately following the present reference we find a general discussion of qualifications for overseers: "If *anyone* desires the office of overseer . . . it is necessary for an overseer to be . . ." (1 Tim 3:1-2).

Also, the entire section in which the present passage is found, beginning in 2:1 (Παρακαλῶ οὖν πρῶτον πάντων), concludes with the statement in 3:14-15 that the writer wrote these things (ταῦτα) for the recipient of this letter to know "how one should conduct oneself in God's household, which is the church of the living God, the pillar and foundation of truth." Finally, the nature of the entire epistle, i.e., that of an epistle concerned to regulate the organization of churches in the post-apostolic era, not just in Timothy's end-of-first-century Ephesus, further enhances the likelihood that the present epistle is designed to provide injunctions and norms that transcend the letter's particular historical-cultural horizon.[71]

These observations strongly caution against singling out v. 15 from the rest of the passage and from considering it as merely situation-bound. While it has become increasingly common in recent years for scholars to limit the applicability of New Testament epistolary passages by classifying them as ad hoc statements, care must be taken not to equate historical particularity with lack of general applicability. This would be reductionistic.[72]

---

[70]Cf. the comments on the use of the OT in the NT gender passages in Köstenberger, "Gender Roles in the NT," 267-71.

[71]This assessment of the structure of 1 Tim 2:1-3:15 differs significantly from that of Gordon D. Fee, "The Great Watershed: Intentionality and Particularity/Eternality: 1 Timothy 2:8-15 as a Test Case," in *Gospel and Spirit: Issues in New Testament Hermeneutics* (Peabody, MA: Hendrickson, 1991), 52-65. Fee's claim that the occurrence of οὖν in 2:1 settles the case by subsuming the entire subsequent section (2:1-3:16) under the purpose of 1:3-4 is not borne out by the actual content of this portion of the letter. In particular, Fee fails to note the general thrust of the statement in 3:14-15. Also, Fee overstates his case, when he takes the entire epistle to be directed exclusivley to correct false teaching. While this is arguably *one* of the purposes of the letter, some of the epistle's general statements (such as 3:1) suggest that the author at least occasionally goes beyond the mere refutation of false teachers to provide positive instruction for the organization of the church as well that need not be mirror-read as indicating a corresponding abuse by false teachers.

[72]Fee, "Great Watershed," 60-62, constitutes a striking case of special pleading in this regard. Proposing to shift the focus from particularity to intentionality, he claims that "[i]t simply cannot be demonstrated that Paul *intended* 1 Timothy 2:11-12 as a rule in all churches at all times. In fact the occasion and purpose of 1 Timothy as a whole, and these verses in particular, suggest otherwise. Nor will it do to appeal to vv. 13-14 as though there were some eternal order in creation, since *neither* Genesis *nor* Paul makes this point." Fee

To use Gordon's hermeneutical framework,[73] while the injunction in 1 Tim 2:15 is couched in language directed toward the author's proto-gnostic opponents (which may account for the unusual use of the term σώζω and other phraseology),[74] the underlying norm of this passage is of permanent validity: women's central domain, as established by creation and confirmed negatively by the fall, is to be found in her involvement in the domestic and procreative sphere, in the natural household. Moreover, if this analysis is correct, it would hold true even if the writer were not Paul but a Pauline follower from a later period, since the principles of normativity outlined above would within the framework of canonical Scripture equally apply to a later author of a biblical document.

While this is a difficult teaching in some respects, it appears to be what 1 Tim 2:15 is saying, and at least this writer does not feel at liberty to shrink from its apparent overt message merely because of the difficulties in implication and application of the passage in contemporary church and culture. It may be ironic that the interpretation that is directly counter-cultural in the present North-American context is one that supports what is generally considered to be a "traditional" or "conservative" stance on the issue of women's roles. But 1 Tim 2:15 is, of course, not the only biblical passage on women's roles, and it remains to discuss its teachings in relation to other pertinent passages such as Gal 3:28 in the concluding section.

---

counsels "obedience to the ultimate concern of the text, even if at times the particulars are not carried over to the 'letter.' " We may respond by asking why Paul *did* refer to creation and the fall in 1 Tim 2:13-14 in order to support his injunction in v. 12, if not to provide substantiation for the normativity of his point. Moreover, to set aside the informing norm underlying the present passage for the sake of "obedience to the ultimate concern of the text" appears to be a precarious expedient indeed. But Fee here merely echoes Marshall, who likewise appeals to the "main thrust of Scripture" or a writer's "real intention" for the purpose of setting aside the overt teaching of certain passages (cf. I. H. Marshall, "An Evangelical Approach to 'Theological Criticism,'" in *The Best in Theology, Volume Three* [ed. J. I. Packer; Carol Stream, IL: Christianity Today, 1989], 45-60, and the more extensive interaction with Marshall in my article on "Gender Passages in the NT," 278). While these writers' categories have the appearance of being nuanced and discerning, they do, in fact, betray considerable subjectivity in judgment that would at least in principle enable them to set aside any passage that does not appear "reasonable" to them in the light of general culture for the sake of their own preferred interpretation. How much better to allow Scripture to be counter-cultural and to challenge one's own views than to domesticate it by not permitting it to say what is incompatible with contemporary culture or a given interpreter's views.

[73]See n. 69 and the discussion above.

[74]See the discussion of the possible proto-gnostic background to the present passage above.

Apart from the gnostic background to 1 Tim 2:15, there also appears to be a possible allusion to Genesis in this portion. But if this is the case, what part of Genesis is referred to: the so-called "proto-evangelion" in Gen 3:15, the reference to the woman's curse in childbirth (Gen 3:16), God's mandate to the man and the woman to be fruitful, to multiply, and to fill the earth and to rule over it (Gen 1:28), or another passage? The answer to this question may provide an important corrective to viewing 1 Tim 2:15 too one-sidedly against its gnostic backdrop and supply us with important clues to the salvation-historical, biblical-theological, and inter-textual canonical framework of the writer of 1 Timothy.

Genesis. It has often been suggested that the writer of 1 Timothy here alludes to Gen 3:16[75] or even to the "protoevangelion" in Gen 3:15. This is seen to be indicated by the allusion to Genesis 3 in 1 Tim 2:14 and by the interpretation of 1 Tim 2:15 in terms of a Messianic typology ("women shall be saved by 'the' childbirth, i.e., Mary's giving birth to Jesus the Messiah"). It has already been argued above that there is no evidence from the context for an allusion to Gen 3:15 in the present passage. But what about Gen 3:16? If one requires verbal parallels between the original passage and a later allusion to it, 1 Tim 2:15 hardly qualifies as an allusion to Gen 3:16, since no direct verbal parallels can be found (LXX: τέξῃ τέκνα). Thus it may at best represent an echo of Gen 3:16, reflecting a perhaps unconscious reference to a passage with related content (i.e., childbearing).[76]

It needs to be argued, however, that the mere fact that 1 Tim 2:14 alludes to Genesis 3 is not decisive for establishing a deliberate reference to Gen 3:16 in the following verse. The consideration of other factors will aid in determining this matter. It should be noted that Gen 3:16 speaks of the fall's negative consequences on the woman's childbearing while 1 Tim 2:15 accentuates its positive ramifications. Should the writer of 1 Timothy therefore be taken to imply that, in the present era of salvation, the effects of the curse will be reversed? On a literal level, of course, this is manifestly untrue, as every woman who has given birth and every husband of such a woman who attended the birth can testify. Even on any other level, raising children and managing a household still subsist in a fallen world, albeit

---

[75]Cf. also G. Schneider in *EDNT* 3:340: "The background is probably the Jewish view that to endure the pains of childbirth suspends the curse in Gen 3:16."

[76]On the distinction between allusions and echoes, see Richard B. Hays, *Echoes of Scripture in the Letters of Paul* (New Haven: Yale University Press, 1989); and Jon Paulien, "Elusive Allusions: The Problematic Use of the Old Testament in Revelation," *BibRes* 33 (1988): 39–41.

supported by God's gracious enablement. While the reversal of the consequences of the fall is surely elaborated upon in many New Testament passages, it is doubtful that this is the writer's point in the present passage. In line with his general concern to protect women from being victimized by false teachers, he enjoins them to adhere to their God-given domestic roles—thus they will escape and be preserved from Satan.

One final possibility remains. If the present passage is found neither to allude to Gen 3:15 or 16, does 1 Tim 2:15 perhaps imply the author's interpretation of the fall narrative? This appears to be supported by the underlying logic connecting 1 Tim 2:14 and 15. Eve, it is said, was deceived and fell into transgression. Christian women, on the other hand, will escape or be kept safe from Satan, if they adhere to their God-given domestic role. Thus, by implication, Eve fell, because she failed to keep her proper domain and, by leaving it, became vulnerable to the serpent's false teaching (cf. 2 Cor 11:2-3). If this interpretation is correct, the writer of 1 Timothy is drawing from his reading of the fall narrative the lesson that Christian women will be kept safe from Satan if they avoid Eve's mistake, i.e., leaving her proper God-given realm (cf. Jude 6).[77] 1 Tim 2:15 thus represents, not an allusion to Gen 3:15 or 16, but an interpretation of the fall narrative. As will be seen below, this understanding also makes the best sense in context with 1 Tim 2:11-12.

Moreover, if there is any theological kinship with Genesis in the present passage, it may be with God's command to the man and the woman in Gen 1:28 to be fruitful and multiply and to fill the earth and rule over it. The passage would thus hark back to the way in which the woman was initially given a share in humankind's rule over God's creation prior to the fall. In this case, it is inaccurate to view 1 Tim 2:15 merely from the perspective that it excludes the woman from all ruling functions in family, church, and society: the woman rather participates in this rule by adhering to her specific God-ordained role as indicated in the original creation account.

The Meaning of τῆς τεκνογονίας in 1 Timothy 2:15a
The term τεκνογονία was apparently extremely rare in Greek literature from classical times to the time of writing of 1 Timothy and beyond.[78] A

---

[77]As 2 Cor 11:2-3, 14-15, Jude 6, and a number of passages in the Pastorals indicate, the leaving of one's proper God-given domain, the rejection of authority, and sexual immorality are properties of Satan and the fallen angels as well as of false teachers, and these, in turn, seek to draw women into their sphere of influence.

[78]We will limit our discussion to instances of the noun τεκνογονία and not

search of the *Thesaurus Linguae Graecae* data base yields only two instances of the pre-Pauline usage of the term. The first extant reference containing τεκνογονία is found in one of Hippocrates' letters (fifth century BC):

> Καὶ πῶς οὐκ ἐλεγχθείης, ἔφην, ὦ ἄριστε; ἡ οὐκ οἴη ἀτοκός γε εἶναι γελῶν ἀνθρώπου θάνατον ἢ νοῦσον ἢ παρακοπὴν ἢ μανίην ἢ μελαγχολίην ἢ σφαγὴν ἢ ἄλλο τι χεῖρον; ἢ τοὔμπαλιν γάμους ἢ πανηγύριας ἢ τεκνογονίην ἢ μυστήρια ἢ ἀρχάς καὶ τιμὰς ἢ ἄλλο τι ὅλως ἀγαθόν; ("But why, my good man, should you not be refuted? Should it not be inappropriate indeed to laugh at a person's death or disease or insanity or madness or melancholy or injury or something worse? Or, conversely, at weddings or festivals or childbearing or religious rites or authorities and offices or any other good thing?")[79]

It is evident that this reference is quite general to childbirths as events in life similar to weddings or other important occasions.

The second reference is found in the Stoic philosopher Chrysippus' *Fragmenta Moralia* (third century BCE):

> καὶ τὸ νομοθετεῖν δὲ καὶ τὸ παιδεύειν ἀνθρώπους, ἔτι δὲ συγγράφειν τὰ δυνάμενα ὠφελεῖν τοὺς ἐντυγχάνοντας τοῖς γράμμασιν οἰκεῖον εἶναι τοῖς σπουδαίοις καὶ τὸ συγκαταβαίνειν καὶ εἰς γάμον καὶ εἰς τεκνογονίαν καὶ αὐτοῦ χάριν καὶ τῆς πατρίδος καὶ ὑπομένειν περὶ ταύτης, ἐὰν ᾖ μετρία, καὶ πόνους καὶ θάνατον ("Moreover [they say] that making laws and training persons, and also composing things which can be of value to those who read letters, belong to those who are zealous both to submit to marriage and to childbirth for its sake and [that of their] homeland, and to endure for her, if necessary, both pain and death").[80]

---

deal with occurrences of the verb τεκνογονεῖν, since the former expression is used in the present passage.

[79]Hippocrates, *Epistulae* 17.105, in *Oeuvres complètes d'Hippocrate* (ed. Littré; Paris: Baillière, 1839 (repr. Amsterdam: Hakkert, 1973), 9:356-57: "Et comment, cher ami, ne serais-tu pas réfuté? Ou penses-tu n'être pas extravagant en riant de la mort, de la maladie, du délire, de la folie, de la mélancolie, du meurtre, et de quelque accident encore pire? Ou, inversement, des mariages, des panégyries (sorte de solennité), des naissances d'enfants, des mystères, des commandements, des honneurs, ou de tout autre bien?" I am grateful to Lawrence Lahey for his assistance with the English translation.

[80]Chrysippus, *Fragmenta Moralia* 611, in *Stoicorum Veterum Fragmenta* (ed. Johannes von Arnim; Leipzig: Teubner, 1903; repr. Stuttgart: Teubner, 1968), 3:158. I am grateful to Lawrence Lahey for his assistance with the English translation.

As in the first reference, childbirth (here is the singular) is found in conjunction with marriage, here as a duty to be submitted to for their own sake and for that of the country.

Moreover, a reference in Aristotle's *History of Animals* needs to be considered where two manuscripts have τεκνοποϊας (*Cod. Marcianus*=Aᵃ and *Cod. Laurentianus*=Cᵃ; followed by the *TLG* data base) and two manuscripts have τεκνογονίας (*Cod. Vaticanus*=P; Dᵃ; followed by the Loeb Classical Library series):

> Μετὰ δὲ τὰ τρὶς ἑπτὰ ἔτη αἱ μὲν γυναῖκες πρὸς τὰς τεκνοποϊας (τεκνογονίας) ἤδη εὐκαίρως ἔχουσιν, οἱ δ'ἄνδρες ἔτι ἔχουσιν ἐπίδοσιν ("After twenty-one years, the females are in good condition to bear children while men still need time for development.").[81]

This reference is to the physical giving of birth to children, which appears to confirm the judgment of the *TLG* data base to follow the more solid manuscript evidence and to read here τεκνοποϊία, a term that refers unambiguously to the physical giving of birth.

Thus there remain two undisputed pre-Pauline references to τεκνογονία in Greek literature. Both instances are rather general; the more recent passage in Chrysippus, however, appears to involve the use of a synecdoche. People are submitting, not merely to marriage and childbirth, but to married life and having children. Incidentally, the objection often raised against taking τεκνογονία as a synecdoche in 1 Tim 2:15, i.e., that in this case the author would have used the term τεκνοτροφέω which is found in 1 Tim 5:10, misses the mark, since the latter term merely specifies the raising of children, a sense required in the latter context, while τεκνογονία, apart from its literal use referring to physical childbirth, may also pertain to the having of a family in a general sense.[82]

In the light of these observations, and particularly the reference by Chrysippus, it seems perfectly permissible to understand τεκνογονία in 1 Tim 2:15 as referring, not merely to the giving of birth to children, but to the having of a family, with all that this entails. The scarcity of the term accentuates the deliberateness of the usage in 1 Tim 2:15a (cf. the verb

---

[81]Aristotle, *History of Animals* 528a.28, in *Aristote: Histoire des Animaux*, Vol. 2, Books V–VII (trans. Pierre Louis; Paris: Les Belles Lettres, 1968), 136; and in Loeb Classical Library series, *Aristotle: History of Animals*, Vol. IX (VII), 425.

[82]Cf. Heinrich Julius Holtzmann, *Die Pastoralbriefe* (Leipzig: Wilhelm Engelmann, 1880), 316, who notes that Chrysostom and Theophylact use τεκνογονία with the sense of child-rearing in general.

form τεκνογονεῖν in 1 Tim 5:14). The generic nature of the reference indicated by the definite article joins with the author's choice of the noun rather than the verb in the present passage in suggesting that a general concept is in view, "procreation," i.e., the woman's participation in the multiplication of the human race. Indeed, *procreatio* is the Latin translation of this term (cf., e.g., the Vulgate).

We may therefore conclude that 1 Tim 2:15 may best be rendered in the following way: "She (i.e., the woman) escapes (or is preserved; gnomic future) [from Satan] by way of procreation (i.e., having a family)."[83] Moreover, in line with 1 Tim 5:14, one should view procreation as merely the core of the woman's responsibility that also entails, not merely the bearing, but also the raising of children, as well as managing the home (synecdoche; cf. also Titus 2:4–5). The sense of the injunction in the present passage is thus that women can expect to escape Satan under the condition of adhering to their God-ordained role centering around the natural household.

Integration of the Interpretation of 1 Timothy 2:15a with 1 Timothy 2:9–15 and Contemporary Implications

How may the preceding interpretation of 1 Tim 2:15 be integrated with a reading of 1 Tim 2:11–15 as a whole, and how does it relate to other passages on the topic? While it is not the focus of the present essay to explore the implications of the suggested interpretation so that our comments need of necessity be brief, a few pertinent comments must be made. We commend the above interpretation of 1 Tim 2:15 even to those who may not agree with our comments on the passage's application below. As we have discussed elsewhere in greater detail, women are enjoined in vv. 11 and 12 to learn submissively rather than to teach or exercise authority in the church.[84] Vv. 13 and 14 supply reasons for this injunction from creation and the fall. V. 15 states women's proper role in terms of lessons to be learned from Eve's failure at the fall. Thus v. 15 moves beyond the fall

---

[83]Dibelius and Conzelmann (*Pastoral Epistles*, 49) cite the following parallel regarding the father's role in *Corp. Herm.* 2.17: "For the procreation of children is held by wise men to be the most important and the holiest function in life" (διὸ καὶ μεγίστη ἐν τῷ βίῳ σπουδὴ καὶ εὐσεβεστάτη τοῖς εὖ φρονοῦσίν ἐστιν ἡ παιδοποιΐα).

[84]For this rendering and interpretation, see Köstenberger, Schreiner, and Baldwin, *Women in the Church*.

to a restoration of the original creation design. The movement is from creation (v. 13) to the fall (v. 14) to a restored creation order (v. 15). All this occurs in a context of setting proper parameters for the legitimate ministry of women in v. 12 (cf. 3:1-2).

If this reading is correct, v. 15 is in fact closely connected to v. 12, where, as stated, women are prohibited from permanent teaching or ruling functions in the church. Similar to the reasons given in vv. 13 and 14, the statement in v. 15 elaborates on the injunction of v. 12: all will be well with women who, unlike Eve, adhere to the domain assigned to them by God. Women, on the other hand, who depart from their God-ordained roles in their lives become vulnerable to Satan, particularly if they assume permanent teaching or ruling functions in the local assembly.[85] The Pastorals contrast this focus on procreation and the domestic sphere by the godly woman resulting in her preservation from Satan with the contempt of marriage and procreation found in the church's environment. Adherence to such teaching led to women's straying from the home, which, in turn, made them an easy prey for Satan, similar to Eve at the fall.

If these lines of thought are correct, the present passage would speak powerfully to a cultural context where many are seeking to "liberate" women from all encumbrances of family responsibilities in order to unleash them on a quest for self-fulfillment apart from such functions. Passages such as the present one appear to indicate that it is precisely by participating in her role pertaining to the family that women fulfill their central calling. Moreover, if the reference to "childbearing" should indeed be understood as synecdoche, even unmarried women are to retain a focus on the domestic sphere and all that it entails.

But what are we to make of Gal 3:28, seen by some as the paradigm passage on the present issue, a hermeneutical lodestar in the Pauline firmament, indeed Scripture's Magna Carta of egalitarian gender roles? If Paul wrote 1 Timothy, did he regress from his earlier "enlightened" stance in Galatians to a traditional patriarchal view in 1 Timothy? Or are we to focus on Gal 3:28, since the passage is formulated more generally, while considering 1 Tim 2:11-15 to be more specific in its application, if not entirely contingent on the original context, so that 1 Tim 2:15 should be read within the larger purview of the statement in Gal 3:28? This is an exceedingly important hermeneutical question. As I have argued

---

[85]We cannot here explore in detail the complex implications for applying this teaching in a contemporary end-of-twentieth-century North-American context. For some helpful basic classifications, see Mary Kassian, *Women, Creation, and the Fall*, 81-83.

STUDIES IN JOHN AND GENDER

elsewhere, the reading of Gal 3:28 just described does, in fact, not bear closer scrutiny in its own literary context, which focuses on the salvation-historical fact that men and women, like Jews and Gentiles, slave or free, are equally heirs of salvation, just as they equally bear God's image (cf. Gal 3:26; cf. also Gen 1:28; 1 Pet 3:7; and 1 Cor 12:13 where Jews and Gentiles, slave or free are mentioned, but not male or female).[86] This passage does therefore not speak of gender roles in the government of the church but of salvation-historical entrance into Christ and the community of believers.

Moreover, Galatians, like 1 Timothy, is part of a specific original historical context, so that there is no warrant for taking Gal 3:28 to be normative while consigning 1 Tim 2:15 to the state of historical and cultural relativity. Contrary to such efforts, the teachings of Gal 3:28 and 1 Tim 2:15 should rather both be considered as normative teachings and be related to one another in the sense that Scripture teaches *both* that women and men have equal status as believers in Christ *and* that they have different roles assigned to them by their Creator. Thus 1 Tim 2:15 would not contradict Gal 3:28 but merely specify aspects of role differentiation within the larger perspective of male-female equality with respect to salvation as taught in Gal 3:28. If this is the case, it would be inadmissible to affirm Gal 3:28 while rejecting 1 Tim 2:11–15. Rather, the latter passage should be equally affirmed and applied as the former.

We part with the concluding observation that much harm has come in recent years from the increasingly antagonistic, even inflammatory, climate in which issues such as this have been discussed. Rather than viewing this question primarily in terms of "confining" women to the home, it may be more productive to focus on the issue of determining the essence of a gender's calling from God, with men and women helping each other to live out their respective roles. The need of the hour is for an increasing number of individuals who model integrated relationships and ministry in the local church as well as in other Christian settings.[87]

---

[86]For a more thorough treatment of this issue, see my "Gender Passages in the NT," especially pp. 273–79.

[87]I am grateful for the assistance of Keith Collins and Scott Shidemantle in the research for this essay and for the helpful responses to an earlier draft of this essay by Brent Kassian, Lawrence Lahey, Peter O'Brien, and Thomas Schreiner.

CHAPTER FIFTEEN

WOMEN IN THE PAULINE MISSION[*]

Paul has been called everything from misogynist to misunderstood with regard to his stance on women in the ministry of the church, and a thorough re-examination of the role women played in the apostle's mission is needed to clear up some confusion. This is especially important since we are not dealing merely with the mission of one important individual, Paul. Ultimately, Paul's mission is *missio Dei,* the mission of God, and the mission of the Holy Spirit *through Paul.* Called and converted by the risen Christ, led by the Spirit, Paul's mission arguably transcends the man and his historical-cultural context. If this is true, it also and especially applies to the role women played in the Pauline mission, and it is here that we can ill afford not to listen and learn from the apostle; for today's churches are in dire need of an authoritative, definitive word on how women (and men) ought to function in the church.

Recent discussions of the role of women in relation to Paul have been plagued by at least three deficiencies.[1] First, primacy has frequently been given, not to Paul's own writings, but to contemporary concerns, and Pauline texts have been used to validate the interpreter's own preconceived notions on this issue. Proper hermeneutical procedure, however, demands that Paul's voice be heard first and foremost rather than being drowned out in the clamor of contemporary voices and concerns. Primacy must once again be given to Paul.

Second, studies on women in relation to Paul have frequently focused on Paul's *teaching* but not his *practice* (that is, how women actually functioned in churches under Paul's jurisdiction) or, less frequently, vice versa.[2] A comprehensive, balanced apprehension of Paul's stance toward

---

[*]This essay is reprinted with permission of InterVarsity Press from "Women in the Pauline Mission," *The Gospel for the Nations* (ed. Peter G. Bolt and Mark D. Thompson; Leicester, UK: InterVarsity Press, 2000), 221–47.

[1]On these and other hermeneutical issues, see my "Gender Passages in the NT: Hermeneutical Fallacies Critiqued," *WTJ* 56 (1994): 259–83.

[2]At the risk of oversimplification it may be said that interpreters advocating limitations on the ministry of women in Scripture tend to focus on the Pauline teaching on women's roles while egalitarian scholars favor descriptive passages.

women's roles must take account of both: how women *should* function in the church according to Pauline teaching (didactic passages on women's roles) and how they actually *did* function in the Pauline churches and mission in keeping with the apostle's instructions (narrative passages and references to specific women in Paul's writings).[3] The present essay will start with the latter question in order not to prejudge doctrinal issues and to safeguard a truly inductive approach toward the descriptive passages as much as possible. After this, the treatment of didactic passages in Paul will provide a framework from which to evaluate the first set of references.

The third problem besetting studies of women in relation to Paul is that women are regularly treated in isolation from men. The reason for this may be that the motivation underlying many such discussions is to magnify the contributions made by women to the life of the early church. However, if women are studied in isolation from men, imbalance and loss of perspective are the inevitable result. Women in the Pauline mission should therefore be studied in relation to men.[4]

In investigating descriptive passages in Paul's writings that show how women functioned in the Pauline churches and mission, this discussion will proceed in chronological order of writing. After this, Paul's explicit teaching on women's roles will be surveyed. Because I have previously written on the Pauline teaching on the role of women, this essay will summarize my findings on the didactic passages, and give more detailed attention to providing a thorough treatment of the descriptive references.

---

[3]For a helpful general treatment along these lines see T. R. Schreiner, "The Valuable Ministries of Women in the Context of Male Leadership: A Survey of Old and New Testament Examples and Teaching," in *Recovering Biblical Manhood and Womanhood* (ed. J. Piper and W. Grudem; Wheaton, IL: Crossway, 1991), 209–24.

[4]See E. E. Ellis, "Paul and His Co-Workers," *NTS* 17 (1970–71): 437–52 and idem, "Coworkers, Paul and His," in *Dictionary of Paul and His Letters* (ed. G. F. Hawthorne, R. P. Martin, and D. G. Reid; Downers Grove, IL: InterVarsity, 1993), 183–89 (note the helpful chart in "Paul and His Co-Workers," 438="Coworkers, Paul and His," 184). See also W.-H. Ollrog, *Paulus und seine Mitarbeiter: Untersuchungen zu Theorie und Praxis der paulinischen Mission* (WMANT 50; Neukirchen-Vluyn: Neukirchener, 1979).

Women in the Pauline Churches and Mission

Data from Paul's Letters[5]

A chronological survey of named women in the Pauline corpus yields the following list:[6]

Table 11: Named Women in the Pauline Corpus

	Epistle	*Names of women*	*Information provided*
	Gal	none mentioned	
	1 Thess	none mentioned	
	2 Thess	none mentioned	
(2)	1 Cor	Chloe (1:11)	some "from Chloe"
		Priscilla (16:19)	church at her house
	2 Cor	none mentioned	
(11)	Rom	Phoebe (16:1)	"our sister," servant/deacon (διάκονος) of church inCenchrea, benefactress/ patroness (προστάτις)
		Priscilla (16:3)	fellow worker (συνεργοί; with Aquila), church at their house
		Mary (16:6)	"worked very hard for you"
		Junia (?) (16:7)	"outstanding among the apostles" (ἀποστολοί; with Andronicus)

(Table continued on following page.)

---

[5]The only woman mentioned in the Book of Acts in relation to Paul's ministry is Priscilla (18:2-3, 18-19, 26). When C. C. Kroeger, "Women in the Early Church," in *Dictionary of the Later New Testament and Its Developments* (ed. R. P. Martin and P. H. Davids; Downers Grove, IL: InterVarsity, 1997), 1216, claims that "[n]o fewer than eleven women are specifically named [in the book of Acts], and five are involved in church-related ministries," she discusses only the involvement of "Mary the mother of Jesus and her female associates" in 1:14 and Dorcas in 9:36-41. On women's roles in Acts see also C. S. Keener, "Woman and Man," in *Dictionary of the Later NT and Its Developments*, 1206-1207.

[6]The order of writing is judged to be: Gal, 1 and 2 Thess, 1 and 2 Cor, Rom, the Prison Epistles (Eph, Phil, Col, Phlm), and the Pastoral Epistles (1 Tim, Titus, 2 Tim). Here, all thirteen are considered as part of the Pauline corpus, and references in them to people and places are taken seriously. Regarding the Pauline authorship of the Pastorals, see my "Ascertaining," 107-108, n. 1. Unnamed women will be considered only if some identifying mark is provided, e.g. "the mother *of Rufus*" (Rom 16:13). The reference to Lois and Eunice (2 Tim 1:5) will not be included in the present study, because these two women had no *direct* involvement in the Pauline mission. Named women *in ancient times*, such as Hagar or Sarah, likewise fall outside the scope of the present investigation.

(Table continued from preceding page.)

Epistle		Names of women	Information provided
		Tryphena and	
		Tryphosa (16:12)	"women who work hard in the Lord"
		Persis (16:12)	"another woman who has worked very hard in the Lord"
		mother of Rufus (16:13)	"who has been a mother to me, too"
		Julia (16:15)	none
		sister of Nereus (16:15)	none
		Olympas (16:15)	none
	Eph	none mentioned	
(2)	Phil	Euodia & Syntyche (4:2)	coworkers (?), "contended at my side in the cause of the gospel"
(1)	Col	Nympha (4:15)	church at her house
(1)	Phlm	Apphia (2)	"our sister" (cf. Rom. 16:1), church at her house (with Philemon)
	1 Tim	none mentioned	
	Titus	none mentioned	
(2)	2 Tim	Priscilla (4:19)	none
		Claudia (4:21)	none

Nineteen passages in Paul's writings refer to a total of seventeen women.[7] Two things are worth observing: First, references to women in Paul's writings are unevenly distributed, with almost two thirds occurring in Romans 16. Without this chapter, our knowledge of the ways in which women functioned in the early church would be rather minimal, at least as far as the biblical record is concerned. Second, references to women in Paul's remaining letters are either entirely absent or very sporadic. The only women mentioned outside of Romans 16 are Chloe and Priscilla (1 Cor); Euodia and Syntyche (Phil); Nympha (Col); Apphia (Phlm); and Claudia and Priscilla (2 Tim). Since the references to Chloe and Euodia and Syntyche are somewhat incidental, and virtually no information is given concerning the other women mentioned outside of Romans 16 (Nympha, Apphia, Claudia), Priscilla alone remains as a woman regarding whom more extensive information is available. We will return to this issue shortly.

---

[7]The only multiple reference pertains to Priscilla (three times). W. Cotter, "Women's Authority Roles in Paul's Churches: Countercultural or Conventional?," *NovT* 36 (1994): 350, n. 2, lists only thirteen women, not mentioning Persis (an oversight?), Junia (considered to be male?), Nympha (Colossians deutero-Pauline? oversight?), and Claudia (Pastorals deutero-Pauline?).

Before proceeding with a detailed study of each of the women mentioned in Paul's letters, it may be helpful to compare the references to women in Paul's letters with those to men. Including multiple references, the picture is as follows:

Table 12: Comparison of References to Women and Men in the Pauline Corpus

Pauline book	Ref.s to women	Ref.s to men	Total
Gal	0	5	5
1 Thess	0	2	2
2 Thess	0	2	2
1 Cor	2	13	15
2 Cor	0	2	2
Rom	11	23	34
Eph	0	1	1
Phil	2	3	5
Col	1	10	11
Phlm	1	9	10
1 Tim	0	1	1
Titus	0	5	5
2 Tim	2	12	14
Total	19	88	107

Of the persons mentioned in relation to the Pauline mission in the apostle's writings, 82% are men and 18% are women. Once multiple references are eliminated, the Pauline epistles identify about five-five men by name as associated with Paul in mission, compared with seventeen women. Of course, this quantitative statistic says nothing about the status of these persons in the early church. Nevertheless, the conclusion can be drawn that, set in perspective, references to women in Paul's letters are rather sparse (especially outside of Rom 16). This shows that the major weight of responsibility borne for the Pauline mission rested on men, a fact that is frequently obscured in studies on the subject which give exclusive consideration to women.[8]

Discussion of References to Women in Paul's Letters
Before delving into the references to women in Paul's letters, it will be helpful to address two issues that pertain to the following discussion in general. These issues are, first, the fragmentary and frequently

---

[8]E.g., Cotter, "Women's Authority Roles"; B. Witherington, *Women in the Earliest Churches* (SNTSMS 58; Cambridge: Cambridge University Press, 1988). A notable exception is P. Richardson, "From Apostles to Virgins: Romans 16 and the Roles of Women in the Early Church," *TorJT* 2 (1986): 232–43.

inconclusive nature of the available data, and secondly, the frequent yet fallacious hermeneutical procedure of drawing simplistic conclusions from a designation applied to a given person involved in the Pauline mission (such as "coworker") in the assigning of that person's overall status (e.g. of "leader"). Regarding the first issue, it must frankly be acknowledged that the information provided by Paul regarding women is frequently (if not regularly) inadequate to form firm conclusions regarding the precise nature of their ministry. This is certainly true of Chloe, Junia, Euodia and Syntyche, and a series of other women whose names appear in lists of greetings with virtually no further identification. The following discussion will seek to exercise restraint in creatively filling in these gaps and focus primarily on explicit textual and contextual cues. A survey of the relevant literature indicates that interpreters committed to women's full participation in the church's ministry, including leadership roles, tend to fill in gaps in ways that magnify the contributions of these women in the greatest way possible.[9] The purpose of this procedure is readily apparent: once a certain woman (and all women mentioned in Scripture) have been elevated to the status of prototypical, paradigmatic "authoritative leaders" in the early church, they can be made models for contemporary egalitarian ministry in the church. But responsible scholarship must distinguish between explicit statements and gaps, and between firm conclusions from explicit data and mere inferences.

The second issue pertains to a fallacious form of argument that is employed with great frequency. It runs as follows: if person A is called X in one passage, and the same designation X is used for another person (person B; in the present case, a woman) in a different passage, it follows that persons A and B have the exact same ministry. But the logic of this kind of argument is demonstrably flawed: if the sky can be said to be grey, and a cat is grey, does it follow that the sky and the cat are the same in every respect? Of course not.[10] *One* shared characteristic among two objects or persons, whether being grey or being Paul's coworkers, does not establish equality between these persons or objects *in every respect.* To argue thus is to commit the fallacy of focusing exclusively on a certain degree of semantic overlap between two terms while ignoring other aspects of a word's range of meaning that come into play by way of context in one

---

[9]See e.g. E. Schüssler Fiorenza, 'Missionaries, Apostles, Coworkers: Romans Romans 16 and the Reconstruction of Women's Early Christian History', *WW* 6 (1986): 420-33.

[10]For the semantic fallacy of confusing sense and reference, cf. Carson, *Exegetical Fallacies* (2d ed.; Grand Rapids: Baker, 1996), 63-64.

instance but not necessarily in another. Thus the mere fact that both Timothy and the one hand and Euodia and Syntyche on the other are called "co-workers" of Paul does not necessarily imply that all had identical ministries. All that can be said is that Timothy, Euodia and Syntyche can be called "co-workers" of Paul in a meaningful sense. But their ministries may very well differ.[11] The strongest piece of evidence for this distinction is the fact that the New Testament calls certain men "co-workers" *of God.*[12] But it stands to reason that no human being can be a "co-worker" on equal terms with God. Thus it is possible to link two people by the term "co-worker" without necessarily implying total equality (or equal authority) between those two persons. Sometimes, the word may refer to lateral "colleagues"; at other times, there may be genuine collaboration, but not on equal terms. Even in the case of Timothy, who is called a "co-worker" of Paul, it would be naive to assume that Paul and Timothy were on an equal footing. Paul frequently takes authority in sending Timothy as his emissary (e.g. Acts 19:22; 1 Cor. 4:17; Phil. 2:19; 1 Thess. 3:2); not once does Timothy send Paul. But Paul can still call Timothy his "co-worker." The conclusion is obvious: when the term "coworker" (or another term potentially conveying the notion of leadership or authority) is applied to a woman in Paul's writings, we cannot necessarily assume on the basis of this designation that this woman functioned as an equal partner of Paul in his mission. This must be established on further contextual and other grounds. Schreiner says it well: "All church leaders would be fellow-workers and laborers, but not all fellow-workers and laborers are necessarily church leaders."[13]

With these preliminary caveats in place, the study of the seventeen women mentioned in Paul's writings may proceed, following the chronological order in which they are mentioned.

---

[11]Cf. Ellis, "Paul and His Co-Workers," 440: "Co-workers may be described as equal to one another, as are Paul and Apollos in I Cor. iii. 8 f., but this is not implicit in the term." Contra e.g. S. J. Grenz, *Women in the Church: A Biblical Theology of Women in Ministry* (Downers Grove, IL: InterVarsity, 1995), 85: "the terms Paul uses in this text [Rom 16] suggest the participation of women in all dimensions of the ministry."

[12]Timothy is called "co-worker of God" in 1 Thess 3:2 (τὸν ἀδελφὸν ἡμῶν καὶ συνεργὸν τοῦ θεοῦ). The same designation is applied to Paul and his associates in 1 Cor 3:9 (θεοῦ γάρ ἐσμεν συνεργοί). Cf. Ellis, "Paul and His Co-Workers," 440, who further points out that Philo, with reference to the plagues on Egypt, can call the insects God's συνεργοί (Philo, *de vita Mosis*, 1.110). Ellis provides further examples on p. 440, n. 3.

[13]Schreiner, "Valuable Ministries of Women," 219.

Chloe. The first woman referred to in Paul's correspondence is a woman named Chloe (1 Cor 1:11). In the introduction to 1 Corinthians, Paul says that he had been informed "by some from Chloe" (ὑπὸ τῶν Χλόης) that there were divisions in the Corinthian church. These people are more likely slaves or freedmen than family members, since in the latter case a father's name would have been used, even if he were deceased.[14] Moreover, in light of the fact that Paul mentions Stephanas, Fortunatus, and Achaicus as the Corinthian church's official representatives (16:15-17),[15] it is probable that those "from Chloe" were people with whom Paul had more informal contact. Perhaps while on business in Corinth, they had gotten acquainted with the divisions plaguing the Corinthian church and mentioned this to Paul (upon their return?) in Ephesus.[16] The scarcity of evidence does not allow any firm conclusions. All that can be said is that Chloe was presumably a well-to do (Christian?) woman, perhaps resident in Ephesus or Corinth.

Priscilla.[17] A second reference in the same letter is to Priscilla (1 Cor 16:19) in connection with her husband Aquila (who is mentioned first here) and the church meeting at their house. Paul, apparently writing from Ephesus (cf. 1 Cor 16:8), passes on Aquila's and Priscilla's greetings from there to Corinth, where he had first met this couple (cf. Acts 18:2-3). Priscilla, together with her husband Aquila, is mentioned again in Rom 16:3, where both are called Paul's "fellow-workers in Christ Jesus" who risked their lives for him.[18] Apparently, Priscilla and Aquila had returned to

---

[14]G. D. Fee, *The First Epistle to the Corinthians* (NICNT; Grand Rapids: Eerdmans, 1987), 54, n. 32, referring to G. Theissen, *The Social Setting of Pauline Christianity: Essays on Corinth* (ed. and trans. J. H. Schütz; Philadelphia: Fortress, 1982), 57. See further Theissen's comments on pp. 93-94.

[15]Cotter, "Women's Authority Roles," 351-52, fails to address this piece of evidence. She thinks Chloe was a wealthy member of the church at Corinth, primarily because she believes the vague reference indicates that Chloe was well-known in the community.

[16]For a similar view, see Fee, *First Epistle to the Corinthians*, 54, n. 34, referring to William Ramsay, "Historical Commentary on the Epistles to the Corinthians," *Expositor* 6th series (1898-99), 103-105.

[17]The diminutive "Prisca" is used in Acts, while "Priscilla" occurs in the epistles.

[18]The term "fellow-workers" (συνεργοί; used elsewhere in Rom 16:9, 21; 1 Cor 3:9; 2 Cor 1:24; 8:23; Phil 2:25; 4:3; Col 4:11; 1 Thess 3:2; and Phlm 24) denotes work in ministry, with the particular kind of ministry not specified. Cf. D. J. Moo, *The Epistle to the Romans* (NICNT; Grand Rapids: Eerdmans, 1996), 920. Witherington, *Women in the Earliest Churches*, 111, claims on the basis of 1 Cor 16:16-18 and 1 Thess 5:12 that the term "co-worker" implies "a leadership

Rome by that time (cf. Acts 18:2). The final reference to Priscilla and Aquila is found in 2 Tim 4:19 where Paul sends greetings to the couple (back in Ephesus?) from his Roman prison.

In four of the six instances where she is mentioned in the New Testament, Priscilla's name appears before that of her husband (Acts 18:18-19, 26; Rom 16:3; 2 Tim 4:19).[19] Scholars have speculated that the reason for this is that Priscilla was converted before her husband, perhaps having led Aquila to faith in Christ, or that she played an even more prominent part in the life and work of the church than her husband.[20] Alternatively, it has been conjectured that "Prisca was the more dominant of the two or of higher social status, and she may either have provided the financial resources for the business or have been the brains behind it."[21] But none of this is explicitly stated in the text.

According to Acts 18:26, the couple invited Apollos to their home and explained to him "the way of God more adequately." Some have concluded from this that Priscilla serves as a paradigm for a woman teacher or preacher. But this claim is unwarranted. All that can be said is that Priscilla, together with and in the presence of her husband, and in the context of their home, helped provide corrective instruction to a man, Apollos.[22] Moreover, the genre of the book of Acts is historical narrative, so that care must be taken not to exaggerate the alleged normative character of Priscilla's practice for all women (even though there is no indication that Luke is

---

function involving some form of authoritative speech," whether "teaching, preaching, or both." But his argument is fallacious, for even if it were said in certain contexts that certain συνεργοί were in positions of "authority" or "leadership" (notoriously slippery terms), it is illegitimate to conclude that this necessarily applies to everyone designated Paul's "co-worker" in his letters. To argue thus is to confuse meaning and reference. See above.

[19]Aquila is mentioned first in Acts 18:2 and 1 Cor 16:19.

[20]C. E. B. Cranfield, *The Epistle to the Romans* (ICC; Edinburgh: T & T Clark, 1979), 2:784.

[21]J. D. G. Dunn, *Romans 9-16* (WBC 38b; Dallas, TX: Word, 1988), 892.

[22]The wording chosen by C. S. Keener, "Man and Woman," in *Dictionary of Paul and His Letters* (ed. G. F. Hawthorne, R. P. Martin, and D. G. Reid; Downers Grove, IL: InterVarsity, 1993), 589, that "Luke portrays her [Priscilla] as a *fellow-minister* with her husband, joining him in instructing *another minister*, Apollos (Acts 18:26)," is misleading, because it generally suggests an *ordained* minister in modern parlance, which (as far as we know) neither of those people was. See already the heading in C. S. Keener, *Paul, Women and Wives: Marriage and Women's Ministry in the Letters of Paul* (Peabody, MA: Hendrickson, 1992), 240: "Priscilla, a woman minister."

critical of what Priscilla did).[23]

Nevertheless, according to the book of Acts and Paul's epistles, Priscilla and Aquila were among Paul's most strategic allies in his Gentile mission (καὶ πᾶσαι αἱ ἐκκλησίαι τῶν ἐθνῶν; Rom 16:4), playing important roles in such major centres as Ephesus, Corinth, and Rome.[24] Together they hosted house churches in their home wherever they went, instructed others such as Apollos, and even "risked their necks" for Paul (Rom 16:4).[25]

Phoebe. Paul's epistle to the Romans contains references to several women.[26] It should be noted that the concluding chapter of Romans includes an unusually large list of people, probably because Paul had not planted or even visited the church before and thus wanted to establish that he knew, either personally or through other means, a significant number of individuals who were now members of the Roman congregation in order to solicit the church's support for his mission to Spain (Rom 15:24).[27]

---

[23]Contra Witherington, *Women in the Earliest Churches*, 156, who claims that, "[b]y including this story [Priscilla and Aquila instructing Apollos], Luke reveals the new roles women ought to be assuming in his view in the Christian community" and that "[b]y the very fact that Luke portrays women performing these various roles, he shows how the Gospel liberates and creates new possibilities for women." It is hard to escape the conclusion that Witherington's analysis is significantly influenced by contemporary agendas while flowing less from an accurate historical apprehension of the "first horizon" of Scripture.

[24]Cf. Witherington, *Women in the Earliest Churches*, 114.

[25]C. C. Kroeger, "Women in the Early Church," 1218, in a section of considerable length, seeks to revive the suggestion made by von Harnack that Priscilla and Aquila might be the authors of the epistle to the Hebrews, complete with the conspiracy theory that "if Priscilla were perceived as the primary author, there might be a tendency to suppress this fact." But this relies on the unconvincing argument that the use of a masculine singular to refer to the writer at Heb 11:32 (διηγούμενον) "may [merely] indicate male input (!) [rather than male authorship]."

[26]For an analysis of Rom 16 in light of ancient inscriptional evidence, see esp. P. Lampe, *Die stadtrömischen Christen in den ersten beiden Jahrhunderten: Untersuchungen zur Sozialgeschichte* (WUNT 2/18; Mohr-Siebeck, 1987), 135–53.

[27]Cf. J. A. Fitzmyer, *Romans* (AB 33; New York: Doubleday, 1993), 734. For a decisive refutation of the view taken by some that Rom 16 is not an integral part of Romans, see Cranfield, *Romans*, 1:5–11. Among the most extensive arguments against the "Ephesian hypothesis" concerning Rom 16 are W.-H. Ollrog, "Die Abfassungsverhältnisse von Röm 16," in *Kirche. Festschrift für Günther Bornkamm zum 75. Geburtstag* (ed. D. Lührmann and G. Strecker; Tübingen: Mohr-Siebeck, 1980), 221–44, esp. 234 (see also Ollrog's comments

The first woman mentioned is Phoebe (Rom 16:1-2), "our sister" (that is, a fellow-Christian) and "a servant (διάκονος) of the church in Cenchrea."[28] Paul commends Phoebe to the Roman church, using the technical epistolary expression for introducing a friend to other acquaintances (Συνίστημι δὲ ὑμῖν).[29] He asks the believers in Rome to give this woman any help she might need, again using the usual expression in a letter of recommendation, "in whatever affair she may need [you or your help]" (παραστῆτε αὐτῇ ἐν ᾧ ἂν ὑμῶν χρῄζῃ πράγματι).[30] The reason for Paul's request is that the woman so commended "has been a great help (πρόστατις) to many people, including me." This may refer to the hospitality extended to Paul when he visited Cenchrea at the occasion of his three-month stay in Corinth (cf. Acts 20:2-3).[31] In the present instance, Phoebe may have been the bearer of Paul's letter to Rome, which would explain why Paul mentions her first in his list of greetings in the concluding chapter of Romans.[32]

The designation διάκονος may be a generic reference to this woman's ministry as a "servant" (cf. e.g. 2 Cor 3:6; 11:23; Eph 6:21; Col 1:7; 4:7). More likely, in light of "the official-sounding nature of the phrase by which Paul identifies her" (a διάκονος of the church at Cenchrea);[33] the use of the masculine term διάκονος;[34] and perhaps also because of the conjoined term πρόστατις,[35] Phoebe served as a deaconess (cf. esp. 1 Tim 3:11).[36]

---

on Paul's intentions in writing Rom 16 on pp. 239-42); and Lampe, *Die stadtrömischen Christen*, 124-35.

[28]The term ἐκκλησία, as in vv. 4, 5, 16, and 23, probably refers to a local congregation, presumably a house church.

[29]Keener, "Man and Woman," 589, notes that twice as many women as men are commended in Rom 16, adding that "[t]his may indicate his [Paul's] sensitivity to the opposition women undoubtedly faced for their ministry in some quarters." Paul may well commend Phoebe, in this instance, for a variety of other reasons than this.

[30]Cf. Fitzmyer, *Romans*, 728, 731.

[31]Ibid., 731.

[32]Ibid., 729.

[33]So S. B. Clark, *Man and Woman in Christ: An Examination of the Roles of Men and Women in Light of Scripture and the Social Sciences* (Ann Arbor, MI: Servant, 1980), 119.

[34]T. R. Schreiner, *Romans* (BECNT; Grand Rapids: Baker, 1998), 787.

[35]Dunn, *Romans 9-16*, 888-89, is probably correct in suggesting that Phoebe's two roles, διάκονος and πρόστατις, should be seen as linked. He is followed by France, *Women in the Church's Ministry: A Test Case for Biblical Interpretation* (Grand Rapids: Eerdmans, 1997 [1995]), 88.

[36]See esp. Clark, *Man and Woman in Christ*, 119-23.

Deacons were set apart for "the practical service of the needy" in the early church (cf. Phil 1:1; Titus 1:9; 1 Tim 3:8-13).[37] They were to be of proven Christian character but, unlike overseers, not required to be able to teach (cf. 1 Tim 3:2 with 1 Tim 3:8-10, 12-13) or to participate in the governing of the church (cf. 1 Tim 2:12; 5:17). Neuer maintains that the office of deaconess "certainly did not involve public proclamation of the word, teaching, or leading the church. Perhaps it involved serving the congregation, by bringing material help to the needy (Rom 16:2), in serving women, the sick, and strangers."[38]

As a wealthy woman, a "benefactress" or "patroness" (προστάτις, the feminine form of προστάτης), Phoebe would have used her financial means to come "to the aid of others, especially foreigners, by providing housing and financial aid and by representing their interests before local authorities."[39] This would have been a needed ministry in a busy seaport

---

[37]Cf. Cranfield, *Romans*, 2:781; Moo, *Epistle to the Romans*, 913; W. Neuer, *Man and Woman in Christian Perspective* (trans. G. J. Wenham; Wheaton, IL: Crossway, 1991 [1981]), 121. See also the comments by Theissen, *Social Setting of Pauline Christianity*, 88-89. Contra F. F. Bruce, *The Book of the Acts* (NICNT; rev. ed.; Grand Rapids: Eerdmans, 1988), 122, who in his discussion of Acts 6 suggests that "it might be better to render it [the term διάκονος] by the more general term 'minister' " and is followed by Keener, *Paul, Women and Wives*, 239; and esp. Ellis, "Paul and His Co-Workers," 442 (following D. Georgi, *The Opponents of Paul in Second Corinthians* [Philadelphia: Fortress, 1986], 27-32), who claims that "the *diakonoi* appear to be a special class of co-workers, those who are active in preaching and teaching. They appear in Paul's circle not only as itinerant workers but also as workers in local congregations, such as Phoebe (Rom. xvi. I)." Ellis reiterates this claim in "Coworkers, Paul and His," 185: "It [the term *diakonos*] is probably best rendered 'minister' since it refers to workers with special activities in preaching and teaching." But Ellis fails to address the absence of the requirement "able to teach" for deacons in 1 Tim 3:8-13, and the rather general nature of the majority of New Testament references to διάκονος just cited. See also the following discussion and note.

[38]Neuer, *Man and Woman in Biblical Perspective*, 121. Contra D. C. Arichea, Jr., "Who Was Phoebe? Translating *Diakonos* in Romans 16.1," *BT* 39 (1988): 409, who contends, without adducing evidence, that διάκονος in Rom 16:1 describes "a person with special functions in the pastoral and administrative life of the church; and such functions would most probably include pastoral care, teaching, and even missionary work."

[39]So Moo, *Epistle to the Romans*, 916. The term προστάτις often refers to the function of "protection," such as in Appius, *BC* 1.11. Cf. also Cranfield, *Romans*, 2:783, who comments that the choice of the expression προστάτις "implies that Phoebe was possessed of some social position, wealth and independence"; and Theissen, *Social Setting of Pauline Christianity*. Witherington, *Women in the Earliest Churches*, 115, argues, on the strength of the use of προϊστάμενος in Rom 12:8, that Phoebe may have held the formal

such as Cenchrea. "Phoebe, then, was probably a woman of high social standing and some wealth, who put her status, resources, and time at the services of traveling Christians, like Paul, who needed help and support."[40] However, this does not mean, as is alleged with some frequency, that patronesses were leaders of houses.[41] Moreover, to call her "president," or even "leader" of the church at Cenchrea, goes beyond the evidence, as does the claim that "Phoebe held a position of considerable responsibility, prominence, and authority in her congregation."[42]

Junia. A controversial reference is that to Junia in Rom 16:7, who, together with Andronicus, is called "notorious among the ἀποστόλοι" (ἐπίσημοι ἐν τοῖς ἀποστόλοις).[43] The accusative Ἰουνιαν could derive either from the nominative Ἰούνια (accusative accented as Ἰουνίαν), in which case the person referred to would be a woman, or Ἰουνιᾶς (accusative accented as Ἰουνιᾶν), a male name.[44] The name is a Latin one trans-

---

position of "a person in charge of the charitable work of the church," but this is pure conjecture.

[40]Moo, *Epistle to the Romans*, 916.

[41]Cf. e.g. Keener, *Paul, Women and Wives*, 240, and the critique in the following note.

[42]Cf. R. R. Schulz, "A Case for 'President' Phoebe in Romans 16:2," *LTJ* 24 (1990): 124-27; the list of commentators given in Fitzmyer, *Romans*, 731; and Keener, *Paul, Women and Wives*, 239. Schulz, in seeking to make his case for "president" Phoebe in Rom 16:2, (1) inappropriately links the verb form προΐστημι with the noun προστάτις; (2) inappropriately equates the meaning of the feminine προστάτις with the masculine προστάτης (cf. Schreiner, "Valuable Ministries of Women," 219-20; the same flaw can be detected in Keener, *Paul, Women and Wives*, 240, whose evidence for his suggested meaning of the term προστάτις consists of an article on προστάτης and two references in Epictetus and Marcus Aurelius likewise featuring προστάτης [p. 252, n. 26]); (3) unduly minimizes the possible connection between προστάτις and the verb παρίστημι (which means "to help") in the same verse (cf. Schreiner, "Valuable Ministries of Women," 219); (4) unduly suggests that προστάτις must mean "leader" or "president" here because it is linked with διάκονος (which, whether it is used here as a technical term or not, bears the original meaning "servant" and was in any case not equivalent to the function of overseer in the early church); and (5) adduces tenuous background information regarding the role of priestesses in (goddess) worship in Greek religion. Moreover, it is puzzling how Schulz can claim that "*prostatis* may be the closest NT word we have to 'president' ": why not terms such as ἐπίσκοπος (Acts 20:28; Phil 1:1; 1 Tim 3:2; Titus 1:7)?

[43]Regarding the latter phrase, see further the comments below.

[44]Both UBS 3 and 4 as well as Nestle-Aland 25th and 26th print the masculine accentuation. Note that a few textual witnesses (esp. p[46] [ca. 200 AD]) read Ἰουλιαν, which Metzger regards as a "clerical error" (cf. Rom 16:15). Cf. B. M. Metzger, *A Textual Commentary on the Greek New Testament* (corr. ed.; New York:

cribed into Greek.[45] It is taken by some to be a shortened form of *Junianus, Junianius,* or *Junilius.*[46] But "[i]f *Iounias* is indeed a shortened form of the common name *Iounianus,* why then does the name *Iunias* never occur?"[47] Indeed, "(1) the female Latin name Junia occurs more than 250 times in Greek and Latin inscriptions found in Rome alone, whereas the male name Junias is unattested anywhere; and (2) when Greek manuscripts began to be accented, scribes wrote the feminine Ἰουνίαν ("Junia")."[48] In 1977, B. Brooten could state that "we do not have a single shred of evidence that the name *Junias* ever existed . . . all of the philological evidence points to the feminine *Junia.*"[49] In the past twenty years, no one has been able to refute these claims, and no further evidence has come to light.[50] In light of these arguments, and the complete lack of evidence for the existence of a male name "Junias," it must be concluded that, until evidence to the contrary is forthcoming, the person referred to

---

UBS, 1975), 539.

[45]So Cervin, "Note Regarding 'Junia(s),' " 464–70.

[46]So *BADG,* 380: "Ἰουνιᾶς, ᾶ, ὁ *Junias* (not found elsewh., prob. short form of the common Junianus; cf. Bl.-D. §125.2; Rob. 172) . . . The possibility, fr. a purely lexical point of view, that this is a woman's name Ἰουνία, ας, *Junia* . . . deserves consideration (but s. Ltzm., Hdb. ad loc.)." However, the assertion by H. Lietzmann, *Die Briefe des Apostels Paulus: I. An die Römer* (HNT 3; Tübingen: J. C. B. Mohr [Paul Siebeck], 1906), 73: "Ἰουνιαν muss wegen der folgenden Aussagen einen Mann bezeichnen, also Ἰουνιᾶς = Junianus," is sheer dogmatism. Bl.-D. §125, 2 cite as possible parallel the shortening of Σιλουανόσ (Paul and 1 Pet 5:12) to Σιλᾶς (Acts) or Σιλέας; V. Fàbrega, "War Junia(s), der hervorragende Apostel (Rom. 16,7), eine Frau?" *Jahrbuch für Antike und Christentum* 27/28 (1984–85): 49, adds the shortening of Ἀντιπᾶς for Ἀντίπατρος (Rev 2:13), of Κλωπᾶς or Κλεοπᾶς for Κλεόπατρος (John 19:25; Luke 24:18), and of Λουκᾶς for the Latin Lucius or Lucanus (Col 4:14; 2 Tim 4:11; Phlm 24). See also M-M, 306 who comment that "Ἰουνιᾶς is probably a contracted form of *Iounianus,* which is common in the inscrr., e.g. *CIL* III. 4020."

[47]Cervin, "Note Regarding 'Junia(s),' " 466. Similarly, R. R. Schulz, "Romans 16:7: Junia or Junias?" *ExpTim* 98 (1986–87): 109: "The Junias theory is an argument from silence."

[48]B. M. Metzger, *A Textual Commentary on the Greek New Testament* (2nd ed.; New York: UBS, 1994), 475. For a survey of patristic exegesis, see esp. Fàbrega, "War Junia(s) . . . eine Frau?" 54–63, who discusses in particular the references in Chrysostom, Theodoret, and Origen.

[49]B. Brooten, "Junia . . . Outstanding among the Apostles (Romans 16:7)," in *Women Priests: A Catholic Commentary on the Vatican Declaration,* ed. L. and A. Swidler (New York: Paulist, 1977), 142–43.

[50]Reference should be made to Brooten's claim ("Junia . . . Outstanding among the Apostles," 144, n. 4) that Migne's edition of the text of the earliest commentator on Rom 16:7, Origen of Alexandria (c. 185–253/54), has *Junia* emended to *Junias,* but that the MSS themselves have *Junia* or *Julia.* To date, I

in Rom 16:7 is a woman named Junia.

Andronicus and Junia are identified as Paul's συγγενεῖς, which could mean " 'fellow-countrymen' [that is, Jews; cf. Rom 9:3], and not 'relations' " [that is, relatives].[51] In this case it is unclear, however, why Paul, in chapter 16, calls (except for Andronicus and Junia) only Herodion (v. 11), Lucius, Jason, and Sosipater (v. 21) Jews, but not Aquila and Priscilla (v. 3), Mary (v. 6), or Rufus and his mother (v. 13).[52] It is therefore more likely that συγγενεῖς μου means "my friends" or "my close associates" as an expression indicating collaboration in ministry, equivalent to the expression ἀγαπητός μου in Rom 16:5, 8-9.[53] This would explain why even Lucius, Jason, and Sosipater, who are commonly suspected not to have been Jews, can be called συγγενεῖς μου by Paul. Andronicus and Junia are further called his "fellow prisoners" (συναιχμάλωτος), a designation elsewhere applied only to Epaphras (Phlm 23) and Aristarchus (Col 4:10). Nothing is known about the specifics of this imprisonment; it is usually assumed that Paul refers to a literal imprisonment, which appears probable, though a figurative use of the term cannot be ruled out.[54]

---

have not been able to obtain these MSS to verify Brooten's claim. But see Fàbrega, "War Junia(s) . . . eine Frau?" 59, n. 51, who points out that the name Junia is found in a commentary written by Hraban of Fulda in c. CE 820, which the latter claims to have taken verbatim from Origen's (Rufinus') commentary (is this the basis for Brooten's claim?). In his extensive discussion (pp. 58-60), Fàbrega also notes that Origen's Romans commentary, written in CE 244, has been preserved only in a Latin version written by Rufinus in CE 404. In this version, Rufinus frequently condenses Origen's comments or even replaces them with his own. Also, Rufinus' interpretation is based not on the Greek, but the Latin, text of the Roman epistle. With reference to the work of E. von der Goltz and O. Bauernfeind, Fàbrega concludes that it is likely that Origen himself did not comment at all on the list of names in Rom 16. The implication of this is that Origen should in future discussions of the issue be excluded as evidence for a patristic interpretation of Ἰουνιαν as male (or, of course, female, for that matter).

[51]So Cranfield, *Romans*, 2:788, referring to W. Sanday and A. C. Headlam, *A Critical and Exegetical Commentary on the Epistle to the Romans* (ICC; Edinburgh: T & T Clark, [5]1902 [1895]), 423. Contra Ellis, "Coworkers, Paul and His," 186, who seeks to make a case that συγγενεῖς in Paul's writings regularly refers to the apostle's literal relatives. Consequently, Ellis conjectures that Andronicus and Junia "were very likely Jerusalem relatives who were missionaries from that church to Rome."

[52]Cf. Fàbrega, "War Junia(s) . . . eine Frau?" 49.

[53]Fàbrega, "War Junia(s) . . . eine Frau?," 50; following W. Michaelis, "συγγενής κτλ.," *TDNT* 7:741-42.

[54]Cf. W. A. Meeks, *The First Urban Christians: The Social World of the Apostle Paul* (New Haven/London: Yale University Press, 1983), 57: "Andronicus and Junia(s) (Rom. 16:7) have also moved from the East, where they were imprisoned with Paul somewhere, sometime, to Rome . . ." Possibly Paul does not

Moreover, Andronicus and Junia are identified as ἐπίσημοι ἐν τοῖς ἀποστόλοις, "notorious among the ἀποστολοί."[55] Most commentators see the reference as inclusive, that is, as including Andronicus and Junia among the circle of ἀποστολοί, whatever meaning is assigned to this term (see below). However, it is possible that the reference is exclusive, that is, Andronicus and Junia are said to be "notorious" (i.e. well known) among the circle of ἀποστολοί (cf. PssSol 2:6: ἐπισήμῳ ἐν τοῖς ἔθνεσιν, "a spectacle among the Gentiles"). If so, Andronicus and Junia could be church workers or Christians whose ministry is not further specified and who are identified as well-known among the apostolic circle (with ἀποστολοί perhaps having a more narrow compass).

Alternatively (and perhaps more likely),[56] "among" may be used in an inclusive sense, in which case this couple would be included among the ἀποστολοί, whichever sense the latter term has. In this case, if Junia is indeed a woman, and if she is called "notorious among the ἀποστολοί," does the presence of a woman "ἀπόστολος" in the New Testament imply, then, that the early church placed no restrictions on the ministry of women?[57] This depends largely on the question of whether "apostle" is

---

mean to indicate that Andronicus and Junia were imprisoned with him at the same time or in the same place but simply that they too had been imprisoned for the faith at some point. Cf. Fitzmyer, *Romans*, 739. For an argument for a figurative use of this expression, see esp. Kittel, "αἰχμάλωτος," *TDNT* 1:196-97.

[55]This is the almost unanimous view of commentators, including Dunn, *Romans 9-16*, 894; Cranfield, *Romans*, 2:789, referring also to R. Schnackenburg, "Apostles Before and During Paul's Time," in *Apostolic History and the Gospel: Biblical and Historical Essays Presented to F. F. Bruce* (ed. W. W. Gasque and R. P. Martin; Grand Rapids: Eerdmans, 1970), 287-303; and Cervin, "Note Regarding 'Junia(s),' " 470, who also notes the Vulgate rendering, "qui sunt nobiles in [i.e. among] apostolis." The term ἐπίσημος is used elsewhere in the New Testament only in Matt 27:16 (referring to the "notorious" prisoner Barabbas) and occurs eight times in the LXX (Gen 30:42; Esth 5:4; 1 Macc 11:37; 14:48; 2 Macc 15:36; 3 Macc 6:1; Pss 2:6; 17:30), generally to denote that which is distinguished or conspicuous as over against that which is insignificant, nondescript or otherwise unnoticed.

[56]For this inclusive sense, see Lucian, *Merc. Cond.* 28.5: "he will be conspicuous among the claques" (ἐπίσημος ἔσῃ ἐν τοῖς ἐπαινοῦσι [2nd cent. CE]); Eusebius, *Praep. Evang.* 10.14: "This man became most distinguished among the Greeks" (ὁ ἀνὴρ ἐπισημότατος ἐν τοῖς Ἕλλησι (4th cent. CE)); Concilium Ephesenum 1.1.7.152.26: "a man prominent among the ἐκκλησιαστικοί" (ἀνὴρ ἀεὶ ἐν τοῖς ἐκκλησιαστικοῖς [5th cent. CE]).

[57]The ideological stake in this question is helpfully acknowledged by Moo, *Epistle to the Romans*, 923. Keener, "Man and Woman," 589, may have a point when he comments that the proposal that Ἰουνιαν in Rom 16:7 represents a shortened form of *Iounianus* or the like "rests on the assumption that a woman could not be an apostle, rather than on any evidence inherent in the text itself."

here used in a narrow or broad sense. Four types of use can be discerned in the writings of the New Testament. First, ἀπόστολος may refer to the Twelve (e.g. Matt 10:2). Second, the term is used for someone like Paul who had seen the Lord and was commissioned by him to a special ministry (e.g. 1 Cor 1:1; 2 Cor 1:1; Col 1:1). Third, the expression may denote an emissary sent out to perform a certain task or convey a particular message (2 Cor 8:23; Phil 2:25). And fourth, ἀπόστολος may refer to an itinerant missionary (e.g. Acts 14:4, 14 of Barnabas).[58]

To which of these does the context in Rom 16:7 point in the case of Andronicus and Junia? At the outset, it is highly unlikely that these otherwise unknown figures are said here to stand out among noted apostles such as the Twelve (an impossibility) or Peter, James, or even Paul.[59] The sense "messenger, emissary" (cf. 2 Cor 8:23: ἀπόστολοι ἐκκλησιῶν; Phil 2:25: ὑμῶν ἀπόστολος) appears more likely.[60] However, the designation "outstanding among the messengers" seems a bit awkward, for the role of messenger tends to be rather inconspicuous, and this description is like designating a person as an "extraordinary usher." The meaning "travelling missionary" is therefore most likely, especially in light of 1 Cor 9:5 (cf. Acts 14:4, 14; 1 Cor 12:28; 1 Thess 2:7; Eph 4:11).[61] In this case, Andronicus and Junia would be identified as "outstanding among (itinerant) missionaries" (an important office in the early church as well as

---

Similarly, France, *Women in the Church's Ministry*, 86–87. See also Brooten, "Junia . . . Outstanding among the Apostles"; and more recently, Grenz, *Women in the Church*, 211.

[58]Cf. Witherington, *Women in the Earliest Churches*, 115, referring to C. K. Barrett, *The Signs of an Apostle* (Philadelphia: Fortress, 1972), 23ff.; and Schnackenburg, "Apostles Before and During Paul's Time," 293–94.

[59]So rightly Ellis, "Coworkers, Paul and His," 186. Contra Dunn, *Romans 9–16*, 894, who exceeds the evidence when he "firmly conclude[s] . . . that one of the foundation apostles of Christianity [viz. Eph. 2:20] was a woman and a wife."

[60]This view is adopted by J. Piper and W. Grudem, "Chapter 2: An Overview of Central Concerns: Questions and Answers," in J. Piper and W. Grudem, eds., *Recovering Biblical Manhood and Womanhood—A Response to Evangelical Feminism* (Wheaton, IL: Crossway, 1991), 81, who ascribe to Andronicus and Junias [sic] "some kind of itinerant ministry," citing as parallels Phil 2:25 and 2 Cor 8:23.

[61]Cf. Cranfield, *Romans*, 2:789, followed by Witherington, *Women in the Earliest Churches*, 115; Moo, *Epistle to the Romans*, 924; Ellis, "Coworkers, Paul and His," 186; France, *Women in the Church's Ministry*, 87; and Lampe, *Die stadtrömischen Christen*, 137. Fàbrega, "War Junia(s) . . . eine Frau?" 53 also cites the German commentators Lietzmann, Schmithals, Schnackenburg, and Wilkens as holding this view.

today), perhaps in part because they were converted before Paul (Rom 16:7), which means that they must have become believers during the very early days of the church.

If this is the case, Andronicus and Junia were a distinguished senior missionary couple, and the designation ἀπόστολος, applied to both of them jointly, does not imply that Junia by herself occupied an authoritative leadership position in a local church or in the early Christian movement.[62] Indeed, if Junia is mentioned in the present passage in tandem with Andronicus (who is unquestionably male) *because she is his wife* (note that other husband and wife pairs in Romans 16 include Priscilla and Aquila in v. 3 and probably Philologus and Julia in v. 15),[63] they would have exercised their travelling ministry jointly rather than independently, similar to Priscilla and Aquila or the pattern mentioned in 1 Cor 9:5, so that even in this function Junia should not be elevated to "apostle" in isolation from (her husband?) Andronicus.[64]

---

[62]Contra Grenz, *Women in the Church*, 96, who claims that "the weight of evidence favors interpreting Junia as an authoritative apostle."

[63]This is called by some the consensus view of ancient commentators until the twelfth or thirteenth century (e.g. G. Lohfink; for a list of references, see Fitzmyer, *Romans*, 737–38). But this is inaccurate, since accented ninth-century minuscule MSS (e.g. 33) already bear the masculine form Ἰουνιᾶν and never the feminine form Ἰουνίαν (cf. P. Lampe, "Iunia/Iunias: Sklavenherkunft im Kreise der vorpaulinischen Apostel [Röm 16:7]," *ZNW* 76 [1985]: 132, n. 1; Fitzmyer, *Romans*, 738). Keener, *Paul, Women and Wives*, 242, appropriately comments that "[i]f Junia is a woman apostle traveling with Andronicus, a male apostle, certain scandal would result if they were not brother and sister or husband and wife. Since most apostles, unlike Paul, were married (1 Cor. 9:5), the early church was probably right when it understood them as a husband-wife apostolic team" (this does not imply endorsement of Keener's use of the terms "apostles" and "apostolic" in this statement). See further J. Jeremias, "Paarweise Sendung im Neuen Testament," in *New Testament Essays: Studies in Memory of Thomas Walter Manson* (ed. A. J. B. Higgins; Manchester: Manchester University Press, 1959), 139, who calls Andronicus and Junias a "Sendbotenpaar der Urgemeinde" in keeping with the Jewish pattern, emulated by both Jesus and Paul, of sending out messengers in pairs.

[64]Cf. Moo, *Epistle to the Romans*, 923, who calls Andronicus and Junia "this husband and wife ministry team." Similarly, Dunn, *Romans 9–16*, 894: "The most natural way to read the two names within the phrase is as husband and wife." Andrew Perriman, *Speaking of Women* (Leicester: Apollos, 1998), 70, n. 29, cites Clement of Alexandria, who wrote that the apostles took their wives with them as "fellow ministers" through whom "the Lord's teaching penetrated into the women's quarters without scandal" (*Stromateis* 3.6.53). Note also Fitzmyer, *Romans*, 739: "They could be considered paired messengers of the gospel, even if husband and wife."

Other Women Referred to in Romans 16. Several other women referred to in Romans are said to have "worked (very) hard" (ἐκοπίασεν) for other believers (Mary; Rom 16:6) or "in the Lord" (Tryphena and Tryphosa, Persis; Rom 16:12). No further information is available for Mary, a common Jewish name in that day. The root underlying the names Tryphena and Tryphosa means "soft" or "delicate," and it is possible that Paul was aware of the irony of attributing hard work to two women thus called. Tryphena and Tryphosa may have been (twin) sisters, since it was common to assign children names from the same Greek root;[65] or these two women were grouped together because of the similarity of their names.[66] Πέρσις means "Persian woman" and was a typical Greek slave name.[67] In the case of each of these women, the reference to their hard work may simply pertain to a variety of good works which were to be the hallmark of a godly woman (cf. 1 Tim 2:10), even though this is not stated explicitly.[68]

Also in Romans, mention is made of Julia (16:15); the (unnamed) sister of Nereus (16:15); and Olympas (16:15). In context, these probably refer to the wife (or, less likely, sister; Julia) and children (Nereus and his sister) of Philologus who is mentioned first, together with another member of their family or particular house church (Olympas) and others (similarly, v. 14).[69] Because these are common names for slaves and freedmen, it is frequently suggested that they were slaves of the imperial household in Rome.[70] The list of names in Paul's letter to the Romans also includes the (unnamed) mother of Rufus (16:13) "who has been a mother to me, too." The Rufus mentioned here may be the person referred to in Mark 15:21 where Simon of Cyrene is identified as "the father of Alexander and Rufus"; but this identification, while plausible, is less than certain. Paul adds that this woman was ἐκλεκτός ἐν κυρίῳ, "chosen in (by) the Lord."

---

[65]Moo, *Epistle to the Romans*, 925, n. 54.

[66]Cf. Cranfield, *Romans*, 2:793.

[67]Ibid.; Lampe, *Die stadtrömischen Christen*, 145.

[68]Cf. Dunn, *Romans 9–16*, 894, who points out that κοπιάω is a general term that does not denote leadership per se. But see A. von Harnack, "Κόπος (Κοπιᾶν, Οἱ Κοπιῶντες) im frühchristlichen Sprachgebrauch," *ZNW* 27 (1928): 1–10, esp. 5, who contends that κοπιᾶν was used by Paul to refer to missionary service as well as to service in the church: "the Christian who works on behalf of others performs 'hard labor' " (my translation); and Lampe, *Die stadtrömischen Christen*, 137, who calls the term a "terminus technicus der Missionssprache."

[69]Ibid., 2:795; Fitzmyer, *Romans*, 742.

[70]See e.g. Dunn, *Romans 9–16*, 898.

Euodia and Syntyche. The final group of references is found in the prison epistles. In Philippians, Paul makes mention of two women named Euodia and Syntyche, who had contended at his side in the cause of the gospel but who now needed to work out their differences with the help of an arbitrator (Phil 4:2). The surprising fact that Paul chooses to identify both women by name may indicate that their disagreement threatened the unity of the entire church. Otherwise, it is hard to explain why Paul would embarrass these women by referring to them by name in a letter to be read aloud to the public assembly. Indeed, the book of Acts indicates that ("prominent") women played a significant part in the newly founded churches in Macedonia (16:14-15, 40; 17:4, 12).

Paul mentions that Euodia and Syntyche had contended (the verb is συναθλέω) at his side in the cause of the gospel (4:3).[71] The fact that the same expression is used in 1:27 (the only other New Testament occurrence of this term) with reference to the entire congregation at Philippi suggests that these two women had participated in Paul's own struggle for the advance of the gospel as had the Philippian church as a whole (cf. 1:30).[72] To have contended together with Paul in (the proclamation of) the gospel and to be called his "co-worker" is a fairly broad designation and does not necessarily imply that Euodia and Syntyche had the same kind of ministry as Paul.[73] Internal evidence suggests that the nature of the Philippians' "partnership in the gospel" with Paul (Phil 1:5) centered significantly around their financial support of his ministry (Phil 4:10-19; cf. 2 Cor 8-9; Rom 15:25-29) and their willingness to suffer with him for the sake of the gospel (Phil 1:30).[74]

---

[71]See further *IPol.* 6:1: "Labor with one another, struggle together, run together, suffer together, rest together, rise up together as God's stewards and assessors and servants" (συγκοπιᾶτε ἀλλήλοις, συναθλεῖτε, συντρέχετε, συμπάσχετε, συγκοιμᾶσθε, συνεγείρεσθε ὡς θεοῦ οἰκόνομοι καὶ πάρεδροι καὶ ὑπηρέται), advice which is addressed to the entire Christian community.

[72]P. T. O'Brien, *Commentary on Philippians* (NIGTC; Grand Rapids: Eerdmans, 1991), 481-82. The suggestion by Cotter, "Women's Authority Roles," 353, that Euodia and Syntyche "belonged to a team of men and women evangelizers" is unduly specific and thus exceeds the evidence.

[73]See already the preliminary observations made above. Note also the early variant καὶ τῶν συνεργῶν μου καὶ τῶν λοιπῶν ("and my coworkers, and the others"; Codex Sinaiticus, p[16]), which, if original, would suggest that the women and Clement are not included in the category of "co-workers." Cf. M. Silva, *Philippians* (BECNT; Grand Rapids: Baker, 1992), 223.

[74]This is argued persuasively by F. X. Malinowski, "The Brave Women of Philippi," *BTB* 15 (1985): 60-64.

In particular, the verbal parallel with 1:27 (συναθλέω) indicates that Paul is thinking of Euodia and Syntyche in the same way as he thought of the community as a whole, that is, as believers who bore courageous testimony to their faith and who shared sacrificially of their financial resources in order to advance the cause of the gospel of Jesus Christ. The claim that Euodia and Syntyche were "important leaders," "two influential church leaders," "two women church leaders," or the like, is therefore overblown.[75]

Other Women Referred to in the Prison Epistles and the Pastorals. In the closing section of Colossians, Paul includes in his greetings a reference to Nympha and the church meeting at her house (Col 4:15).[76] No further information is available. In his letter to Philemon, Paul refers to "our sister" Apphia (Phlm 2), a designation elsewhere in Paul's writings used only with reference to Phoebe in Rom 16:1. Apphia, not a recipient of the letter but merely included in the introductory salutation,[77] has been identified as Philemon's wife from early times.[78] If this is correct, it would explain Paul's mention of her immediately after Philemon, since as Philemon's wife Apphia would wish to know about the situation surrounding the runaway slave Onesimus as well.

Finally, Paul's second letter to Timothy makes mention of a woman named Claudia (4:21). Again, no further information is available.

---

[75]The references are to V. P. Furnish, *The Moral Teaching of Paul* (Nashville: Abingdon, 1979), 105; H. Koester, "Letter to the Philippians," *IDBSup* (Nashville: Abingdon, 1976), 666; and R. Scroggs, "Woman in the NT," *IDBSup* (Nashville: Abingdon, 1976), 966.

[76]There is some uncertainty as to whether this refers to a man or a woman, but on balance a female reference seems to be preferred. Cf. P. T. O'Brien, *Colossians, Philemon* (WBC 44; Waco, TX: Word, 1982), 256; Perriman, *Speaking of Women*, 71–72. On house churches, see also references to Philemon (Phlm 2; see further next note), Lydia (Acts 16:15, 40), Gaius (Rom 16:23), and Aquila and Priscilla (1 Cor 16:19; Rom 16:5).

[77]The reference to the church meeting in "your" (σοῦ) house is singular and refers to Philemon alone; cf. O'Brien, *Colossians, Philemon*, 273. Contra Cotter, "Women's Authority Roles," 351, who claims that Apphia is one of "the main leaders of that otherwise faceless assembly," citing as evidence only that this is the view of E. Schüssler Fiorenza, *In Memory of Her* (New York: Crossroads, 1988), 177.

[78]Cf. E. Lohse, *Colossians and Philemon* (Hermeneia; Philadelphia: Fortress, 1971 [1968]), 190 (followed by O'Brien, *Colossians, Philemon*, 273): "Since her [Apphia's] name follows immediately after Philemon's, one can assume that she is his wife," referring also to Theodoret: "Paul . . . adds the name of the wife . . . to that of the husband" (*Paulus . . . marito . . . jungit uxorem*).

Evaluation. All of Paul's travel companions were male.[79] This follows the precedent established by Jesus.[80] None of the women mentioned in relation to the Pauline mission serves as pastor-teacher or elder. Phoebe apparently functioned as a deaconess and is also called benefactress. If Junia was a woman (which is highly probable), she probably served as an itinerant missionary or, less likely, as a messenger, together with her presumed husband, Andronicus. Priscilla, together with her husband Aquila, had a church meeting in her house, as did Nympha and Apphia (with Philemon). Priscilla is also shown to have had a (leading?) part in instructing Apollos in her home, again together with her husband.

The positions of Euodia and Syntyche in the Philippian church were apparently significant enough to threaten the unity of the entire congregation. These two women were (in all probability) counted among Paul's co-workers and had contended at his side for the gospel (even though it is unclear precisely which form this partnership had taken). Rufus' mother had been like a mother to Paul, at least on one memorable occasion. Other women had worked very hard for other believers in the Lord (Mary, Tryphena, Tryphosa, Persis). Too little is known about Chloe to ascertain her position in relation to the Corinthian church. Julia (possibly the wife of Philologus), the sister of Nereus (Julia's daughter?), and Claudia are mentioned without specific information about the nature of their ministry.

Overall, the listed data indicate that the influence of women was to a significant extent informal and frequently centered around their home. There are instances of women exercising hospitality, including hosting a house church; devoting themselves to a variety of good works; having a part in raising their children in the faith; and, if wealthy, helping others financially, be it with or without a formal position in the church. Some were engaged in missionary work together with their husbands. What is

---

[79]W. Hadorn, "Die Gefährten und Mitarbeiter des Paulus," in *Aus Schrift und Geschichte. Theologische Abhandlungen Adolf Schlatter zu seinem 70. Geburtstage* (Stuttgart: Calwer Vereinsbuchhandlung, 1922), 73.

[80]Luke 8:1-3 is no real exception, for the thrust of this passage is not that women were among those who were part of Jesus' regular travel companions but that some women who had benefited from his ministry supported him and the Twelve in their itinerant work. See D. Bock, *Luke 1:1-9:50* (BECNT; Grand Rapids: Baker, 1994), 713, who notes, with reference to C. H. Talbert, *Reading Luke: A Literary and Theological Commentary on the Third Gospel* (New York: Crossroad, 1982), 92-93, and B. Witherington, "On the Road with Mary Magdalene, Joanna, Susanna, and Other Disciples-Luke 8:1-3," *ZNW* 70 (1979): 243-48, that it was unusual for women to travel with a rabbi in Jesus' day.

more, when reading passages such as the sixteenth chapter of Romans, one gets the impression that women were thoroughly integrated in the Pauline churches, having a vital part in the mission and life of the early Christian community and fulfilling roles of significant, albeit not ultimate, responsibility within the church.[81] This included "missionary work, carrying letters, serving in charitable tasks as deaconesses, providing aid or shelter for traveling apostles, etc."[82] In the exercise of their respective roles, they functioned fully within the parameters of their Graeco-Roman surroundings.[83] The roles exercised by them also conformed to the pattern characteristic of the ministry of Jesus. In the ministries of both Jesus and Paul, men bore the ultimate responsibility for the ongoing mission, with women actively supporting and contributing to that mission.

This concludes the survey of women named in the Pauline epistles in relation to their described function in the Pauline mission. We may now turn to a discussion of Paul's explicit *teaching* regarding the role of women in the church.

Pauline Teaching on Women in the Church

The literature on Paul's teaching regarding women is vast indeed, and the issue continues to be hotly debated in the contemporary church and scholarship. Moreover, the New Testament teaching on women is fre-

---

[81]Cf. Schreiner, "Valuable Ministries of Women," 222: "it is clear that Biblical writers consistently ascribe ultimate responsibility to men for the leadership of the church." Ellis, "Coworkers, Paul and His," 187, may overstate his case when he maintains that "[a] remarkable number of women are mentioned as Paul's associates, both in Acts and in his letters. Some are *called ministers* (*diakonoi*) or coworkers (*synergoi*) or missionaries (*apostoloi*), several of whom were *engaged in ministries of teaching and preaching* (Rom 16:1, 3, 7; Phil 4:2–3; cf. Acts 18:26)" (emphasis added). See the discussion of διάκονος as "minister" and the treatment of Phoebe, Priscilla, Junia, and Euodia and Syntyche above.

[82]Witherington, *Women in the Earliest Churches*, 116.

[83]The primary focus of the present essay is the study of the relevant biblical passages rather than extensive exploration of the ancient cultural background. For a helpful survey, see e.g. Witherington, "Women in First-Century Mediterranean Cultures," in *Women in the Earliest Churches*, 5–23. Cf. also Cotter, "Women's Authority Roles," whose study is, however, marred by her ambiguous use of the terms "authority" and "leadership" and by her one-sided focus on descriptive Pauline passages at the exclusion of didactic portions (for a fuller critique, see my review in *CBMW News* 1/4 [1996]: 14).

quently treated as a test case in hermeneutics.[84] Since I have treated the subject in several publications elsewhere, I will limit myself here to a brief summary of the general contours of Paul's teaching on the subject.[85] We begin with a few programmatic comments.

Prolegomena

Several recent studies give short shrift to explicit Pauline teaching on the present subject.[86] Descriptive references are absolutized, while didactic passages such as 1 Tim 2:9–15 are marginalized as "difficult" or limited in application. However, the problem with this procedure is that it leaves the interpreter without a proper framework for evaluating the descriptive passages discussed above. There exists, of course, the opposite danger of filtering descriptive passages through a pre-established doctrinal grid derived from didactic passages in Paul's writings.[87] The ideal to strive for is

---

[84]Cf. most recently France, *Women in the Church's Ministry*. See also Köstenberger, "Gender Passages in the NT," 259–83.

[85]See esp. A. J. Köstenberger, T. R. Schreiner, and H. S. Baldwin, eds., *Women in the Church: A Fresh Analysis of 1 Timothy 2:9-15* (Grand Rapids: Baker, 1995); Köstenberger, "Syntactical Background Studies to 1 Tim. 2.12 in the New Testament and Extrabiblical Greek Literature," in *Discourse Analysis and Other Topics in Biblical Greek* (ed. S. E. Porter and D. A. Carson; JSNTSup 113; Sheffield: Sheffield Academic Press, 1995), 156–79; id., "Gender Passages in the NT"; id., "The Crux of the Matter: Paul's Pastoral Pronouncements Regarding Women's Roles in 1 Timothy 2:9-15," *Faith and Mission* 14 (1997): 24–48; "Ascertaining Women's God-Ordained Roles: An Interpretation of 1 Timothy 2:15," *BBR* 7 (1997): 107–44.

[86]Cf., e.g., Grenz, *Women in the Church* (see my review in *JETS*).

[87]Examples of this are the insistence of complementarian scholars such as W. Grudem and J. Piper that Junia(s) is a man, despite the fact that there is virtually no evidence to support such a claim, or the refusal by certain conservative interpreters to entertain seriously the possibility that Phoebe indeed functioned as a deaconess merely because their preconceived doctrinal commitments preclude such a possibility. On the first issue, cf. Piper and Grudem, "Overview of Central Concerns," in *Recovering Biblical Manhood and Womanhood*, 79–81; and most recently W. Grudem, "Willow Creek enforces egalitarianism," *CBMW News* 2/5 (1997): 5, where the only two pieces of evidence cited are a debatable reference in Origen (see n. 50 above) and a probably unreliable piece of information from Epiphanius (as Grudem himself points out in a damaging concession, Epiphanius also identified the obvious feminine name "Prisca" in Rom 16:3 as a masculine name; p. 479, n. 19). Also, it is methodologically fallacious for Grudem and Piper to rule out completely from consideration relevant evidence from Latin literature as well as inscriptional evidence. This selective appraisal of the evidence is all the more remarkable as Grudem himself appropriately excoriates egalitarian scholars such as C. C. Kroeger for refusing to concede that κεφαλή regularly denotes "head" with the connotation of authority while maintaining, with evidence that evaporates when checked out, that it means "source." See Grudem's devastating

a balanced analysis of both descriptive and didactic passages in Paul, with enough tentativeness in the process to allow for the findings of the analysis of descriptive passages to inform the study of didactic passages and vice versa. Of course, inerrantist interpreters will expect Pauline teaching on women's roles, correctly interpreted, and the way women actually functioned in the Pauline mission and churches to be found in harmony.[88] Thus, if one starts with an investigation of descriptive passages and ends up with the notion that no clear parameters for women's ministry are evident from these texts, one should be prepared to revisit this issue once Paul's didactic passages have been studied, if such parameters emerge from those texts.[89] But in many instances, this dialectic never takes place.[90]

In fact, didactic passages in Paul deserve to be given full weight, even priority, in the matter. For it would be unreasonable for one to expect to be able to glean a full prescriptive pattern for women's roles in ministry

---

critique of Kroeger, "Head," in the *Dictionary of Paul and His Letters* (ed. G. F. Hawthorne, R. P. Martin, D. G. Reid; Downers Grove, IL: InterVarsity, 1997), 375–77, at the Annual Meeting of the Evangelical Theological Society (November 21, 1997) and his article "The meaning source 'does not exist'," *CBMW News* 2/5 (1997): 1,7–8.

[88]Contra France, *Women in the Church's Ministry*, 89, who concludes his survey of women in the Pauline churches with the comment that "[t]his material, together with the evidence we have cited from other Pauline letters and from Acts, is in such striking contrast with the refusal in 1 Timothy 2.11–12 to allow a woman to teach or to have authority, and with the concept of 'submission,' that it raises sharply the hermeneutical question of where within the varied and apparently conflicting testimony of the New Testament it is right to start to construct our biblical understanding of women's ministry." France's solution to this 'dilemma' is to follow F. F. Bruce (*Commentary on Galatians* [NIGTC; Exeter: Paternoster; Grand Rapids: Eerdmans, 1982], 190) in distinguishing between "basic principles" such as Gal 3:28 and "less basic" texts such as 1 Tim 2:11–15 (ibid., 94). But this procedure is not only highly subjective (as France himself admits, ibid.; what criteria?) but also establishes a "canon within a canon" (also conceded by France, ibid.) that accentuates preferred texts while marginalizing (or altogether ignoring) unwelcome texts. For a critique, see the present author's "Gender Passages in the NT," 273–79.

[89]Keener, "Appendix A: Women's Ministry Elsewhere in Paul," in *Paul, Women and Wives*, 237, acknowledges the tension he feels when he writes, "The biggest problem with interpreting 1 Timothy 2:11–15 as excluding women from teaching roles in the church is that Paul clearly commended women for such roles." But Keener is apparently not prepared to take 1 Tim 2:11–15 at face value and revisit the narrative sections of Paul's writings to see whether it was appropriate for him to read these as indicating "that Paul clearly commended women for such roles [of teaching in the church]" in the first place.

[90]Cf. e.g. Witherington, *Women in the Earliest Churches*; Cotter, "Women's Authority Roles."

according to Paul from incidental references alone. Moreover, the possibility remains, at least in theory, that descriptive passages depict women functioning in roles in ways not permitted by Paul. Normativity must therefore be established rather than assumed. For these reasons descriptive references should be used primarily to illustrate and provide background for Paul's specific teaching on women's roles in the church. Indeed, as will be seen below, Paul indicates certain parameters within which women were (and are) to function in the church, and there is nothing in the descriptive portions of Paul's letters that actually conflicts with Paul's explicit teaching on the subject. But further discussion of this has to await the conclusion of this essay. We must first provide a brief synthesis of Pauline teaching on the roles of women in the church.

Discussion of Didactic Passages in Paul Regarding Women
The major thrust of Pauline teaching on women's roles may be characterized as follows. Paul infers from the creation account in Genesis that God has assigned to the man the ultimate responsibility for the family (cf. Eph 5:21–33 in conjunction with 1 Cor 11:3, 7–8).[91] The man's role as "head" is not a function of the fall; the fall merely led to the man's abuse of his God-given authority in relation to his wife.[92] But even in the church age, Paul affirms that the wife is to submit to her husband who in turn is exhorted to love his wife as Christ loved the church (Eph 5:21–33; Col 3:18–19).

The marriage relationship restored in Christ thus does not lead to a completely "egalitarian" relationship. Rather, the creation ideal, which included the man's bearing of ultimate responsibility for the married couple (viz. the term "helper" applied to the woman in Gen 2:18, esp. in relation to the Pauline statements in 1 Cor 11:8–9 and 1 Tim 2:13),[93] is again made possible and freed from the distortions introduced by sin. It is

---

[91]On Eph 5:21–33, esp. v. 32, see my "The Mystery of Christ and the Church: Head and Body, 'One Flesh,' " *Trin*J 12NS (1991): 79–94.

[92]R. C. Ortlund, Jr., "Male-Female Equality and Male Headship," in *Recovering Biblical Manhood and Womanhood* (ed. J. Piper and W. Grudem; Wheaton, IL: Crossway, 1991), 95–112.

[93]I am aware of the discussion surrounding the Hebrew term for "helper" in Gen 2:18, but remain unconvinced that the expression, in context as well as understood by later Christian interpreters such as the apostle Paul, refers to nothing but the woman's equal position to the man without connotations of functional subordination. Cf. esp. Ortlund, "Male-Female Equality and Male Headship"; and Köstenberger, "Gender Passages in the NT," 271, n. 45.

not authority that is sin, but its abuse.[94] And submission does not imply inferiority, since even Christ chose to submit to the Father with whom he is united as equal in the Godhead (1 Cor 11:3).[95] Paul does not claim to be innovative in this regard; he consistently takes his cue from the foundational narrative of humanity in Genesis 1–3.[96]

What does constitute a Pauline innovation, however, is Paul's extension of the biblical teaching regarding marriage to the roles of men and women *in the church*. Since the church is God's "household" (e.g. 1 Tim 3:15), it follows that the church, as a "family of families," functions according to the pattern established for the family and the household in the beginning.[97] And, as argued above, according to this pattern the man has been given ultimate responsibility. Thus as in the family, so in the church, the man bears ultimate responsibility (cf. the qualification of "faithful husband" [not "wife"] for an overseer in 1 Tim 3:2, esp. in conjunction with 1 Tim 2:12).

Conversely, Paul does not permit a woman to teach or have authority over a man (1 Tim 2:12).[98] Why? Because of the man's priority in creation (1 Tim 2:13) and the woman's "priority" at the fall where the creation pattern was reversed (serpent-woman-man-God rather than God-man-woman-serpent; 1 Tim 2:14). Nevertheless, women have a significant role in managing the household, including childrearing and sup-

---

[94]This seems to be missed by Grenz, *Women in the Church*, 216–18, who writes: "[T]he complementarians' more hierarchical understanding of church structure tends to undermine their good intention to maintain a servant focus. It is difficult to see pastors primarily as servants of God's people when ordination appears to endow a privileged few with power and status" (p. 218).

[95]Cf. J. Cottrell, "Christ: a model for headship *and* submission," *CBMW News* 2/4 (1997): 7–8.

[96]See Köstenberger, "Gender Passages in the NT," 267–71.

[97]Cf. V. S. Poythress, "The Church as Family: Why Male Leadership in the Family Requires Male Leadership in the Church," in *Recovering Biblical Manhood and Womanhood*, 233–47.

[98]Witherington, *Women in the Earliest Churches*, 121–22, did not have the benefit of the evidence presented in Köstenberger et al., *Women in the Church*, particularly Köstenberger, "A Complex Sentence Structure in 1 Timothy 2:12." He correctly points out that in a (unique) passage by Chrysostom (ca. CE 390) the crucial word αὐθεντεῖν apparently means "act the despot" or the like; but he fails to consider that the sentence structure of 1 Tim 2:12 requires αὐθεντεῖν to have a positive connotation. Thus Paul is shown not merely to correct a local abuse in the Ephesian church but to set abiding parameters for the ministry of women in the church: they are "not to teach or have authority over a man."

port of their husband (1 Tim 2:15),[99] as well as ministry to other women (Titus 2:3–5), children, and a variety of good works.

Regarding the faith, there is no difference between men and women: women, like men, become believers through faith in Christ (Gal 3:28).[100] As Peter wrote, both are "fellow-heirs" of grace (1 Pet 3:7). But equality in worth and dignity does not mean equality in function or role. This seems to be the clear implication from Paul's teaching on the role of women and men in the church.

It is neither possible nor necessary here to discuss all the instances where issues pertaining to women are addressed in Paul's letters, such as his teaching on caring for widows (1 Tim 5) or singleness (1 Cor 7), or even the puzzling passage on head coverings (1 Cor 11:2–16), since these issues are at best of marginal significance for women's roles in the Pauline mission. We conclude with some pertinent observations tying together our study of descriptive and didactic passages on women in Paul's letters and the book of Acts.

Conclusion

Paul's teaching on the role of women and the way in which women actually functioned in the Pauline churches are consistent.[101] Paul taught that women were not to serve as pastor-teachers or elders, and there is no evidence in Paul's epistles or Acts that women functioned in such roles in the churches established by Paul. Where the principle of the man's bearing of ultimate responsibility for God's household was not jeopardized, Paul allowed women to serve without further limitation. Thus in 1 Tim 3:11, he lays down qualifications for deaconesses, and in Rom 16:1 we learn that Phoebe apparently functioned in such a role.[102] Women also supported the Pauline mission by exercising numerous other ministries.

The pattern of women's roles in the Pauline mission and churches also coheres with that found in the mission of Jesus. Jesus, too, chose only men for his Twelve; but he ministered to women and was supported by women in a variety of ways. Above all, both Jesus and Paul sought to

---

[99]For a recent interpretation of 1 Tim 2:15, see Köstenberger, "Ascertaining Women's God-Ordained Roles."

[100]On the interpretation of Gal 3:28 in the context of recent discussions of women's roles, see my "Gender Passages in the NT," 273–79.

[101]Cf. Moo, *Epistle to the Romans*, 927.

[102]See Schreiner, "Valuable Ministries of Women," 213–14 and 219–20.

integrate women fully in the community of believers, treating them with dignity and appreciation for their contribution. But they did so demonstrably and precisely without removing all parameters for women's ministry.[103] Frequently, this is not so much explicitly argued as assumed, for Jesus' and Paul's contemporaries generally were not likely to challenge a pattern of ministry that assigned ultimate responsibility for the community of believers to men. Men, not women, were generally regarded as heads of households, and elders in Jewish synagogues, to give but one example, were regularly men rather than women.

What are the implications of these observations for the practice of the contemporary church? While this has not been the primary focus of the present essay, I would be remiss if I failed to acknowledge the significance of the findings of this investigation for contemporary church practice. While it is not the purpose of the book of Acts or Paul's letters to legislate for every conceivable circumstance, I do find several principles that have abiding significance for the role of women in the church. Negatively, women are not permitted to serve in positions of ultimate responsibility over the entire church, such as pastor-teacher or elder. Positively, women may serve in roles of hospitality, missionary work, benevolence of various kinds, private teaching in conjunction with their husbands, ministry to younger women, responsibility for raising children together with their husbands, and other significant ministries.

As in Old and New Testament times, what is to determine women's roles is not the dictates of contemporary culture but the designs of God. God's plan is consistent from the time of creation to the age of the church, and from his pattern for the family to that for God's "household." As the present essay has shown, women made a vital contribution to the Pauline mission; they continue to make an important contribution today.

It is not easy to write on a subject that continues to divide the church. May the present essay help to shed light on this important issue. I conclude with a pertinent observation by E. E. Ellis: "Paul and his colleagues are not called 'teacher' or 'leader' although some of them do teach and lead. For they have one teacher, the Messiah, and they are all brothers.

---

[103]See esp. Neuer, *Man and Woman in Biblical Perspective*, 122: "His [Paul's] attitude is in complete agreement with that of Jesus, who in his teaching and actions recognised the differences between men and women. Jesus and Paul agree that creation and redemption do not conflict with each other; rather they constitute an inseparable unity, since both nature and grace are the work of God. For this reason Jesus and Paul do not abrogate the created order of the sexes in the kingdom of God, or the church, but expressly acknowledge it."

Probably in response to their Lord's command, they eschew titles of eminence. With reference to their task they are the workers, the servants, the special messengers, with reference to one another they are the brothers."[104] We would do well to emulate the example of Paul and the early church. For we who are "in Christ" are all brothers and sisters in Christ, and together strive to fulfill the mission entrusted to the church today, seeking to hasten the coming of our Lord whom we will soon see face to face.

---

[104]Ellis, "Paul and His Co-Workers," 451.

BIBLIOGRAPHY

Bibliography on John

Abbott, Edwin A. *Johannine Vocabulary: A Comparison of the Words of the Fourth Gospel with Those of the Three.* London: Adam and Charles Black, 1905.

——. *Johannine Grammar.* London: Adam and Charles Black, 1906.

Aberbach, Moses. "Relations Between Master and Disciple in the Talmudic Age." *Essays presented to Chief Rabbi Israel Brodie on the occasion of his 70th Birthday.* Ed. Hirsh J. Zimmels et al. London: Soncino, 1967, 1-24.

Alexander, P. S. "Rabbinic Judaism and the New Testament." *Zeitschrift für die neutestamentliche Wissenschaft* 74 (1983): 237-46.

Anderson, Gerald, ed. *The Theology of the Christian Mission.* Nashville: Abingdon, 1961.

Arias, Mortimer and Alan Johnson. *The Great Commission. Biblical Models for Evangelism.* Nashville: Abingdon, 1992.

Ashton, John. *Understanding the Fourth Gospel.* Oxford: Clarendon, 1991.

Barr, James. *The Semantics of Biblical Language.* Oxford: Oxford University Press, 1961.

Barrett, C. K. *The Gospel According to St. John.* 2d ed. Philadelphia: Westminster, 1978.

——. "Christocentric or Theocentric? Observations on the Theological Method of the Fourth Gospel." *Essays on John.* Philadelphia: Westminster, 1982, 1-18.

Bauckham, Richard, ed. *The Gospels for All Christians: Rethinking the Gospel Audiences.* Grand Rapids: Eerdmans, 1997.

——. "For Whom Were the Gospels Written?" *The Gospels for All Christians: Rethinking the Gospel Audiences.* Ed. Richard Bauckham. Grand Rapids: Eerdmans, 1997, 9-48.

Baumgarten, Siegmund Jacob. *Auslegung des Evangelii St. Johannis.* Halle, 1762.

Baur, Ferdinand Christian. *Kritische Untersuchungen über die kanonischen Evangelien.* Tübingen, 1847.

Beale, Greg K., ed. *The Right Doctrine from the Wrong Texts? Essays on the Use of the Old Testament in the New.* Grand Rapids: Baker, 1994.

Beasley-Murray, George R. *John.* Word Biblical Commentary 36. Waco, TX: Word, 1987.

Becker, Jürgen. "Wunder und Christologie. Zum literarkritischen und christologischen Problem der Wunder im Johannesevangelium." *New Testament Studies* 16 (1969/70): 130-48.

Bengel, Johannes Albrecht. *Gnomon Novi Testamenti.* 3d ed. Stuttgart: Steinkopf, 1860 [Tübingen, 1742]. ET Edinburgh: T. & T. Clark, 1860.

Bentley, Jerry H. "New Testament Scholarship at Louvain in the Early Sixteenth Century." *Studies in Medieval and Renaissance History* n.s. 2 (1979): 51-79.

——. *Humanists and Holy Writ—New Testament Scholarship in the Renaissance.* Princeton, NJ: Princeton University Press, 1983.

Berger, Klaus. *Die Amen-Worte Jesu. Eine Untersuchung zum Problem der Legitimation in apokalyptischer Rede.* Beihefte zur Zeitschrift für die neutestamentliche Wissenschaft 39. Berlin: W. de Gruyter, 1970.

Betz, Otto. "Das Problem des Wunders bei Flavius Josephus im Vergleich zum Wunderproblem bei den Rabbinen und im Johannesevangelium." *Jesus. Der Messias Israels. Aufsätze zur biblischen Theologie.* Wissenschaftliche Untersuchungen zum Neuen Testament 42. Tübingen: Mohr-Siebeck, 1987, 409-19.

Beyerhaus, Peter. *Shaken Foundations: Theological Foundations for Mission.* Grand Rapids: Zondervan, 1972.

Bittner, Wolfgang J. *Jesu Zeichen im Johannesevangelium. Die Messias-Erkenntnis im Johannesevangelium vor ihrem jüdischen Hintergrund.* Wissenschaftliche Untersuchungen zum Neuen Testament 2/26. Tübingen: Mohr-Siebeck, 1987.

Blank, Josef. *Krisis. Untersuchungen zur johanneischen Christologie und Eschatologie.* Freiburg im Breisgau: Lambertus, 1964.

Blauw, Johannes. *The Missionary Nature of the Church: A Survey of the Biblical Theology of Mission.* Grand Rapids: Eerdmans, 1974 [1962].

Blomberg, Craig L. *The Historical Reliability of the Gospels.* Downers Grove, IL: Inter-Varsity, 1987.

———. "Where Do We Start Studying Jesus?" *Jesus Under Fire.* Ed. Michael J. Wilkins and J. P. Moreland. Grand Rapids: Zondervan, 1995, 17–50.

———. "The Globalization of Biblical Interpretation: A Test Case—John 3–4." *Bulletin of Biblical Research* 5 (1995): 1–15.

Boismard, Marie-Émile. *Moses or Jesus: An Essay in Johannine Christology.* Philadelphia: Fortress, 1993.

Borgen, P. *Bread from Heaven: An Exegetical Study of the Concept of Manna in the Gospel of John and the writings of Philo.* Novum Testamentum Supplements 10. Leiden: E. J. Brill, 1965.

Bosch, David J. *Paradigm Shifts in Theology of Mission.* Maryknoll, NY: Orbis, 1991.

———. "Reflections on Biblical Models of Mission." *Toward the Twenty-first Century in Christian Mission: Essays in Honor of Gerald H. Anderson.* Ed. James M. Phillips and Robert T. Coote. Grand Rapids: Eerdmans, 1993, 175–92.

Braumann, Georg. "Die Schuldner und die Sündnerin. Luk. VII. 36–50." *New Testament Studies* 10 (1963–64): 487–93.

Bretschneider, Karl Gottlieb. *Probabilia de evangelii et epistolarum Joannis, Apostoli, indole et origine eruditorum Judiciis.* Leipzig, 1820.

Brockway, Allan, et al. *The Theology of the Churches and the Jewish People.* StatemeNew Testament Studies by the World Council of Church [sic] and Its Member Churches. Geneva: World Council of Churches, 1988.

Brown, Raymond E. "The Problem of Historicity in John." *New Testament Essays.* Garden City, NY: Doubleday, 1965, 187–217.

———. "Appendix III: Signs and Works." *The Gospel According to John I–XII.* New York: Doubleday, 1966, 525–32.

———. *The Gospel According to John.* Anchor Bible 29–29A. 2 vols. New York: Doubleday, 1966 and 1970.

———. " 'Other Sheep Not of This Fold': The Johannine Perspective on Christian Diversity in the Late First Century." *Journal of Biblical Literature* 97 (1978): 5–22.

———. *The Community of the Beloved Disciple.* New York: Paulist, 1979.

Bruce, F. F. "The History of New Testament Study." *New Testament Interpretation.* Ed. I. H. Marshall. Exeter: Paternoster, 1977.

———. *The Hard Sayings of Jesus.* Downers Grove, IL: InterVarsity, 1983.

Bühner, Jan-Adolph. *Der Gesandte und sein Weg im 4. Evangelium. Die Kultur-und religionsgeschichtliche Entwicklung.* Wissenschaftliche Untersuchungen zum Neuen Testament 2/2. Tübingen: J. C. B. Mohr, Paul Siebeck, 1977.

Bultmann Rudolf. *Das Evangelium des Johannes.* Göttingen: Vandenhoeck & Ruprecht, 1950.

———. *Theology of the New Testament.* Trans. Kendrick Grobel. New York: Charles Scribner's Sons, 1951 and 1955.

———. *The History of the Synoptic Tradition.* Trans. John Marsh. Oxford: Basil Blackwell, 1963.

———. *The Gospel of John*. Trans. George R. Beasley-Murray et al. Oxford: Basil Black-well, 1971.

Burge, Gary M. *The Anointed Community. The Holy Spirit in the Johannine Tradition*. Grand Rapids: Eerdmans, 1987.

Carson, D. A. "The Function of the Paraclete in John 16:7–11." *Journal of Biblical Literature* 98 (1979): 547–66.

———. *The Farewell Discourse and Final Prayer of Jesus*. Grand Rapids: Baker, 1980.

———. *Divine Sovereignty and Human Responsibility. Biblical Perspectives in Tension*. Atlanta: John Knox, 1981.

———. "Historical Tradition in the Fourth Gospel: After Dodd, What?" *Gospel Perspectives II*. Ed. R. T. France and David Wenham. Sheffield: JSOT, 1981, 83–145.

———. "Understanding Misunderstandings in the Fourth Gospel." *Tyndale Bulletin* 33 (1982): 52–89.

———. *Exegetical Fallacies*. Grand Rapids: Baker, 1984.

———. "The Purpose of the Fourth Gospel: Jn 20:31 Reconsidered." *Journal of Biblical Literature* 106 (1987): 639–51.

———. "Church and Mission: Reflections on Contextualization and the Third Horizon." *The Church in the Bible and the World*. Ed. D. A. Carson. Grand Rapids: Baker, 213–57.

———. "John and Johannine Epistles." *It Is Written: Scripture Citing Scripture*. Ed. D. A. Carson and H. G. M. Williamson; Cambridge: Cambridge University Press, 1988, 245–64.

———. *The Gospel According to John*. Grand Rapids: Eerdmans, 1991.

———. "The Purpose of Signs and Wonders in the New Testament." *Power Religion*. Ed. Michael S. Horton. Chicago: Moody, 1992, 89–118.

Charlesworth, James H. *John and the Dead Sea Scrolls*. New York: Crossroad, 1990.

Chillingworth, William. *The Religion of Protestants: a Safe Way to Salvation*. Oxford, 1638.

Chilton, Bruce D. *A Galilean Rabbi and His Bible: Jesus' Use of the Interpreted Scripture of His Time*. Good News Studies 8. Wilmington, DE: Michael Glazier, 1984.

Chubb, Thomas. *The true gospel of Jesus Christ asserted*. London, 1738.

Cludius, Hermann Heimart. *Uransichten des Christenthums nebst Untersuchungen über einige Bücher des neuen Testaments*. Altona, 1808.

Cohen, Shaye J. D. "Epigraphical Rabbis." *JQR* 72 (1982): 1–17.

Collins, Raymond F. *These Things Have Been Written. Studies on the Fourth Gospel*. Grand Rapids: Eerdmans, 1991.

Cotoni, Marie-Helène. *L'exegèse du Nouveau Testament dans la philosophie française du dix-huitième siècle*. Oxford: Voltaire Foundation at the Taylor Institution, 1984.

Cotterell, Peter and Max Turner. *Linguistics and Biblical Interpretation*. Downers Grove, IL: InterVarsity, 1989.

Cribbs, F. Lamar. "St. Luke and the Johannine Tradition." *Journal of Biblical Literature* 90 (1971): 422–50.

———. "A study of the contacts that exist between St Luke and St John." *Society of Biblical Literature Papers 1973*. Vol. 2. Cambridge, MA: Society of Biblical Literature, 1973, 1–93.

Cullmann, Oscar. *Der johanneische Kreis*. Tübingen: Mohr-Siebeck, 1975.

Culpepper, R. Alan. *The Anatomy of the Fourth Gospel*. Philadelphia: Fortress, 1983.

Cyre, Susan. "Fallout Escalates Over 'Goddess' Sophia Worship." *Christianity Today* 38/4 (1994): 74.

Dalman, Gustaf. *Die Worte Jesu mit Berücksichtigung des nachkanonischen jüdischen Schriftums und der aramäischen Sprache* 2d. Leipzig: J. C. Hinrichs, 1930.

Daube, David. "Responsibilities of Master and Disciples in the Gospels." *New Testament Studies* 19 (1972-73): 1-15.

———. *The New Testament and Rabbinic Judaism.* New York: Arno, 1973.

Davids, Peter H. "The Gospels and Jewish Tradition: Twenty Years After Gerhardsson." *Gospel Perspectives I.* Ed. R. T. France and David Wenham. Sheffield: JSOT, 1980, 75-99.

Davies, W. D. "The Johannine 'Signs' of Jesus." *A Companion to John: Readings in Johannine Theology.* Ed. Michael J. Taylor. New York: Alba, 1977, 91-115.

———. *The Gospel and the Land: Early Christian and Jewish Territorial Doctrine.* Sheffield: JSOT, 1994.

———. "Reflections on Aspects of the Jewish Background of the Gospel of John." *Exploring the Gospel of John. In Honor of D. Moody Smith.* Ed. R. Alan Culpepper and Clifton C. Black. Louisville, KY: Westminster/John Knox, 1996, 43-64.

Dietzfelbinger, Christian. "Die größeren Werke (Joh 14.12f)." *New Testament Studies* 35 (1989): 27-47.

Dodd, C. H. "Jesus als Lehrer und Prophet." *Mysterium Christi: Christological Studies by British and German Theologians.* Ed. G. K. A. Bell and Adolf Deissmann. London: Longmans & Green, 1930, 67-86.

———. *The Interpretation of the Fourth Gospel.* Cambridge: Cambridge University Press, 1953.

———. *Historical Tradition in the Fourth Gospel.* Cambridge: Cambridge University Press, 1963.

Donaldson, J. "The Title Rabbi in the Gospels—Some Reflections on the Evidence of the Synoptics." *Jewish Quarterly Review* 63 (1972-73): 287-91.

Drexler, Hans. "Die große Sündnerin: Lucas 7:36-50." *Zeitschrift für die neutestamentliche Wissenschaft* 59 (1968): 159-73.

DuBose, Francis M. *God Who Sends.* Nashville: Broadman, 1983.

Dunn, James D. G. "John and the Oral Gospel Tradition." *Jesus and the Oral Gospel Tradition.* Ed. H. Wansbrough. Journal for the Study of the New Testament Supplement Series 64. Sheffield: JSOT, 1991, 351-79.

Eckermann, Johann Christoph Rudolf. "Ueber die eigentlich sichern Gründe des Glaubens an die Haupthatsachen der Geschichte Jesu, und über die wahrscheinliche Entstehung der Evangelien und der Apostelgeschichte." *Theologische Beyträge.* Vol. V. Pt. 2. Altona, 1796, 106-256.

———. *Erklärung aller dunkeln Stellen des Neuen TestameNew Testament Studies.* Vol. II. Kiel, 1807.

Eichhorn, Johann Gottfried. *Die Einleitung in das Neue Testament.* Leipzig: Weidmannsche Buchhandlung, 1810.

Eisenman, Robert and Michael Wise. *The Dead Sea Scrolls Uncovered.* New York: Penguin, 1992.

Evans, C. A. "Obduracy and the Lord's Servant: Some Observations on the Use of the Old Testament in the Fourth Gospel." *Early Jewish and Christian Exegesis: Studies in Memory of William Hugh Brownlee.* Ed. Craig A. Evans and William F. Stinespring, Atlanta: Scholars Press, 1987, 221-36.

———. *Word and Glory: On the Exegetical and Theological Background of John's Prologue.* Journal for the Study of the New Testament Supplement Series 89. Sheffield: JSOT, 1993.

Evans, C. Stephen. *The Historical Christ and the Jesus of Faith: The Incarnational Narrative as History.* Oxford: Clarendon, 1996.

Evanson, Edward. *The Dissonance of the Four generally received Evangelists and the Evidence of their Authenticity examined.* Ipswich, 1792. 2d ed. Gloucester, 1805.

Fanning, Buist M. *Verbal Aspect in New Testament Greek.* Oxford Theological Monographs. Oxford: Clarendon, 1990.

Fascher, Erich. "Jesus der Lehrer." *Theologische Literaturzeitung* 79 (1954): 325-42.

Fee, Gordon D. "On the Text and Meaning of John 20.30-31." *The Four Gospels 1992. Festschrift Frans Neirynck.* Bibliotheca ephemeridum theologicarum lovaniensium C. Ed. F. van Segbroeck, C. M. Tuckett, G. van Belle, J. Verheyden. Leuven: University Press, 1992, 2193-2205.

Forestell, J. Terence. *The Word of the Cross. Salvation as Revelation in the Fourth Gospel.* Analecta biblica 57. Rome: Pontifical Biblical Institute, 1974.

Fortna, Robert T. *The Gospel of Signs: A Reconstruction of the Narrative Source Underlying the Fourth Gospel.* Study for the New Testament Monograph Series 11. Cambridge: Cambridge University Press, 1970.

France, R. T. *Jesus and the Old Testament.* London: Tyndale, 1971.

———. "Mark and the Teaching of Jesus." *Gospel Perspectives I.* Ed. R. T. France and David Wenham. Sheffield: JSOT, 1980, 101-36.

Freed, Edwin D. "Variations in the Language and Thought of John." *Zeitschrift für die neutestamentliche Wissenschaft* 55 (1964): 167-97.

Friend, Helen S. "Like Father, Like Son: A Discussion of the Concept of Agency in Halakah and John." *Ashland Theological Journal* 21 (1990): 18-28.

Gerhardsson, B. *Memory and Manuscript: Oral Tradition and Written Transmission in Rabbinic Judaism and Early Christianity.* Uppsala: C. W. K. Gleerup, 1961.

Glasser, Arthur. "Evangelical Missions." *Toward the Twenty-first Century in Christian Mission: Essays in Honor of Gerald H. Anderson.* Ed. James M. Phillips and Robert T. Coote. Grand Rapids: Eerdmans, 1993, 9-20.

Grässer, Erich. *Der Alte Bund im Neuen: Exegetische Studien zur Israelfrage im Neuen Testament.* Wissenschaftliche Untersuchungen zum Neuen Testament 35. Tübingen: Mohr-Siebeck, 1985.

Greenslade, S. L., ed. *Cambridge History of the Bible—The West from the Reformation to the Present Day.* Vol. III. Cambridge: Cambridge University Press, 1983 [1963].

Grigsby, Bruce H. "The Cross as an Expiatory Sacrifice in the Fourth Gospel." *Journal for the Study of the New Testament* 15 (1982): 51-80.

Guthrie, Donald. "The Importance of Signs in the Fourth Gospel." *Vox Evangelica* V (1967): 72-83.

Hahn, Ferdinand. *Christologische Hoheitstitel.* Forschungen zur Religion und Literatur des Alten und Neuen Testaments 83. Göttingen: Vandenhoeck & Ruprecht, 1963.

———. *Mission in the New Testament.* Studies in Biblical Theology 47. London: SCM, 1965.

Harvey, Anthony E. "Christ as Agent." *The Glory of the Christ in the New Testament. Studies in Christology in Memory of George Bradford Caird.* Ed. L. D. Hurst and N. T. Wright. Oxford: Clarendon, 1987, 239-50.

Hasler, Victor. *Amen: Redaktionsgeschichtliche Untersuchung zur Einführungsformel der Herrenworte "Wahrlich, ich sage euch."* Zurich/Stuttgart: Gotthelf, 1969.

Hengel, M. *The Charismatic Teacher and his Followers.* Edinburgh: T. & T. Clark, 1981.

———. *The Johannine Question.* Trans. John Bowden. London: SCM, 1989.

———. *Die johanneische Frage: Ein Lösungsversuch.* Wissenschaftliche Untersuchungen zum Neuen Testament 67. Tübingen: Mohr-Siebeck, 1993.

———. "The Old Testament in the Fourth Gospel." *The Gospels and the Scriptures of Israel.* Ed. Craig A. Evans and William R. Stegner. Journal for the Study of New Testament Supplement Series 104. Sheffield: Sheffield Academic Press, 1994, 380-95.

Herder, Johann Gottfried. *Briefe das Studium der Theologie betreffend.* 1st ed. 1780-81; 2d ed. 1785-86.

———. *Herder's Collected Works.* Ed. B. Suphan. Vol. XIX. Berlin: Weidmannsche Buchhandlung, 1880 [1796-97].

Hesselgrave, David J. *Today's Choices for Tomorrow's Mission.* Grand Rapids: Zondervan, 1988.

———. "Holes in 'Holistic Mission.' " *Trinity World Forum* 15/3 (1990): 1-5.

———. "To John Stott—A Surrejoinder." *Trinity World Forum* 16/3 (1991): 3-4.

———. "The 1993 Parliament of the World's Religions—Our Response to Invitations to Participate." *Trinity World Forum* 18/2 (1993): 1-5.

Hilgenfeld, Adolf. "Die Evangelienforschung nach ihrem Verlauf und gegenwärtigen Stand." *Zeitschrift für wissenschaftliche Theologie* 4 (1861): 1ff, 137ff.

Hornig, Gottfried. *Die Anfänge der historisch-kritischen Theologie: Johann Salomo Semlers Schriftverständnis und seine Stellung zu Luther.* Göttingen: Vandenhoeck & Ruprecht, 1961.

Horst, Georg Konrad. "Über einige Widersprüche in dem Evangelium des Johannis in Absicht auf den Logos, oder das Höhere in Christo" and "Lässt sich die Echtheit des johanneischen Evangeliums aus hinlänglichen Gründen bezweifeln, und welches ist der wahrscheinliche Ursprung dieser Schrift?" *Museum für Religionswissenschaft in ihrem ganzen Umfange.* Ed. H. Ph. K. Henke. Vol. I. Magdeburg, 1804.

Ibuki, Yu. "Die Doxa des Gesandten—Studie zur johanneischen Christologie." *Annual of the Japanese Biblical Institute* XIV. Ed. Masao Sekine and Akira Satake. Tokyo: Yamamoto Shoten, 1988, 38-81.

Jonge, Marinus de. "Signs and Works in the Fourth Gospel." *Miscellanea neotestamentica* 2. Ed. T. Baarda, A. F. J. Klijn and W. C. Van Unnik. Novum Testamentum Supplements 48. Leiden: Brill, 1978, 107-25.

Kane, J. Herbert. *Christian Missions in Biblical Perspective.* Grand Rapids: Baker, 1976.

Käsemann, Ernst. *The Testament of Jesus: A Study of the Gospel of John in the Light of Chapter 17.* Trans. Gerhard Krodel. Philadelphia: Fortress, 1968.

Kiley, Mark. "The Exegesis of God: Jesus' Signs in John 1-11." *Society of Biblical Literature Seminar Papers* 27. Atlanta: Scholars Press, 1988, 555-69.

Kilgallen, John J. "John the Baptist, the Sinful Woman, and the Pharisee." *Journal of Biblical Literature* 104 (1985): 675-79.

Köstenberger, Andreas. "The Missions of Jesus and of the Disciples According to the Fourth Gospel. With Implications for the Fourth Gospel's Purpose and the Mission of the Contemporary Church." Deerfield, IL, 1993.

———. "The Two Johannine Words for Sending: A Study of John's Use of Words with Reference to General Linguistic Theory." Paper presented at the Annual Meeting of the Society of Biblical Literature. Chicago, November 1994.

———. "The Seventh Johannine Sign: A Study in John's Christology." *Bulletin of Biblical Research* 5 (1995): 87-103.

———. "The Challenge of a Systematized Biblical Theology of Mission: Missiological Insights from the Gospel of John." *Missiology* 23 (1995): 445-64.

———. "The 'Greater Works' of the Believer According to John 14:12." *Didaskalia* 6 (1995): 36-45.

———. "Frühe Zweifel an der johanneischen Verfasserschaft des vierten Evangeliums in der modernen Interpretationsgeschichte." *European Journal of Theology* 5 (1996): 37-46.

———. *The Missions of Jesus and the Disciples According to the Fourth Gospel.* Grand Rapids: Eerdmans, 1998.

———. "The Seventh Johannine Sign: A Study in John's Christology." *Bulletin of Biblical Research* 5 (1995): 87-103.

Kraft, Charles H. *Communication Theory for Christian Witness.* Rev. ed. Maryknoll, NY: Orbis, 1991.

Kuhl, Josef. *Die Sendung Jesu und der Kirche nach dem Johannes-Evangelium.* St. Augustin: Steyler, 1967.

Kümmel, Werner Georg. " 'Einleitung in das Neue Testament' als theologische Aufgabe." *Evangelische Theologie* 19 (1959): 4-16.

——. *The New Testament: The History of the Investigation of its Problems.* Trans. S. McLean Gilmour and Howard C. Kee. Nashville: Abingdon, 1972.

Lacomara, A. "Deuteronomy and the Farewell Discourse (Jn 13:31-16:33)." *Catholic Biblical Quarterly* 36 (1974): 65-84.

Lange, Samuel Gottlieb. *Die Schriften Johannis des vertrauten Schülers Jesu.* Vol. II. Weimar, n.d.

Leistner, Reinhold. *Antijudaismus im Johannesevangelium? Darstellung des Problems in der neueren Auslegungsgeschichte und Untersuchung der Leidensgeschichte.* Bern: Herbert Lang, 1974.

Lemcio, Eugene E. *The Past of Jesus in the Gospels.* Society for New Testament Studies Monograph Series 68. Cambridge: Cambridge University Press, 1991.

Lemmer, R. "A Possible Understanding by the Implied Reader, of some of the *coming-going-being sent* Pronouncements, in the Johannine Farewell Discourses." *Neotestamentica* 25 (1991): 289-310.

Levinsohn, Stephen H. *Discourse Features of New Testament Greek.* Dallas, TX: Summer Institute of Linguistics, 1992.

Lindars, Barnabas. "Part III: The New Testament." *The Study and Use of the Bible.* John Rogerson, Christopher Rowland, and Barnabas Lindars. Grand Rapids: Eerdmans, 1988, 229-397.

Loader, William. *The Christology of the Fourth Gospel.* Beiträge zur biblischen Exegese und Theologie 23. Frankfurt am Main: Peter Lang, 1992.

Lohse, Eduard. "Miracles in the Fourth Gospel." *What about the New Testament? In Honor of Christopher Evans.* Ed. Morna D. Hooker and Colin J. A. Hickling. London: SCM, 1975, 64-75.

——. "ῥαββί, ῥαββουνί," *Theological Dictionary of the New Testament* VI: 961-65.

Louw, J. P. "On Johannine Style." *Neotestamentica* 20 (1986): 5-12.

Louw, Johannes P. and Eugene A. Nida. *Greek-English Lexicon of the New Testament based on Semantic Domains.* 2 vols. 2d ed. New York: United Bible Societies, 1988 and 1989.

Luthardt, Christoph Ernst. *St. John the Author of the Fourth Gospel.* Edinburgh: T. & T. Clark, 1875.

——. *St. John's Gospel.* Edinburgh: T. & T. Clark, 1878.

Maccini, R. G. *Her Testimony is True: Women as Witnesses according to John.* Journal for the Study of the New Testament Supplement Series 125. Sheffield: Sheffield Academic Press, 1996.

Malatesta, Edward. *Interiority and Covenant. A Study of εἶναι ἐν and μένειν ἐν in the First Letter of Saint John.* Analecta biblica 69. Rome: Biblical Institute Press, 1978.

Martyn, J. Louis. "Glimpses into the History of the Johannine Community." *L'Évangile de Jean: Sources, rédaction, théologie.* Ed. Marinus de Jonge. Louvain: University Press, 149-75.

——. *History and Theology in the Fourth Gospel.* Rev. ed. Nashville: Abingdon, 1979.

McElhanon, Kenneth. "Don't Give Up on the Incarnational Model." *Evangelical Missions Quarterly* 27 (1991): 390-93.

McPolin, James. "Mission in the Fourth Gospel." *Irish Theological Quarterly* 36 (1969): 113-22.

Meeks, W. A. *The Prophet-King: Moses Traditions and the Johannine Christology.* Studien zum Neuen Testament 14. Leiden: E. J. Brill, 1967.

Meier, John P. *A Marginal Jew.* 2 vols. New York: Doubleday, 1991 and 1994.
Mercer, Calvin. "Ἀποστέλλειν and Πέμπειν in John." *New Testament Studies* 36 (1990): 619-24.
Meye, R. P. *Jesus and the Twelve.* Grand Rapids: Eerdmans, 1968.
Michaelis, Johann David. *Syntagma Commentationum.* Göttingen, 1759-67.
——. *Anmerkungen zum Evangelio Johannis: Anmerkungen für Ungelehrte zu seiner Uebersetzung des Neuen Testaments.* Vol. II. Göttingen, 1790.
Miranda, Juan Peter. *Der Vater der mich gesandt hat: Religionsgeschichtliche Untersuchungen zu den johanneischen Sendungsformeln: Zugleich ein Beitrag zur johanneischen Christologie und Ekklesiologie.* Europäische Hochschulschriften 23/7. Frankfurt am Main: Peter Lang, 1976 [1972].
——. *Die Sendung Jesu im vierten Evangelium: Religions- und theologiegeschichtliche Untersuchungen zu den Sendungsformeln.* Stuttgarter Bibelstudien 87. Stuttgart: Katholisches Bibelwerk, 1977.
Moore, G. F. *Judaism in the First Centuries of the Christian Era.* Vol. III. Cambridge, MA: Harvard University Press, 1962.
Morris, Leon. *Studies in the Fourth Gospel.* Grand Rapids: Eerdmans, 1969.
——. "History and Theology in the Fourth Gospel." *Studies in the Fourth Gospel.* Grand Rapids: Eerdmans, 1969, 65-138.
——. *Jesus is the Christ. Studies in the Theology of John.* Grand Rapids: Eerdmans, 1989.
Moulton, James Hope. *A Grammar of New Testament Greek.* Edinburgh: T & T Clark, 1976.
Neill, Stephen C. and Tom Wright. *The Interpretation of the New Testament 1861-1986.* 2d ed. Oxford/New York: Oxford University Press, 1988.
Nereparampil, Lucius. *Destroy this Temple. An Exegetico-Theological Study on the Meaning of Jesus' Temple-Logion in Jn 2:19.* Bangalore: Dharmaram Publications, 1978.
Neusner, Jacob. "A Life of Rabbi Tarfon ca. 50-120 CE." *Judaica* 17 (1961): 141-67.
——. *The Rabbinic Traditions about the Pharisees before 70.* 3 vols. Leiden: E. J. Brill, 1971.
——. *Rabbinic Literature and the New Testament: What We Cannot Show, We Do Not Know.* Valley Forge, PA: Trinity Press International, 1994.
Nicholson, Godfrey Carruthers. *Death as Departure. The Johannine Descent-Ascent Schema.* Society of Biblical Literature Dissertation Series 63. Chico, CA: Scholars Press, 1983.
Nicol, Willem. *The Semeia in the Fourth Gospel. Tradition and Redaction.* Novum Testamentum Supplements 32. Leiden: Brill, 1972.
Okure, Teresa. *The Johannine Approach to Mission.* Wissenschaftliche Untersuchungen zum Neuen Testament 2/31. Tübingen: Mohr-Siebeck, 1988.
Onuki, Takashi. *Gemeinde und Welt im Johannesevangelium: Ein Beitrag zur Frage nach der theologischen und pragmatischen Funktion des johanneischen "Dualismus."* Wissenschaftliche Monographien zum Alten und Neuen Testament 56. Neukirchen-Vluyn: Neukirchener, 1984.
Osborne, Grant R. "Redactional Trajectories in the Crucifixion Narrative." *Evangelical Quarterly* 51 (1979): 80-96.
——. *The Hermeneutical Spiral: A Comprehensive Introduction to Biblical Interpretation.* Downers Grove, IL: InterVarsity, 1991.
Parker, Pierson. "Luke and the Fourth Evangelist." *New Testament Studies* 9 (1962): 317-36.
Piper, John. *Let the Nations Be Glad! The Supremacy of God in Missions.* Grand Rapids: Baker, 1993.

Popkes, Wiard. "Zum Verständnis der Mission bei Johannes." *Zeitschrift für Mission* 4 (1978): 63-69.

Porter, Stanley E. *Verbal Aspect in the Greek of the New Testament, with Reference to Tense and Mood.* New York: Peter Lang, 1989.

———. *Idioms of the Greek New Testament.* Sheffield: JSOT, 1992.

Pryor, John W. *John: Evangelist of the Covenant People: The Narrative and Themes of the Fourth Gospel.* Downers Grove, IL: InterVarsity, 1992.

Radermakers, Jean. "Mission et Apostolat dans l'Évangile Johannique." *Studia Evangelica* II/1. Texte und Untersuchungen 87. Ed. Frank L. Cross. Berlin: Akademie, 1959.

Reim, Günter. *Studien zum alttestamentlichen Hintergrund des Johannesevangeliums.* Society for New Testament Studies Monograph Series 22. Cambridge: Cambridge University Press, 1974.

———. "Targum und Johannesevangelium." *Biblische Zeitschrift* 27 (1983): 1-13.

Reimarus, Hermann Samuel. *The Goal of Jesus and his Disciples.* Ed. George Wesley Buchanan. Leiden: E. J. Brill, 1970.

Rengstorf, Karl-Heinz. "σημεῖον, et al." *Theological Dictionary of the New Testament* 7:200-269.

———. "ἀποστέλλω, et al." *Theological Dictionary of the New Testament* 1:398-446.

———. "μανθάνω, et al." *Theological Dictionary of the New Testament* 4:390-461.

Rensberger, David. *Overcoming the World: Politics and Community in the Gospel of John.* London: SPCK, 1988.

Reventlow, Henning Graf. *The Authority of the Bible and the Rise of the Modern World.* Trans. John Bowden. Philadelphia: Fortress, 1984.

Ridderbos, Herman N. *The Gospel of John.* Grand Rapids: Eerdmans, 1997.

Riedl, Johannes. *Das Heilswerk Jesu nach Johannes.* Freiburger Theologische Studien 93. Freiburg im Breisgau: Herder, 1973.

Riesenfeld, Harald. *The Gospel Tradition and its Beginnings. A Study in the Limits of "Formgeschichte."* London: Mowbray, 1957.

Riesner R. "Der Ursprung der Jesus-Überlieferung." *Theologische Zeitschrift* 38 (1982): 493-513.

———. *Jesus als Lehrer.* Wissenschaftliche Untersuchungen zum Neuen Testament 2/7. 3d ed. Tübingen: J. C. B. Mohr, Paul Siebeck, 1988.

———. "Jesus as Preacher and Teacher." *Jesus and the Oral Gospel Tradition.* Journal for the Study of the New Testament Supplement Series 64. Ed. Henry Wansborough. Sheffield: JSOT, 1991, 185-210.

Riga, P. "Signs of Glory: The Use of Semeion in John's Gospel." *Interpretation* 17 (1963): 402-10.

Robinson, John A. T. "The Destination and Purpose of St. John's Gospel." *New Testament Studies* 6 (1959/60): 127-31.

———. "The New Look on the Fourth Gospel." *Twelve New Testament Studies.* Studies in Biblical Theology 34. London: SCM, 1962, 94-106.

Rommen, Edward. "Missiology's Place in the Academy." *Trinity World Forum* 17/3 (1992): 1-4.

———. "The De-Theologizing of Missiology." *Trinity World Forum* 19/1 (1993): 1-4.

Ruether, Rosemary Radford. *Faith and Fratricide: The Theological Roots of Anti-Semitism.* New York: Seabury, 1974.

Sanders, E. P. *Jesus & Judaism.* London: SCM, 1985.

Sanders, J. N. *A Commentary on the Gospel According to St. John.* London: Adam & Charles Black, 1968.

Sandmel, Samuel. *We Jews and Jesus.* Oxford: Oxford University Press, 1965.

Schlatter, A. *Die Sprache und Heimat des vierten Evangelisten.* Beiträge zur Förderung christlicher Theologie 6. Gütersloh: C. Bertelsmann, 1902.

——. *Der Evangelist Johannes.* Stuttgart: Calwer, 1930.

——. *The History of the Christ.* Trans. Andreas J. Köstenberger. Grand Rapids: Baker, 1997.

——. *The Theology of the Apostles.* Trans. Andreas J. Köstenberger. Grand Rapids: Baker, 1999.

Schmidt, Daryl D. "Review of Porter, *Verbal Aspect,* and Fanning, *Verbal Aspect.*" *Journal of Biblical Literature* 111 (1992): 417–18.

Schmidt, Johann Ernst Christian. "Versuch über Entstehung der Katholischen Kirche." *Bibliothek für Kritik und Exegese.* Herborn & Hadamar, 1798, 1–35.

——. *Kritische Geschichte der neutestamentlichen Schriften.* Giessen, 1804–1805.

Schnackenburg, Rudolf. "Das Brot des Lebens (Joh 6)." *Das Johannesevangelium IV. Teil: Ergänzende Auslegungen und Exkurse.* Herders theologischer Kommentar zum Neuen Testament. Freiburg/Basel/Wien: Herder, 1984, 119–31.

——. "Der Missionsgedanke des Johannesevangeliums im heutigen Horizont." *Das Johannesevangelium. IV. Teil. Ergänzende Auslegungen und Exkurse.* Herders theologischer Kommentar zum Neuen Testament. Freiburg: Herder, 1984, 58–72.

——. *The Gospel According to St. John.* 3 vols. New York: Crossroad, 1990 [1965].

——. *Jesus in the Gospels.* Louisville, KY: Westminster/John Knox, 1995.

Schnelle, Udo. *Antidocetic Christology in the Gospel of John. An Investigation of the Place of the Fourth Gospel in the Johannine School.* Minneapolis: Fortress, 1992.

Schoeps, H. J. *Paul. The Theology of the Apostle in the Light of Jewish Religious History.* Trans. Harold Knight. Philadelphia: Westminster, 1961 [1959].

Schulz, Anselm. *Nachfolgen und Nachahmen. Studien über das Verhältnis der neutestamentlichen Jüngerschaft zur urchristlichen Vorbildethik.* Studien zum Alten und Neuen Testament VI. München: Kösel, 1962.

Schürer, E. *The History of the Jewish People in the Age of Jesus Christ.* Vol. II. Ed. G. Vermes, F. Millar, and M. Black. Edinburgh: T. & T. Clark, 1979.

Schweitzer, Albert. *The Quest of the Historical Jesus—A Critical Study of Its Progress from Reimarus to Wrede.* Trans. W. Montgomery. New York: Macmillan, 1968 [1906].

Segovia, F. F. *"What is John?" Readers and Readings of the Fourth Gospel.* Society of Biblical Literature Symposium Series 3. Atlanta: Scholars Press, 1996.

Semler, Johann Salomo. *Paraphrasis Evangelii Johannis.* Halle, 1771.

Senior, Donald and Carroll Stuhlmueller. *The Biblical Foundations for Mission.* Maryknoll, NY: Orbis, 1983.

Seynaeve, Jaak. "Les verbes ἀποστέλλω et πέμπω dans le vocabulaire théologique de Saint Jean." *L'Évangile de Jean. Sources, Rédaction, Théologie.* Bibliotheca ephemeridum theologicarum lovaniensium XLIV. Ed. Marinus de Jonge. Leuven: Gembleux, 1977, 385–89.

Shanks, Hershel. "Is the Title 'Rabbi' Anachronistic in the Gospels?" *Jewish Quarterly Review* 53 (1963): 337–45.

Sider, Robert D., ed. *Collected Works of Erasmus.* Vol. 46. Trans. Jane E. Phillips. Toronto/London: University of Toronto Press, 1991.

Silberman, L. H. "Anent the Use of Rabbinic Material." *New Testament Studies* 24 (1978): 415–17.

——. "Once Again: The Use of Rabbinic Material." *New Testament Studies* 42 (1996): 153–55.

Silva, M. *Biblical Words and their Meaning. An Introduction to Lexical Semantics.* Grand Rapids: Zondervan, 1983.

——. "Historical Reconstruction in New Testament Criticism." *Hermeneutics, Authority, and Canon.* Ed. D. A. Carson and J. D. Woodbridge. Grand Rapids: Zondervan, 1986, 112–21.

——. *God, Language and Scripture. Reading the Bible in the light of general linguistics.* Grand Rapids: Zondervan, 1990.

——. "Review of Porter, *Verbal Aspect*, and Fanning, *Verbal Aspect*." *Westminster Theological Journal* 54 (1992): 179-83.

Simon, Richard. *Nouvelles Observations sur le Texte et les Versions du Nouveau Testament.* Paris, 1695.

Smalley, Stephen S. "The Sign in John XXI." *New Testament Studies* 20 (1974): 275-88.

——. *John: Evangelist and Interpreter. History and Interpretation in the Fourth Gospel.* Greenwood, S C: Attic, 1978.

Smith, D. Moody. *Johannine Christianity.* Columbia, SC: University of South Carolina, 1984.

Smith, Robert Houston. "Exodus Typology in the Fourth Gospel." *Journal of Biblical Literature* 81 (1962): 329-42.

Solages, de, B. *Jean et les Synoptiques.* Leiden: E. J. Brill, 1979.

Spinoza, Baruch. *Tractatus Theologico-Politicus.* New York: Dover, 1951.

Stäudlin, Carl Friedrich. "Bemerkungen über den Ursprung der vier Evangelien und der Apostelgeschichte in Beziehung auf die Untersuchungen des Herrn Doctors Eckermann, in seinen theologischen Beiträgen." *Beiträge zur Philosophie und Geschichte der Religion und Sittenlehre.* Vol. V. Pt. 2. Lübeck, 1799.

Stein, Carl Wilhelm. *Authentia Evangelii Johannis, contra S. V. Bretschneideri dubia vindicata.* Brandenburg: J. J. Wiesike, 1822.

Stolz, Fritz. "Zeichen und Wunder. Die prophetische Legitimation und ihre Geschichte." *Zeitschrift für Theologie und Kirche* 69 (1972): 125-44.

Storr, Gottlob Christian. *Ueber den Zweck der evangelischen Geschichte und der Brief Johannis.* Tübingen, 1786.

Stott, John R. W. *Christian Mission in the Modern World.* London: Church Pastoral Aid Society, 1975.

——. "An Open Letter to David Hesselgrave." *Trinity World Forum* 16/3 (1991): 1-2.

——. *The Contemporary Christian: Applying God's Word to Today's World.* Downers Grove, IL: InterVarsity, 1992.

Strack, Hermann L. and Günter Stemberger. *Introduction to the Talmud and Midrash.* Minneapolis: Fortress, 1992.

Strauss, David Friedrich. *The Life of Jesus Critically Examined.* London: SCM, 1973 [1840].

——. *The Christ of Faith and the Jesus of History—A Critique of Schleiermacher's* The Life of Jesus. Ed. Leander E. Keck. Philadelphia, 1977.

Sullivan, Barry. "Ego Te Absolvo: The Forgiveness of Sins in the Context of the Pneumatic Community." Th. M. thesis. Grand Rapids Theological Seminary, 1988.

Teeple, Howard M. *The Literary Origins of the Gospel of John.* Evanston: Religion and Ethics Institute, 1974.

Telford, W. R. "Major Trends and Interpretive Issues in the Study of Jesus." *Studying the Historical Jesus. Evaluations of the State of Current Research.* Ed. Bruce D. Chilton and Craig A. Evans. Leiden: E. J. Brill, 1994, 33-74.

Thiselton, Anthony C. "Semantics and New Testament Interpretation." *New Testament Interpretation.* Ed. I. Howard Marshall. Exeter: Paternoster, 1977, 75-104.

Thomas, J. C. "The Fourth Gospel and Rabbinic Judaism." *Zeitschrift für die neutestamentliche Wissenschaft* 82 (1991): 159-82.

Thompson, Marianne Meye. *The Humanity of Jesus in the Fourth Gospel.* Philadelphia: Fortress, 1988.

——. "Signs, Seeing, and Faith." *The Humanity of Jesus in the Fourth Gospel.* Philadelphia: Fortress, 1988, 53-86.

——. "Signs and Faith in the Fourth Gospel." *Bulletin of Biblical Research* 1 (1991): 89-108.

——. "The Historical Jesus and the Johannine Christ." *Exploring the Gospel of John. In Honor of D. Moody Smith.* Ed. R. Alan Culpepper and Clifton C. Black. Louisville, KY: Westminster/John Knox, 1996, 21-42.

Thüsing, Wilhelm. *Die Erhöhung und Verherrlichung Jesu im Johannesevangelium.* Neutestamentliche Abhandlungen 21. Münster: W. Aschendorff, 1979.

Trotter, Andrew H. "Justification in the Gospel of John." *Right with God: Justification in the Bible and the world.* Ed. D. A. Carson. Grand Rapids: Baker, 1992, 126-45.

Turner, Max. "Atonement and the Death of Jesus in John: Some Questions to Bultmann and Forestell." *Evangelical Quarterly* 62 (1990): 99-122.

Turner, Nigel. *Vol. IV: Style.* In *A Grammar of New Testament Greek.* Ed. James Hope Moulton. Edinburgh: T & T Clark, 1976.

van Unnik, W. C. "The Purpose of St. John's Gospel." *Studia Evangelica I.* Texte und Untersuchungen 73. Ed. Kurt Aland et al. Berlin: Akademie, 1959, 382-411.

Vermes, Geza. *Jesus the Jew.* New York: Macmillan, 1973.

Vogel, Erhard Friedrich. *Der Evangelist Johannes und seine Ausleger von dem jüngsten Gericht.* 2 vols. 1801-1804.

von Wahlde, Urban C. "The Johannine 'Jews': A Critical Survey." *New Testament Studies* 28 (1982): 33-60.

Wegscheider. *Versuch einer vollständigen Einleitung in das Evangelium des Johannes.* Göttingen, 1806.

Wells, David. "The D-Min-Ization of the Ministry." *No God but God: Breaking with the Idols of Our Age.* Ed. Os Guinness and John Seel. Chicago: Moody, 1992, 175-88.

Wells, Edw. *An Help For the more Easy and Clear Understanding of the Holy Scriptures: Being the Gospel of John.* London, 1719.

Wenham, David. "The enigma of the Fourth Gospel: another look." *Tyndale Bulletin* 48 (1997): 149-78.

Whiston, William. *Primitive Christianity Reviv'd.* Vol. III. London, 1711.

Wilkens, Wilhelm. *Zeichen und Werke. Ein Beitrag zur Theologie des 4. Evangeliums in Erzählungs- und Redestoff.* ATANT 55. Zurich: Zwingli, 1969.

Woodbridge, John D. "Richard Simon, le père de la critique biblique." *Le Grand Siècle et la Bible.* Bible de tous les temps 6. Trans. Jean-Robert Armogathe. Paris: Beauchesne, 1989, 193-206.

——. "German Reactions to Richard Simon." *Historische Kritik und biblischer Kanon in der deutschen Aufklärung.* Wolfenbütteler Forschungen 41. Ed. Henning Graf Reventlow, Walter Sparn, and John Woodbridge. Wiesbaden: Harrassowitz, 1988, 65-87.

Yarbrough, Robert W. "Divine Election in the Gospel of John." *The Grace of God, the Bondage of the Will.* Vol. 1. Ed. Thomas R. Schreiner and Bruce A. Ware. Grand Rapids: Baker, 1995, 47-62.

Zipperer, John. "The Elusive Quest for Religious Harmony." *Christianity Today* 37/11 (1993): 42-44.

Bibliography on Gender

Achtemeier, Elizabeth. "Why God is Not Mother." *Christianity Today* 37/9 (1993): 16-23.

Arichea, D. C., Jr. "Who Was Phoebe? Translating *Diakonos* in Romans 16.1." *BT* 39 (1988): 401-409.

Baldwin, Henry Scott. "New Evidence Concerning the Use of 'Αυθεντέω in 1 Timothy 2:12." Paper presented at the 1992 Annual Meeting of the Evangelical Theological Society.

——. "A Difficult Word: 'αυθεντέω in 1 Timothy 2:12." *Women in the Church. A Fresh Analysis of 1 Timothy 2:9-15.* Ed. Andreas J. Köstenberger, Thomas R. Schreiner, and H. Scott Baldwin. Grand Rapids: Baker, 1995, 65-80.

Barclay, William. *The Letters to Timothy, Titus and Philemon.* 3d ed. Edinburgh: Saint Andrew, 1965 [1960].

Barr, James. *The Semantics of Biblical Language.* Oxford: Oxford University Press, 1961.

Barrett, C. K. *The Pastoral Epistles.* London: Oxford University Press, 1963.

——. *The Signs of an Apostle.* Philadelphia: Fortress, 1972.

Bartchy, Scott. "Power, Submission, and Sexual Identity among the Early Christians." *Essays in New Testament Christianity.* Ed. C. Robert Wetzel. Cincinnati: Standard, 1978, 50-80.

Barth, Marcus. "Traditions in Ephesians." *New Testament Studies* 30 (1984): 3-25.

Batey, Richard. *New Testament Nuptial Imagery.* Leiden: Brill, 1971.

Baugh, Steven M. "Feminism at Ephesus: 1 Timothy 2:12 in Historical Context." *Outlook* 42 (May 1992): 7-10.

——. "The Apostle Among the Amazons." *Westminster Theological Journal* 56 (1994): 153-71.

——. "A Foreign World: Ephesus in the First Century." *Women in the Church: A Fresh Analysis of 1 Timothy 2:9-15.* Ed. Andreas J. Köstenberger, Thomas R. Schreiner, and H. Scott Baldwin. Grand Rapids: Baker, 13-52.

Becker, Carol E. *Leading Women.* Nashville: Abingdon, 1996.

Bernard, J. H. *The Pastoral Epistles.* Grand Rapids: Baker, 1980.

Betz, Hans Dieter. *Galatians: A Commentary on Paul's Letter to the Churches in Galatia.* Hermeneia. Philadelphia: Fortress, 1979.

Blenkinsopp, Joseph. *Celibacy, Ministry, Church.* New York: Herder & Herder, 1968.

Bock, Darrell. *Luke 1:1-9:50.* Baker Exegetical Commentary on the New Testament. Grand Rapids: Baker, 1994.

Bockmühl, Markus N. A. *Revelation and Mystery in Ancient Judaism and Pauline Christianity.* Wissenschaftliche Untersuchungen zum Neuen Testament 2/36. Tübingen: Mohr-Siebeck, 1990.

Bokenkotter, Thomas. *Essential Catholicism—Dynamics of Faith and Belief.* New York: Doubleday, 1985.

Boomsma, Clarence. *Male and Female, One in Christ.* Grand Rapids: Baker, 1993.

Bowman, Ann J. "Women in Ministry: An Exegetical Study of 1 Timothy 2:11-15." *Bibliotheca Sacra* 149 (1992): 193-213.

Bristow, John Temple. *What Paul Really Said About Women. An Apostle's Liberating Views on Equality in Marriage, Leadership, and Love.* San Francisco: Harper & Row, 1988.

Bromiley, Geoffrey W. "The Interpretation of the Bible." *The Expositor's Bible Commentary* Vol. 1. Ed. Frank E. Gaebelein. Grand Rapids: Zondervan, 1979, 78-79.

Brooks, James and Carlton Winbery. *Syntax of New Testament Greek.* Wilmington, DE: University Press of America, 1979.

Brooten, Bernadette. "Junia . . . Outstanding among the Apostles (Romans 16:7)." *Women Priests: A Catholic Commentary on the Vatican Declaration.* Ed. Leonard and Arlene Swidler. New York: Paulist, 1977, 141-44.

Brown, Harold O. J. "The New Testament Against Itself: 1 Timothy 2:9-15 and the 'Breakthrough' of Galatians 3:28." *Women in the Church: A Fresh Analysis of 1 Timothy 2:9-15.* Grand Rapids: Baker, 1995, 197-208.

Brown, Peter. *The Body and Society—Men, Women and Sexual Renunciation in Early Christianity.* New York: Columbia University Press, 1988.

Brown, Raymond E. *The Semitic Background of the Term "Mystery" in the New Testament.* Philadelphia: Fortress, 1968.

Brox, Norbert. *Die Pastoralbriefe.* Regensburger Neues Testament. 8th ed. Regensburg: Friedrich Pustet, 1969.

Bruce, F. F. *The Epistle to the Ephesians.* London: Pickering & Inglis, 1961.

——. *The Epistle to the Galatians.* Exeter: Paternoster/Grand Rapids: Eerdmans, 1982.

——. *The Book of Acts.* New International Commentary on the New Testament. Rev. ed. Grand Rapids: Eerdmans, 1988.

——. "Women in the Church: A Biblical Survey." *A Mind for What Matters.* Grand Rapids: Eerdmans, 1990, 259-66, 323-25.

Bultmann, Rudolf. "Is Exegesis without Presuppositions Possible?" *Existence and Faith.* Ed. Schubert Ogden. London: Hodder and Stoughton, 1961, 289-96.

Bürki, H. *Der erste Brief des Paulus an Timotheus.* Wuppertaler Studienbibel. Wuppertal: R. Brockhaus. 4th ed. 1980 [1974].

Callam, Daniel. "Clerical continence in the Fourth Century: Three Papal Decretals." *Theological Studies* 41 (1980): 3-50.

Calvin, John. *Commentaries on the Epistles to Timothy, Titus, and Philemon.* Trans. William Pringle. Grand Rapids: Eerdmans, 1948.

Cambier, J. "Le grand mystère concernant le Christ et son Eglise Ephésiens 5, 22-33." *Biblica* 47 (1966): 43-90.

Caragounis, Chrys C. *The Ephesian Mysterion: Meaning and Content.* Lund: C. W. K. Gleerup, 1977.

Carson, D. A. "Matthew." *The Expositor's Bible Commentary* 8. Grand Rapids: Zondervan, 1984.

——. *Exegetical Fallacies.* 2d ed. Grand Rapids: Baker, 1996.

Cervin, Richard S. "Does *kephalē* Mean 'Source' or 'Authority over' in Greek Literature? A Rebuttal." *Trinity Journal* 10 NS (1989): 85-112.

——. "A Note Regarding the Name 'Junia(s)' in Romans 16.7." *New Testament Studies* 40 (1994): 464-70.

Cholij, Roman. *Clerical Celibacy in East and West.* Leominster, Herefordshire: Fowler Wright, 1988.

Clark, Stephen B. *Man and Woman in Christ: An Examination of the Roles of Men and Women in Light of Scripture and the Social Sciences.* Ann Arbor, MI: Servant, 1980.

Clouse, Bonnidell and Robert G. *Women in Ministry.* Downers Grove, IL: InterVarsity, 1989.

Clowney, Edmund P. "The Biblical Theology of the Church." *The Church in the Bible and the World.* Ed. D. A. Carson. Grand Rapids: Baker, 1987, 13-87.

Cochini, Christian. *The Apostolic Origins of Priestly Celibacy.* San Francisco: Ignatius, 1990.

Cooper, John W. *A Cause for Division? Women in Office and the Unity of the Church.* Grand Rapids: Calvin Theological Seminary, 1991.

Coppens, Joseph. "Le 'mystère' dans la théologie paulinienne et ses parallèles qumrânien." *Littérature et théologie pauliniennes.* Albert Descamps, Béda Rigaux, et al. Recherches bibliques 5. Paris: Declee de Brouwer, 1960, 142-65.

——. *Sacerdoce et Célibat. Etudes Historiques et Théologiques.* Louvain: Editions Duculot, 1971.

Cotter, Wendy. "Women's Authority Roles in Paul's Churches: Countercultural or Conventional?" *Novum Testamentum* 36 (1994): 350-72.

Cottrell, Jack. "Christ: A model for headship *and* submission." *CBMW News* 2/4 (1997): 7-8.

Cranfield, C. E. B. *The Epistle to the Romans.* International Critical Commentary. Edinburgh: T & T Clark, 1979.

Denzler, Georg. *Das Papsttum und der Amtszölibat. Päpste und das Papsttum.* Vol. 5, I & II. Stuttgart: Anton Hiersemann, 1973.

Dibelius, Martin and Hans Conzelmann. *The Pastoral Epistles.* Hermeneia. Trans. Philip
Buttolph and Adela Yarbro. Philadelphia: Fortress, 1972.

Doriani, Daniel. "Appendix 1: History of the Interpretation of 1 Timothy 2." *Women in
the Church: A Fresh Analysis of 1 Timothy 2:9-15.* Ed. Andreas J. Köstenberger,
Thomas R. Schreiner, and H. Scott Baldwin. Grand Rapids: Baker, 1995, 213-67.

Dunn, James D. G. *Romans 9-16.* Word Biblical Commentary 38b. Dallas, TX: Word,
1988.

Ellicott, Charles J. *The Pastoral Epistles of St. Paul.* London: Longmans, Green, Reader, &
Dyer, 1869.

Ellis, E. Earle. "Paul and His Co-Workers." *New Testament Studies* 17 (1970-71):
437-52

———. "Pseudonymity and Canonicity in New Testament Documents." *Worship, Theology
and Ministry in the Early Church: Essays in Honor of Ralph P. Martin.* Ed. Michael J.
Wilkins and Terence Paige. Sheffield: JSOT, 1992, 212-24.

———. "Coworkers, Paul and His." *Dictionary of Paul and His Letters.* Ed. Gerald F. Hawthorne, Ralph P. Martin, and Daniel G. Reid. Downers Grove, IL: InterVarsity, 1993,
183-89.

———. "Pastoral Letters." *Dictionary of Paul and His Letters.* Ed. Gerald F. Hawthorne,
Ralph P. Martin, and Daniel G. Reid. Downers Grove, IL: InterVarsity, 1993, 658-66.

Engberg-Pedersen, Troels. "1 Corinthians 11:16 and the Character of Pauline Exhortation." *Journal of Biblical Literature* 110 (1991): 679-89.

Fàbrega, Valentin. "War Junia(s), der hervorragende Apostel (Rom. 16,7), eine Frau?"
Jahrbuch für Antike und Christentum 27/28 (1984-85): 47-64.

Fairbairn, Patrick. *Pastoral Epistles.* Minneapolis: James & Klock, 1976 [1874].

Falconer, Robert. *The Pastoral Epistles.* Oxford: Clarendon, 1937.

———. "1 Timothy 2:14,15: Interpretative Notes." *Journal of Biblical Literature* 60 (1941):
375-79.

Fee, Gordon D. *The First Epistle to the Corinthians.* New International Commentary on
the New Testament. Grand Rapids: Eerdmans, 1987.

———. *1 and 2 Timothy, Titus.* New International Biblical Commentary. Peabody, MA:
Hendrickson, 1988.

———. "Issues in Evangelical Hermeneutics, Part III: The Great Watershed—Intentionality
& Particularity/Eternality: 1 Timothy 2:8-15 as a Test Case." *Crux* 26 (1990):
31-37=*Gospel and Spirit: Issues in New Testament Hermeneutics.* Peabody, MA:
Hendrickson, 1991, 52-65.

Ferguson, Everett. *Backgrounds of Early Christianity.* Grand Rapids: Eerdmans, 1987.

Fichter, Joseph Henry. *The Pastoral Provisions—Married Catholic Priests.* Kansas City,
MO: Sheed & Ward, 1989.

Fitzmyer, Joseph. "*Kephalē* in I Corinthians 11:3." *Interpretation* 47 (1993): 52-59.

———. *Romans.* Anchor Bible 33. New York: Doubleday, 1993.

Flannery, Austin. *Vatican Council II.* 2 vols. Northport, NY: Costello, 1988 [2d ed.] and
1982.

Fleming, Joy L. E. *A Rhetorical Analysis of Genesis 2-3 with Implications for a Theology
of Man and Woman.* Ph.D. diss. Strasburg, 1987.

Fletcher, Jesse C. *The Southern Baptist Covention: A Sesquicentennial History.* Nashville:
Broadman & Holman, 1994.

Foh, Susan J. *Women and the Word of God.* Grand Rapids: Baker, 1979.

France, R. T. "The Church and the Kingdom of God: Some Hermeneutical Issues." *Biblical Interpretation and the Church: The Problem of Contextualization.* Ed. D. A. Carson. Nashville: Nelson, 1984, 30-44.

———. *Women in the Church's Ministry: A Test Case for Biblical Interpretation.* Grand
Rapids: Eerdmans, 1997 [1995].

Frein, George H. *Celibacy: The Necessary Option.* New York: Crossroad, 1988.

Furnish, Victor. *The Moral Teaching of Paul.* Nashville: Abingdon, 1979.

Gadamer, Hans-Georg. *Truth and Method.* 2d ed. New York: Crossroad, 1982.

Georgi, Dieter. *The Opponents of Paul in Second Corinthians.* Philadelphia: Fortress, 1986.

Giles, Kevin. "The Biblical Case for Slavery: Can the Bible Mislead? A Case Study in Hermeneutics." *Evangelical Quarterly* 66 (1994): 3-17.

Godwin, Joscelyn. *Mystery Religions in the Ancient World.* New York: Harper & Row, 1987.

Gordon, T. David. "A Certain Kind of Letter: The Genre of 1 Timothy." *Women in the Church: A Fresh Analysis of 1 Timothy 2:9-15.* Ed. Andreas J. Köstenberger, Thomas R. Schreiner, and H. Scott Baldwin. Grand Rapids: Baker, 1995, 53-63.

Grenz, Stanley J. and Denise Kjesbo. "Anticipating God's New Community: Theological Foundations for Women in Ministry." *Journal of the Evangelical Theological Society* 38 (1995): 595-611.

——. *Women in the Church: A Biblical Theology of Women in Ministry.* Downers Grove, IL: InterVarsity, 1995.

——. "Putting Women in Their Place." *Academic Alert* 5/1 (Winter 1996): 1-2.

Gritz, S. H. *Paul, Women Teachers, and the Mother Goddess at Ephesus. A Study of 1 Timothy 2:9-15 in Light of the Religious and Cultural Milieu of the First Century.* Lanham, MD: University Press of America, 1991.

——. "The Role of Women in the Church." *The People of God: Essays on the Believers' Church.* Ed. Paul A. Basden and David S. Dockery. Nashville: Broadman, 1991, 299-314.

Groothuis, Rebecca. *Women Caught in the Conflict.* Grand Rapids: Baker, 1994.

Grudem, Wayne. "Does *kephalē* ('Head') Mean 'Source' or 'Authority Over' in Greek Literature? A Survey of 2,336 Examples." *Trinity Journal* 6 NS (1985): 38-59.

——. "The Meaning of κεφαλή ('Head'): A Response to Recent Studies." *Trinity Journal* 11 NS (1990): 3-72.

——. "Asbury Professor Advocates Egalitarianism but Undermines Biblical Authority: A Critique of David Thompson's 'Trajectory' Hermeneutic." *CBMW News* 2/1 (1996): 8-12.

——. "Willow Creek Enforces Egalitarianism." *CBMW News* 2/5 (1997): 1, 3-6.

——. "Catherine Kroeger, InterVarsity, and the Meaning of *kephalē* ('head')." Paper presented at the Annual Meeting of the Evangelical Theological Society. November 21, 1997.

——. "The meaning source 'does not exist.' " *CBWM News* 2/5 (1997): 1, 7-8.

Guthrie, Donald. "Appendix." *The Pastoral Epistles.* Tyndale New Testament Commentary. Grand Rapids: Eerdmans, 1958. Repr. 1984, 211-28.

——. *New Testament Introduction.* Revised ed. Downers Grove, IL: InterVarsity, 1990.

Haas, Guenther. "Patriarchy as an Evil that God Tolerated: Analysis and Implications for the Authority of Scripture." *Journal of the Evangelical Theological Society* 38 (1995): 321-36.

Hadorn, Wilhelm. "Die Gefährten und Mitarbeiter des Paulus." *Aus Schrift und Geschichte. Theologische Abhandlungen Adolf Schlatter zu seinem 70. Geburtstage.* Stuttgart: Calwer Vereinsbuchhandlung, 1922, 65-82.

Hanson, A. T. *The Pastoral Letters.* Cambridge Bible Commentary. London: Cambridge University Press, 1966.

——. *The Pastoral Epistles.* New Century Bible Commentary. Grand Rapids: Eerdmans, 1982.

——. "The Use of the Old Testament in the Pastoral Epistles." *Irish Biblical Studies* 3 (1981): 203-19.

Harnack, Adolf von. "Κόπος (Κοπιᾶν, Οἱ Κοπιῶντες) im frühchristlichen Sprachgebrauch." *Zeitschrift für die neutestamentliche Wissenschaft* 27 (1928): 1-10.

Harper, Michael. *Equal and Different: Male and Female in Church and Family.* London: Hodder & Stoughton, 1994.

Harris, Murray J. "Appendix: Prepositions and Theology in the Greek New Testament." *New International Dictionary of New Testament Theology* 3: 1171-1215.

Harvey, A. H. "The Use of Mystery Language in the Bible." *Journal of Theological Studies* 31 (1980): 320-36.

Hauke, Manfred. *Die Problematik um das Frauenpriestertum vor dem Hintergrund der Schöpfungs- und Erlösungsordnung.* Kappadozier konfessionskundliche und kontroverstheologische Studien 46. Paderborn: Bonifatius, 1982. 3d ed. 1991.

———. *God oder Goddess? Feminist Theolog: What is it? Where does it lead?.* San Francisco: Ignatius, 1994.

Hays, Richard B. *Echoes of Scripture in the Letters of Paul.* New Haven: Yale University Press, 1989.

Hayter, Mary. *The New Eve in Christ.* Grand Rapids: Eerdmans, 1987.

Hendriksen, William. *Exposition of the Pastoral Epistles.* New Testament Commentary. Grand Rapids: Baker, 1957.

Hirsch, E. D., Jr. *Validity in Interpretation.* New Haven and London: Yale University Press, 1967.

Holtz, Gottfried. *Die Pastoralbriefe.* Theologischer Handkommentar zum Neuen Testament. 3d ed. Berlin: Evangelische Ver-lagsanstalt, 1980 [1966].

Holtzmann, Heinrich Julius. *Die Pastoralbriefe.* Leipzig: Wilhelm Engelmann, 1880.

Huizenga, Hilde. "Women, Salvation, and the Birth of Christ: A Reexamination of 1 Timothy 2:15." *Studies in Biblical Theology* 12 (1982): 17-26.

Hurley, James B. *Man and Woman in Biblical Perspective.* Grand Rapids: Zondervan, 1981.

Jagt, Krijn A. Van der. "Women are Saved through Bearing Children (1 Timothy 2.11-15)." *Bible Translator* 39 (1988): 201-208.

Jebb, S. "A Suggested Interpretation of 1 Ti 2.15." *Expository Times* 81 (1970): 221-22.

Jeremias, Joachim. "Paarweise Sendung im Neuen Testament." *New Testament Essays: Studies in Memory of Thomas Walter Manson.* Ed. A. J. B. Higgins. Manchester: Manchester University Press, 1959, 136-43.

———. *Die Briefe an Timotheus und Titus.* Das Neue Testament Deutsch IX. 8th ed. Göttingen: Vandenhoeck & Ruprecht, 1963.

Jewett, Paul K. *Man as Male and Female.* Grand Rapids: Eerdmans, 1975.

Johnston, Robert K. "Biblical Authority & Interpretation: the Test Case of Women's Role [sic] in the Church & Home Updated." *Women, Authority & the Bible.* Ed. Alvera Mickelsen. Downers Grove, IL: InterVarsity, 1986, 30-41.

———. "The Role of Women in the Church and Home: An Evangelical Testcase in Hermeneutics." *Scripture, Tradition, and Interpretation.* Ed. W. Ward Gasque and William Sanford LaSor. Grand Rapids: Eerdmans, 1978, 234-59.

Karris, Robert J. "The Background and Significance of the Polemic of the Pastoral Epistles." *Journal of Biblical Literature* 92 (1973): 549-64.

Kassian, Mary. *Women, Creation and the Fall.* Westchester, IL: Crossway, 1990.

———. *The Feminist Gospel: The Movement to Unite Feminism with the Church.* Wheaton, IL: Crossway, 1992.

Kassing, P. Alfrid. "Das Heil der Mutterschaft." *Liturgie und Mönchtum* (1958): 39-63.

Keener, Craig S. *Paul, Women and Wives: Marriage and Women's Ministry in the Letters of Paul.* Peabody, MA: Hendrickson, 1992.

———. "Man and Woman." *Dictionary of Paul and His Letters.* Ed. Gerald F. Hawthorne, Ralph P. Martin, and Daniel G. Reid. Downers Grove, IL: InterVarsity, 1993, 583-92.

———. "Woman and Man." *Dictionary of the Later New Testament and Its Developments.* Ed. Ralph P. Martin and Peter H. Davids. Downers Grove, IL: InterVarsity, 1205-1215.

Kelly, J. N. D. *A Commentary on the Pastoral Epistles.* Grand Rapids: Baker, 1963.

Kimberley, David R. "1 Tim 2:15: A Possible Understanding of a Difficult Text." *Journal of the Evangelical Theological Society* 35 (1992): 481-86.

Kittel, Gerhard. "αἰχμάλωτος, κτλ." *Theological Dictionary of the New Testament* 1:195-97.

Klein, William W., Craig L. Blomberg, and Robert L. Hubbard, Jr. *Introduction to Biblical Interpretation.* Dallas: Word, 1993.

Knight III, George W. " ᾿Αυθεντέω in Reference to Women in 1 Timothy 2.12." *New Testament Studies* 30 (1984): 143-57.

———. *The Role Relationship of Men & Women.* Rev. ed. Phillipsburg, NJ: Presbyterian and Reformed, 1985.

———. "Husbands and Wives as Analogues of Christ and the Church." *Recovering Biblical Manhood & Womanhood — A Response to Evangelical Feminism.* Ed. John Piper and Wayne Grudem. Wheaton, IL: Crossway, 1991, 165-78, 492-95.

———. *The Pastoral Epistles.* New International Greek Testament Commentary. Grand Rapids: Eerdmans, 1992.

Koester, Helmut. "Letter to the Philippians." *Interpreter's Dictionary of the Bible Supplement.* Nashville: Abingdon, 1976, 665-66.

Köstenberger, Andreas. "The Mystery of Christ and the Church: Head and Body, 'One Flesh.' " *Trinity Journal* 12 NS (1991): 79-94.

———. "A Complex Sentence Structure in 1 Timothy 2:12." *Women and the Church: A Fresh Analysis of 1 Timothy 2:11-15.* Ed. Andreas J. Köstenberger, Thomas R. Schreiner, and H. Scott Baldwin. Grand Rapids: Baker, 1995.

———. "Gender Passages in the NT: Hermeneutical Fallacies Critiqued." *Westminster Theological Journal* 56 (1994): 259-83.

———. "Syntactical Background Studies to 1 Timothy 2.12 in the New Testament and Extrabiblical Greek Literature." *Discourse Analysis and Other Topics in Biblical Greek.* Ed. Stanley E. Porter and D. A. Carson. *Journal for the Study of the New Testament Supplement Series* 113. Sheffield: Sheffield Academic Press, 1995, 156-79.

———. "Review of Cotter, "Women's Authority," *CBMW News* 1/4 (1996): 14.

———. "Ascertaining Women's God-ordained Roles: An Interpretation of 1 Timothy 2:15." *Bulletin of Biblical Research* 7 (1997): 107-44.

———. "The Crux of the Matter: Paul's Pastoral Pronouncements Regarding Women's Roles in 1 Timothy 2:9-15." *Faith & Mission* 14 (1997): 24-48.

Köstenberger, Andreas J., Thomas R. Schreiner, and H. Scott Baldwin, eds. *Women and the Church: A Fresh Analysis of 1 Timothy 2:11-15.* Grand Rapids: Baker, 1995.

Kroeger, Catherine C. "1 Timothy 2:12–A Classicist's View." *Women, Authority and the Bible.* Ed. Alvera Mickelsen. Downers Grove, IL: InterVarsity, 1986, 225-44.

———. "Women in the Church: A Classicist's View of 1 Tim 2:11-15." *Journal of Biblical Equality* 1 (1989): 3-31.

———. "Head." *Dictionary of Paul and His Letters.* Ed. Gerald F. Hawthorne, Ralph P. Martin, Daniel G. Reid. Downers Grove, IL: InterVarsity, 1997, 375-77.

———. "Women in the Early Church." *Dictionary of the Later New Testament and Its Developments.* Ed. Ralph P. Martin and Peter H. Davids. Downers Grove, IL: InterVarsity, 1997, 1215-22.

Kroeger, Richard and Catherine Clark. *I Suffer Not a Woman: Rethinking 1 Tim 2:11-15 in Light of Ancient Evidence.* Grand Rapids: Baker, 1991.

Ladd, George Eldon. *A Theology of the New Testament.* Grand Rapids: Eerdmans, 1987.

Lampe, Peter. "Iunia/Iunias: Sklavenherkunft im Kreise der vorpaulinischen Apostel [Röm 16:7]." *Zeitschrift für die neutestamentliche Wissenschaft* 76 (1985): 132–34.

———. *Die stadtrömischen Christen in den ersten beiden Jahrhunderten: Untersuchungen zur Sozialgeschichte.* Wissenschaftliche Untersuchungen zum Neuen Testament 2/18. Mohr-Siebeck, 1987.

Lea, Henry C. *The History of Sacerdotal Celibacy in the Christian Church.* New York: Russell & Russell, 1957.

Lietzmann, Hans. *Die Briefe des Apostels Paulus: I. An die Römer.* Handbuch zum Neuen Testament 3. Tübingen: Mohr-Siebeck, 1906.

Lincoln, A. T. "The Use of the Old Testament in Ephesians." *Journal for the Study of the New Testament* 14 (1982): 16–57.

Lohse, Eduard. *Colossians and Philemon.* Hermeneia. Philadelphia: Fortress, 1971 [1968].

Longenecker, Richard N. "On the Concept of Development in Pauline Thought." *Perspectives on Evangelical Theology.* Ed. Kennety S. Kantzer and Stanley N. Gundry. Grand Rapids: Baker, 1979, 195–207.

———. *New Testament Social Ethics for Today.* Grand Rapids: Eerdmans, 1984.

———. "Authority, Hierarchy & Leadership Patterns in the Bible." *Women, Authority & the Bible.* Ed. Alvery Mickelsen. Downers Grove, IL: InterVarsity, 1986, 66-85.

Louw, Johannes P. and Eugene A. Nida. *Greek-English Lexicon of the New Testament Based on Semantic Domains.* Vol. 1. New York: United Bible Societies, 1988.

Luter, A. Boyd. "Partnership in the Gospel: The Role of Women in the Church at Philippi." *Journal of the Evangelical Theological Society* 39 (1996): 411-20.

Luther, Martin. *Luther's Works.* Vol. 28: Commentaries on 1 Corinthians 7, 1 Corinthians 15, Lectures on 1 Timothy. Ed. Hilton C. Oswald. St. Louis: Concordia, 1973 [1528].

Malinowski, Francis X. "The Brave Women of Philippi." *Biblical Theology Bulletin* 15 (1985): 60–64.

Marshall, I. H. "An Evangelical Approach to 'Theological Criticism." *The Best in Theology Volume Three.* Ed. J. I. Packer. Carol Stream, IL: Christianity Today, 1989, 45–60.

———. 'Salvation in the Pastoral Epistles.' Paper presented at the Annual Conference of the Society of Biblical Literature, November 1994.

Mason, Mike. *The Mystery of Marriage.* Portland, OR: Multnomah, 1985.

Meeks, Wayne A. *The First Urban Christians: The Social World of the Apostle Paul.* New Haven/London: Yale University Press, 1983.

Metzger, Bruce M. "Paul's Vision of the Church: A Study of the Ephesian Letter." *Theology Today* 6 (1949): 49–63.

———. "A Reconsideration of Certain Arguments Against the Pauline Authorship of the Pastoral Epistles." *Expository Times* 70 (1958): 91-94.

———. *A Textual Commentary on the Greek New Testament.* Corr. ed. New York: United Bible Societies, 1975. 2d ed. 1994.

———. *The Apocrypha of the Old Testament.* New York: Oxford University Press, 1977.

Michaelis, Wilhelm. "συγγενής, κτλ." *Theological Dictionary of the New Testament* 7:736-42.

Michel, Otto. "Grundfragen der Pastoralbriefe." *Auf dem Grunde der Apostel und Propheten: Festgabe für Landesbischof D. Theophil Wurm zum 80. Geburtstag.* Ed. Emil Brunner et al. Stuttgart: Quell-Verlag der Evangelischen Gesellschaft, 1948, 94.

Mickelsen, Alvera, ed. *Women, Authority & the Bible.* Downers Grove, IL: InterVarsity, 1986.

———. "Women in the Church's Ministry. Does 1 Timothy 2:9-15 Help or Hinder?" *Daughters of Sarah* 16/4 (1990): 7-12.

Mistiaen, Veronique. "International News in Brief." *Chicago Tribune* (August 13, 1995): 6/1,8.

Moll, Helmut. *The Church and Women. A Compendium.* San Francisco: Ignatius, 1988.

Moo, Douglas J. "1 Timothy 2:11-15: Meaning and Significance." *Trinity Journal* 1 NS (1980): 62-83.

——. "The Interpretation of 1 Timothy 2:11-15: A Rejoinder." *Trinity Journal* 2 NS (1981): 198-222.

——. "The Problem of Sensus Plenior." *Hermeneutics, Authority, and Canon.* Ed. D. A. Carson and John D. Woodbridge. Grand Rapids: Zondervan, 1986, 175-212.

——. "What Does It Mean Not to Teach or Have Authority Over Men? 1 Timothy 2:11-15." *Recovering Biblical Manhood & Womanhood—A Response to Evangelical Feminism.* Ed. John Piper and Wayne Grudem. Wheaton, IL: Crossway, 1991, 179-93, 495-99.

——. *The Epistle to the Romans.* New International Commentary on the New Testament. Grand Rapids: Eerdmans, 1996.

Morrow, Lance. "A convert's confession." *TIME* (October 3, 1994): 71.

Motyer, Steve. "Expounding 1 Timothy 2:8-15." *Vox Evangelica* 24 (1994): 91-102.

Moule, C. F. D. *An Idiom Book of New Testament Greek.* Cambridge: Cambridge University Press, 1953.

Neuer, Werner. *Man and Woman in Christian Perspective.* Trans. Gordon J. Wenham. Wheaton, IL: Crossway, 1991 [1981].

——. *Mann und Frau in christlicher Sicht.* 5th ed. Gießen: Brunnen, 1993.

O'Brien, Peter T. *Colossians, Philemon.* Word Biblical Commentary 44. Waco, TX: Word, 1982.

——. *Commentary on Philippians.* New International Greek Testament Commentary. Grand Rapids: Eerdmans, 1991.

Ollrog, Wolf-Henning. *Paulus und seine Mitarbeiter: Untersuchungen zu Theorie und Praxis der paulinischen Mission.* Wissenschaftliche Monographien zum Alten und Neuen Testament 50. Neukirchen-Vluyn: Neukirchener, 1979.

——. "Die Abfassungsverhältnisse von Röm 16." *Kirche. Festschrift für Günther Bornkamm zum 75. Geburtstag.* Ed. Dieter Lührmann and Georg Strecker. Tübingen: Mohr-Siebeck, 1980, 221-44.

Ortlund, Raymond C., Jr. "Male-Female Equality and Male Headship." *Recovering Biblical Manhood & Womanhood—A Response to Evangelical Feminism.* Wheaton, IL: Crossway, 1991, 95-112, 479-83.

Osborne, Grant R. "Hermeneutics and Women in the Church." *Journal of the Evangelical Theological Society* 20 (1977): 337-52.

——. "Women in Jesus' Ministry." *Westminster Theological Journal* 51 (1989): 259-91.

——. *The Hermeneutical Spiral: A Comprehensive Introduction to Biblical Interpretation.* Downers Grove, IL: InterVarsity, 1991.

Osburn, Carroll D. " 'Αυθεντέω (1 Timothy 2:12)." *Restoration Quarterly* 25 (1982): 1-12.

Padgett, Alan. "Wealthy Women at Ephesus: 1 Timothy 2:8-15 in Social Context." *Interpretation* 41 (1987): 19-31.

Patterson, Paige. "The Meaning of Authority in the Local Church." *Recovering Biblical Manhood and Womanhood—A Response to Evangelical Feminism.* Ed. John Piper and Wayne Grudem. Wheaton, IL: Crossway, 1991, 248-59, 509-12.

Paulien, Jon. "Elusive Allusions: The Problematic Use of the Old Testament in Revelation." *Biblical Research* 33 (1988): 37-53.

Payne, Philip Barton. "Libertarian Women in Ephesus: A Response to Douglas J. Moo's Article, '1 Timothy 2:11-15: Meaning and Significance.' " *Trinity Journal* 2 NS (1981): 169-97.

——. "οὐδέ in 1 Timothy 2:12." Paper presented at the Annual Meeting of the Evangelical Theological Society, November 21, 1986.

Perriman, Andrew C. "What Eve Did, What Women Shouldn't Do: The Meaning of 'Αυθεντέω in 1 Timothy 2:12." *Tyndale Bulletin* 44 (1993): 129-42.

——. *Speaking of Women.* Leicester: Apollos, 1998.

Perschbacher, Wesley J. *New Testament Greek Syntax.* Chicago: Moody, 1995.

Piper, John and Wayne Grudem, ed. *Recovering Biblical Manhood & Womanhood—A Response to Evangelical Feminism.* Wheaton, IL: Crossway, 1991.

——. "An Overview of Central Concerns: Questions and Answers." *Recovering Biblical Manhood & Womanhood—A Response to Evangelical Feminism.* Ed. John Piper and Wayne Grudem. Wheaton, IL: Crossway, 1991, 60-92, 478-79.

Pisa, Maria Regina. "Es hat ja Priesterinnen gegeben." *Die Presse* (November 13, 1995): 2.

Porter, Stanley E. *Idioms of New Testament Greek.* Sheffield: Sheffield Academic Press, 1992.

——. "What Does it Mean to be 'Saved by Childbirth' (1 Timothy 2.15)?" *Journal for the Study of the New Testament* 49 (1993): 87-102.

——. "Pauline Authorship and the Pastoral Epistles: Implications for Canon." *Bulletin of Biblical Research* 5 (1995): 105-23.

Poythress, Vern Sheridan. "The Church as Family: Why Male Leadership in the Family Requires Male Leadership in the Church." *Recovering Biblical Manhood and Womanhood—A Response to Biblical Feminism.* Ed. John Piper and Wayne Grudem. Wheaton, IL: Crossway, 1991, 233-47, 508-509.

Purvis, Sally B. *The Stained Glass Ceiling.* Louisville, KY: Westminster/John Knox, 1995.

Ramsay, William. "Historical Commentary on the Epistles to the Corinthians." *Expositor* 6th series. London: Hodder & Stoughton, 1898-99.

Ranke-Heinemann, Uta. *Eunuchen für das Himmelreich—Katholische Kirche und Sexualität.* Munich: Knaur, 1989.

Richardson, Peter. "From Apostles to Virgins: Romans 16 and the Roles of Women in the Early Church." *Toronto Journal of Theology* 2 (1986): 232-61.

Rigaux, Béda. "Révélation des Mystères et perfection à Qumran et dans le Nouveau Testament." *New Testament Studies* 4 (1958): 237-62.

Roberts, Mark D. "Women Shall Be Saved: A Closer Look at 1 Timothy 2:15." *TSF Bulletin* (1991): 4-7.

Robertson, A. T. *A Grammar of the Greek New Testament in the Light of Historical Research.* Nashville: Broadman, 1934.

Roloff, Jürgen. *Der erste Brief an Timotheus.* Evangelisch-katholischer Kommentar zum Neuen Testament. Zürich/Neukirchen-Vluyn: Benziger/Neukirchener, 1988.

Sampley, John Paul. *And the Two Shall Become One Flesh: A Study of Traditions in Ephesians 5:21-33.* Cambridge: Cambridge University Press, 1971.

Sanday, W. and A. C. Headlam, *A Critical and Exegetical Commentary on the Epistle to the Romans.* International Critical Commentary. 5th ed. Edinburgh: T & T Clark, 1902.

Scanzoni, Letha and Nancy Hardesty. *All We're Meant to Be: A Biblical Approach to Women's Liberation.* Waco, TX: Word, 1974.

Schillebeeckx, Edward. *Clerical Celibacy under Fire.* London/Sidney: Sheed & Ward, 1968.

Schlarb, Egbert. *Die gesunde Lehre: Häresie und Wahrheit im Spiegel der Pastoralbriefe.* Marburg: N. G. Elwert, 1990.

Schlatter, Adolf. *Die Kirche der Griechen im Urteil des Paulus.* 2d ed. Stuttgart: Calwer, 1958 [1936].

Schnackenburg, Rudolf. "Apostles Before and During Paul's Time." *Apostolic History and the Gospel: Biblical and Historical Essays Presented to F. F. Bruce.* Ed. W. Ward Gasque and Ralph P. Martin. Grand Rapids: Eerdmans, 1970, 287-303.

Scholer, David M. "1 Timothy 2:9-15 & the Place of Women in the Church's Ministry." *Women, Authority & the Bible.* Ed. Alvery Mickelsen. Downers Grove, IL: InterVarsity, 1986, 193-219.

Schöne, Jobst. *Hirtenbrief zur Frage der Ordination von Frauen zum Amt der Kirche.* Groß Oesingen: Verlag der Lutherischen Buchhandlung Heinrich Harms, 1994.

Schreiner, Thomas R. "Head Coverings, Prophecies and the Trinity: 1 Corinthians 11:2-16." *Recovering Biblical Manhood and Womanhood—A Response to Biblical Feminism.* Ed. John Piper and Wayne Grudem. Wheaton, IL: Crossway, 1991, 124-39, 485-87.

——. "The Valuable Ministries of Women in the Context of Male Leadership: A Survey of Old and New Testament Examples and Teaching." *Recovering Biblical Manhood and Womanhood—A Response to Biblical Feminism.* Ed. John Piper and Wayne Grudem. Wheaton, IL: Crossway, 1991, 209-24, 503-506.

——. "An Interpretation of 1 Timothy 2:9-15: A Dialogue with Recent Scholarship." *Women in the Church: A Fresh Analysis of 1 Timothy 2:9-15.* Grand Rapids: Baker, 1995, 105-54.

——. "Review of Grenz and Kjesbo, *Women in the Church.*" *Trinity Journal* 17 NS (1996): 114-24.

——. *Romans.* Baker Exegetical Commentary on the New Testament. Grand Rapids: Baker, 1998.

Schulz, Ray R. "Romans 16:7: Junia or Junias?" *Expository Times* 98 (1986-87): 108-10.

——. "A Case for 'President' Phoebe in Romans 16:2." *Lutheran Theological Journal* 24 (1990): 124-27.

Schüssler-Fiorenza, Elisabeth. "Toward a Feminist Biblical Hermeneutics: Biblical Interpretation and Liberation Theology." *Readings in Moral Theology IV: The Use of Scripture in Moral Theology.* Ed. C. E. Curran and R. A. McCormick. Ramsey, NJ: Paulist, 1984, 354-82.

——. "Missionaries, Apostles, Coworkers: Romans 16 and the Reconstruction of Women's Early Christian History." *Word and World* 6 (1986): 420-33.

——. *In Memory of Her: A Feminist Theological Reconstruction of Christian Origins.* New York: Crossroad, 1988.

Scott, E. F. *The Pastoral Epistles.* Moffatt New Testament Commentary. London: Hodder & Stoughton, 1936.

Scroggs, Robin. "Woman in the NT." *Interpreter's Dictionary of the Bible Supplement.* Nashville: Abingdon, 1976, 966-68.

Silva, Moisés. *Philippians.* Baker Exegetical Commentary on the New Testament. Grand Rapids: Baker, 1992.

Sipe, A. W. Richard. *A Secret World: Sexuality and the Search for Celibacy.* New York: Brunner-Mazel, 1990.

Skarsaune, Oskar. "Heresy and the Pastoral Epistles." *Themelios* 20/1 (October 1994): 9-14.

Smith, D. Moody. "The Old Testament in the New Testament: The Pauline Literature." *It Is Written: Scripture Citing Scripture.* Ed. D. A. Carson and H. G. M. Williamson. Cambridge: University Press, 1988, 265-91.

Snodgrass, Klyne R. "Galatians 3:28: Conundrum or Solution?" *Women, Authority & the Bible.* Downers Grove, IL: InterVarsity, 1986, 161-81.

——. "The Ordination of Women—Thirteen Years Later: Do We Really Value the Ministry of Women?" *Covenant Quarterly* 48/3 (1990): 26-43.

BIBLIOGRAPHY

375

Soden, Hans von. "ΜΥΣΤΗΡΙΟΝ und sacramentum in den ersten zwei Jahrhunderten der Kirche." *Zeitschrift für die neutestamentliche Wissenschaft* 12 (1911): 188-227.

Spencer, Aída Dina Besançon. "Eve at Ephesus (Should women be ordained as pastors according to the First Letter to Timothy 2:11-15?)." *Journal of the Evangelical Theological Society* 17 (1974): 215-22.

Spicq, Ceslaus. *Saint Paul. Les Épitres Pastorales* I. Ébib. 4th ed. Paris: J. Gabalda, 1969.

Stendahl, Krister. *The Bible and the Role of Women—A Case Study in Hermeneutics.* Trans. Emilie T. Sander. Facet Books 15. Philadelphia: Fortress, 1966 [1958].

Stott, John R. W. *The Message of Ephesians.* Downers Grove, IL: InterVarsity, 1979.

——. *Decisive Issues Facing Christians Today.* Old Tappan, NJ: Revell, 1990.

Swartley, Willard M. *Slavery, Sabbath, War, and Women.* Scottdale, PA: Herald, 1983.

Talbert, Charles H. *Reading Luke: A Literary and Theological Commentary on the Third Gospel.* New York: Crossroad, 1982.

Theissen, Gerd. *The Social Setting of Pauline Christianity: Essays on Corinth.* Ed. and trans. J. H. Schütz. Philadelphia: Fortress, 1982.

Thiessen, Terrance. "Toward a Hermeneutic for Discerning Moral Absolutes." *Journal of the Evangelical Theological Society* 36 (1993): 189-207.

Thiselton, Anthony C. *The Two Horizons: New Testament Hermeneutics and Philosophical Description.* Grand Rapids: Eerdmans, 1980.

——. *New Horizons in Hermeneutics.* Grand Rapids: Zondervan, 1992.

Thompson, David L. "Women, Men, Slaves and the Bible: Hermeneutical Inquiries." *Christian Scholar's Review* 25 (1996): 326-49.

Towner, Philip H. *The Goal of Our Instruction: The Structure of Theology and Ethics in the Pastoral Epistles.* Journal for the Study of the New Testament Supplement Series 34. Sheffield: JSOT, 1989.

——. *1-2 Timothy & Titus.* InterVarsity New Testament Commentary Series. Downers Grove, IL: InterVarsity, 1994.

Trummer, Peter. "Corpus Paulinum—Corpus Pastorale. Zur Ortung der Paulustradition in den Pastoralbriefen." *Paulus in den neutestamentlichen Spätschriften. Zur Paulusrezeption im Neuen Testament.* Quaestiones Disputatae 89. Ed. Karl Kertelge. Freiburg: Herder, 1981, 122-45.

Tucker, Ruth A. and Walter Liefeld. *Daughters of the Church.* Grand Rapids: Zondervan, 1987.

Ulrichsen, J. H. "Noen bemerkninger til 1. Tim 2, 15." *Norsk Teologisk Tidsskrift* 84 (1983): 19-25.

Vogt, E. " 'Mysteria' in textibus Qumran." *Biblica* 37 (1965): 247-57.

Waltermann, Leo, ed.. *Über den Zölibat der Priester.* Cologne: J. P. Bachern, 1970.

Waltke, Bruce K. "1 Timothy 2:8-15: Unique or Normative?" *Crux* 28/1 (1992): 22-27.

Wilshire, L. E. "The TLG Computer and Further Research to 'Αυθεντέω in 1 Timothy 2.12." *New Testament Studies* 34 (1988): 120-34.

Witherington, Ben. "On the Road with Mary Magdalene, Joanna, Susanna, and Other Disciples—Luke 8:1-3." *Zeitschrift für die neutestamentliche Wissenschaft* 70 (1979): 243-48.

——. *Women in the Ministry of Jesus.* Society for New Testament Studies Monograph Series 51. Cambridge: Cambridge University Press, 1984.

——. *Women in the Earliest Churches.* Society for New Testament Studies Monograph Series 59. Cambridge: Cambridge University Press, 1988.

——. *Women and the Genesis of Christianity.* Cambridge: Cambridge University Press, 1990.

Wolters, Albert. "Review: *I Suffer Not a Woman.*" *Calvin Theological Journal* 28 (1993): 208-13.

Wood, A. Skevington. "Ephesians." *The Expositor's Bible Commentary* Vol. 11. Grand Rapids: Zondervan, 1978.

Yarbrough, Robert W. "I Suffer Not a Woman: A Review Essay." *Presbyterion* 18 (1992): 25-33.

———. "New Light on Paul and Women?" *Christianity Today* 37/11 (1993): 68-69.

———. "The Hermeneutics of 1 Timothy 2:9-15." *Women in the Church: A Fresh Analysis of 1 Timothy 2:9-15.* Ed. Andreas J. Köstenberger, Thomas R. Schreiner, and H. Scott Baldwin. Grand Rapids: Baker, 1995, 155-96.

Yamauchi, Edwin M. "Gnosis, Gnosticism." *Dictionary of Paul and His Letters.* Ed. Gerald F. Hawthorne, Ralph P. Martin, and Daniel G. Reid. Downers Grove, IL: InterVarsity, 1993, 350-54.

Zscharnack, Leopold. *Der Dienst der Frau in den ersten Jahrhunderten der christlichen Kirche.* Göttingen: Vandenhoeck & Ruprecht, 1902.

GENERAL INDEX